Lecture Notes in Computer Science 12775

More information about this subseries at http://www.springer.com/series/7409

Gabriele Meiselwitz (Ed.)

Social Computing and Social Media

Applications in Marketing, Learning, and Health

13th International Conference, SCSM 2021
Held as Part of the 23rd HCI International Conference, HCII 2021
Virtual Event, July 24–29, 2021
Proceedings, Part II

 Springer

Editor
Gabriele Meiselwitz
Department of Computer Science
Towson University
Towson, MD, USA

ISSN 0302-9743   ISSN 1611-3349   (electronic)
Lecture Notes in Computer Science
ISBN 978-3-030-77684-8   ISBN 978-3-030-77685-5   (eBook)
https://doi.org/10.1007/978-3-030-77685-5

LNCS Sublibrary: SL3 – Information Systems and Applications, incl. Internet/Web, and HCI

This Springer imprint is published by the registered company Springer Nature Switzerland AG
The registered company address is: Gewerbestrasse 11, 6330 Cham, Switzerland

Foreword

Human-Computer Interaction (HCI) is acquiring an ever-increasing scientific and industrial importance, and having more impact on people's everyday life, as an ever-growing number of human activities are progressively moving from the physical to the digital world. This process, which has been ongoing for some time now, has been dramatically accelerated by the COVID-19 pandemic. The HCI International (HCII) conference series, held yearly, aims to respond to the compelling need to advance the exchange of knowledge and research and development efforts on the human aspects of design and use of computing systems.

The 23rd International Conference on Human-Computer Interaction, HCI International 2021 (HCII 2021), was planned to be held at the Washington Hilton Hotel, Washington DC, USA, during July 24–29, 2021. Due to the COVID-19 pandemic and with everyone's health and safety in mind, HCII 2021 was organized and run as a virtual conference. It incorporated the 21 thematic areas and affiliated conferences listed on the following page.

A total of 5222 individuals from academia, research institutes, industry, and governmental agencies from 81 countries submitted contributions, and 1276 papers and 241 posters were included in the proceedings to appear just before the start of the conference. The contributions thoroughly cover the entire field of HCI, addressing major advances in knowledge and effective use of computers in a variety of application areas. These papers provide academics, researchers, engineers, scientists, practitioners, and students with state-of-the-art information on the most recent advances in HCI. The volumes constituting the set of proceedings to appear before the start of the conference are listed in the following pages.

The HCI International (HCII) conference also offers the option of 'Late Breaking Work' which applies both for papers and posters, and the corresponding volume(s) of the proceedings will appear after the conference. Full papers will be included in the 'HCII 2021 - Late Breaking Papers' volumes of the proceedings to be published in the Springer LNCS series, while 'Poster Extended Abstracts' will be included as short research papers in the 'HCII 2021 - Late Breaking Posters' volumes to be published in the Springer CCIS series.

The present volume contains papers submitted and presented in the context of the 13th International Conference on Social Computing and Social Media (SCSM 2021), an affiliated conference to HCII 2021. I would like to thank the Chair, Gabriele Meiselwitz, for her invaluable contribution to its organization and the preparation of the proceedings, as well as the members of the Program Board for their contributions and support. This year, the SCSM affiliated conference has focused on topics related to computer-mediated communication, experience design in social computing, and social network analysis, as well as social media applications in marketing and customer behavior, learning and education, and health and wellbeing.

I would also like to thank the Program Board Chairs and the members of the Program Boards of all thematic areas and affiliated conferences for their contribution towards the highest scientific quality and overall success of the HCI International 2021 conference.

This conference would not have been possible without the continuous and unwavering support and advice of Gavriel Salvendy, founder, General Chair Emeritus, and Scientific Advisor. For his outstanding efforts, I would like to express my appreciation to Abbas Moallem, Communications Chair and Editor of HCI International News.

July 2021   Constantine Stephanidis

HCI International 2021 Thematic Areas and Affiliated Conferences

Thematic Areas

- HCI: Human-Computer Interaction
- HIMI: Human Interface and the Management of Information

Affiliated Conferences

- EPCE: 18th International Conference on Engineering Psychology and Cognitive Ergonomics
- UAHCI: 15th International Conference on Universal Access in Human-Computer Interaction
- VAMR: 13th International Conference on Virtual, Augmented and Mixed Reality
- CCD: 13th International Conference on Cross-Cultural Design
- SCSM: 13th International Conference on Social Computing and Social Media
- AC: 15th International Conference on Augmented Cognition
- DHM: 12th International Conference on Digital Human Modeling and Applications in Health, Safety, Ergonomics and Risk Management
- DUXU: 10th International Conference on Design, User Experience, and Usability
- DAPI: 9th International Conference on Distributed, Ambient and Pervasive Interactions
- HCIBGO: 8th International Conference on HCI in Business, Government and Organizations
- LCT: 8th International Conference on Learning and Collaboration Technologies
- ITAP: 7th International Conference on Human Aspects of IT for the Aged Population
- HCI-CPT: 3rd International Conference on HCI for Cybersecurity, Privacy and Trust
- HCI-Games: 3rd International Conference on HCI in Games
- MobiTAS: 3rd International Conference on HCI in Mobility, Transport and Automotive Systems
- AIS: 3rd International Conference on Adaptive Instructional Systems
- C&C: 9th International Conference on Culture and Computing
- MOBILE: 2nd International Conference on Design, Operation and Evaluation of Mobile Communications
- AI-HCI: 2nd International Conference on Artificial Intelligence in HCI

List of Conference Proceedings Volumes Appearing Before the Conference

1. LNCS 12762, Human-Computer Interaction: Theory, Methods and Tools (Part I), edited by Masaaki Kurosu
2. LNCS 12763, Human-Computer Interaction: Interaction Techniques and Novel Applications (Part II), edited by Masaaki Kurosu
3. LNCS 12764, Human-Computer Interaction: Design and User Experience Case Studies (Part III), edited by Masaaki Kurosu
4. LNCS 12765, Human Interface and the Management of Information: Information Presentation and Visualization (Part I), edited by Sakae Yamamoto and Hirohiko Mori
5. LNCS 12766, Human Interface and the Management of Information: Information-rich and Intelligent Environments (Part II), edited by Sakae Yamamoto and Hirohiko Mori
6. LNAI 12767, Engineering Psychology and Cognitive Ergonomics, edited by Don Harris and Wen-Chin Li
7. LNCS 12768, Universal Access in Human-Computer Interaction: Design Methods and User Experience (Part I), edited by Margherita Antona and Constantine Stephanidis
8. LNCS 12769, Universal Access in Human-Computer Interaction: Access to Media, Learning and Assistive Environments (Part II), edited by Margherita Antona and Constantine Stephanidis
9. LNCS 12770, Virtual, Augmented and Mixed Reality, edited by Jessie Y. C. Chen and Gino Fragomeni
10. LNCS 12771, Cross-Cultural Design: Experience and Product Design Across Cultures (Part I), edited by P. L. Patrick Rau
11. LNCS 12772, Cross-Cultural Design: Applications in Arts, Learning, Well-being, and Social Development (Part II), edited by P. L. Patrick Rau
12. LNCS 12773, Cross-Cultural Design: Applications in Cultural Heritage, Tourism, Autonomous Vehicles, and Intelligent Agents (Part III), edited by P. L. Patrick Rau
13. LNCS 12774, Social Computing and Social Media: Experience Design and Social Network Analysis (Part I), edited by Gabriele Meiselwitz
14. LNCS 12775, Social Computing and Social Media: Applications in Marketing, Learning, and Health (Part II), edited by Gabriele Meiselwitz
15. LNAI 12776, Augmented Cognition, edited by Dylan D. Schmorrow and Cali M. Fidopiastis
16. LNCS 12777, Digital Human Modeling and Applications in Health, Safety, Ergonomics and Risk Management: Human Body, Motion and Behavior (Part I), edited by Vincent G. Duffy
17. LNCS 12778, Digital Human Modeling and Applications in Health, Safety, Ergonomics and Risk Management: AI, Product and Service (Part II), edited by Vincent G. Duffy

http://2021.hci.international/proceedings

13th International Conference on Social Computing and Social Media (SCSM 2021)

Program Board Chair: **Gabriele Meiselwitz,** *Towson University, USA*

- Francisco Alvarez, Mexico
- Andria Andriuzzi, France
- Karine Berthelot-Guiet, France
- James Braman, USA
- Adheesh Budree, South Africa
- Adela Coman, Romania
- Panagiotis Germanakos, Germany
- Hung-Hsuan Huang, Japan
- Aylin Ilhan, Germany
- Ayaka Ito, Japan
- Carsten Kleiner, Germany
- Takashi Namatame, Japan
- Hoang D. Nguyen, Singapore
- Kohei Otake, Japan
- Daniela Quiñones, Chile
- Cristian Rusu, Chile
- Christian W. Scheiner, Germany
- Pavel Strach, Czech Republic
- Jacqui Taylor-Jackson, Australia
- Simona Vasilache, Japan
- Giovanni Vincenti, USA
- Yuanqiong Wang, USA
- Brian Wentz, USA

The full list with the Program Board Chairs and the members of the Program Boards of all thematic areas and affiliated conferences is available online at:

http://www.hci.international/board-members-2021.php

HCI International 2022

The 24th International Conference on Human-Computer Interaction, HCI International 2022, will be held jointly with the affiliated conferences at the Gothia Towers Hotel and Swedish Exhibition & Congress Centre, Gothenburg, Sweden, June 26 – July 1, 2022. It will cover a broad spectrum of themes related to Human-Computer Interaction, including theoretical issues, methods, tools, processes, and case studies in HCI design, as well as novel interaction techniques, interfaces, and applications. The proceedings will be published by Springer. More information will be available on the conference website: http://2022.hci.international/:

General Chair
Prof. Constantine Stephanidis
University of Crete and ICS-FORTH
Heraklion, Crete, Greece
Email: general_chair@hcii2022.org

http://2022.hci.international/

Contents – Part II

SCSM in Health and Wellbeing

Contents – Part I

Experience Design in Social Computing

SCSM in Marketing and Customer Behavior

Influencer Engagement Rate Under Scalable Machine Learning Approaches

Maram AlAnezi and Meznah Almutairy[✉]

Imam Muhammad Ibn Saud Islamic University, Riyadh, Saudi Arabia
mmfalanzi@sm.imamu.edu.sa, mrmutairy@imamu.edu.sa

Abstract. Digital advertising is used to leverage Internet technologies to deliver advertisements to consumers. For an advertisement to reach a large number of audience, business owners usually relay on social media influencers to deliver advertisements messages. However, there are a large number of influencers and it is critical step for business owners to select influencers to be hired. One important measure that has been used to assist the process of selecting an influencer is the influencer engagement rate. Engagement rate measure aims to evaluate how well an influencer can attract potential customers. The current engagement rate measures depend on a simple information such as number of followers, posts, or comments on an influencer account. In this paper we propose a more sophisticated engagement rate measure based on a carful analysis of potential customers reaction to an influencer advertisements posts. The new measure works only on advertisements posts. Also, it take into account the polarity of the comments on these posts, not only their count. To efficiently compute the new engagement rate measure over large size of data, we propose machine learning (ML) approaches to generate necessarily information to compute the new engagement rate measure. We use ML approaches, in particular classifications, in two stages. First, we use classification to efficiently classify a post to an advertisement and none advertisement post. Next, we use ML based sentiments analysis approach to determine the polarity of the comments on an advertisement post. The new measure could be used to measure users engagement to any post and in a wide range of social media platforms. We tested the new engagement rate measure using Instagram influencer accounts, in specific Instafamous accounts. Compared to the current measures, our results show that this new ML based engagement rate measure suggests significantly different ranked list of potential influencers. This ranked list of influencers are more aligned with the business needs and the accepted practices in measuring successful advertisers.

Keywords: Text classification · Sentiment analysis · Machine learning · Engagement rate · Instagram marketing · Social media marketing

© Springer Nature Switzerland AG 2021
G. Meiselwitz (Ed.): HCII 2021, LNCS 12775, pp. 3–14, 2021.
https://doi.org/10.1007/978-3-030-77685-5_1

1   Introduction

Social media platforms have became an important virtual site for people to gather in. Social media allowed the creation and sharing of content with users and thus allowed organizations and companies to understand the needs of users. Thus, recent marketing strategies, that are carried out mainly via digital advertising, have became a major channel to attract the potential of customers and increase business profit. Companies and marketers use social media platforms not just to share information about products to customers, but also to communicate with the customer about the products allowing for more successful marketing results [5].

Instagram is a social media platform that enables their users to upload pictures and videos and share them with their followers or with a specific group of friends. Instagram supports both web and mobile application over all classical operating systems. Instagram is known to be one of the main platforms for advertising since it had more than 400 million users in 2015. According to the statistic published on the official website of Instagram, the number of monthly active users has reached one billion [8]. One major reason for Instagram to be the major digital channel choice for advertising is the fact that customers like to do business with or through people they know, like, and trust. Thus, Instagram influencers, such as Instafamous, usually show consumers who are they, what they love, and what they do. When a customer can visually make a trusted connection to an influencer, this connection will translate to sales and collaboration to what an influencers could provide. Thus, it is essential step for business owners to hire influencers to deliver advertisements messages in today digital marks.

For business owners to hire influencers, it is very critical to evaluate how an influencer is successful in achieving advertising/marketing goals. There any many tools that could suggest a long list of influencers such Gabstats and Social blade [1,12,14]. However, it is not clear how these lists are created in the first place since most of them are closed box tools. More importantly, it is not clear if these lists, in particular, are based on influencers ability to deliver a successful advertisements. Many digital marketing strategies [3,6] suggest that calculating post engagement rate for an influencer is reasonable measure for advertising success. Engagements rate could be computed in different ways such as counting the number of followers of an account or counting the number of likes and/or comments on a post. For example a recent work [14] propose to determine the engagement rate of influencers by computing popularity (number of followers) and the media influential rate. They propose to calculate (i) comment engagement rate (average number of comments per post), (ii) like engagement rate (average number of likes per post), and (iii) video engagement (the average number of video views per post). They use these rates to compute to weighted media influential rate, with giving each rate in the sum a different wight.

However, all these ways are not necessarily the best way to truly capture the customers' engagement, or their reactions, to an advertisement post.

In this paper we propose a new engagement rate measure based on an in depth analysis of users' comments to adversing posts. In addition, we propose an efficient method to compute this new engagement rate measure based on ML approaches. In particular, for a given list of potential influencers' accounts, classification is utilized to filter posts and to analyze user comments. For the new measure, we ensure that engagement rate is computed from the advertisement posts only. When computing the engagement rate, we distinguish between the counts of positive, negative, and irrelevant comments. This is a significantly different than just counting all existence comments, regardless of its semantic to the post, as in most of the engagement rate measures [3]. In our new measure, the engagement rate is increases only with the count of positive comments and decreases with the count of negative comments while the count of irrelevant comments have no impact.

In order to ensure efficient computation, we use ML approaches in two stages. First, we use classification to efficiently classify a post to an advertisement and none advertisement post. Next, to determine the polarity of the comments on an advertisement post, we use ML based sentiments analysis approach. In each of the above steps, we propose some refining process to better reach the goal of each stage. Details will be described later in the paper.

We believe our work can provide an important insight for brands who would like to effectively hire a set of influencers and maximize their advertising effect [13]. The new measure is generic and could be used to measure users engagements to any post. It is also could be used to enhance other existing work such as in [14]. It is not limited to digital advertising application, but could be used in a wide range of applications. Although, we use Instagram social platform in our work, the measure can be used for any social media platforms.

2   Related Work

Advertising is a critical step of marketing that presents products or services to customers. In traditional advertising, the goal is to focus on how to sell a product to customers and increase the business profit. In Forbes, a global media company that focuses on business, investing, and entrepreneurship, Dave Lavinsky said "traditional advertising is achieved through newspapers, magazines, telephone books, radio, and TV where these ads are typically placed for a fee which corresponds to the size of the ad and the medium in which it is published." It is a one-way communication channel where the focus is on how to satisfy expected customers needs. On the other hand, in digital advertising [10], the focus is on how efficiently reach customers and understand their needs to improve products and increase profit. Digital advertising uses social networks' platforms to build two-ways communication with customers. It facilitates reaching the right audience to convince them in the brand in a direct communication. Thus, traditional advertising became far from competition. The current wildly used social media platforms are Facebook, Google+, Instagram, Twitter and Pinterest [5]. When consider digital marketing, and in particular digital advertising, Instagram is by far the key social media platform.

In order for an advertising to reach-out a large number of audience, social influencers have attracted a great attention as new marketing channels. Many respected companies, such as NIKE or Starbucks, try to advertise their products through social influencers. Social influencers are usually recognized as social media user who have expertise in specific areas and have a large number of followers with similar interests [13]. Typical influencers are known as social media celebrities. In [7], authors differentiate between two types of celebrities: traditional celebrity and Instafamous. Traditional celebrity is a known person who has an active account and has many followers because of their work led to their access to those followers, such as musicians, athletes, actors and models. Those traditional celebrities have been widely selected be the face of any marketing campaign. Recently a new type of celebrities, called Instafamous, became a strong alternative option for the traditional ones. Instafamous have more active followers because they tend to communicate directly with the audience, show regular life style, and share many of their moments and their experiences, making the audience feel that Instafamous are more friends rather than stars. Because of that, Instafamous are closer to the audience and gain thier trust easily. Without loose of generality, in our experiments we focus on Instafamous accounts. The proposed new engagement rate measure and the proposed ML approach to compute it efficiently can be used for any type of influencers account or even ordinary user account.

In digital advertisements, as in Instagram advertisements, hiring a social influencer to advertise products and services is a costly process. For a company to cut down this cost, it tries to find the most successful social influencer in advertisements. Thus, it is very critical to evaluate the influencers ads and measure their success to achieve marketing goals. However, with the rapid increase in the number of users and marketers that are active in social media, it is difficult for companies to decide on the right influencer to cary the marketing campaign. Precisely, they struggle to answer the question of how to measure the impact of social marketing campaigns and then find the best influencer. One of the most effective ways to answer this question is to measure engagement rate for an influencer account.

The ads over a social network platform are usually delivered to the audience as digital posts, such as images and short videos. To evaluate an influencer impact on social media, users engagement over an influencer posts are computed. There are many suggestions have been proposed to compute engagement rates [6]. Bond [3] suggests that measuring the success of an ads are based on calculating post engagements. Measures proposed so far could be classified mainly into two types. The first type serve the influencer to learn about his/her posts impact level. For example, a post engagement can be computed from the total of number of likes, comments, sends, saves and interactions (profile visits, website clicks, and emails) divided by the number of impressions (the total number of times the content is displayed to people on Instagram, including repeat views). This type usually include mainly personal data and are available for public. Thus, it does not support comparing impact of different influencers' accounts. The second type of engagement rate measures use only data publicly available, and thus, they are more suitable for influence comparisons. Many of these measure rely only on the number of followers, average number of likes and/or comments to evaluate an influencer impact. These measures depend on a simple public data usually supported by the social media platform. In our work we propose a more sophisticated engagement rate measure based on deeper understanding of user reactions to advertisement posts in particular. In order to achieve that we propose to use ML algorithms to extract this complex information to be incorporate to the new engagement rate measure.

3 Influencer Engagement Rate

In this section we describe how to evaluate the impact of a social influencer on his/her followers. This is done by computing an influencer engagement rate which try to quantify the reactions of followers to influencer posts. We describe two common social influencer rate measures. Then we propose our new engagement measure. Then for all these measure we describe how to compute the rate of engagement.

For a given Influencer (e.g. Instafmous) account I with F followers, and a given time interval $T = (t_s, t_e)$ where $t_s \leq t_e$, Let $P_{I,T} = \{p\}$ refers to the set of posts that are posted on the account I within interval T and let $|P_{I,T}| = N$ refer to the number of posts. If t_p refer to the time of posting a post p, then $P_{I,T}$ defined as:

$$P_{I,T} = \{p | p \in I, t_s \leq t_p \leq t_e\} \tag{1}$$

Let define for each post p the number of its likes L_p and the number of its comments C_p. Two engagement measures, $Eng1$ and $Eng2$ have been proposed for a given set of posts as follows:

$$Eng1(P) = \sum_{p \in P} L_p \tag{2}$$

$$Eng2(P) = \sum_{p \in P} (L_p + C_p) \tag{3}$$

Our proposed measure is similar to $Eng2$ but instead of simply taking the count of the comments, we differentiate between the types of comments. In specific, we only increases the comments count when the comments are positive toward a post. If the comments are negative, then this decreases the measure. Irrelevant comments are removed from the computations. More formally the proposed engagement rate measure is:

$$Eng3(P) = \sum_{p \in P} (L_p + PC_p - NC_p) \tag{4}$$

where PC_p and NC_p refers to positive and negative comments for a post p respectively.

To compute the rate of engagement, the engagement values are divided by the number of followers F and the number of considered posts N. More formally we define engagement rates for the above three measures are follows:

$$EngRate1(P) = Eng1(P)/(F \times N) \tag{5}$$
$$EngRate2(P) = Eng2(P)/(F \times N) \tag{6}$$
$$EngRate3(P) = Eng3(P)/(F \times N) \tag{7}$$

The engagement rate is computed from a selected time interval. The time interval is usually set to be recent and a one month long. However, it is recommended to pick the posts that are at least $1\sim2$ weeks old. In this case, a post could have enough time to receive followers' reactions. It is possible to compute the engagement rate from a selected number of posts instead of time interval. In this case the number of posts will be equal to all considered influencers' accounts.

4   Scalable Machine Learning Approach

Most of the social media platform gives a simple statistics such as count of likes and comments. In order to compute the $EngRate3$ efficiently, we use ML approaches, in specific classification. Without loose of generality, we use Multinomial Naive Bayes algorithm as our core classifier.

4.1   Multinomial Naive Bayes Classification Algorithm

Multinomial Naive Bayes (MNB) classifier is a specialized version of Naive Bayes classifier. It has been used successfully to handle text documents using word counts as it's underlying method of calculating probability. Naive Bayes is based on Bayes? theorem. It is called Nave because of the simplification assumption used that features in the dataset are mutually independent. Occurrence of one feature does not affect the probability of occurrence of the other feature. The distribution of each feature is assumed to be a multinomial distribution [2].

We illustrate how Multinomial Naive Bayes works on text documents [4] as follows. In text classification, we are given a description $d \in X$ of a document, where X is the document space; and a fixed set of classes $C = \{c_1, c_2, \ldots, c_J\}$. Classes are also called categories or labels. Typically, the document space X is some type of high-dimensional space, and the classes are human defined for the needs of an application. For example in our application, labels are used to identify if a post being an ads post or none-ads post. Also, labels are used to identify if the polarity of a comment on a post whether it is positive, negative, or irrelevant. We are given a training set D of labeled documents $<d, c>$, where $<d, c> \in X \times C$. Using a learning method or learning algorithm, we then wish to learn a classifier or classification function γ that maps documents to classes: $\gamma : X \to C$. The pseudo code for both training and applying MNB classifier is described below.

TrainMultinomialNB (C, D)

---

1   V ← ExtractVocabulary (D)
2   N ← CountDocs (D)
3   **for each** c ∈ C
4   **do** Nc ← CountDocsInClass (D,c)
    a. prior[c] ←Nc/N
    b. $text_c$ ← ConcatTextOfAllDocsInClass (D, c)
    c. **for each** t ∈ V
    d. **do** T_{ct} ← CountTokensOfTerm ($text_c$, t)
    e. **for each** t ∈ V
    f. **do** condprob[t][c] ← $(T_{ct}+1)/ \sum_{t'}(T_{ct'}) + 1$
5   **return** V, prior, condprob

ApplyMultinomialNB (C, D)

---

1   W ← ExtractTokensFromDoc (V, d)
2   **for each** c ∈ C
3   **do** score[c] ← log prior[c]
    a. for each t ∈ W
    b.do score[c] += log condprob[t][c]
4   **return** $argmax_{c \in C} score[c]$

4.2 Posts Classification

In order to compute the engagement rate from advertisements posts only, we propose to classify the posts, using its description, to an ads post and none-ads post. By default, Instagram classifies the posts into so many classes such as Beauty, Fashion, Technology, Events, Food and Drinks, Health and Other-adds. We do not use Instagram classes for may reasons. Firstly, the number of possible classes are large and this increases the computational needs of the classifier and does not serve our need. We only need to know of it is an ads post or not. Secondly, and more importantly, it is not used to differentiate the ads from none-ads posts. It is usually meant to describe a topic (e.g. fashion), without investigating if this post is for advertising purpose or for other purposes (e.g. personal or educational). It is worth mentioning that our work could be extended to have deeper level of classifications where an advertisements posts could be further classified to classes. This will enable understand the influence of an ads on specific business sector.

In our experiments, we consider both Arabic and none Arabic Instafamous accounts. Most of the limited existing NLP libraries, which support Arabic, does not perform well when working with Arabic text. This is because Arabic language is a challenging language to work with especially for slang. Therefore, we create a training data sets of Arabic posts where we manually choose the class labels for a post based on its description. Then we feed that to the Multinomial Naive Bayes classifier. The classifier reach an accuracy of 79% using our labeled training posts' descriptions set.

4.3   Comments Classification

We propose to analyze sentiments to determine the polarity of the comments on Instagram post. Instead of using traditional rule based sentiments analysis, we use classification algorithms. In [9] authors showed that ML techniques have improved accuracy of sentiment analysis. In particular, Naive Bayes algorithm found to be quite fast and accurate for sentiment analysis.

Similar to posts classification, we also created our Arabic training data sets. In this tanning set, for each post and for each comment associate with this posts, we manually labeled the comments to be positive, negatives, or irrelevant. Then we feed that to the Multinomial Naive Bayes classifier. The classifier reach an accuracy of 80% using our labeled training comment sets.

5   System Architecture

In this section we describe our System Architecture Design, Data-Flow, and Flow Chart.

There are many types of the architecture design such as layered architecture, pipe architecture, repository architecture, and client-server architecture. Since the software communicate with the Instagram server over the Internet, client-server architecture is the most a appropriate architecture design for our software. Figure Fig. 1 shows the flowchart of the System Architecture Design.

The data processing is the core of our work. Figures Fig. 2 and 3 show how the data flows in the system including the learning process and results reporting.

6   System Implementation

In this section we describe the system implementation requirements and implementation details. We developed and ran our experiments using MacBook laptop. We implemented the software using Python since it is being credited as one of the fastest growing programming language [11] and heavily used in machine learning. We used JavaScript for calculating the engagements rates and for data visualization. We used PHP for connecting and retrieving data from the SQL database. Finally, the following Tools and Technologies are used to run our program:

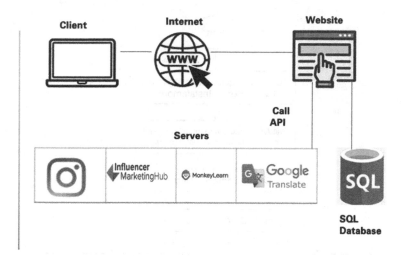

Fig. 1. System architecture design

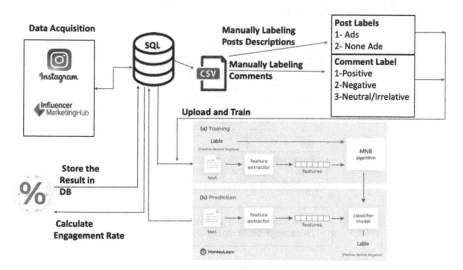

Fig. 2. The system of data flow.

Influencer Marketing Hub Tool: Provide influencers on Instagram Based on the number of followers and their nationalities. We used 1000 influencers on Instagram based on the highest number of followers and that they speak Arabic or English.

Google Translate Tool: Our data consists of English and Arabic therefore, we use Google trans- late API for translating Arabic posts and comments to English for more accurate analysis.

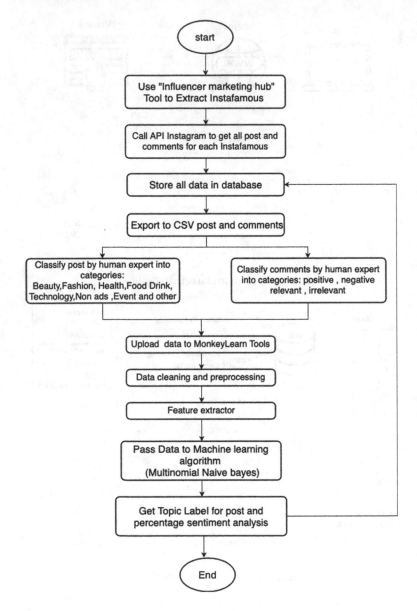

Fig. 3. Flowchart of the system.

MonkeyLearn Tool: Text classification service which provides the user to upload their data set to train an algorithm. Monkey-Learn used to train custom machine learning models to get topic, sentiment, intent, keywords and more.

7   Conclusion

In this paper we propose a sophisticated engagement rate measure based on a careful analysis of potential customers reaction to an influencer advertisements posts. The measure aligned better with business needs and accepted practices in measuring successful advertisers. The new measure works only on advertisements posts and takes into account the polarity of the comments on these posts, not only their counts. To efficiently compute the new measure, we proposed machine learning approaches, in particular classification, to generate necessarily information to compute the measure. The measure is generic and could be used for a wide range of social media applications. Our experimental results using Instagram influencer, or Infamous, accounts show that this new ML based engagement rate suggests significantly different ranked list of potential influencers. This open a new way to identify and find social influencers.

Acknowledgment. The authors would like to thank Thana Abdullah AlSaadoun and Manar Abdulrahman Almujalle for assistance with labeling data sets of the model training and suggesting the classification algorithm. Special acknowledgment for Engineering Naif AlShehri for the valuable insights and review.

References

1. https://influencermarketinghub.com
2. Bhangle, R.S., Sornalakshmi, K.: Twitter sentimental analysis on fan engagement. In: Rajsingh, E.B., Veerasamy, J., Alavi, A.H., Peter, J.D. (eds.) Advances in Big Data and Cloud Computing. AISC, vol. 645, pp. 27–39. Springer, Singapore (2018). https://doi.org/10.1007/978-981-10-7200-0_3
3. BOND, A.: How to build a successful instagram ad campaign with only 5 dollars a day
4. Manning, C.D., Raghavan, P., Schutze, H.: An Introduction to Information Retrieval. Cambridge University Press, Cambridge (2009)
5. Durmaz, Y., Efendioglu, I.: Travel from traditional marketing to digital marketing. Global J. Manage. Bus. Res. **16**, 34–40 (2016)
6. Hoffman, D.L., Fodor, M.: Can you measure the ROI of your social media marketing? MIT Sloan Manage. Rev. **52**(1), 41 (2010)
7. Hwa, C.: The impact of social media influencers on purchase intention and the mediation effect of customer attitude. Asian J. Bus. Res. **7**, 19–36 (2017)
8. Instagram: Our story -instagram press @online (2019). https://instagram-press.com/our-story/
9. Singh, J., Singh, G., Singh, R.: Optimization of sentiment analysis using machine learning classifier. Hum.-Centric Comput. Inf. Sci. **7**(1), 32 (2017)
10. Lavinsky, D.: Is traditional marketing still alive? (2017). https://www.forbes.com/sites/davelavinsky/2013/03/08/is-traditional-marketing-still-alive/#6ec0ea4c3806
11. Nagpal, A., Gabrani, G.: Python for data analytics, scientific and technical applications. In: 2019 Amity International Conference on Artificial Intelligence (AICAI), pp. 140–145 (2019)

12. Ranpariya, V., Chu, B., Fathy, R., Lipoff, J.B.: Instagram influencer definitions and the need for dermatologist engagement on social media. J. Am. Acad. Dermatol. **83**(6), e449–e450 (2020)
13. Kim, S., Han, J., Yoo, S., Gerla, M.: How are social influencers connected in Instagram? In: Ciampaglia, G.L., Mashhadi, A., Yasseri, T. (eds.) SocInfo 2017. LNCS, vol. 10540, pp. 257–264. Springer, Cham (2017). https://doi.org/10.1007/978-3-319-67256-4_20
14. Yew, R.L.H., Suhaidi, S.B., Seewoochurn, P., Sevamalai, V.K.: Social network influencers? Engagement rate algorithm using Instagram data, pp. 1–8 (2018)

Action-Aware Restricted Stream Influence Maximization Model to Identify Social Influencers

Meznah Almutairy[(⊠)], Hailah Alaskar, Latifah Alhumaid, and Rawan Alkhalifah

Imam Muhammad Ibn Saud Islamic University, Riyadh, Saudi Arabia
mrmutairy@imamu.edu.sa, {halaskar,lalhumaid,rkalkhalifah}@sm.imamu.edu.sa

Abstract. The problem of *influencer identification* is an important problem in social network analysis, due to the impact of influential users one the opinions of their audience. Most of the existing approaches to identify influencers are developed for static networks, whereas the social networks are time-sensitive and evolving over time. Therefore, identifying influencers over a *dynamic*, or *stream*, social network is more adequate for such problem. However, the amount of work proposed for dynamic networks are limited. Recent work proposed that identifying influencers with respect to some analysis-specific *restrictions* (e.g. influencers' locations or Influence context) produces a more concrete analyses. Current models proposed to identify influencers are based on capturing the number of social actions triggered by an influencer's social action. These models do not differentiate between social actions' types and treat them indistinguishably. However, the type of an action a user select to do captures an important clues in how as user is influenced. In this paper we propose to solve *Action-Aware Restricted Stream Influence Maximization* (ARSIM) problem that identifies the most influential social network users in real-time. We extend the *Action-based* dynamic model [5] to incorporate actions' types into the model. The model does not only differentiate between the actions' types, it gives the option to weight these actions differently; facilitating new approaches to identify influencers. We run the model with respect to a given set of commonly used restrictions. We adopted a sliding window to update efficiently the model in real time. The model is generic and can be used with any social network platform, actions types, and restrictions. We run our experiments using Twitter data where we differentiate between four action types: (tweet, retweet, reply and quote tweet) and with respect to location, topic and/or language restrictions. Our results shows that our new model is able to identify significantly different influencers based on the given actions wights. This should open the gate for more sophisticate and deeper understanding for influencers impact types over the social network. The model is generic and can be used in any type of social network.

Keywords: Action-Aware · Stream Influence Maximization · Real-time analysis · Social networks

© Springer Nature Switzerland AG 2021
G. Meiselwitz (Ed.): HCII 2021, LNCS 12775, pp. 15–28, 2021.
https://doi.org/10.1007/978-3-030-77685-5_2

1   Introduction

Online social networks, or social networks for short, have evolved into a place where public opinion is shaped by the influence of some users over others. Thus, analyzing this relation of influence between users is of a growing importance on many levels, some of which are for governmental purposes, such as political matters, and others are commercial, such as marketing and targeted advertising. Influence Analysis over social networks is the basis of these applications. The first step to achieve this analysis is to identify influencers in a large amount of social relations [4]. Traditionally, social network analysis is conducted over a static network [8], where the set of users and their relations are fixed. However, in real applications, these relations have significant different changes over time, and thus old influencer may no longer have significant impact on public opinion. On the other hand, new influencers may take over the change of public opinion. Therefore, when identifying influencer, real-time analysis is more appropriate. Although, the real-time analysis is the right way to go, many challenges are encountered at this setting. This includes the large size of the data, the continuous change in the users and their relations, and the need to efficiency, update the analysis as respond to the new data arriving and the pruning for old data.

In the recent years, there has been interest in finding social influencers given some required restrictions [4,6]. For example, influencers may be defined with respect to some geographical locations. Alternatively, influencers may be defined with respect to some context or topics of interest. Therefore there have been some attempts to incorporate these restrictions when finding social influencers. However, not all the systems support real-time identification and obey given restrictions in an efficient matter. The ones that could support that are all commercial and their approach to find influencers are not clear raising the question about software output the validity. All models proposed to identify influencers are based on the counting the number of a social actions (e.g. as tweeting, retweeting, replays) triggered by an influencer's social action. These proposed models do not differentiate between social actions types and treat them indistinguishably as a generic action type. We believe the type of an action a user selects to do over a social network captures an important semantic in how the user is influenced. Also, we believe the type of an action is not only important but also should be weighted differently allowing for further influencers identification from different perspectives.

In this paper we propose to solve *Action-Aware Restricted Stream Influence Maximization* (AR-SIM) problem that identifies the most influential social network users in real-time. We extend the *Action-based* dynamic model [5] to incorporate actions' types into the model. The proposed model do not only differentiate between the actions' types but it also weights these actions differently, which significantly expand the possible options to find influencers from various perspectives according to its impact type over a social network. In our system, we run the model with respect to a given set of user combined restrictions. We adopted a sliding window to run update the model in real time. We run our experiments using Twitter data with respect to location, topic and/or language restrictions. Our results shows that our new model is able to identify significantly different influencers based on the given actions wights and combined restrictions. This should open the gate for more sophisticate and deeper understanding for influencers impact over the social network. The model is generic and can be used in any type of social network and tradition models can be derived from our model by simple set the weights to be equal and ignore the action types. For purposes of concentrating and simplicity, we mainly conduct the analysis using Twitter data.

The paper is organized as follows. First we describe relevant work. Next, we propose *AR-SIM* problem explain in details the system architecture and implementation. Finally, experiment results are presented and discussed.

2   Related Work

Much effort has been put into the problem of identifying influencers in social networks. In this section, we summarize the most relevant literature and how they approached this problem.

A social network is generally represented as a graph data structure $G = \{V, E\}$ [4,5,7,8]. Depending on the underlying analysis, V and E may capture different features of a social network. For example, V could represent the set of users and E represents the set of the actions between those users [7], or vice versa [5,8]. Alternatively, V could represent the set of social actions and E represents the causality of those social actions [5,8]. In both cases, the graph could be traversed and/or statistics could be collected to conduct the intended analysis.

A social networks is classically classified into *static* or *dynamic*. Both of them are usually represented as graphs. In static network, the assumption is that the graph structure is fixed and then any analysis is built on top of this fixed structure. On the other hand, in dynamic network, the graph structure could change where new nodes and edges can be added and/or deleted.

2.1   Influence Maximization Problem

In a social network, Influence Maximization (IM) aims to find the set of social network users that maximize the influence value in the network. In the classical version of IM problem, *Static Influence Maximization*, most of the existing solutions depend on the influence probabilities between users to compute the influence value from the social actions. In this case the set of users with high probabilities to influence a largest group of users are identified as a solution to IM problem. Classical IM methods have one major limitation, they assume the social influence between users is static, that makes influence probabilities determined based on the historical user actions, which do not support the fast evolving and the highly dynamic of the social network. Thus, we believe this static network assumption is not valid when solving IM problem in real-time.

IM methods that account for the dynamics of the social network are named *Stream Influence Maximization* (SIM). These methods are efficient and effective to track influencers in real-time. SIM methods track the social influences along current available social actions and obtain updated list of influencers continuously. To solve SIM problem, some work adopt the *Sliding Window* model, which captures the short-term memory of social influences where past influences are replaced with new influences with respect to the allowed time window [5,6]. More information in how handle social stream is presented in Sect. 2.3.

Most of IM solutions identifying the influencers for general purpose [5,7,8]. Recently there have been an interest on solving IM using the set of actions that are only related to a *restricted topic*, e.g. hashtag or keyword [3,4], or originated by users in a *restricted location*, e.g. tweets/retweets with locations [6]. We refer to this version of as *Restricted Influence Maximization* problem.

In our system we support the two main types restrictions: topic-restricted and location-restricted. We also consider language-restricted since it useful in some scenarios like find the trending topics for the local language only in a location without restrict by topic. We allow the user of our system to create any combination of these restrictions. This problem can naturally can be extended to a stream setting since the restriction are used to filter the input used to build dynamic model.

2.2 Diffusion Models

Diffusion Models are used to capture the spread of an idea or a piece of information throughout a network. They are also known as an influence propagation models. Originally there were two basic diffusion models, *Linear Threshold* (LT) and *Independent Cascade* (IC) [2]. Under LT model, a node switches to being active if sufficient number of its neighbors become active and thus is considered receiver-oriented (i.e. neighbors target a node). Unlike the LT model, the process of IC model is considered sender-oriented (i.e. node targets neighbors). In both models, the process also terminates when no activations are possible and again the influence spread is the number of expected active nodes at the end of the process.

Recently, other diffusion models have been proposed to support efficient influence spread computation in dynamic settings such as *Flow-based* [4] and *Action-based* model [5]. In Flow-based model, the nodes are the users and the edges are the direction flow of the information. Nodes can influence one another by tracking the information flow paths. Since actions are reflective of the diffusion process, Action-based model defines influence propagation simply based on actions performed by users.

When working with a static network, the first two models are more appropriate, because they are designed based on given probabilities for a user influence, this can be a problem on its own and has been studied by Goyal et al. [1]. In a stream setting, these probabilities are highly dynamic and change rapidly. Recomputing these probabilities is computationally expensive. Thus, the last two models are more appropriate as they are more efficient for a dynamic setting, and also support context-aware and location-aware queries.

2.3 Handling a Social Stream

There are some approaches that have been proposed to handle the social stream. Because diffusion models capture the spread of information throughout a network, the approach to handle the stream must be consistent with the diffusion model used. Below is a short summary for the approaches that alined with diffusion model described above in Sect. 2.2

Yang et al. [7] proposed *Polling-based* under LT\IC diffusion model. They consider a weighted graph where the nodes are users and the edges are actions performed by users (e.g. a user v has an edge directed to u if v retweeted from u). The edge weight represents the number of retweets between v and u under the LT model, or the probability that v retweets from u under the IC model. A social stream then can be represented as a series of updates on the edge weights.

Zhuang et al. [8] proposed *Probing-based* under IC diffusion model. They consider the graph where the nodes are users while the edges are the actions. They keep a summary of the stream by saving the topological updates on the graph (e.g. edge/node insertions/deletions).

Subbian et al. 2016a and 2016b [3,4] proposed *Tree-based* method under the Flow-based diffusion model. They propose to keep a summery of the stream by creating a tree data structure of flow paths with relevant weights that are computed according to the transmission of massages containing the keyword. The update this summery when a new contents arrives. Subbian et al. [3] recomputes the summary from scratch every time for each content arrives, making their approach computationally expensive. When the updated version by Subbian et al. 2016a [4], updates the summary incrementally by updating the flow paths weights only when a new social content gets transmitted, then add it to the flow path in the tree.

Wang et al. 2017 and Wang et al. 2018 [5,6] proposed by *Sliding Window* method under the Action-based diffusion model. They consider the graph where the nodes are the actions performed by the users, an edge exists between actions if one action triggers the other. They model the social stream as social actions which are generated by actor activities, a summary is created by keeping the most N recent actions in the sliding window. The Sliding Window is used in our system and is explain in detail in Sect. 3

3 Action-Aware Restricted Stream Influence Maximization Problem (AR-SIM)

In this section we start with illustration for the need for incorporating the action types when solving Influence Maximization Problem. Next we formalize the new problem and the model.

3.1 Motivation for the Action-Aware Influence

Recently, there has been an interest to find top influential users given a set of restrictions. The restrictions serve in identifying influencers for certain purposes instead of the general case. We refer to this problem as Restricted Stream Influence Maximization Problem R-SIM. In our system we consider three types of restrictions keyword, language and location. In this work we solve an extended version of R-SIM problem that differentiate the types of actions in the data stream. We call this version *Action-Aware Restricted Stream Influence Maximization Problem* (AR-SIM).

The new version distinguishes between the actions types since these actions represent, for an influenced user, different feelings and needs, and thus should be captured differently. To describe this consider a Twitter social stream data, which has four major action types: *Tweet, Retweet, Quote and Reply*. The user may select one of the four types based on some reasons. A user may use Retweet action to spread a tweet to his/her audiences or show an agreement and support with a posted tweet. It is possible that a user pick to Reply to a tweet to be active, positively or negatively, on a tweet thread to present their friendship and loyalty or to gain followers from that account. On the other hand The Quote usually show an interest to discuss further the tweet. In all cases, there is large room for social behavioral specialist to understand deeper the behavior and the impact of influencer.

3.2   AR-SIM Model Formalization

Below we describe AR-SIM and the model formally along illustration examples. We extend the formalization use in [5] to fit out actions-aware model.

Action Stream: We consider a social action stream over a social network with a user set U. We *model* the social stream using unbounded *time-sequence social actions* that are generated by user activities. More formally, we represent an action of user $u \in U$ at time t who is influenced by an earlier action $a_{t'}$ at time t' $(t' < t)$, and an action weight V that represented by a value from 0 to 1 based on the action type as $a_t = (u, a_{t'}, V)$. Then, a social action stream S is modeled by $S = <...., a_t = (u, a_{t'}, V), ..>$.

Figure 1 shows a social stream with action types where each symbols means: Retweet(R), Tweet(T), Quote(Q) and Reply(P). For example $a_1 = (u_1, nil, T)$ as a_1 an action that performed by user u_1 who has Tweet(T) action type with no previous action and $a_2 = (u_2, a_1, R)$ as a_2 an action that performed by user u_2 who has Retweet(R) action type with respond by previous action a_1. Then the social action stream S modeled as $S = <a_1 = (u_1, nil, T), a_2 = (u_2, a_1, R), ...>$.

Time Bounded Stream: To capture only recent stream actions we adopt *sliding window approach*. We consider N as a window size and W_t as sliding window at time t. Figure 1 shows how to adopt sliding window using previous social stream example. The window size N is set to be $N = 8$, and two examples of sliding windows on the stream are shown W_8 at time 8 and W_10 at time 10, highlighted in blue and red boxes respectively.

Weighted Influence Set: We define the influence set of a user as follows: The influence set of a user $u \in U$ at time t, denoted as $I_t(u)$, is the set of users who are

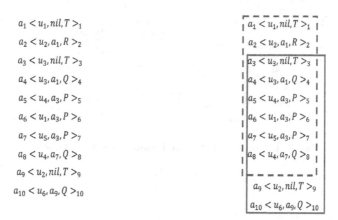

Fig. 1. An example of a social stream with distinguished action types with and without sliding windows (Color figure online)

influenced by u wrt. the sliding window at time t (i.e., W_t). Equivalently, $I_t(u) = \{v|(u, v)_t\}$. Traditional Influence set treats all actions equally. In our work, we augmented each action with a weight, and thus, we extend traditional Influence set to be weighted influence set. Action type weight are used to calculate the influence scores based on the action type values. The influence set contains a set of tuples, each tuple has user u and the highest action weight that user u has received wrt. the window at a time. In our experiments we the weight could be any real value from 0 to 1. When the weights are all set to 1, then we treat action equally and we get the tradition influence set.

Figures 2 and 3 show two influence sets at time 8 and 10 that display the difference between influence score for top_k (k = 1) users with action type and without action type. We assume the weights of the action types as the follow: 1, 0.75, 0.50 and 0.25 for Retweet, Quote, Tweet and Reply respectively. The tables shows the difference between the influence set values before and after considering the action weights. For Example, at W_8 $I_8(u_1)$ with type weight is equal to 2.25, on the other hand, the W_8 $I_8(u_1)$ without type weight is equal to 3, where each action is equal to 1. And at W_{10} $I_10(u_3)$ with type weight is equal to 1.25, where without the type weight is equal to 4. This difference will change significantly the result of the top influencers based on the action types.

Influence Value: Influence value measured by $f(I_t(S))$ where $I_t()$ is the "weighted" cardinality of the set of users at time t. In particular we take the sum of weighted cardinalities for all the influences sets of all users. More formally, for a given $k > 0$, to find the set of at most k users who collectively achieve the largest influence value S_t^{opt}. We compute the *influence value* for both single user and set of users to identify the most k influential users. For example the *influence value* for single user u_1 is $I_t(u_1) = \{u_1, u_2, u_3\} = 2.25$. As shown in Fig. 4, the *influence value* for set of users u_1 and u_3 is $I(u_1, u_3) = |I(u_1)| + |I(u_3)| = |\{u_1, u_2, u_3\}| + |\{u_1, u_3, u_4, u_5\}| = 3.50$. And the most k users when $k = 2$ is

User	$I_8(u)$	$I_8(u)$, without type weight	$I_8(u)$, with type weight
u_1	$\{(u_1,3), (u_2,5), (u_3,4)\}$	3	2.25
u_2	$\{(u_2,5)\}$	1	1
u_3	$\{(u_1,2), (u_3,3), (u_4,2), (u_5,2)\}$	4	1.25
u_4	$\{(u_4,2)\}$	1	0.25
u_5	$\{(u_4,2), (u_5,2)\}$	2	0.50
u_6	$\{\}$	0	0

Fig. 2. Examples of weighted influence sets at time 8

User	$I_{10}(u)$	$I_8(u)$, without type weight	$I_8(u)$, with type weight
u_1	$\{(u_1,3), (u_3,4)\}$	2	1.25
u_2	$\{(u_2,3), (u_6,4)\}$	2	1.25
u_3	$\{(u_1,2), (u_3,3), (u_4,2), (u_5,2)\}$	4	1.25
u_4	$\{(u_5,2)\}$	1	0.25
u_5	$\{(u_4,4), (u_5,2)\}$	2	1
u_6	$\{(u_6,4)\}$	1	0.75

Fig. 3. Examples of weighted influence sets at time 10

User	$I_8(u)$	$I_8(u)$, with type weight
u_1	$\{(u_1,3), (u_2,5), (u_3,4)\}$	2.25
u_2	$\{(u_2,5)\}$	1
u_3	$\{(u_1,2), (u_3,3), (u_4,2), (u_5,2)\}$	1.25
u_4	$\{(u_4,2)\}$	0.25
u_5	$\{(u_4,2), (u_5,2)\}$	0.50
u_6	$\{\}$	0

Fig. 4. An example of top k influence sets at time 8 where $k = 2$

$S_8^{opt} = \{u_1, u_3\}$, $f(I_8(S_8^{opt})) = 3.5$. To find the set of top k users, we simple sort the users based on their influence value and then take top k one to form the final list.

4   System Architecture

To identifying the most influential users in Twitter, the software passes through five main stages as shown in Fig. 5. The stages are listed in details below.

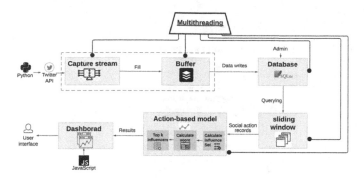

Fig. 5. System architecture.

Stage I - Capturing Data Stream: In this stage the system capture the stream by using Twitter API with Tweepy python library. The stream is filtered based a given restriction or/and list of restrictions (e.g. keyword or/and list of keywords) that is provided by the user. Next, the filtered stream is buffered continuously until either the maximum number of actions is buffered or a maximum time update time limit is exceeded. At this time stream information is flushed to the system database for later processing.

Stage II - Saving Data Stream: The system saves the data stream on SQLite database. The data in the database is organized into three parts of data (as shown in Fig. 6): the older data that used to build the model, the current data within a window, and, the new arriving data from the stream. To keep the size of the database as small as possible, the old data is usually removed when it is no longer has an impact on identifying influencers (illustrated in late stages). To identify the current influencers, the current data is used by model where the current data us defined by the set of data within a window of time. Finally, the new data is saved as we need to balance between handling the stream at different speed and the required computations to identify influencers.

Stage III - Recognizing Current Data: To maintain sufficiently low computational complexity, the system Identify influencers on only some reasonably recent data. The system create a sliding window that contains the most recent actions (possibly leaving out some very recent ones). The window is defined by two user-specified parameters: a window size N and an update interval M, where both N and M are units of time. The window size N controls how many data need to be considered to find influencers. The update interval M controls how frequent the window slides to a new position, leaving out old data points and creating space for new ones.

Stage IV -Identify Influencers: For every new shift in the window, the system updates the model as follows. It inserts the new actions to the model, removes the old ones from the model and their influence set, and compute the influence score.

Fig. 6. Database conceptual orgnization.

Stage V - Visualize the Influence Results: The system displays a dashboard that measure the influence of identified influencers. A JavaScript library is used to implement a dashboard that contain a graph, chart, and diagrams representing the influencers relation with their *influencee* and influence scores.

Stage VI - Parallel Processing and Threading: Since the system is real time system, the system utilizes the parallel processing for efficiency. The system run each stage in the software in parallel with the other stages. There are two ways to implement parallelism: Multiprocessing and Multi-threading, the main difference is multi-threading enables sharing the memory between all threads, while with processes that's not the case.

5   Experiment Results and Discussions

As stated earlier, *AR-SIM* is an extended version of the Stream Influence Maximization problem *SIM*. Wang et al. [5], *SIM* developers, have defined an influencer as a user who performs an action that triggers many actions by other users. In our case, when the weights assigned are equal for all different actions, then our *AR-SIM* is identical to *SIM* model.

Later, Wang et al. 2018 [6] added a location restriction to firstly minimize the influencer results and hence gives a more targeted analysis based on the selected location, and secondly to handle the stream more efficiently. For our solution, we add more restrictions (keyword, location, and language) to the SIM problem. Further, we allow a user to create a complex restrictions from the basic ones using logical operators such as "and", "or" over more than on possible values for a restrictions. We also include other none traditional restrictions, such as a lower threshold on an influencer number of followers, and whether an account is verified.

We evaluate the effectiveness of our proposed solution *AR-SIM* with several real-world scenarios. We focus on two aspects: the impact of incorporate actions types into the model and the ability to handle complex restrictions.

5.1   The Impact of Actions' Types

First, we test the action types consideration and the difference results between identifying the influencers using our proposed model *AR-SIM* and the general *SIM* for the same dataset and the same restrictions. Figure 7 (a) shows the results of the general *SIM* model which all the actions have the same priority "action weight: 1". In contrast, Fig. 7 (b) shows the results of *AR-SIM* model, which considering the action weights as the following: Tweet: 0.25, Retweet: 1, Reply: 0.75, and Quote: 0.50. Note that our selection of the weights suggests, for example, that "Retweet" action shows a strong influence level while "Quote" action is about less influence by half compared to "Retweet". To understand the impact of *AR-SIM* model, we compare the discovered top four influencers from *SIM* model and *AR-SIM* while fixing the time interval, i.e., fixing the dataset. Next we study how the models are handling the stream in real time.

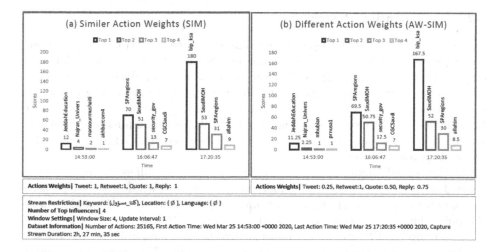

Fig. 7. The impact of action types experiment results.

When time interval is fixed, we can see that all the computed influence scores using *AR-SIM* model are less than the computed score using *SIM* for the same influencer in all three time intervals considered. This is expected since our selections for the actions weights are no more than 1. By investigating the first time interval, we can see clearly how *AR-SIM* changes the significant of an influence level. For example, the gap in the score between 2nd influencer and 3rd influencer has decreases from 2 to 1.25. This suggest that their influence is more closer in our model that simple model. In addition, the gap in the score between 3rd influencer and 4th influencer has decreases from 1 to 0, suggesting those influencer have similar influence level. In some cases it is possible that the gap is large to the point where the order of influencer is changed significantly and some may not be any more in the top list. The results confirm that differentiating the types of social actions, by considering different weight, leads in quantifying and evaluating significantly the social influence. This suggesting that the list of discovered influencers could be significantly different.

For consecutive period of times, the influence scores changed causing influencers to appear or disappear. For example in *SIM* model Fig. 7 (a) the influencers (SaudiMOH) has in second period (B) score (51), and third period (C) has score (53). This suggest that three is new social actions related to SaudiMOH Tweet, causing it to be still a real time influencer in interval (C). On the other hand, the influencer (JeddahEducation) disappeared in the second period (B). This suggest that there is no more new social actions related to JeddahEducation's original tweet, and thus is no more an influencer. As in *SIM*, using *AR-SIM* model, Fig. 7 (b), theses scores also changes over time, but obviously using the computed scores by *AR-SIM* model. The results confirm that the model response effectively to the changes over time and report only active influences.

5.2   Implementing Restrictions

We test *AR-SIM* model/system using different stream restrictions (location, language, and keyword) and other parameters (See Fig. 8). These restrictions are aim to tune the influence analysis to a target needs, and to reduce computational cost. These restriction serve as stream filtering and appears to use the user as search parameters. Beside the mentioned restrictions, the search can be tuned further with user defined action weights, select only verified influencers accounts, set the number of top influencers, and the window settings (which defined the duration of real time analysis).

In the top-left figure, we use a single keyword, use different weights, pick verified account with at least 1000 followers, and set the window size is 4 where the updates is in every 1 min. The stream is captured for about 2 h and 27 min. We build the model and update it with a total of 25,165 tweets.

In the top-right figure, we use multi keywords, use equal weights, and the set window size is 8 where the updates is in every 1.5 min. The stream is captured for about 3 h and 17 min. We build the model and update it with a total of 7,465 tweets.

In the bottom-left figure, we use multi keywords, set the language to Arabic, use equal weights, and set the window size is 4 where the updates is in every 0.5 min. The stream is captured for about 8 h and 38 min. We build the model and update it with a total of 4,140 tweets.

In the bottom-right figure, we use multi keywords, set the langue to Arabic, set the location to "Riyadh", pick verified account with at least 2000 followers, use equal weights, and set the window size is 6 where the updates is in every 3 min. The stream is captured for about 8 min. We build the model and update it with a total of 9,732 tweets.

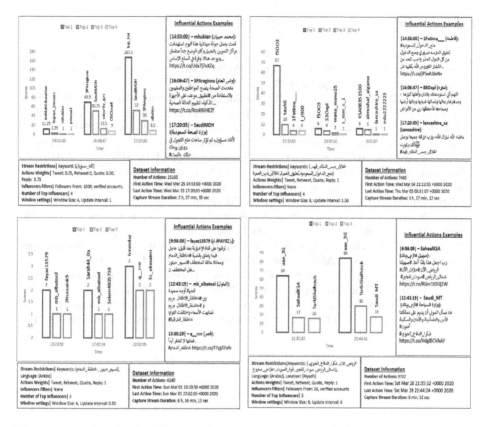

Fig. 8. Examples of *AR-SIM* model/system outputs using different stream restrictions and other user defined options.

6   Conclusion

In this paper, we extend and solve a new version of Stream Influence Maximization *SIM* problem, that is *Action-Aware Restricted-Stream Influence Maximization* problem. We extend the *Action-based* model to represent and weight different social actions. We adopted *Sliding window* model to a capture only the recent actions for real-time analysis. We designed and implemented a system that identifies the most influential users in real-time. The system allows the user to restrict the search using keyword, language and location.

It will be useful to extend this work to include model other than action-aware. For simplicity, we focused on solving the problem with handling sliding windows with a single action shift at a time. It is possible to extend the work with handling multiple action shifts at a time. We aim to explore better approaches to save and handle the stream. We focused only in Twitter data, however, a complete system should also consider other popular social network platforms.

References

1. Goyal, A., Bonchi, F., Lakshmanan, L.V.: Learning influence probabilities in social networks. In: Proceedings of the Third ACM International Conference on Web Search and Data Mining, pp. 241–250. ACM (2010)
2. Kempe, D., Kleinberg, J., Tardos, É.: Maximizing the spread of influence through a social network. In: Proceedings of the Ninth ACM SIGKDD International Conference on Knowledge Discovery and Data Mining, pp. 137–146. ACM (2003)
3. Subbian, K., Aggarwal, C., Srivastava, J.: Mining influencers using information flows in social streams. ACM Trans. Knowl. Discov. Data (TKDD) **10**(3), 26 (2016)
4. Subbian, K., Aggarwal, C.C., Srivastava, J.: Querying and tracking influencers in social streams. In: Proceedings of the Ninth ACM International Conference on Web Search and Data Mining, pp. 493–502. ACM (2016)
5. Wang, Y., Fan, Q., Li, Y., Tan, K.L.: Real-time influence maximization on dynamic social streams. Proc. VLDB Endow. **10**(7), 805–816 (2017)
6. Wang, Y., Li, Y., Fan, J., Tan, K.L.: Location-aware influence maximization over dynamic social streams. ACM Trans. Inf. Syst. (TOIS) **36**(4), 43 (2018)
7. Yang, Y., Wang, Z., Pei, J., Chen, E.: Tracking influential individuals in dynamic networks. IEEE Trans. Knowl. Data Eng. **29**(11), 2615–2628 (2017)
8. Zhuang, H., Sun, Y., Tang, J., Zhang, J., Sun, X.: Influence maximization in dynamic social networks. In: 2013 IEEE 13th International Conference on Data Mining, pp. 1313–1318. IEEE (2013)

Multimodal Analysis of Client Persuasion in Consulting Interactions: Toward Understanding Successful Consulting

Yasushi Amari[1], Shogo Okada[1(✉)], Maiko Matsumoto[2], Kugatsu Sadamitsu[2], and Atsushi Nakamoto[2]

[1] Japan Advanced Institute of Science and Technology, Nomi, Ishikawa, Japan
{y_amari,okada-s}@jaist.ac.jp
[2] Future Corporation, Shinagawa-ku, Tokyo, Japan
{m.matsumoto.rb,k.sadamitsu.ic,a.nakamoto.kh}@future.co.jp

Abstract. To analyze successful consulting processes using multimodal analysis, the aim of this research is to develop a model for recognizing when a client is persuaded by a consultant using multimodal features. These models enable us to analyze the utterances of highly skilled professional consultants in persuading clients. For this purpose, first, we collect a multimodal counseling interaction corpus including audio and spoken dialogue content (manual transcription) on dialogue sessions between a professional beauty counselor and five clients. Second, we developed a recognition model of persuasion labels using acoustic and linguistic features that are extracted from a multimodal corpus by training a machine learning model as a binary classification task. The experimental results show that the persuasion was 0.697 for accuracy and 0.661 for F1-score with bidirectional LSTM.

Keywords: Social signal processing · Multimodal interaction · Consulting interaction · Persuasion

1 Introduction

Professional consultants need to satisfy the requirements of the clients by providing appropriate advice via interaction. In addition, sufficient educational training is required to obtain sufficient consulting skills. To support the skill training for counseling and consulting, this paper focuses on the analysis of the counseling skills of professional counselors. In recent years, many studies have focused on social signal processing [26] (SSP) for developing recognition models of physiological aspects or cognitive performance based on the integration of findings of social physiology and multimodal sensing technology. Common approaches in this research develop recognition models of skill scores annotated by third party coders or participants in the interaction using multimodal features observed in conversation. Though the advantage on the application side of the approach is

© Springer Nature Switzerland AG 2021
G. Meiselwitz (Ed.): HCII 2021, LNCS 12775, pp. 29–40, 2021.
https://doi.org/10.1007/978-3-030-77685-5_3

to predict skill levels and detect people with highly developed skills by using pre-trained recognition models, it is still difficult to analyze how consultants with highly developed skills persuade clients using multimodal time-series data.

To analyze the successful consulting process using multimodal analysis, the aim of this research is to develop a recognition model for when a client is persuaded by a consultant using multimodal features. These models enable us to analyze the utterances of highly skilled professional consultants that persuaded the client. For this purpose, first, we collect a multimodal counseling interaction corpus including audio and spoken dialogue content (manual transcription) on dialogue sessions between a professional beauty counselor and five clients. In addition, we asked these clients (participants) to annotate the persuasion label per utterance. Second, we developed a recognition model of persuasion labels using acoustic and linguistic features that were extracted from a multimodal corpus by training the machine learning model as a binary classification task. The main contributions of this paper are as follows:

Corpus with Client Persuasion. In this paper, we collected a dialogue corpus on beauty counseling in a real situation. The multimodal corpus with persuasion labels was annotated by clients in the counseling interaction settings and is available for analyzing how counselors persuade clients (Sect. 3).

Recognition Model of Client Persuasion. With the dataset, we focus on developing an utterance-based recognition model of client persuasion. The recognition setting of a client's persuasion is unexplored in previous research (Sect. 6.1).

Analysis of Effective Consultant Linguistic Features for Recognizing Client Persuasion. We clarify which linguistic feature of consultant is effective for recognizing when a client has been persuaded (Sect. 6.3).

2   Related Work

The objective of this research is to develop a recognition model of client persuasion to identify the trigger used by a professional consultant to persuade a client. The overall goal of this research is to extract the essence (skills) of how the consultant persuades the client. Many studies focus on automatic assessment communication skills models. The research can be classified from the viewpoint of communication situations and the types of skills. Studies that focus on communication skills in a monolog situation, including public speaking [2,17,27], and social media [16], have been carried out. Other directions for research studies include modeling communication skills in dyadic interactions, including job interview settings [14], group interactions [9,15,18], and human-computer (including robot and virtual humans) interactions [8,22,23]. As target variables related to communication skills, interpersonal communication skills [14,15,23], empathy skills [9], listening skills [22], leadership [18], and public speaking skills [2,17,27] are used. This study's objective is not to analyze the communication process of a person with highly developed skills but to develop a model to predict the skills of participants.

The role of counseling is similar to that of consultation. To develop an automatic analysis model of empathy with behavioral signal processing [28] and implementing counselor agents that are used for physiological health care, many studies have focused on analyzing the behavior of counselors. The skills for listening to patient stories with empathy are required for professional counselors. Therefore, analyzing the multimodal behavior for representing empathy is the central challenge in this research. Xiao et al. proposed a prediction model of counselor empathy measures in motivational interviewing [29]. DeVault et al. [4] presented a virtual human interviewer system designed to create an engaging face-to-face interaction where the user feels comfortable talking and sharing information. Using a corpus collected using the agent system [4,24] presented an analysis of behavioral cues that indicate an opportunity to provide an empathetic response by using a multimodal deep neural network. The common objective in many studies is to model the empathetic response and empathy in the communication process. The objective is different from that of this research because the objective of this paper is to model the persuasion of clients on consultations for face makeup.

3 Data Corpus

3.1 Dyadic Consultant-Client Dialogue Setting

To analyze consultation dialogue by a professional consultant, a female beauty consultant with professional experience of more than 60 years and who engaged in beauty consultant education participated in this experiment. 5 female participants were recruited as clients for the consultation. These participants were counseled for the first time by the consultant. Consultation dialogue data of a total of 5 sessions were recorded using wearable microphones (AmiVoice Front PM01). The average session time was 12.9 min. The objective of the consultation session was to propose the appropriate makeup methodology to clients through counseling based on the client's personality and preference. Following the consulting session, clients are wearing makeup by the consultant. In particular, the main goal of this consultation was to provide the clients with a unique and new point of view on makeup application based on the expertise of the consultant. The makeup method proposed by the counselor was not always accepted by the clients as appropriate, and the consultant had to convince the client with explanations based on evidence and past experience.

3.2 Annotation

We asked clients to annotate when they were persuaded after the consultation session by watching recorded speech data with manual transcription. In this study, to annotate the label to the accurate segment interval, utterances of the consultant and client were segmented manually, and dialogue contents were scripted by two coders. When a short pause with less than 2 s existed between consequent utterances of the consultant, we merged these consequent utterances into a segment. Utterances of the client were also chunked as one segment in the same manner when such a short pause was observed. We defined the chunked segment as the subject of annotation (a sample for machine learning), and coders (clients) annotated whether they were persuaded by the utterances of the consultant. We define the segment (the unit of sample) as a exchange, which consists of client utterance followed by consultant utterance. The number of persuaded scene labels annotated by each client is shown in Table 1. The exchange-level annotation is available as labeled data to develop a recognition model of the persuaded scene, to analyze the linguistic and acoustic features used in the persuasion. The minimum number was 64, the maximum number was 142, the total number of persuasion labels was 223 and total number of samples was 525.

Table 1. Number of persuaded scene labels per client

Client	Convinced scene	Total	Convinced/Total
A	23	92	0.250
B	14	64	0.219
C	43	101	0.426
D	81	126	0.643
E	62	142	0.437
Total	223	525	0.425

4   Multimodal Feature Extraction

We extracted the acoustic features from audio data, which were segmented manually. We also extracted the linguistic features based on manual transcription. All feature values were normalized using the Z-score method. We summarize the details of the feature set in Table 2.

4.1   Acoustic Features

The acoustic features were extracted from the speech signal of an utterance segment. We used the audio processing tool OpenSMILE[1] to extract the acoustic features. The features of 1,582 dimensions included in the INTERSPEECH 2010 Paralinguistic Challenge feature set [19] were extracted using this tool. These features included the loudness as the normalized intensity, mel-frequency cepstral coefficients 0–14, the logarithmic power of the mel-frequency bands 0–7 (distributed over a range from 0 to 8 kHz), the 8-line spectral pair frequencies computed from 8 LPC coefficients, the envelope of the smoothed fundamental frequency contour, and the voicing probability based on the fundamental frequency.

---

[1] https://www.audeering.com/opensmile/.

Table 2. Summarize the details of the feature set for each modality

Modality	Features
Acoustic	PCM loudness
	MFCC [0–14]
	log Mel Freq. Band [0–7]
	LSP frequency [0–7]
	F0 by sub-harmonic sum
	F0 envelope
	Voicing probability
	Jitter local
	Jitter DDP
	Shimmer local
Linguistic	Word count per PoS type
	Number of letters in words
	Word repetition
	Content of the vocabulary
	Word sentiment
	Linguistic features of previous utterance

4.2 Linguistic Features

We extracted linguistic features from manual transcription data. The linguistic features were extracted from the transcriptions using the Japanese morphological analysis tool MeCab [12] because all of the participants were Japanese and spoke in Japanese. First, the sentence was segmented into word sets by the tool. Second, the PoS type and filler were automatically annotated to each word in the word set. The same linguistic feature set was extracted for the consultant and clients. The linguistic features are as follows:

Word Count Per PoS Type: We counted the spoken words for each grammatical construction or PoS: "noun", "proper noun", "verb", "conjunction", "adjective" and "interjection". In addition, the word "filler" was counted. The number of features was 7.

Number of Letters in Words: To capture the length of the spoken words, we counted the characters (called "Hiragana") in words. The number of characters captures how many words with many characters participants spoke.

Word Repetition: Word repetition is effective for delivering important information. When a word appeared in an utterance more than once during the session, the number of occurrences of the part-of-speech for that word was counted. The parts of speech counted were nouns, verbs, and adjectives. The number of features was 3.

Content of the Vocabulary: We extracted the features based on a word-embedding method to analyze the content of the vocabulary in the consultation. The word-embedding model was trained on the Japanese Wikipedia corpus [21]. The feature extraction procedure was as follows: Vector V_{w_i} in the (embedded) vector space of word w_i by using the model was summed for all words in an utterance, where symbols, particles, and auxiliary verbs were removed from the word set. The average and variance in each element in V for all spoken utterances were calculated as features. The dimension of the vector space was set to 200, and thus, the number of features was 400 (mean and variance of 200 elements in a vector).

Word Sentiment: In consulting sessions, consultants often advise with positive language expression. From this background, the sentiment of words is an effective feature for capturing the positive or negative words used in a consultation. For this purpose, we used the Japanese Sentiment Polarity Dictionary [6,11] of words annotated with their semantic orientation to analyze the sentiment orientation of words in spoken dialogue. We extracted the word sentiment features as follows: We counted the number of word w_i in the utterance, which was found in the dictionary word set by matching word w_i with the word set. Let the number of words with a positive orientation be N_{pos} and that with a negative orientation be N_{neg}, the sentiment feature l_s was calculated as $(N_{pos} - N_{neg})/(N_{pos} + N_{neg})$. If words in the dictionary were not included in utterance, $l_s = 0$. In addition, N_{pos} and N_{neg} are also used as features.

Linguistic Features of the Previous Utterance: We extracted all feature sets except the word2vec feature from the previous utterance $(t - 1)$ as the feature set of the current utterance (t) considering the time-series dependency of the spoken utterance.

5 Experiment

Three research questions are addressed in order to analyze multimodal features that were effective in recognizing whether a client was persuaded during counseling.

[**RQ1:**] Which features of consultant or client are effective to improve the recognition performance?
[**RQ2:**] Does temporal context in dialogue contribute to estimate the persuasion label?
[**RQ3:**] Which linguistic features of consultant contribute to detect client persuasion?

5.1 Preprocessing and Evaluation

To preprocess for classification modeling, we reduced the number of dimensions of features using PCA. PCA was performed for specific feature groups with a high dimensional vector. The specific feature groups were composed of (i) acoustic features, (ii) the mean of word2vec, and (iii) the variance in word2vec. PCA was performed for a total of six feature groups (each feature (i)–(iii) extracted from the consultant and clients). We set a cumulative contribution rate of 95% as the threshold for dimension reduction. After dimension reduction, the number of acoustic features was 232 for counselor and 248 for clients. The number of word2vec features was 183 for counselor and 110 for clients. In addition, the feature selection with the Kolmogorov-Smirnov (KS) test was conducted with a significance level of 5% in all datasets. To evaluate the model, cross-validation testing by leave-one-client-session-out was conducted. We report the accuracy and F1-score of the test results as classification accuracy.

5.2 Machine Learning Models

We used a linear support vector machine (SVM) [3] model as the base model to compare the contributions of multimodal features or features from both participants. To explore an accurate model with high classification accuracy and explore how the temporal context is effective for this task, the linear SVM model was compared with random forest (RF) [1], XGBoost [25], and Feed forward deep neural network (DNN), long-short term memory (LSTM) [7] and bidirectional LSTM (BLSTM) [5]. The hyper parameters of SVM, RF and XGBoost were optimized using a 4-fold cross-validation (CV) scheme in training dataset. The detail of hyper parameter tuning is given in Appendix A.

DNN was composed of feed-forward neural network with multiple fully connected layers and with dropout [20] (rate $= 0.5$) after each layer. The network architecture is composed of two middle layers, 128 units per layer. We set the batch size to 64 and the number of epochs to 50. For implementation of LSTM and BLSTM, a single LSTM hidden layer with 128 units is used to extract feature from the sequence input data with T exchanges, followed by a dropout [20] (rate $= 0.3$). The LSTM layer was followed by a fully connected layer to learn the LSTM output, followed by two fully connected layer. A output layer is used for estimating labels. We set the batch size to 128 and the number of epochs to 100. And set the learning rate to 0.004. For DNN, LSTM and BLSTM, binary cross-entropy function is used as a loss function, ReLU [13] for the activation function, and Adam [10] is used as the optimization. The learning rate of Adam is set to 0.001 for DNN and 0.004 for LSTM and BLSTM.

6   Experiment Result

We compared the classification performance of the multimodal features and analyzed the contribution of each modality in recognizing whether a client is persuaded during counseling. "Acoustic" and "linguistic" are represented as A and L, respectively.

6.1   Classification Results

Table 3 shows the binary classification accuracy and F1-score of the SVM trained with the multimodal feature set of both participants. All results with each modal feature per participant (consultant or client) were better than that of the majority baseline. In Table 3, the best accuracy and F1-score for models that were trained using the consultant feature set of 0.670 and 0.575 using acoustic features, respectively. The best accuracy and F1-score for models with the client feature set were 0.653 and 0.597 using multimodal features, respectively. The best accuracy and F1-score of the models with the feature set of consultant and client were 0.670 and 0.608, respectively, which were the best accuracy and F1 score in all models.

Comparing the accuracy between unimodal models, the acoustic features were more effective than linguistic features on both accuracy and F1-score measures in all experiments. This result shows that the acoustic features were more important than the linguistic features to this task. Comparing the accuracy between the unimodal model and multimodal model, multimodal fusion improved the best unimodal accuracy when features from clients were used (0.634 to 0.653) and when features from both participants were used (0.651 to 0.670), respectively. Conversely, the multimodal fusion did not improve the accuracy when features from the counselor were used, and the acoustic model obtained the best accuracy. Comparing the accuracy between the consultant model and client model in unimodal models, better accuracy and F1-score were obtained by the consultant models than those obtained by the clients in both models with acoustic and linguistic feature sets. These results show that although the persuasion label was annotated by the clients, multimodal features observed from the consultant were effective in recognizing the client's persuasion.

Answer to RQ1: The feature set of consultant was more effective than the client. In addition, the recognition performance was improved by fusing the consultant and client feature sets.

Table 3. Binary classification results with the multimodal feature set of counselor and clients. The majority baseline for accuracy was 0.575.

Modality	Consultant			Client			Consultant + Client		
	A	L	A+L	A	L	A+L	A	L	A+L
Accuracy	**0.670**	0.596	0.650	0.634	0.577	0.653	0.651	0.575	**0.670**
F1-score	0.575	0.485	0.551	0.525	0.476	0.597	0.565	0.506	**0.608**

6.2   Comparison of Machine Learning Models

Table 4 shows the binary classification accuracy and F1-score of the SVM, random forest, XGBoost, DNN, LSTM and BLSTM trained with the multimodal feature set that is extracted from both the consultant and client. LSTM and

BLSTM are trained with time-seres features of T exchanges which is defined in Sect. 3.2. The comparison among models enable us to analyze appropriate model for this task and the importance of time-series features (temporal context) to classify the client's persuasion.

Table 4. Binary classification results of SVM, random forest, XGBoost, DNN, LSTM and BLSTM.

Classifier	SVM	Random forest	XGBoost	DNN	LSTM	BLSTM		
					$T = 6$	$T = 4$	$T = 5$	$T = 6$
Accuracy	0.670	0.532	0.686	0.691	0.594	0.651	0.690	**0.697**
F1-score	0.608	0.450	0.604	0.623	0.532	0.642	**0.661**	0.654

Table 4 shows that the best accuracy was 0.697, which is obtained by BLSTM with six exchanges ($T = 6$) and second best accuracy was obtained by DNN (0.691). The best F1-score of persuasion label was 0.661, which was obtained by BLSTM with $T = 5$. It means that deep neural network techniques promise to improve the classification performance. BLSTM with $T = 6$ improved the accuracy of LSTM with $T = 6$ by 0.103, so it is found that using both past and future temporal contexts in dialogue is effective to classify the persuasion label. On the comparison of F1 score between DNN and BLSTM, BLSTM which is trained with temporal contexts ($T = [4, 5, 6]$) improved the F1-score of DNN by 0.019, 0.038 and 0.031, respectively.

Answer to RQ2: The temporal context in advice of the consultant is a key factor whether clients are persuaded.

6.3   Linguistic Feature Analysis of Consultant

To analyze how linguistic features are observed from professional consultant on persuading the client, BLSTM ($T = 6$), which has the highest accuracy in Sect. 6.2 was trained by removing a linguistic feature group of consultant one by one. The groups are linguistic features are "Word count per PoS type", "Number of letters in words", "Word repetition", "Content of the vocabulary", and "Word sentiment". If the evaluation metrics consisting of accuracy and F1-score degraded, the removed feature group was effective for the classification. In contrast, if the evaluation metrics improved, the removed feature group was not effective for classification. Table 5 shows the accuracy and F1-score of the BLSTM trained with linguistic feature of consultant, after each feature group was excluded. "Diff" denotes the difference in accuracy and F1-score between when all feature groups were used and when one feature group was removed. In Table 5, the feature group of the "Content of the vocabulary" was the most effective (accuracy: +0.118, F1-score: +0.088) in recognizing the label. In addition, the feature groups that contributed to both accuracy and F1-score were "Number of letters in words", "Content of the vocabulary" and "Word sentiment".

Moreover, to analyze features in these two groups, we perform the Mann-Whitney U test on "Number of letters in words" and positive words count as a representative of "Word sentiment". As a result, the p-value for "Number of letters in words" was 0.0007 and the p-value for positive words count was 0.0010. The mean value of "Number of letters in words" for the "no persuaded" and "persuaded" was 41.5 and 47.5, respectively. That of positive words count was 0.9 and 1.3, respectively. The results show that clients are more likely to be persuaded when the values of the number of characters in a utterance and positive words count are high. This indicates that clients tend to be persuaded when the consultant often use many words or long words and words with positive polarity. The box plot for these two features are shown in Appendix B.

Answer to RQ3: "Content of the vocabulary" was the most effective features to detect client persuasion. The amount of words and the polarity of words were also important to persuade the client.

Table 5. Contribution of each linguistic feature group for persuasion label classification.

	Accuracy		F1-score	
Consalutant L	0.602		0.481	
Removed features	Accuracy	Diff	F1-score	Diff
Word count per PoS type	0.592	+0.010	0.507	−0.026
Number of letters in words	0.579	+0.023	0.426	+0.055
Word repetition	0.590	+0.011	0.506	−0.024
Content of the vocabulary	0.484	+0.118	0.394	+0.088
Word sentiment	0.587	+0.015	0.451	+0.031

7 Conclusion

We presented a recognition model of client persuasion for analyzing how the client is persuaded in the consultation process by a professional consultant with a novel consultant interaction corpus. The best results were obtained when the BLSTM-trained multimodal features of the consultant and client were used simultaneously with 0.697 for accuracy and 0.661 for F1-score. In addition, we clarified which linguistic feature of consultant is effective for recognizing when a client has been persuade with ablation test. The important future direction is to collect data from consultants with various kinds of experiments and compare how to persuade the clients.

Acknowledgements. We sincerely appreciate Be · Fine Co. ltd. and Ms. Teruko Kobayashi who is the professional beauty counselor.

References

1. Breiman, L.: Random forests. Mach. Learn. **45**, 5–32 (2001)
2. Chen, L., Feng, G., Joe, J., Leong, C.W., Kitchen, C., Lee, C.M.: Towards automated assessment of public speaking skills using multimodal cues. In: Proceedings of the ACM International Conference on Multimodal Interaction, pp. 200–203 (2014)
3. Cortes, C., Vapnik, V.: Support vector networks. Mach. Learn. **20**, 273–297 (1995)
4. DeVault, D., et al.: SimSensei kiosk: a virtual human interviewer for healthcare decision support. In: Proceedings of the International Conference on Autonomous Agents and Multi-agent Systems, pp. 1061–1068 (2014)
5. Graves, A., Schmidhuber, J.: Framewise phoneme classification with bidirectional LSTM and other neural network architectures. Neural Netw. **18**, 602–610 (2005)
6. Higashiyama, M., Inui, K., Matsumoto, Y.: Learning sentiment of nouns from selectional preferences of verbs and adjectives. In: Proceedings of the Annual Meeting of the Association for Natural Language Processing, pp. 584–587 (2008)
7. Hochreiter, S., Schmidhuber, J.: Long short-term memory. Neural Comput. **9**(8), 1735–1780 (1997)
8. Hoque, M.E., Courgeon, M., Martin, J.-C., Mutlu, B., Picard, R.W.: MACH: My automated conversation coach. In: Proceedings of the ACM International Joint Conference on Pervasive and Ubiquitous Computing, pp. 697–706 (2013)
9. Ishii, R., Otsuka, K., Kumano, S., Higashinaka, R., Tomita, J.: Analyzing gaze behavior and dialogue act during turn-taking for estimating empathy skill level. In: Proceedings of the ACM International Conference on Multimodal Interaction, pp. 31–39 (2018)
10. Kingma, D., Adam, J.B.: A method for stochastic optimization. In: Proceedings of the International Conference on Learning Representations, pp. 1–15 (2015)
11. Nozomi, K., Kentaro, I., Yuji, M., Kenji, T.: Collecting evaluative expressions for opinion extraction. J. Nat. Lang. Process. **12**(3), 203–222 (2005)
12. Kudo, T., Yamamoto, K., Matsumoto, Y.: Applying conditional random fields to Japanese morphological analysis. In: Proceedings of the Conference on Empirical Methods in Natural Language Processing, pp. 230–237 (2004)
13. Nair, V., Hinton, G.E.: Rectified linear units improve Restricted Boltzmann machines. In: Proceedings of the International Conference on Machine Learning, pp. 807–814 (2010)
14. Nguyen, L.S., Frauendorfer, D., Mast, M.S., Gatica-Perez, D.: Hire me: Computational inference of hirability in employment interviews based on nonverbal behavior. IEEE Trans. Multimed. **16**(4), 1018–1031 (2014)
15. Okada, S., et al.: Estimating communication skills using dialogue acts and nonverbal features in multiple discussion datasets. In: Proceedings of the ACM International Conference on Multimodal Interaction, pp. 169–176 (2016)
16. Park, S., Shim, H.S., Chatterjee, M., Sagae, K., Morency, L.-P.: Computational analysis of persuasiveness in social multimedia: a novel dataset and multimodal prediction approach. In: Proceedings of the ACM International Conference on Multimodal Interaction, pp. 50–57 (2014)
17. Ramanarayanan, V., Leong, C.W., Chen, L., Feng, G., Suendermann-Oeft, D.: Evaluating speech, face, emotion and body movement time-series features for automated multimodal presentation scoring. In: Proceedings of the ACM International Conference on Multimodal Interaction, pp. 23–30 (2015)

18. Sanchez-Cortes, D., Aran, O., Mast, M.S., Gatica-Perez, D.: A nonverbal behavior approach to identify emergent leaders in small groups. IEEE Trans. Multimed. **14**, 816–832 (2012)
19. Schuller, B., Steidl, S., Batliner, A., Burkhardt, F., Devillers, L., Müller, C., Narayanan, S.: The interspeech 2010 paralinguistic challenge. In: Proceedings of the Annual Conference of the International Speech Communication Association, pp. 2794–2797 (2010)
20. Srivastava, N., Hinton, G.E., Krizhevsky, A., Sutskever, I., Salakhutdinov, R.: Dropout: a simple way to prevent neural networks from overfitting. J. Mach. Learn. Res. **15**(1), 1929–1958 (2014)
21. Suzuki, M., Matsuda, K., Sekine, S., Okazaki, N., Inui, K.: A joint neural model for fine-grained named entity classification of wikipedia articles. IEICE Trans. Inf. Syst. **E101.D**(1), 73–81 (2018)
22. Tanaka, H., Negoro, H., Iwasaka, H., Nakamura, S.: Listening skills assessment through computer agents. In: Proceedings of the ACM International Conference on Multimodal Interaction, pp. 492–496 (2018)
23. Tanaka, H., et al.: Automated social skills trainer. In: Proceedings of the ACM International Conference on Inteligent User Interface, pp. 17–27 (2015)
24. Tavabi, L., Stefanov, K., Gilani, S.N., Traum, D., Soleymani, M.: Multimodal learning for identifying opportunities for empathetic responses. In: Proceedings of the ACM International Conference on Multimodal Interaction, pp. 95–104 (2019)
25. Tianqi, C., Carlos, G.: XGBoost: a scalable tree boosting system. In: Proceedings of the International Conference on Knowledge Discovery and Data Mining, pp. 785–794 (2016)
26. Vinciarelli, A., Pantic, M., Bourlard, H.: Social signal processing: survey of an emerging domain. Image Vis. Comput. **27**(12), 1743–1759 (2009)
27. Wörtwein, T., Chollet, M., Schauerte, B., Morency, L.-P., Stiefelhagen, R., Scherer, S.: Multimodal public speaking performance assessment. In: Proceedings of ACM International Conference on Multimodal Interaction, pp. 43–50 (2015)
28. Xiao, B., Imel, Z.E., Georgiou, P., Atkins, D.C., Narayanan, S.S.: Computational analysis and simulation of empathic behaviors: a survey of empathy modeling with behavioral signal processing framework. Curr. Psych. Rep. **18**(5), 1–11 (2016)
29. Xiao, B., Imel, Z.E., Georgiou, P.G., Atkins, D.C., Narayanan, S.S.: "rate my therapist": Automated detection of empathy in drug and alcohol counseling via speech and language processing. PLOS ONE **10**(12), 1–15 (2015)

Advertising on the Web: Soft Narration or Hard Promotion

Karine Berthelot-Guiet[(⊠)]

Celsa Sorbonne Université, Paris, France
karine.berthelot-guiet@sorbonne-universite.fr

Abstract. Brands are ubiquitous for the last years, they are present in almost every space on the web and especially in social computing, social networks and social media. Their presence is linked to different aims and accompanied by comments. The professional point of view focuses on the idea that social media provide the possibility of a conversation based on transparency, equality, and proximity. Computer systems and algorithms have been developed, refined and expressly designed to facilitate the identification of "consumers" as they navigate and supposedly allow the production and broadcasting of a tailor-made advertising message.

What form of advertising is finally presented on the web? A first set appears to work more on the inventiveness than on the algorithm to reach a public between *unadvertising* and *hyperadvertising*. In both cases, advertising tends to work on the spectacular side, with complex and refined narratives. A second appears to go back to the beginning of marketing and advertising in terms of narration, design and discourse. On the web, social networks and replay and streaming platforms, advertising hype is making a great and maybe regretful comeback. On the other hand, advertising falls back on pure promotion. At the same times, advertising finds old flaws, outside the regulatory systems: we see "réclame" reappearing on social networks. This communication will aim to analyze contemporary forms of advertising forged by and for the machines of the web

Keywords: Brand · Digital advertising · Social media · Advertising literacy · Native advertising · Advertising hype

1 Introduction

Brands are ubiquitous for a long time, especially in the last decades in all media, including the Internet; they are present in almost every space on the web, especially in social computing, social networks, and social media [1, 10, 11, 14–16]. Their presence serves several purposes, and accompanying comments are diverse. The professional perspective focuses mainly on the idea that social media provide a conversation based on transparency, equality, and proximity between the brands and their consumers/publics [15, 19, 24].

Advertising on the web has been around for more than 20 years, which allows us to take a step back from the now recurring and common productions. We can see how, years after years, metamorphoses and hybridizations coming one after another, along

© Springer Nature Switzerland AG 2021
G. Meiselwitz (Ed.): HCII 2021, LNCS 12775, pp. 41–53, 2021.
https://doi.org/10.1007/978-3-030-77685-5_4

with the fact that web users are developing skills and abilities regarding digital advertising literacy [1, 10, 11, 18, 20–22]. They have acquired a capacity to identify and appreciate brand discourses and show an ability to identify the traits of marketing and advertising discourses as such [10, 23].

Simultaneously, computer systems and other algorithms have been developed, refined, and expressly designed to facilitate the identification of "consumers" as they navigate and supposedly allow the production and broadcasting of a tailor-made advertising message. This is what marketing and advertising professionals commonly talk about in dedicated forums and publications. The promise of the ultimate algorithm, of ultra-pertinent advertising, of the perfect match between product and consumer, of artificial intelligence at the consumer society's service, all appear to be already well-established professional myths [18, 19, 22, 29].

What forms of advertising are present on the web?

A first set appears to work more on the inventiveness than on the algorithm to reach a public: at least two solutions have occurred in professional uses: one is about erasing a maximum of classical advertising features, called unadvertising, the other one is about optimizing advertising quality and/or trying to find new media or transforming things into a media for advertising, called hyperadvertising. In both cases, advertising tends to work on the spectacular side, with complex and refined narratives [11, 15].

A second appears to go back to the beginning of marketing and advertising in terms of narration, design, and discourse. On the web, social networks, and replay and streaming platforms, advertising hype makes a great and somewhat unfortunate comeback. On the other hand, advertising falls back on pure promotion. Platform and social networks put us face to face with the promotional offers that algorithmic calculations consider relevant; no narration or so little, a product demonstration at best. The brand, the product, the price, in their raw state, in order to trigger the famous Pavlovian reflex. At the same time, advertising finds old flaws outside the regulatory systems: we see "réclame" reappearing on social networks. "Réclame" was a widespread form of advertising in French newspapers of the nineteenth century; the advertisement misled the reader by taking the form of a small article or short story written by the journalist holding the column. It could make the reader believe that it was news and not advertising [14, 16, 26–28].

This communication will aim to analyze contemporary forms of advertising promoted by and for the web machines.

2 A History of Brand Discourses on the Web a History of

2.1 From Advertising Banners to Brand Conversations: New Advertising Formats on the Web

Internet advertising officially appeared on an American site as a banner in 1994, developed very quickly, and became an important area for brand communication and a major, if not the only, growth driver for advertising agencies [14]. As early as 1995, the Yahoo! site included advertising. In 1996, the first advertising banner appeared in France. In 1998, Hewlett Packard offered the first interactive advertising. At the same time, systems for identifying "advertising effectiveness" on the web were designed. In 2000, the first advertising on cell phones started in Finland, and the "pop up" format appeared as well as "flash" and "rich media". The standards for online advertising began to be set, and the IAB[1] defined the rectangle and the skyscraper. Formats constantly evolved under the impetus of new computer systems. Thanks to an agreement with Yahoo!, Google became the leader in the online advertising market. In 2000, internet advertising spending accounted for 0.5% and was mainly in banner design and placement. In 2008, banners and sponsored links were prominent with the emergence of new possibilities related to web 2.0: blogs, online games, sites like Second Life, community sites, cell phone advertising.

In the mid-2000s, the idea of "brand content" and the notion of "conversation" with brands appeared on the advertising market [15]. As early as 2006, Maurice Lévy, CEO of Publicis, the first advertising French group, introduced the term; in 2007, Havas put it forward, and, in 2008, Publicis included "conversation" in its annual report. Advertisers widely promote the emergence of a new communications paradigm. Driven by a group of American consultants, the marketing and commercial communication environment started to experience a massive conversion to the virtues of conversation, thought of as a sort of communicational panacea, adorned with all the qualities that advertising was not supposed to have. The conversation is promoted as a pacified, egalitarian communication that would put brands and consumers on the same hierarchical level. Under the combined action of all kinds of agencies, brands will, therefore, if they don't always know why or really have something to say, start to produce Facebook pages, Twitter and other Instagram accounts to participate in the coveted conversation.

"Brands are in conversation", "markets are conversations", "marketing is conversational": all these are bits and pieces of a discourse that is now commonplace in the professional field of marketing and communication. What does this prolix display of conversation tell us about market communication? What is the nature of this conversational marketing? What communicational norms and imaginaries are at work? What does this hypermediated chatter tell us about the profession, advertising, and its discourse?

The commercial vogue of conversational marketing calls for an investigation into the nature of the conversation produced. From a linguistic point of view, the conversation is a paradoxical communicational activity that everyone thinks they know, that everyone practices without thinking about it, which seems obvious and straightforward, whereas it is complex, codified, hierarchical, and agonistic. Professionals in commercial communication and marketing define conversation as both the most natural activity in the world and the object of a necessary mastery permitted or promised to brands by implementing various professional tools [12, 13, 15].

A text produced by Anglo-Saxon consultants and entitled the Clue Train Manifesto[2] is known by professionals as the initiator of the brand conversation. This text describes a pre-capitalist conversation as real, direct, which has disappeared with the advent of the industrial era and the appearance of mass production and consumption. The argument postulates the disappearance of all this in the industrial era, until the appearance and the rise of the Internet, and above all of "2.0" version of the network, which allows the production of content and exchange through intermediary applications. The "web

---

[1] International Advertising Bureau.

[2] https://www.cluetrain.com.

conversation" inherits the attributes given to its great ancestor; it is just as irenic and idealized. Moreover, this conversation is built as opposed to the communication of influence, namely advertising and "public relations", renamed "flacks" and "huckters". It goes even further by stating, from the human/market perspective, "We are immune to advertising. Just forget it".

In the first place, the conversation is related to an ancient state, to an idealized commercial exchange stage, before the industrial era, in which selling was, supposedly, the conclusion of a conversation between people in a place called a market. From this irenic and idealized vision of conversation (and selling), the authors produce the conclusion that has become famous in the field of marketing: "markets are conversations". Therefore, the conversation is an ideal place for exchange where truth is the order of the day. From then on, the need for brands to take these conversations into account, or even enter into them, not to say lead them, is put forward by the authors. The path is thus mapped out for consulting agencies that must enable brands to enter the conversation, which is a hybrid production, largely consensual, both innate (for consumers) and to be learned (for brands), a communication that is intended to be in a horizontal, free from hierarchical positions and power or influence. Marketing web conversations are opposed to the top-down verticality of advertising, supposedly linked to brands' dominant hierarchical position [15].

Conversation allows us to analyze the rise, in contemporary brand discourses, of a partition between "form" and "content" that tends to dissociate the advertising essence of messages, their principle of influence or advertising, and the advertising form of the message, in the classical sense of the term. This is particularly important since brands and advertising evolve in a continuing context of consumer suspicion against marketing, advertising, and brands [28].

Faced with a problematic social reception, some brands keep "classic" advertising and develop other forms of communication whose common denominator, under the abundant diversity of proposals, is the avoidance of the usual advertising forms and the search for redenomination or even "redefinition" of the communication activity carried out in this way. Among these forms, we find brand blogs, consumer magazines, the remuneration of private individuals' blogs by brands, the production of "brand films", brand museums, games, advertising "co-production" platforms, and so on. All of them allow brands to speak out without advertising. Marketing professionals praise them as transparent, immediate, without mediation, enabling to reset the information versus communication partition into an "information-communication" versus advertising one, highlighting participation and conversation. The recurring themes are interactivity, immateriality, and democracy, which turn out to be among the most common utopias linked to the web [13, 15].

Thus, marketing and advertising professionals produce an ideological discourse on the communicational proposals of brands that give precious indications on the communicational thought on which they rely. Conversational products such as social media accounts are "humanizing" brands since they enable embodiment and a kind of human-to-human communication. Allegedly "transparent" and "informational," these communication products seek to avoid suspicion and propose a redefinition of the limits of information and communication; the brand discourse is communicational while remaining outside the notion of influence, therefore advertising.

2.2 Soft Narrations: Brand Conversations and Advertising Show Between Unadvertising and Hyperadvertising

Brand conversations take place in a global evolution of advertising and brand discourses, on and outside the web, that also happened during the last 20 years. Advertising evolves in a general context of continuous transformation. This professional field effectively identifies new techniques, technologies, supports, and media likely to serve the advertising message by allowing renewal of the discourse, increased visibility, and strong contemporaneity [1–4, 11, 13, 22, 27].

Brand managers, both in companies and in the agencies that advise them, face a complex economic and social context that is, to some extent, unfavorable to brands in general and advertising in particular. Contemporary media readily echo a general attitude of suspicion and opposition to advertising [16, 28]. Brands are judged by their actions and those of the companies that own them. It is frequent and socially valued to declare that one does not like advertising. Furthermore, all the more so since we live in societies and environments where advertising is omnipresent and rhythms, or at the very least, accompanies daily life.

Simultaneously, the advertising inter-profession has developed a strong shared belief that traditional forms of advertising are less and less adapted to the rise of anti-advertising in the general public, the saturation of traditional advertising spaces. Moreover, this professional sector relies on the activity of agencies which must regularly find growth relays to maintain a viable economic activity [11, 16, 22].

In this overall context, two types of strategies have emerged in professional practices:

– the first, uncovered and worked on by Caroline Marti [15, 24, 25], consists in minimizing advertising forms by erasing them as much as possible: this is unadvertising,
– the second, on the contrary, maximizes the advertising aspects [10, 11, 13, 15], either through a quantitative work consisting of producing new media or transforming into media or through a qualitative work that works qualitatively on advertising, often through a strong aestheticization and hypertrophied semiotization: this is hyperpublicitarisation.

These denominations result from transversal research results that give a name and a logic to varied professional productions, often produced on an ad hoc basis. From a professional perspective, unadvertising and hyperadvertising are product placement, brand content, sponsorship, programming, conversational marketing, etc. [15].

Unadvertising is a combination of communication strategies designed to avoid or minimize the classic forms of advertising:

- By entering into pre-existing media forms (product placement whether on television, in the cinema, or games or television programming). Sponsorship of television programs is also part of this.
- By adopting forms of communication that are supposed to redistribute communicational roles as in social networks or media.
- By imitating either existing media productions (consumer magazines, branded web series such as Easy to Assemble by Ikea, branded games), or cultural productions or devices such as for branded films, branded books, or branded exhibitions and museums.

Hyperadvertising works essentially on the hypertrophy of advertising aspects. It is not a question of hiding the nature of the message, but, on the contrary, of maximizing the advertising presence. When this work is quantitative, it is, in general, a search for continuous media creation in order to transform elements of daily life into ephemeral or perennial advertising media. When the work is qualitative, it increases the message's semiotic densification through creative and/or sophisticated aesthetic work. New formats are being experimented with, such as exceptionally long television commercials, requiring exceptional film work, magazine advertisements printed on very high quality, heavyweight and extremely glossy paper, etc.

What are the devices proposed over the last fifteen years under the name of conversation? These productions have the metacommunicative capacity to discourse on "brand conversation" while putting it into action. Conversation in marketing productions, be it a blog or a dedicated space (site, forum, social networks), is an activity that involves individuals who communicate in a participative way. This conversation appears as pacified or peaceful in appearance; its themes are light. In the first period, the spaces dedicated to brand conversations seemed to delegate the discourse to the participants. However, formally, they were made up of numerous visual and thematic frameworks that did not leave much freedom of intervention beyond giving an opinion on one or more products, recipes, or discovering new aspects of the brand.

Brand conversation devices are designed to serve the market transaction [15, 24]. Those who wish to participate must register, fill out a database and participate in questionnaires. The brand is omnipresent visually and symbolically because it is the source of all the discourses. This is particularly flagrant on social media. The proposed conversation is instead a series of questions/stimulus-answers; it takes place in a closed space, made of delimitations, text zones nested one inside another, and entirely framed by the brand's signs. The conversation produced by the brands is always hierarchical because the brand tries to keep the lead voice. The invitation to enter into the conversation, multiplied by the repetition of the injunctions to speak, is more important than the exchanges' reality.

Conversation between brands and consumers mostly takes place now through social networks. It evolves between several modalities: soliloquy when the brand is not followed, dissensus for brands often criticized (a new form of long-term crisis communication), pure sales pitch for brands that use social networks for hard selling (couponing, sales promotions, putting the consumer to work through numerous mini-surveys). Ideal brand conversation, as describes by professionals, is finally very exceptional.

Most of the time, comments on brands social networks accounts are not dialogues between a public/consumers and the brands or even between commentators, especially since most social network systems isolate the comments; they do not give them to read by automatically closing access to their content to propose instead a quantification of "like", "share" and "comments". These systems create almost the opposite of a conversation since they convert into numbers, and therefore into a quantified audience, what should be qualitative and dialogical. However, the large number of users registered to follow these social media branded pages encourages us to take seriously what happens within these spaces [11]. It is, indeed, essential to understand what all or part of these registrants is doing if they are not conversing with brands. Therefore, we propose to consider contemporary forms of communication on social networks from an advertising show's angle.

Some Facebook, Instagram, and TikTok brand accounts look more like hyperadvertising productions where the brands are omnipresent with discursive contents very strongly linked to their advertising discourse. The advertising show is blatant, and it can be for brands like M&M the primary goal of these accounts much more than conversation. Some participants qualify the "authors" of these messages as marketing and advertising professionals: "Simultaneous faint, candle falls to the floor.... the absolute best M&M commercial ever!!!!!!", "every time it hits... yo u're crazy about advertisers", "another shot of Buzzman ca". Brands can even broadcast old commercials, entering the field of patrimonialization.

The hyper-advertising nature of these branded communications attracts participants who are willing to receive voluntarily, several times a week, freely and consensually, advertising content from brands they have chosen. We cannot know if all of them are consumers and/or buyers of these brands, but they are undoubtedly voluntary consumers of their advertising discourse and signs. Brands provide a consenting public, which has signed up for this purpose, a daily form of advertising show.

The consumption of the signs of the brand is even, in some cases, accompanied by an evaluation by the same public of the advertising quality of the messages produced. Commentators demonstrate aesthetic, narrative, or even strategic judgment capacities regarding what they consider to be good advertising depending on the brand concerned. The advertising show is accompanied by amateur criticism of advertising productions that bears witness to an advertising culture. This type of comment does not remain a dead letter as the M&M's brand chose to highlight during the final of the last Super bowl (a key moment in advertising in the United States). The brand produced its usual annual advertising film and a film featuring film critics giving an extremely complimentary speech about a film you do not see until one of them reminds you that it is just an advertisement and is put in its place by the others. The game about the confusion between short films and commercials available on the Facebook page and the YouTube channel mmschocolate is central.

3 Advertising and Algorithm: The Return of the Repressed

3.1 Advertising Hyperadvertising: Paradox and Necessity

The forms of hyperpublicitarization *a priori* set aside traditional advertising or coexist with it. However, an essential question arises: how to ensure that these devices, unadvertised as hyperadvertised, have an audience. Indeed, who, apart from people who are already loyal to a brand, will pick up these messages on the web or take the trouble to find them out? Among the possible answers, one is to choose shocking or humorous or aesthetic messages, hoping that Internet users will relay them via their own networks, which is called virality.

We propose to analyze a solution that is less expected; it is the one that consists in resorting to advertising, which thus endorses its double meaning of "making known, making public" and "promotion." We will qualify this unexpected turnaround, borrowing a psychoanalytical expression, as "return of the repressed." Thus, some television, press, and billboard advertisements primarily intend to let people know what the brands offer under the aegis of the unadvertised/hyperadvertised and where their productions are visible, in order to try to give them receivers.

Indeed, it is not easy for brand managers to ensure an audience for their hyperadvertising proposals, however aesthetic and neat they may be. It is more likely to reach people who are already sufficiently attached to a brand, often requalified as "fans" or "ambassadors" by brands, to search the web for new communication proposals. In other words, the unadvertised or hyperadvertised forms would then only find as an audience people who are already sufficiently convinced by the brand to consult dedicated sites, browse them long enough and go and look for additional elements on Youtube, for example. The question is how to attract other people?

Several means coexist; one of them is producing funny enough films, or shocking, or intriguing enough to trigger a "rumor" that professionals in the field currently call "buzz" that will spread. Internet users then become a media for the advertising message because they talk about it and even ensuring themselves the diffusion through links or the inclusion of the commercials in their social network accounts. Simpler forms of diffusion exist by using emails between friends or acquaintances containing a link to a brand message.

In addition to these forms of dissemination, professionals in charge of brand discourses are, paradoxically and frequently, relying on good old advertising, in the press, on television, and on billboards to ensure that their audience is aware of their alternative proposals for large and small advertising shows. This can take many forms:

- The message retains a classic and expected advertising form and additional content online, with its URL; this is the case for the press advertisements of the Louis Vuitton brand inviting readers to watch online "L'invitation au voyage" (late 2012); knowing that the movie starred David Bowie, which the press advertising did not indicate.
- The message is a classic "teasing" advertising, giving access to a part of the message, long enough to entice and make the viewer watch the rest of it, as in the television campaign for Axe brand men's hair styling products (2013–2014#PREMIEREIMPRESSION). The online content was men hairdressing tutorials using the brand's

products with a strongly offbeat tone, always highlighting the supposed seduction value linked to the use of the brand's products.
– The message takes the advertising form of a classic movie poster, thus consecrating the message's spectacular form.

We are witnessing a complexification of the advertising system where traditional advertising coexists with unadvertised or hyperadvertised forms and the advertising that should incite people to watch them.

3.2 Online Advertising: Return of the Hype

Alongside the phenomena of unadvertising and hyperadvertising, the first forms of advertising on the Web have continued to evolve, not so much in the forms as in the means used to put the right ads in front of the right people. As a result, online advertising, for which advertisers pay for "media space", has undergone a revolution with algorithms [10, 18, 21, 29]. Indeed, to the simple advertising on websites or displays, to the purchase of keywords came to be added the purchase of automated advertising space, or programmatic, managed by algorithms which calculate "in real-time" which advertisement will suit best to the Net user according to his/her course on the Web. This intrusion of machines and calculation into the advertising equation has given both companies and their advertising agencies a glimpse of the Holy Grail: understanding what is going on in the consumers' head and only offering them what is likely to please them and make them buy. The secret idea of brain manipulation is reappearing on the horizon [16].

As a result, any web browsing without an adblocker software plunges us into a world that is both familiar, because the ads we see are related to our interests, and extremely monotonous because most algorithms build a universe based on the idea of "sameness" and don't allow to be surprised or really discover. Moreover, whenever you spend much time online, the sensation of ad hype quickly becomes overwhelming. Whether you are on Google, Safari, influencer sites, sales sites, health forums, media sites, apps, Facebook, Instagram, TikTok, Pinterest, etc., the sale offers are all the same. The feeling of harassment is not far away, and the discomfort can be substantial. Furthermore, these advertisements are often close to pure promotion. These ads are visually disturbing while offering poor content: the brand name, a minimalist visual, a strong incentive to grasp the promotion, to "see more," or to "go for it." These ads are devoid of creative work and bring us back to the feeling that we are a click machine.

The sensation of hype can also be due to the imposed and excessive viewing of the same commercial in a limited time. Replay viewing platforms and systems such as Youtube mainly generate this effect, as Internet users come to consume/binge watch videos one after the other, relaunching the viewing of the same ads, episode after episode. No commercial, even a successful and creative one, can survive this type of treatment without triggering an intense annoyance at any future viewing.

3.3 Native Advertising: Is "Réclame" Back ?

Web 2.0 generates new possible blurring of the classic markers of advertising. These masked digital advertising forms provoked the re-appearance of advertising forms of "deception," such as the ancient "réclame" problem. [10].

Online advertising is awkward because it is ubiquitous, repetitive, uncreative, and intrusive; when the forms produced are spectacular and desirable, however, they must be advertised to find an audience. Another solution seeks to solve the equation by bypassing the problem and melting advertising into the online medium's style in which it is placed. Thus, native advertising [11] appears the most recent avatar of a form of advertising born with the beginnings of advertising in the press called "réclame" in French. In between, the history of advertising forms in France is no stranger to deceptive forms; we can find today in the hybrid and sometimes difficult to differentiate, for the non-specialist, forms of advertising that are sponsorship, programming, consumer magazines, and the "traditional" advertorial [10, 14–16, 26, 27].

Historically, advertising forms have not always been labeled as such due to a lack of regulation. It has been especially true for a kind of advertising, very much in vogue between 1850 and 1930, known as "réclame" or "fait-Paris payé". It was presented in the form of a relatively short article, an "advertisement disguised as an article, an editorial advertisement whose purpose was to mislead the reader". It cost twice as much, in terms of buying space, as other forms of advertising because it was thought that the trust subscribers placed in their newspaper made it very efficient. Walter Benjamin [8, 9] describes press advertisement both in its economic functioning, forms, and the problems the "réclame" caused in the nineteenth and early twentieth centuries. Emile de Girardin, a significant promoter of these transformations, introduced, in 1836, in his newspaper *La Presse* advertisements, serials, and copy sales. As a result, it intertwined journalistic, literature, and advertising logics: "On information, advertisements, and feuilletons: the idler must be furnished with sensations, the merchant with customers, and the man in the street with a worldview. From this cohabitation are born literary forms formatted by the market and advertisements that form the passage between information and artistic production, notably "réclames"/advertisements or "disguised ads", first "a small notice slipped into the newspaper towards the end, and generally paid for by the bookseller"; then a problematic form linked to great financial scandals, which the French press finally managed to stop thanks to the growth of the advertising market in general [8].

This form of advertising is now prohibited and must be specified as such by a mention such as advertising, advertorials, advertorials, editorials, etc. However, the notion of deception is difficult to erase, and native advertising plays on the limits with "réclame" low profile advertising mode, melted in publishing spaces [11]. Native advertising, also named "sponsored content," "proposed advertising," "contextual advertisement", like old "réclame," seeks to blend in with digital media discourses: it looks and sounds the same, deals with the same kind of topics. Like the old "réclame," native advertising is supposed to ensure credibility because of its journalistic and informational appearance. The oldest and most controversial form of hidden advertising reappears under new clothes, maybe more sophisticated. However, the operating principle remains the same: the context benefits the brand since the reader is concentrated on the interest of the content more than in questioning the source of information.

The moral problem posed by "réclame" was solved in the French early twentieth century by the moralization imposed by both the press and advertising self-regulation, and this kind of advertising is prohibited and must be marked as such by a mention such as advertising, infomercial, or advertorial. Although this is the case on social networks, the constant emergence of new digital communication forms makes blurring challenging to identify. As pointed out by the French advertising self-regulation authority (ARPP), increased difficulties are emerging concerning the early identification of advertising discourse. Indeed, a text entitled "Information and advertising: clarifying the nature of the issuer" shows to what extent contemporary forms of digital brand communication raise three types of question in terms of advertising ethics: "The question of identifying the issuer, the nature of the information emitted, its status (information, advertising, communication, spontaneous expression)". Therefore, the profession is perfectly aware that many digital advertising productions may be "likely to sow doubt in the minds of consumers" [14].

4   Conclusion: The Age of Suspicion

It turns out that the digital Eldorado that advertisers and brand managers hoped for is complex and rapidly changing. The possibilities seen as infinite and extraordinary opened up by algorithms, and the learning machine often bring advertising back to forms worthy of its early beginnings, between repetition/masking, poverty of content, and blurring of the boundaries between advertising and non-advertising. Machines cannot create the perfect ad without people setting it up to do so. Moreover, the question of the definition of good advertising and even the definition of advertising itself seems to be the heart of the problem.

From the point of view of professionals working in the fields related to advertising, its definition is relatively easy and circumscribed; it refers to the explicit identification of the transmitter and the advertising nature of the discourse in established media, which are also identified in a closed set including the digital field. If we follow the professional definition of advertising, it is easily identifiable since it is mandatory to differentiate it from the other media discourse components.

Is it that simple for the vast majority of "non-advertising professionals" who encounter many brand-related occurrences and discourses in their daily lives and tend to recharacterize most communications put into circulation by a brand as "advertising"? This makes it possible to fully understand the commonly held idea that advertising is misleading and influences people without their knowledge. Advertising is accused of intentionally seeking to mislead its receivers/consumers by using forms of communication that are not frank, which is very common in web advertising as seen with native advertising.

This indifferentiation in the minds of non-professionals is so broad that any branded commercial communication act falls within the common understanding of the term "advertising," including brand discourses on the Internet, particularly in social networks, television sponsorships, and other street actions building a kind of global advertising space. To curate advertising, it is still necessary to specify which definition is used: if marketing professionals accept it from their perspective, it is not sure that viewers see the difference. The advertising show on the web needs to mature enough to forget that machines alone can do the job without the human quick of regulation and creativity?

References

1. Andriuzzi, A., Michel, G.: Social media conversations: when consumers do not react positively to brands' kindness to others. In: Meiselwitz, G. (ed.) Social Computing and Social Media. Communication and Social Communities. HCII 2019. Lecture Notes in Computer Science, vol 11579. Springer, Cham (2019). https://doi.org/10.1007/978-3-030-21905-5_21
2. Barthes, R.: L'imagination publicitaire, Points et perspectives de la recherche publicitaire, IREP, Paris, pp 87–88 (1967)
3. Barthes, R.: Elements of Semiology. Hill and Wang, New York (1968)
4. Barthes, R.: Mythologies. The Noonday Press, New York (1991)
5. Barthes, R.: Le message publicitaire. In: Œuvres Complètes, T. Éditions du Seuil, Paris (2002)
6. Baudrillard, J.: The System of Objects. Verso, London (1996)
7. Baudrillard, J.: The Consumer Society: Myths and Structures. Sage, London (1998)
8. Benjamin, W.: The Arcades Project. The Belknap Press of Harvard University Press, Cambridge (2002)
9. Benjamin, W.: The Writer of Modern Life. Essays on Charles Baudelaire. The Belknap Press of Harvard University Press, Cambridge (2008)
10. Berthelot-Guiet, K.: The digital "advertising call": an archeology of advertising literacy. In: Meiselwitz, G. (eds.) Social Computing and Social Media. Participation, User Experience, Consumer Experience, and Applications of Social Computing. HCII 2020. Lecture Notes in Computer Science, vol 12195. Springer, Cham (2020). https://doi.org/10.1007/978-3-030-49576-3_21
11. Marti, C., Berthelot-Guiet, K.: Advertising or not advertising: representations and expressions of advertising digital literacy on social media. In: Meiselwitz, G. (eds.) Social Computing and Social Media. Communication and Social Communities. HCII 2019. Lecture Notes in Computer Science, vol 11579. Springer, Cham (2019). https://doi.org/10.1007/978-3-030-21905-5_32
12. Berthelot-Guiet, K., Marti de Montety, C., Patrin-Leclère, V.: Sémiotique des métamorphoses marques-médias. In: Berthelot-Guiet, K., Boutaud. J.-J. (eds.) Sémiotique mode d'emploi. Le Bord de l'eau, Lormont (2015)
13. Berthelot-Guiet, K.: Analyser les discours publicitaires. Armand Colin, Paris (2015)
14. Berthelot-Guiet, K.: 80 ans d'autorégulation publicitaire. In: Wolton, D. (ed.) Avis à la publicité. Cherche-midi, Paris (2015)
15. Berthelot-Guiet, K., Marti de Montety, C., Patrin-Leclère, V.: La Fin de la Publicité ? Tours et Contours de la Dépublicitarisation. Bord de l'eau, Lormont (2014)
16. Berthelot-Guiet, K.: Paroles de Pub La Vie Triviale de la Publicité. Éditions Non Standard, Le Havre (2013)
17. Bull, A.: Brand Journalism. Routledge, London, New York (2013)
18. Eugeni, R.: The post-advertising condition. A socio-semiotic and semio-pragmatic approach to algorithmic capitalism. In: Meiselwitz, G. (eds,) Social Computing and Social Media. Communication and Social Communities. HCII 2019. Lecture Notes in Computer Science, vol 11579. Springer, Cham (2019). https://doi.org/10.1007/978-3-030-21905-5_23
19. Flichy, P.: The Internet Imaginaire. The MIT Press, Cambridge (2008)
20. Erdem, N.: Argumentative study on digital advertising literacy. In: Taskiran, N.O. (ed.) Handbook of Research on Multidisciplinary Approaches to Literacy in the Digital Age. IGI, Hershey (2019)
21. Hellín Ortuño, P.A.: The cultural component in advertising analysis. a non-numerical vision of the programmatic advertising. In: Meiselwitz, G. (ed.) HCII 2019. LNCS, vol. 11579, pp. 346–360. Springer, Cham (2019). https://doi.org/10.1007/978-3-030-21905-5_27
22. Herpin, N.: Sociologie de la consommation. La Découverte, Paris (2001)

23. Malmelin, N.: What is advertising literacy? Exploring the dimensions of advertising literacy. J. Vis. Literacy **29**(2), 129–142 (2010)
24. Marti de Montety, C., Patrin-Leclere, V., La conversion à la conversation, le succès d'un succédané. Communication & Langages, 169 (2011)
25. Marti, C.: Les mediations culturelles de marques: une quête d'autorité. ISTE editions, London (2019)
26. Martin, M.: Histoire de la publicité en France. Presses Universtaires de Paris Ouest, Nanterre (2012)
27. Martin, M.: Trois Siècles de Publicité en France. Odile Jacod, Paris (1992)
28. Sacriste, V.: Les français et la publicité. Une longue tradition de contestation, La publicité aujourd'hui, La revue du CIRCAV, pp. 13–30. L'Harmattan, Paris (2009)
29. Trindade, E.: Algorithms and advertising in consumption mediations: a semio-pragmatic perspective. In: Meiselwitz, G. (ed.) HCII 2019. LNCS, vol. 11579, pp. 514–526. Springer, Cham (2019). https://doi.org/10.1007/978-3-030-21905-5_40

The Impact of Social Media Marketing on Impulse Buying

Adheesh Budree[✉], Warren Driver, Abongile Pandle, and Gandidzanwa Tanaka

University of Cape Town, Western Cape, Cape Town, South Africa
Adheesh.budree@uct.ac.za

Abstract. Research on the use of social media has shown that it tends to influence if not alter human perceptions while purchasing and added frequently targeted marketing on these platforms has also impacted on consumer buying behavior. This paper, through a rigorous systematic literature review, evaluated the topic of Social Media Marketing and critically examines the effect it has on consumer behavior, and particularly impulse buying. The search strategy used to conduct the literature review was primarily targeted towards discovering academic publications via accepted databases and literature search engines. The basis for published literature reviewed was taken from a basket of top Information Systems journals. Several themes were found to influence impulsive purchases as driven by social media marketing. These included purchasing behaviors, social media influencers, and brand loyalty where it was found that companies often exploit the vulnerabilities of the consumer psyche to maximize successful online impulse sales using social media marketing as stimulant. Both social and eCommerce technology proved to be major contributors to this phenomenon to the extent that available research considers them to be independent impulsive purchase stimuli in their own standing.

Keywords: Social media · eCommerce · Social media marketing · Impulse buying

1 Background

The spawn and dominance of social networking websites over the last two decades has paved the way for the subsequent digitization of many human interactions [44]. The increase in use of this technology by the billions in just the past decade created an online market that cannot be ignored by businesses, which has led to mass advertising on these platforms [15].

Research on the use of social media has shown that it tends to influence if not alter human perception of brands [5, 51] and the added marketing on these platforms also impacts consumer behavior [47]. Impulse buying can be defined as the impromptu purchase of a product or service [9], while Social Media Marketing (SMM) is the use of social media platforms and websites to promote a product or service [25].

This paper, through a rigorous systematic literature review, evaluated the topic of SMM and critically examines the effect it has on consumer behavior, and particularly

© Springer Nature Switzerland AG 2021
G. Meiselwitz (Ed.): HCII 2021, LNCS 12775, pp. 54–65, 2021.
https://doi.org/10.1007/978-3-030-77685-5_5

impulse buying. The search strategy used to conduct the literature review was primarily targeted towards discovering academic publications via accepted databases and literature search engines. The basis for published literature reviewed was taken from the basket of top Information Systems journals (Oosterwyk et al. 2019).

2 Literature Review Method

In order to adequately identify and assess literature relevant to the topic area, a systematic literature review was conducted. As showing in Fig. 1 below, the search strategy that was used to conduct the literature review was primarily targeted towards discovering articles, published papers in journals, and conference proceedings via widely accepted databases and literature search engines. These included Google Scholar, Gartner and Statista. The basis for published literature was taken from the basket of top IS journals, as identified by Oosterwyk et al. (2019), as well as literature from:

- International Journal of Market Research
- International Journal of Entrepreneurial Research
- European Journal of Business and Management
- International Journal of Quality and Service Sciences
- International Journal of Commerce and Finance

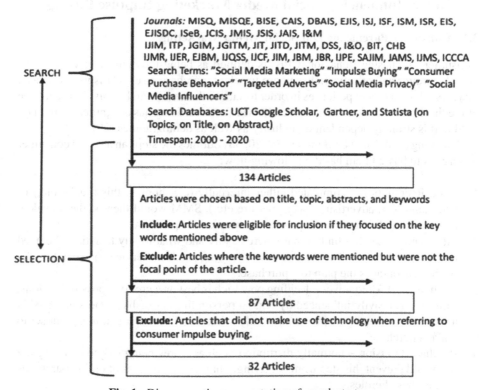

Fig. 1. Diagrammatic representation of search strategy

- Journal of Interactive Marketing
- Journal of Brand Management
- Journal of Business Research
- International Journal of Production Economics
- South African Journal of Information Management,
- Journal of the Academy of Marketing Science
- International Journal of Management Studies,
- International Conference on Computing, Communication and Automation

The literature was reviewed on the dimensions of their topic, title, and abstract. The review process of the collected literature also entailed the inclusion and exclusion criteria and broadened the literature collection based on the examination of a backward and forward search (cited papers and the ones citing it). As a result, 134 peer-reviewed papers were included in the initial collection in which the papers were published over the timespan of 2000–2020. In the few cases where the topic, title, and abstract were insufficient for the selection process, the introduction and conclusion were reviewed to ensure significant papers were not unfairly excluded.

The following sections highlight the key findings from the literature review conducted, and thereafter conclusions from these findings are drawn.

3 Factors Influencing Social Media Marketing Impulse Buying

3.1 Consumer Purchasing and Social Media Marketing

Consumer Purchasing Behavior (CPB) is defined as being the manner in which individuals, groups and organizations choose to select, purchase, use and dispose products, services, ideas and/or experiences in order to satisfy their needs and wants [42]. The type of media (Print, Broadcast and/or Social) used for advertising has a significant effect on CPB and is strongly dependent on industry as well as demographics [29].

The long established CPB model [19, 20, 38] outlines the steps an average consumer undergoes to buy an item has the following flow:

1. Need Recognition – stimulated either internally (e.g. hunger, thirst, ache etc.) or externally (e.g. advertising, peer pressure etc.). SMM would then be the prevalent external stimuli initiating the process to impulsively purchase.
2. Information Search – finding out where to buy and what to buy to satisfy the need recognized in step 1. The relative ease of seeing products/services on social media further encourages the path to a purchase.
3. Evaluation of Alternatives - deciding on which is best on a group of possible options. This step is heavily influenced by what a person likes or dislikes and since SMMs are already targeted, the person sees only what they like and are at this point set to make a purchase.
4. Purchase Decision – normally disruption such as stores being closed or being too far would prevent this step from occurring, but the effectiveness of online purchases evades these hurdles.

5. Post-Purchase Behavior – In traditional purchases where the need recognition was not stimulated by an SMM advert, this step would be what deters the next impulsive purchase but since SMM ensures consumers see only what they like, they are left in a position where they are most likely to commit to another purchase if financially able to do so.

[25] defined Social Media Marketing (SMM) as being the use of social media and platforms and websites to promote a product or service. In an attempt to investigate the effect of brand content stimuli on consumer's psychological reactions, [35] found that invocation of consumer interactivity with companies and their products is precisely what makes SMM work well. [2] concur in their categorization of Customer Relationship Management as being one of the central themes of social media marketing in their review of over 144 existing publications on the field.

The growth of the global SMM market from $60 to over a $100 billion in just the past 3 years serves as empirical evidence to sustain the effectiveness of Social Media Marketing [45]. [17] further observed that an increasing number of companies are adopting an SMM strategy for their marketing in the form of twitter accounts after having acknowledged the impact of commercial tweets on revenue growth.

In the context of SMM, [21] found that step 2 of the CPB model had little impact on the consumer whereas step 3 had the greatest. [32] commissioned a content-coded study of over 100 000 Facebook messages across 782 companies and made the key finding that consumers exhibit a repulsive response towards product/service driven content and that this was why companies oft adopt a more emotional, philanthropic and alternatively persuasive SMM approach; the intention being to maximize a successful sale on step 4 of the CPB model.

3.2 Impulse Buying and Social Media

Impulse Buying refers to the purchasing of a product or service without previously planning to do so but have been persuaded by some stimuli such as an advert or simply doing so out of whim [9].

According to [13], marketing presence on the different social media channels triggers impulse purchasing among consumers due the increase of accessibility to products and services as this facilitates an easy purchase process. The study also observes a correlation between lack of consumer planning and the tendency to purchase impulsively. For example, Facebook uses a specific targeted strategy that links consumers to their likes or current topics of interest. Most people that sign up to Facebook have the intention to connect with people and brands that they "like". This exposes the user to stimuli that may trigger the process of impulsive purchasing [33].

According to [41], there are two main phycological motivations as to why targeted marketing urges users to buy products or services impulsively, viz, (1) the hedonic and (2) the utilitarian. The hedonic motivation accounts for the experimental purchasers who are most likely to buy a product when they have experienced instant pleasure or satisfaction from it [50]. The utilitarian motivation, on the contrary, refers to users who are task-orientated and have the intention or desire to purchase products and/or services efficiently depending on whether they find the good/service necessary to have (Zheng et al. 2019). Categorization in this manner helps practitioners test the effectiveness of advertising campaigns and to understand users' motivation under different stimuli in order to predict their responses [41, 50].

One of the tests carried out is that of how consumers feel when browsing the internet in order to access information. Browsing is defined as the "in-store examination of a retailer's merchandise for informational and/or recreational purposes without an immediate intent to buy" [8]. When consumers engage in hedonic browsing and they experience a positive effect of emotion when they come across a specific good or service, they will buy the product impulsively. When consumers engage in utilitarian browsing, they need to realize the purchase goal, by finding high quality information in order to make a purchase decision. According to studies these consumers make purchase decisions based on information given from other users as it reduces risk of a poor product purchase; this is called Word-of-Mouth marketing [50].

3.3 Social Media Influencers (SMIs)

The growth of Social Media has enabled the creation of personas whose interaction with certain products/services in SMM have impacted the purchase behavior of consumers; These personas are widely referred to as "influencers" [26]. The practice itself is not new but its effect has recently caught the eye of both industry and academia; the result of which was a stimulated increase of investment in the personas and in their research [30].

[34] undertook a study to determine the impact of SMIs on purchase intention and they found that influencers indeed sway the purchase intention of consumers. A contrary outcome is that of [12] who observed, while examining the effect on the tourism industry of rural Greece, that the impact of SMI therein was mostly generational. Both studies, however, still concurred that an influence to buy impulsively was sparked by SMIs whenever consumers engaged with the products they promote.

3.4 Brand Equity/Power

Central to any marketing strategy is the inescapable reality of what the consumer perceives to be the actual value of a product/service as influenced by the brand name; an effect called Brand Equity [39]. [27] commissioned a study to explore the effect of this phenomenon in relation to consumer behavior as enabled by SMM efforts on luxury brands. They made the following key findings:

- SMM incorporates five key aspects, viz, (1) entertainment (2) interaction (3) trendiness (4) customization and (5) word-of-mouth; all of which are equally important from the consumer's point of view.
- There is a strong correlation between a brand's equity and any effort to undertake SMM; that is to say, companies that have greater brand equity are most likely to influence their customers to buy their products through SMM than those with lesser brand equity. Thus, CPB is influenced by brands.

- Companies who treat social media as more of a brand image building tool rather than a platform for advertising are more likely to succeed in their SMM efforts; sustaining the observation of [32] and [21].

The consensus from these studies is that consumers who are loyal to a certain brand are likely to impulsively purchase products more often from such brand if continuous SMM engagement is present.

4 Technology Platforms and Impulse Buying

[37] observed, while investigating online shopping prevalence in Japan, that the total cost of buying a product is lower than its brick-and-mortar purchase and this is inclusive of time spent as well as the overall perceived effort. This relative ease suggests that SMM alone cannot be fully credited to impulsive purchases, in lieu, this impact can also be attributed to the supporting electronic commerce technology that makes online purchases possible.

4.1 Social Media Technology

Social Media takes various forms which may be classified in many different ways. For the purpose of this paper, the different platforms are categorized following the 13-type typology used by [1] in their measure of the degree of social media use in the corporate field of work.

Social networks connect people that know each another, share common interests or would like to engage in similar activities. Users have an individual profile; they can be found by other users using their full name, and they upload pictures and videos. Companies use social networks by creating a corporate profile in order to position certain brands and to inform and support existing or to win new customers. The level and frequency of engagement as well as the brand power of these companies is known to compel users to buy products even if they had no prior intention of doing so.

1. **Video Sharing Platforms** – allow users to upload and share personal, business or royalty-free videos and to watch them legally. Most websites offer the opportunity to comment on specific videos. Companies use these social media to share commercials, to test unconventional promotional videos or to save costs, which are much lower compared to TV advertising. The videos are often targeted, and this is encouraging impulsive purchases for those users who see them.
2. **Messaging Applications** – which, taking from the name, enable instant/live messaging (mostly via text but also image, video and VoIP ready). Companies intending to use these applications as marketing tools often do so by recommending their products/services to users who have indicated interest in previous similar products and this in turn maximizes chances of buying out of whim. SMI's also leverage the status features to promote products/services to an audience they have influence over, thereby increasing their chances of making unplanned purchases.

3. **Discussion Forums** – a virtual discussion platform where users can ask and/or answer other users' questions and exchange thoughts, opinions or experiences. Communication here does not happen in real time, like in a chat, but is time delayed and usually visible to the public. The link between discussion forums and Impulsive purchases exists in the form of answers where a mere recommendation that has the most community likes persuades a reading consumer to "try-out" a certain product or service even if they had only meant to learn more about it.

There are many used per category throughout the world for different purposes, but for the scope of this paper focus is on the leading platform per category measured by geographic spread popularity and/or number of users globally [14].

Social Networks
Facebook
Founded in the year 2004, Facebook leads all known Social Media platforms with over 2.4 billion active users worldwide [14]. The company reported in 2017 that it had reached over 3 million active advertisers and a revenue growth of over 47% from the 2016 financial year [22]. Facebook's advertising strategy involves recommended posts on users' news feed, fan pages, content "liked" by friends and the common practice of "following" available as a feature in most social networks [24]. The effectiveness of Facebook's approach can be easily observed from its financial growth [23] over the years but most recently it has gone through a series of PR issues which may have impacted on its annual returns [24]. It however remains the leading social media platform and businesses in their hundreds of millions continue to see it as a valuable advertising space [23].

Media Sharing Networks
YouTube
YouTube is a video streaming service owned by Google LLC that first became operational in the year 2005. As of January 2020, it has over 2 billion active users and retains 2nd place [3] as the most popular website globally (second only to its parent company's flagship product Google Search Engine). YouTube has a similar approach to cable television advertising but differs in that the ads are now targeted based on the users perceived interest. This perceived interest is gathered from the user's usage data such as videos watched, channels subscribed to. Users may sign-up to become youtubers (video content creators) with channels (groupings of videos based on some typography such as gaming, movies, music etc.) on which other users may subscribe (follow the channel content). The spike in revenue from $8.1 to $15.1 billion in the past 2 years is a key indicator as to the effectiveness of the approach [5].

Messaging Applications
WhatsApp
With over 2 billion active users worldwide [14], WhatsApp remains the leading instant messaging service and continues to attract an increasing audience of users. WhatsApp does not do any formalized advertising (a common practice of most instant messaging apps) but the advent of influencers and influences gives it enough credibility to be on this

list. The volume of photos, videos and messages shared daily (in the millions) constitute a market that influencers predominantly tap into via the "status update" feature [23].

Discussion Forums
Quora
A website community of more than 300 million active users, valued at $2 billion as of 2019, that allows questions to be asked, answered, edited and organized by its community of users [40]. Companies market their products through the question and answer approach offered and this engagement influences consumer purchasing [49].

4.2   E-commerce Technology

Online shopping allows consumers to directly buy goods and/or services from a seller over the internet using a web browser [48]. Impulse buying is mostly stimulated by the relative ease of online purchasing as enabled by the various online payment technologies such as PayPal, MasterCard, Visa, Stripe and SnapScan to name a few [6]. It is the case that buying something impulsively is often caused by the urge to instantly gratify a need/want triggered by some advert and this wouldn't work well if the means to purchase such an item were not embedded or closely linked to the advert itself [43].

There therefore are three aspects that make this e-commerce offering encourage an impulsive purchase spurred by SMM, viz, (i) the capability of viewing products/services online via websites, (ii) the ability to pay online and (iii) the option of having your products physically delivered to you [7].

Business-to-Consumer (B2C)
According to [46], the overall revenue growth credited to online transactions in South Africa has increased by an average of 4% in the past 3 years to gross a net total of $3.8 billion in the year 2020; for the combined industries of Fashion, Electronics, Toys, Hobby & DIY, Furniture & Appliances and Food & Personal Care. This indicates that an increasing number of businesses are investing in selling their products and services online. Consumers shop online via desktop computers, laptops, tablet computers, smartphones and smart speakers all of which afford the comfort of shopping from home accompanied by a reduced presence of demotivators that often lead to a consumer cancelling a purchase [31] and this alternative shopping experience encourages impulse buying.

e-Payment
[18] commissioned an exhaustive study of approximately a million transactions from a leading fashion retailer and found that the existence of deferred payment as an online payment method option increases the likelihood of a successful purchase (conversion rate). They found this phenomenon to be habitual and not restricted by gender and demographics because it acts as a form of insurance for those consumers who fear wasting money on fraudulent online transactions [16]. Whereas this assurance is good

for business and the average consumer, it does however present a problem for those consumers susceptible to purchasing impulsively [11].

Delivery

Most businesses that sell their products online offer internal shipping to the consumer's home or a specified address or may charge a courier levy on the price [10]. This step proved most crucial in the online shopping experience to the point that dedicated food delivery companies such as Meituan-Dianping, Uber Eats, Instacart, Seamless, Grub hub etc. were spawned in just the span of the past 2 decades [28]. [45] reports an annual growth of 11% on the global revenue of this industry and [36] argued that the availability of such convenience foods would increase food waste due to the newfound ease of buying out of whim.

5 Conclusion and Recommendations

The topic of impulse buying as impacted by SMM was critically explored with the aid of existing literature on social media marketing, consumer psychology and e-commerce trends. Several themes were seen to influence consumer impulsive purchases as driven by SMM and these included CPB, social media influencers, and Brand Equity where it was found that companies often exploit the vulnerabilities of the consumer psyche to maximize successful online sales using SMM as stimulant.

The supporting technology which we classified into two types, namely, the SMM platform and E-Commerce proved to be major contributors to the phenomenon to the extent that available research considers them to be independent impulsive purchase stimuli in their own standing.

The implications of this paper's findings to academia, organizations and legislative bodies are as follows:

- There is a need investigate the regulation of SMM in as far as its potential to encourage impulse buying.
- Studies must be conducted to understand the link between SMM & E-Commerce technology which may also need to be reassessed in the context of curbing impulsive purchases.
- Existing research indicate a possible exacerbation of pre-existing habitual/psychological conditions, with SMM acting as one of the stimulants and therefore the investigation of treatment therapies may need to be refined or developed anew.

References

1. Aichner, T., Jacob, F.: Measuring the degree of corporate social media use. Int. J. Mark. Res. **57**(2), 257–276 (2015)
2. Alalwan, A.A., Rana, N.P., Dwivedi, Y.K., Algharabat, R.: Social media in marketing: a review and analysis of the existing literature. Telemat. Inform. **34**(7), 1177–1190 (2017)

3. Alexa: Competitive analysis, marketing mix and traffic - Alexa. Alexa Website Rankings. youtube.com (2020). https://www.alexa.com/siteinfo/youtube.com
4. Alphabet: Annual report 2019, vol. 13. Alphabet Inc. (2019)
5. Balakrishnan, B.K.P.D., Dahnil, M.I., Yi, W.J.: The impact of social media marketing medium toward purchase intention and brand loyalty among generation Y. Procedia-Soc. Behav. Sci. **148**, 177–185 (2014)
6. Bezovski, Z.: The future of the mobile payment as electronic payment system. Eur. J. Bus. Manag. **8**(8), 127–132 (2016)
7. Bilgihan, A., Kandampully, J., Zhang, T.C.: Towards a unified customer experience in online shopping environments. Int. J. Qual. Serv. Sci. **8**, 102–119 (2016)
8. Bloch, P.H., Richins, M.L.: Shopping Without Purchase: an Investigation of Consumer Browsing Behavior. ACR North American Advances, Duluth (1983)
9. Business Dictionary: What is impulse buying? Definition and meaning - BusinessDictionary.com. Business Dictionary, 20 February 2020 (2020). http://www.businessdictionary.com/definition/impulse-buying.html
10. Cao, Y., Ajjan, H., Hong, P.: Post-purchase shipping and customer service experiences in online shopping and their impact on customer satisfaction. Asia Pac. J. Mark. Logist. (2018)
11. Chan, T.K.H., Cheung, C.M.K., Lee, Z.W.Y.: The state of online impulse-buying research: a literature analysis. Inf. Manag. **54**(2), 204–217 (2017)
12. Chatzigeorgiou, C.: Modelling the impact of social media influencers on behavioural intentions of millennials: the case of tourism in rural areas in Greece (2017)
13. Chen, J.V., Su, B., Widjaja, A.E.: Facebook C2C social commerce: a study of online impulse buying. Decis. Support Syst. **83**, 57–69 (2016)
14. Clement, J.: Global social media ranking 2019|Statista. Statista (2020a). https://www.statista.com/statistics/272014/global-social-networks-ranked-by-number-of-users/
15. Clement, J.: Number of social media users worldwide 2010–2021|Statista. Statista (2020b). https://www.statista.com/statistics/278414/number-of-worldwide-social-network-users/
16. Clemons, E.K., Wilson, J., Matt, C., Hess, T., Ren, F., Jin, F.: Online trust: an international study of subjects' willingness to shop at online merchants, including the effects of promises and of third party guarantees. In: 2016 49th Hawaii International Conference on System Sciences (HICSS), pp. 5220–5229 (2016)
17. Cui, R., Agrawal, G., Ramnath, R.: Towards successful social media advertising: predicting the influence of commercial Tweets. arXiv Preprint arXiv:1910.12446 (2019)
18. Deufel, P., Kemper, J.: Online payment method selection: the habitual choice of deferring payment (2018)
19. Dewey, J.: How we think. DC Heath and Company, Boston (1910). OCLC 194219
20. Engel, J.F., Kollat, D.T., Blackwell, R.D.: Consumer Behavior. Holt, Rinehart, and Winston, New York (1968)
21. Ertemel, A.V., Ammoura, A.: The role of social media advertising in consumer buying behavior. Int. J. Commer. Financ. **2**(1), 81–89 (2016)
22. Facebook: Facebook annual report 2017 (2017)
23. Facebook: Facebook – financials (2020a). https://investor.fb.com/financials/default.aspx
24. Facebook: Facebook annual report 2020 (2020b)
25. Felix, R., Rauschnabel, P.A., Hinsch, C.: Elements of strategic social media marketing: a holistic framework. J. Bus. Res. **70**, 118–126 (2017)
26. Freberg, K., Graham, K., McGaughey, K., Freberg, L.A.: Who are the social media influencers? A study of public perceptions of personality. Public Relat. Rev. **37**(1), 90–92 (2011)
27. Godey, B., et al.: Social media marketing efforts of luxury brands: influence on brand equity and consumer behavior. J. Bus. Res. **69**(12), 5833–5841 (2016)

28. He, Z., Han, G., Cheng, T.C.E., Fan, B., Dong, J.: Evolutionary food quality and location strategies for restaurants in competitive online-to-offline food ordering and delivery markets: an agent-based approach. Int. J. Prod. Econ. **215**, 61–72 (2019)
29. Hee, O.C., Yen, W.S.: The influence of advertising media towards consumer purchasing behavior in the food and beverage industry in Malaysia. Int. J. Hum. Resour. Stud. **8**(2), 148–163 (2018)
30. Khamis, S., Ang, L., Welling, R.: Self-branding, 'micro-celebrity' and the rise of social media influencers. Celebr. Stud. **8**(2), 191–208 (2017)
31. Kukar-Kinney, M., Scheinbaum, A.C., Schaefers, T.: Compulsive buying in online daily deal settings: an investigation of motivations and contextual elements. J. Bus. Res. **69**(2), 691–699 (2016)
32. Lee, D., Hosanagar, K., Nair, H.S.: Advertising content and consumer engagement on social media: evidence from Facebook. Manag. Sci. **64**(11), 5105–5131 (2018)
33. Leong, L.Y., Jaafar, N.I., Ainin, S.: The effects of Facebook browsing and usage intensity on impulse purchase in f-commerce. Comput. Hum. Behav. **78**, 160–173 (2018). https://doi.org/10.1016/j.chb.2017.09.033
34. Lim, X.J., Radzol, A.R.M., Cheah, J.H., Wong, M.W.: The impact of social media influencers on purchase intention and the mediation effect of customer attitude. Asian J. Bus. Res. **7**(2), 19–36 (2017)
35. Lou, L., Koh, J.: Social media advertising effectiveness: a conceptual framework and empirical validation. Asia Pac. J. Inf. Syst. **28**(3), 183–203 (2018)
36. Mallinson, L.J., Russell, J.M., Barker, M.E.: Attitudes and behaviour towards convenience food and food waste in the United Kingdom. Appetite **103**, 17–28 (2016)
37. Miyatake, K., Nemoto, T., Nakaharai, S., Hayashi, K.: Reduction in consumers' purchasing cost by online shopping. Transp. Res. Procedia **12**(2016), 656–666 (2016)
38. Nicosia, F.M.: Consumer Decision Processes. Prentice-Hall, Engle-wood Cliffs (1966)
39. Oxford Dictionary: Brand equity def - Google search (n.d.). Accessed 23 May 2020. https://www.google.com/search?client=firefox-b-d&q=Brand+Equity+def
40. Schleifer, T.: Question-and-answer site Quora still exists, and it's now worth $2B - Vox. Vox Media (2019). https://www.vox.com/recode/2019/5/16/18627157/quora-value-billion-question-answer
41. Setyani, V., Zhu, Y.Q., Hidayanto, A.N., Sandhyaduhita, P.I., Hsiao, B.: Exploring the psychological mechanisms from personalized advertisements to urge to buy impulsively on social media. Int. J. Inf. Manag. **48**, 96–107 (2019)
42. Shih, S.P., Yu, S., Tseng, H.C.: The study of consumers' buying behavior and consumer satisfaction in beverages industry in Tainan, Taiwan. J. Econ. Bus. Manag. **3**(3), 391–394 (2015). https://doi.org/10.7763/joebm.2015.v3.215
43. Sinarta, Y., Buhalis, D.: Technology empowered real-time service. In: Stangl, B., Pesonen, J. (eds.) Information and Communication Technologies in Tourism 2018, pp. 283–295. Springer, Cham (2018). https://doi.org/10.1007/978-3-319-72923-7_22
44. Statista: Social media usage worldwide. Statista (2019). https://www-statista-com.gate3.library.lse.ac.uk/study/12393/social-networks-statista-dossier/
45. Statista: Social media advertising - worldwide|Statista Market Forecast. Statista (2020a). https://www.statista.com/outlook/220/100/social-media-advertising/worldwide
46. Statista: Social media advertising - worldwide|Statista Market Forecast. Statista (2020b)
47. Stephen, A.T.: The role of digital and social media marketing in consumer behavior. Curr. Opin. Psychol. **10**, 17–21 (2016)
48. Wikipedia: Online shopping - Wikipedia. Wikipedia Articles (2020). https://en.wikipedia.org/wiki/Online_shopping

49. Yang, L., Amatriain, X.: Recommending the world's knowledge: application of recommender systems at Quora. In: Proceedings of the 10th ACM Conference on Recommender Systems, p. 389 (2016)
50. Zheng, X., Men, J., Yang, F., Gong, X.: Understanding impulse buying in mobile commerce: An investigation into hedonic and utilitarian browsing. Int. J. Inf. Manag. **48**, 151–160 (2019)
51. Ali, Z., Shabbir, M.A., Rauf, M., Hussain, A.: To assess the impact of social media marketing on consumer perception (2016)

Notes on Advertising Logic in Food Applications

Eneus Trindade[(✉)]

University of Sao Paulo, Sao Paulo, Brazil
eneustrindade@usp.br

Abstract. The objective of this article is to understand the way of communicative interaction of applications currently used in the sectors of material culture food in the city of São Paulo, Brazil, in order to reflect on the types of functionalities and logics that these devices establish in the mediatization of consumption and the cultures in which they operate via processes of interaction. At the same time, one observes such applications with a new dimension of work in advertising with their institutionality and promocionalities.

Keywords: Food · Advertising · Mediations · Consumption · Applications

1 Introduction

The purpose of this article is to understand the way of communicative interaction of applications currently used in the sectors of material food consumption, in order to reflect on the types of functionalities and logics that these devices establish in the mediatization of consumption and cultures in which they are inserted through interaction processes. At the same time, we see such applications as a new dimension of advertising work with their institutional and promotional logic.

Applications are software designed to perform a group of functions, tasks or activities coordinated for some type of benefit, utility of interest tousers and they can be web applications, which act on the interface via browsers with access addresses, without the need to be installed on the operating system or mobile that work installed on the operating systems of mobile devices such as smartphones, for example, being able to expand its functionalities by having the functionalities of the mobile device and it can be paid or free, distributed/marketed on commercial digital platforms. The applications operate in a kind of economic intermediation with consequences for the productive lives of work and consumption.

Work in service applications (apps) is seen as an expansion of advertising work, since they generate forms of production and consumption, of messages, of values, under the aegis of a media brand, the app itself, with their circuits and devices, typical of the advertising universe, that is, they serve the self-promotion and institutionalization of their brands for this intermediation of consumption.

Such a finding is a symptom of communication for current consumption that suffers from a paradoxical phenomenon: the depublicitarization of traditional advertising formats and hyperpublicitarization of consumption, as treated by some French researchers

G. Meiselwitz (Ed.): HCII 2021, LNCS 12775, pp. 66–85, 2021.
https://doi.org/10.1007/978-3-030-77685-5_6

[2], with a view to the propagability, visibility and commercial profitability in broad meanings of human life, provoking direct and indirect mediatizations, that is, direct when the action of the device transforms the processes of that cultural manifestation, or indirect, when the processes of cultural manifestation are endorsed or reinforced by the media devices without any transformation of the manifestation in itself [8].

In this sense, it is observed that the advertising agency is par excellence the communicational work device that promoted this communicational mediation for consumption. Today with startups, driven by the logic of neoliberal creative economies, such companies emerge and act with this agency function in the digital communication mediation of ways of consuming, expanding the sense of agency beyond the sense of the traditional advertising agency and working on institutionalization and promotion of app brands in their consumption, configuring themselves as media brands that mediate innumerable possibilities and whose functionalities allow us to perceive this strong advertising character of applications.

The idea of brand-media is not limited to the notion of media as the set of means in which brands would be conveyed. It is considered that the mediation of the brand, due to its condition to conform to industrial/communicational formats and also due to its ability to blend between discursive genres of cultures, demarcating an evolutionary capacity of brand signs, which is highly hybridizing and of high potential for propagation and circulation as a mediatizing action. The brand-media shows an ecosystemic condition of adaptation and dynamics of regulated/mediated social life in the relations between brands and consumers [15, 21].

It is in this context, that this reflection can contribute to answer some problems. The mediation of the algorithms is based on predetermined calculations and schedules that guide, through the app interface, the possibilities of most recurring and expected uses and consumptions for consumers. However, the local contexts of uses make us think of updates to these schedules, via filtering processes that provide reconfigurations of the algorithms, through machine learning, in view of the expected and effective uses and consumptions of a given platform or app.

In what measures does the mediation of contexts interfere with production logics? How are the interfaces of these apps? What have they modified by this mediatization of the productive and consumption logic of the sectors of material life where they operate? These are issues relevant to the communicational field that need to be understood, for the advancement of training and scientific thinking in the area. These discussions were initially formulated in another opportunity [20] and allowed the formulation of a semiopragmatics of the digital interaction of the relationships between app brands and consumers.

It is in this perspective that we delimit here the questions prior to the study of apps in the food sector, seeking to map their functionalities and understand indications of the logic that such uses bring to the consumption culture of the sector in the context of São Paulo, seeking to contribute to the reflection of communication and consumption in the mediation of algorithms in the cultural life of São Paulo about food.

We observe that in this reflection, circulation and interactions themselves will not be studied. But its possibilities in the perspective programmed for the interactions. These processes seek to generate inferences about some mediatizing logic, from the measurement of the algorithm in the consumption of food, considering its potentialities in relation to the more general uses and consumptions in the context of the city of São Paulo, as well as the most popular apps iFood, Uber Eats, Rappi, Apptite and LivUp (the latter, as an example of a more conceptual business model distinct from the others). Thus, it is envisaged to know the views of the production logic and the industrial format of the studied apps from their functionality and utilities, such as technological mediation [22].

2   Materials and Methods

This reflection addresses the expansion of advertising logic and agency by apps, in the material culture of consumption, through examples of food; discusses its direct and indirect mediatizing logic [8], observes functionalities, aspects of its media circulation, based on the understanding of the role of the mediation of the algorithms, such as mediation of consumption, aiming at the constitution of a semiopragmatic theoretical perspective of these communication and consumption phenomena, to subsidize future studies that can understand the imaginary about apps and their algorithms by the subject-consumers, but before this stage, in a project like the one described here, it is necessary as a structuring basis and starting point for the diagnosis of the problems presented here of the potential of the interactions in their predicted functionalities.

For this research, the selection of five apps from the food sector most relevant to the context of food consumption in São Paulo were foreseen, considering the type of mediation they operate (purchase, trends, etc.), reputation, visibility, profitability and the number of users in the context of the city of São Paulo. It was observed the affordances allowed by the apps and its functionalities are described in detail, as well as to conceive aspects of the interactions [9], because for Eric Landowski the interactions are an aspect that transcend the discursive narrative logic and allow to access the meanings of interactions in a socio-semiotic context of the lived practices. Such interactions are summarized in four sense regimes: a) the programmed interaction, the one in which the interactants perform their actions reactively, within the expected expectations of the interactional environment, comprising a logic of regularities of interaction situations; b) the inter-action in the manipulation, which induces the interactant to act in accordance with the interests of the meaning-emitting pole, seeking to make the results efficient within the most anticipated or most frequent regularities; c) adjustment when regularities are tensioned by a randomness that, in turn, tension between logics of an intentionality that contradict themselves, in relation to the logic of the sensitive, of tastes and allow adjustment, negotiations, for this sensitive aspect; d) and finally, the accidental interaction that is established outside the regularities, are the situations not foreseen to the interaction, which leads to the possibility of an event, outside the control of the emitting pole.

The French researcher points out that semiotics, in Greimas' proposition, has always occupied itself with the programmed and manipulative dimension of the senses and that it has given little space to accidental and adjustment, which is just the space of aesthetic experience, in terms of communication lived in media uses and consumptions with cultural products, including brand messages and advertising. Algorithms as devices of digital/numerical humanity do not escape these regimes of interactions [20]. The algorithmic interaction considers the regimes of programming, manipulation, adjustment and accident, the latter two being, liable to veirification from the circulation processes and the media uses and consumptions of digital platforms and apps that, due to the AI (artificial intelligence) conditions, adjust to the possibilities of the data identified in the real dynamics of the interactions, through machine learning processes. Here, this type of observation will not be carried out, but we will understand the mechanisms of functionalities where such regimes can manifest themselves with greater potential.

It is also worth noting that access via apps did not allow identifying the number of users in the city of São Paulo and, initially, five interviews with entrepreneurs/collaborators of the studied apps were also planned, in addition to evaluating how the algorithms of these apps are adjusted. against consumption and machine learning. But the pandemic did not allow for that.

So, the focus of the discussion here will be on the features and powers for interactions. It should be noted that the apps to be presented in this work follow Srnicek's classification [17] on the formats of Platform Capitalism and are understood here as applications for Lean Platforms (of services), by intermediating services, at the same time that they accumulate functions of advertising apps, although this is not their first nature. And they work in the dimension of the GIG/collaborative or so-called shared economy, also called the economy of intermediation, it is worth mentioning that, in all the denominations given here, it is possible to criticize such an economic perspective, as they reduce employability and on their basis they work, most of the time, depending on the informal work of couriers, not presenting a fair income division and favoring underemployment and the informal economy [18].

The apps were observed as to their main objectives, functionalities, environment (Android, iOS, WEB), Public; Services offered free of charge, whether the app is free or paid, interface and way of working on the platform. We opted to work with free apps, due to the greater ease of access and possible current use.

In the food sector after a dense mapping of the current food context in the city of São Paulo, five food applications were chosen - iFood, Rappi, UberEats, Apptite and LivUp - inserted in the São Paulo community, for further investigation and organization of possible confluences with the topic under discussion. These platforms were mainly selected for their degree of maturity and market penetration; for approaching the promise of value and the way they seek to change the food consumption of the population in a broad way.

iFood is a food delivery application, designed and formulated in Brazil in 2011; today, it has operations in other countries in Latin America, with products and solutions for all food occasions, with the greatest coverage of operations among all applications in the Brazilian territory - being able to exert great influence on eating habits.

Rappi, on the other hand, is a Colombian delivery app created in 2015, which differs by having a 'anything' option, in a logic of substituting the consumer in the execution of a task (including that of removing a food in restaurant, which becomes its main focus).

The American UberEats carries the logistics and concept of the parent brand Uber, being a solution for the food delivery market. The three companies mentioned operate in a very similar way.

Appetit was launched as a promise of a 'humanized' delivery app, centered on the restaurant and user experience, counting on its network of partners only recognized chefs, with a promotional call and guerrilla tactics less present in its marketing logic.

Finally, LivUp, founded in 2016, is a foodtech (according to the Latin America Institute of Business -LAIOB, foodtechs are considered companies that use the combination of technological resources to transform the way of producing, selling, consuming and serving all types of food as the website says http://www.laiob.com/blog/o-que-e-foodtech/). The companyBrazilian company that offers pre-prepared frozen food, for heating and consumption, focused on organic and healthy food so that people eat the quality meal that in theory 'they would not have time to prepare', as announced on its website https://www.livup.com.br/.

3 Functionalities, Strengths of Interactions and Advertising Logic in the Researched Apps

It is important to note that this part of the work is written based on data from the research report [14], carried out under the guidance of the author of this article, which brings all the mapping of discussions on ways of working and the logic of potential interactions. The descriptive results point to the following descriptions.

iFood's main objectivepromote the purchase of food entirely online, without interface with attendants. The public is made up of economically active men and women, interested in consuming food/meals delivery.

The main features of this app consist of the action of the free access to the menu of the partner restaurants and through the application, you can place an order for these dishes, have an estimate of the time needed for delivery (based on your location), choose between different payment options and confirm the order - without making calls or speaking to attendants. The application works in a geolocation format, showing the end consumer a mapping of the restaurants closest to their delivery address. The app works on compatibility on operating systems iOS, Android and Web, which allows users to access it on various mobile devices or not, its installation is free from distribution platforms to operating systems or the web.

The services offered in the app allow the creation of an own profile in the application, with the possibility of filtered search (by restaurant, cuisine, price, evaluation, etc.). There is the option of choosing delivery by courier or pickup, directly at the purchase establishment. There is also the interaction of the apparent adjustment effect by ´customization´, that is, the option of adding or removing ingredients from the dishes at the end of the order. The application allows the real-time tracking of the order placed until its delivery/withdrawal, creating a synchronicity effect in the delivery tracking. There are features and information sent to the user's profile in the app that aim to encourage the use of promotional coupons provided in the profile messages or to be inserted later, manually in the 'coupons' tab,

There is a tool for evaluating the delivery person after completing the order, plus the option of 'Tip', if the consumer wants to pay an extra amount of one, three or five Brazilian reais for delivery, to those who work on delivery as an incentive to the work of deliverers and allow the reputation of the delivery service to be verified. There is still available, the functionality in the 'Help' tab, with real-time support via app, for accidental occurrences in the interaction, something out of the expected. This being the only space in which the app's actions can manifest an unscheduled, manipulative or adjustment feature.

The services offered after purchase within the app, manifest themselves in extra services for an additional price in the app and are configured by 'iFood Plus', an exemption program for the payment of delivery fees by charging a monthly subscription, which gives users, depending on the chosen contracting plan, the right to: (i) unlimited orders delivered per month; or (ii) a predetermined number of order deliveries per month. These are actions of loyalty to the iFood brand in its institutionalization process.

It is observed that on the checkout tab, depending exclusively on the partner restaurant, sustainable packaging options can be offered for an additional price, this being another action to adjust the expectations of consumers with some environmental awareness.

In your interface iFood is an application that is simple to use, with a white background on all pages of the app, and that is differentiated along the categories or promotional lists that the user enters. When clicking on the application, we see a red screen with the iFood logo and then the home screen.

On this screen, we can choose between the options of 'Delivery' or 'Withdrawal'; in both options, below, we see a box for selecting the preferred address and it is based on it that the application will show what is available in each region.

Next, we have a search bar for 'item or store', which works with Search Engine Optimization methodology that gathers the strategies that involve the creation of relevant content to attract users to a destination.

Below the search bar, there are banners from key categories, such as 'Market', 'Promotions', etc., which, when clicked, open new 'homes' with lists of promotions and partners focused on each of these categories. An advertising hyperextension of the app.

Below, we have the biggest banners of the home, which function as a virtual showcase where the main current promotional lists are presented. Then, you can view the last restaurants ordered by the user in that location, so that you can quickly make a new purchase.

Still on the main page, two finite carousels with geolocalized promotions are shown, one of them, the 'Delivery Rocket', for deliveries that take up to 30 min after placing the order online and another that bears the name 'Good and cheap food', with dishes at the moment's promotions.

Below, we have a section of culinary categories, such as Brazilian, Healthy, Lunch, which when clicked, take you to a list of selected cuisine restaurants. Next, we see the 'Famous on iFood' section, with a carousel of logos of the most requested restaurants on the platform that are close to the consumer, followed by a 'iFood Gourmet' banner, self-styled as 'selection of excellent restaurants' - which is a list of premium restaurants close to the user. This stratification of tastes and types of food guides meanings of food consumption, creating possibilities for adjustments to consumer interests.

And finally, we have the 'Restaurants' tab, with infinite scroll and the possibility of filters and sorting according to the consumer's needs (ex.: restaurants that offer free delivery fee, payment methods accepted by the restaurant, which have less time best rated, etc.).

Once the user selects a restaurant, he is taken to his virtual 'menu', which is nothing more than the list of dishes and side dishes offered by that restaurant, with their respective values. When selecting one (or more) dish (s), the consumer can place a note on that item, asking to add or remove certain ingredients, and then it is directed to the checkout tab.

There are two ways of working within the app: the do Deliveryman He works as a kind of self-employed professional on demand. The iFood x Deliveryman relationship in this scenario is more of a commercial partnership than a job, since there is no employment relationship between the company and the delivery person, still less a regulation provided by law that ensures labor rights for users of the platform.

To become a delivery person, another application called iFood for Deliverers must be downloaded, which is intended for those who want to work in the delivery business in partnership with iFood partner restaurants. When registering on the platform and providing personal data, the delivery person is able to accept delivery orders to iFood customers. It is possible to work independently or linked to a specific establishment. When registering, the delivery person has the option to choose the city where he wants to make deliveries and which ones he wants to make, in addition to consulting debts and credits for racing and access the iFood support service. The delivery app is only available for Android. Access to iOS connotes a condition of class and uses and consumption not consistent with the condition of delivery personnel.

The other is that Restaurant owner: to be part of the network of partner restaurants, you need to have a registration number as a legal entity for your restaurant and also internet access at your workplace to receive online orders. The registration itself is carried out by selecting one of the available plans. After iFood's approval, the responsible person must configure the rest of the restaurant's information on the platform, such as: accepted payment methods, opening hours, menu items, so that this information is available to customers in the application.

In this tab, he can choose the payment method (of which that restaurant offers), check the delivery time of that dish and add promotional coupons. When validating all information, he clicks on a "Checkout" button and is directed to a status page to track delivery.

The advertising functionalities and automations aimed at loyalty/institutionalization, sales promotion, associated with geolocation tools, show the use of an advanced algorithm with a good data optimization capacity, in its machine learning, to target offers and incentives adapted to consumer groups with similar profiles.

The food delivery service application studied has a direction for advertising work, manifested in the traces of the interactivity of the interfaces and functionalities of the iFood brand.

Rappi's main objective the delivery services of food and home products in Brazil - from any establishment in the city, in an agile way, both for the financial operations of purchase and delivery of the products, and in the ways of making these deliveries feasible, in São Paulo, the unlocking of urban modes (alternative modes of transport such as scooters, bicycles).

The app's audience is made up of economically active men and women of various age groups. The main features and differentials are access to a delivery service that stands out for delivering absolutely anything. The platform offers restaurant menus, supermarket items, from different types of stores (such as pet shops, pharmacies, among others). In the 'Anything' option, the user can order any type of product, as long as it fits in the courier's bag. This means that, within the same application, consumers can buy and receive beauty products, ready-to-eat foods wherever they want or even ask them to deliver a belonging they forgot at home and whatever else they need.

Rappi, like iFood, works on operating system compatibility iOS, Android and Web, which allows users to access it on various mobile devices or not, its installation is free from distribution platforms to operating systems or the web. Services offered in this app are as follows: Access to services and features is through the creation of an own profile in the application; there is the possibility of filtered search (by restaurant or other stores); there is the possibility of personalization: option to add or remove ingredients from the dishes at the end of the order (adjustment effect interaction); there is the property of scanning QR codes in stores associated with financial transactions within the application itself; there is real-time monitoring of the order made until its delivery/withdrawal.

There are promotional features such as the use of promotional coupons available via the app or manually entered in the 'coupons' tab; there is the assessment of the delivery person after the order is completed, which allows verifying the reliability of the service performed by delivery people, which favor the reputation of the Rappi brand; has a 'Help' tab available in the app, with real-time support via the application. Before the prohibition of these devices, it also had devices for locating and unlocking scooters in partnership with 'Yellow' and 'Grin', shared urban modals platforms.

Features as services offered after purchase, within the app and as extra services, for an additional price in the app, the 'Rappi Prime' service, which is a membership with a monthly or annual payment, through which the freight service is free and offered in all orders made through the Rappi platform paying with a credit card registered in the app, except for services made from the vertical Delivery. Among its interfaces and interactions, Rappi is a simple to use application, with a white background on all pages of the app. And what differentiates along the uses are the categories or promotional lists that the user can access. When clicking on the application, we see a white screen with the brand icon and then the home screen.

At first, we have three apparent functionalities: an icon that goes back to an abstract human figure in pictogram, where the user can access his profile and modify his information, request help and view his transaction history in the application; a tab for entering the user's current location, since the application works in a geolocation format (showing the final consumer a mapping of the restaurants closest to their delivery address); and finally, a 'Coupon' icon, where when clicking, the user can insert promotional coupons (promotional feature of the app).

Next, we see a tab called 'Rappi Pay', which works as a kind of Rappi 'bank account' - that is, the consumer has access to his balance in reais, according to promotions or initiatives that return money within the application itself, as well as a history of your transactions.

In the central part of the screen, still in this 'payments' section, we have a QR code, which when clicked, opens a camera inside the application to scan scooters and other urban modals, which Rappi has a partnership with; and also that it makes it possible to scan codes at partner stores and restaurants for payment within the application itself. Finally, it shows the user's balance on the left.

Below this section, still in the 'home', are shown several banners that simulate the main categories served by the application (e.g.: Supermarkets, Restaurants, Currency Exchange, Pets, Pharmacy, etc.). When clicking on any of these banners, except "Restaurants", one is redirected to a page that concentrates, in that sequence, a search tab with a filter option for 'products' or 'stores'; Banners with 'Deals of the day' (promotional dimension of the app); and a list with the logos of the main partners in the category (co-branding strategy between the Rappi brand and its partner brands.

By clicking on the restaurant banner, a search bar with a filter option (lower prices, shortest delivery time, highest consumer rating) is shown next, a merry-go-round with the main culinary categories (hamburger, sushi, sweets, etc.), a banner carousel with recommended promotions, a tab for best-selling restaurants, and finally, a 'Recommended for' tab for the user, as an endless list of recommended restaurants for the consumer. They are all advertising devices of endorsement, promotional for sales.

Once the user selects a restaurant or store, he is taken to his virtual menu, which is nothing more than the list of products, dishes and side dishes offered by that restaurant, with their respective values. The consumer also adds what he wants in the 'Anything' section.

When selecting the desired products, you are then directed to the checkout tab. In this tab, he can choose the payment method (of which that restaurant offers), check the delivery time of that dish and add promotional coupons. When validating all information, he clicks on a 'Checkout' button and is directed to a status page to track delivery.

As for the ways of working in the app, as well as in iFood, there are two ways of working in the application: that of the Delivery Person who works as a kind of self-employed professional on demand. Rappi's relationship with the Delivery Man in this scenario is also a commercial partnership, since there is no employment relationship between the company and the delivery person, still less a regulation provided by law that ensures labor rights for users of the platform. To become a delivery person, another application called Rappi Deliverers must be downloaded, which is intended for those who want to work in the delivery business in partnership with Rappi. When registering on the platform and providing personal data, the delivery person is able to accept delivery requests to Rappi customers. When you register, the delivery person has the option of choosing the city where he wants to make deliveries and which ones he wants to make, in addition to consulting debits and credits for racing and accessing Rappi's support service. The delivery app is only available for Android. Once again, the iOS operating system is associated with the uses and inputs of activities not consistent with those of the delivery personnel.

Work as restaurant owner, to be part of the network of partner restaurants, you need to have a business registration with a legal entity number for your restaurant and also internet access at your workplace to receive online orders. Bearing in mind that, in the case of Rappi, even if a restaurant is not registered and with 'a location' within the platform, delivery personnel can go to establishments through 'Anything' and take orders.

As in iFood, Rappi mixes advertising principles of promotionality and loyalty and institutionalization of the application's brand. Its differential is being able to deliver anything, but most of its deliveries are for food services.

The UberEats has as main objective to offer food delivery service (being a branch of the Uber business portfolio), which brings together menus from several restaurants registered for online purchase via app. Your audience is also made up of economically active men and women of various age groups. The main features are given free access to the menu of partner restaurants and both through the uberEats app and through a pop-up within the uber parent brand app itself (which offers ride-hailing services (manages to place a delivery order) of food, having an estimate of the time needed for this delivery, based on your location), choosing between different payment options and confirming the order - without making calls or talking to attendants. The main difference is that in the pop-up within the uber app, a more simplified version of UberEats is run, with less functionality. The app works in geolocation format, showing the end consumer a mapping of the restaurants closest to their delivery address.

Its operation is compatible with operating systems iOS, Android and Web, which allows users to access it on various mobile devices or not, its installation is free from distribution platforms to operating systems or the web. The sherbs offered in this allow the creation of an own profile in the application, which can be integrated into the Uber account itself, if you are already a user; allows the possibility of filtered search (by restaurant, cuisine, price, evaluation, etc.); offers the option of choosing delivery by courier or pick up, directly at the purchase establishment; offers the possibility of personalization or customization: option to add or remove ingredients from dishes at checkout (adjustment interaction effect); allows real-time monitoring of the order placed until its delivery/withdrawal; allows the use of promotional coupons available manually inserted in the 'coupons' tab, ensuring the aspect of the app's promotional.

A 'Help' tab is available, with real-time support via the app, here the possibility of accidental interaction is manifested. Services offered after in-app purchase or extra services for an additional price in the app: in the checkout tab, depending exclusively on the partner restaurant, sustainable packaging options can be offered for an additional price, this device also generates the adjustment effect interactions through the app interface.

The app's interfaces, roughly speaking, feature a simple to use application, with a white background on all the pages of the app, and that will be differentiated along the categories or promotional lists that the user enters. When clicking on the app, we see a black screen with the UberEats logo and then the home screen. On this screen, the first function is to describe the location you are in, since we are talking about an application that uses geolocation for its provision of offers of restaurants and dishes. Next, we have home filtering options, to be arranged according to the user's preference. Among them, for example, we have the option of restaurants to 'withdraw' on the spot, price, most popular, etc. Next, we have a kind of virtual showcase, with a carousel of banners that rotate the best current offers.

Then there is a tab titled 'Uber Rewards', focused on rewards for ride-hailing Uber users within the feed app. Finally, we see an infinite sequence of restaurants that are grouped into merry-go-rounds, according to common themes (e.g., popular near you, special offers, etc.). Once the user selects a restaurant, he is taken to his virtual 'menu', which is nothing more than the list of dishes and side dishes offered by that restaurant, with their respective values. When selecting one (or more) dish (s), the consumer can place a note on that item, asking to add or remove certain ingredients, and then it is directed to the checkout tab. In this tab, he can choose the payment method (of which that restaurant offers), check the delivery time of that dish and add promotional coupons. When validating all information, he clicks on a 'Checkout' button and is directed to a status page to track delivery. The ways of working are similar to the previous apps in the profiles of deliverers and responsible/restaurant owners.

The Apptite's main objective is to connect artisanal food producers (chefs) to consumers through delivery. A different option from previous apps. The public responds to economically active men and women, located in the middle and upper classes: Itaim Bibi, Moema, Brooklin, Campo Belo, Vila Olímpia, Vila Nova Conceição, Tatuapé, Jardins, Centro, Morumbi, Butantã, Pinheiros, Perdizes, Paraíso, Vila Mariana, Pompéia, Vila Madalena, Santana, Ipiranga, Mooca and Lapa. The user has free access to the app. In it you can access the menus of accredited Chefs and manage to schedule delivery of artisanal meals made for delivery, in low demand, by local chefs, without making calls or speaking with attendants.

The application works in a geolocation format, showing the end consumer a mapping of the restaurants closest to their delivery address platform compatibility, unlike other applications this only works on iOS and Android, so it is restricted to mobile devices. The services offered by the app are provided through the creation of your own profile within the application that offers the possibility of filtered ordering (by nearby chefs, by cuisine, less shipping, etc. The option of choosing to schedule the order receipt.

There is also the possibility of personalization: option to add or remove ingredients from the dishes (interaction adjustment effect). Allow the use of promotional coupons made available manually inserted in the 'Coupons' tab, which expresses the advertising action of the app. And a 'Help' tab is available, with real-time support via the app, for unforeseen accidental interactions. There are no additional services or after purchase within the app.

In the interfaces the application's home page shows, at the top, a calendar with the option of scheduling the moment when you want to receive your order, followed by a space to fill in your address, since the application uses geolocation to dispose of your content, and a 'coupons' tab for inserting promotional codes within the app. Next, we see a 'filter' button, with home ordering options, be it for 'quick dishes', 'less shipping', 'nearby chefs', etc. Below, we see the virtual showcase of the app, with a carousel with three banners: 'recommended for you', which when clicked, is directed to a list of dishes similar to your last orders (interactive manipulation of the app to your consumption profile). In the item 'My favorites', which when clicking the consumer is taken to a selection of his most requested dishes. 'Share and get discounts', a tab to share a unique code for each user so your friends can get discounts. Promotional action of the app. Below, there is an infinite sequence of dishes that are grouped in carousels, according to common themes (e.g.: free shipping, incredible discounts, best sellers, etc.).

The ways of work signaled by the app are that of Courier. In a kind of self-employed professional on demand. The Apptite x Delivery relationship in this scenario, as in the previous apps, is more of a commercial partnership than a job, since there is no employment relationship between the company and the delivery person. When registering on the platform and providing personal data, the delivery person is able to accept delivery requests to Apptite customers and receives for delivery.

The other function and which creates the differential of the app's offer, is working as a Chef to be part of the network of partner restaurants, you need to submit your interest to the platform and wait for approval from Appetit, which selects only 'quality' restaurants, according to the platform. The Chef must configure the information of his dishes on the platform, such as: accepted payment methods, opening hours, menu items, so that this information is available to customers in the application.

LivUp, the last app studied, has the main objective to offer healthy frozen food delivery service, ready to quickly heat up in the microwave and eat. The public consists of economically active men and women interested in healthy meals. The main features of app are to give the user access, free of charge to the app, to menus with kits, dishes and individual items for all meals of the day, and can assemble each one according to their preference and needs. It saves time when cooking, since the consumer receives all meals 'practically' ready. Meals are produced entirely with organic products. There is the flexibility to set up meals via the App - from snacks, sweets, snacks and receiving them all at once at the place scheduled by the consumer. With deep-freezing, food flavor, texture and nutrients are guaranteed.

The application is compatible with operating systems iOS, Android and Web, which allows users to access it on various mobile devices or not, its installation is free from distribution platforms to operating systems or the web.

The services offered are provided through the creating your own profile in the application. There is the possibility of filtered search (by restaurant, cuisine, organic food, more orders, etc.); There is the option to choose delivery by courier or pick up, directly in one of LivUp's spaces; There is the interactive effect of adjustment for customization: option to assemble meal kits, combining different types of food in each one. There is also the possibility of using promotional coupons made available manually inserted in the 'coupons' tab, also featuring advertising features. There is the functionality 'Help' tab is available, with real-time support via the app, for accidents not provided for in the app's interface programming.

There are no services offered after in-app purchase or extra services for an additional price. The interfaces in the app home page a bar with four icons: 'What are you hungry for?' menu, which opens a list with clickable categories of: kits, dishes, main portions, side dishes, snacks and drinks. When you click on each of these options, a new list of subcategories opens, and when you click on one of these (for example, 'vegetarians' within the 'kits' category, you are directed to a kind of options menu within of the category; magnifying glass: opens a 'hungry for what?' search bar; profile: tab for managing your profile, including insertion of payment methods, support section, etc.; bag: tab to track the items added to the present moment for the consumer to complete the purchase.

In the sequence, we see a carousel of icons of the highlighted categories (ex.: our organics, more orders, created by chefs, etc.).

Below, there is an infinite sequence of dishes that are grouped in carousels, according to common themes (e.g.: individual items, dishes, sugar-free sweets, etc.).

Finally, the app's ways of working are all of them belong to the company itself and are due to LivUp's employment ties and internal selection processes, from parcel deliverers to food producers. The productive chain in the business model is more fair in the distribution of income compared to the other studied apps that use the economy of intermediation based on precarious work relationships. There is a coherence with the conceptual proposal of the app's brand in its institutionalization and its practices.

4   Some Processes to Highlight

It can be noticed from the studies that, with the advancement of technology in the culture of consumption, there were transformations in the modus operandi of things; this from relationships at work to the ways in which people eat and understand food.

With the relative popularization of the internet, in the Brazilian context and in the city of São Paulo, several tools appear and are built based on narratives to facilitate people's lives. In this context, both concepts of mediation (analysis of the way in which the mediated logics are reflected in the subjects, cultures and their communication) and mediatization (referring to a reflection of the internal logic of the communicational and media organisms, considering contexts and influencing cultures) are essential for understanding how the analyzed apps act on the current society. It seems that mediations respond to what people do with communication. And mediatization answers questions about what types of operations, structures and logical processes that the media institute values in cultures and societies.

From the mediatization it is noticed that the apps present a direct mediatization about the eating habits. Food and the act of eating now pass through lenses capable of seeing only their dietary function and the aesthetics of consumption, a fact that is reinforced by dietary trends [19] that point us to the foods of the future being frozen, of long validity, highlighted by a singular consumption that ignores commensality traits, or it comes second in advertising appeals as a nostalgic argument. The sense of buying food in natura disappears, its preparation and the rituals at the table, showing that cultural mediation of food is being transformed with the purchase of ready-made foods via applications.

The research report that underlies the empirics of this article [14] shows the algorithms of the studied applications as a structural element of the dynamics of the digital ecosystem, since mapping, indexing and categorizing the data produced by modern processors implies calculations to establish relationships between these data, to the point of being able to establish an almost instantaneous organization of uses and consumptions in network spaces via artificial intelligence, it is a precursor action for a de-structuralization and re-structuralization of what we understand in the logic of consumption.

This phenomenon, of Big Data, which dominates the discourse of contemporary technology, caused the turning of the algorithm in the communication infrastructures and the material cultures mediated by it [7, 13], which made the advertising brands to depend on computational routines to control the information they acquire, produce and disseminate. In the application environment, of digital media, a multitude of algorithms cooperate, but also compete with each other in the performance of tasks: from the selection of content considered most relevant to individual members of the public, to the control of the circulation of information and content inserted and circulated on media platforms [13].

In other words, we are talking about an increasingly passive and environmental data collection, widespread and correlative, supported by the identification of biases and in which contexts these biases occur. All this for the creation of such numerical identities. To materialize this concept, just look at the ad served by Experian in the United Kingdom in 2017, entitled 'Meet your Data Self' (Multinational information and database management company, operating in 44 countries, in Brazil the company acts as Serasa Expirian). In a humorous tone, the film makes clear how the use of data creates a pre-character (see Fig. 1), previously non existent, based on its consumption data; it demonstrates how the company, in a convenient way, leverages the use of its database, to give an opinion and decide for it, before itself. Therefore, there is no longer a well-defined separation between what is human action and what is the action of the apparatus. When interacting, we build and reinforce the algorithm, while we also remake our offline identity: our purchases happen from the ads that arrive from our online route; and our daily agendas are guided by the circulation of information of which we are also gear [1].

Fig. 1. Screen capture of Experian's "Meet your Data Self" ad (2020).

In order to do advertising, in this sense, the distinctions between broadcast media systems are clear, where brand-advertisers produced attention relationships by buying media spaces, from this new algorithmic media system, where brand-advertisers need to establish relationships that algorithms are able to recognize - so they can feed back and reproduce themselves in an endless cycle. In other words, it is the movement from the media to the software [12]. And it is in this way that computers are modeling reality - through data structures and algorithms - and that can also be applied to media as soon as they are digitally represented. That is, since the moved media are digital data controlled by the specific cultural software, it makes sense to think of any objective of the applications, of the new media, they are due to specific data structures and/or specific algorithms that it incorporates [12].

Thus, the construction of the interfaces of the selected food applications is explored, in order to point out how algorithmic incorporations occur and their resulting impacts on the culture of material consumption. These interfaces act as a kind of behavioral engineering. It can be seen from the research that the homogenization of the way food applications operate, even in different niches, is mainly due to the centralization of offers in a geolocalized way that adds to the use of AI in the way the apps are made available. and in the way in which application companies constitute their labor relations and make their procedures viable.

According studies about interfaces [6], behavior generates behavior. Thus, we cannot separate what the buyer offers the seller from what the seller offers to the buyer; and so on. This concept, from the affordances theory [6], is relevant to the study of applications, especially power applications, as we talk about interfaces that suggest the availability of something that does not change according to the need of the observer changes, but that is attached and available according to that same need. To better explain this concept, consider the interfaces of the apps analyzed in the present study: they are the virtualization of consumption temples, with thousands of catalogs arranged in one place, suggesting infinite possibilities in their carousels, banners, flashing buttons, that when clicked direct consumers to more and more lists of purchase options, ranging from ready meals to frozen, market products to the fair, in short. In this way, they mediate consumer orders, delivering their wishes to a predefined location.

What is meant, therefore, is that they are platforms that, regardless of whether availability is perceived, met or not met, do not change as the observer's needs change, but, being invariable, they are always there to be perceived [6]. Therefore, the concept of utility technology [3], collaborates to point out this space/interface, of food apps, as capable of satisfying consumers' food desires regardless of their real need, based on the understanding that the offer is available all the time, just a few clicks away, on the screen of a mobile device. The key point of this discussion, therefore, is the fact that this discovery of the interface mediated by the applications, becomes invariable given its power of market regulation, which allows the provision of food independently from a single supplier.

In short, the concept of utility technology [3] concerns the understanding of the interfaces and connected devices that combine the design of experience, also known as 'choice architecture', with elements of gamification and online sociability, added to the analysis BigData, and allow the design of behavioral engineering [3].

All of this leads us to point to apps, as brand-advertisers, platforms that advertise beyond symbolic persuasion; in fact, the behavior of consumers who browse its interface, mediated by such an architecture of choice, provide the necessary feedback to feed back and modify its entire structure in order to enhance consumption - through, of course, Big Data analysis.

And so, to think about consumption mediated by food applications, it is necessary to reframe the role of the consumer in the face of applications: we are talking about brand-advertisers that develop inviting interfaces, suggesting that participants are rational subjects (that is, endowed with knowledge and possibility of consumption) are free and able to exercise their individuality of purchase, even though they are operating within a clearly defined rules space and with dozens of incentives; which map each click (including what is not clicked) to think and modify the way, time and need for how people eat.

The potential interactions of the apps on the presented interfaces are, as you can see, programmed to avoid accidents or risks. The effects of adjustment experiences are not adjustments, they are programmed, but they make the consumer assimilate the functionality of removing ingredients, menu options, restaurants, based on the architecture of the choices as an adjustment. Accidents are only foreseen in the help functions. All of this associated with the machine learning mechanisms of the algorithmic data of these applications create mechanisms for advertising actions, via carousels, coupons with promotional codes, which manipulate small data, possibilities of more specific niche audiences, creating another adjustment effect, with an appearance of personalization,

The work of artificial intelligence algorithms processes personal/registration data, sensitive data, usage and consumption data on platform features, apps, track terms, images that allow the organization of data entry and exit in favor of institutional strategic fixation actions of brands and sales promotions (dumping– promotions at lower prices, setting up an immediate purchase opportunity), while nourishing the conditioning by repetition, loyalty of behaviors identified as consumption patterns of geolocalized groups, creating loop effects that stimulate individuals to the repetition of clicks, views and, above all, repeated purchase actions in retail, in constant flow. This demonstrates the complexity of the automated processing of these personal tracks that is distributed in different stages and formats. In order to maintain consumer interests, a Loop is created by the algorithm, that is, a dynamic that begins with the production of this personal data by the consumer himself (e.g.: opening a pizzeria menu in the application), and is completed with the receipt of a retroactive communication in the form of a personalized offer, which encourages actions that generate new personal data (e.g., receiving an e-mail marketing). In other words, the more you consume, the more consumption incentive actions are generated, forming a Big Data Loop that is able to feed back and create infinite new needs.

It is in this way, with calls that do not seek charm that worked in advertising, that we are bombarded all the time: "Delicious food, free delivery, discount, double dishes and more? Only if it is now". It is worth noting the way in which the synchronicity of these tactics worked by the apps raises the notion of hyper consumption to maximum potential [11]. Big Data, in short, allows applications to catalyze the spiral of contemporary anxiety, depressions, shortages, the difficulty of living [11].

iFood, UberEats and Rappi stand out in these processes, as they have a wider audience. These aspects, which by the business model of LivUp and Apptite are less intense in the loop processes, but all do not dispense with dumping actions always necessary.

The advertising logic and, therefore, communicational, is constitutive of the apps, conditioning the presence of professionals, who think within the digital logics, institutional actions and, above all, promotional actions, which in the face of the manipulation regime seek to prospect new customers, with promotions in the register and first purchases, maintain and retain consumer-users and increase sales.

As we discussed, material consumption, interwoven with algorithmic culture, creates a lifestyle where the more you consume, the more incentive actions for consumption are generated, creating a Loop of infinite new needs, influenced by applications and platforms that, taking advantage of the urgency of work life, the overvaluation of industrialized food - and, consequently, better mediatized, create calculable audiences liable to all this logic of mad consumption. In other words, we discuss an ongoing process where, several changes are triggered in the way we move, buy, transfer and choose products, mediated by companies from the 'new economy' (startups, applications, platforms, etc.), which break with the understanding of what work is, due to a supposedly more practical life appropriate to the time of work.

For characterization purposes, we recognize this process as the work platform, through which we observe a rearrangement of labor relations, in which the applications-platforms, which although they are often used as synonyms, they make differences. Application designates software installed on mobile devices, the articulation of the platform goes beyond the application installed individually on each person's cell phone and their technical materiality are non-human, fundamental actors. By expanding the focus in relation to platforms, in this sense, we understand them as digital infrastructures, which act simultaneously as means of production and means of communication, proving to be useful both for working and for interacting. In this way, they act in the production processes in favor of the capital circulation process and, in the communicational processes, contributing to the acceleration of this circulation.

Thus, we understand the platform work mediated by the food app as constituents of management and control modes, in addition to different developments that intermingle in the very forms of sociability among deliverers, tactics of political organization and appropriations of algorithmic mediation by them. For the possibility of existing in the way they were imagined, the platforms disfigure the symbolism and the role of work in modern society, stressing their infrastructures, regulations and relationships. Are food apps a reference for a new work model? Fed by a service provider who starts the day without having any idea how much he will be able to earn, he is always waiting for a next job that does not know why he came or not for him, why he has a certain value; pedaling tirelessly to earn less than a minimum wage. These are issues to be addressed by the area.

5　Final Considerations

The illusory promise of the fetishization of social discursivization about algorithms application's is that the individual is free and makes choices, but in this game of algorithmic mediations that are not built, everything is programmed and there is not much consumer perception about what it means your data privacy. This discursivization creates an algorithmic imagery of neutrality and objectivity, associated with magical menanisms, such as divination about what the consumer wants. But the rules of the game are only clear and defined for those who develop them and not necessarily for users, who for the most part do not have a clear perception of the algorithmic functioning [4].

We reinforce this point when we visit the privacy codes of the analyzed apps, which hide in small letters and legal language, the way they appropriate each and every digital trace left by the consumer. Let us see, for example, some lines referring to the terms that every user accepts when registering on the UberEats platform, contained in its Privacy Policy [16]: Collection of accurate or approximate location data of the device; Collect this data when the Uber app is running in the background on the user's device; Collect data through cookies, pixels, tags and similar technologies that create and maintain unique identifiers; Collect data and information about the devices used to access our services, including hardware models, device IP address, operating systems and versions, software, preferred languages, unique device identifiers, advertising identifiers, serial numbers, transaction data mobile network device and data [...] with the function of "improving our products and services and for analysis".

It is also mentioned that information collected from users may be shared with third parties and service providers, to "[...] help provide our services or conduct data processing on our behalf [...]". We have no doubts about the real needs of collecting so much data, as well as their real intentions to share with third parties, who say they 'collaborate in improving the application', demonstrating the interdependence of users' personal information in the aggregated data networks.

Let us not forget to pay attention to the fact that it is not only individual/personal data that is being stored in databases; in the case of the analyzed platforms, data on restaurants, markets, producers, partner suppliers are also mediated, as well as, of course, delivery personnel, who have the role of connecting supply to demand. This is because the relationships and correlations between the various data are stored using metadata (also known as tags); these, categorizing other data, as a means of organizing, hierarchizing, dynamizing and evaluating, have become increasingly important as social, political and economic instruments.

There is no consumer awareness of the right to data privacy, although in Brazil in September 2020, the regulatory framework of the General Data Protection Law was approved [10]. A sign of civilizing progress, but one that depends on a virtuous cycle of laws and consolidations of institutions for its effective inspection and implementation in brazilian context.

As we have shown throughout the corpus, the mediation of the algorithms is based on predetermined calculations and schedules, which, guided by the ingeniously calculated application interface, create possibilities for uses and consumptions that overflow the purchase of products and/or contracting their services.. In other words, the transformation occurs not only in eating habits, but also in the production logic itself. It is a broader mathematical order, which goes back to all aspects of social life, reorganizing everyday life and quantifying it in probabilistic logics.

If food is culturally inscribed by the symbolic dimension that this act occupies in the life of civilizations, it is noticeable that food applications, today central to everyday life, are transforming the logic of communicational mediations of consumption and their rituals, mediating new consumption habits, promotions, indications of purchase options, based on calculations about the user-consumer uses that allow strategies that enable new dimensions of the institutional relationship and meaning links between brands and consumers. This article is a theoretical-methodological contribution to the treatment of these empirical phenomena in the life of (i) material culture.

The history of food gains new contours with the platform of capital and the mathematization of eating habits, in this case. In Fladrin and Montanari [5] when organizing the texts that deal with the history of food, they end with the reflection that deals with the McDonaldization of the world. Today the phenomenon studied in food apps shows the platform of food life, as a new chapter of mediatized food cultures, launching new opportunities and challenges for researching the semioprammatic of these communicative forms. It was in this sense that this reflection sought to show a way to understand the phenomena of material consumption, in the logic mediated by digital applications and their numerical mediation in its broad consequences for societies.

Sometimes re-emphasizing what can be understood as a fair economic social practice, now warning about the dangers of the deinstitutionalization of productive life, work, and the economy with a focus only on mediatized consumption, precariousness of labor bonds, which will not sustain society within a fairer civilization plan in its entire chain from production to consumption.

It was also pointed out the presence of advertising logic in every corpus studied, which configures the intrinsic relationship between capitalism, communication, work and consumption, based on the applications observed as an important research agenda in the field of media studies and communication.

Only LivUp seems to be looking for a business model option that considers the production-consumption chain as a whole and within fair practices, but a more in-depth study would be necessary to verify the consistency of this proposal. In any case, LivUp appears to be an exception among the other apps studied, but it shows that the logic of the mediatized economy in platform capitalism can serve two paths and that there are alternatives beyond the appropriation of private personal data, with possibilities of uses. propogandistic logics, not necessarily advertising/commercial, that may give space to other values and practices of material consumption with a view to the new civil possibilities necessary for this moment of humanity.

References

1. Arruda, M.: Nova tropicália: uma desterritorialização da internet algorítmica (New tropicália: a deterritorialization of the algorithmic internet). In: Anais ... XXXIX Congresso Brasileiro de Ciências da Comunicação (XXXIX Brazilian Congress of Communication Sciences), São Paulo (2016). https://portalintercom.org.br/anais/nacional2016/resumos/R11-0380-1.pdf. Accessed Feb 2021
2. Berthelot-Guiet, K., Marti, C., Patrin-Lecrère, V.: Sémiotique des métamorphoses Marques-Médias. In: Berthelot-Guiet, K., Boutaud, J.-J., Jean-Jacques (Org.) (eds.): Sémiotique mode d'emploi. Le Bord L'Eau, Paris. Collection Mondes Marchands, pp. 255–291 (2014)
3. Brodmerkel, S., Carah, N.: Brand Machines, Sensory Media and Calculative Culture. Palgrave Macmillan, London (2016)
4. Bucher, T.: The algorithmic imaginary: exploring the ordinary affects of Facebook algorithms. Inf. Commun. Soc. 20(11), 30–44 (2017). https://doi.org/10.1080/1369118X.2016.1154086. Accessed Feb 2021
5. Flandrin, J.L, Montanari, M.: História da alimentação (History of food 2. From the Modern Age to the presente). Terramar, Lisbon (2001)

6. Gibson, J.J.: The theory of affordances. In: Shaw, R., Bransford, J. (eds.) Perceiving, Acting, and Knowing: Toward an Ecological Psychology, pp. 67–82. Lawrence Erlbaum, Hillsdale (1977)
7. Gillespie, T.: The relevance of algorithms. In: Media Technologies: Essays on communication, Materiality, and Society, Cambridge (2014). http://governingalgorithms.org/wp-content/upl oads/2013/05/1-paper-gillespie.pdf. Accessed Feb 2021
8. Hjarvard, S.: The Mediatization of Culture and Society. Routledge, London/New York (2013)
9. Landowski, E.: Interações arriscadas (Risky interactions). Estação das Letras and Cores, São Paulo (2014)
10. General Law on Protection of Personal Data in Brazil. http://www.planalto.gov.br/ccivil_03/_ato2015-2018/2018/lei/L13709compilado.htm. Accessed Feb 2021
11. Lipovetsky, G.: A Felicidade Paradoxal: um ensaio sobre a sociedade do hiperconsumo. (Paradoxical happiness: an essay on the hyperconsumption Society). Editions 70, Lisbon (2007)
12. Manovich, L.: Novas mídas como tecnologias e ideias: dez definições. (New media as technology and idea: Ten definitions). In: Leão, L. (org.) (ed.) O Chip e o caleidoscópio: refelcções sobre as novas mídias. (The chip and the kaleidoscope: Reflections on new media. Senac, São Paulo (2005)
13. Mckelvey, F.: Algorithmic media need democratic methods: why publics matter. Can. J. Commun. **39**, 597–613 (2014)
14. Oliveira, J.V.: Mediações algorítimicas no consumo da cultura material: mapeando aplicativos de alimentação, funcionalidades e lógicas. (Algorithmic mediations in the culture of material consumption: mapping food applications - functionalities and logic), p. 73. Research Reporte. ECA/USP, São Paulo (2020)
15. Perez, C.: O ecologia publicitária: o crescimento sígnico da publicidade. (Advertising ecology: the signic growth of advertising). In: Perez, C., Castro, M.L.D., Pompeu, B., Santos, G.F.C. (Orgs.) (eds.) Ontologia Publicitária: epistemologia, práxis e linguagem. (Advertising Ontology. Epistemology, Praxis and Language), GPs collection, pp. 111–124. INTERCOM, São Paulo (2018)
16. Privacy Policy Uber Eats. https://help.uber.com/en-US/riders/article/informa%C3%A7%C3%B5es-do-aviso-de-privácia?nodeId=e1f427a1-c1ab-4c6a-a78a-864f47877558. Accessed Feb 2021
17. Srnicek, N.: Platform Capitalism, 1st edn. Polity, Cambridge (2016)
18. Schor, J.B.: After the Gig: How the Sharing Economy Got Hijacked and How to Win It Back. University of California Press, Oakland (2020)
19. Report of Wunderman Thompson, Future 100 2.0.20. https://intelligence.wundermantho mpson.com/trend-reports/the-future-100-2-0-20/. Accessed Feb 2021
20. Trindade, E.: Algorithms and advertising in consumption mediations: a semio-pragmatic perspective. In: Meiselwitz, G. (ed.) HCII 2019. LNCS, vol. 11579, pp. 514–526. Springer, Cham (2019). https://doi.org/10.1007/978-3-030-21905-5_40
21. Trindade, E., Perez, C.: The consumer between mediations and mediatization. Famecos Mag. **26**(2), 32066 (2019). https://revistaseletronicas.pucrs.br/ojs/index.php/revistafamecos/article/view/32066
22. Trindade, E., Perez, C.: From communicational mediations to numerical mediation in consumption: a trend for research. In: IX Propesq PP-National Meeting of Researchers in Advertising, 2018, São Paulo. Anais IX Propesq PP-National Meeting of Researchers in Advertising: Science and Attitude. ECA/USP, pp. 112–127 (2019b)

Studying the Influence of Social Media Use on Sales Performance: The Role of Relational Mediators

Romain Franck[✉] and Maud Dampérat

University of Lyon, UJM-Saint-Etienne, COACTIS, Saint-Etienne, France
{romain.franck,maud.damperat}@univ-st-etienne.fr

Abstract. Based on a relationship marketing approach, this paper studies the impact of social media use on sales performance and its underlying mechanisms. A conceptual model is proposed and empirically tested from the perspective of salespeople in B2B settings. The proposed model includes both the direct influence of social media use on sales performance, and its indirect influence through relational mediators (i.e., adaptive selling behavior and relationship quality). To test the proposed model, we use structural equation modeling with a sample of 199 French B2B salespeople. The proposed model is validated, allowing us to confirm the direct and indirect role of social media use on sales performance and to better understand the underlying mechanisms associated with relational mediators.

Keywords: Adaptive selling behavior · B2B sales · Relationship marketing · Relationship quality · Sales performance · Social media use

1 Introduction

A strategic question for marketing and sales departments is whether they should promote the use of social media by salespeople, which involves investing in these technologies and in training [1]. With the development of social media, salespeople are constantly connected to their customers and managers [2]. Being active on social media allows salespeople to be present earlier in the buyer's trajectory, thereby giving them a better chance of participating in the development of business solutions for customers. By becoming aware of customers' views early on, salespeople increase their chances of winning business [3]. The way of selling in B2B is evolving: salespeople can meet prospects, propose offers, and make sure that customers follow updates through social media. Yet if some salespeople appreciate the use of social media, others display more reluctance on the grounds that only face-to-face meetings are able to create long-lasting relationships. This lack of a common viewpoint may be due to the fact that the use of social media is still relatively new in B2B relationships and that empirical research in the academic literature is extremely limited [4]. Thus there is a need for research in B2B settings on the influence of social media use on sales performance and its relational underlying mechanisms.

© Springer Nature Switzerland AG 2021
G. Meiselwitz (Ed.): HCII 2021, LNCS 12775, pp. 86–97, 2021.
https://doi.org/10.1007/978-3-030-77685-5_7

To understand the influence of social media use, various theoretical approaches have been adopted, mainly information and communication approaches. Some studies indicate that social media can be used for gathering information to acquire a better understanding of customers [5], build a network, and interact with stakeholders [5, 6]. According to Andzulis, Panagopoulos [7], networks on social media can be used to build awareness and gain referrals, and active use of social media can help salespeople improve their communication with customers. Other studies note that salespeople try to enhance their reputation by joining communities, sharing posts or blogging [5, 8], or by exerting social influence in online communities [9]. Yet the relational mechanisms through which the use of social media influences salespeople's performance has yet to be studied.

Few studies focus on social media use from a relationship marketing standpoint. Among those that do, Itani, Agnihotri [10] show the influence of social media use on adaptive selling behavior. However, the role of social media use that modifies touch points and the development of the buyer-seller relationship has been little studied. Indeed, Palmatier, Dant [11] show in a meta-analysis the central and mediating role played by relationship quality. Thus further studies are called for to help understand the role that social media play through adaptive selling behavior and the effect of enhanced relationship quality on sales performance.

Based on relationship marketing [11], we study the influence of social media use on sales performance in B2B settings. We also seek to understand the underlying mechanisms that could explain the influence of social media use on sales performance. Thus we examine the mediating effect of relational mediators (i.e., adaptive selling behavior and relationship quality) between social media use and sales performance. The originality of this paper lies in its addressing: (1) the influence of social media use on both adaptive selling behavior and relationship quality; (2) the mediating role of relationship quality between social media use and sales performance; and (3) the twofold mediation of adaptive selling behavior and relationship quality between social media use and sales performance.

2 Literature Review

2.1 Social Media in B2B Sales

Social media are associated with different technologies able to provide users with services such as networking, online search, and analytics O'Reilly and Battelle [12]. According to Kaplan and Haenlein [13], social media comprise a group of internet-based applications that build on the ideological and technological foundations of Web 2.0, and that enable the creation and exchange of user-generated content. Mangold and Faulds [14] have highlighted the importance of social media for various components of a company's integrated marketing communications strategy, including direct customer communication, such as personal selling.

Social media can be used at all stages of the sales process, from prospecting to relationship monitoring. They are considered to be an essential part of a company's sales process because they allow salespeople to interact with customers, and create social capital that encourages them to interact, engage and build relationships with customers [15]. Social media such as LinkedIn may assist in identifying genuine decision makers and buyers within an organization. Itani, Agnihotri [10] argue that both sales management and salespeople view social media as an effective global tool for increasing connectivity, building personal and long-term relationships with customers.

2.2 Relationship Marketing and Relational Mediators

Relationship marketing is well established in B2B sales [16]. Morgan and Hunt [17] define relationship marketing as "all marketing activities aimed at establishing, developing and maintaining good relationships". Most research and managerial practices assume that relationship marketing efforts generate stronger relationships with customers, thereby increasing seller performance, sales, market share, and profits [17, 18]. Relationship marketing emphasizes the importance of buyer-seller relationships, that improve the efficiency of business relationships [19] and develop business relationships over the long term [20, 21].

The quality of the relationship between buyer and seller is recognized as a key relational mediator, and is conceptualized by three dimensions: (1) trust, i.e. confidence in an exchange partner's reliability and integrity [22]; (2) commitment, i.e. the enduring desire to maintain a valued relationship [23]; and (3) relationship satisfaction, i.e., the customer's affective or emotional state toward a relationship, typically evaluated cumulatively over the history of the exchange [18]. Overall, relationship quality is defined as an assessment of the strength of a relationship. It is conceptualized as a composite or multidimensional construct capturing the different but related facets of a relationship [24, 25].

3   Conceptual Model and Hypotheses Development

3.1   Sales Performance and Social Media Use

We define sales performance as the extent to which technology affects the salesperson's ability to produce good sales results [26]. Achieving sales objectives in terms of both quality and quantity involves issues such as generating new customers, meeting specific sales objectives, improving territorial penetration, and selling profitable products. According to Zallocco, Pullins [27], firms look beyond the transaction-based concepts of unit sales and immediate revenue when measuring and evaluating sales performance. The salesperson is best positioned to know the details of the many requirements of the job, how well she or he actually performs, and what might be accomplished [28]. In the context of industrial selling, buyers use social media for their purchases by comparing products, researching the market, and building relationships with sellers. Social media are becoming major players in all types of communication, particularly in B2B, and create unique potential for better sales performance.

H1: Social media use positively influences sales performance.

3.2   Adaptive Selling Behavior and Social Media Use

Adaptive selling behavior is defined as "the modification of sales behaviors during a customer interaction or between customer interactions based on perceived information about the nature of the sale" [29]. Salespeople who have practiced adaptive selling in the past will be predisposed to continue to do so. The reason salespeople are more able to adapt is because they have a clearer understanding of customer information. In essence, better information improves the seller's ability to adapt by providing meaningful information models from increasingly complex and readily available market data [30].

H2: Social media use positively influences adaptive selling behavior.

3.3   Relationship Quality and Social Media Use

According to Mullins, Ahearne [31] relationship quality perceived by the seller is as a combination of the seller's perception of the customer's trust, satisfaction, and commitment to the firm. Previous studies [11] show that relationship quality is based on three dimensions: commitment [32], trust [11] and satisfaction [18]. We use sellers' perception of relationship quality, as they know the real level of relational characteristics of customers [33]. According to Ellis and Beatty [34], customers obtain social benefits when salespeople connect with them at a personal level (i.e., social behavior). We hypothesize that social media should increase buyer-seller connections and help build trust and commitment.

H3: Social media use positively influences relationship quality.

3.4   Relationship Between Relational Mediators

According to Park, Kim [35], little research has focused on the relationship between adaptive selling behavior and the quality of the relationship. This gap in the literature is surprising given that one of the goals of adaptive selling behavior is to strengthen the bonds between salespeople and customers [36, 37]. Adaptive selling allows sellers to tailor messages to their buyers, and should therefore improve their ability to build relationships with customers [38].

H4: Adaptive selling behavior positively influences relationship quality.

3.5   Relational Mediators and Sales Performance

Adaptive selling behavior results in long-term effectiveness when the benefits of the approach outweigh the costs – that is, when the sales generated by the practice of adaptive selling outweigh the cost of selecting and training salespeople to collect relevant information from their customers and to use that information appropriately [36]. It appears that adaptive selling behavior is especially appropriate when the seller has the necessary resources, when purchasing tasks are complex and can result in large orders, and when customer relationships are not conflictual and are expected to continue in the future. Salespeople can use the information they collect about prospects or customers before or during interaction so as to customize the content and the format of their messages for more effective communication [39]. Thus social media as a source of information should result in better sales performance.

H5: Adaptive selling behavior positively influences sales performance.

According to Palmatier, Dant [11], relationship marketing is based on the assumption that building strong relationships positively influences the outcomes of exchanges, and researchers recognize that exchanges vary across a spectrum from transactional to relational [40]. Providing improved benefits in turn prompts customers to repeatedly buy the products offered by the seller, to do more business with the seller by purchasing additional products, and to recommend the products to others. Thus, we expect relationship quality to have a greater impact on sales performance.

H6: Relationship quality positively influences sales performance.

3.6   The Mediating Effects of Relational Mediators

According to Jaramillo, Locander [38], adaptive selling can enhance the salesperson's ability to build quality relationships with buyers and thereby increase job performance. Román and Iacobucci [41] find positive effects of adaptive selling on both customers' satisfaction with the salesperson and on the salesperson's performance outcome. The existing literature displays varied findings regarding the effect of adaptive selling behaviors on salespeople's performance [10]. In a business interaction, the effective use of social media improves the seller's ability to anticipate and respond to buyers' concerns and objections, and in turn builds relationships and increases sales performance.

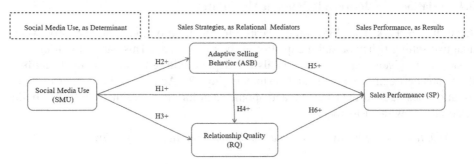

Fig. 1. The proposed model

H7: The relational mediators (a) adaptive selling behavior and (b) relationship quality have a mediating role between social media use and sales performance.

4   Methodology

Figure 1 presents the proposed model.

4.1 Sample

The sample comprised 199 French B2B salespeople based on a Qualtrics panel. Demographic characteristics of the sample are presented in Table 1. The sample comprises 45.5% men and 54% women (0.5% did not comment). Sales professionals were made aware that the research was being conducted for scholarly purposes.

Table 1. Sample description

Age	18 and 34 years old	44.2%
	35 and 54 years old	45.2%
	More than 55 years old	10.6%
Company size	1 to 9 employees	14.6%
	10 to 49 employees	22.1%
	50 to 249 employees	17.6%
	250 to 4999 employees	28.1%
	More than 5000 employees	17.6%
Job title	Commercial	40.2%
	Sales manager	27.1%
	Key accounts manager	4.5%
	Business manager / business developer	11.1%
	Technical sales	11.1%
	Business engineer	6%

4.2 Measurement Scales

For social media use, we used a 3-item 7-point scale adapted from Agnihotri, Dingus [4]. For adaptive selling behavior, we used a 3-item 7-point scale adapted from the ADAPTS scale developed by Spiro and Weitz [36]. We focus on ADAPTS's facet 6 corresponding to the current behavior of sellers. For sales performance, we used a 3-item 7-point scale adapted from Behrman and Perreault Jr. [28] and Boorom, Goolsby [42]. For relationship quality as perceived by the salesperson, we used a tridimensional scale including trust, satisfaction and commitment, presenting all 2-item 7-point scales as developed by Mullins, Ahearne [31].

4.3 Measurement Evaluation

To assess the quality of the measurement scales, we followed a two-step procedure following the recommendations of Steenkamp and Van Trijp [43]. The first step was to study the correlations in order to purify the scales. Items with correlations less than 0.30 were removed. The second step consisted of a confirmatory factor analysis (CFA) evaluated on the basis of the indices recommended by Hu and Bentler [44]. Based on these recommended indices, the measurement model is satisfactory: $Chi^2/81 = 1.504$; RMSEA $= 0.05$; TLI $= 0.962$; CFI $= 0.971$; SRMR $= 0.049$. The standardized coefficients, critical ratio and p-value of each item are presented in Table 2.

Table 2. Results of the measurement model

Constructs	Codifications	λ stand	t-value	p. value
Social Media Use (SMU)	SMU1.	0.771	-	-
	SMU2.	0.848	11.586	0.000
	SMU3.	0.844	11.563	0.000
Adaptive Selling Behavior (ASB)	ASB1.	0.717	-	-
	ASB2.	0.835	8.515	0.000
	ASB3.	0.626	7.599	0.000
Relationship Quality (RQ)	CO1.	0.901	-	-
	CO2.	0.829	12.360	0.000
	SAT1.	0.872	-	-
	SAT2.	0.863	13.030	0.000
	COMM1.	0.931	-	-
	COMM2.	0.666	7.824	0.000
Sales Performance (SP)	SP1.	0.770	-	-
	SP2.	0.801	10.564	0.000
	SP3.	0.814	10.661	0.000

The analysis of reliability, convergent validity and discriminant validity highlights the satisfactory results for each construct. The convergent validity of the constructs is confirmed with average variance extracted (AVE) values greater than 0.50, in accordance with the recommendations of Fornell and Larcker [45]. Likewise, discriminant validity is established, since the average variance extracted from each construct is greater than the correlation squares, which are well below the threshold of 0.50. The detailed results are presented in Table 3.

Table 3. Reliability, convergent validity, and discriminant validity

Constructs	AVE	Squared correlations			
		SMU	ASB	RQ	SP
SMU	**0.68** (a)	*0.82* (b)			
ASB	**0.53**	0.08 (c)	*0.73*		
RQ	**0.72**	0.02	0.17	*0.84*	
SP	**0.75**	0.17	0.21	0.12	*0.80*

(a) The average extracted variance by construct is presented in the second column and is in bold.
(b) The alpha coefficients are presented in the diagonal and are in italics.
(c) The squares of the correlations between constructs are presented in the lower triangle.

5 Results

5.1 Direct Effects Testing

The proposed model and its related hypotheses (H1 to H4) was tested using the structural equations using maximum likelihood method with AMOS 27. Based on Hu and Bentler [44] indices, the structural model is satisfactory: $Chi^2/81 = 1.504$; RMSEA = 0.05; TLI = 0.962; CFI = 0.971; SRMR = 0.049. Results show that social media use positively and significantly influences sales performance (H1: $y = 0.30$; p = 0.000) and adaptive selling behavior (H2: $y = 0.28$; p = 0.001), but has no significant influence on relationship quality (H3: $y = 0.018$; p = 0.835). Thus H1 et H2 are confirmed, but H3 is not. Adaptive selling behavior positively and significantly influence relationship quality (H4: $\beta = 0.403$; p = 0.000). H4 is confirmed. Sales performance is positively and significantly influenced both by adaptive selling behavior (H5: $\beta = 0.296$; p = 0.002) and relationship quality (H6: $\beta = 0.193$; p = 0.027). H5 and H6 are confirmed (Table 4).

Table 4. The results of the proposed model

			λ stand	t-value	p. value
H1	Social Media Use	→ Sales Performance	.30	3.701	.000
H2	Social Media Use	→ Adaptive Selling Behavior	.28	3.201	.001
H3	Social Media Use	→ Relationship Quality	.02	.208	.835
H4	Adaptive Selling Behavior	→ Relationship Quality	.40	4.100	.000
H5	Adaptive selling Behavior	→ Sales Performance	.30	3.139	.002
H6	Relationship Quality	→ Sales Performance	.19	2.204	.027
	Fit Measures:				
	Khi^2/df	121.851/81 (1,504)			
	RMSEA	0,050			
	TLI	0,962			
	CFI	0,971			
	SRMR	0,049			

5.2 Indirect Effects Testing

Regarding the mediating role of adaptive selling behavior and relationship quality, we followed the recommendations of Zhao, Lynch Jr. [46] and of Preacher and Hayes [47], leading us to perform the bootstrap test of the indirect effect via structural equations. The results show that the indirect effect of adaptive selling behavior is statistically significant (b = 0.113; p = 0.005) with a 95% confidence interval (b between 0.037 and 0.235) excluding the value zero. Likewise, the indirect effect of adaptive selling behavior and relationship quality is statistically significant and positive on collective creative efficiency (b = 0.108; p = 0.005; with b between 0.048 and 0.196) (Table 5).

Table 5. The indirect effects

	λ. stand	Lower bounds	Upper bounds	p. value
SMU → ASB → SP	.113	0.037	0.235	0.005
SMU → ASB → RQ → SP	.108	0.048	0.196	0.005

6 Discussion

The main objective of this study was to broaden the understanding of the benefits of using social media use by empirically examining its effects on two key constructs: the quality of the customer relationship and the performance of sellers. The results confirm our conceptualization of the influence of social media use in B2B sales, as most of the hypotheses were confirmed. In line with our hypotheses, the use of social media has a positive and direct influence on sales performance, and an indirect influence through adaptive sales behavior. Our results also shows that adaptive selling has a significant direct influence on the quality of relationships and the performance of sellers.

Surprisingly, however, we find that salespeople's use of social networks does not improve the quality of relationship with their customers. It seems that social media do not create a social bond and are only a source of information for sellers. Marshall, Moncrief [2] found that sales managers and salespeople view social media as an effective tool for increasing connectivity, building personal and long-term relationships with customers, and maintaining global relationships. However, our results call into question the nature of the social bonds that social media actually offer.

Limitations and Research Perspectives
There are several limitations to our study that may affect the reliability of the results. First, all measures were self-reported by the salesperson. While a dyadic sample would be preferable, sample accessibility was limited to sellers only. However, Agnihotri, Dingus [4] argue that "in general contact employees are good sources of information on customer attitudes [48] and a perceptual measure can be used when an accurate objective measure is not available [49]".

It could be interesting to explore the implications for the sales force of the rise in what are known as "social media" and the "always-on" communication technology usage patterns associated with them, as well as the "dark side" of the use of social media on salespeople's job satisfaction. Some face a problem known as "social media fatigue", in which they feel anxious about being overwhelmed by social media [50]. Social media are a new tool for some salespeople and can, in this sense, constitute an additional cognitive load and therefore lead to an overload, with the accompanying risk of burnout and dissatisfaction at work.

We have found that it is not enough that salespeople simply use social media to increase their business performance; instead, salespeople need to understand how using social media can improve different selling behaviors which, in turn, have direct effects on performance. For example, as Itani, Agnihotri [10] suggested, researchers should try to understand how salespeople use different social media tools and other CRM technologies at the same time, and the effect that simultaneous use can have on performance.

References

1. Julienne, E., Damperat, M., Franck, R.: Customer Relationships and Digital Technologies: What Place and Role for Sales Representatives? Augmented Customer Strategy: CRM in the Digital Age, pp. 149–166 (2019)
2. Marshall, G.W., et al.: Revolution in sales: the impact of social media and related technology on the selling environment. J. Pers. Sell. Sales Manag. **32**(3), 349–363 (2012)
3. Ancillai, C., et al.: Advancing social media driven sales research: establishing conceptual foundations for B-to-B social selling. Ind. Mark. Manag. **82**, 293–308 (2019)
4. Agnihotri, R., et al.: Social media: influencing customer satisfaction in B2B sales. Ind. Mark. Manag. **53**, 172–180 (2016)
5. Lacoste, S.: Perspectives on social media ant its use by key account managers. Ind. Mark. Manag. **54**, 33–43 (2016)
6. Bocconcelli, R., Cioppi, M., Pagano, A.: Social media as a resource in SMEs' sales process. J. Bus. Ind. Mark. **32**, 693–709 (2017)
7. Andzulis, J.M., Panagopoulos, N.G., Rapp, A.: A review of social media and implications for the sales process. J. Pers. Sell. Sales Manag. **32**(3), 305–316 (2012)
8. Rollins, M., Nickell, D., Wei, J.: Understanding salespeople's learning experiences through blogging: a social learning approach. Ind. Mark. Manag. **43**(6), 1063–1069 (2014)
9. Wang, Y., et al.: The impact of sellers' social influence on the co-creation of innovation with customers and brand awareness in online communities. Ind. Mark. Manag. **54**, 56–70 (2016)
10. Itani, O.S., Agnihotri, R., Dingus, R.: Social media use in B2b sales and its impact on competitive intelligence collection and adaptive selling: examining the role of learning orientation as an enabler. Ind. Mark. Manag. **66**, 64–79 (2017)
11. Palmatier, R.W., et al.: Factors influencing the effectiveness of relationship marketing: a meta-analysis. J. Mark. **70**(4), 136–153 (2006)
12. O'Reilly, T., Battelle, J.: Web Squared: Web 2.0 Five Years On. O'Reilly Media, Inc., Newton (2009)
13. Kaplan, A.M., Haenlein, M.: Users of the world, unite! The challenges and opportunities of social media. Bus. Horiz. **53**(1), 59–68 (2010)
14. Mangold, W.G., Faulds, D.J.: Social media: the new hybrid element of the promotion mix. Bus. Horiz. **52**(4), 357–365 (2009)
15. Agnihotri, R., et al.: Bringing "social" into sales: the impact of salespeople's social media use on service behaviors and value creation. J. Pers. Sell. Sales Manag. **32**(3), 333–348 (2012)
16. Guenzi, P., Pardo, C., Georges, L.: Relational selling strategy and key account managers' relational behaviors: an exploratory study. Ind. Mark. Manag. **36**(1), 121–133 (2007)
17. Morgan, R.M., Hunt, S.D.: The commitment-trust theory of relationship marketing. J. Mark. **1994**(58), 20–38 (1994)
18. Crosby, L.A., Evans, K.R., Cowles, D.: Relationship quality in services selling: an interpersonal influence perspective. J. Mark. **54**, 68–81 (1990)
19. Zaheer, A., McEvily, B., Perrone, V.: Does trust matter? Exploring the effects of interorganizational and interpersonal trust on performance. Organ. Sci. **9**(2), 141–159 (1998)
20. Jap, S.D.: "Pie sharing" in complex collaboration contexts. J. Mark. Res. **38**(1), 86–99 (2001)
21. Mummalaneni, V., One more exploration into buyer-seller relationships: some conceptual foundations and research propositions. In: Business Marketing: An Interaction and Network Perspective, pp. 233–261 (1995)
22. Doney, P.M., Cannon, J.P.: An examination of the nature of trust in buyer-seller relationships. J. Mark. **61**, 35–51 (1997)
23. Anderson, E., Weitz, B.: The use of pledges to build and sustain commitment in distribution channels. J. Mark. Res. **29**(1), 18–34 (1992)

24. Palmatier, R.W., et al.: Les facteurs qui influencent l'efficacité du marketing relationnel: une méta-analyse. Recherche et applications en marketing **22**(1), 79–103 (2007)
25. Wulf, K.D., Odekerken-Schröder, G., Iacobucci, D.: Investments in consumer relationships: a cross-country and cross-industry exploration. J. Mark. **65**(4), 33–50 (2001)
26. Sundaram, S., et al.: Technology use on the front line: how information technology enhances individual performance. J. Acad. Mark. Sci. **35**(1), 101–112 (2007)
27. Zallocco, R., Pullins, E.B., Mallin, M.L.: A re-examination of B2B sales performance. J. Bus. Ind. Mark. **24**(8), 598–610 (2009)
28. Behrman, D.N., Perreault Jr., W.D.: Measuring the performance of industrial salespersons. J. Bus. Res. **10**(3), 355–370 (1982)
29. Weitz, B.A., Sujan, H., Sujan, M.: Knowledge, motivation, and adaptive behavior: a framework for improving selling effectiveness. J. Mark. **50**(4), 174–191 (1986)
30. Hunter, G.K., Perreault Jr., W.D.: Sales technology orientation, information effectiveness, and sales performance. J. Pers. Sell. Sales Manag. **26**(2), 95–113 (2006)
31. Mullins, R.R., et al.: Know your customer: how salesperson perceptions of customer relationship quality form and influence account profitability. J. Mark. **78**(6), 38–58 (2014)
32. Jap, S.D., Ganesan, S.: Control mechanisms and the relationship life cycle: implications for safeguarding specific investments and developing commitment. J. Mark. Res. **37**(2), 227–245 (2000)
33. Vosgerau, J., Anderson, E.: A social perception view of business relationships in the service sector. In: ACR North American Advances (2004)
34. Ellis, K.L., Beatty, S.E.: Customer relationships with retail salespeople: a conceptual model and propositions. In: ACR North American Advances (1995)
35. Park, J.E., et al.: How does sales force automation influence relationship quality and performance? The mediating roles of learning and selling behaviors. Ind. Mark. Manag. **39**(7), 1128–1138 (2010)
36. Spiro, R.L., Weitz, B.A.: Adaptive selling: conceptualization, measurement, and nomological validity. J. Mark. Res. **27**, 61–69 (1990)
37. Weitz, B.A.: Relationship between salesperson performance and understanding of customer decision making. J. Mark. Res. **15**(4), 501–516 (1978)
38. Jaramillo, F., et al.: Getting the job done: The moderating role of initiative on the relationship between intrinsic motivation and adaptive selling. J. Pers. Sell. Sales Manag. **27**(1), 59–74 (2007)
39. Franke, G.R., Park, J.-E.: Salesperson adaptive selling behavior and customer orientation: a meta-analysis. J. Mark. Res. **43**(4), 693–702 (2006)
40. Anderson, J.C., Narus, J.A.: Partnering as a focused market strategy. Calif. Manag. Rev. **33**(3), 95–113 (1991)
41. Román, S., Iacobucci, D.: Antecedents and consequences of adaptive selling confidence and behavior: a dyadic analysis of salespeople and their customers. J. Acad. Mark. Sci. **38**(3), 363–382 (2010)
42. Boorom, M.L., Goolsby, J.R., Ramsey, R.P.: Relational communication traits and their effect on adaptiveness and sales performance. J. Acad. Mark. Sci. **26**(1), 16–30 (1998)
43. Steenkamp, J.-B.E., Van Trijp, H.C.: The use of LISREL in validating marketing constructs. Int. J. Res. Mark. **8**(4), 283–299 (1991)
44. Hu, L.-T., Bentler, P.M.: Fit indices in covariance structure modeling: sensitivity to underparameterized model misspecification. Psychol. Methods **3**(4), 424 (1998)
45. Fornell, C., Larcker, D.F.: Structural equation models with unobservable variables and measurement error: algebra and statistics. Sage Publications, Los Angeles (1981)
46. Zhao, X., Lynch Jr., J.G., Chen, Q.: Reconsidérer Baron et Kenny: mythes et vérités à propos de l'analyse de médiation. Recherche et Applications en Marketing (French Edition) **26**(1), 81–95 (2011)

47. Preacher, K.J., Hayes, A.F.: SPSS and SAS procedures for estimating indirect effects in simple mediation models. Behav. Res. Methods Instrum. Comput. **36**(4), 717–731 (2004)
48. Bitner, M.J., Booms, B.H., Mohr, L.A.: Critical service encounters: the employee's viewpoint. J. Mark. **58**(4), 95–106 (1994)
49. Dess, G.G., Robinson Jr., R.B.: Measuring organizational performance in the absence of objective measures: the case of the privately-held firm and conglomerate business unit. Strateg. Manag. J. **5**(3), 265–273 (1984)
50. Han, B.: Social media burnout: definition, measurement instrument, and why we care. J. Comput. Inf. Syst. **58**(2), 122–130 (2018)

Prediction for Private Brand Items Purchase Behavior of Hair Salons Using Bayesian Survival Analysis

Yuho Katagiri[1]([✉]), Kohei Otake[3], and Takashi Namatame[2]

[1] Graduate School of Science and Engineering, Chuo University, Hachioji, Japan
[2] Faculty of Science and Engineering, Chuo University, 1-13-27, Kasuga, Bunkyo-ku, Tokyo 112-8551, Japan
nama@indsys.chuo-u.ac.jp
[3] School of Information and Telecommunication Engineering, Tokai University, 2-3-23, Takanawa, Minato-ku, Tokyo 108-8619, Japan
otake@tsc.u-tokai.ac.jp

Abstract. In Japan, the number of beauty salons has been increased and reached over 250,000 at the end of 2018. On the other hand, there are some salon management problems such as price reduction and customer decrease. In such situations, it is an important not only to serve salon services, but to promote private brand (PB) items in addition to treatments. In this study, we analyzed purchase interval of PB items and predicted the purchase in a hair salon chain. First, we created explanatory variables using ID-POS data of the hair salon chain. Secondly, we selected explanatory variables using Cox proportional hazard model. Then, we performed Bayesian survival analysis to evaluate purchase interval considering customers' heterogeneity. As a result, we could grasp appropriate timing when customers had highly purchase motivation and applied marketing measures to effective promotion.

Keywords: Bayesian survival analysis · Purchase interval · Hair salons

1 Introduction

According to the Ministry of Health, Labor and Welfare, the number of beauty salons has been increased and reached about 251,000 at the end of 2018 in Japan [1]. On the other hand, the scale of the hair salon market decreases and there are some management problems such as price reduction and customer decrease [2].

The primary business of hair salons is to provide treatments such as cutting and coloring. However, it is difficult to increase sales more than ever with the current human resources because these services need time. In such situations, it is an important policy to promote Private Brand (PB) items that do not take much time in addition to treatments.

According to our study, there are some exist studies. Iwata et al. [3] constructed a model that predicts hair salon chain customer defection with registration information,

© Springer Nature Switzerland AG 2021
G. Meiselwitz (Ed.): HCII 2021, LNCS 12775, pp. 98–109, 2021.
https://doi.org/10.1007/978-3-030-77685-5_8

purchase history at the previous visit and so on. As a result, they grasped actions specific to customers who defected.

Konishi [4] analyzed visiting interval for hair salon customer who took cut, color or treatment using Cox proportional hazard model. From the result, they showed application possibility of direct marketing.

Although these studies discussed marketing measures to prevent defection, they did not consider measures to maintain sales that focused on PB items.

Also, in our previous research [5], we analyzed the characteristics of customers who bought PB items using customer demography and purchase history. As a result, they discussed how to promote PB items effectively. However, there are still issues to promote at appropriate time because we did not consider about purchase interval.

In this study, we analyzed purchase interval of PB items and predicted the purchase timing. The result of our study will be helpful to know the best timing to approach to customer and to manage inventory.

2 Datasets

In this study, we used ID-POS data of 3 large stores among 12 stores of a hair salon chain in urban area in Japan. In this study, we train the first 9 months' data, and validate the result with the rest 3 months' data.

Tables 1 and 2 show the datasets and analysis subject.

Table 1. Datasets used in this study

Dataset	Details
Member registration information data	Member ID, first time visit, zip code, the propriety of direct mail, sex, age
Purchase history data with customer information	Member ID, visit date/time, sales amount, purchased PB item (menu) etc.

Table 2. Analysis subject

Analysis subject	Details
Store	3 large stores
Customer	1,978 customers who bought PB items twice to twenty times during the training data period
Training data	Data of Table1 from 7/1/2015 to 3/31/2017
Test Data	Data of Table1 from 4/1/2017 to 6/30/2017

3 Analysis

In this section, we explain our analyzing procedure.

First, we created explanatory variables that would affect purchase interval. Secondly, we selected explanatory variables using Cox proportional hazard model because Bayes model cannot select explanatory variables sequentially like a general survival analysis. Then, we constructed two different Bayesian survival models and compared the accuracy of these.

3.1 Explanatory Variables

To analyze customers' purchase interval of PB items, we prepared some variables about purchase characteristics. Especially as to loyalty variables, we also used the "clumpiness" that mean the irregularity of event occurrence.

RFM is one of the most common method used to analyze customer value. Although it has been widely used as concise and useful, it cannot identify irregular and frequently purchase [6, 7].

Then we used "clumpiness" that was defined as the degree of nonconformity to equal interval [8]. Clumpiness can capture the non-uniformity purchase behavior. The formula for "clumpiness" is as follows and we calculated clumpiness for each customer with training data.

First, we defined t_i as the timing of the i th purchase when the customer purchased n times out of the N purchase occasion. Also x_i is shown in Eq. (1).

$$x_i = \begin{cases} \frac{t_1}{N+1} (i = 1) \\ \frac{t_i - t_{i-1}}{N+1} (i = 2, 3, \cdots n) \\ \frac{N+1-t_n}{N+1} (i = n+1) \end{cases} \tag{1}$$

Here, the x_i is standardized t_i.

Furthermore, we defined H_p as indicates the non-uniformity of purchase timing of consumer p.

$$H_p = 1 + \frac{\sum_{i=1}^{n+1} \log(x_i) x_i}{\log(n+1)} \tag{2}$$

Additionally, we performed a random purchase simulation M times on the stipulation that the customer purchased times n out of the N purchase occasion. Then, we set the $\alpha\%$ quantile of the empirical distribution as the threshold value H_0. The clampiness C_p is shown on Eq. (3).

$$C_p = \begin{cases} 1 (H_p \geq H_0) \\ 0 \ (otherwise) \end{cases} \tag{3}$$

($C_p = 1$: clumpiness, $C_p = 0$: no clumpiness)

In this study, we set purchase occasion $N = 640$ (7/1/2015 –3/31/2017), simulation times $M = 20000$, $\alpha\%$ quantile $= 0.10$. Table 3 shows the number of customer who has clumpiness.

Table 3. Number of clumpiness customer

Clumpiness	No clumpiness
147	1831

Other than this, we used customers' behavior and personal attributes from the record of ID-POS data. Finally, we created 27 variables including clumpiness. Details of the variables are shown in Table 4.

Table 4. Details of the explanatory variables

Category	Variable name	Data type
Behavior at the last and the before visit	Touch-up	0 or 1
	Cut	0 or 1
	Color	0 or 1
	Coupon	0 or 1
	Straightened	0 or 1
	Treatment	0 or 1
	Perm	0 or 1
	Blow shampoo hair set	0 or 1
Choice probability of treatment	Touch-up	Decimal
	Cut	Decimal
	Color	Decimal
	Coupon	Decimal
	Straightened	Decimal
	Treatment	Decimal
	Perm	Decimal
	Blow shampoo hair set	Decimal
Payment of the previous visit	Sales	Integer
	Discount amount	Integer
	PB item	0 or 1
	Choose stylist	0 or 1
Loyalty	Accumulate sales	Integer
	Accumulate sales of PB item	Integer
	Number of purchase PB item	Integer
	Clumpiness	0 or 1
Demography	Age	Category
	Sex	Category
	Permission of DM	Category

3.2 Variables Selection

We mainly analyzed with Bayes survival model in this study. However, Bayes model cannot select explanatory variables sequentially like a general survival analysis. Therefore, we selected explanatory variables using Cox proportional hazard model with stepwise method based on AIC before performing Bayes survival analysis [9].

We used the purchase interval as the objective variable and Table 4 as candidate explanatory variable. Then, we performed Cox proportional hazard model with training data.

Table 5 shows the result of Cox proportional hazard model.

Table 5. Result of Cox proportional hazard model

Variable name	coef	Pr(>|z|)
Buy PB item previous visit	1.01	2.00E–16***
Number of purchase PB item	0.21	2.00E–16***
Clumpiness	−0.98	2.00E–16***
Accumulate sales (¥1000)	0.00	3.49E–08***
Blow shampoo hair set	0.38	1.74E–07***
Cut (the visit before last time)	0.53	2.63E–07***
last time Cut & the visit before last time Cut	−0.49	1.92E–06***
Coupon	−1.89	8.47E–06***
Treatment	0.34	6.19E–05***
Permission of DM	0.12	1.30E–04***
Perm	−0.47	1.40E–04***
Choose stylist (previous visit)	0.29	2.30E–04***

$***p < 0.001, **p < 0.01, *p < 0.05$

Table 5 shows that the loyalty variables significant effect on purchase interval. From the result, we used top 4 loyalty variables from the perspective of significance test as explanatory variable in proposed model.

3.3 Proposed Model

Outline of Models. In This Study, We Created a Bayesian Survival Model Assumed a Weibull Distribution to Express Parameters of Each Individual and Group [10]. Survival Analysis is One of the Method to Analyze Time Until an Event Such as Death or Failure Occurs.

Assuming the time t until the event occurs follows a Weibull distribution, Probability density function, Hazard function and Survival function are shown on Eqs. (4), (5) and (6).

$$f(t) = \left(\frac{m}{\eta}\right)\left(\frac{t}{\eta}\right)^{m-1} \exp\left\{-\left(\frac{t}{\eta}\right)^m\right\} \tag{4}$$

$$h(t) = mt^{m-1}\eta^{-m} \tag{5}$$

$$S(t) = \exp\left\{-\left(\frac{t}{\eta}\right)^m\right\} \tag{6}$$

Here, m and η mean shape and scale parameter, respectively. Moreover we expand Eq. (5) as follows.

$$h(t) = mt^{m-1}\eta^{-m} = \frac{m}{\eta^m}t^{m-1} = m\lambda t^{m-1} \tag{7}$$

Then, we defined λ incorporating the effect of covariates as follows.

$$\lambda = \exp\left\{\beta_0 + \sum\nolimits_{i=1}^{p} x_i\beta_i\right\} \tag{8}$$

Here, β_0 means intercept, β_i means coefficient and x_i means covariates. From the above, scale parameter η is calculated as follows.

$$\eta = \exp\left\{-\frac{\beta_0 + \sum_{i=1}^{p} x_i\beta_i}{m}\right\} \tag{9}$$

In this study, we used Markov Chain Monte Carlo methods (MCMC) to estimate parameters with No-U-Turn-sampler (NUTS) sampler [12].

Then, we aggregated "Number of purchase PB item", "Accumulate sales (¥1000)" and "Buy PB item previous visit" for each clumpiness group.

As shown in Figs. 1 and 2, the "no clumpiness" customer had greater number of purchase and sales than the "clumpiness" customer, and the both of variance are wide.

Furthermore, Table 6 shows that the ratio of "Yes" is higher than the other one in "clumpiness" customer. On the other hand, in "no clumpiness" customer group, the ratio of "Yes" is lower than the other.

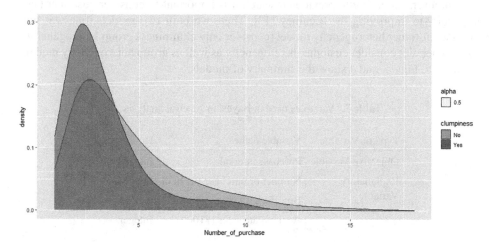

Fig. 1. Result of aggregation "Number of purchase PB item"

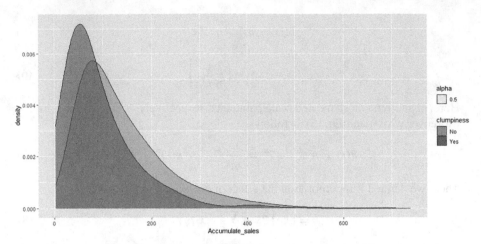

Fig. 2. Result of aggregation "Accumulate sales (¥1000)"

Table 6. Result of aggregation "Buy PB item previous visit"

		Buy PB item previous visit	
		Yes	No
Clumpiness	Yes	69.8%	30.2%
	No	47.8%	52.20%

As above result, the tendency of each variable is different between two clumpiness groups. Therefore, we grasped "clumpiness" as well-identifying group, and estimated parameters for the each group.

Moreover, according to previous research it is important to consider customer heterogeneity to improving the accuracy [13]. Then, we built two models, one was not consider customer heterogeneity model (consider only clumpiness group heterogeneity) and another was consider customer heterogeneity as well as group heterogeneity model.

Table 7, Figs. 3 and 4 show the summary of models.

Table 7. Variables used in Bayesian survival analysis

Type of Variable	Variable name	Data type
Objective Variable	Purchase interval	Integer
Explanatory Variable	Number of purchase PB item	Integer
	Buy PB item previous visit	0 or 1
	Accumulate sales (¥1000)	Integer

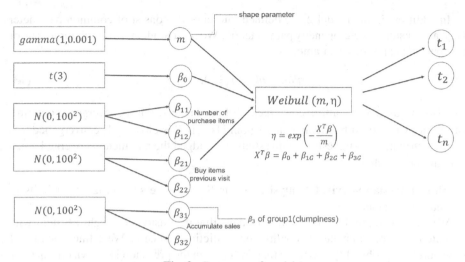

Fig. 3. Summary of model 1

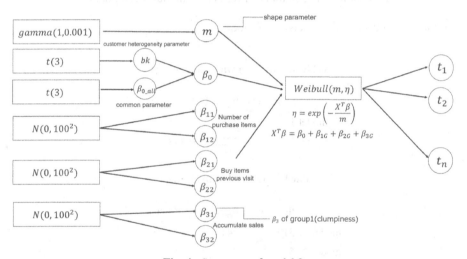

Fig. 4. Summary of model 2

In this study, we used gamma distribution as shape parameter's prior distribution [9].

$$m \sim \text{gamma}(1, 0.001) \tag{10}$$

Also, we used Student's t-distribution as intercept's prior distribution [11], and normal distribution as each coefficient prior distribution in model 1.

$$\beta_0 \sim 10 \times t(3) \tag{11}$$

$$\beta_{iG} \sim N(0, 100^2) \tag{12}$$

In addition, in the model 2, we defined intercept β_0 consist of common parameter β_{0_all} and customer heterogeneity parameter bk. We used Student's t-distribution as prior distribution [11] of these parameters.

$$\beta_{0\_all}, bk \sim t(3, 0, 10) \tag{13}$$

Also, we used $\hat{R}$ to confirm convergence of parameters. $\hat{R}$ is a convergence determination index proposed by Gelman and Rubin [14]. If $\hat{R}$ is close to 1, convergence to a steady distribution is suggested. In this study, we judged the parameter converged when $\hat{R}$ should be less than 1.1.

Result of Bayesian Survival Analysis. In this Section, we summarize our results of bayesian survival analysis.

We calculated purchase probability of days that the customer bought PB item with estimated value of parameters to confirm the prediction precision. We defined the flg $= 1$ if the purchase probability was more than 50%. Then the precision is shown on Eq. (14).

$$\text{Precision} = \text{The number of flg is } 1/\text{ The number of data} \tag{14}$$

Tables 8 and 9 show the precision of models.

Table 8. Precision with training data

	flg $= 0$	flg $= 1$	Precision
model 1	5327	2487	0.355
model 2	5092	2722	0.348

Table 9. Precision with test data

	flg $= 0$	flg $= 1$	Precision
model 1	319	241	0.430
model 2	516	0	0.000

From Tables 8 and 9, we found that the model 2 was better than model 1 from performance. Table 9 shows that model 2 correctly predict with a 43% in contrast model 1 did not correctly predict at all with the test data.

Tables 10 and 11 show the result of the Bayesian survival analysis.

Table 10. Result of the Bayesian survival analysis model 1

Clumpiness	Variable	Mean	Sd
All	Shape	1.561	0.000
Yes	Number of purchase PB item (β_1)	0.189	0.001
	Buy PB item previous visit (β_2)	−0.289	0.002
	Accumulate sales (¥1000) (β_3)	−0.003	0.000
No	Number of purchase PB item (β_1)	0.214	0.000
	Buy PB item previous visit (β_2)	0.943	0.000
	Accumulate sales (¥1000) (β_3)	0.000	0.000

Table 11. Result of the Bayesian survival analysis model 2

Clumpiness	Variable	Mean	Sd
All	Shape	2.831	0.031
Yes	Number of purchase PB item (β_1)	−0.427	0.149
	Buy PB item previous visit (β_2)	2.801	0.348
	Accumulate sales (¥1000) (β_3)	−0.017	0.005
No	Number of purchase PB item (β_1)	0.220	0.017
	Buy PB item previous visit (β_2)	2.378	0.049
	Accumulate sales (¥1000) (β_3)	−0.010	0.001

As shown in Tables 10 and 11 "Number of purchase PB item (β_1)"and "Buy PB item previous visit (β_2)" in "clumpiness" customer have opposite sign between model 1 and model 2. Additionally, there are differences in "Buy PB item previous visit (β_2)" value.

Moreover, from Table 10, he standard deviation of parameters in model 2 were larger than model 1.

4 Discussion

First, we discussed the precision and standard deviation. Tables 8 and 9 showed that the model 2 was better than model 1 in performance. As a result, we found that there were individual differences in each customer. Also, it was important to consider customer heterogeneity as well as "clumpiness" to improve the precision.

Moreover, from Table 10, the standard deviation of almost all parameters are 0 in model 1. We assumed that the parameters value were close customers average because we did not consider customer heterogeneity in model 1.

On the other hand, Table 11 showed that the standard deviation were larger than result of model 1. As a result, we assumed that there were customer who had different purchase behavior from customers' average especially in "clumpiness" customer.

From the above result, we found it was possible to express the differences of purchase behavior due to values and personality that each customer held inside by considering customer heterogeneity. For that reason, we had been able to improve the precision in model 2.

Second, we discuss the result of model 2 follows.

According to the Table 11, "Number of purchase PB item (β_1)" and "Buy PB item previous visit (β_2)" in "no clumpiness" customer were estimated positive values. Therefore, we assumed that customers with the number of purchase was large or bought items previous visit would buy PB item in short interval in "no clumpiness" customer.

On the other hand, in "clumpiness" customer, "Number of purchase PB item (β_1)" was estimated negative values. Consequently, we found that purchase interval of "clumpiness" customer would get longer as number of purchase grew. Therefore, we assumed that the "clumpiness" customer had contrasting feature between general customers in the number of purchase PB item.

We assumed that the model built in this study would help to know the best timing to promote PB items. Specifically, we predict the date that purchase probability is over 50% in each customer. Then, we promote PB items by such as DM based on the result of prediction. The recommendation when customer have highly purchase motivation will encourage repeat purchasing and leads to get customers' loyalty.

Also, we could apply inventory management through verify the number of customer who had 50% purchase probability during a month.

5 Conclusion

In this study, we tried to construct Bayesian survival models for estimating purchase probability to make use of effective promotion or manage inventory. We constructed two models that one was not consider customer heterogeneity and another was consider customer heterogeneity. As a result, we found that it was effective to consider customer heterogeneity for improving accuracy of model.

Moreover, we found that customers who bought PB items in short term had differences between "clumpiness" customer and "no clumpiness" customer. For example, "no clumpiness" customer who bought PB items many times would buy short interval. On the other hand, purchase interval of "clumpiness" customer would get longer as number of purchase grew.

Also, the precision of Bayesian survival models built in this study were not satisfactory. Therefore, there is room for improvement. Purchasing PB items will occur when customer will come hair salon to treatment such as cutting. Consequently, it is necessary to construct Two-Phase Decision-Making Model of visiting and purchasing for future work.

Moreover, we need to consider more information such as there cord of purchase item in part period in addition to "clumpiness".

Acknowledgment. We thank a hair salon company for permission to use valuable datasets. This work was supported by JSPS KAKENHI Grant Number 19K01945.

References

1. Ministry of Health: Labor and Welfare, Statistical Information White Paper Overview of Health Administration Administrative Report in Heisei 30 31 Dec 2019. https://www.mhlw.go.jp/toukei/saikin/hw/eisei_oukoku/18/. (in Japanese)
2. Yano Economic Research Institute: 2019 Edition beauty care marketing general press release 27 June 2016. https://www.yano.co.jp/press-release/show/press_d/2148. (in Japanese)
3. Iwata, M., Otake, K., Namatame, T.: Analysis of the characteristics of customer defection on a hair salon considering individual differences. In: Meiselwitz, G. (ed.) HCII 2019. LNCS, vol. 11579, pp. 378–391. Springer, Cham (2019). https://doi.org/10.1007/978-3-030-21905-5_29
4. Konishi, Y.: A duration analysis of hair salon consumers' behavior and prediction of revisit rates. Proc. Inst. Statist. Math. **54**(2), 445–459 (2006). (in Japanese)
5. Katagiri, Y., Otake, K., Namatame, T.: Analysis of customers of beauty salons-focus on item purchase customers-. Abs. Ann. Conf. Jpn. Soc. Manage. Inf. **28**(2), 96–99 (2019). (in Japanese)
6. Niimi, J., Hoshino, T.: Prediction of the Customer Activity with Using the Improved Measure of Clumpiness Capturing Competitive Usage and Early Churn under Limited Information. Jpn. J. Behav. **92**(47), 27–40 (2020). (in Japanese)
7. Nakayama, Y.: A recent development in customer relationship management : the clumpiness measure of non-uniform visit/purchase intervals. Konan Bus. Rev. **57**(2), 161–181 (2016). (in Japanese)
8. Zhang, Y., Bradlow, E.T., Small, D.S.: Predicting customer value using clumpiness : from RFM to RFMC. Mark. Sci. **34**(2), 195–208 (2015)
9. Yamaguchi, K.: An analysis of website visit behavior by a hierarchical Bayesian model considering the time variation of frequency. J. Mark. Sci. **22**(1), 13–29 (2014). (in Japanese)
10. Y. Tsuda, K. Kaito, K. Yamamoto and K. Kobayashi, "Bayesian Estimation of Weibull Hazard models for Deterioration Forecasting", *Journal of Japan Society of Civil Engineers*, Vol. 62, No. 3, pp. 473–491 (2006) (in Japanese)
11. Clarke, R.T.: Estimating trends in data from the Weibull and a generalized extreme value distribution. Water Resour. Res. **38**(6), 1–10 (2002)
12. Gilks, R.W., Richardson, S., Spiegelhalter, J.D.: Markov Chain Monte Carlo in Practice, pp. 131–143. Chapman & Hall/CRC, Boca Raton (1996)
13. Jain, D.C., Vilcassim, N.J.: Investigating household purchase timing decisions: a conditional hazard function approach. Mark. Sci. **10**(1), 1–23 (1991)
14. Gelman, A., Rubin, D.B.: Inference from iterative simulation using multiple sequences. Statist. Sci. **7**(4), 457–472 (1992)

First Steps in the Entrepreneurial Practice of Marketing

Cristian G. Popescu[1](✉) and Raluca Ion[2](✉)

[1] Faculty of Administration and Business, The University of Bucharest, Bucharest, Romania
cristian.popescu@faa.unibuc.ro
[2] The Bucharest University of Economic Studies, Bucharest, Romania
raluca.ion@eam.ase.ro

Abstract. During a long period of marketing practice, we have decided to write this article, especially seeing the problems of entrepreneurial beginnings from Romania, and from other countries from EU. In this article are highlighted the entrepreneurial mistakes encountered during my entrepreneurial activity, but also due to a long activity in the marketing theory, that it should be thought, adapted at all entrepreneurial levels. Even if it seems difficult to understand by some investors in various fields of activity, however, entrepreneurial marketing is very complex, and requires very good knowledge in the applicability of marketing combined with other fields of economics. Thus, Romanian entrepreneurs have a relatively good thinking, but in general they only consider the short-term strategy, and from here in the same terms all other components of economic disciplines. Hence a whole series of problems that arise in the development of an enterprise, especially in the second stage, when, after entering the market and the enterprise must develop on the market. Through this article I highlight the wrong decisions from a strategic point of view, with concrete examples, which are very common in Romania, but also in other countries, in entrepreneurial practice, mistakes that are widespread. I could say that, in my practice as an entrepreneur and as a theorist, in the last years I started to give more pro bono consultancy to entrepreneurs and their startups rather than to "negotiate" something with them, at least at a first discussion to help them develop their businesses. So, through quantitative research I aim to achieve as objectives the information of entrepreneurial specialists, but also of specialists in marketing theory, about the current mistakes in the application of marketing, especially where there are mistakes of economic calculations that can be very difficult be correct later.

Keywords: Marketing entrepreneurship mistakes · Creative games · Mistakes in applying theory of marketing

1 Introduction

SMEs and entrepreneurship overview.

Small and medium-sized enterprises (SMEs) comprise most of the Europe's economy, as they account for 99% of all firms (European Commission, 2021). SMEs employ

© Springer Nature Switzerland AG 2021
G. Meiselwitz (Ed.): HCII 2021, LNCS 12775, pp. 110–119, 2021.
https://doi.org/10.1007/978-3-030-77685-5_9

about 100 million people, and their contribution to Europe's GDP exceeds 50%. Considering the figures above, they play an essential role to European Union's prosperity, as well as their high resilience to external shocks.

As reports shows (European Commission, 2019), in 2018, there were more than 25 million SMEs in the EU, 93% of them were micro-SMEs. The SMEs comprise 99.8% of all enterprises in the EU non-financial business sector, accounting for 56.4% of value added and 66.6% of employment. In dynamics, in 2018, the number of SMEs grew by 2.1%, the value added by 4.1% and the employment by 1.8%. It can be observed that micro SMEs lead this growth, as they recorded the highest value added and employment increase of all SMEs- size classes. The annual changes vary among member states. Romania registered a change of 2.8% in the SME's number, 14.5% in value added and 2.6% in employment (Eurostat, DIW Econ).

There were 25,079,312 SME's in EU-28, in 2018, employing 146,784,592 people and generating value added of 7,723,625 million euros (Eurostat, National Statistical Offices, DIW Econ). The number of SMEs has grown by 2.0% in 2018 after increasing by 1.5% in 2017. In Romania, there were 589,495 SMEs in 2019, of which 90% micro-SMEs. Their number grew over the last 10 years, as seen in Fig. 1.

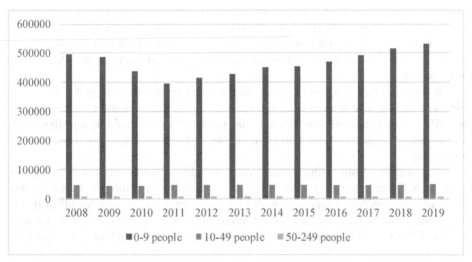

Fig. 1. Number of SMEs in Romania, 2008–2019 Source: authors' compilation based on data of the National Institute of Statistic of Romania, tempo.online.ro, 2021.

The SMEs economic activity grew as well as their number. In Fig. 2, the values of SMEs' turnover are illustrated, for the period 2008–2019. Its value reached 963,450 million lei (about 196,622 million euros) in 2019, increasing by 10%.

EU, through its policies, empower SME's and support entrepreneurship in different forms and directions. Thus, the framework European Entrepreneurship Competence support EU citizens and organizations by developing entrepreneurial learning and the

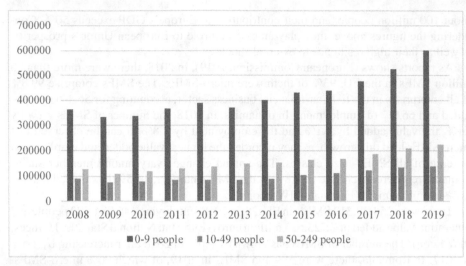

Fig. 2. SMEs turn over in Romania, 2008–2019 (mil.lei) Source: authors' compilation based on data of the National Institute of Statistic of Romania, tempo.online.ro, 2021.

entrepreneurial mindset. EU also fosters entrepreneurship by supporting start-ups, transfers of business, and second chance. Specific groups, such as women or young people, are also envisaged through entrepreneurial learning skills and Erasmus for Young Entrepreneurs.

Furthermore, the European Commission launched the SME's strategy for a sustainable and digital Europe (European Commission, 2020), considering three pillars: to build the SME's capacity and to support them for the transition to sustainability and digitalization; to reduce regulatory burden and to improve market access; and to improve access to financing.

The objective of improving market access is relevant in the context of this piece of research. Considering their wide variety in terms of business models, size, age, and entrepreneurs' profiles, it seems difficult to draw a common strategy for all of them. They come from liberal professions and micro businesses in the services sector and go to middle-range industrial companies, from traditional crafts and foods to high-tech start-ups.

Many SMEs enter the market and face difficulties from different reasons. Cardon (et al. 2011) explored the failure accounts which are attributed to both mistakes made by entrepreneurs, and to misfortunes outside their control. Santarelli and Vivarelli (2007) analyzed the entry mistakes that beginner entrepreneurs make with their attitude "try and see". They observed that the new founders "visit" a sectorial niche searching for business opportunities and later on, they discover whether their entry decision was right or wrong and may decide to exit. Aldrich and Martinez (2007) explored the entrepreneurial process and entrepreneurs' behavior for better understanding of entrepreneurial success. Wolcott and Lippitz (2007) proposed models for corporate entrepreneurship that help entrepreneurs to avoid costly trial-and-error mistakes when selecting and constructing the program for their objectives, considering two main drivers – resource authority and organizational ownership. Four main profiles result – the enabler, the opportunist, the producer and the advocate. They observed that beginners are more likely to make mistakes and go down paths that prove to be infeasible. They considered that the challenge is "to marry the openness of a beginner with the wisdom that comes from experience" (Wolcott, Lippitz, 2007, p. 18).

This piece of research is an empirical study aiming to identifying the main mistakes that beginner entrepreneurs make when entering the markets.

The ideas gathered in this article are about the major problems that we identified among Romanian entrepreneurs who came to us, after a long period of negotiations with these entrepreneurs, who for the most part enter the Romanian market with a food products portfolio, limited products, generally being producers, but they can be also importers of some products from the EU. We did not have the same problems with service activities for two reasons: usually commercial activities that provide services are supported by a pricing strategy compared to services provided, much more adaptable and more flexible to the dynamics of such markets due to higher profit, but also higher demand in general on such markets. Returning to the market of products that I knew in particular, I would say that these are food and non-food products that can be made by Romanian entrepreneurs, or which have a demand significantly higher on the Romanian market. Commenting on the trend in recent years on food policy, we could say that Romanians are following the same trends as Western Europe, but with a gap of several years. For example, statistics show that the growth trend in the consumption of organic products was also registered in Romania, even during the crisis period of 2009–2012, the positive trend was maintained. In the study below, we want to show what really happens when a Romanian entrepreneur enters the market by the simplest method he would have at the time of entering the market, namely selling products to direct consumers, having a number limited of products at the beginning and which, then wants to expand its product range gradually, but also from a quantitative point of view, wants in a development stage of 1–2 years after opening the business to sell more entering new markets sales. We did the study among many entrepreneurs who have been contacted in the last years. Although there are many more entrepreneurs in Romania who fall into the same profile, they did not centralize their data, but given the profile below, in general, the problems faced by Romanian entrepreneurs can be generalized, with small exceptions, which we will list as well.

2   Description of the Entrepreneurial Problem

The main problem of Romanian entrepreneur identified by us is the wrong strategic thinking when entering on the market of Romanian entrepreneurs. Thus, when they think of entering the Romanian market, manufacturing a product or importing it directly, Romanian entrepreneurs want to sell those products as soon as possible, and they do so by the easiest method for any entrepreneur at the beginning of the business, by selling their products to the final consumers. It is a correct method, which gives them the opportunity to enter into possession of a cash flow is faster (than through any intermediary), they consider a direct contact with consumers, so it is easy for them to manage their business, it develops once with the growth of the market represented by the final consumers, allowing them to know very well the consumers and mainly the market. Basically, at the beginning of the business they think and "live" the experience of entering the market of their business, but in the next step, entering new markets, or covering a larger geographical territory, they face the approach of indirect sales channels, represented by one or more intermediaries. Due to the setting of limited strategies for selling their products, entrepreneurs will seek to set unmotivated, rigid, and discouraging prices for the final consumers of intermediaries, which will naturally lead to either a refusal from intermediaries that carefully analyze the product market to be developed, or the final results are not in line with the expectations of both parties. As a subsequent natural effect, it would be to block the development of that entrepreneur, at least until the rethinking of the initial strategy that did not work, problems that will generate an economic cap limited or even a sharp decline in sales (V-shaped chart).

Sales chart when there are entrepreneurial problems regarding strategic mistakes - model (OX - period, OY - sales evolution) (Fig. 3).

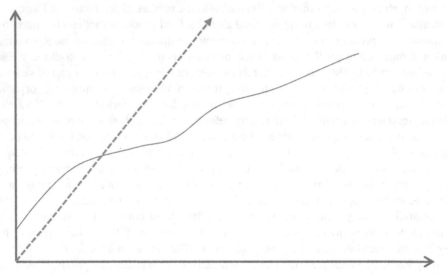

Fig. 3. Sales chart when there are entrepreneurial problems regarding strategic mistakes - model (OX - period, OY - sales evolution)

The dashed line represents the evolution of sales naturally for an economic activity that follows a well-executed marketing strategy, and the continuous line represents an activity of an enterprise that does not have a marketing strategy, and the entrepreneur's knowledge does not give the best economic results.

3   Detailing the Problems

If we were to outline a profile of the entrepreneur who faces mistakes in applying the marketing strategy, we would highlight some of their characteristics:

- average age over 30 years;
- have worked before entering the field of business, usually in a field of routine activity;
- have their own business, usually manufacturing or importing a limited portfolio of products; - entered the market through a direct sales channel, usually working online directly with their customers;
- in the first period of their activity their business is doing well, on average one year, selling only to direct consumers, only 10% sell to a mega-account intermediary (Mega-Image);
- do not have theoretical economic knowledge about business development, although some of them graduated from economic faculties (30%);
- they have products sought on the market, usually food (80%) and which want to expand their range of products;

The problems that entrepreneurs face in negotiating the expansion of the product market are:

- the impossibility of the correct negotiation by both parties of equal selling prices to the final consumers identified on both sales channels (direct and indirect) due to too low prices charged by the contractor, not adapted to the new indirect sales channels, which assume at least 20% from the profit margin to return to an intermediary, and for entrepreneurs who sell fresh food (10%), they can negotiate a profit margin of less than 10–15%;
- strategic mistakes in approaching the market, mostly focused on price, but which also have effects on distribution and promotion policies, and later on product policy;
- the impossibility of the Romanian entrepreneurs to substantially modify the price strategy, without affecting their own business, their own consumers;
- substantial modification of the initial pricing strategy, which will have a definite effect on sales (see the description of the entrepreneurial problem);
- not taking into account the position of negotiator of the entrepreneur, far below that of the intermediate negotiator, who is usually already present on the market, knows very well the prices and competing products, and seeks a benefit after negotiation. This often happens due to the fact that most competitors on food and non-food products, being present on the shelf of the intermediary, have a history, and listing a new entrepreneur with a portfolio of competing products involves increasing the range of competing products on the shelf of the intermediary, which is not necessarily an advantage. So the entrepreneur must expect to come up with a development strategy on new markets favorable to the intermediate negotiator;
- in general, the non-adaptation of a coherent product development strategy considering the entry on new markets, and which can be followed in a negotiation with an intermediary, being very well known the limits of the entrepreneur's negotiation (being disproportionate positions to the detriment of the entrepreneur, will must know the minimum price negotiation limits);
- ignorance of the real reasons why the intermediary will not finally list the contractor's products, because the intermediary will only ask for lower prices (not listing the contractor's products usually resulting from a market research showing that the

contractor's prices to final consumers are lower than the intermediary after applying the reductions noted above);

- the ignorance or non-adaptation of the marketing terror, or the impossibility of its adaptation to the real situation in which the entrepreneur was at the moment of starting the business;
- ignorance of the price/product strategies of the intermediate negotiator, specific to each product, but which must be researched in advance by the entrepreneur, and for which it is very difficult for him to achieve them due to limited knowledge in the field of application marketing;
- the impossibility of adopting correct product/price strategies in a disproportionate negotiation between a small and insignificant Romanian producer and a chain of stores represented by a negotiator of this intermediary who will obviously aim to win regardless of the economic condition of the producer, existing only economic reasoning, being excluded those of business ethics;
- not establishing an initial marketing strategy considering the subsequent variants of market development and not only the immediate, accessible ones, for reporting to a direct sale to the final consumer;
- blocking the negotiations and the impossibility of developing the business or accepting some conditions imposed by the intermediary, which will lead to the exit of the entrepreneur from the market, sometimes through the bankruptcy of the entrepreneur.

Problems faced by intermediary negotiators:

- the impossibility of negotiating final competitive, motivational prices for intermediate negotiators, who, although they need Romanian products, being sought on the market, are forced not to introduce them due to competitive issues (usually compared to products already listed by the intermediate negotiator);
- the impossibility to describe the problems to be faced by the entrepreneur regarding the observance of a correct pricing policy, which should motivate the listing of the products in the network of the intermediary's stores;
- often negotiates only the value component of a product, i.e. focuses on the lowest price, not considering the qualitative component of the product, being necessary and sufficient an evaluation, often subjective, of the attributes of the products to be listed, such as the appearance of the packaging, etc., but the qualitative assessment of the ingredients such as for example in terms of the effects of harmful substances on human health are not taken into account. On the contrary, if the product does not have a minimum validity of 3 months, it will, most of the time, not be listed, being considered "perishable" and dangerous;
- not taking any risk on the part of the negotiator generates a frustration in time for the Romanian entrepreneur, who with small exceptions, will cover all store losses, materialized by returns due to shelf life, physical degradation in stores, or other imposed actions, such as falling prices, the introduction of abusive taxes after listing the products for various reasons, etc.;
- pursuing economic efficiency parameters based on the advantages created by this obvious disproportionality of negotiating positions, between a representative of an

intermediary who, in general, has over 90% of the food trade in large urban areas are provided by large store chains

(https://www.zf.ro);

The evaluation of the market by the intermediary is done after a first, and the communication of the non-listing of the products by the same intermediary negotiator usually comes after his request for a higher price decrease, over the limit calculations made by the entrepreneur. It ultimately leads to the blocking of negotiations and the non-listing of the entrepreneur's products. Finally, the real reason for not listing the products is not communicated to the contractor by the intermediary negotiator, but this could be deduced by the contractor.

4 Initial Dates of Entrepreneurial Errors

On the day when the entrepreneur decides to enter the Romanian market, as a first step described above, it would be to address the final consumers due to obvious advantages, described above, of which the most important would be the direct contact with the consumer and the takeover direct market feedback.

In our example we will list an imported product, from the list of the 10 entrepreneurs we have faced in the last year. This product is a dehydrated product, Romanian dehydrated apples. This product has the advantage of a low degree of processing, according to the Romanian legislation, when the finished product is identified with the raw material entered in the production process; the production process not significantly changing the raw material is called processing.

Thus, the product has the advantage that it is natural (not to be confused with the ecological product, which requires a quality standard imposed by law). The packaging is a heat-sealable bag at one end and with the possibility of resealing the bag after opening it (unsealing). The label is large, visible, with a picture of an apple or other fruit that is in the package, cut, a significant and well represented picture, made with a design with a positive impact on the consumer. The ingredients are few, the fruit cut and dehydrated, in our case apple, and some natural spices for taste (usually ground cinnamon). The label describes the processing of apples, always cut into thin slices and then dehydrated by a production process patented by the Romanian entrepreneur. The production process itself is not much different from the known one, the dehydration by hot air currents, only that the machine made by the Romanian entrepreneur is different, uses a thermally controlled air of up to 30–35 °C to not compromise the finished product. It is considered a Raw-Vegan product if the dehydration process uses a constant temperature below 40 °C. In practice, a similar process of dehydration by osmosis is also known, but this is not the case in our example.

The selling price of the entrepreneur with whom he presented himself for listing is 5.5 lei, at a quantity of 100 gr (excluding VAT, delivery/purchase price, with delivery to the store, DDP). After an evaluation of the market we notice that the product is sold on the manufacturer's website at 6.9 lei, and a similar product on the shelf, in other stores is between 9–15 lei, but considering that the product is Romanian, so having advantages and disadvantages, the prices of similar Romanian products, whose brand is unknown, must be compared. Basically the comparison was made with these products.

Given that it is a product known but less used by Romanians (who prefer fresh apples), but by the fact that there are many competing products on the market, we can say that price is an important factor in consumer choice. The entrepreneur's product has as an innovative element cinnamon powder, which can be important for consumers in choosing this product, but can also be a brake on the sale of the product.

The reference is the price chosen by the entrepreneur as the price to the final consumer of 6.9 lei.

From a simple evaluation, being taken as a benchmark the price to the final consumer of 6.9 lei per bag of 100 g of finished product delivered to the negotiator's stores, there is a profit margin of the entrepreneur of 19.5% (VAT being 5–9% in Romania for food products). Given that the intermediary does not resell the product to a retailer, then its profit margin should be equal to the intermediary's margin + the retailer's margin, ie a minimum of 25–30%.

The contractor is asked by the intermediate negotiator a price reduction of 25–30% margin, ie a purchase price of around 4 lei (which means a little more than 30%, to reach a price negotiation maximum purchase of about 4.5 lei, pursued as the intermediate negotiator). After a discussion, the contractor confesses that the negotiation limit price is 5 lei (including VAT), which means 4.58 lei purchase price for the intermediary, probably due to the production costs that the contractor has.

A similar product, on specialized sites with packaged food, has a higher price, as I showed over 9 lei. Setting a price well below market level by the entrepreneur on a direct distribution channel gives him an immediate advantage to develop in the short term, but limited to a small market to which he has access, but blocks the development of medium and long term business, when he/she wants to sell the products on indirect distribution channels.

Among the usual mistakes made by Romanian entrepreneurs would be those related to marketing theory. Thus, Romanian entrepreneurs without experience and without practical knowledge, calculate their selling price (PV) per unit of finished product starting from the Commercial Addendum (CA), taking into account the production costs (CP) as follows:

$$PV = CP * AC$$

In our case we will have the following example:

5 lei production cost (−9% VAT) = 4.59 lei.

PV to the final consumer is 6.9 lei, at which if we apply a 30% discount (margin) then it reaches a purchase price (PA) of 4.47 lei.
Thus, in fixing the PV, the entrepreneur set a CA of about 38.3%, only that this represents 27.6% profit margin.

The mistake made by the entrepreneur is the wrong calculation of the profit margin (MP), according to the formula of the commercial addition, which does not give him a horizon of knowledge and interpretation of the limits of his negotiation:

$$PV = CP/(1-MP)$$

Calculating the selling price according to the wrong formula of the commercial addition will have more disadvantages than advantages, among the disadvantages being:

- being the simplest and most convenient for the entrepreneur, this formula will not give him the possibility to make an evaluation in percentage regarding the price reduction that he can grant to an intermediary before or at the moment of a negotiation;
- the calculation of the CA will not help the entrepreneur even in his own evaluation of a price strategy, because the possible price reductions are also related to the profit margin;
- results a whole series of strategic blockages that the entrepreneur may have, both on product development and on the survival of the company's activity.

5 Conclusion

Given the above, we believe that the Romanian entrepreneur, even if he has knowledge in developing competitive products on the domestic market and the community, can initially enter the market with the precarious knowledge he has about marketing, but in time, if not informed, he may lose in the development of his company. There is an unhealthy mentality of Romanians that hinders the development of business in general, by the fact that they consider that "they know it all" and apply the theory of wrong marketing. Therefore, very much in the negotiations we have with Romanian entrepreneurs, we made to give them free advice, than to make a negotiation itself./we prefer than to let them negotiate on their own.

References

1. Aldrich, H.E., Martinez, M.A.: Many are called, but few are chosen: an evolutionary perspective for the study of entrepreneurship. In: Cuervo, Á., Ribeiro, D., Roig, S. (eds.) Entrepreneurship, pp. 293–311. Springer Berlin Heidelberg, Berlin, Heidelberg (2007). https://doi.org/10.1007/978-3-540-48543-8_14
2. Cardon, M., Stevens, C., Potter, R.: Misfortunes or mistakes?: Cultural sense making of entrepreneurial failure. J. Bus. Ventur. **26**(1), 79–92 (2011)
3. Eurostat, National Statistical Offices, DIW Econ (2020)
4. European Commission: SME's strategy for a sustainable and digital Europe, Brussels (2020). https://ec.europa.eu/info/sites/info/files/communication-sme-strategy-march-2020_en.pdf
5. European Commission: Annual Report on European SMEs 2018/2019 Research & Development and Innovation by SMEs (2019). (file:///C:/Users//Downloads/EAAK19001ENN.en.pdf)
6. National Institute of Statistics of Romania (2021)
7. Santarelli, E., Vivarelli, M.: Entrepreneurship and the process of firms' entry, survival and growth. Ind. Corp. Chang. **16**(3), 455–488 (2007). https://doi.org/10.1093/icc/dtm010
8. Wolcott, R., Lippitz, M.: The four models of corporate entrepreneurship. MIT Sloan Manag. Rev. **49**(1), 75–83 (2007)
9. https://www.zf.ro/zf-24/cum-isi-impart-retailerii-alimentari-harta-bucurestiului-magazinele-19059914

Customer Visit Prediction Using Purchase Behavior and Tendency

Retsuya Saito[1]([✉]), Kohei Otake[2], and Takashi Namatame[3]

[1] Graduate School of Science and Engineering, Chuo University, 1-13-27, Kasuga, Bunkyo-ku, Tokyo 112-8551, Japan

[2] School of Information and Telecommunication Engineering, Tokai University, 2-3-23, Takanawa, Minato-ku, Tokyo 108-8619, Japan
otake@tsc.u-tokai.ac.jp

[3] Faculty of Science and Engineering, Chuo University, 1-13-27, Kasuga, Bunkyo-ku, Tokyo 112-8551, Japan
nama@indsys.chuo-u.ac.jp

Abstract. Over the last few decades, consumers' preferences and lifestyles have changed significantly. In such market, the number of products and services aims to mass marketing have become less effective. Therefore, personalization tailored to individual characteristics, certain segments, and one-to-one marketing focusing on individuals are becoming important. Therefore, customer relationship management, retaining existing customers and costs for acquiring new customers are important for both of academic and business field. However, for that purpose, it is essential to grasp customer behavior in more detail and use it for analysis. Therefore, in this study, we estimate the potential clusters of customers and customers' purchase behavior. Concretely, we use pLSA and XGBoost which become popular machine learning methodologies. In this study, we set the number of store visits per month for objective variable and show a prediction model of it. Then we compare the model that incorporates the result of predicting the probability of the latent cluster as an explanatory variable with the model that incorporates a general explanatory variable.

Keywords: Customer Behavior · pLSA · XGBoost

1 Introduction

In today's market, consumers' preferences have been diversified, the number of products and services aims to mass marketing have become less effective. In addition, while advances in technological capabilities have made it possible to obtain various data in stores such as retail stores, there is also the problem that a large amount of diverse data cannot be used for customer analysis. From the above, it can be said that in such a modern market, it is an important issue to provide services from the perspective of personalization tailored to individual characteristics and micromarketing focused on specific segments.

© Springer Nature Switzerland AG 2021
G. Meiselwitz (Ed.): HCII 2021, LNCS 12775, pp. 120–129, 2021.
https://doi.org/10.1007/978-3-030-77685-5_10

In past, when a company manages customers, the customer's characteristics are grasped by continuously collecting point cards and purchase history at the time of visit, and the customer's marketing measures are taken. In mature market economy, it is generally known that the cost of acquiring new customers is high, and CRM that emphasizes relationships with existing customers is widespread. This method is widely used not only real stores such supermarket, but in omni-channels that use the Internet such as EC. A useful marketing strategy for customer management is to classify customers to some homogeneous segmentations whose customers have similar preferences. This methodology aims to improve customer satisfaction and create sustainable demand by segmenting customers into some categories and providing services suitable for each customer segment. Marketing methods based on these categories focus on customer-specific characteristics such as customer purchase patterns and daily store visit times. In addition, by extracting the latent class of purchasing behavior of existing customers, it is considered possible to predict the purchasing behavior of customers who visit the store infrequently.

2 Purpose of This Study

In this study, we discuss the possibility of improving the prediction accuracy of customers' purchase behavior to consider the potential needs of customer behavior using POS data with ID of a supermarkets. As mentioned in the previous section, it is known that the cost of retaining existing customers is lower than the cost of acquiring new customers and new strategies. So, marketing measures for existing customers are an important issue. So, it is a useful means to understand customer behavior in more detail and use it for analysis.

Customer behavior can be flexibly predicted by machine learning such as deep learning, and it is expected to be used more and more in the field of marketing in recent years. Some researches have already been done to add user characteristics to explanatory variables. For example, on e-commerce sites, there is a lot of research using clickstream data. Clickstream data is often used to predict customer behavior because it records the user's search behavior in detail. Bucklin et al. [1] focused on diversity of customers by using Click stream data and used economic indicators such as Hirschman-Herfindahl Index (HHI) [2] as variables in addition to the features that have been often used [3, 4]. Next, transaction data is often used to a machine learning model for predicting customer behavior in stores [5]. Ishigaki et al. [6] proposed a latent class models related to product categories and customer lifestyles from transaction data and customer life survey data. The study used Bayesian networks to model relationships to identify class product categories that could be purchased under different conditions such as seasons, customer lifestyles, and time zones. There are many other studies that incorporate the concept of latent classes into machine learning [7], however few studies consider their usefulness as explanatory variables.

3 Datasets and Analysis Method

In this study, we analyze the ID-POS data of a supermarkets chain in Japan. The data period is from April 1, 2014, to March 30, 2016. The subjects of this study are 15,783 customers who have purchased at the supermarket more than once in total from April 1, 2014 to February 28, 2016. In addition, if there are multiple purchase records in a day, put them together at once.

We summarize the items of data in Table 1.

Table 1. Data description

Data	ID-POS Data
Duration of data	April, 1, 2014–March 31, 2016
Number of customer	15,783
Transaction data detail (total of 10,815,884)	Data about purchaces per user per receipt · User_id · Receipt_id · Date · Hour · Item_id · Quantity · Price · Item_category (Four categories)

3.1 Extreme Gradient Boosting

In this study, we create a model using XGBoost (eXtreme Gradient Boosting) [8], which is an ensemble learning that combines Gradient Boosting and Random Forest. This model optimizes the model by using gradient boosting. Also, since it is ensemble learning by boosting, the weak learner created one before is learned and the gradient is determined. In addition, a regularization term, which is a penalty term, is used to avoid overfitting to the data.

This study predicts the number of purchases in the next month. We get the transaction data for 24 months for each customer from the usage data and divide the period into the first 23 months and the rest months. In order to predict the future behavior of customers, 23 months are used as training data and rest 1 month is used as test data. Here, in evaluating the effectiveness of the latent variables, we are creating multiple prediction models with different combinations of input variables. For latent variables, we create a total of three comparative models in order to evaluate the effectiveness as an alternative to the most frequent variable, which is generally expressed in one-hot-encoding, the comparison model is based on 'the basic variable and the most frequent variable', 'the basic variable and the latent variable' and 'the basic variable, the most frequent variable and the latent variable'. In addition, the parameters used in the model are tuned to the optimum parameters by grid search.

3.2 Probabilistic Latent Semantic Analysis

We consider that customers are classified into some latent cluster [9] and generate categories. We target X customers and Y of the top 1000 items sold, and set the variables representing customer i and items j as x_i ($i = 1, ...X$) and y_j ($j = 1, ..., Y$). Also, we set Z be the number of latent customer categories, and z_k ($k = 1, ..., Z$). Here, we model the co-occurrence probability $P(x_i, y_j)$ of x_i and y_j is modeled as shown in (1). Let $\boldsymbol{x}, \boldsymbol{y}$, and $\boldsymbol{z}$ be vectors containing each.

$$P(x_i, y_j) = \sum_{k=1}^{Z} P(x_i|z_k)P(y_j|z_k)P(z_k) \tag{1}$$

If the frequency of simultaneous occurrence of x_i and y_j is N_{ij}, the log-likelihood is (2).

$$\begin{aligned}
l &= \sum_{i=1}^{X}\sum_{j=1}^{Y} N_{ij} \log P(x_i, y_j) \\
&= \sum_{i=1}^{X}\sum_{j=1}^{Y} N_{ij} \log \left\{ \sum_{k=1}^{Z} P(z_k)P(x_i|z_k)P(y_j|z_k) \right\}
\end{aligned} \tag{2}$$

The log-likelihood of this latent class model can be maximized by the EM algorithm. The conditional probabilities that need to be estimated are $P(\boldsymbol{x}|\boldsymbol{z})$, $P(\boldsymbol{y}|\boldsymbol{z})$ and $P(\boldsymbol{z})$. If the initial value is given to each probability as a random number, the conditional probability is calculated from the transformation of (2) as follows.

$$\begin{aligned}
P(x_i|z_k, y_j) &= \frac{P(x_i, y_j, z_k)}{P(x_i, y_j)} \\
&= \frac{P(x_i|z_k)P(y_j|z_k)P(z_k)}{\sum_{k=1}^{Z} P(x_i|z_k)P(y_j|z_k)P(z_k)}
\end{aligned} \tag{3}$$

From method of Lagrange multipliers, the optimal solution that maximizes the conditional probability of formula (3) iterative computation steps can be calculated as follows.

$$P(x_i|z_k) = \frac{\sum_{j=1}^{Y} N_{ij}P(z_k|x_i, y_j)}{\sum_{i=1}^{X}\sum_{j=1}^{Y} N_{ij}P(z_k|x_i, y_j)} \tag{4}$$

$$P(y_i|z_k) = \frac{\sum_{i=1}^{X} N_{ij}P(z_k|x_i, y_j)}{\sum_{i=1}^{X}\sum_{j=1}^{Y} N_{ij}P(z_k|x_i, y_j)} \tag{5}$$

$$P(z_k) = \frac{\sum_{i=1}^{X}\sum_{j=1}^{Y} N_{ij}P(z_k|x_i, y_j)}{\sum_{i=1}^{X}\sum_{j=1}^{Y}\sum_{k=1}^{Z} N_{ij}P(z_k|x_i, y_j)} \tag{6}$$

Each conditional probability can be estimated by executing this iteration until the likelihood converges.

In this study, we target 15,783 customers, and in addition to estimating the latent cluster between customers and products, we estimate the relationship between customers and store visit times, and customers and store visit day of the week in the same way. In addition, the number of latent classes is evaluated based on AIC (Akaike's Information Criterion) and BIC (Bayesian Information Criterion), and the number of classes is determined.

4   Results

In this section, we discuss how the accuracy of using latent variables in predicting the number of future visits of a customer improve. Regarding the latent variable, we model the relationship between the purchased item, the time of arrival, the day of the week of arrival and the customer, and use them in the analysis by putting the probability of belonging of each customer into the variable.

4.1   Latent Variable

The purpose of this study is to improve the accuracy by estimating the latent class between the customer and the item by pLSA and using it as a variable for predicting the number of customer visits. We also discuss the effectiveness of using latent variables in terms of variable interpretation. Here, the values of AIC and BIC in the optimal number of latent classes of the model of customer and item, customer and visit time, customer and visit day of the week, and AIC and BIC in the number of classes before and after that are shown Tables 2, 3 and 4.

Table 2. The number of latent classes of items

Number of class	AIC	BIC
7	8353223.81	8393575.19
8	8346023.79	8393282.93
9	8340034.12	8394201.01

Based on the above results, the number of latent classes of items is set to 8.

Based on the above results, the number of latent classes of visit time is set to 5.

Based on the above results, the number of latent classes of visit day of week is set to 9. The interpretation of each latent class is also shown in Tables 5, 6, 7 and 8.

Although the characteristics of the purchased products can be grasped, no correlation is found with the unit price of the products.

From the characteristics of the latent class, it can be seen that the probability of belonging to the latent class during the visit time is summarized in the time such as morning or evening. From this result, it is considered that the visit time is useful for grasping the characteristics of the customer's lifestyle.

Table 3. The number of latent classes of visit time

Number of class	AIC	BIC
4	431520.16	425653.94
5	430112.45	424286.85
6	430075.94	424290.96

Table 4. The number of latent classes of visit day of the week

Number of class	AIC	BIC
8	320877.37	314974.40
9	320334.09	314444.74
10	320334.25	314458.52

Table 5. Characteristics of each latent class in the items

Class no.	Characteristics of purchased items
1	Vegetable products with the highest sales volume
2	Seasonings, fresh foods, foodstuffs
3	Alcoholic beverages, snacks, snack products
4	Vegetables and fruits products
5	Fruits, sweets, and confectionery products
6	Foods from animals and processed products
7	Side dish, lunch box
8	Products with the highest sales volume

Table 6. Characteristics of each latent class in visit time

Class no.	Characteristics of visit time
1	Time zone from 18:00 to 21:00
2	Time zone from 14:00 to 18:00
3	Time zone from 09:00 to 11:00
4	Time zone from 21:00 to 23:00 and 19:00 to 20:00
5	Time zone from 11:00 to 15:00

Table 7. Characteristics of each latent class in visit day of week

Class no.	Characteristics of visit day of week
1	Visit on Monday and Sunday
2	Visit on Monday and Friday
3	Visit on Tuesday and Friday
4	Visit on Saturday
5	Visit on Monday and Tuesday
6	Visit on Wednesday
7	Visit on Monday and Thursday
8	Visit on Sunday
9	Visit on Thursday and Friday

Depending on the customer, the days of the week they visit are not fixed, and it is thought that there are weeks when they visit the store many times a week, and there are weeks when they come to the store less often due to eating out. However, the customer is expressed by the probability of belonging to each latent class, so it does not definitely limit the day of the week of visit.

4.2 Analysis Results

First, we show the explanatory variables used in this study in Table 8. Here, we define the period used for training data as t_1 and the period used for test data as t_2. In this study, we use a regression analysis model by GLM (Generalized Linear Regression) to make predictions by the parametric statistical model used for comparison, and use the estimated value by maximum likelihood estimation. The analysis used the cumulative number of purchases as the objective variable and made predictions using a Poisson regression model. RMSE was calculated by applying 80% of the original data to the training data and the remaining 20% to the test data.

Next, Table 9 shows the results of predicting the number of purchases using XGBoost and GLM. Here, pattern 1 is a model that uses basic and mode as variables, pattern 2 is a model that uses basic and latent, and pattern 3 is a model that uses basic, mode and latent.

The biggest improvement in the RMSE value is when using the XGBoost model, where only latent variables are added as explanatory variables to the basic variables. Comparing the XGBoost and GLM predictions from the Table 9, the accuracy of XGBoost is constantly improving.

Table 8. Explanatory variables used in the model

Variable name		Explanation
Buy_times$_{t_2}$	Target	Objective variable: Cumulative number of purchases during the t_2 period
Buy_times$_{t_1}$	Basis	Cumulative number of purchases during the t_1 period
Interval		Average number of days visited during t_1 period (logarithm)
Min price		Minimum purchase amount during t_1 period
Max price		Maximum purchase amount during t_1 period
Diff price		The difference between the maximum and minimum prices of item purchased during the t_1 period
Diff days		The difference between the date of last visit and February 28, 2016
Item avg		Average number of items purchased during t_1 period
Most hour	Mode	Most visited time during t_1 period
Most week		Most visited day of week during t_1 period
Buying items	Latent	Probability that a user belongs to a latent class of items classified by pLSA
Visit time		Probability that a user belongs to a latent class of visit time classified by pLSA
Visit week		Probability that a user belongs to a latent class of visit week classified by pLSA

Table 9. RMSE result comparison

Prediction method	Pattern 1	Pattern 2	Pattern 3
XGBoost	2.43	1.92	2.04
GLM	2.70	2.25	2.18

5 Discussion

Firstly, from the results of analysis, it can be seen that the RMSE is most improved for XGBoost when the basic variables and the latent variables are used. In addition, regarding GLM, in some analysis results, the prediction accuracy may be improved in other models than in the case of using basic variables and latent variables. However, in the XGBoost model, the best results are obtained when we used the basic variables and the latent variables. From this result, it is considered that the accuracy of GLM, which is a simple model, is not improved because the characteristics of variables are not fully captured.

Next, we describe the usefulness of the latent variables used in this study. In the retail industry, in order to improve service quality and manage products appropriately, it is desirable to quantitatively understand what kind of customers need what kind of products. In the retail industry, in order to improve service quality and manage products appropriately, it is desirable to quantitatively understand what kind of customers need for what kind of products. Therefore, one-hot-encoding is often used. This method is an important method that is also used for categorical data, but it may be occur a problem that the data tends to be sparse. On the other hand, the expression of latent classes by pLSA used in this study models the relationship between customer and product, customer and time, etc. by assuming a latent class. This method can express the probability of belonging of the latent class in each customer in a low dimension. The significance of the latent is that the hobbies and behavior patterns of customers can be estimated from the limited behavior in the store. As a conventional quantitative variable, it is possible to consider how often the store is visited and how many products are purchased on average. It is not always useful as a variable for predicting customer behavior because it may increase in proportion to the difference in product prices for each store visit time and the number of purchases. However, regarding the potential expressed by the probability of dependence on purchasing tendency, such as how much it depends on the product, we think that it is possible to extract information on purchasing behavior that is more than a mere quantitative variable such as the number of products purchased. In addition, by using latent variables for analysis, it is possible to place an order for products according to the visit time and the day of the week when each customer has a high probability of belonging to the latent class.

6 Conclusion

In this study, in order to consider the diversification of customer values and lifestyles in purchase behavior, we discussed the usefulness of the variables by defining the latent and incorporating it as a variable for analysis. We proposed to use pLSA as a method for expressing latent variables. This is because we thought that it would be appropriate as a method to replace the dummy variables that are generally used when expressing customer information. This time, we evaluated the usefulness of the latent variable by predicting the number of customer visits using XGBoost. As a comparison of the models, we created a model that combines the basic variables and mode variables that have been used conventionally. In addition, the regression model by GLM was used for the prediction by the parametric statistical model, and the estimated value by the maximum likelihood estimation was used. RMSE was used as the evaluation index, and the results obtained showed that RMSE was most improved for XGBoost when the basic variable and the latent variable were used. From this, the effectiveness of the latent variable was shown.

However, in this study, we did not consider environmental factors such as the weather when visiting the store. It is empirically clear that there is a decision to visit the store due to the influence of such environmental factors. In addition, this time, the analysis was performed using transaction data in the actual store, but it is considered necessary to evaluate the validity of the latent variable in the click stream data of the EC site.

Acknowledgement. *This work was supported by JSPS KAKENHI Grant Number 19K01945.*

References

1. Bucklin, R.E., et al.: Choice and the internet: from clickstream to research stream. Mark. Lett. **13**(3), 245–258 (2002). https://doi.org/10.1023/A:1020231107662
2. Davis, P., Garcés, E.: Quantitative Techniques for Competition and Antitrust Analysis. Princeton University Press, Princeton (2009)
3. Niimi, J., Hoshino, T.: Predicting the consumers behavior with using the variety of user access patterns. Jpn. J. Appl. Stat. **44**(3), 121–143 (2015). (in Japanese)
4. Niimi, J., Hoshino, T.: Predicting purchases with using the variety of customer behaviors, analysis of the purchase history and the browsing history by deep learning. Trans. Jpn. Soc. Artif. Intell. **32**(2B), 1–9 (2017). (in Japanese)
5. Matsumura, N., Izumi, K., Yamada, K.: A marketing simulation of a retail store with the consumer reactions to out-of-shelf based on a POS data. Jpn. Soc. Artif. Intell. **31**(2F), 1–8 (2016). (in Japanese)
6. Ishigaki, T., Takenaka, T., Motomura, Y.: Customer behavior prediction system by large scale data fusion in a retail service. Jpn. Soc. Artif. Intell. **26**(6D), 1–9 (2011). (in Japanese)
7. Tsukasa, T., Takenaka, T., Motomura, Y.: Improvement of prediction accuracy of the number of customers by latent class model. Jpn. Soc. Artif.Intell. 25(1B3-2), 1–4 (2011). (in Japanese)
8. Chen, T., Guestrin, C.: XGBoost: a scalable tree boosting system. In: Proceedings of 22nd ACM SIGKDD International Conference on Knowledge Discovery and Data Mining, pp. 785–794 (2016)
9. Hofmann, T.: Probabilistic latent semantic indexing. In: Proceedings of the Fifteenth Conference on Uncertainty in Artificial Intelligence, pp. 289–296 (1999)

Verification of Probabilistic Latent Semantic Analysis Clustering Solution Stability and Proposal of Optimal Initial Values Setting Method

Shinnosuke Terasawa[1](✉), Kohei Otake[2], and Takashi Namatame[3]

[1] Graduate School of Science and Engineering, Chuo University, 1-13-27, Kasuga, Bunkyo-ku 112-8551, Tokyo, Japan
[2] School of Information and Telecommunication Engineering, Tokai University, 2-3-23, Takanawa, Minato-ku 108-8619, Tokyo, Japan
otake@tsc.u-tokai.ac.jp
[3] Faculty of Science and Engineering, Chuo University, 1-13-27, Kasuga, Bunkyo-ku 112-8551, Tokyo, Japan
nama@indsys.chuo-u.ac.jp

Abstract. pLSA is a useful method to know the characteristics of customer or item in marketing. In this study, we proposed a method to set the initial values more efficiently than the existing method for the problem that the final solution depends on the initial values set in the EM algorithm used by pLSA to estimate the solutions. We focused on the dimensional compression and clustering that are the characteristics of pLSA, and thought that the stability of the solution of pLSA would be improved by reflecting it in the initial values. Therefore, first, we performed correspondence analysis and k-means cluster analysis on the original data to express the features of dimensional compression and clustering. Next, we compared the performance of the pLSA results with the initial values of the proposed method and the initial values of the conventional method using random numbers. As a result, it was shown that the proposed method also converges to the same log-likelihood as the conventional method, and that the proposed method is superior in terms of convergence speed and stability.

Keywords: pLSA · Optimization · Correspondence analysis · k-means clustering analysis · EM algorithm

1 Introduction

In this chapter, we mention the problem of pLSA, and the purpose of this study.

1.1 Background

Probabilistic Latent Semantic Analysis (pLSA) is one of the dimensional compression methods with some latent class proposed by Hoffman [1]. The essence is a method of

© Springer Nature Switzerland AG 2021
G. Meiselwitz (Ed.): HCII 2021, LNCS 12775, pp. 130–146, 2021.
https://doi.org/10.1007/978-3-030-77685-5_11

extracting the latent classes that are common features behind row and column elements of matrix data. Therefore, pLSA is used as a clustering method. Furthermore, among the clustering methods, pLSA has three major features as below.

The first is that it can handle high-dimensional data. In conventional clustering, the similarity between data is calculated and close data are collected. Therefore, as data becomes higher dimensions, overall distance apart, hardly to obtain the reasonable results. However, pLSA can handle high-dimensional data because it compresses the dimensions of the data before clustering.

The second is that clustering can be performed simultaneously from both rows and columns. In conventional clustering, columns (rows) are clustered based on rows (columns), so clustering can only be performed from one direction. However, pLSA extracts latent classes that are common to rows and columns, and clusters the elements of rows and columns into latent classes, so clustering can be performed simultaneously from both of rows and columns.

The third is that pLSA is soft clustering. k-means clustering analysis and hierarchical clustering, which are typical clustering methods, are called hard clustering, and each element can belong to only one cluster. However, since pLSA calculates probability of belonging to each class of each row and column element, it is possible to accurately express even an element having multiple meanings.

However, it is known that the solution of pLSA is not stable because it depends on the initial values of the EM algorithm for estimating the solution [2]. Therefore, in many cases when pLSA is used, the initial values are generated by the random numbers and the best solution is adopted [3]. And there is a possibility that pLSA outputs some results that produce different interpretations from the same data.

1.2 Purpose of This Study

In this study, we focused on the initial values dependence of pLSA described in the previous section. In pLSA, the dependence on the initial values is a big problem, and in order to find a stable and valid solution, it is necessary to devise at the phase of setting the initial value. Therefore, we propose a method for setting initial values in order to find a more efficient and stable solution with pLSA. Then, we evaluate and compare the results of pLSA for the case of generating with conventional random numbers and the proposed method and confirm its usefulness.

2 Latent Class Analysis and pLSA

In this chapter, we explain about the latent class analysis including pLSA.

2.1 Latent Class Model

Latent class analysis (LCA) is a method for testing theories about unobserved (hypothesized) categorical variables that are measured (imperfectly) by observed categorical variables [4]. Factor analysis and mixture analysis are included in the latent class model. In addition, the useful points of using latent variables are described in [5] as follows.

There are many advantages to using latent variables, the main of which are that they fit the principle of savings and that they can be diluted. The former makes it easier to obtain a simpler interpretation by reducing the relationships between many observations to a relatively small number of latent variables, and the latter makes it easier to obtain a simpler interpretation of the relationships between latent variables with measurement errors removed. Each means that the estimation tends to be more accurate.

In other words, using latent variables has the advantages of dimensional reduction and improvement of the explanatory power of observed variables. From these points, the latent class model is used as a topic model in the field of handling high-dimensional data such as natural language processing. Specific methods include LSA (Latent Semantics) [6], pLSA, LDA (Latent Dirichlet Allocation) [7]. pLSA is an improved method of LSA by probabilistic processing, and LDA is a method developed as an extended version of pLSA.

2.2 LSA

LSA is one of the methods for estimating topics based on matrix singular value decomposition (SVD), and is also called Latent Semantic Indexing (LSI). LSA uses singular value decomposition to reduce dimensions, and in the reduced vector space, near concepts are plotted near and distant concepts are plotted far [8]. The specific method of singular value decomposition is to decompose, where Σ is a diagonal matrix, an arbitrary matrix X into orthogonal matrices U and V as shown in Eq. (1). Each element of the angular matrix Σ is called a singular value [9]. Each element of Σ can be rearranged as $\hat{\sigma}_1 \geq \hat{\sigma}_2 \geq \cdots \geq \hat{\sigma}_r$. The dimension can be compressed by cutting from the singular value with less influence, that is, $\hat{\sigma}_r$. The smaller the number of singular values to be cut, the closer to the original matrix, and the larger the number of singular values to be cut, the higher the degree of dimensional compression.

$$
X = U \Sigma V^\top = U \begin{pmatrix} \hat{\sigma}_1 & & O \\ & \ddots & \\ O & & \hat{\sigma}_r \end{pmatrix} V \tag{1}
$$

By reducing the dimensions in this way, the similarity between words-words, word-documents, and documents-documents can be obtained from high-dimensional document data [10].

2.3 LDA

While pLSA is a method that outputs the probability calculated from training data, LDA is a method that calculates the probability assuming a probability distribution called a directory distribution [2]. Due to this characteristic, pLSA tends to cause overfitting of training data and is not suitable for estimating the probability of new data, but LDA calculates the probability assuming distribution, so it is suitable for estimation. Therefore, pLSA is suitable for extracting latent factors of actually observed data, and LDA is suitable for new prediction.

2.4 pLSA

pLSA probabilistically calculates this latent class z, assuming that there is a common feature latent semantic class z behind the row element x and the column element y. The co-occurrence probability $P(x, y)$ of x and y is expressed using the latent class z, and outputs the random variables $P(z)$, $P(x|z)$, $P(y|z)$ as final result. The co-occurrence probability $P(x, y)$ can be modeled as in Eq. (2), and the log-likelihood function L is as in Eq. (3), where $N(x, y)$ is the frequency of simultaneous occurrences of x and y.

$$P(x, y) = \sum_z P(x|z)P(y|z)P(z) \tag{2}$$

$$
\begin{aligned}
L &= \sum_x \sum_y N(x, y)\log P(x, y) \\
&= \sum_x \sum_y N(x, y)\log \sum_z P(x|z)P(y|z)P(z) \\
&= \sum_x \sum_y N(x, y)\log \sum_z P(z|x, y)\frac{P(x|z)P(y|z)P(z)}{P(z|x, y)}
\end{aligned}
\tag{3}
$$

To estimate $P(z), P(x|z), P(y|z)$ with maximum likelihood estimation, that maximize this log-likelihood function L. At this time, using Jensen's inequality, the log-likelihood L of Eq. (3) is converted as Eq. (4). And, by maximizing the lower limit that indirectly maximizes the log-likelihood [10].

$$
\begin{aligned}
L &\geq \sum_x \sum_y \sum_z N(x, y)P(z|x, y)\log\frac{P(x|z)P(y|z)P(z)}{P(z|x, y)} \\
&= \sum_x \sum_y \sum_z N(x, y)P(z|x, y)\log P(x|z)P(y|z)P(z) \\
&\quad - \sum_x \sum_y \sum_z N(x, y)P(z|x, y)\log P(z|x, y)
\end{aligned}
\tag{4}
$$

Furthermore, the EM algorithm is used to estimate the parameters that maximize the lower limit of the log-likelihood. EM algorithm is separated into E-step and M-step. E-step calculates $P(z|x, y)$ by using Eq. (5) and fixing the first term of the Eq. (4). M-step calculates $P(z), P(x|z), P(y|z)$ by using Eq. (6)–(8) and $P(z|x, y)$ calculated by E-step. Keep iterating steps E and M until the log-likelihood converges. At this time, the log-likelihood L_h, when the number of iteration is h, is calculated by Eq. (3) and obtained $P(z), P(x|z), P(y|z)$ in h-th M-step. Therefore, it is judged EM algorithm has converged, when the value of $L_h - L_{h-1}$ is smaller than the threshold value.

$$P(z|x, y) = \frac{P(x, y, z)}{P(x, y)} = \frac{P(x|z)P(y|z)P(z)}{\sum_z P(x|z)P(y|z)P(z)} \tag{5}$$

$$P(x|z) = \frac{\sum_y N(x, y)P(z|x, y)}{\sum_x \sum_y N(x, y)P(z|x, y)} \tag{6}$$

$$P(y|z) = \frac{\sum_x N(x, y)P(z|x, y)}{\sum_x \sum_y N(x, y)P(z|x, y)} \tag{7}$$

$$P(z) = \frac{\sum_x \sum_y N(x, y)P(z|x, y)}{\sum_x \sum_y \sum_z N(x, y)P(z|x, y)} \tag{8}$$

2.5   Initial Values Dependence of pLSA

As mentioned in the previous section, the solution of pLSA is obtained by maximum likelihood estimation using the EM algorithm. However, the EM algorithm requires to set the initial values, $P(z)$, $P(x|z)$, $P(y|z)$, for fix the first term of the Eq. (4) in the first iteration of E-step. Therefore, it is known that the final solution of pLSA tends to depend on the initial values set here [2].

3   Proposed Methods

In this chapter, we describe the proposal of the initial values creation method to avoid the initial values dependence of pLSA and the methods used for the performance evaluation of pLSA.

3.1   The Object of Creating Initial Values

pLSA is a method of performing soft clustering by probabilistically expressing close elements as the same latent class at the same time from the viewpoint of rows and columns. Therefore, we propose an initial value setting method in order to converge more efficiently and obtain a stable solution by grouping close elements together at the initial values creation phase. Specifically, the distance between elements is probability expressed and the initial values, $P(x|z)$ and $P(y|z)$ are created. We use correspondence analysis as a method to obtain the coordinates of each element, k-means clustering analysis as a method to grouping close elements together, inner product as a method to obtain similarity between center of gravity coordinates of each cluster and coordinates of each element, softmax function as a method to convert to probability as the initial values.

3.2   The Method of Creating Initial Values

The flow of initial values creation is shown below.

1. We perform correspondence on the co-occurrence matrix to calculate the canonical correlation coefficient, row score, and column score. Align the number of dimensions at this time with the number of latent classes of pLSA.
2. Calculate the coordinates of each element by multiplying the row (column) score of each element by the canonical correlation coefficient.
3. Perform k-means clustering analysis on the coordinates of each row element and column element. The number of clusters at this time is also the same as the number of latent classes of pLSA.
4. Calculate the center of gravity coordinates of each cluster, and calculate the inner products of each element and the center of gravity of each cluster.
5. Use the softmax function, for the obtained inner product, so that the sum of each element in the latent class is 1.
6. Use the obtained matrix as the initial values $P(x|z)$ and $P(y|z)$.

Correspondence Analysis. Correspondence analysis is a method of projecting data into a small number of dimensions to create a new axis by dimensional contraction of multidimensional qualitative data. Correspondence analysis calculates the row and column quantification scores in the contracted dimension and the canonical correlation coefficient. In addition, the coordinates of each element can be calculated by multiplying the calculated quantification score by the canonical correlation coefficient [11].

k-Means Clustering Analysis. The algorithm for clustering n observation into k cluster is as follows.

1. Arbitrarily set k representative coordinates.
2. Calculate the Euclidean distance from each n observation to each representative point, and make the cluster of each observation the cluster of the closest representative point.
3. Calculate the center of gravity of the data for each cluster and use it as a new representative point.
4. If the representative point does not move, the process ends. After moving them, repeat from step 2.

Softmax Function. The softmax function is a function that transforms a n -dimensional real vector so that the sum of each element is 1 and the range is [0, 1]. The equation of the softmax function is shown in the Eq. (9).

$$f(x_i) = \frac{\exp(x_i)}{\sum_{j=1}^{l} \exp(x_i)} \qquad (9)$$

3.3 Matching the Cluster Number

In order to evaluate the stability of pLSA due to the difference in initial values, it is necessary to match the cluster numbers of each result. Therefore, the cluster number of the first result is fixed, and the cluster numbers of the second and subsequent times are assigned using the optimization method. At this time, $P(x, y|z) = P(x|z)P(y|z)$ holds in the result of n-th time. Since the cluster number of the first result is fixed, sim_l that similarity of the latent class i of the first result and the latent class j of the l-th result is defined as an Eq. (10).

$$sim_l(i, j) = \sum_x \sum_y \{P(x, y|z = i, n = 1) \circ P(x, y|z = j, n = l)\} \qquad (10)$$

For all combinations of i and j in the l-th time, the ones arranged in the $m \times m$ matrix are the first result and the l-th time similarity SIM_l. Furthermore, as a variable of the allocation problem, V such as the Eq. (11) is created using the binary variable $t_{(i,j)}$. When $t_{(i,j)} = 1$, the latent class i of the first result and the latent class j of the l-th result are the same class.

$$V = \begin{pmatrix} 1 & \cdots & 0 & \cdots & 0 & t_{(1,1)} & \cdots & t_{(1,j)} & \cdots & t_{(1,m)} \\ \vdots & \ddots & \vdots & & \vdots & \vdots & \vdots & & \ddots & \vdots \\ 0 & \cdots & 1 & \cdots & 0 & t_{(i,1)} & \cdots & t_{(i,j)} & \cdots & t_{(i,m)} \\ \vdots & & \vdots & \ddots & \vdots & \vdots & & \vdots & & \ddots & \vdots \\ 0 & \cdots & 0 & \cdots & 1 & t_{(m,1)} & \cdots & t_{(m,j)} & \cdots & t_{(m,m)} \end{pmatrix} \tag{11}$$

Assuming that the k-th line of V is V_k, the allocation problem is shown below.

The objective function Eq. (12) is the maximization of the similarity of the first result of pLSA and the l-th result of pLSA. Equation (13) and Eq. (14) are equality constraints which means of each are total of V_k becomes 2 and the sum of each column from the $(m + 1)$-th column to the $2m$-th column of V is 1. In other words, allocating one l-th result latent class j equivalent to the first result latent class i and one latent class j as a result of the l-th result. Equation (15) means that $t_{(i,j)}$ is binary variable.

$$\max \quad VV = \sum_{k=1}^{m} \left(V_k^T \times V_k \right) \circ SIM_l \tag{12}$$

$$\text{subject to} \quad \sum_{i=1}^{m} t_{(i,j)} + 1 = 2j = 1, \ldots, m \tag{13}$$

$$\sum_{j=1}^{m} t_{(i,j)} = 1i = 1, \ldots, m \tag{14}$$

$$t_{(i,j)} \in \{0, 1\}i, j = 1, \ldots, m \tag{15}$$

This allocation problem works for each result.

3.4   The Performance Evaluation for pLSA

The performance of pLSA is evaluated from the following three viewpoints.

i.   Log-likelihood at EM algorithm converged
ii. Number of iterations until the EM algorithm converged
iii. Commonality of elements with higher probabilities between $P(x|z)$ and $P(y|z)$.

In first viewpoint, we evaluate validity of pLSA results. Results of pLSA are estimated by maximum likelihood estimator to maximize log-likelihood L in the Eq. (3).

In second viewpoint, we measure the number of iterations as a convergence speed, because maximum likelihood estimator for pLSA using EM algorithm that iterate until results are converged.

In third viewpoint, we use Jaccard coefficient as a commonality of elements with higher probabilities between $P(x|z)$ and $P(y|z)$. The Jaccard coefficient measures commonality of between finite sample sets, and it is defined as Eq. (16). In other words, Jaccard coefficient is higher mean that results of pLSA are stable.

$$J(A, B) = \frac{|A \cap B|}{|A \cap B|} \tag{16}$$

4   Experimental Analysis

In this chapter, we evaluate performance and make comparisons between pLSA using initial values generated by random numbers and created by proposal method.

4.1   The Summary of Data

We use ID-POS data of a supermarket. Table 1 shows summary of the data.

Table 1. Columns of dataset

Term	January 1, 2015 ~ December 31, 2015
Target customer	134,058
Product category	26 (ex. 'Vegetables', 'Fruits', ...)
Number of purchase transactions	62,975,264

4.2   The Flow of Experiment

We show the flow of experiment below.

1. Create the co-occurrence matrix with rows are 'Customer ID', columns are 'Product category' and elements are 'The number of purchases by each customer in each category ($\in \mathbb{N}$)'.
2. Create initial values by using proposal method from the created co-occurrence matrix.
3. Perform pLSA 10 times for each of the two types initial values which show below. In this paper, the number of latent classes is 4.

   a. Generate initial values from random numbers for every 10 times of pLSA
   b. Create and fix $P(x|z)$ and $P(y|z)$ as initial values by using proposal method, and generate only $P(z)$ from random numbers for every 10 times of pLSA.

4. Matching cluster number of the results of 10 pLSA for each of the two initial values.
5. Evaluate the performance of every 10 times results of pLSA that using two types initial values.
6. Compare evaluation values with two types of initial values setting methods.

4.3   Experimental Results

In this section, Conduct experiments and summarize the results according to the flow of the evaluation experiment described in the previous section.

Creating Initial Values. We create the initial values of proposal method from co-occurrence matrix which created from the ID-POS data mentioned in Sect. 4.1. Specific results are shown in order.

1. As a result of performing correspondence analysis on the co-occurrence matrix, Table 2 shows the canonical correlation coefficient, Table 3 shows the row score, and Table 4 shows the column score. The number of dimensions at this time was set to 4 to match the number of dimensions

Table 2. Canonical correlation coefficient

	V1	V2	V3	V4
Canonical correlation coefficient	0.397	0.356	0.289	0.235

Table 3. Row score

	V1	V2	V3	V4
1	−0.212	0.819	0.695	0.171
2	−1.399	1.139	−0.532	0.334
3	−1.352	0.980	−0.753	0.752
4	−0.271	−0.396	0.530	0.479
5	0.563	2.026	0.095	0.351
6	0.180	1.122	−1.238	−1.682
7	0.039	−1.130	2.565	0.784
8	−1.108	0.752	−1.298	0.224
9	1.130	−2.709	0.106	2.017
10	0.003	−1.287	2.919	2.793
⋮	⋮	⋮	⋮	⋮

Table 4. Column score

	V1	V2	V3	V4
1	−0.902	0.793	−0.392	0.415
2	−0.062	0.178	−0.125	−0.929
3	−0.877	0.345	−0.465	0.643
4	0.110	−0.629	−0.397	−0.662
5	−0.893	0.949	−0.946	0.251
6	0.304	0.420	−1.414	−1.019
7	−0.719	0.688	−0.936	−0.149
8	−0.419	0.503	−0.230	−0.063
9	−0.561	0.520	−0.050	−0.008
10	−0.639	0.685	0.000	0.251
⋮	⋮	⋮	⋮	⋮

2. We calculated the coordinates of each element by multiplying the row score and column score of each element by the canonical correlation coefficient. Furthermore, the coordinates of each row element and column element are clustered by the k-means clustering analysis, and the row direction results are shown in Table 5 and the column direction results are shown in Table 6. The number of clusters at this time is also 4 classes in order to match the number of latent classes of pLSA.

Table 5. Coordinates and cluster number (row direction)

	V1	V2	V3	V4	Cluster number
1	−0.084	0.292	0.201	0.040	3
2	−0.555	0.406	−0.154	0.078	3
3	−0.537	0.349	−0.218	0.177	3
4	−0.108	−0.141	0.153	0.112	3
5	0.224	0.722	0.027	0.082	3
6	0.071	0.399	−0.358	−0.395	3
7	0.015	−0.402	0.742	0.184	1
8	−0.440	0.268	−0.375	0.053	3
9	0.448	−0.965	0.031	0.473	4
10	0.001	−0.458	0.844	0.656	1
⋮	⋮	⋮	⋮	⋮	⋮

Table 6. Coordinates and cluster number (column direction)

	V1	V2	V3	V4	Cluster number
1	−0.358	0.282	−0.113	0.097	2
2	−0.025	0.063	−0.036	−0.218	2
3	−0.348	0.123	−0.134	0.151	2
4	0.044	−0.224	−0.115	−0.155	4
5	−0.354	0.338	−0.273	0.059	2
6	0.121	0.150	−0.409	−0.239	2
7	−0.285	0.245	−0.271	−0.035	2
8	−0.166	0.179	−0.066	−0.015	2
9	−0.223	0.185	−0.014	−0.002	2
10	−0.253	0.244	0.000	0.059	2
⋮	⋮	⋮	⋮	⋮	⋮

3. We calculated the coordinates of the center of gravity of each cluster and the inner product of each element and the center of gravity of each cluster. Table 7 shows the results in the row direction, and Table 8 shows the results in the column direction.

Table 7. Inner product of elements and the center of gravity of each cluster (row direction)

	1	2	3	4
1	0.036	−0.501	0.051	−0.199
2	−0.347	−0.585	0.180	−0.278
3	−0.354	−0.366	0.174	−0.252
4	0.043	0.069	0.008	−0.042
5	0.069	−0.605	0.039	−0.235
6	−0.200	−0.473	0.026	0.047
7	0.395	0.015	−0.061	−0.090
8	−0.388	−0.204	0.141	−0.126
9	0.337	1.758	−0.202	0.389
10	0.486	0.427	−0.051	−0.193
⋮	⋮	⋮	⋮	⋮

Table 8. Inner product of elements and the center of gravity of each cluster (column direction)

	1	2	3	4
1	−0.268	0.123	−0.274	−0.122
2	−0.007	0.019	−0.183	0.014
3	−0.434	0.097	−0.086	−0.098
4	−0.225	−0.033	0.185	0.064
5	−0.210	0.145	−0.236	−0.142
6	0.325	0.037	0.055	−0.018
7	−0.218	0.118	−0.187	−0.100
8	−0.079	0.066	−0.197	−0.059
9	−0.164	0.074	−0.257	−0.064
10	−0.135	0.087	−0.292	−0.087
⋮	⋮	⋮	⋮	⋮

4. We used softmax function on the calculated inner product so that the sum of elements in each cluster becomes 1. Use the calculated value of row direction as initial value $P(x|z)$ and value of the column direction as initial value $P(y|z)$. Shown in Table 9 and Table 10.

Table 9. Initial Value $P(x|z)$

	1	2	3	4
1	0.000007161	0.000000645	0.000007931	0.000005688
2	0.000004883	0.000000593	0.000009021	0.000005253
3	0.000004849	0.000000739	0.000008964	0.000005390
4	0.000007207	0.000001142	0.000007593	0.000006655
5	0.000007401	0.000000582	0.000007834	0.000005482
6	0.000005654	0.000000664	0.000007734	0.000007268
7	0.000010255	0.000001081	0.000007085	0.000006341
8	0.000004686	0.000000869	0.000008677	0.000006116
9	0.000009672	0.000006179	0.000006154	0.000010235
10	0.000011230	0.000001633	0.000007159	0.000005721
⋮	⋮	⋮	⋮	⋮

Table 10. Initial Value $P(y|z)$

	1	2	3	4
1	0.00719	0.04283	0.02576	0.03432
2	0.00933	0.03860	0.02820	0.03933
3	0.00609	0.04174	0.03108	0.03515
4	0.00750	0.03663	0.04078	0.04136
5	0.00762	0.04379	0.02676	0.03366
6	0.01301	0.03930	0.03577	0.03810
7	0.00755	0.04259	0.02810	0.03507
8	0.00868	0.04047	0.02781	0.03656
9	0.00798	0.04076	0.02619	0.03639
10	0.00821	0.04132	0.02531	0.03555
⋮	⋮	⋮	⋮	⋮

Matching Cluster Number. Matching the cluster number according to the Sect. 3.3. Table 11, Table 12 show the results of allocation problem. Regarding how to read the tables, the cluster number j in the result of the $n = l$-th time, which equivalents to the cluster number i, becomes 1. In other words, the cluster number $j = 3$ in the $n = 2$ time of the Table 11 is matched as the same class as the cluster number $i = 4$ in the first result.

Table 11. Result of matching cluster number (random initial values)

n	j	i				n	j	i			
		1	2	3	4			1	2	3	4
1	1	1	0	0	0	6	1	0	0	1	0
	2	0	1	0	0		2	1	0	0	0
	3	0	0	1	0		3	0	0	0	1
	4	0	0	0	1		4	0	1	0	0
2	1	1	0	0	0	7	1	0	0	0	1
	2	0	1	0	0		2	0	0	1	0
	3	0	0	0	1		3	1	0	0	0
	4	0	0	1	0		4	0	1	0	0
3	1	0	1	0	0	8	1	0	1	0	0
	2	1	0	0	0		2	1	0	0	0
	3	0	0	0	1		3	0	0	0	1
	4	0	0	1	0		4	0	0	1	0
4	1	0	1	0	0	9	1	0	1	0	0
	2	1	0	0	0		2	1	0	0	0
	3	0	0	0	1		3	0	0	0	1
	4	0	0	1	0		4	0	0	1	0
5	1	0	0	1	0	10	1	0	0	1	0
	2	1	0	0	0		2	0	1	0	0
	3	0	0	0	1		3	0	0	0	1
	4	0	1	0	0		4	1	0	0	0

Log-likelihood and Number of Iteration. We evaluate the performance of pLSA according to the evaluation indexes (i) and (ii) described in Sect. 3.4. Table 13 shows the log-likelihood at the time of convergence due to the difference in the initial values, and Table 14 shows the number of iterations until convergence for comparison.

Table 12. Result of matching cluster number (proposed initial values)

n	j	i 1	2	3	4	n	j	i 1	2	3	4
1	1	1	0	0	0	6	1	0	1	0	0
	2	0	1	0	0		2	0	0	1	0
	3	0	0	1	0		3	0	0	0	1
	4	0	0	0	1		4	1	0	0	0
2	1	0	0	1	0	7	1	0	1	0	0
	2	1	0	0	0		2	0	0	0	1
	3	0	1	0	0		3	0	0	1	0
	4	0	0	0	1		4	1	0	0	0
3	1	0	1	0	0	8	1	0	1	0	0
	2	0	0	0	1		2	0	0	0	1
	3	0	0	1	0		3	0	0	1	0
	4	1	0	0	0		4	1	0	0	0
4	1	0	1	0	0	9	1	0	1	0	0
	2	0	0	0	1		2	0	0	0	1
	3	0	0	1	0		3	0	0	1	0
	4	1	0	0	0		4	1	0	0	0
5	1	0	1	0	0	10	1	0	1	0	0
	2	0	0	0	1		2	0	0	1	0
	3	0	0	1	0		3	0	0	0	1
	4	1	0	0	0		4	1	0	0	0

The average of 10 times in Table 13 shows that the log-likelihoods are almost equal, although the proposed method is slightly higher. This means that the proposal method can get the valid result equivalent to the conventional method.

Thus, the result of pLSA by using proposed initial values is able to reach valid interpretation.

We compared the number of iterations until EM algorithm converges between the conventional method and proposed method of initial values, and Table 14 shows that the average of 10 times of proposed method is approximately 40% less than the conventional method. Thus, this proves that the number of iteration of the EM algorithm can be reduced by summarizing elements with similar tendencies in the phase of creating initial values like the proposal method. In other words, the proposal method can be considered superior to the conventional method, from a viewpoint of the number of iterations in EM algorithm.

Table 13. Comparison of log-likelihood due to differences in initial values

	Random initial values	Proposed initial values
1	−863991350	−863387649
2	−863452515	−863421387
3	−864156758	−863390718
4	−864149980	−863389534
5	−863397470	−863387196
6	−863404655	−863394058
7	−863390474	−863396422
8	−863394910	−863387588
9	−864127118	−863388145
10	−863413711	−863390203
Average	−863687894	−863393290

Table 14. Comparison of the number of iterations due to differences in initial values

	Random initial values	Proposed initial values
1	414	163
2	974	687
3	327	222
4	254	216
5	410	167
6	424	312
7	220	273
8	295	191
9	347	160
10	479	164
Average	414.4	255.5

Jaccard Coefficient. We compared the Jaccard coefficients of each cluster of $P(x|z)$, $P(y|z)$ at two initial values as the stable of pLSA. In this paper, since we use the Jaccard coefficient for 10 times results, The numerator of Eq. 16 is the sum of the total number of common elements in all 45 combinations of 1st to 10th times, and the denominator is the elements appearing in all 45 combinations of 1st to 10th times. This is done for each cluster and the average of them is the Jaccard coefficients. The numbers of upper elements be 100 and 5 for A and B, respectively. Table 15 shows the results.

Table 15. Jaccard coefficients of each cluster of $P(x|z)$, $P(y|z)$

		Random initial values (A)	Proposed initial values (B)	Difference $(B - A)$
$P(x\|z)$	Cluster 1	0.215487	0.7814	0.565913
	Cluster 2	0.211058	0.354753	0.143694
	Cluster 3	0.130239	0.536931	0.406692
	Cluster 4	0.166189	0.593464	0.427275
	Average	0.180743	0.566637	0.385894
$P(y\|z)$	Cluster 1	0.509524	0.688095	0.178571
	Cluster 2	0.319841	0.514903	0.195062
	Cluster 3	0.31067	0.585185	0.274515
	Cluster 4	0.294356	0.720635	0.426279
	Average	0.358598	0.627205	0.268607

The rightmost column of Table 15 shows that all the values obtained by subtracting the Jaccard coefficient of the conventional method from the proposed method are positive. Thus, since the proposed method has less fluctuation in the elements with higher probabilities, it is proved that pLSA using the proposed initial values is more stable than conventional method.

5 Conclusion

In this paper, we aimed to improve performance of pLSA by changing the setting method of initial values for the problem of initial values dependency intrinsic in pLSA. In order to serve the purpose, we focus on the fact that pLSA is a method of collecting elements that are close to the result of dimension compression, and we thought that we can obtain the stable and valid result by summarizing elements with similar tendencies in the phase of creating initial values. So we suggested the method, mention in Sect. 3.2, using correspondence analysis, k-means clustering analysis and softmax function.

Furthermore, we evaluate and compare the performance of pLSA at the conventional initial values and proposed initial values, and we conducted the evaluation experiment in order to examine the usefulness of proposed method.

We used performance evaluation index of pLSA log-likelihood as validity, the numbers of iteration as efficiency and Jaccard coefficient as stable.

It is proved that the proposal method can obtain valid result equivalent to the conventional method from Table 13. And we could show that pLSA using proposed initial values is superior in terms efficiency of stability from Table 14 and Table 15.

Therefore, we suggest the initial values creation method in this paper as setting method of initial values of pLSA.

However, we used k-means clustering analysis in the phase of initial values creation, hence, there is a possibility that the proposed initial values are reflected initial values dependency of k-means clustering analysis. So we have to rethink about the method of grouping the closer elements.

In the proposal method, we created $P(x|z)$, $P(y|z)$ as the initial value, but $P(z)$ was generated by random numbers. Therefore, it is not able to decide the result uniquely. This means that the initial value $P(z)$ reflect on the interpretation of pLSA result. So we have to consider the method of $P(z)$ creation from initial values $P(x|z)$, $P(y|z)$.

Acknowledgement. This work was supported by JSPS KAKENHI Grant Number19K01945.

References

1. Hoffman, T.: Probabilistic latent semantic analysis. In: Proceedings of Uncertainty in Artificial Intelligence, UAI 1999, pp. 289–296 (1999)
2. Analytics Design Lab Inc. pLSA (Probabilistic Latent Semantic Analysis), http://www.analyticsdlab.co.jp/column/plsa.html. Accessed 6 Feb 2021
3. Nishio, Y.: A latent class analysis using association between consumer values and behaviors. In: The 32nd Annual Conference of the Japanese Society for Artificial Intelligence (2018). (in Japanese)
4. Rindskopf, D.: Latent class analysis. In: The SAGE Handbook of Quantitative Methods in Psychology, Chap. 9, pp.199–216, SAGE Publication (2009)
5. Miwa, S.: Introduction to Latent Class Model. Theory Method (Jpn. Assoc. Math. Sociol.) **24**(2), 345–356 (2009)
6. Deerwester, S., Dumais, S.T., Furnas, G.W., Landauer, T.K., Harshman, R.: Indexing by latent semantic analysis. J. Am. Soc. Inf. Sci. **41**, 391–407 (1990)
7. Blei, D., Ng, A., Jordan, M.: Latent Dirichlet allocation. J. Mach. Learn. Res. **3**, 993–1022 (2003)
8. MIERUCA ([Technical explanation] Latent semantic analysis (LSA)~From singular value decomposition (SVD) to document retrieval~), https://mieruca-ai.com/ai/lsa-lsi-svd/. Accessed 6 Feb 2021
9. Agricultural Information Science (LSI). https://axa.biopapyrus.jp/machine-learning/topic-model/lsi.html. Accessed 6 Feb 2021
10. MIERUCA ([Technical explanation] Algorithm and application of stochastic latent semantic analysis (PLSA)), https://mieruca-ai.com/ai/plsa/. Accessed 6 Feb 2021
11. Nakamura, N.: Data science learned in R 2 Multidimensional data analysis method. Kyoritsu Shuppan (2009)

Consumer Attitude and Behavior During Black Friday and Cyber Monday

Diego Yáñez[1]([⊠]), Cristóbal Fernández-Robin[1], Gonzalo Améstica[1], and Scott McCoy[2]

[1] Universidad Técnica Federico Santa María, Valparaíso, Chile
{diego.yanez,cristobal.fernandez,gonzalo.amestica}@usm.cl
[2] Mason School of Business, Williamsburg, VA, USA
scott.mccoy@mason.wm.edu

Abstract. This study aims to analyze consumer behavior during Cyber Monday and Black Friday in Chile through an information technology acceptance model. An extended technology acceptance model was created to which the Technology Continuance Use Theory was incorporated. The variables used to explain continuance intention (CI) were attitude towards shopping (A), subjective norms (NS), perceived risk (PR), perceived usefulness (PU), shopping enjoyment (SE) and convenience (C). To obtain the data necessary for the structural equation model proposed, a survey was created on the SurveyMonkey platform. The survey was disseminated through social networks during May and June 2019. The results indicated that convenience (C) positively influences shopping enjoyment (SE) (.543). Then, shopping enjoyment is the variable that influences the most attitude (.496), which is directly related, with a standardized regression coefficient of .874, to the purchase continuance intention on Cyber Monday and Black Friday. Consequently, saving time and money by doing online shopping generates a pleasure or enjoyment perception in consumers, which has a positive effect on the perception of making purchases during these events and therefore on the intention to continue buying. Other results, conclusions, and theoretical and practical recommendations are further discussed along the paper.

Keywords: E-commerce · Consumer behavior · Cyber monday · Black friday

1 Introduction

The growth of electronic commerce has been significant during the last 5 years, minimizing that of face-to-face sales [6]. Globally, China and the United States lead online sales, exceeding 500 billion dollars annually. Among Latin American countries, Chile ranks second, with annual online sales for almost 6 billion dollars [22].

In the United States two events account for the highest percentage of online sales in the country [29], namely Black Friday and Cyber Monday. The first emerged in 1950, when retail stores lowered their prices and extended their hours [12]. Given the success of the event, it expanded worldwide in 2000, becoming an online event that mobilizes

© Springer Nature Switzerland AG 2021
G. Meiselwitz (Ed.): HCII 2021, LNCS 12775, pp. 147–158, 2021.
https://doi.org/10.1007/978-3-030-77685-5_12

one the highest sales around the world. This led to the creation of a similar event called Cyber Monday in 2005 [26].

In Chile, both events, Cyber Monday and Black Friday, were incorporated to promote online shopping. Cyber Monday became one of the most important online shopping events in the country, obtaining a historical record in sales that exceeded 233 million dollars in 2018. This is equivalent to 23% more than the sales of the previous year (2017), a trend that has been repeating year after year [14]. The results indicate that 66% of Chilean consumers know about the event and that 51.63% were willing to participate in 2018.

The great popularity that these events have had both globally and nationally and the constant increase in consumer purchases invite us to reflect on the motives of consumers to participate in these events, as well as the reasons behind the steady increase in online purchases and the decrease in face-to-face purchases. To answer these questions, it is imperative to analyze the variables that influence the use of these events.

2   Literature Review

2.1   Cyber Monday/Black Friday in Chile

The last Cyber Monday in Chile took place in the first days of October 2018 and included 281 brands. A historical record in sales was obtained, exceeding $ 233 million dollars, which is equivalent to an increase of 23% compared to the event of the previous year (2017). Among the categories that concentrated consumer preferences were clothing, footwear, and accessories, sports and outdoors, home improvement, health and beauty, technology, travel and tourism, with a focus on chain-stores, supermarkets, as well as a

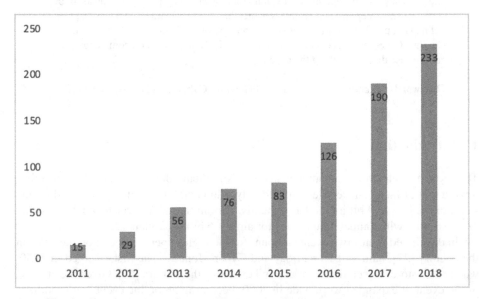

Fig. 1. Historical sales in CyberMonday events in billion USD (data source [14]).

great interest in the real estate and automotive industries [14]. Figure 1 shows the large increase in sales on Cyber Monday, which have increased 15 times since 2011.

The Black Friday in Chile has been held since 2014, and this year it will take place on November 29. According to the existing statistics, 66% of Chileans know what Black Friday is and 51.67% were willing to participate in the 2018 shopping party. According to [5] most consumers will buy online (50.36%), and a large part will choose to purchase both online and at physical stores (42.45%), whereas a minority will only buy at traditional stores (7.19%). Compared to 2017, the percentage of users who chose only physical stores was higher (11.84% compared to 7.19% currently registered) [5].

In contrast to a normal Friday, the increase in sales in Chile on Black Friday is 564%. The average Chilean buyer is willing to pay $ 271 USD in total for purchases on this event. That places Chile at the top of the ranking of Latin American countries, above Argentina ($ 253 USD), and Mexico ($ 239 USD) [5].

Like the case of Cyber Monday, the five most popular product categories for sales on Black Friday are clothing, electronics, footwear, cosmetics, and perfumes and household appliances [5].

2.2 New Technology Acceptance Models

The growing development and use of technology in recent years has led to remarkable progress as well as an increase in studies about consumer behavior. These studies have developed models that attempt to explain user behavior when facing new technologies, generating a research trend applicable to different fields. The models developed have been studied in great depth to better explain the phenomenon under study. In this case, the TAM model and Technology Continuance Theory were used.

Technology Acceptance Model (TAM). The Technology Acceptance Model (TAM) developed by Davis in 1989 is based on the theory of reasoned action. It was specially designed to predict the acceptance of information systems by users in organizations [34].

According to Davis [15], the main purpose of TAM is to explain the factors that determine the use of ICTs (Information and Communication Technologies) by a significant number of users. Therefore, to predict the use of ICT, the model is based on two main characteristics:

Perceived Usefulness: the degree to which people believe that using a particular system will improve their job performance.

Perceived Ease of Use: the degree to which people believe that they will make less effort to perform their tasks by using a particular system.

In addition, the model postulates that there are external variables that influence those already mentioned directly and indirectly on the intention and attitude towards the use of a technology.

Technology Continuance Theory. The Technology Continuance Theory (TCT) is used to describe the attitude and continuance intent to use an information system. It is said to represent an improvement of the TAM model, as it is suitable for the entire acceptance life cycle. It also provides greater explanatory basis for intention to use, merging attitude and satisfaction in a continuance model. In this way, the dependent variable to be explained becomes the Continuance Intention [21].

Previous research [20] suggests that perceived risk and subjective norms are significant constructs for predicting attitude and continuous Intent to Use and that they could be added to TCT.

2.3   Research Model and Hypothesis

The model under study was developed based on two pieces of research. The first one was carried out by Swilley and Goldsmith [29] and provided the structure necessary to model the interactions between variables. The following variables were preserved in the model: Convenience, Perceived Usefulness and Shopping Enjoyment. The second study was conducted by Weng et al. [33] and was adapted to the context of Cyber Monday and Black Friday using the variables, Attitude, Perceived Risk, Subjective Norms, and Continuance Intention. The variables of both studies were extracted with their respective questionnaires, forming the model presented in Fig. 2.

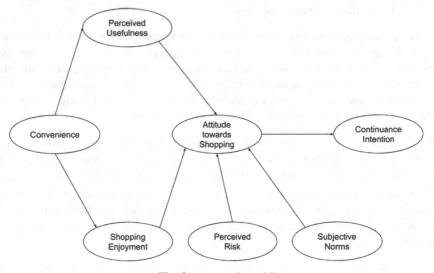

Fig. 2. Proposed model.

The two studies above were carried out in order to model the Intention of Purchase Continuity during Cyber Monday and Black Friday based on Attitude, which is predicted by Perceived Risk and Subjective Norms. Likewise, the Attitude of a consumer is influenced by Perceived Usefulness and Shopping Enjoyment. Both are predicted by Convenience.

Convenience (C). Consumers yearn to shop in an environment that saves them time, reduces search costs, and allows them to find products efficiently [8, 11]. Rohm and Swaminathan [25] define Convenience as the saving of time and effort experienced when purchasing goods and services. Convenience is the main reason for buying online [7, 18], and the intention to buy online is greater due to convenience [9, 10] as consumers can make purchases at any time [28]. Convenience acts as a predictor of purchase motivations, which are represented by the usefulness of online shopping and the enjoyment of the same [11].

H1: Convenience is positively related to Perceived Profit on Cyber Monday/Black Friday online purchases.

H2: Convenience is positively related to Enjoying Shopping on Cyber Monday/Black Friday.

Perceived Usefulness (PU). Perceived Usefulness is defined as the degree to which people believe that the use of a particular system will improve their performance at work [15]. Perceived Usefulness is related to the perception that people have of how much a product or technology enhances the performance of an action [33]. Shih [27] argues that Perceived Usefulness significantly determines attitudes towards online purchases. Likewise, Vijayasarathy [32] states that Utility significantly predicts attitude towards online purchases, and attitude towards online purchases strongly influences the intention to make online purchases.

H3: Perceived Usefulness has a positive influence on Attitude towards online purchases on Cyber Monday/Black Friday.

Shopping Enjoyment (SE). Babin et al. [3] refer to Enjoyment as a hedonic motivation for shopping. Hedonic motivation is the fun or pleasure derived from the use of a technology, which plays a very important role in the acceptance and use of technology [33]. According to Arnold and Reynolds [2], pleasure motivates shopping and influences attitudes towards shopping. Ha and Stoel [16] state that Enjoyment influences attitudes towards online shopping since buyers who enjoy a website are more likely to buy from that site at an event such as Cyber Monday and Black Friday.

H4: The Enjoyment of Shopping has a positive influence on the Attitude towards online purchases on Cyber Monday and Black Friday.

Attitude (A). Attitude is the degree of perception, positive or negative, of people about the performance of an objective behavior [15]. The attitude of a consumer is used to determine the behavior of users towards the use of a specific service. As people show a positive perception of a new system and technology, they are more enthusiastic about using it [19].

H5: The Consumer Attitude towards Cyber Monday/Black Friday is positively related to Continuance of Intention to Use.

Perceived Risk (PR). Perceived Risk is defined as the consequence and uncertainty related to consumer decisions [4]. Risk is perceived through uncertainty in a purchase situation, when a technology fails to deliver the expected service and this results in a loss to the consumer [33]. Consumers' perceptions of risk can negatively influence their attitude towards participating in Cyber Monday/Black Friday events.

H6: Perceived Risk of Cyber Monday/Black Friday by consumers is negatively related to Attitude.

Subjective Norms (SN). The Subjective Norms refers to the perceived social pressure to perform or not a behavior [1]. In other words, the Subjective Norms is related to the normative opinions of the environment towards the performance of a behavior. Hsu and Lu [17] affirm that subjective norms have a great influence on the intentions and attitudes of individuals regarding certain types of behavior. Most new consumers decide to participate in Cyber Monday/Black Friday based on usage and recommendations from family, friends, or colleagues.

H7: The Subjective Norms is positively related to Consumer Attitude towards Cyber Monday/Black Friday.

Continuance Intention (CI). Continuance Intention is defined as the probability that the Individual uses the system [24]. In this case, the TAM model has been applied to study Continuance Intention. Liao et al. [21] state that the continuous use of a long-term information system is determined by internal psychological judgment, that is to say, attitude. In this way, the user's attitude is a stable, lasting, and vital predictor of the Continuance Intention. The model under study seeks to explain the dependent variable, Continuance Intention of Cyber Monday/Black Friday consumers, which is based on their Attitude, which in turn, is predicted by external factors (Perceived Risk and Subjective Norms).

3 Methodology

To conduct this study, a first literature review on electronic commerce and the emergence of Cyber Monday and Black Friday was carried out. In addition, how these events have evolved and affected the population at a global and national level was also researched, as well as the factors that affect consumers when they make a purchase, in order to understand the growth trend of online sales on Cyber Monday and Black Friday in recent years.

The model used corresponds to an extension of the TAM model proposed by Swilley and Goldsmith [29], complemented with the model developed by Weng et al. [33], which incorporates the Technology Continuance Theory. Based on this, a survey that included questions to assess demographic profile, online shopping habits and the variables of the research model was developed. The survey created is presented in Annex 1.

Subsequently, the questionnaire was applied through the SurveyMonkey platform, sharing it on different Social Networks, using a non-probabilistic convenience sampling. A total of 398 surveys were obtained, of which 69.85% were considered valid for the study. Once information was gathered, structural equation modeling (SEM) was conducted using the SPSS Amos v26 software. First, the reliability of the measurement scale was assessed through Cronbach's Alpha and employing the IBM SPSS Statistics v23 software. Second, the fit of the model was studied, and regression estimators were analyzed. Conclusions are drawn on the hypotheses and research objectives based on the results.

4   Results

Three-hundred ninety-eight surveys were applied. The ones in which people claimed to have ever bought on Cyber Monday or Black Friday were considered valid. Therefore, 278 valid responses were obtained, equivalent to 69.85% of the applied surveys, which also meant that 278 out of 398 made a purchase on the Cyber Monday or Black Friday event.

Of the total respondents, 58.94% were female and 41.06% were male. The age of the respondents ranged between 18 and 60 years, with 83.65% aged between 18 and 29 years, and an average sample age of 26 years. The next bracket goes from 30 to 39 years and accounts for 10.58% of the sample. People who were between 50 and 59 years old represent 3.95% and those between 40 and 49 years old constitute 1.92% of the total. Regarding marital status, 89.9% were single, which is related to the age bracket with the highest frequency in the sample, and 8.65% are married, while 1.44% are divorced or separated. As for the educational level of the respondents, 48.31% reported having finished university studies, while 43.96% completed high school. In terms of occupation 71.20% were students, in accordance with the information above, and most of the sample was inferred to be undergraduate or graduate students, since they claim to have completed secondary or higher education.

Regarding frequency of online purchasing, 20.19% of users buy online once a month. In both shopping events, 18.75% stated that they buy online once every 2 months, or once every 3 months. Additionally, 17.79% of those surveyed usually shop online once every 6 months, while only 10.58% do so two or more times a month. In this sample, the preferred shipping form for online shopping is in-store pick-up with 52.97%, as opposed to 47.03% who prefer home delivery. The payment method most frequently used by the sample is debit card or bank transfer with 57.69%, followed by credit card with 39.42%. The trend, with 52.88% of responses, is to buy technology, followed by men's, women's, or children's fashion, which accounts for 49.52%. Electronics are in third place with the highest purchase frequency, specifically 41.35% of the sample. Finally, 32.21% and 25.48% of the sample prefers buying travel and sports-related products, respectively.

4.1   Technology Continuance Modeling

The software SPSS Amos version 26 was used to calculate the structural equation model. The model consists of seven latent variables, which are subdivided into three exogenous (independent) and four endogenous (dependent).

The latent exogenous variables are Convenience (C), Perceived Risk (PR) and Subjective Norms (SN) while the latent endogenous variables are Perceived Usefulness (PU), Shopping Enjoyment (SE), Attitude (A) and Continuance Intention (CI).

The factors of each variable explain it through items, which correspond to directly measurable observable variables. In this case they were defined in the applied survey.

The purpose of the model is to predict the dependent variable Continuance Intention (CI), directly influenced by Attitude (A), which is predicted by independent variables (Perceived Risk [PR] and Subjective Norms [NS]) and dependent variables (Perceived Usefulness [PU], and Shopping Enjoyment [SE]). The last two variables mentioned are predicted by Convenience (C).

4.2 Construct Reliability

The reliability of the model constructs was confirmed through Cronbach's alpha analyses. Loewnthal [23] states that the limit value of this indicator should be 0.6, because each construct has less than 10 items. The results obtained when calculating the Cronbach's alpha of each construct are presented in Table 1.

Table 1. Scale reliability analysis.

Item	Cronbach's alpha
Convenience	.731
Perceived Usefulness	.802
Shopping Enjoyment	.855
Attitude	.850
Perceived Risk	.826
Subjective Norm	.863
Continuance Intention	.762

4.3 Results of the Structural Equations Model (SEM)

Table 2 shows the result of the structural equation model obtained from the SPSS Amos software.

Table 2. Scale reliability analysis.

Item	Standardized Estimate	p-value
SE ← C	.543	***
PU ← C	.659	***
A ← SN	.228	***
A ← PR	−.75	.140
A ← PU	.149	.049
A ← SE	.396	***
CI ← A	.874	***

The coefficient of determination R^2 of the endogenous latent variables is obtained from the results. Predecessor variables explain 76% of variance in Continuance Intention (CI). The variance in Attitude (A) is 38% explained by the variables that predict it. Regarding Perceived Usefulness (PU) and Shopping Enjoyment (SE), 43% and 29% of their variation, respectively, is explained by the latent exogenous variable Convenience (C).

When analyzing the significance of the variables, Convenience (C) is significant when predicting Shopping Enjoyment of (SE) and Perceived Usefulness (PU), since they have a p-value lower than 0.05. Regarding the prediction of Attitude (A), the latent variables that significantly affect it are Subjective Norms (SN), Perceived Usefulness (PU) and Shopping Enjoyment (SE), whereas Perceived Risk (PR) is not significant to Attitude (A) (p-value higher than 0.05). Only Attitude (A) affects Continuance Intention (CI) and results significant for the prediction of the same. If one variable is significant to another, the hypothesis involved is accepted. Therefore, hypotheses H1, H2, H3, H4, H5 and H7 are accepted, whereas hypothesis H6 is rejected.

In terms of the relationships between latent variables, Attitude (A) towards Shopping over Continuance Intention (CI) has the highest standardized regression coefficient (0.87). Furthermore, a weaker relationship is obtained between Perceived Risk (PR) and Attitude (A). The negativity of this case lies in the fact that the more risk an individual perceives when making an online purchase on Cyber Monday/Black Friday, the lower his attitude and therefore Continuance Intention to participate in the events above.

5 Conclusions

This research study was carried out with the objective of modeling the consumer behavior during Cyber Monday and Black Friday in Chile, particularly to identify the factors that influence and are more related to the continuity of the intention to purchase.

The variables used to explain the Continuance Intention of purchase (CI) were Attitude towards Shopping (A), Subjective Norms (SN), Perceived Risk (PR), Perceived Usefulness (PU), Enjoyment of Shopping (SE) and Convenience (C). These variables were extracted from two studies, the first proposed by Swilley and Goldsmith [29] and the second proposed by Weng et al. [33]. The variables were complemented to create the proposed model that corresponds to an extended TAM in which the Technology Continuance Theory was applied.

The results of the sample were analyzed to explain the relationships between the different latent variables that compose the model. It is concluded that:

Attitude is the endogenous latent variable that predicts the variable under study, the continuance intention to purchase. The causal relationship obtained between these two variables had a standardized regression coefficient of 0.87. The items that measure this construct show that Chilean consumers prefer buying online during Cyber Monday/Black Friday over making purchases in person. The positive result of the relationship between the variables above indicates that the intention to continue shopping in the events under study will be greater as long as the Chilean consumer is more inclined to buy online rather than at a physical store. In addition, it is valid to consider a national context in which year after year online sales increase in large quantities.

Subjective Norms and Perceived Risk are external factors that affect Attitude towards shopping. Of these two factors, Subjective Norms has a greater causal relationship towards Attitude (0.23). This construct refers to the perception that users have about what their family, friends or colleagues think they should buy during Cyber Monday/Black

Friday. Despite being positive, the value obtained is low, which is explained by the indifference shown by most of those surveyed to this construct. In turn, Perceived Risk is inversely related to Attitude (-0.07), since the more risk the consumer perceives about the security of online purchases and the payment process on Cyber Monday/Black Friday, the less favorable the Attitude towards employing them. In this way, the small magnitude of this relationship is justified by the respondents' disagreement with the perception of risk in online purchases on the days of the events under study. Furthermore, this factor turned out not to be significant for the prediction of Attitude. To summarize, the perception of Risk does not influence the Attitude towards these online shopping events, and consequently, it does not affect the Intention to buy on Cyber Monday and Black Friday either.

Perceived Usefulness and Shopping Enjoyment are the endogenous variables that impact Attitude. The one that best relates to the latter is Shopping Enjoyment (0.50). The items that constitute this construct suggest that the Chilean consumer is entertained, excited, likes and feels good when buying online on Cyber Monday/Black Friday. This directly influences Attitude towards Shopping, which is quite logical because, if the user has fun shopping, clearly his attitude will be in favor of this activity.

Perceived Usefulness has a weak relationship with Attitude (0.15). With this factor, the Chilean consumer's perception about Productive Utility was measured, as well as how it affected the Attitude when buying online during the events in question. The items of this construct measured whether the events were useful to buy what was desired, or improved the skills, efficiency and productivity of the buyer, in addition to the utility in purchases. Despite the direct relationship between Perceived Usefulness and Attitude, the reason for the weak relationship between these variables may be that for Chilean consumers to exhibit a positive attitude towards shopping, it was not necessary that purchases during the event improved their skills, efficiency, productivity, or utility. It should be noted that the item number 1 of this construct, which measured the utility to buy what is desired, was not significant for the analysis. The non-significance of this item can be related to the fact that many times a consumer, during the events under study, does not satisfy their needs to acquire a consumer good or service, but rather satisfies shopping needs, buying products with better deals.

Finally, the exogenous variable Convenience has a slightly higher impact on Perceived Usefulness (0.66) than on Shopping Enjoyment (0.54). These results are reasonable since the assessment of convenience was based on measuring the influence of time and the benefits of buying online on Cyber Monday/Black Friday. It must be noted that items 2 and 3 were not significant for the measurement of Convenience, as they assessed savings and time consumption during online purchases of the events under study. Their non-relevance is related to the fact that due to the large number of deals on Cyber Monday and Black Friday, the user can spend a more hours shopping online than going to a store and buying the desired product.

Regarding Continuance Intention, the respondents stated being willing to continue shopping online, and substituting acquisitions in physical stores for online purchases on the days of Cyber Monday and Black Friday. Furthermore, they assured their intention to make as many possible online purchases as possible. Once again, the responses obtained are associated with the increase in online sales both nationally and globally.

Therefore, it is concluded that there is a sequence of variables that contribute to an excellent relationship between Attitude towards Shopping and the Continuance Intention to purchase. The convenience of Cyber Monday and Black Friday for more than 70% of users directly increases the Utility that Chilean consumers perceive in terms of the productivity generated by online purchases. Convenience also has a positive impact on Shopping Enjoyment, that is to say, the experience of buying online on the days of the events under study becomes entertaining, exciting and pleasant. Both variables (Utility and Enjoyment) directly influence the Attitude of the Chilean consumer towards shopping during these days, making them prefer to buy online over going to a physical store. The Subjective Norms also impact the Attitude, being the consumer's family, friends or colleagues who influence the attitude towards purchasing during these events. Consequently, the Attitude towards Shopping correctly predicts the Continuance Intention.

References

1. Ajzen, I.: The theory of planned behaviour. Organ. Behav. Hum. Decis. Process. **50**(2), 179–211 (1991)
2. Arnold, M.J., Reynolds, K.E.: Hedonic shopping motivations. J. Retail. **79**, 77–95 (2003)
3. Babin, B.J., Darden, W.R., Griffin, M.: Work and/or fun: measuring hedonic and utilitarian shopping value. J. Cons. Res. **20**(4), 644–656 (1994)
4. Bauer, R.A.: Consumer behavior as risk taking. In: Robert, S.H. (ed.) Dynamic Marketing for a Changing World, pp. 389–398. American Marketing Association, Chicago (1960)
5. Black Friday 2018 Chile. https://black-friday.global/es-cl/. Accessed 26 Jan 2021
6. Bourlier, A., Gomez, G. http://blog.euromonitor.com/2016/10/estrategias-para-la-expansion-mercadosemergentes-utilizando-e-commerce.html. Accessed 26 Jan 2021
7. Burke, R.: Do you see what I see? The future of virtual shopping. J. Acad. Mark. Sci. **25**(4), 352–360 (1997)
8. Brown, L.G.: The strategic and tactical implications of convenience in consumer product marketing. J. Cons. Market. **6**, 13–20 (1989)
9. Chiang, K.: Effects of price, product type, and convenience on consumer intention to shop online. In: American Marketing Association Conference Proceedings, Chicago, IL Winter, pp. 163–169 (2001)
10. Chiang, K., Dholakia, R.R.: Factors driving consumer intention to shop online: an empirical investigation. J. Cons. Psychol. **13**(1/2), 177–183 (2003)
11. Childers, T.L., Carr, C.L., Peck, J., Carson, S.: Hedonic and utilitarian motivations for online retail shopping behavior. J. Retail. **77**, 511–535 (2001)
12. CNN Chile. https://www.cnnchile.com/tendencias/la-verdadera-historia-tras-el-black-friday_20181123/. Accessed 26 Jan 2021
13. Cupani, M.: Análisis de Ecuaciones Estructurales: conceptos, etapas de desarrollo y un ejemplo de aplicación. Revista tesis **1**(1), 186–199 (2012)
14. CyberMonday. https://www.cybermonday.cl/info.html. Accessed 26 Jan 2021
15. Davis, F.: Perceived usefulness, perceived ease of use and user acceptance of information technology. MIS Quart. **13**(3), 319–340 (1989)
16. Ha, S., Stoel, L.: Consumer e-shopping acceptance: antecedents in a technology acceptance model. J. Bus. Res. **62**, 565–571 (2009)
17. Hsu, C.L., Lu, H.P.: Why do people play on-line games? An extended TAM with social influences and flow experience. Inform. Manage. **41**(7), 853–868 (2004)

18. Jarvenpaa, S.L., Todd, P.A.: Is there a future for retailing on the internet? In: Peterson, R.A. (ed.), Electronic Marketing and the Consumer, pp. 139–154. Sage, Thousand Oaks (1997)
19. Lee, M.C.: Explaining and predicting users' continuance intention toward e-learning: an extension of the expectation–confirmation model. Comput. Educ. **54**(2), 506–516 (2010)
20. Liao, C., Chen, J.L., Yen, D.C.: Theory of planning behavior (TPB) and customer satisfaction in the continued use of e-service: an integrated model. Comput. Hum. Behav. **23**(6), 2804–2822 (2007)
21. Liao, C., Palvia, P., Chen, J.L.: Information technology adoption behavior life cycle: toward a Technology Continuance Theory (TCT). Int. J. Inf. Manage. **29**(4), 309–320 (2009)
22. Linio. https://www.linio.com.ar/sp/indice-ecommerce. Accessed 26 Jan 2021
23. Loewnthal, K.M.: An Introduction to Psychological Tests and Scales. UCL Press, London (1996)
24. Prieto, J.C.S., Migueláñez, S.O., García-Peñalvo, F.J.: Utilizarán los futuros docentes las tecnologías móviles? Validación de una propuesta de modelo TAM extendido. Revista de Educación a Distancia (52) (2017)
25. Rohm, A.J., Swaminathan, V.: A typology of online shoppers based on shopping motivations. J. Bus. Res. **57**(7), 748–757 (2004)
26. Saura, J.R., Reyes-Menendez, A., Palos-Sanchez, P.: Un Análisis de Sentimiento en Twitter con Machine Learning: Identificando el sentimiento sobre las ofertas de# BlackFriday. Revista Espacios **39**(16), 75 (2018)
27. Shih, H.: An empirical study on predicting user acceptance of e-shopping on the web. Inf. Manage. **41**, 351–368 (2004)
28. Swaminathan, V., Lepkowska-White, E., Rao, B.P.: Browsers or buyers in cyberspace? An investigation of factors influencing likelihood of electronic exchange. J. Comput. Mediat. Commun. **5**(2) (1999)
29. Swilley, E., Goldsmith, R.E.: Black Friday and Cyber Monday: understanding consumer intentions on two major shopping days. J. Retail. Cons. Serv. **20**(1), 43–50 (2013)
30. Tele13. https://www.t13.cl/noticia/tendencias/cyber-monday-2019-fecha? Accessed 26 Jan 2021
31. Venkatesh, V., Thong, J.Y., Xu, X.: Consumer acceptance and use of information technology: extending the unified theory of acceptance and use of technology. MIS Quart. 157–178 (2012)
32. Vijayasarathy, L.: Predicting consumer intentions to use on-line shopping: the case for an augmented technology acceptance model. Inf. Manage. **41**, 747–762 (2004)
33. Weng, G.S., Zailani, S., Iranmanesh, M., Hyun, S.S.: Mobile taxi booking application service's continuance usage intention by users. Transp. Res. Part D: Transp. Environ. **57**, 207–216 (2017)
34. Yong Varela, L.A., Rivas Tovar, L.A., Chaparro, J.: Modelo de aceptación tecnológica (TAM): un estudio de la influencia de la cultura nacional y del perfil del usuario en el uso de las TIC. Innovar. Revista de Ciencias Administrativas y Sociales **20**(36) (2010)

Social Computing in Learning
and Education

The Challenges and Policy Issues Faced by Saudi HEIs When Adopting or Formulating Social Media Policies

Faowzia Alharthy[✉] and Yuanqiong Wang

Computer and Information Sciences Department, Towson University, Towson, MD 21252, USA
{falharthy,ywang}@towson.edu

Abstract. The purpose of the study is to investigate and clarify the factors that affect Saudi higher education institutions' adoption and formulation of effective policies on social media. A focus group was conducted to explore the critical challenges and issues preventing Saudi higher education from creating and formulating a clear social media policy. Focus group sessions were held online, which involved administrators and policy makers from the higher education in Saudi Arabia. Data were analyzed using qualitative research methodology, specifically, the manual thematic analysis approach with the support of NVivo software. Factors perceived in this study as the major reasons and challenges for not having a clear social media policy included lack of policy makers, awareness, management support, and resources. The findings suggest that Saudi higher education institutions (HEIs) need to enhance their social media policy and may need to consider outsourcing to gather the desirable resources to formulate and implement a clear social media policy.

Keywords: Social media policies · Higher education institutions · Lack of policy

1 Introduction

The Ministry of Education of Saudi Arabia webpage [1] lists 78 public and private universities and colleges in the kingdom. A review of websites from these institutions show that the majority of Saudi higher education do not have clear social media policies on their websites [2]. Alharthy, Wang, and Alfreda [2] found that 65 of the Saudi universities are not equipped with effective policies to minimize the possible negative outcomes of social media integration. Social media have become valuable tools in the education field [3]; however, there are many ethical and security concerns associated with their use [4]. Some unlawful activities and several ethical problems can result from being minimally aware of ethical and security considerations, or from the lack of social media policies. Thus, the higher education should have the policies and guidelines that provide rules intended to outline decisions and actions [5]. Hrdinová, Helbig, and Peters [5] suggested that social media policy should include some components to be an effective and inclusive policy such as ethical principles, security risk, account management, acceptable and unacceptable use, professional or personal social media accounts, content and post,

© Springer Nature Switzerland AG 2021
G. Meiselwitz (Ed.): HCII 2021, LNCS 12775, pp. 161–173, 2021.
https://doi.org/10.1007/978-3-030-77685-5_13

employees conduct, and privacy settings. These are some of the elements that should be contained in the social media policy, which in turn will help the educational institution to define what will be acceptable and unacceptable behaviors on social networking sites and how to use these sites. Researchers have discussed different challenges faced by higher education when adopting or creating social media policy in educational settings [6]. Al-Khalifa and Garcia [7] found that a lack of administrative support and sufficient resources were regarded as significant barriers to social media integration in higher education. Alsufyan, Aloud [8], Castagnera and Lanza [9], Kim, Sohn and Choi [10], and Pookulangara and Koesler [11] reported similar findings, which highlighted barriers that prevent the adoption of social media policy in higher education such as lack of management support, lack of resources, and lack of awareness of the importance of social media policy in educational contexts.

The use of social media in higher education in most countries is under exploration, especially with regard to adoption and usage policy [12]. In addition, social media policies in higher education are currently unable to keep up with the rapidly changing social networking technologies [13, 15]. Social media policies in higher education are currently a subject of discussion in many countries [16]. To date, there have been no research studies conducted which explore the challenges and policy issues viewed by administrators and policy makers from the higher education in Saudi Arabia. Therefore, the purpose of this paper is to 1) understand the challenges and policy issues faced by Saudi HEIs when adopting social media into its organization; 2) assess which factors affect Saudi Arabian HEIs' intentions when formulating social media policies.

2 Methodology

A focus group study was carried out in the effort to answer the research questions presented in the introduction section. Administrators and policy makers from Saudi Arabia HEIs were recruited by recommendation of the Deanship of Scientific Research from the selected institutions. The researcher reached out to 12 members, and 8 of them agreed to participate. The participants were chosen based on their position and their experience in the research issues. The researcher chose Slack, an online workspace that allows groups working together, to be used as the platform for the focus group sessions. The focus group study lasted one week involving both asynchronous and synchronous communications.

Before the start of the focus group session, an email invitation was sent to each participant individually. The invitation email included a nickname and a link that let the participants join the Slack Workspace, where the questions and instructions for the sessions were posted. The participants joined the Slack Workspace using the nickname provided to protect their own identity. Once logged into the Slack, the participants were able to reply with individual comments on each of the posts with strict confidentiality. There were eight open-ended questions for the participants to respond to initially. The participants were given a week to construct and post their responses to all the questions. A one-hour synchronous meeting was scheduled to be done on the last day of the week for the discussion and exchange of views between the participants and the researcher.

All the responses posted in the system during the discussion period were collected as the transcript for analysis.

The manual thematic analysis approach was used to analyze the qualitative data extracted from the focus group with the support of NVivo 12 software [18]. The researcher analyzed the data by reading all the transcripts and assigning codes to important points shared by respondents on each question. The codes were identified, sorted, and integrated into different categories. Each category represented a group of codes that share some relevance to each question. One of the ways of categorizing and coding qualitative data is the "focus prompt" [19], which is a phrase that guides the generation of codes to represent the relevant information in the data.

Based on the interview questions, the researcher planned to address and identify information by reviewing the characteristics of the interview questions and then converting each research question to the "focus prompt" to conform to the codes [19]. Interview question one was not coded because it was used to define the participants in terms of their job position and practical experience. The selection of the participants was anonymous; without identifying any personal information about them, this question was to ensure that they were qualified to participate.

Regarding the second question, the participants were asked whether their educational institutions have a policy of using social media or not, and if the answer was no, what was the reason for the absence. This question was coded as yes, there is a policy, or no. The third question contained the participant's viewpoint on the importance and applicability of social media in the educational process. The coding of these questions was yes or no with some of its benefits mentioned. From the participants' point of view, the benefits of using social media as an educational tool were coded into four categories. Its focus prompt was stated as accessibility, communication & collaboration, improving self-learning, and popularity.

The interview question number four was, "Which challenges do you face in formulating and implementing social media usage policies in academic settings?" Stating its focus prompt as the factors that affect the Saudi policymakers' adoption and formulation of social media policy are lack of awareness, lack of leadership and support, lack of policy and policy makers, and lack of resources.

In the fifth question, the participants were asked about the current experience and skills of students and professors in using social media, if it was sufficient or not. So, this question was coded as yes or no. If the answer was no, they were then prompted to answer, what are the improvement steps taken by the university to raise the skill and experience of students and teachers, if any? From the participants' point of view, the answers were coded into three steps: training, encouragement, and raising cognitive and social awareness of the importance of social media in the educational process.

For the interview question number six, the focus prompt was "list three major reasons for not having a clear social media policy." In addition, the focus prompt for the second part of the question was the improvement suggestions for each reason. Stating its focus prompt as the major reasons for not having a clear social media policy in Saudi higher education are lack of awareness, lack of management support, lack of policy and policy makers, lack of resources, and privacy and security concerns. As for the improvement suggestion, its focus prompt was as follows: increase the awareness of the social media effects and importance in the education process, clearly divide responsibilities, create social media policy, and provide more resources. The seventh question was to find out which Saudi universities have the most engaging use of social media. It was coded as yes with the mention of the university name, or no, I do not know.

The final question was the focus group recommendations for establishing a clear social media policy to make the most of social media use. This question was not coded; rather, it was a simple compilation of the participants' recommendations. The general theme of the recommendations involved how to create a clear social media policy and what the most important points are that should be included in this policy. Down below is the mind map for representing a node hierarchy for each question and the two-researcher reviewed overall summary codes of the major findings as a validity check (Fig. 1).

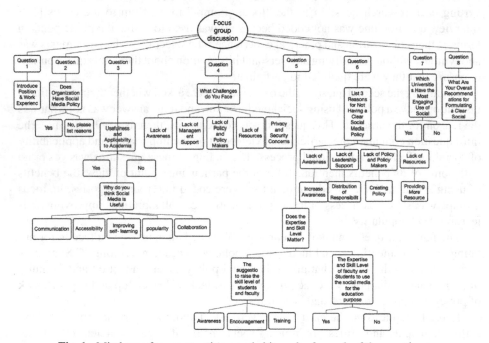

Fig. 1. Mind map for representing a node hierarchy for each of the questions.

3   Findings

The focus group interview consists of 8 questions and the largest amount of data was collected form the fourth and sixth questions as the main focus of this study was to investigate and clarify the factors that affect the Saudi HEIs' social media adoption and formulation of effective policies for educational purposes. Matrix coding queries were used to see how codes were used in different contexts and how many times they appeared. They also show the coding references, which means the number of coding references for this code. The resulting node matrix shows how many times this code appeared in data, which does not mean how many participants mentioned this code. For example, what do participants say about challenges and policy issues in formulating and implementing social media usage policies in academic settings? Down below will be the analysis using matrix coding queries, and the analysis will be question by question.

Q.1. Please introduce your position and share your specific work experience within that position. (Do not include ID information).

The first question in the focus group discussion was about the job position of the participants and their work experience. The reasoning behind this question was to ensure that the participants fit the criteria and were qualified to participate in the focus group. The discussion revolved around the critical challenges and the issues preventing Saudi higher education from having a clear social media policy in their institutions. The researcher chose a variety of administrators and decision-makers who work in Saudi educational institutions such as the Ministry of Higher Education. There are also many Saudi educational systems out of the country, such as the Saudi Arabian Cultural Mission (SACM) in the U.S. The researcher also selected members with experience and knowledge in the field of research. Thus, the focus group would be in a position to discuss and agree on a specific set of issues and challenges that Saudi educational institutions face regarding establishing a policy of using social media sites.

Q.2. Does your organization currently have a social media policy? If not, please share the reasons why.

The result of the second question shows that seven out of eight of the participants had no social media policy in their organization, while only one participant had a policy. Furthermore, four of the seven participants disclosed that their organizations are in the process of making a social media policy while the other participants provided no information regarding the missing policy. The reason behind not having a social media policy in their respective institutions can be referred to in question 6.

Q.3. Why do you think social media is useful in educational settings? Do you think there is a need to integrate social media in current academic practices?

All the participants agreed that social media policy is important and applicable in academic practices. Table 1 below shows some of the educational approaches and benefits of social media in the educational setting that the interviewers mentioned: accessibility, communication, collaboration, improving self- learning, and popularity. Also, the table shows that accessibility and communication were sited the most by the participants while improving self-learning, popularity, and collaboration were sited the least.

Table 1. The benefits of social media in the educational settings "Matrix coding queries results".

	Accessibility	Communication	Improving self-learning	Collaboration	Popularity
Why is social media useful	8	7	5	3	4

Note: The number of coding references for each code

Q.4. Which challenges do you face in formulating and implementing social media usage policies in academic settings?

Table 2 below shows which challenges are faced by Saudi HEIs when they adopt or integrate the social media policy. The findings from the focus group discussion highlighted the lack of policy elements which are lack of awareness, lack of management support, lack of policy and policy makers, lack of resources, and privacy and security concerns. From the interviews and discussions, one key factor that was highlighted as the most important challenge was lack of policy and policy makers. One other finding that the participants often pointed out was the lack of management support followed by the privacy and security concerns. This was followed by the lack of awareness, in which the practice of social media is relatively new in the region and many individuals still confuse formal versus informal use. Based on the participants' answers, they all agreed that the lack of resources was the least important challenge faced by Saudi HEIs while adopting a social media policy.

Table 2. The challenges faced by Saudi HEIs "Matrix coding queries results"

	Lack of Awareness	Lack of management support	Lack of policy and policy makers	Lack of resources	Privacy and security concerns
The lack of policy elements	2	5	7	1	4

Q.5. Does the expertise and skill level of faculty and students suffice to use social media for educational purposes? If not, is your institution considering any steps for improvement?

Table 3 below shows that five of the eight participants disagreed that the current experience and skill level of the faculty and students allows for implementation of social media for educational purposes while three of them agreed.

Table 3. The expertise and skill level of faculty and students "Matrix coding queries results"

	No	Yes
The expertise and skill level of faculty and students is sufficient	5	3

Regarding the steps of improvement, the participants were considering factors such as increased awareness of the social media effects in the education process, encouragement of the use of social media platforms, and training plans for faculty and students to keep them updated with technological risks and developments. Therefore, training and encouragement to the students and the faculty should be put in place to ensure that there is maximum awareness of the use of social media in the education setting. The table below shows that the increase of awareness of social media importance was cited the most by the participants, followed by the encouragement, while training was cited the least. This is because the participants believe that awareness is necessary for effective implementation and a positive attitude towards technology (Table 4).

Table 4. The suggestions to raise skill level of students and faculty "Matrix coding queries results"

	Increased awareness	Encouragement	Training
Steps of improvement	4	3	1

Q.6. Please list three major reasons for not having a clear social media policy. Also, share improvement suggestions for each.

From the discussions, the main key factors that participants believe are the reasons for not having a policy are lack of awareness, lack of leadership and support, lack of policy makers, and lack of resources. The table below shows that lack of awareness of the important role that the implementation of social media policy plays, the lack of people who are specialized in educational strategies and who can formulate the policy, and not having enough human and financial resources were the three major reasons for not having a clear social media policy. Another finding was that participants suggested that the Saudi HEIs had no clear policy due to the lack of leadership and support, which indicates the lack of clear division of duties between the HEIs and the ministry of education in Saudi Arabia. In other words, Saudi HEIs should not wait until the ministry of education writes the policies for them; they have to initiate the first steps in creating social media policy (Table 5).

Table 5. The reasons for not having a policy "Matrix coding queries results"

	Lack of awareness	Lack of leadership support	Lack of policy and policy makers	Lack of resources
Reasons for not having a clear social media policy	6	4	5	3

The data obtained from this study provides useful insights into the needs of the Saudi HEIs to increase the awareness of the social media effects and importance in the education process, have a clear division of responsibilities, create social media policy, and provide more resources. The table below shows that the increase of awareness was the highest improvement suggestion while the other suggestions had the same level of importance (Table 6).

Q.7. Which universities have the most engaging use of social media? What is attractive about their approach to social media?

The result of this question shows that all the participants reported to have no idea which universities had the most engaging use of social media in Saudi Arabia because

Table 6. The improvement suggestions for each reason "Matrix coding queries results"

	Increase awareness	Distribution of responsibility	Creating policy	Providing more resources
Improvement suggestions for each	4	3	3	3

none of the participants had the correct information to answer this question, nor do they have a common knowledge database among educational institutions to share information. In addition, another reason is that there needs to be more research done in this area.

Q.8. Overall, what are your recommendations for formulating clear social media policies to ensure active and productive usage of these sites for learning purposes?

Saudi Arabia can ensure active and productive usage of social media by establishing and creating a clear policy. As a result, higher education and the ministry of higher education must work together to create, develop, and adapt effective social media policy. Stated below are the respondents' opinions about the formulating social media policies:

Look for the best practices of such platforms in educational settings nationally and internationally [Participant 2]

Benefiting from other universities who have adopted and implemented a clear policy by learning from the example they set. [Participant 5]

It should cover how to adopt a tone of voice, the importance of consistency and analytics, while (in a Saudi context) [Participant 5]

As is clear from the previous comments, in order to create a comprehensive policy that understands the needs of the new generation, this policy should be dynamic to keep pace with the rapid developments in the field of technology. This policy also must include students, faculty, and staff and explain to them in detail what they can and cannot do in terms of actions, laws, and guidelines. Participants also recommend that HEIs develop social media policies with rules and guidelines that address the unique challenges faced by these institutions instead of relying on governmental policies that are too broad for adequate use in higher education.

Make it dynamic so it accommodates the changing, evolving and emerging social networking technologies, so HEI's do not need to revise and change their social media policies so frequently as a result of the natural and expected changes in these platforms [Participant 2]

Policies should empower educators and provide the students with freedom and flexibility of learning in a safe environment [Participant 1]

Policies should protect the privacy and integrate of all parties involved and provide them with a safe communication environment [Participant 1]

Policies should ensure equal opportunities to all social media users [Participant 1]

Policies should indicate clearly the responsibilities of educators and when not to speak on behalf of the upper management [Participant 1]

Understand the newer generation's needs (especially that Generation Z is fast approaching) and cater to their needs when writing the policy [Participant 2]

It should be clear, active, fast responding and speaks in youth language [Participant 3]

Policies should clearly stipulate the code of conduct between teachers, students and other involved individuals [Participant 1]

The recommendations down below specified the importance of having a committee in which there are experts in developing a policy that will guide the safe use of social media in higher education in line with the needs of the new generation. These experts should also be informed of international best practices that would be useful in the development of social media policy for Saudi higher education.

Have a committee for formulating clear social media policies that incorporate representatives of stakeholders [Participant 1]

Include technological experts in the design process [Participant 1]

Have teams which draw up acceptable use policies for social media that apply to all university staff, forbidding content that is offensive, promotes illegal activity or infringes copyright etc. [Participant 6]

Universities should hire people who have higher degrees in education in order to formulate and establish these policies. [Participant 4]

As is clear from the focus group comments, there is the problem that some administrations and policymakers are from a different generation. Leaders of HEI must understand the difference between their generation and the new generation. They need to adapt to deliver the education models the newer generation needs. Some participants also mentioned that training and extensive workshops about the importance of developing social media policies would resolve this problem.

Have a committee which includes members with different backgrounds and age to build a strategy on implementation. [Participant 7]

Training must be provided especially to older generations to eliminate user-resistance to technology. [Participant 8]

Committees must be formed to study and embrace best practices [Participant 8]

People must be educated through extensive workshops about the importance of developing social media policies. [Participant 8]

Finally, the Ministry of Higher Education and higher education institutions should work together to establish a policy for the use of social media, train educators and employees how to use them, and enforce laws and the rules in case of any violation. As some participants recommended, they should start developing social media policies aimed at raising awareness of productive social media usage among potential users.

Policies should include clear guidance on reporting incidents [Participant 1]

Policies should include clear procedures for monitoring and evaluation of the content [Participant 1]

Policies should include guidelines on copyrights and fair use [Participant 1]

Spreading awareness and educating of its importance and the risks may arise as a result of the absence of a clear policy [Participant 5]

Offering guidance on questions of modesty when it comes to photography and how to correctly refer to members of the Royal Court. [Participant 6]

Map it to our current regulations and internet usage policies. [Participant 8]

Briefly, study best practices, training, minimize user resistance. [Participant 8]

4 Discussion

This study investigated the challenges and policy issues faced by Saudi HEIs when adopting or formulating social media policies. The respondent's answers support previous research which indicated that a majority of participants agreed that their organizations had no social media policy [2]. They all strongly believe that social media is useful in educational settings for several reasons such as accessibility, communication & collaboration, improving self-learning, and popularity.

In addition, five of the eight participants disagreed that the current experience and skill level of the faculty and students allows the implementation of social media usage in educational settings, while three of them agreed. Therefore, they proposed three suggestions to raise the efficiency and skill level of students and faculty. The participants suggested establishing intensive training courses to increase the level of awareness among both students and faculty, while also encouraging and motivating them to use social media. Results in this question support the other findings of Alqahtani and Issa [20], which revealed the lack of awareness raised as a barrier to social media use and how training and knowledge would resolve this problem. In this respect, training faculty and students is needed to make the best use of social media and encouraging creative ways of learning. When the participants were asked which university has the most engaging use of social media, the participants' answers showed that they do not have the information to make that conclusion for several reasons. They include lack of Arabic interfaces in social media platforms as well as the lack of having a common knowledge database among educational institutions. Therefore, there needs to be more research done in this area.

One other finding that the participants commonly pointed out was the lack of management support needed for keeping up with the rapid change in social media and its application. This result is compatible with results of [15, 16] which showed that most of the higher education institutions are currently unable to keep pace with the rapid developments in the field of technology and to make policies for use that are able to develop in line with this continuous development. Therefore, creating a scalable social media policy will help solve this problem.

In addition, when the participants were asked to list the three major reasons for not having a clear social media policy, they cited the same reasons and challenges in the fourth question, including a lack of awareness, a lack of policy makers, and a lack of resources. Results in the present study support the other findings of Tess [5] and Al-Khalifa and Garcia [4], which revealed that a lack of administrative support and sufficient resources were regarded as significant barriers to integrate a clear policy in higher education.

However, the lack of resources was the least important challenge faced by Saudi higher education institutions. The participants believe that the shortage of qualified human resources to establish a policy of using social media is more important than the shortage of financial or technical resources. The majority believe that most Saudi universities are equipped with the latest technologies, which constantly are updated. Accordingly, participants see the policy maker as the most important component in making a social media policy in Saudi HEIs. This finding is either due to the lack of people who are experts and specialists in creating the policy or lack of their awareness. Or, due to that, policy makers are unaware of the usefulness of social media in the educational process and how integrated social media is in the new generation. So, having a committee for creating clear social media policies that incorporate representatives of stakeholders should be encouraged by the Ministry of Education in Saudi Arabia.

In addition, they added another reason, which is that Saudi HEIs derive their policy from the Ministry of Education and that they do not have sufficient powers to create their own policy, as is the case in some developed countries such as the United States. It is suggested that Saudi HEIs do not wait until the ministry of education writes the policies for social media use for them but they need to enhance and outsource the desirable resources to formulate and implement a clear social media policy.

5 Conclusion

As a result, decision-makers in the Ministry of Higher Education should create an effective and inclusive social media policy. It should be submitted to higher education institutions as a guide and template for their use. In addition, the Ministry of Higher Education should work with experts in social media policies to formulate a clear policy and develop it so that it remains relevant to this rapidly changing field. Furthermore, Saudi universities need to have a line of communication between universities and the ministry of education regarding newly adopted or developed policies. Also, policy makers in the Ministry of Higher Education must ensure that these policies are developed and implemented by Saudi universities and that the regulations are implemented when misuse occurs by any one of the users, whether they are students, faculty, or employees. By formulating effective social media policies that could address the negative outcomes associated with social media usage, policy makers may be persuaded to increase the motivation for adopting social media for enhancing teaching and learning methodologies [18]. To date there have been no research studies conducted which explore the challenges and policy issues viewed by administrators and policy makers from the higher education in Saudi Arabia. Because of that, there needs to be more research done in this area. Future research should focus on how to write an effective responsible social media policy and decide, what would an inclusive social media policy look like? Finally, to address these challenges, the government has already implemented many steps like the scholarship program, which aims to better equip the new generation to face these challenges. In addition, in their 2030 vision, they plan to make an overhaul of their education system by focusing on integrating technology, and creating actionable steps to amend current and non-existent social media policies.

References

1. The Ministry of Education - University Education: Public and private universities and colleges (2020). https://www.moe.gov.sa/en/HigherEducation/governmenthighereducation/StateUniversities/Pages/default.aspx. Accessed Jan 2020
2. Alharthy, F., Wang, Y., Dudley, A.: An analysis of the current policies for social media use in Saudi higher education. In: Meiselwitz, G. (ed.) Social Computing and Social Media. Participation, User Experience, Consumer Experience, and Applications of Social Computing. HCII 2020. LNCS, vol 12195. Springer, Cham (2020). https://doi.org/10.1007/978-3-030-49576-3_33
3. Straumsheim, C., Jaschik, S., Lederman, D.: Faculty Attitudes on Technology. Inside, Washington, DC (2015)
4. Fowler, F.C.: Policy studies for educational leaders: an introduction (2009)
5. Tess, P.A.: The role of social media in higher education classes (real and virtual)–a literature review. Comput. Hum. Behav. **29**(5), A60–A68 (2013)
6. Hrdinová, J., Helbig, N., Peters, C.S.: Designing social media policy for government: eight essential elements. Center for Technology in Government, University at Albany, Albany, NY (2010)
7. Al-Khalifa, H.S., Garcia, R.A.: The state of social media in Saudi Arabia's higher education. Int. J. Technol. Educ. Mark. **3**(1), 65–76 (2013)
8. Alsufyan, N.K., Aloud, M.: The state of social media engagement in Saudi universities. J. Appl. Res. High. Educ. **9**(2), 267–303 (2017)
9. Castagnera, J.O., Lanza, I.V.: Social networking and faculty discipline: a Pennsylvania case points toward confrontational times, requiring collective bargaining attention. J. Collect. Bargain. Acad. **2**(1), 5 (2010)
10. Kim, Y., Sohn, D., Choi, S.M.: Cultural difference in motivations for using social network sites: a comparative study of American and Korean college students. Comput. Hum. Behav. **27**(1), 365–372 (2011)
11. Pookulangara, S., Koesler, K.: Cultural influence on consumers' usage of social networks and its' impact on online purchase intentions. J. Retail. Consum. Serv. **18**(4), 348–354 (2011)
12. Sánchez, R.A., Cortijo, V., Javed, U.: Students' perceptions of Facebook for academic purposes. Comput. Educ. **70**, 138–149 (2014)
13. Yuan, L., Powell, S.J.: MOOCs and open education: implications for higher education (2013)
14. Viberg, O., Grönlund, Å.: Cross-cultural analysis of users' attitudes toward the use of mobile devices in second and foreign language learning in higher education: a case from Sweden and China. Comput. Educ. **69**, 169–180 (2013)
15. Dyer, M.M., Carver, M., Miller, J.K.: An analysis of states' policies regarding social media use in education. Dissertation, Saint Louis University (2016)
16. Fowler, Frances C.: Policy studies for educational leaders: an introduction (2009)
17. Siau, K., Nah, F.F.-H., Teng, L.: Acceptable internet use policy. Commun. ACM **45**(1), 75–79 (2002)
18. Welsh, E.: Dealing with data: using NVivo in the qualitative data analysis process. In: Forum Qualitative Sozialforschung/Forum: Qualitative Social Research, 31 May 2002, vol. 3, no. 2 (2002)

19. Kane, M., Trochim, W.M.: Concept mapping for applied social research. Sage Handbook Appl. Soc. Res. Meth. 435–474 (2009)
20. Alqahtani, S., Issa, T.: Barriers to the adoption of social networking sites in Saudi Arabia's higher education. Behav. Inf. Technol. **37**(10–11), 1072–1082 (2018)

Analyzing the Student eXperience Concept: A Literature Review

Sandra Cano(✉) ⓘD, Cristian Rusu ⓘD, Nicolás Matus ⓘD, Daniela Quiñones ⓘD, and Ivan Mercado

Pontificia Universidad Católica de Valparaíso, Av. Brasil 2241, 2340000 Valparaíso, Chile
{sandra.cano,cristian.rusu,daniela.quinones,
ivan.mercado}@pucv.cl

Abstract. Customer eXperience (CX) refers to people's expectations and perceptions when interacting with a brand/company, through systems, products and services that this offers. Student eXperience (SX) is a particular case of CX, as students interact with several products, systems and services that an educational institution offers. This article presents a review of the literature published during the last 10 years (from 2011 to 2020), indexed in three databases (Scopus, Science Direct, and IEEE Xplore). We are analyzing the SX concept, its dimensions, and the SX evaluation methods. We focused our study on undergraduate higher education students, trying to answer three research questions: what is SX?, what are the SX dimensions?, and what methods are used to evaluate SX? Literature related to SX is abundant and it shows a growing tendency. Most of the studies are related to the Social Science field. Our study offers an overview of the research on SX and offers a basis for future, specific research.

Keywords: Student experience · Customer experience · Literature review · Higher education

1 Introduction

Customer eXperience (CX) refers to people's expectations, emotions and interactions with a brand/company, through systems, products and services. The company and its customers benefit from the improvement of the different points of interaction between them as well as the improvement of the nature of these interactions. The brands obtain increased commitment from their customers, the customers have a better experience and increased satisfaction, ultimately resulting in positive feelings and emotions. Proper CX administration can lead to a differential advantage for service organizations [1].

The CX requires analyzing both the points of contact between the customer and a company (touchpoints) and the customer's journey. Touchpoints are the instances in which the customer comes into contact, physically or logically, with an organization; it includes the channel used for the interaction, and the specific task being completed [2]. Another important element when it comes to CX is the concept of Customer Journey Map (CJM). This allows visualizing the process that a person goes through in order to

© Springer Nature Switzerland AG 2021
G. Meiselwitz (Ed.): HCII 2021, LNCS 12775, pp. 174–186, 2021.
https://doi.org/10.1007/978-3-030-77685-5_14

accomplish a certain goal [3]. This journey can be complemented with an emotional diagram, which tells us how the emotions and feelings of the customer fluctuate during the process. It should be noted that all customers are different, since not all have the same perceptions and expectations about a system, product or service, just as all have different needs to satisfy.

Considering that students come into contact with educational organizations by interacting with a wide range of products, systems and services through different touchpoints, and have particular customer journeys, it is possible to analyze students as customers. With the aforementioned, we can conceive the concept of Student eXperience (SX) as a particular case of CX. Also, this particularized type of CX (under educational settings) can be associated with particular needs.

Nowadays, the advance of technology is transforming the teaching and learning. Therefore, is being fundamental to evaluate the quality in higher education and the SX. The experiences are related with digital technologies and online services that are used to enable, enhance and engage the student throughout their journey, and interaction with the university.

The proper definition and understanding of the SX concept, as well as the elements that compose and influence it are vital to improve the students CX. The concept of SX has been addressed in the literature but does not have yet a widely agreed definition. This may be a problem in scientific research on SX. As with the concept, there is no general agreement on the factors that influence the SX. Understanding the dimensions of a problem allows us to better address them in order to solve it. This is also the case with both CX and SX. Despite the lack of general agreed definition, it is possible to partially consolidate the SX concept, as well as the associated factors that influence it. Our study compiles definitions and concepts that are explicitly or implicitly present in works that deal with both the experiences of the students and their own characteristics. It tries to answer the following research questions: (1) What is SX?, (2) What are the SX dimensions?, and (3) What methods are used to evaluate SX?

The purpose of our literature review is to deconstruct the concept of SX based on bibliographic evidence, as well as to analyze the elements of which they are composed and the factors that influence it. In this way, we want to consolidate the concept of SX to serve as a baseline for future research. We point out that this research is focused on higher education students, specifically undergraduate students. Section 2 presents relevant concepts, as User eXperience (UX), CX and SX. Section 3 describes the procedure that we have followed. Section 4 answers the 3 research questions. Finally, Sect. 5 highlights conclusions and future work.

2   Background

2.1   User eXperience

User eXperiences (UX) is the result of subjective perceptions of the use of the goods and services, that are used in a given context. The ISO standard 9241–210 defines UX as follows: "person's perceptions and responses resulting from the use and/or anticipated use of a product, system or service". It is remarkable that this experience includes all the user emotions, beliefs, preferences, perceptions, physical and psychological responses, behaviors and accomplishments that occur before, during and after use [4].

2.2 Customer eXperience

Although the term Customer eXperience (CX) has been widely discussed it does not have a clear, standardized definition. This term is important when referring to the satisfaction of customers, since it relates their experiences with the use of the various products, systems or services that a company offers. CX has been considered as "the physical and emotional experiences occurring through the interactions with the product and/or service offering of a brand from point of first direct, conscious contact, through the total journey to the post-consumption stage" [5]. CX can be considered as an extension of the UX concept, that refers to customer's interactions with all products, systems and services that a company/organization offers.

To truly understand the complex nature of CX, it has been decomposed in dimensions. Gentile, Spiller and Noci (2007) consider that CX has six dimensions: emotional, sensorial, cognitive, pragmatic, lifestyle and relational. The emotional component involves the affective system, through the generation of moods, feelings and emotions. The sensorial component involves the stimulation that affects the senses. The cognitive component is involved with thinking or conscious mental processes. The pragmatic component is involved with the practical act of doing something. The lifestyle component is involved with the values and the beliefs of a person and the adoption of a certain lifestyles and behaviors. The relational component is related to the person, social contexts, relationships with other people [6].

Touchpoints are vital elements in designing the Customer Journey Map (CJM). They have been defined as a representation of: "(…) a specific interaction between a customer and an organization. It includes the device being used, the channel used for the interaction, and the specific task being completed." [2]. Unlike the official channels that the company uses for the client to interact with them, the touchpoints can be both planned or not.

CJM is a CX tool widely used to visualize the experiences, feelings and sensations of customers while they interact with a certain service, product or system. Its main elements are the touchpoints, that have been defined as: "(…) a visualization of the process that a person goes through in order to accomplish a goal". Although there is no consensus on its structure, a CJM have the following 5 key elements: (1) Actors, which are the people or users who experience the journey and who the CJM focuses on; (2) Scenario+Expectations, which describe the actual or anticipated interactions of the user on their journey, as well as the expectations of such interaction; (3) Journey Phases, which are the different high-level stages in the journey; (4) Actions, Mindsets and Emotions, which are behaviors, thoughts, and feelings the user/persona has throughout the journey and that are mapped within each of the journey phases; (5) Opportunities, which are the insights gained from mapping. They tell us how the user experience can be optimized [3]. CJM can be complemented with an emotional journey. Its function is to represent the emotional state of the customers and to analyze the fluctuation of their feelings throughout the journey.

2.3   Student eXperience

Taking into consideration the previous explanation of the CX concept it is possible to observe that the client may be particularized depending on the type of products and services that the company/organization provide. In this way, we refer to the Student eXperience (SX) as a customer's perceptions when consumes products and/or services, not only educational, provided in a specific educational context, by an educational institution.

In order to correctly understand SX, we need to identify its dimensions/factors, and to construct a proper SX model. We have to understand students' need, to identify their interactions with the educational institution, the products, systems and services involved, and students' perceptions. CJM is a powerful tool when analyzing SX.

3   Research Method

To guide this research, a literature review method was performed based on a framework of literature review in software engineering proposed by Kitchenham [7], which includes the following 3 phases:

- Planning the review, which involve the definition of the research questions;
- Conducting the review, which involves the development of the review, study selection and data extraction; and
- Reporting the review, which involve the presentation and discussion of the results of the review.

3.1   Research Questions

We oriented the literature review to the following topics: (1) the topics addressed by the research; (2) the factors regarding the SX; and (3) the methods that analyze SX aspects. Table 1 presents the 3 research questions that guided our study.

Table 1.   Research questions utilized in the review.

Id	Research Question (RQ)
RQ1	What is SX?
RQ2	What are the SX dimensions?
RQ3	What methods are used to evaluate SX?

3.2   Literature Search

For this research we examined the literature published within the last 10 years (from 2011 to 2020), indexed in three databases: Scopus, Science Direct, and IEEE Xplore. In all three databases we searched for two following keywords: "Student experience" and "Higher education". The number of studies indexed in each database is described in Table 2.

Table 2. Search results in databases using the keywords "student experience" and "higher education".

Database	Number of articles	% Articles
Scopus	1962	63%
Science Direct	130	4%
IEEE Xplore	1025	33%

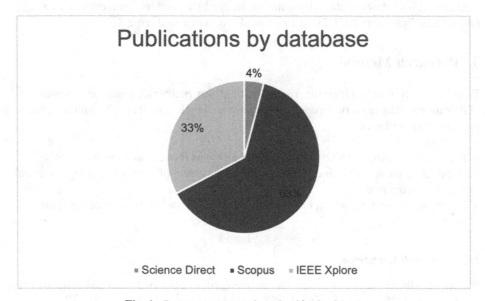

Fig. 1. Papers percentage by scientific databases.

Figure 1 presents the percentage of studies indexed in each database. Scopus offers by far the largest number of studies while Science Direct offers the fewest.

Figure 2 indicates the area of knowledge associated to the 1962 documents indexed in Scopus database. By far, most studies are associated to Social Sciences (1654). SX studies associated to Computer Sciences is still relatively low.

Figure 3 indicates that most of the documents found in Science Direct database are also related to Social Science (105). Only 4 documents are associated to Computer Science.

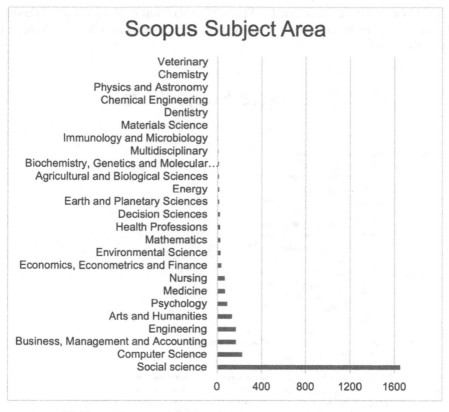

Fig. 2. Subject area distribution of the documents found in Scopus.

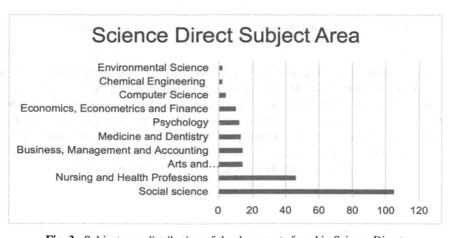

Fig. 3. Subject area distribution of the documents found in Science Direct.

We found 971 documents in IEEE Xplore (Fig. 4), most of them related to Further Education (552). In this case, a significant number of documents are related to Computer Aided Instruction.

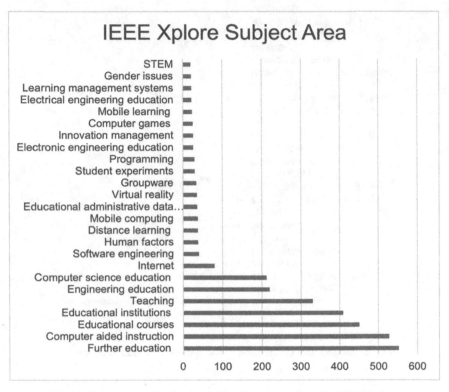

Fig. 4. Subject area distribution of the documents found in IEEE Xplore.

Figure 5 shows a growing tendency can be observed in the number of publications that contain the terms "Student experience" and "Higher education" over the years. This shows a growing interest in SX in higher education. Although the year 2021 is not contemplated in the search time range, we can infer that the number of articles published until the end of the year will exceed those published the previous year, thus maintaining the upward trend. This is due to the fact that as of the date of this document (January 2021), 43 articles have already been published among the databases consulted.

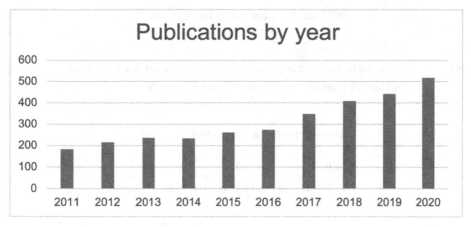

Fig. 5. Total number of publications per year indexed in the three databases.

Figure 6 indicates that 20% of the documents are open access, while the remaining 80% requires some type of subscription.

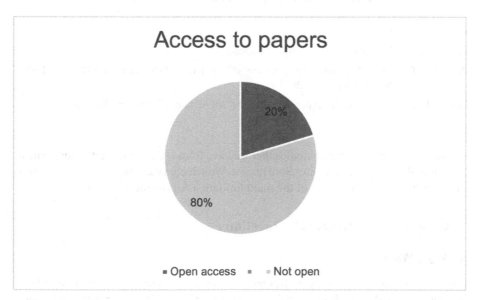

Fig. 6. Access to the publications.

3.3 Studies Selection

We searched for studies focusing on SX, in all areas, and including all types of research methods. The inclusion criteria are described in Table 3. As indicated in Table 4, the study was limited to SX in higher education, at undergraduate level.

Table 3. Inclusion criteria for this review.

Id	Inclusion Criteria (IN)
IN1	Focusing in understanding aspects the Student eXperience (case studies)
IN2	All field/disciplines, and all type of research methods

Table 4. Exclusion criteria for this review.

Id	Exclusion Criteria (EX)
EX1	Articles focused on other levels than undergraduate

As shown in Table 5, three search strings (SS) were utilized: SS1 to search in Science Direct, SS2 to search in Scopus, and SS3 to search in IEEE Xplore. Filters were applied to search for these terms in the metadata and not in the full texts.

Table 5. Search strings used in electronic databases.

Id	Search String (SS)
SS1	"Student Experience" AND "Higher Education"
SS2	TITLE-ABS-KEY ("Student Experience" AND "Higher Education") AND PUBYEAR > 2010 AND PUBYEAR < 2021
SS3	("All Metadata" Student experience) AND ("All Metadata": Higher education)

Due to the huge number of studies that we have found (2,000+), we did not perform yet a full analyze, a systematic literature review. We selected the articles that we analyzed in a subjective way. This is one of the main limitations of our study.

4 Answering the Research Questions

4.1 RQ1: What is SX?

In this literature review various studies have been examined in order to find definitions of the term SX. Although this search did not pay off, it is possible to construct an implicit definition by analyzing the topics and study cases treated in the articles that use these terms. It is for this reason that we look for the dimensions that comprise the use of the term SX, as well as the methods used by these articles. As this is not a systematic review, we cannot rule out the existence of an explicit definition of SX in the literature. However, regarding the articles analyzed, it should be pointed out that no formal definitions of the SX concept were observed.

Although there is no formal definition of the term, it could be observed that the articles used the concept "Student experience" interchangeably to refer to the experiences of the students regarding the topics covered by them. The experiences of the students include social interactions, emotions, feelings, expectations, perceptions, use of technology and the adoption of teaching-learning & assessment methodologies. In this way, it is evident that the term SX is used in a large number of situations and is ubiquitous in the life of the higher education student, being present in situations both inside and outside the university campus. An example of this was evident in 2020, where due to the COVID-19 virus, students stopped attending their institutions in person and saw their academic life affected by external problems, seeing their time to study reduced or increased, and/or experiencing effects of job loss [8].

It is evident how the experiences of the students are something inherently subjective and not static; these can change and can be influenced by a large number of factors, both external and specific to the students and their environment. Due to the very nature of these experiences, most of the selected studies analyze them from a qualitative approach.

It should be mentioned that despite the different topics covered in each of the articles, it is common for the term to refer to elements that desirably want to be improved. Furthermore, given the nature of the term, most of the articles focus on the academic and/or pedagogical experiences of the students directly related to the classroom, teaching or modules [9–12].

4.2   RQ2: What are the SX Dimensions?

The term SX is ubiquitous in the students' life, and it is related to multiple aspects of their academic and personal life. It is for this reason that in order to understand the dimensions of the concept it is necessary to approach it holistically.

The studies analyzed treat the term SX mainly as an educational aspect, giving a lot of importance to the pedagogical field. In this way, the authors talk about how the educational experience of students improves when they rethink the way in which they are taught and evaluated [9], or in which they are recommended which modules they should take [10]. In this educational dimension, the role of technology to enrich student learning is also discussed; tools such as Audience Response Systems (ARS) [11] or gamification tools [12] improve the educational experiences of students by promoting their participation. Student participation is mentioned as an important element in the educational field, as it keeps them motivated and improves their experiences through social and academic interactions. It is in this aspect that the identification of variables referring to students' experience becomes important to predict the degree of their institutional commitment [13].

It is important to mention that the role of non-strictly educational academic services is addressed to improve the SX, since they provide them with important support, guide them academically and reduce the university dropout rate [14]. Also, in case of having negative experiences, these services can correct these situations and increase their satisfaction; that is why it is important to develop the quality services that meet students' needs [15]. A clear example of the development of quality services in higher education can be seen in an article that seeks to improve student engagement with library services and to improve the customer relationship, demonstrating the impact of library services on the experience of students [16].

It should be noticed that student experience will vary based on multiple factors, such as gender, family background, culture, and age. The experiences are mainly affected by the expectations of the students. The case of exchange students is remarkable, as they have different cultural background and expectations; their experiences depend on the fulfillment of these expectations and integration in their new environment [17]. It is also important to observe the impact of genders and their level of studies, with respect to expectations [18]. This allows us to suppose that the experiences of the students are not something static, just as their expectations and perceptions are not.

The studies also refer to experiences that are completely distant from the academic sphere or the classroom. It is mentioned the case of students who, due to COVID-19, are studying online, and feel frustration and negative feelings due to lack of interaction or discomfort caused by lack of habit with the remote mode [19]. It also mentioned how students who have been infected with the virus have been affected economically or at work [8], and in this way they have been affected in the academic sphere. This makes it clear that the experience of students is related to broad aspects of their lives. Finally, the case of sites that facilitate the realization of academic fraud is presented. Such sites promotionally use negative aspects of the SX to encourage them to consume their services [20]. This indicates that students' perception is intimately linked to their experiences and those are malleable and not static.

4.3 RQ3: What Methods are Used to Evaluate SX?

Although no formal definition of the SX concept is made, studies deal with topics that influence or are influenced by the experiences of the students. In this way it is interesting to observe what methods these studies use to carry out their goals. It highlights that the qualitative approach is more common that que quantitative one. For instance, a work is dedicated to analyze the study path of the students, by taking the study modules that suit them best, thus improving their educational experience [10]. Another example is the case of a study that analyze the hostile marketing practices of websites that offer academic fraud services at the expense of the disclosure of negative aspects of student experiences. For this, the study reviewed these websites on several occasions [19].

Most of the analyzed studies are using surveys, questionnaires and interviews to collect data of interest, the study subject being in all cases the students who attended the institutions that carried out the studies. The surveys focus on multiple elements, such as: Collaborative learning, Student-faculty interaction, Time allocation, Commitment to research, Campus climate and diversity, Community and civic engagement, Co-curricular activities, Uses of technology, Academic experience, Safety, Housing, Social experience, Facilities, Industry connections, Student well-being, Overall satisfaction, Skills development, Student engagement, Teaching quality, Student support, Learning resources, and Overall quality [21].

It is important to note that most of the studies analyzed made the students participate in their research, considering their personal opinions. This certainly sets a precedent for the way in which research must be conducted when we consider factors that influence or are influenced by SX. A clear example of student participation to improve SX was a study that conducted semi-structured individual interviews with 90 students to ask them about their assessment experiences. The results of the study show the importance of the evaluation processes for SX [22].

5 Conclusions and Future Work

In view of the number of articles that are published year after year in relation to the term "Student experience" it is possible to assume that there is an increasingly important concept both in society and in the academic sphere. This shows the importance of consolidating or achieving an approximation to a formal definition of the term, in order that the articles made in the future have a solid theoretical basis.

After analyzing the selected articles in this review, it was possible to see that there is no formal definition of the term SX, but this is not an impediment to extract an implicit definition from it. This is due to the fact that the selected studies refer indistinctly to the different aspects that are related to the experiences of the students, depending on the different study cases. In this way, in all the articles referring to the subject, it is intended to improve the students' experiences, both academically and in areas that escape the classroom. This is basically due to the fact that students do not stop being students when they leave the classroom, therefore their experiences do not limit to the academic sphere and also permeate in the psychological and social spectrum.

Having said the above, it is evident that the dimensions that comprise the SX are multiple, and the factors that influence it are also varied. As mentioned in previous sections, given the ubiquitous and broad nature of the term, a holistic approach is necessary to understand the concept. Among some dimensions that encompass the term according to the articles analyzed is the field of academic services, technology as an element to facilitate learning, teaching and evaluation methods. Factors that can influence the experience of students are also mentioned, such as: physical health, financial status, family background, working habits, sex, years of study, and culture. These factors have been shown to be strongly related to the expectations of students and to influence their perceptions. The correct management of the SX is important for the well-being of the students because, as seen in the articles analyzed, it enables improvements in learning, institutional commitment and their mental health.

As future work, we intend to carry out a systematic literature review on the SX concept, in order to consolidate a conceptual framework for future research in the area.

Acknowledgement. The study has been supported by the project UE2020.12.INV.FIN.INF.02, financed by Pontificia Universidad Católica de Valparaíso (Chile).

References

1. Sujata, J.: Customer experience management: an exploratory study on the parameters affecting customer experience for cellular mobile services of a telecom company. Procedia – Soc. Behav. Sci. **133**, 392–399 (2014)
2. Nielsen Norman Group. https://www.nngroup.com/articles/channels-devices-touchpoints/. Accessed 30 Jan 2021

3. Nielsen Norman Group. https://www.nngroup.com/articles/journey-mapping-101/. Accessed 29 Jan 2021
4. ISO 9241–210: Ergonomics of human-system interaction—Part 11: Usability: Definitions and concepts, International Organization for Standardization, Geneva (2018)
5. Hill, N., Roche, G., Allen, L.: Customer Satisfaction. The Customer Experience Through the Customer's Eye. 1st edn. Cogent Publishing, London (2007)
6. Spiller, N., Noci, G.: How to sustain the customer experience: an overview of experience components that co-create value with the customer. Eur. Manage. J. **25**(5), 395–410 (2007)
7. Kitchenham, B.A.: Procedures for undertaking systematic reviews. Joint Technical report. Computer Science Department, Keele University and National ICT Australia Ltd. (2004)
8. Aucejo, E., French, J., Ugalde Araya, M.P., Zafar, B.: The impact of COVID-19 on student experiences and expectations:evidence from a survey. J. Public Econ. **191**, 104271 (2020)
9. Moraa, H., Signes-Ponta, M.T., Fuster-Guillóa, A., Pertegal-Felices, M.L.: A collaborative working model for enhancing the learning process of science & engineering students. Comput. Hum. Behav. **103**, 140–150 (2020)
10. Edwards, C., Gaved, M.: Understanding student experience: a pathways model. In: L@S 2020: Proceedings of the Seventh ACM Conference on Learning @ Scale, pp. 265–268. Virtual event, USA (2020)
11. Wood, R., Shirazi, S.: A systematic review of audience response systems for teaching and learning in higher education: the student experience. Comput. Educ. **153**, 103896 (2020)
12. Ab. Rahman, R., Ahmad, S., Hashim, U.R.: The effectiveness of gamification technique for higher education students engagement in polytechnic Muadzam Shah Pahang, Malaysia. International Journal of Educational Technology in Higher Education **15**, 41 (2018)
13. Hall, P.B., Milligan, M.: Factors influencing the institutional commitment of online students. Internet Higher Educ. **20**, 51–56 (2014)
14. Ciobanu, A.: The role of student services in the improving of student experience in higher education. Procedia – Soc. Behav. Sci. **92**, 169–173 (2013)
15. Hefer, Y., Cant, M.C.: Students' perception and satisfaction towards customer service in higher education institutions. Corpor. Owner. Control **12**, 599–605 (2014)
16. Grieves, K., Halpin, M.: Developing a Quality Model at University Library Services Sunderland. Perform. Measure. Metr. **15**, 50–57 (2014)
17. Wen, W., JieHao, D.H.: International students' experiences in China: Does the planned reverse mobility work? Int. J. Educ. Dev. **61**, 204–212 (2018)
18. de Jagera, J., Gbadamosi, G.: Predicting students' satisfaction through service quality in higher education. Int. J. Manage. Educ. **11**, 107–118 (2013)
19. Piyatamrong, T., Derrick, J., Nyamapfene, A.: Technology-mediated higher education provision during the COVID-19 pandemic: a qualitative assessment of engineering student experiences and sentiments. J. Eng. Educ. Transf. **34**, 290–297 (2021)
20. Crook, C., Nixon, E.: How internet essay mill websites portray the student experience of higher education. Internet Higher Educ. **48**, 100775 (2021)
21. Brightspot strategy. https://www.brightspotstrategy.com/student-experience-survey-choose-assessment/. Accessed 08 Feb 2021
22. Carless, D.: Students' experiences of assessment for learning. In: Carless, D., Bridges, S.M., Ka Yuk Chan, C., Glofcheski, R. (eds.) Scaling up Assessment for Learning in Higher Education. TEPA, vol. 5, pp. 113–126. Springer, Singapore (2017). https://doi.org/10.1007/978-981-10-3045-1_8

Exploring Factors of an Inclusive Textbook Access Program in Computer Technology Courses

Michele Clements[✉] and James Braman[✉]

Community College of Baltimore County, Baltimore, MD 21237, USA
{mclements,jbraman}@ccbcmd.edu

Abstract. Many factors contribute to student success in college-level courses. One major factor is student access to required course materials. There is a growing number of students who, for several reasons, do not have access to materials or choose not to purchase textbooks. The negative impact of textbook cost is well known and documented and often a significant contributor to not purchasing course materials. In this paper, we explore the use of an inclusive textbook access program for several computer courses at a large community college. As part of this project, we present student feedback on this initiative and examine perceptions on textbook use and purchasing habits. The research helps gain insight into having the textbook built into the cost of the course and the impact of having access to a digital copy of the text on the very first day of class.

Keywords: Textbooks · Inclusive access · Student success · Course materials

1 Introduction

Many factors play a role in student success in a college-level course. One major factor contributing to student success is having access to course materials, specifically the required textbook. While some courses may require additional readings, videos, or use of other materials, the main textbook is generally essential and purposefully selected. There are numerous reasons why a student would not have access or could not obtain access to a required textbook. One major factor is cost. Some students may not be able to afford the textbook, lack adequate funding to purchase course materials, or need to make other spending priorities. The negative impact of textbook cost is well known and documented and is often a major contributor to students not acquiring a textbook. One large study found that 66% of students surveyed noted they did not purchase the required textbook due to cost [1]. Another study found that 85% of students wait until the first day of class or do not buy the course materials, with nearly 91% citing cost as the major factor in deciding not to purchase the required text [2].

There are other factors, including student perception of the level of relevance of course materials. Students may assume that the materials are "not really needed" or that textbook material is "irrelevant" to them, or simply full of "seductive details" only

© Springer Nature Switzerland AG 2021
G. Meiselwitz (Ed.): HCII 2021, LNCS 12775, pp. 187–198, 2021.
https://doi.org/10.1007/978-3-030-77685-5_15

meant to hold attention but not convey content they need to learn [3]. There may be some perception that the textbook material can be "skipped" as they can get by using course notes and other online resources. Additionally, there may be the idea that the course materials are not of high quality and that purchasing the book is a waste of money and time. Other reports highlight the perception that students do not feel that the costs are warranted [4]. Complicating these issues are course materials that may be packaged with electronic resources, interactive components, or simulations. These components are aimed at helping to provide additional educational resources, simulate course software, or simplify content. In other instances, eBook versions of materials are required with the aim of increasing engagement with the course to boost reading [5].

Inclusive access programs focus on textbook access and improving the retention, engagement, and overall success in college courses by providing equitable access to required materials on the very first day of class. Through inclusive access, students can start doing coursework immediately. These programs are sometimes referred to as "day-one access", "digital discount", "inclusive access", "all students acquire", "enterprise solutions" and "First Day" [6]. For the purposes of this paper, the program will be referred to as *inclusive access*. Despite the various names for inclusive access programs, the goal is the same: to provide an additional option to students for obtaining textbook materials in a convenient and cost-effective way that may be integrated into the course through the learning management system (LMS). Students are automatically signed up for course materials and charged as part of the cost of tuition [7]. There has been a drastic increase in the number of inclusive access programs since the Department of Education allowed institutions to include books and other supplies within the normal tuition or fees [7].

Despite the apparent benefits of inclusive access, students can still opt-out of the program. Typically, if students do not opt-out, they are automatically charged for the course materials as part of tuition costs or subsequently billed. The most significant advantage for students is that publishers offer volume discounts, which result in considerable cost savings. It is important to note that students always have the option to opt-out of the inclusive access during the opt-out period, which is typically two weeks. There is potential for legal issues if this is not an option or not made clear [7]. Inclusive access programs have been expanded into information technology courses to help combat the typically higher costs of textbooks and additional materials. Indiana University reported students saved an estimated 3.5 million between 2016 through 2017 [8]. Inclusive access usually includes an eBook instead of an actual printed copy of the book, which is a driving force in reducing costs. Typically, eBooks cost less, which has been a significant factor in addressing the increasing costs of textbooks. Higher textbook prices disproportionally impact community college students when compared to four-year institutions. It is estimated that 50% of community college students use financial aid to purchase textbooks compared to 28% of students at four-year public institutions and 22% at 4-year private institutions [9]. Reducing the cost may allow students to buy materials sooner. This is particularly helpful as course materials and assignments can be addressed during the first day of class, and tasks can be started right away. Students potentially save time by not buying the wrong book or the need to search for electronic content in an eBook and can also utilize additional electronic resources and study tools [10].

This paper aims to investigate the impact of an inclusive access program in computer science and information technology courses at the Community College of Baltimore County. We report on student feedback obtained through a survey as part of a pilot study. In this project, the aim is to examine the following research questions as part of a preliminary research initiative. R1: What potential impact does the inclusive access textbook program have on student success, motivation, and self-reported course performance? And, R2: Has the inclusive access textbook program influenced textbook purchasing habits?

2 Background

During the fall 2019 semester, the Computer Science and Information Technology (CSIT) department at the Community College of Baltimore County decided to utilize a new textbook access program. This was in collaboration with the college bookstore, Barnes and Nobel [11]. Their inclusive access program is referred to as First Day. The CSIT department was motivated to utilize this program due to the significant cost savings for students and the convenience of having inclusive access of the course textbook embedded into the course. Students would have access to an eBook version of the traditional physical book as an embedded link in the LMS. The text could also be accessed outside of the LMS if needed and could be accessed once the course was over for a limited about of time. Students could still purchase the printed textbook at the bookstore or through other book vendors if they wished and had the ability to opt-out of the program. The initial rollout was in several highly enrolled, general education courses within the department. These included CSIT 101 - Technology and Information Systems, CSIT 111 - Logic and Object-Oriented Design, and CSIT 120 - Diversity in a Technological Society. After receiving very positive initial feedback from both students and faculty, the program was expanded to other courses by the spring 2020 semester, including CSIT 210 - Introduction to Programing, CSIT 211 – Advanced programing, CSIT 214 - C+ + Programming, and CSIT 216 - Python Programming. These additional courses represent most of our programming courses and are typically taken by those majoring in Computer Science, Information Technology, Management Information Systems, or other related majors.

In addition to the positive feedback, another primary motivation was the continued cost savings for students. Implementation of the inclusive access program during the fall 2019 semester resulted in an estimated cost savings of more than $78,000 for students enrolled in the initial rollout of the general education courses. The program was expanded to include four upper-level programming courses during the spring 2020 semester and is continuing to grow. The total cost savings for students throughout 2020 was more than $249,000. Table 1 illustrates the estimated enrollment of the courses between the fall 2019 semester through fall 2020. Courses noted with "N/A" were not included in the inclusive access program during that particular semester. Following this data, Table 2 shows the estimated cost savings for 2020.

Informal feedback received from faculty after the first semester was mostly positive. Based on this initial feedback, we wanted to collect real data from students to answer the proposed research questions. Section 3 describes the survey and reports of the collected feedback.

Table 1. Estimated enrollment for courses using the First Day Program

Courses	Fall 2019	Winter 2020	Spring 2020	Summer 2020	Fall 2020
CSIT 101	897	95	729	179	943
CSIT 111	362	40	310	88	484
CSIT 120	259	47	278	90	300
CSIT 210	N/A	N/A	169	48	162
CSIT 211	N/A	N/A	79	29	80
CSIT 214	N/A	N/A	62	N/A	63
CSIT 216	N/A	N/A	N/A	N/A	19

Table 2. Estimated cost savings for 2020 through the First Day Program

Class	Original cost	First day cost	Cost difference	Registered for 2020	Estimated cost savings
CSIT 101	$100	$65	$35	1851	$68,110.00
CSIT 111	$106.65	$22	$84.65	882	$78,047.30
CSIT 120	$99.85	$37	$62.85	668	$44,937.75
CSIT 210	$173.30	$41.15	$132.15	379	$50,084.85
CSIT 211	No additional costs for students who purchased the book for CSIT 210 – The same book is used for CSIT 211				
CSIT 214	$127.99	$65.05	$62.94	125	$7,867.50
CSIT 216	$101.32	$86.65	$14.67	19	$278.73
Total savings					**$249,326.13**

3   Methods and Results

3.1   Research Design

To gain feedback on the First Day program within the CSIT Department, a survey was administered to several sections of courses that were part of the inclusive access program at the end of the Fall 2020 semester. The survey was electronic and was distributed through SurveyMonkey. There were 240 total responses to the survey. After removing invalid entries and data from those self-reporting under the age of 18, 231 responses were used from the survey and analyzed. Open-ended questions were coded and simplified, then classified by similar responses. 187 responses (80.95%) were obtained from CSIT 101 Technology and Information Systems, 12 responses (5.19%) from CSIT 111 Logic and OO Design, 25 responses (10.28%) from CSIT 120 Diversity in a Technological Society, 1 response (0.43%) from CSIT 210 Introduction to Programing, 3 responses (1.30%) from CSIT 211 – Advanced programing, 1 response (0.43%) from CSIT 214 C+ + Programming and 2 responses (0.87%) from CSIT 216 Python Programming.

3.2 Survey Results

The top reported majors noted by 211 respondents (91.34%) included: general studies, information technology, computer science, psychology, business administration/management, biology, education, accounting, and engineering. Regarding age, 146 (63.2%) of respondents were in the age range of 18 to 24, 48 (20.78%) were between the age of 25 and 34, 23 (9.96%) were between the age of 35 and 44, 10 (4.33%) were between the age of 45 and 54, with a remaining 4 (1.73%) reported being above 55 and older. We also asked participants how many semesters they had been enrolled at the college. From 230 responses, 72 (31.30%) reported that this was their first semester, 31 (13.48%) reported attending for two semesters, 55 (23.91%) reported attending for three semesters, 28 (12.17%) reported attending for four semesters. The remaining 44 (19.31%) have been at the college for five or more semesters. Additionally, 91 (39.57%) reported attending college part-time, 137 (59.57%) full-time, and 2 (0.87%) noting "other" as their enrollment status.

After the demographic questions, the survey continued by asking specific questions focused on the inclusive access program labeled in the survey questions as First Day. Q6 asked "Have you heard of the First Day program before this course?". From 229 responses, 81 of the participants (35.37%) responded "Yes" while the remaining 148 of the participants (64.63%) reported "No." Following was Q7 which asked, "Do you agree that the First Day Program was clearly explained in your course?". The results are summarized in Table 3 below. In addition, Q8 asked, "Did having the digital version of the textbook through the First Day program help you to be successful in the course?". The results are summarized in Table 4 below. There was an option to leave additional comments about the textbook, which are outlined in Table 5. These results will be discussed in detail later in this paper. In addition to the listed comments, five participants noted that they were unaware that they were using a textbook in the course. Three comments pointed out that the interactive web components or videos that were embedded in the digital textbook were helpful in the course.

Table 3. Summary of question 7 clarity of explanation

Options	Frequency (n = 231)
Strongly agree	78 (33.77%)
Agree	84 (36.36%)
Neither agree nor disagree	48 (20.78%)
Disagree	16 (6.93%)
Strongly disagree	5 (2.16%)

Next, Q9 in the survey asked, "The First Day program usually included an eBook. How does the use of an eBook affect your study habits in a course?". This was an open-ended question. Table 6 summarizes the classified feedback obtained from this question. There were 204 responses; however, multiple part responses were possible and tallied

Table 4. Helpfulness rating of the digital textbook

Options	Frequency (n = 228)
Extremely helpful	86 (37.72%)
Very helpful	76 (33.33%)
Somewhat helpful	49 (21.49%)
Not so helpful	12 (5.26%)
Not at all helpful	5 (2.19%)

Table 5. Additional comments corresponding to question 8

Additional comments reported from Q8
"It was very convenient due to the fact that you can download on your smartphone and study anywhere"
"I usually opt out since I prefer physical copies, but I kept the e-books this time because of COVID-19 and it was very convenient"
"I was a returning (many years later) student and was very confused in the beginning on the course"
"I have a personal preference for physical copies of books, and the eBook itself is not great in terms of quality. All that being said, it is quite nice to not have to buy a book"
"Nice and easy access to reading and studying material"
"Allowed me to not have to worry about leaving the book as it is accessible on any computer that I may access"
"We didn't have to go to bookstore and the book was available to us the first day of class"
"Sorry, I am old fashioned, and I prefer paper books that I can refer to again in the future. Reading course material only on a small device or a desktop is difficult. I like the flexibility of having paper books"
"I wish there was an option to buy physical copy for discounted price"
"I still don't know what this is to be honest. I am really grateful for discounted, online textbooks (or free which seems to be an upcoming trend) but I have wondered the entire course what "First Day" was and where the book is. I have no clue how to find it or why I paid for it"

as separate responses. Responses that were undecipherable, blank, or comments not relatable to study habits were not included. Next, the survey asked in Q10, "Do you use outside materials to help you study or to learn course materials?". There were 231 responses to this question, where 45 (28.13%) said "Yes", 88 (38.10%) said "No", 78 (33.77%) reported "Sometimes". Fifteen participants who responded "yes" (15.15%) listed which resources they use and have been summarized in Table 7 below. Participants could list more than one response. Q11 asked, "How likely would you have been to purchase the textbook for the class? (If not part of First Day)". Responses are summarized in Table 8.

Participants had the option of noting additional comments, which are noted in Table 9. As a related question, Q12 asked, "Have you ever decided not to purchase a textbook for a course because of the cost?". All 231 participants responded to this question and 107 (46.32%) responded "Yes", 99 (42.86%) responded "No", and the remaining 25 (10.82%) responded as "Unsure". Q13 asked, "If you had the choice, select the choice below about purchasing your course textbook." The options included: I would prefer to have the textbook cost included in my tuition, I would prefer to purchase the textbook from the bookstore myself, I would prefer to purchase the textbook on my own, and I have no opinion. The results are summarized in Table 10.

Table 6. Generalized comments about study habits

General comments	Frequency
More convenient/available/accessible	47
No difference	35
Helpful/very helpful	20
eBook easier to use	20
Easier to study/easier to stay organized	18
Prefer printed books/paper	15
Harder to study with eBook/at the computer for long time periods	14
Used various built in eBook features	13
Ok/fine/good for studying	10
Did not use	10
Prefer eBooks	7
Can be used on multiple devices (e.g., phone)	6
Hard to study without internet	1
More distractions online/at computer	1
Difficulty navigating the eBook	1
Poor quality eBook	1

Next, the survey asked in Q14, "Should the First Day program continue to be an option for CSIT courses?". Table 11 summarizes the responses to this question. A majority of the 231 participants, 187 (80.95%) responded "Yes" to the question, 7 (3.03%) responded "No," and 37 (16.02%) replied, "Unsure." In the next section, we provide a discussion of the survey results.

4 Discussion

The feedback from this preliminary survey was insightful in understanding some factors of using the inclusive textbook access program in several computer courses offered by the

Table 7. Outside materials used as study aides

Reported resources	Frequency (n = 15)
YouTube	12
Quizlet	10
Google	6
Internet/various websites	5
Non textbooks/other references	2
Stackoverflow.com	1
Course notes	1
Google scholar	1
Chegg.com	1
College library	1
Making flashcards	1

Table 8. Textbook purchasing preferences

Options	Frequency (n = 231)
Very likely	68 (29.44%)
Likely	74 (32.03%)
Neither likely nor unlikely	47 (20.35%)
Unlikely	24 (10.39%)
Very unlikely	18 (7.79%)

Computer Science and Information Technology department at the Community College of Baltimore County. One theme that emerged was that most participants reported not knowing about the inclusive access program before the current course. This most likely will change as students continue to take classes that utilize the inclusive access program. Fortunately, most participants stated that the explanation of the program was presented clearly. As part of the explanation of inclusive access, instructors are provided a set of instructions to post as part of the course materials, including instructions for how to opt-out. It is suggested that this same information be posted as an announcement. Additionally, instructors introduce First Day during class sessions and how to use the digital eBook to access content, review features, and incorporate any study components that are part of the eBook platform. Taking these steps may be related to the high rating of helpfulness reported by most participants and worth exploring in future research. Participants also reported that the convenience of having the textbook always accessible to them, which could be an element that improves study habits, was also helpful. There were several responses that participants preferred printed materials or a combination of

Table 9. Additional comments about purchasing eBooks

Additional comments
"I would love to buy eBook like this one if they sell it"
"I wish that I can buy the textbook for the class if it is available"
"Only if required"
"I always buy physical copies of the books"
"Depends on how essential the book is to complete my course work"
"Frankly, you can find the books online on pdf's usually or don't need the book at all. Still haven't purchased a book"
"There is no textbook for this class"
"Paying for books is a scam"
"Not sure depends on the rigor of the class"
"I probably would have had to no matter what"
"It depends on if an eBook was offered"
"If it is required, I'm going to need to buy it"
"I would have been very upset if I would have had to purchase something that i never used"
"I wish I knew what this was and that it had been explained better. I don't even know where to find it"
"If it was not discounted or free, then I would be hesitant about it but would ultimately have to get it because of the class I need it for"
"Whether I did pay or not, I would have if I had too"

Table 10. Textbook purchasing preferences

Options	Frequency (n = 229)
I would prefer to have the textbook cost included in my tuition	134 (58.52%)
I would prefer to purchase the textbook from the bookstore myself	24 (10.48%)
I would prefer to purchase the textbook on my own	30 (13.10%)
I have no opinion	41 (17.90%)

eBook and printed materials. Those that preferred print resources felt that they learned better through this medium.

When asked specifically, "How does the use of an eBook affect your study habits in a course?", this open-ended question revealed several factors. An overwhelming majority preferred the eBook and noted that it was convenient, always available, and accessible, and more comfortable to use. At the same time, some participants reported feeling no difference in the effect of study habits between inclusive access with the eBook compared to having a more traditional textbook approach. Despite the convenience, there were

Table 11. Likert scale responses for continuing

Options	Frequency (n = 230)
Strongly agree	117 (50.87%)
Agree	81 (35.22%)
Neither agree nor disagree	30 (13.04%)
Disagree	0 (0%)
Strongly disagree	2 (0.87%)

some concerns regarding the need to access the materials through the computer for long periods of time, the concern due to eye strain and headaches, and the preference to have printed materials. Others liked to be able to use the materials through cell phones and other devices. There was also a concern of potential issues using the materials if there was no Internet access. These concerns emphasize the continued need for multiple options. Interestingly when asked about using outside materials along with the eBook, 61.9% reported either "Yes" or "Sometimes." More research is needed to explore why, what specific types of, and reasons that outside materials are being used.

Regarding textbook purchasing habits, 46.32% of students reported in our survey that they had decided at some point not to purchase a course textbook due to the price. As noted previously, one survey reported that 66% of students did not purchase the required textbook due to cost [1]. It is unknown what specific cost threshold was influential for making students choose not to make the purchase. It is possible that cost in combination with other factors such as other spending priorities were used in the decision not to purchase the required materials. However, 58.52% reported that they would prefer to have the textbook cost included in the cost of tuition. This is most likely due to the reduced price and convenience. This is similar to another survey where students reported interest in participating in inclusive access programs to be able to have access to digital materials at more affordable prices [2]. Other research indicates that students felt that participating in inclusive access programs provides more convenient access to course materials. They benefited academically by developing a better understanding of the content, increased engagement, and preparedness because they had early access [12]. One survey reported students felt that their grades were impacted negatively by not having access [2].

The feedback reported in our survey was primarily positive and in favor of inclusive access due to convenience, cost, availability, flexibility, and having a positive impact on study habits. It is not too surprising that the results of Q14, "Should the First Day program continue to be an option for CSIT courses?" were that most participants, 187 (80.95%) responded "Yes", 7 (3.03%) responded "No" and 37 (16.02%) responded "Unsure". In the future, it will be important to examine the "why" of the positive responses more closely.

5   Future Work and Conclusion

As discussed, many factors play a role in student success and access to required textbooks is one major factor. This preliminary study examined an inclusive access textbook program in several computer courses. Overall, the aim was to explore the potential impact of the program on student success, motivation, self-reported course performance, and the influence on textbook purchasing habits. The feedback helped move us toward answering our research questions. However, more research is needed to dig deeper into other influential factors and other contributors that impact purchasing decisions.

A more detailed survey is planned in the future that expands on these issues to answer and address our research questions further. The results so far indicate a positive impact on success based on having the course materials provided through this program and a positive view on having the textbook costs built into the course. A goal of the inclusive access program is to have every student have equal access to materials at the beginning of the course. It has been shown that student success increases when students have access to the correct required materials through inclusive access [13]. In future iterations of this project, we plan on examining grades and other learning outcomes in courses that use inclusive access compared to past semesters that did not. We also plan to expand this comparison with a wider view of course selections. One weakness of this study was that most of the feedback was obtained through those registered in CSIT 101. Having a broader response from other course sections and a variety of courses will be advantageous.

There is also the need to explore the views of faculty. We are particularly interested in any course changes that were made due to the program or if activities during the first or second week of the semester have changed over the last several semesters for courses using inclusive access. Has the ability to work with the required material on the first day positively impacted instructors who must usually wait a few days or who are hesitant to assign specific readings or assignments on the first day of class because students have difficulties delays getting the textbook? Additionally, research is needed on the impact of interactive materials included as part of the course. Some instructors create their own interactive materials [14], whereas others rely on the publisher's materials. We also intend to explore the impact of student study habits concerning textbook access and using eBooks.

In conclusion, access to course materials is essential to be successful in a college-level course. Despite many options available to obtain course materials, we have presented preliminary feedback from students using an inclusive access textbook program from several computing courses. The results have been positive overall, and we have gained insights on what elements have been beneficial and impactful. We plan to investigate other factors that influence success rates in relation to equitable textbook access and other ways to improve inclusive course design. It has been made clear over this past year, with many institutions shifting to distance learning due to COVID-19 and the reliance on the course material, that these issues are of increasing importance.

References

1. Martin, M., Belikov, O., Hilton, J., Wiley, D., Fischer, L.: Analysis of student and faculty perceptions of textbook costs in higher education. Open Praxis **9**(1), 79–91 (2017)
2. VitalSource: Study confirms costs lead students to forgo required learning materials; grades suffer as a result (2017). https://press.vitalsource.com/study-confirms-costs-lead-students-to-forgo-required-learning-materials-grades-suffer-as-a-result
3. Maloy, J., Fries, L., Laski, F., Ramirez, G.: Seductive details in the flipped classroom: the impact of interesting but educationally irrelevant information on student learning and motivation. CBE—Life Sci. Educ. **18**(3), ar42 (2019)
4. Whitford, E.: Textbook trade-offs. Inside Higher Ed (2018). https://www.insidehighered.com/news/2018/07/26/students-sacrifice-meals-and-trips-home-pay-textbooks
5. Liberatore, M.: High textbook reading rates when using an interactive textbook for a Material and Energy Balances course. Chem. Eng. Educ. **51**(3), 109–118 (2017)
6. Ruth, D.: OpenStax textbooks now available through bookstore digital access programs (2017). https://openstax.org/blog/openstax-textbooks-now-available-through-bookstore-digital-access-programs
7. McKenzie, L.: The true cost of inclusive access. Inside Higher Ed (2019). https://www.insidehighered.com/news/2019/02/05/college-hot-water-over-inclusive-access-programs-and-student-choice
8. Indiana University: Indiana University's eText program saves students over $3.5 million (2017). https://itnews.iu.edu/articles/2017/indiana-universitys-etext-program-saves-students-over-3.5-million.php
9. Senack, E., Donoghue, R.: Covering the cost: why we can no longer afford to ignore high textbook prices. Student Organizing, Inc.- Covering the Cost (2016). https://www.luminafoundation.org/wp-content/uploads/2017/08/covering-the-cost.pdf
10. Jensen, K., Nackerud, S.: The evolution of affordable content efforts in higher education: programs, case studies, and examples (2018). https://doi.org/10.24926/86666.0101
11. CCBC Bookstore. https://www.ccbcmd.edu/Resources-for-Students/Bookstore.aspx
12. Erhorn, S., Frazee, J., Summer, T., Pastor, M., Brown, K., Cirina-Chiu, C.: SDSU's immediate access program: providing affordable solutions [PowerPoint slides] (2017). https://slideplayer.com/slide/12799931/
13. Ruel, C.: How inclusive access purchasing programs can lower the cost of higher education (2017). https://hub.wiley.com/community/exchanges/educate/blog/2017/01/12/how-inclusive-access-purchasing-programs-can-lower-the-cost-of-higher-education-and-more
14. Vincenti, G., Hilberg, J.S., Braman, J.: Student preferences for consuming supplemental instructional material in CS0/CS1/CS2 courses. In: Proceedings of the 26th International Conference of the Society for Information Technology and Teacher Education (SITE), Las Vegas, Nevada USA (2015)

Online Learning and Student Satisfaction in the Context of the COVID-19 Pandemic

Cristóbal Fernández-Robin[✉], Gonzalo Améstica, Diego Yáñez, and Edgard Toledo

Universidad Técnica Federico Santa María, Valparaíso, Chile
{cristobal.fernandez,gonzalo.amestica,diego.yanez,
edgard.toledo}@usm.cl

Abstract. The end of the new normal that has resulted from the pandemic is uncertain. Meanwhile the effects of the introduction of new ways of doing things in the field of academic pedagogy are being studied from different perspectives. Within the series of trials and errors in the introduction of new technological teaching systems, greater amount of research is required, especially in populations of adult students who have suffered a deeper impact due to the pandemic, since their lives have changed by carrying out parenting, study and work processes from their homes.

Initially, a review of various models that study learning acceptance and student satisfaction was carried out. From them, a series of variables and dimensions were selected developing 5 hypotheses that were arranged to be measured by an information collection instrument that was applied through an online survey to a non-probabilistic sample of 148 adult students. Then, a structural equation model was used to explore online learning acceptance and satisfaction. The model utilizes 3 dimensions: perceived online support services, perceived ease of use, and perceived utility.

The main results made evident the key role of the perceived utility of online learning acceptance and student satisfaction. A second finding was the low importance of perceived ease-of-use in accepting online learning and student satisfaction. The authors concluded that several changes can be observed in the perception of students and in how they accomplish satisfaction and learning acceptance, if these are compared to previous studies.

Keywords: Information and communication technologies · Online education · Student satisfaction · Learning acceptance · Educational support

1 Introduction

The COVID 19 pandemic has affected the life of much of the planet for 10 months already. In several countries the process has been complicated, violent and extensive. It has impacted normality, establishing a new order, way of living, working, and relating to other people.

In this new normal, alternatives have had to be sought in order to limit the social and economic impacts, with the hope that a possible economic reactivation can bring

© Springer Nature Switzerland AG 2021
G. Meiselwitz (Ed.): HCII 2021, LNCS 12775, pp. 199–210, 2021.
https://doi.org/10.1007/978-3-030-77685-5_16

back the conditions prior to the pandemic in the medium or short term. All industries are making efforts to adapt to these new circumstances, and education is no exception.

Different authors have reviewed this topic, and the conclusion is similar: a way forward is required during the pandemic that uses the available information technologies to minimize the impact on the learning processes of different generations. However, knowing how this advancement should be developed is not yet possible, as there are many aspects that should still be studied (Moorhouse 2020). Some initial analyses are worth highlighting. (Joseph Crawford et al. 2020) review examples of actions taken at the international level, in an attempt to provide an answer based on the comparison of different alternatives. Sahu (2020) identifies the relevant challenges of the case, namely the change from face-to-face classes to online classes, the development of assessments, international students, international travel restrictions, mental health, and the University support services. On the last point, the creation of a multidisciplinary team is recommended in order to make decisions based on the greatest amount of information possible.

These conclusions are similar to those reached by other authors (Bao 2020), for which the importance of online instructional design and its relationship with student learning are emphasized, as well as the effectiveness in the delivery of instructional information, the support provided by the teachers and their assistants, high-quality participation in order to increase the degree and depth of student learning, and the existence of a contingency plan.

Under this new paradigm, the incorporation of online methodologies has had mixed outcomes, whose performance requires further study to assess their impact today and tomorrow. The extensive outbreak of the Coronavirus disease has created an opportunity to research how traditional face-to-face teaching has been transferred to online education platforms, an issue that directly affects the quality of education (Chen et al. 2020). Now is the time to embrace these practices and resources in the best way possible to improve the teaching and learning process. However, the entire context of online learning has much to improve upon (Ghazal et al. 2018). Therefore, a fundamental objective is to ensure the best possible integration of ICT into the process, thus improving the learning outcomes.

In recent years, the use of ICT in the educational environment and especially in university education has been increasing. Online education or e-learning is understood as the process of using electronic technologies to access educational materials in non-traditional ways (Vululleh 2018). Therefore, it involves different types of tools and methods, which demonstrates its potential to connect people and resources, promote self-directed learning, increase student and teacher interactivity, enhance collaborative effort, remove geographic barriers, generate self-confidence and provide opportunities for critical thinking, among others (Ghazal et al. 2018, Lee 2010).

There are different discussions about the relationship between learning outcomes, online learning acceptance and student satisfaction, typical for TAM (Lee 2010, Lee et al. 2011). Consequently, this study aims to measure the Online Learning Acceptance and Student Satisfaction (OLAS) in a population of adult students who have been affected by the COVID-19 pandemic at the family, work, economic and social levels. To this end, 3 variables that help in the prediction of these constructs through interactions of both direct and indirect types are conceived. These are the Perceived Service Quality (PSQ) of online support services, Perceived Ease of Use (PEOU) and Perceived Usefulness (PU). Based on the literature on the topic, 5 hypotheses are proposed (see Fig. 1):

- H1: PSQ positively influences the PEOU of online learning.
- H2: PSQ positively influences the PU of online learning.
- H3: PEOU positively influences OLAS.
- H4: PU positively influences OLAS.
- H5: The PSQ positively influences OLAS.

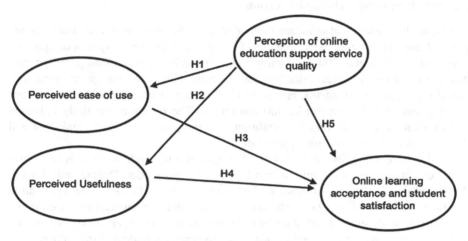

Fig. 1. Structural model used by Lee research.

With this objective, the theoretical background that supports the study is first introduced, addressing the results of several works that have been conducted on the subject. Subsequently, research methodology is described, explaining the procedure for data collection and analysis. The following chapters deal with the findings of the study, and finally, its key conclusions and recommendations are presented.

2 Theoretical Framework

2.1 Use and Acceptance of ICT in Higher Education

Online education has contributed to promoting self-directed learning in students (Ghazal et al. 2018), enabled new ways of communication and work (Muñoz-Miralles et al. 2016), and become a valuable and motivating element for students (Ferro et al. 2009, Vega-Hernández et al. 2018). However, even if there are benefits associated with the incorporation of ICT in higher education, the effect of these will largely depend on the degree to which the implemented technologies are accepted and employed by users (Kumar Sharma et al. 2014, Tarhini et al. 2013). In this line, little research has been conducted on educational websites or e-learning tools and programs linked to higher education.

Among the studies developed is the work of Selim (2003), who proposed an acceptance model of a course website using the constructs of ease of use and perceived usefulness, concepts established by Davis (1989) in his Technology Acceptance Model (TAM). This model was extended by Venkatesh and Davis (2000) by including two more constructs, social influences and cognitive instrumental processes. In this way, Selim (2003) concluded that the usefulness and ease of use of the course website proved to be key determinants of its acceptance and use as an effective and efficient learning technology.

2.2 Satisfaction with Online Education

In general, the factors that influence user satisfaction in an e-learning environment are grouped into six dimensions: student, teacher, course, technology, system design, and environmental (Sun et al. 2008). Adapting these approaches, Teo and Wong (2013) examined the variables that affect e-learning satisfaction, which are tutor quality (teacher), perceived usefulness (student), perceived ease of use (technology), course delivery (design) and enabling (environmental) conditions. The results of the study indicated that in addition to facilitating the conditions, all the predictors had a significant and direct relationship with e-learning satisfaction.

In the same vein, Ghazal et al. (2018) proposed a research model that integrates variables obtained from the Information System success model (Delone and McLean 2003) and the TAM model to research how certain success factors in the application of educational software can boost student experience and user satisfaction. In short, the results of the study showed that characteristics of students (computer anxiety, technological experience and computer self-efficacy), classmates (attitude and interaction), and course (quality and flexibility) were vital elements to maintain a positive and satisfying user experience.

Other studies explain satisfaction with online courses directly through perceptions of support (Song et al. 2004, Mullen and Tallent-Runnels 2006, Lee 2010, Lee et al. 2011). In this sense, the research developed by Lee et al. (2011) confirms that when students perceive peer and technical educational support, they consider courses to be a support for their learning and therefore are more likely to be satisfied with online courses.

2.3 Perception of Quality in Online Education

Another aspect that educational institutions, especially universities, have paid attention to is improving the quality of their online education programs. In this sense, the literature shows that the Information System success model (Delone and McLean 2003) is employed in some cases to find the determinants of success in electronic learning systems. Thus, the system, information and service quality are identified as statistically significant and positively related to online learning systems (Lin 2007, Wang et al. 2007, Machado-Da-Silva et al. 2014).

System quality refers to the individual perception of stability, responsiveness, and ease of use of an information system (DeLone and McLean 2003). Some authors believe that the quality of the system is the main factor in the acceptance of a technology (Lin and Lu 2000; Lee and Lee 2008), since the findings show a significant relationship between the quality of the system, the usefulness perceived by students and the ease of use of the technological system (Ghazal et al. 2018).

Second, information quality refers to the quality of the content delivered through the information system to users, in terms of relevance, timeliness, accuracy, integrity, sufficiency, consistency, accessibility, understandability, and format (DeLone and McLean 2003, Roca et al. 2006). Regarding the relationship between the quality of information and the perceptions of ease of use and usefulness of the system, results are mixed. While several studies demonstrate the existence of this relationship (Al-Busaidi 2012, Cheng 2012, Lwoga 2014, Gay 2016), the work by Ghazal et al. (2018) concludes that there is no relationship effect between these variables.

Finally, service quality refers to the quality of the support provided to the end users of the system (Ghazal et al. 2018). Its measures include effectiveness, reliability, responsiveness, guarantee, and availability of technical support (DeLone and McLean 2003). Like system and information quality, the influence of service quality on the perceived usefulness of individuals and on the perceived ease of use of an online system (that is to say, on the acceptance of e-learning) has received widespread theoretical support (Saeed et al. 2003, Cho et al. 2009, Lee 2010, Wang and Chiu 2011, Cheng 2012, Ramayah and Lee 2012); However, some research considers that service quality only has significant effects on the perceived usefulness of the students regarding the online system (Pai and Huang 2011, Ghazal et al. 2018).

3 Methodology

In this work, a descriptive and cross-sectional study was conducted.

The study considered students from professional education programs (known as tertiary education) in industrial engineering during evenings at a private university in Chile. This group stands out for having a previous academic degree, which is usually related to a previous occupation. Typically, this sample of students is older than students attending classes during the mornings. The students were considered the population and unit of analysis of this work.

Convenience sampling was used, a non-probabilistic sampling, was used for selecting the sample. The study considered a total of 148 students from two of the main regions of Chile, who participated in the survey through a web system during the months of July and August 2020, that is to say, while much of the country was under quarantine. This sample represents 46% the total population of students in the program described above. The sample is constituted of 76% males and 24% females.

3.1 Data Collection Instrument and Stimuli

The instrument used was based mainly on studies by different authors (Lee 2010). From these, a series of stimuli arranged under 4 latent variables, three dependent variables (Perception of Ease of Use, PEOU; Perceived Usefulness, PU; student Online Learning Acceptance and Satisfaction, OLAS), and one independent variable (Perceived Service Quality, PSQ, of online education support). In addition, stimuli were added under a structure for the evaluation of support services, information, coordination, communication platforms and content management, teachers and assistants. Finally, a student self-evaluation variable regarding the program was also considered.

All stimuli were organized in a self-administered questionnaire through the web system and are presented in Table 1.

Table 1. Stimuli used in data collection instrument.

Perceived ease of use	
1	I find it easy to use the online learning system to do what I want it to do
2	I find the online learning system is clear and understandable for me
3	It is easy for me to become skillful at using the online learning system
4	I find the online learning system easy to use
Perceived utility	
1	Using online learning system improves my ability to accomplish academic tasks
2	Using online learning system increases my productivity in accomplishing academic tasks
3	Using online learning system enhance my effectiveness in accomplishing academic tasks
4	I find online learning system useful in my study completion
Online learning acceptance and student satisfaction	
1	If I need to study for advanced degree, I would expect to use the university online learning system
2	If asked, I would likely recommend the university online learning system as an ideal learning platform
3	For future advanced degrees, I would probably use the university online learning system
4	Overall, I am satisfied with the university online learning system
Perception on online education support service quality	
1	When I register for online courses, I expect to have adequate feedback and support services from the program
2	When I register for online courses, I expect to have adequate feedback and support services from the university
3	When I register for online courses, I expect to have adequate feedback and support services from academic program managers
Online education services and support evaluation	
1	Program support and feedback
2	University support and information services
3	Academic program managers support
4	Zoom platform performance
5	Online course management platform performance
6	Overall faculty evaluation
7	Overall teaching assistant evaluation
8	Self-evaluation for performance

All these stimuli, including those related to the evaluation of the training program on key performance variables associated with the different stages experienced by students, were measured using a 7-level Likert scale that ranged from "Totally disagree = 1" up to "Strongly agree = 7".

3.2   Factor Analysis Through Structural Model

Perception stimuli were analyzed using a structural model, checking its goodness of fit through the Chi-square test. The CFI and RMSEA indices were used to review the fit of the model and the defined hypotheses.

The evaluation variables were used to improve the reading of the model results. All analyses were developed with the SPSS and AMOS platforms.

For measuring scale consistency, Cronbach's alpha coefficient was employed, which yielded adequate results in all cases: PEOU 0.908; PU 0.959; PSQ 0.983; OLAS 0.966.

4   Results

An analysis was performed through a structural model (Escobedo Portillo et al. 2016) (Byrne 2009). Maximum likelihood was used to estimate the values of the model components. From the proposed model, an acceptable goodness of fit was achieved, as defined by different studies (Byrne 1994).

The CMIN or Chi-square value is considered non-significant, which would indicate an acceptable model, that is to say, the observed covariance matrix is similar to that estimated by the model. The CMIN/DF value is 4.185, which is also considered acceptable (Schumacker and Lomax 2004). In the case of GFI, a value of 0.822 is obtained, which is also considered quite adequate. The NCP also meets expectations for the independent model. The ECVI, which shows how the model would fit another similar sample, also has an adequate value (Kaplan 2000).

Table 2 shows the measures of incremental adjustment and parsimony. For the incremental adjustment measures, which compare the model with another specific one, generally good values were obtained, especially in the CFI and IFI tests, the latter has been recommended for limited samples like the one used in this study (Bollen 1989). At the parsimony level, the model behaves quite well, yielding a PRATIO of 0.81 (Escobedo Portillo et al. 2016).

Table 2. Incremental adjustment and parsimony measures.

Model	CMIN	CMIN/DF	GFI	NCP	ECVI
Proposed	355.765	4.185	0.822	270.765	2.896
Saturated	0	–	1	0	1.633
Independent	3234.903	30.809	0.151	3129.903	22.21

For the incremental adjustment measures, which compare the model with another specific one, good values were obtained in general, particularly in the CFI and IFI tests, the latter has been recommended for limited samples like the one used in this study (Bollen 1989). At the parsimony level, the model behaves quite well, yielding a PRATIO of 0.81 (Escobedo Portillo et al. 2016). Table 3 shows these measurements.

Table 3. Incremental adjustment measures by model comparison.

Model	NFI Delta1	RFI rho1	GFI Delta2	CFI	PRATIO
Proposed	0.89	0.864	0.914	0.913	0.81
Saturated	1	–	1	1	0
Independent	0	0	0	0	0

In summary, the fit of the model seems to be adequate for its analysis in the context of the hypotheses initially proposed (Cheung and Rensvold 2002).

4.1 Hypothesis Review

All hypotheses were tested using the data provided by the sample. For null hypothesis 1 "There is no relationship between PSQ and PEOU" an adequate significance was obtained ($p < 0.001$), which allows for rejecting the null hypothesis, and accepting the possibility of a positive influence of PSQ on PEOU.

Null hypothesis 2 "There is no relationship between PSQ and PU" maintained a low significance ($p = 0.015$), but not enough to reject it.

In the case of null hypothesis 3 "There is no relationship between PEOU and OLAS", a low significance was obtained ($p < 0.01$), which would allow, in the opinion of the researchers, for considering the rejection of the null hypothesis. In this case, there would be a positive influence of PEOU on OLAS. The same positive influence would occur between PU and OLAS when rejecting the null hypothesis 4 "There is no relationship between PU and OLAS" ($p < 0.001$).

Finally, null hypothesis 5 "There is no relationship between PSQ and OLAS" did not present an adequate significance and therefore could not be rejected.

All these relationships are presented in Table 4.

The application of the model to the sample suggests the existence of direct and indirect effects on student satisfaction and acceptance of online learning. The main factor of interest in this case would be perceived usefulness, followed by the perception of ease of use for online learning systems. The exogenous variable perceived quality of online education support was relevant in one of the proposed hypotheses, positively influencing the perception of ease of use, which implies an indirect effect on student satisfaction and acceptance of online learning.

4.2 Review of Measures of Dispersion

An analysis of the observed variables allows us to identify a low dispersion in the data of the variables associated with the perceived quality of online education support. This

Table 4. Results of the structural equation analysis for the hypothesis.

		Estimate regression weights	S.E	C.R	P
PEOU	←PSQ	0.279	0.077	3.608	***
PU	←PSQ	0.208	0.086	2.422	0.015
OLAS	←PSQ	−0.011	0.042	−0.271	0.787
OLAS	←PEOU	0.124	0.046	2.674	0.007
OLAS	←PU	1.025	0.061	16.891	***

*** means that p-value is less than 0.001 (P = 0.001)

lower dispersion can be explained by the increase in the need for consultations from support services, due to the current quarantine, which has increased the normal use of these learning systems. The analysis of covariances shows how the relationship between the perceived quality of online education support and student satisfaction and acceptance of online learning is high, always greater than 0.6 (average covariance of 0.68).

5 Conclusions

This study analyzed the relationship and impact of the perceived quality of online education support on the perception of students of online learning systems, and then how this influences the acceptance of online learning and student satisfaction with these systems in the context of a rapidly changing and uncertain scenario due to the current pandemic. In addition, the total impact on student satisfaction and acceptance of online learning was analyzed, based on the perceived quality of online education support. The results are of interest and disagree with previous studies, which is explained by the impact of the pandemic on the social, economic and educational spheres.

The first important result is that the PSQ variable significantly and positively affects the PEOU variable. Then, the PEOU variable significantly and positively influences the OLAS variable, which is also significantly and positively impacted by the PU variable. PU, in turn, is the most relevant predictor of student satisfaction and acceptance of online learning.

The research failed to show the significant direct impact of the PSQ variable on OLAS and PU.

These results are in contrast with previous research. The researchers suggest that these differences could be explained by: 1.) the current pandemic and, 2.) the local context in relation to online education. The pandemic has modified the delivery and assessment of content by different educational programs, in order to achieve the learning outcomes expected by the students. This scenario of uncertainty affects the perception of students, making practical aspects such as the ability to perform tasks, the level of productivity and effectiveness, and the usefulness of the online system with respect to the study process more relevant. Regarding the local context, emphasis is placed on the previous face-to-face condition of the programs in relation to the sample under study, which is therefore affected by the modification of the teaching and learning format, an element that is not measured in previous research. The population was still adapting to

208 C. Fernández-Robin et al.

these changes at the time of the survey, which gives unique importance to longitudinally contrasting the future conditions of the sample.

The study incorporated the factor of perceived quality of online education support, in order to identify its role in the acceptance of online learning and student satisfaction in the transitory context of pandemic. The results showed an indirect influence of this factor, through its impact on the perception of ease of use. Students will increase their satisfaction and acceptance of online learning, while positively perceiving ease of use, and this variable will be perceived positively to the extent that there is a positive perceived quality of the support given to the online education of students.

The relevance of support is traditionally related to the role of teachers and assistants in the educational process. This study sought to place a greater emphasis on the role of support independent of teachers, but this resulted in a lesser importance of the PSQ variable.

In this way, in the context of abrupt social and educational changes, due to the greater social involvement of the population studied, the factor that has the greatest influence on the satisfaction and acceptance of online learning is perceived usefulness. This finding is consistent with previous research and reinforces the idea that, during the pandemic, online education technologies will positively affect student satisfaction and acceptance of online learning, as long as these systems improve the capacity, productivity and effectiveness of the student in the fulfillment of their academic work.

References

Al-Busaidi, K.A.: Learners' perspective on critical factors to LMS success in blended learning: an empirical investigation. Commun. Assoc. Inf. Syst. 30(1), 2 (2012)

Bao, W.: COVID-19 and online teaching in higher education: a case study of Peking University. Hum. Behav. Emerg. Technol. 2(2), 113–115 (2020). https://doi.org/10.1002/hbe2.191

Bollen, K.A.: A new incremental fit index for general structural equation models. Sociol. Methods Res. 17(3), 303–316 (1989). https://doi.org/10.1177/0049124189017003004

Byrne, B.M.: Structural Equation Modeling with EQS and EQS/WINDOWS: Basic Concepts, Applications, and Programming. SAGE, Thousand Oaks (1994)

Byrne, B.M.: Structural Equation Modeling With AMOS: Basic Concepts, Applications, and Programming, 2nd edn. Routledge, London (2009)

Chen, T., Peng, L., Yin, X., Rong, J., Yang, J., Cong, G.: Analysis of user satisfaction with online education platforms in China during the COVID-19 pandemic. Healthcare 8(3), 200 (2020)

Cheng, Y.M.: Effects of quality antecedents on e-learning acceptance. Internet Res. 22(3), 361–390 (2012)

Cheung, G.W., Rensvold, R.B.: Evaluating goodness-of-fit indexes for testing measurement invariance. Struct. Equ. Model. 9(2), 233–255 (2002). https://doi.org/10.1207/S15328007SEM0902_5

Cho, V., Cheng, T.E., Lai, W.J.: The role of perceived user-interface design in continued usage intention of self-paced e-learning tools. Comput. Educ. 53(2), 216–227 (2009)

Davis, F.D.: Perceived usefulness, perceived ease of use, and user acceptance of information technology. MIS Q. 319–340 (1989)

Delone, W.H., McLean, E.R.: The DeLone and McLean model of information systems success: a ten-year update. J. Manag. Inf. Syst. 19(4), 9–30 (2003)

Escobedo Portillo, M.T., Hernández Gómez, J.A., Estebané Ortega, V., Martínez Moreno, G.: Modelos de ecuaciones estructurales: Características, fases, construcción, aplicación y resultados. Ciencia & Trabajo **18**(55), 16–22 (2016). https://doi.org/10.4067/S0718-244920160001 00004

Ferro, C., Martínez, A.I., Otero, M.D.C.: Ventajas del uso de las TICs en el proceso de enseñanza-aprendizaje desde la óptica de los docentes universitarios españoles. Edutec: Revista Electrónica de Tecnología Educativa **29**, a119–a119 (2009)

Gay, G.H.E.: An assessment of online instructor e-learning readiness before, during, and after course delivery. J. Comput. High. Educ. **28**(2), 199–220 (2016). https://doi.org/10.1007/s12 528-016-9115-z

Ghazal, S., Al-Samarraie, H., Aldowah, H.: "I am still learning": modeling LMS critical success factors for promoting students' experience and satisfaction in a blended learning environment. IEEE Access **6**, 77179–77201 (2018)

Crawford, J., et al.: COVID-19: 20 countries' higher education intra-period digital pedagogy responses. J. Appl. Learn. Teach. **3**(1), 1–20 (2020). https://doi.org/10.37074/jalt.2020.3.1.7

Kaplan, D.: Structural Equation Modeling Foundations and Extensions. Sage Publications, Thousand Oaks (2000)

Kumar Sharma, S., Kumar Chandel, J., Madhumohan Govindaluri, S.: Students' acceptance and satisfaction of learning through course websites. Educ. Bus. Soc. Contemp. Middle East. Issues **7**(2/3), 152–166 (2014)

Lee, J.K., Lee, W.K.: The relationship of e-Learner's self-regulatory efficacy and perception of e-Learning environmental quality. Comput. Hum. Behav. **24**(1), 32–47 (2008)

Lee, J.W.: Online support service quality, online learning acceptance, and student satisfaction. Internet High. Educ. **13**(4), 277–283 (2010)

Lee, S.J., Srinivasan, S., Trail, T., Lewis, D., Lopez, S.: Examining the relationship among student perception of support, course satisfaction, and learning outcomes in online learning. Internet High. Educ. **14**(3), 158–163 (2011)

Lin, J.C.C., Lu, H.: Towards an understanding of the behavioural intention to use a web site. Int. J. Inf. Manage. **20**(3), 197–208 (2000)

Lin, F.H.: Measuring online learning systems success: applying the updated DeLone and McLean Model. Cyberpsychol. Behav. **10**(6), 817–820 (2007)

Lwoga, E.: Critical success factors for adoption of web-based learning management systems in Tanzania. Int. J. Educ. Dev. ICT **10**(1), 4–21 (2014)

Machado-Da-Silva, N.B., Meirelles, D.S.F., Filenga, D., Filho, B.M.: Student satisfaction process in virtual learning system: Considerations based in information and service quality from Brazil's experience. Turk. Online J. Distance Educ. **15**(3), 122–142 (2014)

Moorhouse, B.L.: Adaptations to a face-to-face initial teacher education course 'forced' online due to the COVID-19 pandemic. J. Educ. Teach. **46**, 609–611 (2020). https://doi.org/10.1080/ 02607476.2020.1755205

Mullen, G.E., Tallent-Runnels, M.K.: Student outcomes and perceptions of instructors' demands and support in online and traditional classrooms. Internet High. Educ. **9**(4), 257–266 (2006)

Muñoz-Miralles, R., et al.: The problematic use of Information and Communication Technologies (ICT) in adolescents by the cross sectional JOITIC study. BMC Pediatr. **16**(1), 1–11 (2016)

Pai, F.Y., Huang, K.I.: Applying the technology acceptance model to the introduction of healthcare information systems. Technol. Forecast. Soc. Chang. **78**(4), 650–660 (2011)

Ramayah, T., Lee, J.W.C.: System characteristics, satisfaction and e-learning usage: a structural equation model (SEM). Turk. Online J. Educ. Technol.-TOJET **11**(2), 196–206 (2012)

Roca, J.C., Chiu, C.M., Martínez, F.J.: Understanding e-learning continuance intention: an extension of the technology acceptance model. Int. J. Hum. Comput. Stud. **64**(8), 683–696 (2006)

Sahu, P.: Closure of universities due to coronavirus disease 2019 (COVID-19): impact on education and mental health of students and academic staff. Cureus (2020). https://doi.org/10.7759/cureus.7541

Saeed, K.A., Hwang, Y., Mun, Y.Y.: Toward an integrative framework for online consumer behavior research: a meta-analysis approach. J. Organ. End User Comput. (JOEUC) 15(4), 1–26 (2003)

Schumacker, R.E., Lomax, R.G.: A Beginner's Guide to Structural Equation Modeling. Psychology Press, London (2004)

Selim, H.M.: An empirical investigation of student acceptance of course websites. Comput. Educ. 40(4), 343–360 (2003)

Song, L., Singleton, E.S., Hill, J.R., Koh, M.H.: Improving online learning: student perceptions of useful and challenging characteristics. Internet High. Educ. 7(1), 59–70 (2004)

Sun, P.C., Tsai, R.J., Finger, G., Chen, Y.Y., Yeh, D.: What drives a successful e-learning? An empirical investigation of the critical factors influencing learner satisfaction. Comput. Educ. 50(4), 1183–1202 (2008)

Tarhini, A., Hone, K., Liu, X.: User acceptance towards web-based learning systems: investigating the role of social, organizational and individual factors in European higher education. Procedia Comput. Sci. 17, 189–197 (2013)

Teo, T., Wong, S.L.: Modeling key drivers of e-learning satisfaction among student teachers. J. Educ. Comput. Res. 48(1), 71–95 (2013)

Vega-Hernández, M.-C., Patino-Alonso, M.-C., Galindo-Villardón, M.-P.: Multivariate characterization of university students using the ICT for learning. Comput. Educ. 121, 124–130 (2018)

Venkatesh, V., Davis, F.: A theoretical extension of the technology acceptance model: four longitudinal field studies. Manage. Sci. 46(2), 186–204 (2000)

Vululleh, P.: Determinants of students' e-learning acceptance in developing countries: an approach based on Structural Equation Modeling (SEM). Int. J. Educ. Dev. ICT 14(1), 141–151 (2018)

Wang, H.C., Chiu, Y.F.: Assessing e-learning 2.0 system success. Comput. Educ. 57(2), 1790–1800 (2011)

Wang, S.Y., Wang, Y.H., Shee, Y.D.: Measuring e-learning systems success in an organizational context: scale development and validation. Comput. Hum. Behav. 23(4), 1792–1808 (2007)

Activity Comparison of the Participants Using Japanese as L2 and Their L1 in Group Discussion

Hung-Hsuan Huang[1]($\boxtimes$), Zi-Yu Pei[2], and Kazuhiro Kuwabara[2]

[1] Faculty of Informatics, University of Fukuchiyama, Fukuchiyama, Japan
hhhuang@acm.org
[2] College of Information Science and Engineering, Ritsumeikan University, Kusatsu, Japan

Abstract. In order to supplement the decreasing working population, there are more and more foreigner workers working in Japanese society. In such a situation where small numbers of foreigner workers need to work with Japanese people as the majority, inefficiency of the group occurs due to language or cultural barriers. This work-in-progress project collects a data corpus for understanding the problems may occur in this "unbalanced" group work and aims to provide computer aided support in the future. We collected 8.5 h of the task-oriented conversation of small groups in the following settings: one Chinese speaker/three Japanese talking in Japanese (C-J), four Chinese speakers talking in Chinese (C-C), and four Japanese talking in Japanese (J-J). In this specific paper, we analyzed a subset (9 15-min discussion sessions) of the data corpus to see the activity changes between C-J and C-C settings.

Keywords: Multiparty interaction · Group discussion · Multimodal interaction · L2 learner · Conversation analysis

1 Introduction

In developed countries, the declining birthrate and aging population are progressing. Especially in Japan, the ratio of the population over 65 years old has been already as high as 28.1% and is expected to over 1/3 by 2036. On the other hand, the total population is expected to continuously decrease to be less than 100 million from current 126.4 million by 2053 [3]. In order to supplement the decreasing working population, Japanese government has started to relax the regulations on introducing foreign workers. The increase of foreigner workers in Japanese society can be expected in near future. In such a situation, foreigner workers are the minority and have to collaboratively work with Japanese colleagues who are the majority. The working environment is optimized for the Japanese, the rules of the company were also established by the Japanese. Not only the language barrier, the differences in habits, the way of thinking, or communication styles oriented from cultural backgrounds may inhibit efficient team work.

© Springer Nature Switzerland AG 2021
G. Meiselwitz (Ed.): HCII 2021, LNCS 12775, pp. 211–222, 2021.
https://doi.org/10.1007/978-3-030-77685-5_17

Our project is aiming to develop an environment for both foreigner and Japanese people to practice the collaborative work in an unbalanced situation where Japanese participants are the majority and the task itself is Japanese favored. In this environment, the avatars of trainees can interact with autonomous agents in realtime and with multiple modalities like facial expressions, gestures, and voice. In order to develop believable models of the agents, reliable ground truths from empirical results are required.

This paper reports the activity analysis of L2 Japanese speakers in group tasks using Japanese language and their native language (Chinese). This work is based on the corpus collected in an experiment to acquire multimodal sensory data in collaborative tasks with unbalanced setup of cultural backgrounds. These data are supposed to be used for developing foreigner/Japanese behavior generation/detection models in a training environment with virtual agents. From our knowledge, there is no such dataset available and we believe the data collected can provide valuable resources for developing tools in supporting unbalanced groups. This paper presents the design of data recording experiment, the summary of the collected corpus, and preliminary analysis on the change of behaviors of non-native participants between the sessions of their first and second languages.

2   Related Works

In the computer science field, there have been research works on machine learning based on nonverbal features, including such features as speaking turn, voice prosody, visual activity, and visual focus of attention on the interaction of small groups. Aran and Gatica-Perez [1] presented an analysis of participants' personality prediction in small groups. Okada et al. [10] developed a regression model to infer the score for communication skill using multimodal features, including linguistic and nonverbal features: voice prosody, speaking turn, and head activity. Schiavo et al. [11] presented a system that monitors the group members' nonverbal behaviors and acts as an automatic facilitator. It supports the flow of communication in a group conversation activity. There are works in exploring the barriers of L2 speakers in group discussion [12] or on their behavior changes between the group discussion in L1 and L2 languages [13]. But most of them are about using English as the L2 language. Although there are a number of research works on Japanese language learning in the fields of linguistics and language education [8], we found few works from computer science field.

This work distinguishes previous one with the following settings:

- Unbalanced composition of L1/L2 speakers in the members of small groups.
- Comparable data of the sessions in Chinese-speaker/Chinese-speaker, Chinese-speaker/Japanese, and Japanese/Japanese combinations so that the behavior changes of both of Japanese and Chinese-speaker participants can be analyzed.
- Data corpus collection and analysis on Japanese as 2nd language in computer science field where sensory data is recorded and meant for machine learning tasks.

3   Experiment Design

In order to extract the characteristics of unbalanced groups, we conducted the experiment to compare unbalanced groups with homogeneous groups. Participants are formed to be groups in the following conditions:

Unbalanced groups: collaborative decision-making discussions were conducted by four participants, three native Japanese speakers and one native Chinese speakers who speaks Japanese as second language. The language used is Japanese only. Chinese-speaking participants are required to be living in Japan for at least one year, passed Japanese Language Proficiency Test (JLPT) level N2, and be confident to talk in Japanese fluently.

Homogeneous groups: composed of native Japanese or Chinese speakers only. The languages used are the participants' native languages (Japanese or Mandarine Chinese).

Chinese speakers are chosen as the foreigner participant because they are the majority of foreigner students in Japan (Chinese and Taiwanese, 41% in 2018) [6]. All subjects are recruited in Kyoto University including students and office staff. Considering the potential wider range of foreigner students and the easiness for people in the same generation to talk, the range of the participants are limited to between 18 to 29. All groups are composed with equal number of male and female participants to prevent gender bias in the results.

In order to identify the causes of the differences of participants' behaviors, the following factors are considered in the selection of discussion topics: the categories and the knowledge level. For the categories of topics, we considered the factor that whether there are prior candidates to choose from in making the final decision. Following the previous work [9], two typical categories of topics were selected in investigating this factor, ranking style and brain-storming style of problems. In addition to that, we also wanted to investigated the effects of knowledge level on the topic, and therefore two topics were selected for each category.

One topic which is supposed to be more favored to Japanese subjects, i.e. a topic which they are supposed to know better. This setting is for simulating the situation when a foreigner has to work on a task which he or she has less knowledge than his/her Japanese partners. The is supposed to happen often in Japanese companies. The other topic which is supposed to be fair to both cultural backgrounds is selected as the baseline for comparison. In addition to the factors being investigated in this work, the possibility of being discussed by both of young Japanese and Chinese participants, and of being evaluated group performance based on the discussion results are considered in selecting the topics. As the results, the following discussion topics were selected.

Ranking Style Topics: participants are asked to collaboratively rank the items from a given list based on their importance or goodness. For this category of discussion.

– Ranking of anime titles: participants are asked to predict the top-five rankings from a list of 15 Japanese anime titles based on their popularity. The correct answers are the scores of these titles on a Japanese SNS site where its members can discuss and score anime titles [1]. On this site, popular titles have at least several hundreds of evaluation and can be considered as a reliable source. This is supposed to be a Japanese-favored topic because all of these titles are Japanese ones and the scores are placed by Japanese anime fans.
– Winter survival exercise: this is a classic task in the research field of group dynamics [7]. The participants are asked to rank top-five important ones from a list of 15 items with an assumption that they met an airplane crash in winter mountains. Item scores determined by experts are available for evaluating this task. This task is supposed to be fair to all of the participants.

Brain-Storming Style Topics: participants are asked to collaboratively deliberate as many ideas as possible without prior candidates. In this work, the preparation of a debate is decided to be the brain-storming task. The participants are asked to discuss the supporting and defending points from a point of view as they are preparing to debate it with another team. Because reliable sources of the evaluation of group performance on this type of task are not available, the count of deliberated supporting/defending points can be used as an objective metric of group performance. Therefore, all experiment sessions have to be conducted with the same point of view on each topic. We set it to be the side of *positive* opinion of the topics.

– Deregulation for introducing foreign workers: the participants are instructed to discuss this issue from the view point of its effect on Japanese society. This topic is supposed to be a Japanese-favored topic.
– Justice of animal experiments: the participants discuss the trade-off between advance of medical technology and the right of animals.

The setup of the recording environment is shown in Fig. 1. The experiment participants sit around a 1.2 m × 1.2 m square table. Two video cameras are used to capture the overall scene. Everyone of them had a dedicated WebCam (Logitech Brio Ultra HD) to capture his or her face in large size in 1920 × 1080 resolution 60 Hz frame rate. Four additional WebCam (Logitech C920) are attached at diagonal direction of the table to compensate the center ones in the case when the participants face to the sides. These cameras have 1920 × 1080 resolution and capture at 30 fps. For each trial the data set contains 15 min of four face camera recordings and four corner recordings. In addition to the eight WebCams, two high-resolution (4K) video cameras (Sony FDR AX-700) are used to capture

The participants also wear motion capture suites (Noitom Perception Neuron 2.0), and their body movements including fingers are recorded. In five out of the 18 experiment sessions motion data was recorded at 60 fps with 33 sensors. The sensor data was interpreted with a human body model by the bundled Axis Neuron software and translated into a BVH file containing the 3D coordinates

---

[1] https://www.anikore.jp/pop_ranking/.

for 72 body parts 60 Hz. Each participant wore a headset microphone (Audio-Technica HYP-190H) which was connected to an audio digitizer (Roland Sonar X1 LE).

4   Experiment Procedures

All subjects were recruited in Kyoto University, nearly all of them are students with one exception, an office staff. Nine native Chinese speakers (three males and six females, mean age: 25.1) and 33 Japanese participants (18 males and 15 females, mean age: 22.7) were recruited in Kyoto University for the experiment. Considering the potential wider range of foreigner students and the easiness for people in the same generation to talk, the age range of the majority of the participants is from 18 to 29 with only two exceptions (one is 31 and one is 36). Chinese-speaking participants were required to have been living in Japan for at least one year, passed Japanese Language Proficiency Test (JLPT) level N2 and above, and self-declared that they can communicate in Japanese fluently.

Fig. 1. Setup of the data corpus recording experiment

The experiment was conducted in the in-subject way, that is, the participants participated in two experiments, in an unbalanced group and in a homogenous group (Japanese or Chinese speaking). These participants were formed into 17 groups: eight mixed ones, seven Japanese-only ones, and two Chinese speaker-only ones. All groups are composed of the participants in the same gender or equal number of male and female participants to prevent gender bias in the results. The differences of group dynamics may be caused by the balance of member's cultural background and may be caused by the personal traits. After the introduction of the whole experiment, the big-five [4] personality test of each participant is conducted. They then discuss on two assigned topics, one is a ranking style topic and the other one is in brain storming style. Each discussion session is limited to 15 min. An alarm clock is placed in front of each participant to help them to conclude the discussion with allowed time slot. After the experiment, they filled questionnaires which evaluate the performance of the group and the individual participants.

5   Analyzed Dataset

From the nature of this project and the collected data corpus. The first interesting research questions are:

- Did the Chinese-speaker participants changed their behaviors when they are discussing in L1 language (Chinese) and in L2 language (Japanese)?
- If they did, what they changed and how they changed?

Therefore, in this specific paper, we focus on the analysis of the activities of Chinese speakers in unbalanced condition (hereafter C-J sessions) and in homogeneous condition (hereafter C-C sessions). Due to the complexity of the controlled factors like native languages of the participant, balance of genders, duplication of discussion topics, two-time experiments and so on in composing the experiment groups. Not all participants could participate the experiment for exactly two times (one C-C or J-J experiment and one C-J experiment). Some of them participated for only once. Among the main target of this project, the nine Chinese-speaker participant, seven of them completed the two settings of experiments. In this paper, we focus on these seven participants and analyzed a subset of the collected data corpus. They were organized in two C-C experiments. Participants S1, S4, and S5 are in the same C-C group while the other one participant in this group could not make to participate another C-J experiment. On the other hand, participants S2, S3, S6, and S7 are in the same C-C group. In addition to the two C-C sessions, participant S1 S7 also participated in seven C-J experiments individually. 19 individual native Japanese speakers participated in these C-J experiments. Two of them participated twice in C-J experiments. In order to prevent the duplication of discussion topics, they did not participate J-J experiments. One of the two experiment sessions, brain-storming style discussion is analyzed in this work. This sums up to a subset of the data corpus which is comprised of two C-C sessions and 7 -J sessions where seven Chinese-speaker participants joined one C-C experiment and one C-J experiment each, and the Japanese participants of C-J sessions are different individuals in most of the cases.

Table 1 shows the summary of the analyzed subset of the data corpus regarding to how they uttered during the C-C experiments and C-J experiments. The voice activities of the subjects are detected by the tool, Praat [2] using default parameters. Considering the length of experiment sessions, 15 min ($= 900$ s), the participant S1 and S7 can be observed to be active in both C-C and C-J settings while the other participants were not. Especially S6 was nearly not participating in the C-J session. He had a silent period up to 623 s which is longer than 2/3 of the whole session. This is probably due to low-confidence (or low proficiency) in the communication using Japanese language.

Table 1. Summary of the analyzed subset of the data corpus. *Utterance* columns show the basic statistical information of the utterances of Chinese-speaker subject S1-S7 in the Chinese-speaker only sessions (C-C rows) and unbalanced ones (C-J rows). *Silent* columns show the corresponding information in the periods when the subject did not speak. "num" denote number of times while "total," "min," "max," "mean," and "std" denote the total, minimum, maximum, mean, and standard deviation of the duration in seconcs

		Utterance						Silence			
		num	total	min	max	mean	std	min	max	mean	std
C-C	S1	233	333.51	0.06	10.09	1.43	1.58	0.30	17.60	2.48	3.43
	S2	44	54.43	0.35	4.70	1.24	0.90	0.44	124.17	19.16	29.71
	S3	63	130.93	0.41	7.32	2.08	1.49	0.27	259.08	10.95	36.80
	S4	63	112.39	0.06	7.18	1.78	1.46	0.34	120.85	12.46	23.52
	S5	44	149.66	0.14	23.38	3.40	4.06	0.31	84.26	15.72	21.57
	S6	72	168.46	0.26	27.33	2.34	3.41	0.08	122.70	9.99	20.06
	S7	180	437.92	0.11	23.05	2.43	3.06	0.30	24.69	2.69	3.92
C-J	S1	268	398.76	0.16	7.98	1.49	1.20	0.11	20.19	1.89	2.82
	S2	110	77.91	0.06	3.66	0.71	0.77	0.34	138.61	7.58	15.17
	S3	54	80.81	0.15	5.28	1.50	1.91	0.30	36.92	3.28	4.70
	S4	141	161.58	0.12	5.68	1.15	1.04	0.18	55.75	5.28	9.26
	S5	65	150.08	0.18	8.54	2.31	2.00	0.22	206.10	11.59	34.49
	S6	17	17.81	0.14	3.07	1.05	0.89	0.42	623.42	50.10	149.37
	S7	233	356.84	0.17	7.50	1.53	1.25	0.10	21.10	2.43	3.25

Table 2 shows the ratio of C-J rows over C-C rows in Table 1 and make it easier to observe the behavior changes of the participants between the two settings. Following the observations in Table 1, participant S6's activity dropped dramatically in the discussion with Japanese participants. Interestingly, although there is no obvious difference in the total amount of utterances between the two settings, it can be observed that the participants tended to speak shorter utterances more frequently in the discussion with Japanese participants than with Chinese speakers. This can be caused by the nature characteristics of Japanese language comparing to Chinese language, or due to the lower ability to compose long sentences in speaking a L2 language. Regarding to the silent periods, there is also tendency that the participants had shorter silent periods. Combing with the previous observation, the communication occurred in C-J experiments tend to be progressed more dynamically, shorter utterances, shorter silence, and change turns more frequently.

Figure 2 depicts the speaking activities in comparing with other participants in the same group. Considering that there are four participants in each group, if all of the participants contributed to the discussion equally, then the ratio should be around 1/4 (=25%). From the graph, it can be observed that S1

Table 2. Ratio of C-J rows over C-C rows of Table 1

	Utterance						Silence			
	num	total	min	max	mean	std	min	max	mean	std
S1	115.0%	119.6%	285.7%	79.1%	103.9%	75.8%	34.5%	114.7%	75.9%	82.4%
S2	250.0%	143.1%	18.2%	77.9%	57.3%	85.0%	78.9%	111.6%	39.6%	51.0%
S3	85.7%	61.7%	36.7%	72.2%	72.0%	128.9%	111.8%	14.3%	30.0%	12.8%
S4	223.8%	143.8%	214.3%	79.1%	64.2%	71.1%	52.3%	46.1%	42.4%	39.4%
S5	147.7%	100.3%	122.9%	36.5%	67.9%	49.3%	70.5%	244.6%	73.7%	159.9%
S6	23.6%	10.6%	55.0%	11.2%	44.8%	26.1%	525.0%	508.1%	501.2%	744.5%
S7	129.4%	81.5%	152.7%	32.5%	63.0%	40.8%	32.9%	85.5%	90.4%	82.8%
Avg	139.3%	94.4%	126.5%	55.5%	67.6%	68.2%	129.4%	160.7%	121.9%	167.5%

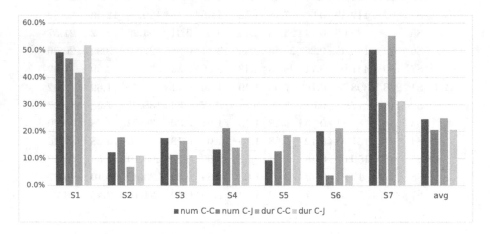

Fig. 2. Comparison with other participants in the same group. The graph shows the ratio between the total number and total duration of utterances of the Chinese-speaker participants, S1-S7 and the total values of all four participants in each session

and S7 spoke around 50% of the total amount of their groups in C-C sessions. Both of them were the participants who spoke most even in the C-J sessions. This may come from their personality that they are more open to the others and are active in collaborating with others. Also, their proficiency in Japanese can be considered high so that they could also keep the roles in the discussion with native speakers. However, there are obvious drops of S7 in C-J session but there were no dramatic differences in S1. This may happen because relatively lower ability of S7 in Japanese language or may come from the influences of the Japanese participants. It is difficult to tell the reason why this happen merely from the data. Not depicted in the graph but from the raw data, the percentages of the amount of utterances of the three Japanese participants in S1's C-J session were 16.1%, 17.4%, and 14.6%. On the other hand, the percentages in S7's case were 33.7%, 20.7%, and 14.4%. The discussion was more equally distributed among all of the participants in the later group. Also considering the fact that the situation where single participant occupied 50% of the time did not happen in Japanese (J-J) groups. It may imply that participant S7 was better collaborating with other Japanese participants.

6   Analysis Based on Dialogue Acts

Qualitative analysis of what the types of the utterances were can provide more insights in how the communication among the participants were actually done during the experiment. The utterances were then annotated with dialogue acts (DAs) according to ISO 24617-2 [5] standard. After the annotation, not all but 26 dialogue acts were observed in the nine sessions. In order to analyze the contributions to the discussion, we further divide the dialogue acts into the following four categories.

Task: the DAs that are related to make the discussion task in progress. From the distribution of this category, how well individual participants were contributing to the discussion are expected to be able to be observed. This category include the following DAs: *Agreement, Disagreement, Answer, Completion, Inform, Question, Check-Question, Set-Question, Suggest*

Feedback: the DAs that are related to feedbacks to other participants or ask for from other participants. These DAs are expected understand the responsiveness and therefore the engagement in the task of individual participants. This category includes the following DAs: *Allonegative, Allopositive, Autonegative, Autopositive*

Turn Management: the DAs that are related to turn management. These DAs are expected to be able to see the activeness of the participants during the discussion. This category includes the following DAs: *Turn Grab, Turn Keep, Turn Release, Turn Take*

Others the other DAs that are not belonged to either of the three categories above. *Apology, Accept Apology, Init-Greeting, Return-Greeting, Opening, Thanking, Self-Correction, Stalling*

Table 3 shows the summary of the DAs of Chinese-speaker participants in each category. Others category does not reveal useful information related to the analysis and is omitted here. From the data, all participants except S1 decreased the ratio of task oriented utterances in C-J sessions. Three of them decreased to be around 50% of C-C sessions. This may imply that they could not contribute to the discussion as the situation where they can use their native language. Turn manage utterances are also observed to decrease significantly in C-J sessions from most of the participants (S2-S6). This suggested that the turns were switched much less smooth in C-J sessions. On the other hands, all participants except S1 increased the ratio in their feedbacks in the experiment with Japanese participants. Combining with the observation above, this may imply that they are less active to obtain the initiative in the discussion and may be more collaborative to the other participants in C-J experiment. This may also imply that they switched communication styles in the two cultures where Chinese are often

Table 3. Summary of the dialogue acts in each category. The columns named "C" or "J" show the data of "C-C" sessions and "C-J" sessions. "#" columns show the number of utterances and "%" columns mean the ratio of the number of utterances in that category within individual subjects. J/C columns show the ratio of "J %" columns and "C %" columns

	Task					Feedback					Turn Management				
	C #	C %	J #	J %	J/C %	C #	C %	J #	J %	J/C %	C #	C %	J #	J %	J/C %
S1	123	53.9	188	71.5	132.5	75	32.9	30	11.4	34.7	11	4.8	20	7.6	157.6
S2	18	43.9	22	22.0	50.1	17	41.5	67	67.0	161.6	5	12.2	4	4.0	32.8
S3	41	65.1	28	57.1	87.8	4	6.3	12	24.5	385.7	12	19.0	1	2.0	10.7
S4	33	54.1	68	48.9	90.4	14	23.0	53	38.1	166.1	13	21.3	5	3.6	16.9
S5	27	61.4	29	46.0	75.0	1	2.3	18	28.6	1257.1	15	34.1	3	4.8	14.0
S6	41	56.9	5	29.4	51.6	16	22.2	10	58.8	264.7	12	16.7	1	5.9	35.3
S7	101	58.0	73	32.6	56.1	55	31.6	114	50.9	161.0	9	5.2	14	6.3	120.8

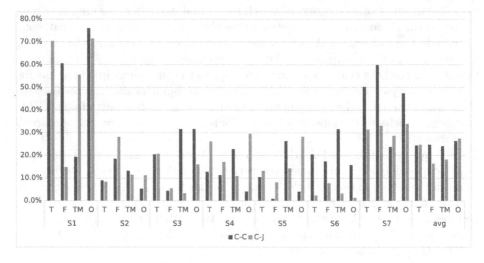

Fig. 3. Percentage of the numbers of utterances done by each the Chinese-speaker participants in each group regarding to utterance categories. "T", "F", "TM", and "O" denotes Task, Feedback, Turn Management, and Others categories respectively

considered individualistic and Japanese are often considered collectivistic. Overall, S1 and S7 were active in the discussion while S2-S6 are less active, this may cause by the both personality and language proficiency. Among S1 and S7, S1 seems to have the tendency of one-way communication, i.e. speak by herself, and was less attentive to the other participants. From these data, S7 is perceived to have high communication skill among these participants.

Figure 3 shows the ratio of number of utterances in each category among all participants in the group. Again, if their utterances are equally to the others, the ratios will be around 25%. From this graph, S1 and S2 are observed to dominating their groups in the C-C condition. S1 became even stronger in C-J condition and may even overwhelmed the Japanese participants (more than 70% of tasked oriented utterances were done by this single person in a four-people group). S7 decreased his dominance in C-J session and seemed to better adopted himself in Japanese style communication. S2 and S3 did not show much different roles in C-J sessions, while S4 and S5 could contribute even more than in C-J condition. This may because there were no dominating partners in the C-J session. Comparing to other participants, S6's activity had a dramatic drop in C-J session. He is the one who needs support among the seven participants.

7   Conclusions

Most participants largely changed their behaviors between the two conditions, talking in their L1 (Chinese) with other Chinese speakers and talking in L2 (Japanese) with native Japanese speakers. However, from the small dataset, it is hard to find unified tendency among the participants, and there were diversities in their behavior changes. This may be caused by their personality, language proficiency, understanding of Japanese culture, knowledge of the discussion topics, and the communication partners. However, from the analysis of their activities, the cues for their language proficiency and how well they can communicate with native Japanese speakers could be found. Among the seven analyzed participants, two were leading the discussion in both Chinese and Japanese settings, one significantly dropped his performance, and the other four decreased their activities to some degree.

Future direction of this work is to find the what kinds of computer aided support can be realized in what kind of situations during collaborative work of unbalanced group members. A short-term goal is to find the moments where non-native speakers have difficult in expressing their thoughts and provide handily hints in runtime. We are now working on the classification of the causes of short pauses of the participants, the participant know what to say but cannot find an appropriate word or expression, the participant is deliberating a new idea, or the participant is just listening to the others from multimodal low-level signals. In order to work on such detection task, the data corpus is still small, it is necessary for us to conduct more experiments to increase the number of groups for more generalized results. Further investigation on individual modalities may provide interesting findings of how the participants changed in details. For example, acoustic analysis may find the hesitation of the participant and further help to provide support to he or she.

Acknowledgements. This research is partially supported by KAKENHI: Grant-in-Aid for Scientific Research (A), Grant No. 19H01120.

References

1. Aran, O., Gatica-Perez, D.: One of a kind: Inferring personality impressions in meetings. In: Proceedings of 15th ACM International Conference on Multimodal Interaction (ICMI 2013), Sydney, Australia, December 2013
2. Boersma, P., Weenink, D.: Praat: doing phonetics by computer [computer software] version 6.0.40. http://www.praat.org/, May 2018
3. Cabinet Office, Government of Japan: Annual report on the ageing society: 2019. Technical report, July 2019
4. Claes, L., Vandereycken, W., Luyten, P., Soenens, B., Pieters, G., Vertommen, H.: Personality prototypes in eating disorders based on the big five model. J. Pers. Disord. **20**(4), 401–416 (2006)
5. Ishii, C.T., Liu, C., Ishiguro, H., Hagita, N.: Head motions during dialogue speech and nod timing control in humanoid robots. In: Proceedings of the 5th ACM/IEEE International Conference on Human-Robot Interaction (HRI 2010), pp. 293–300 (2010)
6. (JASSO), J.S.S.O.: Survey results of enrollment status of foreign students in fy2018. Technical report, January 2019
7. Joshi, M.P., Davis, E.B., Kathuria, R., Ken Weidner I, C.: Experiential learning process: exploring teaching and learning of strategic management framework through the winter survival exercise. J. Manag. Educ. **29**(5), 672–695 (2005)
8. Mori, Y., Hasegawa, A., Mori, J.: The trends and developments of L2 Japanese research in the 2010s. Lang. Train. **54**(1), 90–127 (2020)
9. Nihei, F., Nakano, Y.I., Hayashi, Y., Huang, H.H., Okada, S.: Predicting influential statements in group discussions using speech and head motion information. In: 16th International Conference on Multimodal Interaction (ICMI 2014), Istanbul, pp. 136–143, November 2014
10. Okada, S., Nakano, Y., Hayashi, Y., Takase, Y., Nitta, K.: Estimating communication skills using dialogue acts and nonverbal features in multiple discussion datasets. In: 18th ACM International Conference on Multimodal Interaction (ICMI 2016), Tokyo, pp. 169–176, November 2016
11. Schiavo, G., Cappelletti, A., Mencarini, E., Stock, O., Zancanaro, M.: Overt or subtle? Supporting group conversations with automatically targeted directives. In: Proceedings of the 19th International Conference on Intelligent User Interfaces (IUI 2014), pp. 225–234 (2014)
12. Stroud, R.: Second language group discussion participation: a closer examination of 'barriers' and 'boosts'. In: Proceedings of the International Conference on Education and Learning (ICEL), Tokyo, January 2017
13. Yamamoto, S., Taguchi, K., Ijuin, K., Umata, I., Nishida, M.: Multimodal corpus of multiparty conversations in L1and L2 languages and findings obtained from it. Lang. Resour. Eval. **49**, 857–882 (2015). https://doi.org/10.1007/s10579-015-9299-2

Serious Games in STEM: Online Collaborative Design of a Lunar Simulator

Chantil Hunt Estevez, Joshua Jones, Sujan Shrestha, and Giovanni Vincenti[✉]

University of Baltimore, Baltimore, MD 21201, USA
{chantil.huntestevez,gvincenti}@ubalt.edu

Abstract. Development logs and video game streaming can be used as a tool to improve the quality of student projects and create a high-quality product that can be utilized by a general audience for STEM engagement purposes. University of Baltimore's Lunar Surface navigation simulator was designed to fulfill NASA SUITS 2021 challenge requirements. Our goal was to design a user interface that could help lost individuals navigate through unknown terrain while using augmented reality. Participants were prompted to explore a virtual world using a menu designed for augmented reality technology and later leave feedback to help our team refine the design. This experience shows how the effort associated with collecting feedback through live streaming and remote user testing can lead students to have an improved educational experience and produce a high-quality final product.

Keywords: Codesign · Social media · Virtual Reality · Student engagement

1 Introduction

Development logs and video game streaming can be used as tools to engage and motivate students as they complete curricular and extra-curricular work. University of Baltimore's Lunar Surface Navigation Simulator was designed to fulfill the requirements for the NASA SUITS (Spacesuit User Interface Technologies for Students) 2021 Design Challenge; specifically for Human-In-The-Loop Testing (HITL) via remote online hosting sites like Itch.io. Our goal was to design a user interface (UI) that would help lost individuals navigate through unknown terrain while using an augmented reality (AR) headset.

This manuscript describes how development logs paired with online platforms and video games can be used to engage the individuals on STEM themes. We explore the ways web based publishing and streaming platforms like Itch.io and Twitch can be used to promote student engagement in a remote environment. Finally, we discuss how video games can be used as a learning tool in support of curricular activities designed to let students master an educational topic, boosting engagement and comprehension via unorthodox web-based verbal communication and technical documentation.

© Springer Nature Switzerland AG 2021
G. Meiselwitz (Ed.): HCII 2021, LNCS 12775, pp. 223–235, 2021.
https://doi.org/10.1007/978-3-030-77685-5_18

2   Background

In the last decade, public and private entities have increasingly shared data related to their focus of operations. In some cases the main driver is transparency, such as with governments [6], in other cases the interest aligns with the organization's operations [8], and in yet other cases it is a mix of both [10]. No matter what is the reason that pushes an organization to release data, the variety and contextualization of what is available becomes a treasure trove for academic settings [15], especially in terms of student engagement [17].

The subject of this paper is related to the NASA SUITS[1] Design Challenge, which is one of seven Artemis open challenges created to engage students in research and development efforts to take the first woman and the next man to the Moon by the year 2024. This challenge in particular focuses on the space suit as a system rather than just a piece of garment, aiding astronauts in the performance of their tasks while on an Extra-Vehicular Activity (EVA), or space walk. Every year the challenge offers a new scenario, meant to engage students who are not necessarily specialized in fields related to space exploration, thus not constrained by years of "lessons learned" and consequently fostering unbridled creativity and out-of-the-box thinking.

The outreach aspect associated with SUITS brought front and center the pervasive effect that social media has had on education and its integration in nearly every aspect of the classroom [1]. Whether social media technology is part of the pedagogy or simply the means that teachers and students utilize to collaborate [16], its role is undeniably here to stay. Even though it is not enough to just add a social media component to a course in order to improve the students' experience [7], often times even courses that do not utilize explicitly social media will benefit from informal online communities [5]. Implementing a social media component to courses for adult students, such as the predominant population at our institution, fosters problem-solving and learning [11].

3   ARGOS

An interdisciplinary team of students from the University of Baltimore has participated to the NASA SUITS Design Challenge since academic year 2018-19. The team create ARGOS, or Augmented Reality Guidance and Operations System [14]. The original version of the system includes three main components, as shown in Fig. 1. The most important element is the Extra-Vehicular Activity (EVA) simulator, which represents the Heads Up Display (HUD) that the astronaut on a spacewalk would wear. This system is implemented on a Magic Leap 1 AR device. The second element is a telemetry simulation, which is responsible for emulating the data stream that a space suit may generate. Lastly, we have an Intra-Vehicular Activity (IVA) simulator, which mimics assistive operations that other astronauts within the station or personnel at NASA's Mission Control Center may provide to the EVA operator.

---

[1] https://microgravityuniversity.jsc.nasa.gov/nasasuits.cfm.

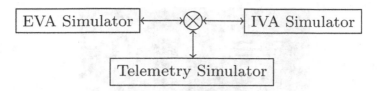

Fig. 1. Schematic overview of the main components and connectivity in ARGOS.

The original contribution has become an evolving platform that now hosts several technologies, including an augmented reality application that can be controlled by the user as well as remotely through a mobile application, different systems that provide data communications, processing, and storage. Table 1 summarizes the evolution of the system in response to the main challenge posed by the NASA SUITS technical leads.

Table 1. Main technical task associated with the last three years of NASA SUITS and the technical features implemented in ARGOS.

Year	Main challenge	ARGOS features
2018–19	Technical Repair	Step-by-Step Repair Guidance
		3D Animations for each Repair Step
		Remote HUD Assistance and Control
2019–20	Scientific Sampling	Step-by-Step Sampling Guidance
		Wireless Breadcrumb Network
2020–21	Lunar Surface Navigation	HUD Navigational Guidance System
		Containerized Distributed Processing System
		Self-Contained Positioning System

As the tasks change, the user interface has to adapt as well. One of the main requirements of the Challenge is that students perform user testing. During previous years, we were able to do so effectively, since our institution has several facilities dedicated to User Experience. Last year, we created a user interface that was extremely effective in teaching novices how to collect geological samples using the AR system [20], as shown in Fig. 2.

This year, however, given restrictions imposed in response to COVID-19 to educational institutions [9], we had to shift our operations to account for contact-free user testing. Even with the best precautions, the Magic Leap 1 device sits tightly around the user's head, covering the eyes and sitting on the bridge of the nose. Even though Augmented and Virtual Reality (VR) are quite different [2] and a review of user experience research methodologies for AR devices [3] confirmed the impossibility of such testing for our timeline and resources, eventually we chose to use the video game/simulation route [4], which allowed for

Fig. 2. Scientific Sampling example on the ML1. The design of the UI is by Claudia Yee [20] and the implementation by Michael Vandi (manuscript in the works).

satisfactory results even though we are utilizing a different medium since many of the measurable goals overlap [13]. Consequently, we decided to entrust the simulation described in this paper as a way to test the usability of our UI that may help astronauts explore the Lunar surface.

3.1   Academic Context

Over the last two years, several courses at our institution have contextualized the assignments related to the subject matter around open challenges, creating an engaging way that students prefer to typical projects for regular and capstone courses [18]. The project presented in this article does the opposite, where students decided to take an open challenge, NASA SUITS in this case, and utilize it as the subject of their project. This fact further supports the great engagement that open challenges may generate in students.

Table 2. Assignments and deliverables for the *Games for Learning* course.

Assignment	*Deliverable(s)*
Prototype Design	UI design, storyboard, paper/digital prototype
Instructional Design Document	Game instructions, procedures, and guidelines
Game Development	A fully working game
Usability Testing	Usability testing methods and results

The course that sets the context for this project is "Games for Learning," which is one of the electives associated with the "Serious Games" requirement for the degree in *Simulation and Game Design* at the University of Baltimore. The students were part of the course in the Fall 2020 semester, and four assignments, reported in Table 2, required students to incrementally develop a fully working product throughout the semester.

3.2 Lunar Surface Navigation Simulator

Our Lunar Surface Navigation Simulator, shown in Fig. 3, was designed to meet the requirements for the course described earlier and to fulfill NASA SUITS 2021 challenge requirements. Specifically our group decided to use this simulation to conduct Human In The Loop Testing via remote online hosting sites like Itch.io. Our goal was identify ways we could help lost individuals problem-solve through unknown terrain while using a simulated environment. Created in Unity URP (Universal Render Pipeline), the navigation system was polished thanks to player feedback during development. Participants were prompted to explore a Lunar Surface model using a menu designed for AR technology. All feedback received during the development and testing phases further helped our team refine our design of the AR solution.

Fig. 3. Latest iteration of the simulation. Used for user testing and posted on Itch.io for free browser play at https://unachanti.itch.io/astrobees.

4 Integrating Scientific Data into the Simulation

In order to recreate the site missions within the simulation, we sought to reference data that was gathered from previous Apollo missions[2]. In this data set, NASA had provided images of the foot trails left by astronauts in the Apollo 17 mission, as they wandered from their starting point to a location of interest, and back. In these images of the Apollo 17 mission, "the foot trails, including the last path made on the moon by humans, are easily distinguished from the dual tracks left by the lunar rover, which remains parked east of the lander" [12]. These images were used to reference how a minimap could be used as a guide to help IVA operators and astronauts orient those walking on the lunar surface. A program based on artificial intelligence (AI) was utilized to map potential routes while avoiding obstacles, like craters and large rock formations.

---

[2] https://www.nasa.gov/mission_pages/LRO/news/apollo-sites.html.

Utilizing NASA's open source CGI Moonkit[3], we recreated the surfacetexture and map of the Lunar Surface. The primary goal of these image maps is to help recreate a 3D render of the moon as accurately as possible. These images were captured using Orbiter Cameras and Lasers[4] to measure the height and face of the Lunar surface. Thanks to the engineers and scientists responsible for recording and releasing this data set of the Lunar Reconnaissance Orbiter (LRO) mission to the public, we were able to recreate the moon. This feature helped us create a visual narrative to promote our work for the NASA SUITS challenge within a Remote Unity Simulation.

A 3D model library gathered and archived by NASA's team of engineers and artists is available for all those who wish to have and utilize 3D model references[5]. Through this library one can find a variety of models that range from 3D Apollo Mission Maps to theoretical designs of tools that could one day be used in future missions. The simulation benefited from using this library as a reference for accurate 3D model development and detailed mapping.

To project and visually inform players of the site location they are on and maintain the thematic narrative of space exploration, the simulation also included models directly derived from NASA 3D library. Among the models used from the 3D model library, was the Deep Space Habitat (DSH)[6] model sourced from The Habitat Systems Project. The DSH model was created by a team of experts to "develop sustainable living quarters, workspaces, and laboratories for next-generation space missions."[7] For the simulation, this model was used to communicate the starting location of the player as well as orient the Mapping AI. Alongside the DHS model, A Space Exploration Vehicle model (SEV)[8] was added to orient the players and AI mapping functionality to a secondary location. The Space Exploration Vehicle was used as a placeholder to a rover model, for a simulated repair task.

5 Collaborative Design Process

A collaborative design process is essential in the development of a product. However, given the societal context that COVID-19 has materialized during the implementation of ARGOS, we were forced to resort to different strategies for engaging potential users. We ultimately chose to leverage social media to implement a distributed co-design model based on [19] with modifications that were necessary for the context of this project. This section describes the evolution of the simulation and reports some measurables related to the live streaming sessions.

---

[3] https://www.nasa.gov/feature/goddard/2019/cgi-moon-kit-as-a-form-of-visual-storytelling.
[4] https://svs.gsfc.nasa.gov/4720.
[5] https://nasa3d.arc.nasa.gov/images.
[6] https://nasa3d.arc.nasa.gov/detail/nmss-hdu.
[7] https://www.nasa.gov/exploration/technology/deep_space_habitat/.
[8] https://nasa3d.arc.nasa.gov/detail/nmss-sev.

5.1   The Evolution

Before development began, we created a paper prototype, shown in Fig. 4, to quickly visualize how certain UI elements would look within the simulation. In this prototype, we visited how a basic menu system would react to button interactions and scenarios. Imagining how an astronaut would travel with a direct line of communication with Earth and a scenario where the player would be without any connection to Earth was pivotal for the development of further iterations.

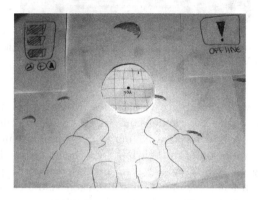

Fig. 4. Paper Prototype of the Simulation. The initial stages of development began conceptualizing the mechanics on paper.

Problem-solving became the learning principle used for the first iteration of Simulation Development, shown in Fig. 5. The rules of the game were for the players to orient themselves using only a minimap and a compass as tools to travel to 10 sites before time ran out. Prior to play, users were informed of how to play the simulation as a means to aid their conceptual knowledge pools, then observed to better understand the individual's methods of problem-solving. Although individuals who playtested applied themselves in different methods, completing the mission proved to be difficult and distracting for everyone who tried. We identified the method used to communicate directions as the source of the problem.

This outcome, however, motivated players to try again. Upon second play, we engaged with users in learning community mockups, where we as playtesters would audibly cue and read out loud the instructions to those individuals. Doing so, the individuals reported they were able to engage better and situate their problem-solving skills to their prior knowledge, which ultimately helped them boost their score. However, none were able to collect all sites successfully.

In the third iteration of development, shown in Fig. 6, much of the design changed after user feedback from previous iterations. This prototype solidified the problem solving learning principle as a base to understand user interaction. We chose to expand the button functionality of the game to observe player

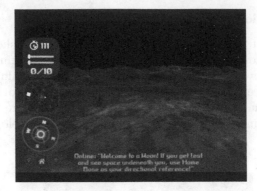

Fig. 5. Second Iteration of the Simulation. Created to test Navigation and comprehend how people learn via Video Games.

decision making as well as enhance visual cues. Much of the UI was revamped and re-designed for easier comprehension. In this version, the simulation was still oriented on site collecting as a means to map and orient players to their location. If the user were to fail in their mission, the game would simply prompt the player to try again as in previous iterations. However, despite updates that were made, users still felt the simulation still lacked visual cues that would help orient themselves inside the world without the minimap.

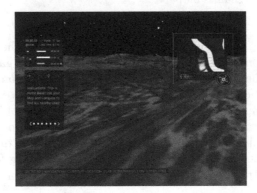

Fig. 6. Third Iteration of the Simulation. A prototype designed to help conceptualize Navigation Features.

The latest iteration of the Lunar Surface Simulator, shown in Fig. 7, focused on a distinct lens from previous versions. In contrast to previous attempts, this version was released on Itch.io for HTML5 browser play, along with options to download for those without browser compatibility. All feedback gathered from past iterations pointed to a glaring issue within the Navigation system itself. In order to address the human centered design flaw, we devised a multistep plan in order to aid players with varying preferences of GPS-like orientation. To further enhance the minimap system, an AI was programmed to follow a path and read the height of unknown topography, as a laser would, in order to determine a best route for the player. This AI program collaborated with Unity's Navigation Tool to avoid significant obstacles that could injure the player. A second option for navigation was also offered for those who preferred visual orientation cues in the world, and a compass arrow model was created to pop-up and orient a player upon selecting a pre-saved location they desired to reach.

Fig. 7. Fourth Iteration of the Simulation. Using AI to help players navigate across the Lunar Surface.

5.2   Streaming Events

Participants were prompted to explore this virtual environment using a menu designed for AR technology and later leave feedback to help our team refine development for a course project. All feedback received during the development and testing phases further helped our team refine our project efforts. The bulk of the feedback from social media was collected over three live streaming sessions on Twitch, where participants were able to interact with the developers. A summary of the participation for each event is reported in Table 3.

The data shows a satisfactory engagement with potential users. The amount of viewers may be considered low based on empirical comparison with other live streaming events geared towards the general population, however it was a significant number when trying to conduct a meaningful and constructive collaborative design process. Since only one student was managing the live stream as well as collecting data, the pace was not overwhelming and the amount of feedback and suggestions was reasonable to track by a single person.

Table 3. Data about the live streaming sessions on Twitch.

Session	Avg Viewers	Max Viewers	Unique Viewers	Chat Messages	Duration
1	3	6	8	41	1 h 23 min
2	3	5	14	93	3 h 00 min
3	2	4	16	26	2 h 27 min
Totals			38	160	6 h 50 min

6   Discussion

The primary outcomes associated with this project involve two main goals: collecting user feedback to improve the overall product, and the "lessons learned" from the students carrying out the project. We believe that both goals were met successfully and the overall process can be replicated at other institutions and to obtain similar benefits.

6.1   User Feedback

The 160 comments that were collected during the live stream sessions gave helpful feedback to the developers. A review of the data shows that there were three main topic areas: technology, user experience, and STEM engagement.

Technology. The simulation was created in Unity, which offers a feature to export a project into a format that can be easily utilized through web browsers. However, the end product is not consistent on different platforms. For this reason, some feedback was dependent on the platform in use. The main issue that was reported was that the navigation map was not being displayed properly or at all. Another issue was the way the pointer affected the simulation. As everyone has different pointing devices, such as a mouse or a touchpad, along with different individual mannerisms, some users had difficulties adapting to the mechanics.

User Experience. The second main category of feedback was associated with the interface. Several comments report that the size and type of fonts were not legible clearly, and that some icons were not interpreted properly. These comments were particularly helpful in modifying the simulation to include more legible fonts as well as intuitive visual elements. One user also reported that the way the map was represented made them misinterpret their actual direction, leading them to a crater. We considered this a major issue, since the simulation utilizes realistic data and ranges of motion, which means that falling into a crater would probably mean that the astronaut may not be able to get out of it on their own.

STEM Engagement. The comments also indicated that this simulation sparked an interest in the subject matter. In particular, some participants commented on the lighting in relation to full exposure to sunlight, as well as how shades may be affected. One comment suggested that the simulation should include ways to interact with the environment, so that the user may learn how objects and forces behave when there is lower gravity. These comments were particularly encouraging, as the main long-term goal of this simulation is to let enthusiasts explore the Lunar surface, giving them a realistic and educational depiction of what astronauts may experience.

6.2   Students' Experience Report

A very significant aspect of this work is the effect that the collaborative design approach had on the students who were ultimately responsible for the simulation. Both students are working on an undergraduate degree in Simulation and Game Design. The first report comes from Chantil Hunt Estevez, the lead of this project.

> My tasks for this simulation were focused on the development and implementation of scientifically accurate models and assets for the game. The simulation was a development created to prove a theory, and then became the very backbone for remote user testing for UB's AstroBees in the 2021 NASA SUITS Challenge. I am not much of a programmer, which is why I took advantage of open source tutorials that helped greatly in the learning and development stages of this project. Thanks to the wonderful remote collaboration of a small team of developers we were able to make a product that served as a useful feedback engine.
>
> Going into Simulation and Video Game design, I would have never imagined the utility of Simulations and Games for Learning. The public development of this simulation became a great way to reach out to people via virtual gaming spaces, such as Itch.io and Twitch. We were able to gather great feedback on our progress and ideas because of the ways we interacted with the people. Itch.io in particular became the best ground to receive constructive feedback on our Simulation from people all over the world during a global pandemic. Working on this project has been a rewarding learning experience that opened up a lot of ideas of the potential of video games and virtual social spaces as a means to interact with people on topics regarding STEM.

Joshua Jones is the second student involved with the development of this project. He had a significant role as he took on a considerable amount of programming over a short time span, far beyond what is typically required in university-level undergraduate courses.

> My contribution to the Lunar Surface Navigation Simulation was tailored to back-end programming. Developing with C# programming language, on Unity object-oriented scripting. During this process, I construct

scripts that give game objects within the simulation engine their behavior; Using Object-oriented programming(OOP). In a collaborative effort during the programming process, implementation of player animation was developed by 3D modeler Chantil. From this, development of an animator controller script was created to give specific user/player related input distinctive movement. After programming each script, multiple iterations of testing and compiling was conducted to ensure proper functionality.

While designing scripts using Object-oriented programming(OOP), I learned the importance of commenting behind my own work. In large projects like this it is imperative to leave comments that your colleague can follow and understand your contribution. To help improve, correct or build upon especially when teleworking and developing a project through software from different locations. I would want programmers to understand that there are a variety of ways to manipulate a script into performing a task, make sure that you write a script that is readable, does not affect the program outside the intended purpose and easily can be read and contributed to without difficulty.

Both students demonstrate that the complexity of the project was significant but did not deter them from pursuing it. They both had to adapt quickly to a changing work environment because of COVID-related closings, as well as requirements. Overall their performance was exemplary, and the product they created is a great asset not only for our institution but also for enthusiasts who wish to learn more about the Lunar surface and what it actually looks like.

7   Conclusions

The project as well as the way in which the students decided to carry out the development process offers an insight into how collaborative design may be successfully injected into undergraduate education. The outcomes reported directly by the students as well as the overall quality of the final product speak highly of how remote user testing over social media can lead to greater engagement in the subject matter and an outstanding educational experience.

References

1. Abe, P., Jordan, N.A.: Integrating social media into the classroom curriculum. About Campus **18**(1), 16–20 (2013)
2. Azuma, R.T.: A survey of augmented reality. Presence: Teleoperators Virtual Environ. **6**(4), 355–385 (1997)
3. Dünser, A., Billinghurst, M.: Evaluating augmented reality systems. In: Furht, B. (ed.) Handbook of Augmented Reality, pp. 289–307. Springer, New York (2011). https://doi.org/10.1007/978-1-4614-0064-6_13
4. Gee, J.P.: What video games have to teach us about learning and literacy. Comput. Entertain. (CIE) **1**(1), 20–20 (2003)

5. Hamilton, W.A., Garretson, O., Kerne, A.: Streaming on twitch: fostering participatory communities of play within live mixed media. In: Proceedings of the SIGCHI Conference on Human Factors in Computing Systems, pp. 1315–1324 (2014)
6. Janssen, M., Charalabidis, Y., Zuiderwijk, A.: Benefits, adoption barriers and myths of open data and open government. Inf. Syst. Manag. **29**(4), 258–268 (2012)
7. Krutka, D.G., Nowell, S., Whitlock, A.M.: Towards a social media pedagogy: successes and shortcomings in educative uses of Twitter with teacher candidates. J. Technol. Teach. Educ. **25**(2), 215–240 (2017)
8. Mangal, A., Kumar, N.: Using big data to enhance the bosch production line performance: a Kaggle challenge. In: 2016 IEEE International Conference on Big Data (Big Data), pp. 2029–2035. IEEE (2016)
9. Marinoni, G., Van't Land, H., Jensen, T.: The impact of Covid-19 on higher education around the world. IAU Global Survey Report (2020)
10. Mergel, I.: Open innovation in the public sector: drivers and barriers for the adoption of Challenge.gov. Public Manag. Rev. **20**(5), 726–745 (2018)
11. Mondahl, M., Razmerita, L.: Social media, collaboration and social learning-a case-study of foreign language learning. Electron. J. E-learn. **12**(4), 339–352 (2014)
12. Neal-Jones, N., Zubritsky, E., Cole, S.: NASA spacecraft images offer sharper views of apollo landing sites (2017). https://www.nasa.gov/mission_pages/LRO/news/apollo-sites.html
13. Sánchez, J.L.G., Vela, F.L.G., Simarro, F.M., Padilla-Zea, N.: Playability: analysing user experience in video games. Behav. Inf. Technol. **31**(10), 1033–1054 (2012)
14. Soto Medico, J.P., et al.: ARGOS: a platform for student engagement. In: Proceedings of the 21st Annual Conference on Information Technology Education, p. 298 (2020)
15. Tavegia, S., Braman, J., Vincenti, G., Yancy, B.: Enhancing database courses through the EDNA project: a preliminary framework for the extraction of diverse datasets and analysis. In: Meiselwitz, G. (ed.) HCII 2019. LNCS, vol. 11579, pp. 227–237. Springer, Cham (2019). https://doi.org/10.1007/978-3-030-21905-5_18
16. Tay, E., Allen, M.: Designing social media into university learning: technology of collaboration or collaboration for technology? Educ. Media Int. **48**(3), 151–163 (2011)
17. Vincenti, G.: Engaging IT students through the NASA suits design challenge: an experience report. In: Proceedings of the 20th Annual SIG Conference on Information Technology Education, p. 22 (2019)
18. Vincenti, G.: Open challenges as a way to engage students: an experience report from three undergraduate courses. In: Proceedings of the 21st Annual Conference on Information Technology Education, pp. 200–205 (2020)
19. Walsh, G., Foss, E.: A case for intergenerational distributed co-design: the online kidsteam example. In: Proceedings of the 14th International Conference on Interaction Design and Children, pp. 99–108 (2015)
20. Yee, C.: Wearable augmented reality in procedural tasks: designing an interface used to deliver step-by-step instructions to support novice users in unfamiliar tasks (2020)

Safeguarding Academic Integrity in Crisis Induced Environment: A Case Study of Emirati Engineering and IT Students in a Private University in the UAE

Ajrina Hysaj[1]([✉]) [iD] and Sara Suleymanova[2] [iD]

[1] UOWD College, University of Wollongong in Dubai, Dubai, UAE
Ajrinahysaj@uowdubai.ac.ae
[2] University of Dubai, Dubai, UAE
ssuleymanova@ud.ac.ae

Abstract. This paper discusses the challenges faced by Emirati students enrolled in a private university in the United Arab Emirates. In particular, the study focuses on the development of their academic writing skills. It uses data collected from composition papers written in a semester through the online platform. The data was collected from undergraduate engineering and information technology students and it reports findings of a study examining the effectiveness of promoting Arabic speakers' development of critical and analytical thinking skills using a content with a content-based approach. The data is discussed in relation to development of academic language in an English course through application of skills in an essay format. This study attempts to highlight the value of content-based approach through instructional practices and designing of online authentic assessment tasks. Two groups of engineering and computer science students participated in three different written assessments in the study. Six essay topics were designed considering students linguistic and societal factors. Data were collected via online assessments. The findings revealed significant improvements in the students' academic writing scores and considerable reduction in plagiarism cases was also found. The quantitative and qualitative examination show positive impact of active participation in the online learning platform. Based on these findings, instructional suggestions and caveats are provided.

Keywords: Emirati students · Academic writing · Content-based learning · Online assessment · Plagiarism

1 Introduction

COVID-19 enforced unprecedented circumstances on the education sector throughout the world. The unparalleled conditions created by the pandemic, were followed by unpreceded measures taken by governments and societies around the globe. Educators, policy makers and management of education institutions were the frontline of the pandemic, similar to the health practitioners. The decisions were difficult, time was

G. Meiselwitz (Ed.): HCII 2021, LNCS 12775, pp. 236–245, 2021.
https://doi.org/10.1007/978-3-030-77685-5_19

extremely expensive as the health of children, students, teachers, and administration staff was in jeopardy. Following the advice of WHO (World Health Organisation) education system adjusted to distance learning and teachers around the globe mostly with no prior training on the online platform started live sessions on Zoom, Adobe Connect or WebEx and many other applications. Nevertheless, live sessions did not require an enormous amount of preparation and were not the elephant in the room. The most challenging and time-pressing decisions were related to the fundamentals of teaching and learning processes e.g. preparation of online material, methods of interactions between teachers and students, or students with each other, adaptation of assessment tasks, alignment of curriculum design with the design delivery and training of teachers for a successful and fruitful online experience.

UAE is famous for many reasons e.g. being a haven for architects and engineers of different fields, being a unique business hub, and being home to a large number of federal and private universities international or locally founded. Furthermore, the UAE leadership prides itself for supporting the communities and offering the utmost assistance to citizens and expatriates. All of these dynamics in one way or the other interconnect and create a nurturing environment that nourishes development and prosperity. UAE like other developing economies of the Gulf States is home to a large number of foreign labors from all over the world, who are actively involved in the progress of the nation. As the foreign force outnumbers the local population by two folds to say the least, English language has spread through the years as a lingua franca at all aspects of the society. However, the leadership of the UAE has always emphasised the importance of Arabic and Muslim culture; therefore, English and Arabic are both formal languages in the UAE. However, considering the unprecedented circumstances of Covid 19 and the drastic measures taken my educators worldwide, this paper will analyse the adaptation of online activities and assessment tasks to encourage active participation and to curb plagiarism instances amongst Emirati students enrolled in engineering and information technology courses in a private university based in the United Arab Emirates.

2   Literature Review

2.1   Academic Writing and Emirati Students – Challenges of Linguistic and Societal Nature

Academic writing is one of the greatest challenges for undergraduate and post-graduate students worldwide. Emirati students in the UAE may have studied in English medium or Arabic medium high schools. Moreover, as English is widely spoken in the UAE and its citizens are familiar with the language, they can generally get by even if they do not have any formal education in English language. Emirati undergraduate students wishing to study in an English medium university, require taking IELTS, TOEFL or EmSAT tests and obtaining an overall score as specified by the university they want to enroll.

Academic writing is justifiably seen to be of great value, but despite its rigorous and precise format it may, ironically, not always receive the attention it deserves inside and outside the classroom. As Arabic and English languages have different modes of textual organization, Arabic speakers have increased difficulty in writing academic pieces of work [1, 14, 17]. Another study by Randal and Samimi [27] emphasised that challenges for writing in English include (i) how to differentiate between compounds and modifiers (ii) distinguishing between spoken and written styles in English texts; (iii) differences in alphabets and b) differences in writing styles, and (iv) in that Arabic tends to have more metaphoric phrases and lengthier sentences than English does. Moreover, in the study by Al Fadda [2], students consider particularly difficult to negotiate the difference between spoken and written forms of English language, as well as formalizing a coherent paragraph or determine which skills are important for professional academic writing; and how to avoid grammatical mistakes in their writing.

2.2 Content Based Online Authentic Writing Assessment

Content based teaching and assessing is not new to the ESL (English as a Second Language) field, primarily because it contains sustainable pedagogical and pragmatic teaching approaches. For instance, if we as academic writing teachers are aiming at development of our students writing skills, we can in no way consider this process as a mechanical one that comes as of mere practice of vocabulary and grammar skills. While improvement in vocabulary and grammatical abilities are highly valuable in any language, their acquisition needs to be backed up by development of critical and analytical thinking as well as sustainable content-based material.

The concepts of development of critical and analytical thinking skills have been around since late 90s through the works of Tütünis [31] and continued with studies of Pally [25], Liaw [22], Stam [29] and Singh [30]. Although, critical and analytical thinking skills are difficult to be developed due to their complexity and abstract nature; they are crucial for thought enhancement and linguistic application in an academic setting. Most of the major and minor assessments in academic settings are of written nature. Furthermore, even the spoken tasks require an array of critical and analytical thinking skills. EFL (English as First Language) students are not immune to the difficulties imposed on them while producing written academic pieces of work. This phenomenon makes the analysis of content-based teaching and learning even more pressing.

ESL and EFL teachers of academic English writing skills have explored content-based approach targeting improvement of students' critical and analytical thinking and writing skills. Findings by Liaw [22] emphasised correlation between content-based teaching and advancement of critical and analytical thinking skills. As indicated in the article [27] "language in its entirety has many different and disparate aspects" (p. 10). The domains that classify the attributes of language can be physical, physiological and psychological. Hence, the domains of language belong to the individual and to the society where the individual resides. People construct thoughts depending on the languages they speak; therefore, language as a way of thinking and learning is more than a pedagogical catchphrase [29]. Interrelatedness between development of thinking and language requires appropriate consideration for the sake of students and educators [13, 23]. The content-based approach is a learning method that can facilitate language learning through instructional practice. The ESL learners when studying in an English medium university [7, 12] in particular need this support to progress in their studies.

Pally [25] concluded that instructions carried out through a sustained content-based (CBI) facilitate learning of analytical/critical thinking skills, mainly as a result of confronting authentic academic tasks where the set of skills is modelled, explained and practiced. However, the provided instructions require conformity with a constant practice, to be sustainable and fruitful for the learners. Another component of academic writing skills' class is the appropriate development and application of rhetorical conventions that simulate university courses. University students tend to display higher levels of active engagement with assessment topics that represent their culture. For example, if educators design, writing assessments based on students' cultural belonging; consequently, their interest and familiarity levels are higher [13, 27]. Understandably, the outcome of an increasingly active involvement with the assessment tasks results in higher grades and improvements of student's academic satisfaction [12–14]. Nevertheless, it is worth mentioning that the effort put by students is conditional to their unique personalities and sets of skills, being it cognitive or organizational. Students who are considerate of instructions provided prior to the task completion, model the language as informed and find interest in assessment topics can discover their own views and support them efficiently.

2.3 Curbing Plagiarism in the Online Platform

Educators worldwide have been analysing issues related to plagiarism for over three decades. Nevertheless, as our study was based in the UAE we focused on understanding the issue from cultural and linguistic perspectives in relation to Arabic speakers, as it is the case of our Emirati students. Significant studies related to plagiarism instances in the UAE written by Khan and Balasubramanian [18], Khan and others [19, 20] and Hysaj and ElKhouly [16], have concluded that some of the factors involved in the rampant lack of academic integrity in the region are spread of technology, ghost-writing and E-cheating. According to Pecorari and Petric [26] the blend of cultural and language issues, increases the potential for the plagiarism to take place. However, findings of Heckler and Forde [11] indicate that facilitating the process of learning can potentially bring changes to values and beliefs supporting a long-lasting learning culture and curbing instances of plagiarism. Therefore, our role as academic writing teachers should be to work towards a systematic and inclusive educative approach, by creating awareness to students about plagiarism but more importantly by teaching them academic writing skills. The motivation behind motives why students plagiarise includes the practices and behaviors that could be due to cultural, psychological or any other individual related factors. Nevertheless, as concluded by a qualitative research conducted by Devlin and Grey [10], better engagement of teachers with students is an effective way toward minimizing and marginalizing instances of plagiarism [14, 16]. Another issue worth analysing in regards to plagiarism is students' identity [5, 15]. As mentioned in the work of Lea and Street [21] creation of classroom and assessment tasks by bearing in mind students' identity encourages participation and improves the quality of the work produced. Distance learning if anything, only makes plagiarism more difficult to detect and it opens the door to ghost writing and E-cheating. Moreover, according to Rowe [28] and Burgoon et al. [6] people cheat when they feel distant from the assessor or the teacher. Therefore, creation of simpler, inclusive and culturally appropriate assessment tasks becomes a necessity for every educator [4, 6]. Furthermore, as mentioned in the studies by McKeeven [24], Culwin and Lancaster [9] online plagiarism systems should serve as similarity detection systems and not as online policing systems.

3 Methodology

This study was conducted to analyse how the different type of essay questions can have an impact on the student's performance through an online delivered course. The samples were collected from two sections of an English course in the general curriculum program offered at the University in the Spring term for the Academic year 2019–2020. The students generally take this course in their second semester at the Bachelor of Science program with concentration in either in Electrical Engineering or Information System Security. Both sections were taught by the same instructor. Three different writings were analysed. For each of the written assessments, a sample between 52 to 58 students work were collected and analysed. The level of students on the course is somewhere between IELTS band 6 to 6.5, which equals to the B2 level under the Common European Framework of References for Languages (CEFR).

For each writing, students were given a selection of topics to choose from and were asked to write approximately around 250 words essay. The allowed time was no more than 40 min per writing and all the writings were in class assessments. The marking criteria used for the writings was divided into three main categories as below:

1) Task fulfillment that includes content, organization and flow, essay structure and paragraphs with details including examples.
2) Vocabulary that is adequate range, limited repetition, correct word forms and spellings.
3) Grammar that is clarity and grammatical correctness of sentences, punctuation and linkers.

The grading scale used was from 0 being the lowest to 10 marks being the highest. Two major methodologies were used in analyzing the data, one being the quantitative and the other being qualitative. The former was used to design the tables below, which show the quantitative data sampled for each writing with grading scale and the numbers indicate how many students scored the marked grades for both classes of the same course. See tables below:

Table 1. Writing 1, Explanatory essay-Participants: 57

Grading scale	0–1	1–2	2–3	3–4	4–5	5–6	6–7	7–8	8–9	9–10
Class 1	1	0	0	0	1	0	5	8	12	4
Class 2	2	0	0	0	0	1	1	8	10	3

The quantitative approach in data analysis was used in the grading process of each of the writings by using the marking criteria mentioned in the previous paragraph, along with the comparison of the essay questions with the students' performances. The question types selected for each of the writings change in style from Writing 1 to Writing 3. The first writing being an explanatory essay, whereas the other two were comparative essays.

Table 2. Writing 2, Comparative essay-Participants: 52

Grading scale	0–1	1–2	2–3	3–4	4–5	5–6	6–7	7–8	8–9	9–10
Class 1	0	0	0	0	0	1	5	6	10	5
Class 2	1	0	0	1	0	0	1	3	10	9

Table 3. Writing 3, Comparative essay-Participants: 58

Grading scale	0–1	1–2	2–3	3–4	4–5	5–6	6–7	7–8	8–9	9–10
Class 1	0	0	0	1	1	0	1	6	10	14
Class 2	0	0	0	0	1	2	8	4	5	5

The explanatory essay writing assessment had two given topics for students to choose from and follow the essay structure with a clear introduction, body and a conclusion. The topics were mainly general and broad in nature. See the two given topics below for each of the 3 written assessments:

Topics for Writing 1:

1. *The recent developments in technology, such as the smartphone or tablet, have changed lives. Explain/discuss how technology has improved the quality of life.*
2. *Explain how a certain company or group of people you know that is doing something to help improve the environment. Think how they are impacting the community, environment, etc.*

Topics for Writing 2:

1. *There have been many changes in the way we interact with each other due to the current pandemics, in the past few months. Compare and contrast the advantages and disadvantages of the current situation and its effects on the UAE society.*
2. *What are some of the effects of the UAE's increase in tourism? Compare and contrast some of the positive and the negative aspects of it in terms of business, people, environment, etc.*

Topics for Writing 3:

1. *Arabic is the official language of the UAE, however, in most higher education institutes English is the main language of instruction. Compare and contrast the advantages and the disadvantages of studying in English to Arabic.*
2. *Due to economic globalisation in the UAE, people most of the time interact in English. Should everyone learn to speak English to be more successful or having access to*

translation would be sufficient? Compare and contrast the advantages of knowing English in the UAE.

4   Results

The results provide clear indication of reduction in the plagiarism rate. In the first writing (see Table 1), 3 students out of 57 plagiarised and therefore, obtained 0 grade out of 10, however, in Writing 2 (see Table 2) the figure went further down to 1 plagiarism and to 0 plagiarism cases in the third writing assignment (see Table 3). This is indicative of the fact that students were more inclined to google the essay questions that were more general in nature in Writing 1 and easy to obtain data on the given topic, whereas the questions are very specific and personal in the other two writings and consequently difficult to search for answers elsewhere. The rate of plagiarism was partial around 30%, which was majorly irrelevant to the question in writing 2 and was under graded between 3–4 out of 10. In addition, it must be observed that another factor in the reduction of plagiarism could be due to the fact that students were more aware of the penalties and the academic consequences.

Another major analysis was observed which was the fact that the first writing had more students who could not complete the word count of 250 words and said that they ran out of ideas to write. This led to lower scores in the writing mark where they scored between 3 to 5 marks out of 10 (refer to Table 1). Nevertheless, this was not an issue in the second or the third writing, where at times students would write even more than the word limit and reach between 300 to 350 words in the same given time, within the same allowed time of 40 min. The questions that were more tailored for the Emirati students and their concerns specifically in Writing 2 and Writing 3, students performed better in critically analysing the question that they were more familiar with and more comfortable to discuss in depth. Though there is a natural tendency for students to improve in their language skills over a course of time during the semester, the link between plagiarism and unfinished work seems to indicate a great connection to the question types and prior knowledge which students possess.

The third writing was a comparative essay and had more content-based questions where the context was aimed at the UAE and its people. Two further topics were given to students to select and compose their writing. The first option was on the current concern around the pandemic and the lockdown at the time the writing was given and the second choice was about the UAE's boom in tourism. Both of which have had a huge impact on the UAE's society in recent times. The last given assessment was another comparative essay. Again, the questions were very much focused on the issues that have a direct influence on the targeted students and their setting. Both of the topics were set around the question of language situation in the UAE and its influence on its people. The results provide positive statistical inference suggesting that above two third of students did not opt to plagiarize after the first assessment and instead focused on improving their writing skills, especially the content and sentence structure. Nonetheless, over two thirds still had issues with essay and paragraph structure, despite being able to organize their thoughts in a more appropriate format.

5 Discussion

This research clears the way for understanding Emirati undergraduate students' attitudes towards the teaching methods of writing utilised in their academic writing course. It seems that students are encouraged to adhere to the rules of institutions in regards to academic integrity more when offered an active role in the game of learning to write academically [3]. Furthermore, Emirati students seem to be open to learning and assessing through online platform to a considerable extent. From a pedagogical perspective, this creates conditions for increased reliability on the online platform since students are able to retain the information [5], develop critical thinking [4, 7] and avoid the breach of academic integrity [1]. As the theoretical background of online teaching and learning offers solid basis for online delivery adaptation of materials and authentic assessments, its utilisation serves the purpose of facilitating learning without applying undue pressure on the learners. After understanding that these teaching methods are pedagogically appropriate, the next step is to work towards continuous improvement of the alignment between learning objectives, diversity of online activities and assessment tasks.

Based on the findings provided by this study, it is evident that personalizing teaching and assessment tasks, through content-based learning considering students' cognitive, linguistic and collective requirements, can guarantee better teaching and learning results. Another recommendation is in regards to the role of teachers as facilitators of learning. Understanding of the course adaptation process is crucial and complicated; therefore, teachers need to be empowered with knowledge and tools prior to applying changes to the curriculum in the face-to-face or online platforms. According to Adnan [1], it is important to pay attention to the voice of teachers when transitioning from face to face to the online platform. Moreover, teachers should consider the cultural aspect as valuable in regards to teaching and learning when handling non-traditional delivery methods as culture plays an important role in the process of teaching and learning.

6 Conclusion and Recommendations

To conclude, this study affirms that content-based teaching allows students to develop their cognitive set of skills without undue pressure. Moreover, it provides them with confidence in their academic writing abilities and it eliminates the need to plagiarize. Nevertheless, considering the fact that students, who plagiarised on the first essay, were marked '0' this may have had an impact on the straightforwardly noticeable reduction in plagiarism instances in the other essays. Furthermore, this may have had an impact not only on the students who failed but also on other students that realised the institution's zero tolerance plagiarism policy. The results of this study offer the platform to consider content-based teaching and assessing in other universities who cater to multicultural students. In other words, the affirmation drawn by this study may serve as a starting point of analysing content-based learning and teaching in the distance learning platform. The formative feedback provided by the teacher has been very important in the process; nevertheless, the results also display that students felt connected with the content of their essays and felt at ease answering them. In other ways, they did not feel intimidated by many academic writing components e.g. content, structure, language and vocabulary all at once. They had enough possibilities of understanding the concepts one at a time and were not propelled to plagiarize. This study showed that Emirati undergraduate Engineering and IT students prefer to write about topics familiar to them and most importantly appealing to their cultural and linguistic background.

References

1. Adnan, M.: Professional development in the transition to online teaching: the voice of entrant online instructors. ReCALL **30**(1), 88–111 (2018)
2. Al Fadda, H.: Difficulties in academic writing: from the perspective of King Saud University postgraduate students. Engl. Lang. Teach. **5**(3), 123–130 (2012)
3. Alschuler, A.S., Blimling, G.S.: Curbing epidemic cheating through systemic change. Coll. Teach. **43**(4), 123–125 (1995)
4. Bretag, T.: Challenges in addressing plagiarism in education. PLoS Med. **10**(12), e1001574 (2013)
5. Boston, W., Ice, P., Burgess, M.: Assessing student retention in online learning environments: a longitudinal study. Online J. Distance Learn. Adm. **15**(2), 1–6 (2012)
6. Burgoon, J.K., Stoner, G.A., Bonito, J.A., Dunbar, N.E.: Trust and deception in mediated communication. In: 36th Annual Hawaii International Conference on System Sciences, pp. 11-pp. IEEE (2003)
7. Carmichael, E., Farrell, H.: Evaluation of the effectiveness of online resources in developing student critical thinking: review of literature and case study of a critical thinking online site. J. Univ. Teach. Learn. Pract. **9**(1), 4 (2012)
8. Chu, H.C.J., Swaffar, J., Charney, D.H.: Cultural representations of rhetorical conventions: the effects on reading recall. Tesol Q **36**(4), 511–541 (2002)
9. Culwin, F., Lancaster, T.: Plagiarism issues for higher education. Vine **31**, 36–41 (2001)
10. Devlin, M., Gray, K.: In their own words: a qualitative study of the reasons Australian university students plagiarize. High Educ. Res. Dev. **26**(2), 181–198 (2007)
11. Heckler, N., Forde, D.: The role of cultural values in plagiarism in higher education. J. Acad. Ethics **13**, 63–75 (2014)
12. Hysaj, A., Elkhouly, A., Qureshi, A.W., Abdulaziz, N.: Analysis of engineering students' academic satisfaction in a culturally diverse university. In: IEEE International Conference on Teaching, Assessment, and Learning for Engineering (TALE), pp. 755–760 (2018)
13. Hysaj, A., Elkhouly, A., Qureshi, A.W., Abdulaziz, N.: A study of the impact of tutor's support and undergraduate student's academic satisfaction. Am. J. Humanit. Soc. Sci. Res. (AJHSSR) **3**(12), 70–77 (2019)
14. Hysaj, A., Hamam, D., et al.: Exploring the affordance of distance learning platform (DLP) in COVID19 remote learning environment. In: Stephanidis, C., et al. (eds.) HCII 2020. LNCS, vol. 12425, pp. 421–431. Springer, Cham (2020). https://doi.org/10.1007/978-3-030-60128-7_32
15. Hysaj, A., Hamam, D.: Analysis of engineering students' academic satisfaction in a culturally diverse university. In: 2020 IEEE International Conference on Teaching, Assessment, and Learning for Engineering (TALE), pp. 334–339, December 2020 (2020)
16. Hysaj, A., Elkhouly, A.: Why do students plagiarize? The case of multicultural students in an Australian University in the United Arab Emirates. In: ENAI Conference (2020)
17. Hysaj, A., Suleymanova, S.: The analysis of developing the application of critical thinking in oral and written discussions: the case of Emirati students in the United Arab Emirates'. In: IEEE International Conference on Teaching, Assessment and Learning for Engineering (TALE), pp. 855–860. IEEE (2020)

18. Khan, Z.R., Balasubramanian, S.: Students go click, flick and cheat... e-cheating, technologies and more. J. Acad. Bus. Ethics **6**, 1 (2012)
19. Khan, Z.R.: E-cheating and calculator-technology. In: Elleithy, K., Sobh, T., Iskander, M., Kapila, V., Karim, M., Mahmood, A. (eds.) Technological Developments in Networking, Education and Automation, pp. 115–119. Springer, Dordrecht (2010). https://doi.org/10.1007/978-90-481-9151-2_20
20. Khan, Z.R., Al-Qaimari, G., Samuel, S.D.: Professionalism and ethics: is education the bridge? In: Information Systems and Technology Education: From the University to the Workplace, pp. 214–241. IGI Global (2007)
21. Lea, M.R., Street, B.V.: Student writing in higher education: an academic literacies approach. Stud. High. Educ. **23**(2), 157–172 (1998)
22. Liaw, M.L.: Content-based reading and writing for critical thinking skills in an EFL context. Engl. Teach. Learn. **31**(2), 45–87 (2007)
23. Mallia, J.: Strategies for developing English academic writing skills. Arab World Engl. J. (AWEJ) **8**(2), 3–15 (2017)
24. McKeever, L.: Online plagiarism detection services saviour or scourge? Assess. Eval. High. Educ. **31**(2), 155–165 (2006)
25. Pally, M.: Skills development in 'sustained' content-based curricula: case studies in analytical/critical thinking and academic writing. Lang. Educ. **15**(4), 279–305 (2001)
26. Pecorari, B.: Petrić, Plagiarism in second-language writing. Lang. Teach. **47**(3), 269–302 (2014)
27. Randall, M., Samimi, M.A.: The status of English in Dubai. Engl. Today **26**(1), 43–50 (2010)
28. Rowe, N.C.: Cheating in online student assessment: Beyond plagiarism. Online J. Distance Learn. Adm. **7**(2), 1–10 (2004)
29. Stam, G.A.: Changes in patterns of thinking with second language acquisition. Doctoral dissertation, University of Chicago, Department of Psychology: Cognition and Communication (2006)
30. Singh, M.K.M.: International graduate students' academic writing practices in Malaysia: challenges and solutions. J. Int. Stud. **5**(1), 12–22 (2005)
31. Tütünis, B.: Content-based academic writing. Internet TESL J. **6**(7) (2000)

Efficacy of Group Work in the Online Platform: An Exploration of Multicultural Undergraduates' Attitudes in Online Academic Writing Classes

Ajrina Hysaj[1]([✉]) [iD], Doaa Hamam[2] [iD], and Sandra Baroudi[3] [iD]

[1] UOWD College, University of Wollongong in Dubai, Dubai, UAE
Ajrinahysaj@uowdubai.ac.ae
[2] Higher Colleges of Technology, Dubai, UAE
dhamam@hct.ac.ae
[3] Zayed University, Dubai, UAE
sandra.baroudi@zu.ac.ae

Abstract. Group work in online classes can be a challenging task for both teachers and students. Teachers need to make sure that the group task is designed carefully to achieve its learning objectives, and students need to learn how to work efficiently as members in a group to achieve their targets and meet deadlines. This paper addresses the efficacy of group work in academic writing online classes, and it aims at exploring multicultural students' attitudes towards working in groups in online academic writing classes. Fifty-nine students were surveyed using a Likert-scale survey, from which five students were interviewed using semi-structured interviews to explore their attitudes towards group work in the online writing classes. The findings revealed that students generally had positive attitudes towards group work in online academic writing classes; however, some students reported that technical issues caused problems at times. Results also revealed that the benefits of this experience outweighed the disadvantages. The study's findings can be useful for practitioners and curriculum designers as they shed light on the benefits of group work in online academic writing classes and the challenges students may face during these classes.

Keywords: Academic writing · Online platform · Group work · Multicultural students

1 Introduction

Humans are social beings who learn together in educational institutions, work in organisations or companies and live in communities. All these environments may be subject to individual preferences, family choices, social or economic status. All environments; the chosen or the destined ones require people to collaborate extensively, tolerate generously and participate actively. Therefore, the concept of group work is highly interconnected with the existence of social beings. One of the environments where students are required

© Springer Nature Switzerland AG 2021
G. Meiselwitz (Ed.): HCII 2021, LNCS 12775, pp. 246–256, 2021.
https://doi.org/10.1007/978-3-030-77685-5_20

to work in groups, negotiate ideas, agree to differ, take the lead to finish tasks, and make friends for life is in higher education classrooms. The experience that most students have while in higher education is learning to be independent, take appropriate actions, be accountable for, and learn from other individuals' experiences while interacting with them, in a diverse and changing society [45]. The diversity prevalent in multicultural classrooms is a challenge for many who are new to it and exciting to those who recognise its importance and stand up to the challenge aiming at academic and personal development. Any educator needs to consider multiculturalism when designing online activities or academic writing assessment tasks [17]. Considering the positive and drawbacks of multicultural groups is beneficial to the educators as it helps create a supportive and encouraging atmosphere. However, most importantly, it is beneficial to the students who would approach the group work with more realistic expectations. Since students are social beings, this consideration would help them set realistic goals while working with others, learn from the experience and then set higher personal and academic goals in the future [12, 13, 35, 44, 46]. Furthermore, students would learn to pay attention to factors like time and stress management. Cohen and Lotan [7] described group work as a collaborative type of work that a small group of students partake, aiming to complete well-defined tasks and without the teacher's direct supervision. Classrooms characterised by multiculturalism are nurturing environments for academically and linguistically heterogeneous students and offer an encouraging and yet challenging atmosphere for a successful and fulfilling group work experience. The purpose and the goals aimed to be achieved through group work tasks in the online or face-to-face platforms are the force that drives the type and content of group tasks [18, 29].

2 Literature Review

2.1 Psychological and Psycholinguistic Rationale for Group Work in the Online Platform

The force majeure of COVID 19 created unprecedented circumstances worldwide disrupting all major activities with all countries imposing partial or general lockdowns; aiming to constrain the spread of the deadly virus. According to a review by Brooks et al. [5], which analysed 3166 research papers, most people experienced post-traumatic stress symptoms, confusion and anger after being in quarantine. As a result of full or partial lockdowns, most schools and universities worldwide started applying remote learning, and curricula were adapted to suit the online platform. Educators and students experienced a swift change from face-to-face to online learning, and as expected, the first reactions were confusion, resistance to change and lack of resilience [5]. Although the stress was powerful, educators had to take the lead and guide their students towards a successful learning experience in remote learning.

Groups are by definition complex and multi-layered, and as highlighted by Barnes, Ernst and Hyde [2], they are successful if they have a common goal and can draw boundaries, which subsequently create an atmosphere of mutual understanding and unity. Explicably, boundaries help ease any external or internal factor and allow the group members to work within the appropriate environment to learn. Learning from others while working together is an integral part of human existence, and it is commonly experienced in group work in the education field [16, 39, 41, 42]. As seen, all these authors analysed the theory of the American philosopher John Dewey on the ways that people learn, considering learning as a social factor and not only an educational one. According to Dewey, some of the most long-lasting benefits of group work are at the core of learning: reflective learning, experiential learning, and inquiry-based learning. This consideration empowers learning with social behaviour aspects and creates an atmosphere of learning through doing, learning through thinking and learning through exploring [12]. These learning layers are multiplied in groups due to other people's presence and individual behaviour and experience [13, 35, 44, 46].

Group work in face-to-face or online classes requires collaboration between the group members, negotiation of thought, acceptance of others' opinions and most importantly a positive and encouraging atmosphere that facilitates working through cognitive, academic and personal learning experiences [8]. Therefore, it is an appropriate learning platform backed by sound pedagogical arguments [4, 10, 27, 30, 31, 34]. Group work has long been considered as a good platform for language acquisition through the interlanguage talk and the negotiation of group work tasks [4, 6, 24, 28, 31–33]. The transference of linguistic abilities amongst ESL or EFL students naturally occurs when working in groups. However, a study by Izumi and Izumi [26] highlighted that the syntactic formation of appropriate grammatical forms of words requires input production more than it requires output production of words, emphasising the need that L2 learners have to create a mapping of meaning prior to output production. This process requires L2 learners to engage in syntactic processing through reflection and experiential learning.

2.2 Perspectives of Multicultural Students on Online Learning and Group Work

Higher education institutions are an optimal environment worldwide to nurture the positivity of multiculturalism and prepare students for a globalised professional world. Multiculturalism has been researched by many researchers worldwide, as it presents a variety of challenges and opportunities. The investigation of multicultural students' perspectives of communication with teachers and peers, sheds light on the differences between cultures and nations and their effects on the respective learners' learning process. A study by Benediktsson and Ragnarsdottir [3] revealed that multicultural students prefer a student-centered approach and highlight the value of communication, despite holding different opinions regarding group work. The theoretical framework preferred by multicultural students, according to this study, is that of constructivism, which puts the learner in the centre of the teaching and learning processes. Application of culturally responsive learning and assessment activities require exploration of multicultural students' perspectives on learning and teaching. For instance, an exploratory case study by Popov et al. [43] revealed that challenges experienced my multicultural students when working in groups reflect their individual and collective cultural influences. Furthermore, some challenges were considered harder for some students and easier for the others, and the ANOVA analysis displayed the tendency that most multicultural students have to differ in cross-cutting and culture-related issues. Therefore, the exploratory factor analysis highlighted the viewpoint of Hofstede's individualist and collectivist cultural dimension, suggesting that students' cultural background highly influences their perceptions of the importance of group work challenges.

According to Masika and Jones [36], effective group work requires recognising and accepting students' identities as part of the group work learning experiences. Students' identities are as crucial as their engagement with the group work; one without the other is difficult- if not impossible- to be achieved [22, 25]. Students' belonging and active engagement in the learning process are reflected in universities' retention levels and has attracted the interest of management and educators for over two decades [1, 14, 37, 40, 48]. The sudden implementation of online learning makes it even more vital that students' identities and active participation in the online platform are investigated and analysed [25]. Online learning contexts require augmentation of interaction possibilities amongst group members during lessons by utilising the breakout rooms in platforms like Zoom or WebEx. These increased interactions in the online platform can instill a sense of belonging and be transferred from the success in group work to the educational institution's connection and society.

2.3 Does Group Work Affect Multicultural Students?

According to Blatchford et al. [4], group work adds a different context to the learning experience by constructing knowledge, acquiring learning, and designing a social ped-agogy of successful learning. The concepts of co-learning have gained momentum not only because of the positive outcome experience when students work in groups while in university, but also because of their relevance in the business world and societal settings. The spread of technology and the utilisation of avatars in creating a virtual reality very similar to the face-to-face one creates a platform where the information is available; however, the co-learning which is extremely valuable does not occur. For example, mul-ticultural students may read about other cultures, but cannot benefit from that knowledge as much as by communicating with people from other cultures. Moreover, while working with people from other cultures, students obtain various types of information and con-struct meanings and create a mental correlation of paradigms, problems and solutions [20, 22]. According to Hoyles, Healy and Pozzi [19], one of the crucial factors of group work is developing students' autonomy and achieving the synergy between group mem-bers, because independence and interdependence are valuable for a successful group work task completion, and professional life.

One associated problem of group work is the inequality in the distribution of work amongst the group members. According to Davies [11], one of the considerable disad-vantages of multicultural group work is that it may encourage 'free riders' when learn-ers choose between altruism and selfishness. Some solutions to resolve this issue are acknowledging the complexity of the assessment tasks by rewarding the effort contribu-tion and minimising group size. Another suggestion offered is implementing incentives for productive group members and penalties for unproductive group members. Design-ing group work tasks and their marking matrix requires careful consideration to ensure the successful application of a well-integrated conceptual design and a fruitful learning experience. Therefore, it is evident that there are several advantages and disadvantages of group work in the classroom, and it is clear that several factors influence the efficacy of group work. To explore the efficacy of group work in the online writing classes, this study addresses the following research questions; what are the multicultural students' attitudes towards group work in online academic writing classes? What are participants' experiences and challenges during the online group work?

3   Methodology

This study used mixed method design to answer the research questions and obtain a better understanding of the topic studied [9, 15]. As such, the quantitative data followed a descriptive survey design to explore students' attitudes towards the online group work, while the qualitative data followed an exploratory approach to generate subjective views and obtain an overall picture about the participants' experiences and challenges during the online group work [9]. The survey was developed by the researchers to examine 1) Students' attitudes towards online group work 2) Psychological and psycholinguistic rationale for group work. Participants scored their answers based on a 5 Likert scale ranging from 1 to 5 where 1 = Strongly agree and 5 = Strongly disagree. Percentages were extracted to show differences in participants' scores on each item. As for the qualitative data, semi-structured interviews were conducted with five students. Interviews were done in the university site, they were audio-recorded, and lasted for 30 min each. Participants were asked to answer a total of ten open-ended questions. These questions explored their overall experience in the online group work. Examples of these questions are: What are the pros and cons of group work in the online platform? How did you manage to work in your group with your team? What are the challenges you faced during the process? and others. The students were informed with the purpose of the study, and that their participation was voluntary. Responses were analyzed based on an inductive analysis strategy to construct categories or themes from raw data [9]. Hence, two themes were identified: the disadvantages and the advantages of group work in the online platform. The study's timeframe was around 12–13 weeks. A purposeful convenient sampling technique was adopted to ease the accessibility to participants and help the researcher discover, understand and gain insights about the topic [38]. A total of 59 multicultural students' who were enrolled in academic writing classes in a university in the UAE were invited to participate in the study by their instructor. Students came from different nationalities and backgrounds and their mean age was 20 years old.

4   Results

4.1   Students' Survey

Online Learning Perspective
The students' attitudes towards online perspective were generally positive. However, some students (31.3%) reported that they feel disadvantaged because of the technical issues they face when attending classes. Others (29.2%) reported difficulty understanding instructions for academic writing content and structure through the online platform using several technological tools. Students revealed that they had positive and facilitated experience in the online writing classes for the other survey items. Therefore, although many students stated that they learned new technical skills in the online classes, it seems to be technical issues that are causing challenges. The detailed percentages for the first part of the survey are presented in Table 1.

Table 1. Students' attitudes towards online group work

Survey item	1	2	3	4	5
I believe that online teaching helped me learn new technological skills that I will need in the future	22.4%	26.5%	26.5%	18.4%	6.1%
I always try to learn new applications since they are required in the online platform	20.8%	27.1%	20.8.1%	4.2%	6.3%
I require a high level of self-confidence related to technical skills to learn online successfully	31.3%	37.5%	10%	5%	0%
I do not feel at a disadvantage due to technological issues while attending lessons in the online platform	22.9%	20.8%	20.8%	31.3%	4.2%
I believe it is easy to understand instructions for academic writing content and structure through the online platform using several technological tools	14.6%	22.9%	20.8%	29.2%	12.5%
I am familiar with the technological tools that can help me improve academic writing skills in the online platform	27.1%	41.7%	16.7%	8.3%	6.3%

4.2 Psychological and Psycholinguistic Rationale for Group Work

For the second part of the survey which is the psychological and psycholinguistics rationale for group work, a relatively low percentage of students 14.3%–14.6% reported that they did not enjoy group work in the online platform and did not think it helped with individualized instructions. 14.3% of students disagreed that group work stimulates the development of life-long collaborative skills and 22.9% disagreed that the online platform offers a variety of opportunities for language acquisition through group discussions and live sessions. However, the rest of the survey items' results indicated positive attitudes towards group work in the online writing classes. More details are presented in Table 2.

Table 2. Psychological and psycholinguistics rationale for group Work

Survey item	1	2	3	4	5
I enjoyed the group work in the online platform	34.7%	24.5%	8.2%	14.3%	18.4%
I believe that group work helps individualise instruction	33.3%	25%	8.3%	14.6%	18.8%
I believe that group work promotes a positive affective climate	29.2%	33.3%	16.7%	8.3%	12.5%

(continued)

Table 2. (*continued*)

Survey item	1	2	3	4	5
I believe that through group work we improve our negotiation skills highly required in the business world	35.4%	39.6%	6.3%	4.2%	14.6%
I believe that group work increases work accuracy due to a variety of cognitive and research skills present in the group	31.3%	43.8%	6.3%	4.2%	14.6%
I believe that group work helps in completing the task on time without an overwhelming effort and stress	33.3%	27.1%	12.5%	12.5%	14.6%
I believe that online group work stimulates deeper learning because we are introduced to issues and search for solutions though online sources	25%	37.5%	12.5%	8.3%	16.7%
I believe that online group work stimulates development of life-long collaborative skills since we are introduced to issues and search for solutions through group negotiations	22.9%	45.8%	10.4%	6.3%	14.6%
I believe that online learning offers a variety of opportunities for language acquisition through group discussions and live sessions	22.9%	25%	22.9%	6.3%	22.9%

In general, students did not face many issues when attending online writing classes except for some technical issues, and they had positive attitudes towards the overall process of working in groups in online writing classes.

4.3 Students' Interviews

Five students were interviewed for this research study, and their answers were thematically divided. Several subthemes emerged during the interviews, but two main broad themes were identified: the disadvantages and the advantages of group work in the online platform. For the disadvantages, three out of five students reported that technical issues could be frustrating at times. The other two students did not face many challenges in this respect. Two students complained about the lack of cooperation from their peers. A student mentioned that sometimes, the group members did not meet the required deadlines or respond promptly to their peers. One student also mentioned that since his colleagues came from different backgrounds, it was challenging to work together because of cultural differences. Another student mentioned that making assumption was a problem; he believed that he worked harder than others and was disappointed because the other group members did not work hard enough to achieve their mutual goals. Another student also stated that the group team leader did not have enough leadership skills to manage the group, distribute tasks, follow up, and resolve conflict. That eventually led to lower grades for the whole group.

On the other hand, all students reported many advantages for group work in the online platform, four out of the five students stated that they enjoyed working with their peers and that group work motivated them to finish their work on time. They also focused on the work quality because others were going to read it and give their feedback. They were also relieved because their peers could explain to them the difficult parts of the task when needed. All students reported that because the classes were online, they felt socially isolated, and that is why it was good that they had to interact with others on a regular basis and work together as a group. Most students mentioned that they had learnt new skills from their peers, and one student mentioned that his peers were more approachable than the teacher and that facilitated getting any information by merely texting the other group members or making a post in the discussion group. Another student reported that she felt more comfortable interacting with the group's members online because of her shy nature. She was able to communicate more when she contacted her peers through the online platform. Finally, most students mentioned that their teachers' feedback was precious to their learning process.

5 Discussion

As opposed to the findings of the review done by Brooks et al. [5], this current study revealed that students in the higher education level were quick adapters to the online learning environment, and expressed positive attitudes and perceptions towards group work in the online platform. Students not only enjoyed the online group activities but indicated that their knowledge and skills in learning and using new technological platforms have increased. As a consequence, their self-confidence which is related to technical skills improved and their interactions and engagement were enhanced. Hence, and based on both the constructivist and social learning theory, we believe that these interactions and participations have enriched the group work experience and paved the way for successful online learning environment. Additionally, the online group work proved to promote a positive and effective climate between students from different backgrounds. Similar to the findings of Hoyles, Healy and Pozzi [19], this study's results revealed that the multicultural aspect did not hinder the effectiveness of the group work, on the contrary, majority of students worked in synergy and collaborated in order to achieve the given task successfully.

Despite some obstacles faced by students (i.e., lack of collaboration and cooperation from few peers and technical issues), they have generally benefited from this experience towards the improvement of their academic writing skills. This is because group work offered students opportunities for language acquisition through pairs and groups discussions. In alignment with Blatchford et al. [4], Izumi and Izumi [26], and Long [33], our results showed that online group work facilitated the transference of linguistic abilities amongst EFL students. During the group work, students were engaged in negotiations and live discussions that have enriched their linguistic skills and stimulated their deeper learning. Furthermore, participants of this study reported difficulty understanding instructions for academic writing content and structure through the online platform. Therefore, a well-designed group activity with clear instructions and guidelines allows learners to benefit from the accumulated knowledge and application through group work. According to Croy [10], implementing a well-designed online instruction aligned with the course outline is a substantial component of teaching and learning that would construct students' knowledge and develop their responsibility towards their learning. Another important factor of successful online teaching is students' feedback about their group work and online presence [25]. This indicates a certain level of engagement with the lessons and the subject matter. Furthermore, since students are different individuals, and one size never fits all, consideration of students' individual needs is expected and inevitable for a productive teaching and learning process [21, 22]. Finally, the most crucial online teaching and learning factor is the students' evaluative feedback about the online lessons, online tools, and their respective applications.

6 Conclusion and Recommendations

Although most factors related to group work are the same across the board, psychological and psycholinguistic ones deserve special attention regarding academic writing skills classes while working in groups in the online platform. Moreover, lack of technological skills is another substantial factor influencing how students think and react when considering learning through the online platform. Academic writing skills require well-informed linguistic and content organised assessment tasks to ensure successful teaching and learning [22]. Moreover, cultural clashes may occur during group work, but they seem rare among multicultural students born and raised in a multicultural society. Finally, multiculturalism requires more in-depth analysis when considering online learning, especially as more universities move towards a blended or online learning approach, as culturally responsive teaching is still an intermittent phenomenon in many universities.

References

1. Anderman, L.H.: Academic and social perceptions as predictors of change in middle school students' sense of school belonging. J. Exp. Educ. **72**(1), 5–22 (2003)
2. Barnes, B., Ernst, S., Hyde, K.: An Introduction to Group Work: A Group-Analytic Perspective. Macmillan International Higher Education, London (2017)
3. Benediktsson, A.I., Ragnarsdottir, H.: Communication and group work in the multicultural classroom: immigrant students' experiences. Eur. J. Educ. Res. **8**(2), 453–465 (2019)
4. Blatchford, P., Kutnick, P., Baines, E., Galton, M.: Toward a social pedagogy of classroom group work. Int. J. Educ. Res. **39**(1–2), 153–172 (2003)
5. Brooks, S.K., et al.: The psychological impact of quarantine and how to reduce it: rapid review of the evidence. Lancet **395**, 912–920 (2020)
6. Clarke, M.A., Silberstein, S.: Toward a realisation of psycholinguistic principles in the ESL reading class. Lang. Learn. **27**(1), 135–154 (1977)
7. Cohen, E.G., Lotan, R.A.: Designing Group Work: Strategies for the Heterogeneous Classroom. Teachers College Press, New York (2014)
8. Cowie, H., Smith, P., Boulton, M., Laver, R.: Cooperation in the Multi-Ethnic Classroom: The Impact of 1994 Cooperative Group Work on Social Relationships in Middle Schools. Routledge, Abingdon (2018)
9. Creswell, J.W.: Research Design: Qualitative, Quantitative, & Mixed Methods Approaches. Sage Publications, Thousand Oaks (2014)

10. Croy, S.R.: Development of a group work assessment pedagogy using constructive alignment theory (2018)
11. Davies, W.M.: Group work as a form of assessment: common problems and recommended solutions. High. Educ. **58**(4), 563–584 (2018)
12. Dewey, J.: Experience and education. In: The Educational Forum, vol. 50, no. 3, pp. 241–252. Taylor & Francis Group (1986)
13. Fishman, S.M., McCarthy, L.P.: John Dewey and the Challenge of Classroom Practice. Teachers College Press, New York (1998)
14. Fong Lam, U., Chen, W.W., Zhang, J., Liang, T.: It feels good to learn where I belong: School belonging, academic emotions, and academic achievement in adolescents. Sch. Psychol. Int. **36**(4), 393–409 (2015)
15. Fraenkel, J.R., Wallen, N.E.: How to Design and Evaluate Research in Education. McGraw-Hill, New York (2009)
16. Giles, D.E., Jr., Eyler, J.: The theoretical roots of service-learning in John Dewey: toward a theory of service-learning. Mich. J. Community Serv. Learn. **1**(1), 7 (1994)
17. Hamam, D.: A study of the rhetorical features and the argument structure of EAP essays by L1 & L2 students. J. Asia TEFL **17**(2), 699–706 (2020)
18. Holtham, C.W., Melville, R.R., Sodhi, M.S.: Designing student group work in management education: widening the palette of options. J. Manag. Educ. **30**(6), 809–817 (2006)
19. Hoyles, C., Healy, L., Pozzi, S.: Interdependence and autonomy: aspects of group work with computers. Learn. Instr. **2**(3), 239–257 (1992)
20. Hysaj, A, Elkhouly, A., Qureshi, A.W., Abdulaziz, N.: Analysis of engineering students' academic satisfaction in a culturally diverse university. In: IEEE International Conference on Teaching, Assessment, and Learning for Engineering (TALE), pp. 755–760. IEEE (2018)
21. Hysaj, A., Elkhouly, A., Qureshi, A.W., Abdulaziz, N.A.: Study of the impact of tutor's support and undergraduate student's academic satisfaction. Am. J. Hum. Soc. Sci. Res **3**(12), 70–77 (2019)
22. Hysaj, A., Hamam, D.: Does delivery method matter for multicultural undergraduate students? A case study of an Australian University in the United Arab Emirates. In: Meiselwitz, G. (ed.) HCII 2020. LNCS, vol. 12195, pp. 538–548. Springer, Cham (2020). https://doi.org/10.1007/978-3-030-49576-3_39
23. Hysaj, A., Hamam, D.: Exploring the affordance of distance learning platform (DLP) in COVID19 remote learning environment. In: Stephanidis, C., et al. (eds.) HCII 2020. LNCS, vol. 12425, pp. 421–431. Springer, Cham (2020). https://doi.org/10.1007/978-3-030-60128-7_32
24. Hysaj, A., Hamam, D.: Academic Writing skills in the online platform-A success, a failure or something in between? A study on perceptions of higher education students and teachers in the UAE. In: IEEE International Conference on Teaching, Assessment and Learning for Engineering (TALE), pp. 334–339. IEEE (2020)
25. Hysaj, A., Suleymanova, S.: The analysis of developing the application of critical thinking in oral and written discussions: the case of Emirati students in the United Arab Emirates. In: IEEE International Conference on Teaching, Assessment and Learning for Engineering (TALE), pp. 855–860. IEEE (2020)
26. Izumi, Y., Izumi, S.: Investigating the effects of oral output on the learning of relative clauses in English: issues in the psycholinguistic requirements for effective output tasks. Can. Mod. Lang. Rev. **60**(5), 587–609 (2004)
27. Kamberelis, G., Dimitriadis, G.: Focus Groups. Routledge, London (2013)
28. Kay, J., Lesser, R., Coltheart, M.: Psycholinguistic assessments of language processing in aphasia (PALPA): an introduction. Aphasiology **10**(2), 159–180 (1996)
29. Kinsella, K.: Designing group work that supports and enhances diverse classroom work styles. Test **6**(1), 24–30 (2009)

30. Laurillard, D.: The pedagogical challenges to collaborative technologies. Int. J. Comput.-Support. Collab. Learn. **4**(1), 5–20 (2009). https://doi.org/10.1007/s11412-008-9056-2
31. Long, M.H., Porter, P.A.: Group work, interlanguage talk, and second language acquisition. TESOL Q. **19**(2), 207–228 (1985)
32. Long, M.H.: Task, Group, and Task-Group Interactions, pp. 30–50. Eric (1990)
33. Long, M.H.: In defense of tasks and TBLT: nonissues and real issues. Annu. Rev. Appl. Linguist. **36**, 5–33 (2016)
34. Lusted, D.: Why pedagogy? Screen **27**(5), 2–16 (1986)
35. Martin, J.: The Education of John Dewey: A Biography. Columbia University Press, New York (2003)
36. Masika, R., Jones, J.: Building student belonging and engagement: insights into higher education students' experiences of participating and learning together. Teach. High. Educ. **21**(2), 138–150 (2016)
37. McMahon, S.D., Wernsman, J., Rose, D.S.: The relation of classroom environment and school belonging to academic self-efficacy among urban fourth-and fifth-grade students. Elem. Sch. J. **109**(3), 267–281 (2009)
38. Merriam, S.B.: Qualitative Research: A Guide to Design and Implementation. Jossey-Bass, San Francisco (2015)
39. Miettinen, R.: The concept of experiential learning and John Dewey's theory of reflective thought and action. Int. J. Lifelong Educ. **19**(1), 54–72 (2000)
40. Neel, C.G.O., Fuligni, A.: A longitudinal study of school belonging and academic motivation across high school. Child Dev. **84**(2), 678–692 (2013)
41. Ord, J., Leather, M.: The substance beneath the labels of experiential learning: the importance of John Dewey for outdoor educators. J. Outdoor Environ. Educ. **15**(2), 13–23 (2011)
42. Ord, J.: John Dewey and Experiential Learning: developing the theory of youth work. Youth Policy **108**(1), 55–72 (2012)
43. Popov, V., Brinkman, D., Biemans, H.J., Mulder, M., Kuznetsov, A., Noroozi, O.: Multicultural student group work in higher education: an explorative case study on challenges as perceived by students. Int. J. Intercult. Relat. **36**(2), 302–317 (2012)
44. Sharan, Y., Sharan, S.: Expanding Cooperative Learning Through Group Investigation. Teachers College Press, New York (1992)
45. Stephenson, J.: The concept of capability and its importance in higher education. In: Capability and Quality in Higher Education, pp. 1–13 (1998)
46. Ültanır, E.: An epistemological glance at the constructivist approach: constructivist learning in Dewey, Piaget, and Montessori. Int. J. Instr. **5**(2) (2012)
47. Uwah, C.J., McMahon, H.G., Furlow, C.F.: School belonging, educational aspirations, and academic self-efficacy among African American male high school students: implications for school counselors. Prof. Sch. Couns. **11**(5), 296–305 (2008)
48. Wenger, E.: A social theory of learning. In: Contemporary Theories of Learning, pp. 209–218 (2009)

Design, Implementation and Evaluation of a Technical Platform that Supports Spanish Speaking Children with Intellectual Disabilities Learn English as a Second Language

Luis Rojas[1]([✉]) [iD], Katrina Sorbello[2] [iD], Patricia Contreras[3] [iD], and Juan Felipe Calderon[4] [iD]

[1] Universidad San Sebastián, Facultad de Ingeniería y Tecnología, Santiago, Chile
[2] The Stella Way 17 Enford Street, Hillcrest, QLD, Australia
[3] Escuela Especial de Desarrollo de La Reina, Larrain 6374, Santiago, Chile
[4] Universidad Andres Bello, Facultad de Ingeniería, Quillota 980, Viña del Mar, Chile

Abstract. Recent Chilean legislation established a curriculum focused on children with cognitive deficits, adapting the original English curriculum to a specialized one that can be used in Special Education Needs (SEN) schools. However, currently, Chilean SEN schools are not making use of these methods to support students to learn a new language such as English. Furthermore, the research of similar mobile applications available indicated a focus on native English speaking children with intellectual disabilities, however, did not support Spanish speaking children. Therefore, this study was created to observe the impact of mobile activities in English language instruction in the setting of a Chilean SEN school. The proposed solution was designed, developed, and implemented in conjunction with specialist teachers. Prototypes of the mobile application were installed on tablets specifically for this study and deployed in an experimental group. Students were assigned to two groups, control and experimental, where the same pre and post-tests were conducted. This included activities such as writing an English word from the image displayed, matching an image with the associated English word, and completing the missing letters of an English word (which was proven to be the most difficult activity). This experiment resulted in a significant impact on the learning achieved in the experimental group. The Cohen D resulted in 0.92 with a p-value of <0.001. Furthermore, the analysis of the standard deviation of time usage in each activity provided insights into the difficulty levels supporting modifications of future activities.

Keywords: Learn english · Second language · Intellectual disabilities · Special Education Needs

1 Introduction

Today software platforms have played an important role in society, facilitating access to information and providing tools for people with intellectual disabilities. These applications support students to learn in a didactic way and with new methods, to better develop

© Springer Nature Switzerland AG 2021
G. Meiselwitz (Ed.): HCII 2021, LNCS 12775, pp. 257–269, 2021.
https://doi.org/10.1007/978-3-030-77685-5_21

their thinking skills and abilities [1, 2]. In the initial years of education, it is relevant to instill training in the use of English as a second language [3–5]. In these years, the brain is more susceptible, enabling students to learn faster, more easily, and achieve better performance in the future [6]. This is especially relevant in children with cognitive deficits because it allows them to generate early stimulation. However, teaching English as a foreign language to people with intellectual disabilities (ID) presents complications, requiring specific techniques and methods [7].

Recently, Chilean legislation, through Decree 83/15, established technical-pedagogical norms to carry out a curriculum focused on children with cognitive deficits, adapting the original English curriculum to a specialized one that can be used in Special Education Needs (SEN) schools. However, currently, these schools are not making use of these methods to learn a new language such as English. Therefore, the main objective of this work is to address the problem of poor development of English language comprehension in Spanish-speaking children with cognitive deficits at an early age; through the design, implementation, and evaluation of a software platform to support the process of learning.

This work aims to describe and analyze the process of design, construction, and implementation of Inclusive2L. Design-based research, widely used in learning sciences, was used as a methodology. As a source scenario for the design requirements and subsequent implementation, a Chilean SEN school was engaged, with whom the pedagogical and technological design was co-constructed, to adapt to the needs and particular characteristics of the target students. With this, the development of a set of interactive activities to be carried out individually was procured. The evaluation and reflection process consisted of two stages: usability evaluation and learning achievement evaluation. For this, a 6-month experimentation was carried out, using a pre-post pseudo-experimental design with a control group. Regarding usability, the quantitative analysis of the effectiveness and efficiency attributes was analyzed. Meanwhile, in the pedagogical field, the efficacy and impact of technology in achieving the learning objectives were defined.

This paper is organized as follows. Section 1 introduced the motivation of our work through the problem identified and the proposed solution. Section 2 presents related work. Section 3 describes the details of our proposed solution. Section 4 describes the experiment accomplished to implement and evaluate the proposed solution in a real environment. Section 5 reports the learning and user outcomes obtained. Finally, Sect. 6 presents conclusions and future work.

2 Related Work

The purpose of this section is to present the condition of relevant applications related to the topic addressed by this project. Therefore, representative applications designed for working with children with ID who are learning English as a second language will be investigated.

The Abaplanet [8] application, developed by the Lovaas Foundation [9], provides learning activities, aimed at children with Autism Spectrum Disorders (ASD) and those with other SEN. The application utilizes play activities and the Applied Behavior Analysis (ABA) method in exercises such as matching or receptive language. In addition, it has an intelligent system to adapt the level of the learning sessions according to the student's progress. In this way, the application records the activity carried out by the student and also assesses learning [10]. However, none of its adapted activities allow for English language learning for Spanish-speaking children with ID.

The Learn English for Kids [11] application is aimed at teaching English to children and is available for free on iOS and Android platforms. This application provides various images to help with vocabulary, audio files to practice listening, and recording functions to practice speaking. Teaching is done through lessons that are structured first with easy words and phrases, which gradually become more difficult.

Similarly, Special Words [12] enables teaching various English words to native speakers. The application is intended for children with SEN, ensuing a simple and intuitive interface. In addition, it presents a way to engage children with technology using both traditional and holistic teaching methods [13]. The application provides activities to develop and stimulate different skills, such as manual-vision coordination, improvement in fine motor skills, communication, speech stimulation, expanding the child's vocabulary and personal, social and emotional development. Notably, the words, photos and audio can be customized to make it a more friendly environment for the child to develop different skills.

However, the proposed English activities of these applications ([11] and [12]) are focused on native English speaking children, proving difficult to adapt to children with ID where Spanish is their native language.

Lingvist [14] is an application that adapts in real time to the user and the learning habits. This is done through linguistic analysis methods, that is, the application adapts to the existing knowledge of the learner, providing personalised lesson plans. In this way, the language learning experience is contextualised for the individual users needs. The application has additional features such as monitoring of user statistics, voice recognition system, grammar aids providing flexibility, virtual voices to replicate words, examples of real situations created by expert linguists, grammatical challenges and a simple to understand interface [15]. However, despite these attributes, the application does not provide elements to adjust its contents to the learning needs of children with ID.

The PICAA [16] application provides various activities for children with SEN, designed as a classroom support application. The user interface and educational contents have been designed to be adaptable to the needs and abilities of the student. The application offers individualized teaching with the customization to support group activities, stimulating the execution of activities. This provides the opportunity to personalize the learning experience for each individual user.

Similar to the Lingvist application, PICAA stimulates vocabulary, memory and eye-hand coordination improvements by incorporating teaching methods of word and image association, puzzles and exploration, order and memory activities, vocabulary comprehension, and cause and effect learning [10]. While this application provides various activities to support the education of children with SEN, it does not offer activities to learn English as a second language.

Azahar [17] is a set of free and customizable applications that allow people with ASD and ID to improve their communication and planning tasks, in order to enjoy their leisure activities. Azahar is composed of a set of 10 applications, with different contents including concepts of time, personal communication, access and management of music, hours of the day, and stimulating games. These applications use the Treatment and Education of Autistic and Related Communication-Handicapped Children (TEACCH) methodology and are available for computers and some Android applications. Amongst the characteristics presented in the Azahar project, pictograms, photos and voices are also utilized. Similar to PICAA, this application provides content and materials suitable for students with learning disabilities however is not focused on learning English as a second language.

Generally, it is evident that these English teaching applications offer suitable activities that support the learner in forming comprehension and expression skills. Furthermore, apart from The Learn English for Kids, all applications contain monitoring tools that provide a record of progress. Additionally, the applications adapted to work with a neurodevelopmental disorder [8, 12, 16] and [17], such as ASD, SEN and ID, are customizable, except for the PICAA application. However, these proposals focus on native English speaking students or do not provide adaptations for children with ID. However, unfortunately for this study, the applications explored are not intended for Spanish speaking students with ID who are learning English as a second language.

When working with children with ID, the American Association on Intellectual and Developmental Disabilities (AAIDD) notes that it is critical to consider factors such as the child's environment and culture, as well as linguistic diversity and cultural differences in the way people interact, communicate, move and behave. Therefore, it is evident that the explored applications do not consider the adequacy nor the suitability of its materials and methods for English language learning in Spanish-speaking children with ID.

3   Proposal

To address the aforementioned limitations, a software platform with activities adapted to teach the English language to Spanish-speaking children with ID is proposed. Specifically focusing on the impact of implementing didactic instructions via a mobile application in an SEN school.

The proposed activities were designed by specialists in SEN. The proposal was implemented and validated in a real environment during an academic semester, in an SEN school located in Santiago, Chile.

Using a mobile application, each student independently completed activities for the development of skills in the areas of listening and reading, and comprehension and spoken expression. The teacher has access to all activities and designs customized plans based on the students' ID level. Also, parents and guardians have access to the individual student results obtained via the mobile application.

The proposed solution was developed through four phases before being released for testing. Firstly, a study was carried out on the ID present in SEN schools, including an investigation of the current teaching methods implemented by ID specialist teachers.

Secondly, design guidelines [18, 19] and methodologies [20] were outlined to guide the development process of the proposed mobile application. Thirdly, from these two phases, activities were designed in conjunction with a specialist in SEN. It was vital at this stage that the activities achieved the topic of this study, that is, activities designed to have a positive impact on learning English as a second language for Spanish speaking students with ID.

The fourth phase was to create a prototype from the aforementioned design activities, which were installed on tablets owned by the school. This allowed for constant feedback from teachers, students, and parents or guardians.

Finally, a control group and an experimental group were established, carrying out a pre-test and a post-test, to see the impact of the application on the students' learning process throughout the semester.

3.1 Activity Description

The activities were co-created with specialists, following a learning methodology according to the children's needs. These activities focused on the development of the four English language skills: listening, speaking, reading, and writing. Additionally, the activity design of the proposed application endeavors that children acquire cognitive skills that enable them to organize and internalize the information they obtain through language practice.

Resembling the benefits of customizable lessons in the related work section, the mobile application facilitates customizable plans. The ID specialist teachers assign activities to students' tablets that have difficulty levels ranging from low to difficult. The detailed configuration the teacher deployed was determined by both the student's ID level and their preferred activity type (based on previous performance).

The activities types carried out consisted of the following tasks:

- Write the word: the student must write the concept illustrated by the image using the keyboard of the tablet.
- Match: the student must match a written word with its associated image.
- Complete with the missing letter: the student must complete a word with the associated missing letter.

3.2 Software Description

The software platform monitors various interactions (i.e. attempts, decisions, times, and clicks) of individual students in the activities (i.e. colors, family, and greetings). This permits access to relevant information about the children's learning process and the possibility of monitoring, evaluating, and making timely decisions about the activities that were proposed by the teachers.

The purpose of this application is to digitalize activities that are carried out with traditional tools such as paper, pencil, and blackboards. The advantage is to have all activities and their associated records unified within a single application. An important factor in the decision to use a mobile application is its degree of accessibility [21] ensuring its ease of use for students with ID.

Amongst the characteristics of the mobile application is:

- Activities executor: contains the activities that each student must undertake, according to the units of the corresponding subject. The student has two possibilities to advance:

at their own pace, or the teacher's discretion. The teachers reviewed the student's progress to intervene with adaptations as appropriate.

- Activity log: stores the results of the students' execution to evaluate their performance.
- Vocabulary: a fixed repository of visual and auditory material, with the vocabulary that the students can use in the activities. The repository was organized into categories of vocabulary which was constantly available for the student to access.

In the construction of the application the following resources were used:

- Balsamiq Mockups 3 is a tool to design interface mockups, which was used to design the prototypes of the interfaces of the mobile application.
- Unity is a multiplatform video game engine, which uses scripting for objects called "GameObjects". This engine was used to develop the software platform, due to its ease of orienting and working with the objects required for the activities.
- Google Cloud Platform (GCP) is a platform that amalgamates Google applications for web development. Therefore, this platform was used to manage the database. Within this platform 3 resources were used, which are:
- Storage was used to store the ".sql" file generated in "MySQL Workbench 8.0 CE".
- SQL was used to mount the ".sql" file that is in "Storage" and manage the database.
- Compute Engine was used to have a virtual machine directly connected to the database and, thus, be able to work as a "root" user and all related permissions.

Final Interface Design. This section presents an array of final interfaces to illustrate concrete examples of the designed activities. Notably, the design decisions (i.e. typeface, size, background color, images, extension, and contrasts) were conducted per the guidelines provided by SEN specialists.

As can be identified in Fig. 1, the activity instructions were presented in Spanish alongside an image, facilitated by the Spanish translation of the English word to be completed. The student is provided with a selection of vowels to complete the English word. This activity (Fig. 1) has an associated medium level. In cases of a low or difficult level, the number of missing vowels would decrease or increase (respectfully). Additionally, the difficult level does not include the Spanish translation after the instructions.

If the student's response is correct, the word will be completed and the vowel button will turn green. On the contrary, if the student's response is incorrect, the word will not be completed, and the selected vowel would turn red, indicating that it is not the correct vowel to complete the word. Finally, when completing the word, a window will be displayed on the image, which consists of a correct message and an 'ok' button, to proceed to the next activity.

An activity to match and associate words with pictures is presented in Fig. 2. The activity instructions were presented in Spanish followed by a selection of English words and their associated images that the student was required to join.

When completing the activity, if the student response is correct when the word is matched with its associated image, both will disappear from the screen. However, incorrectly matching a word to an image (for example, the student matches the word "Lion" to the image of a sheep) will prevent the two selected objects from disappearing.

Fig. 1. Activity to complete the word with the missing letter/s.

Fig. 2. Activity to match the word with the associated image.

The activity is regarded at a difficult level. For lower levels, the words and images are decreased. For example, a medium level will display four words with associated images, while at the lower level only 3 options will be available. Finally, by completing the activity correctly all words and pictures will disappear and the same feedback as the previous activity in Fig. 1 will follow.

4 Implementation and Evaluation

In order to validate the proposal, a pre-post quasi-experimental study with two groups was designed:

- Group A: with the technological intervention (9 students).
- Group B: without the technological intervention (6 students).

All students across both groups correspond to the 6th-grade level, all with intellectual disabilities. To evaluate the impact on learning, an initial test was applied to both groups, prior to the intervention, and an equivalent final test. The tasks of the initial and final test were divided into 5 items, which represent the 5 units of the course to be evaluated:

I. Colors

  1. Join the color and associated name together with a line.
  2. Color each star according to the indicated color.
  3. Write the color of each shape on the provided line.

II. Greetings

  1. Look at the picture and mark the correct option with a cross.
  2. Name the type of greeting displayed in each image.
  3. Look at the image and paint the correct option in each option.

III. Numbers

  1. Match the number and associated name together with a line.
  2. Write the number and circle the associated number.
  3. Listen and write the numbers heard.

IV. Family

  1. Write the name of the images displayed.
  2. Listen to the name of the family members and circle the correct. choice in each option.

V. Animals

  1. Write the animal name of the images displayed.
  2. Match the animal and associated name together with a line.

3. Listen to the names of the following animals and mark a cross on the associated images.

To evaluate the success of the activities, the results between pre and post-tests for both groups were compared respectfully. To effectively compare the results, the Student's t-test was applied to observe the distribution of results and identify significant differences. Additionally, to quantify the effect size of the differences observed the Cohen's D statistic was implemented.

5 Results

This section describes and analyzes the learning results obtained during the implementation of the mobile application (Sect. 5.1). Furthermore, the usage times of the designed activities are reviewed in detail (Sect. 5.2).

5.1 Learner Results

For the analysis, group A (with technological intervention) included 9 students while group B (without technological intervention) included 6 students. All students of the two groups completed the pre and post-test, with a maximum score of 75 points.

The highest score of the pretest for group A was 72 points, while the lowest was 18 points. The average score was 46.44 (SD = 5.55), which is greater than the expected 50% of the ideal test score (36 points). Whereas for group B, the highest score was 74 points while the lowest was 5 points. Group B has an average of 36.33 (SD = 26.65), which shows a greater dispersion in the results for this group.

In regards to the post-test, in group A, the highest score was 74 points while the lowest was 36, with an average of 59.67 (SD = 12.82). In group B the highest score was 61 points, and the lowest 26, with an average of 47.50 (SD = 15.63).

A summary of the results can be seen in Table 1, where an increase in the averages for both groups was attained. Furthermore, a decrease in the respective standard deviations demonstrates a higher concentration of students scoring an average result.

Table 1. Descriptive summary of learner results.

	Pre test		Post test	
	Mean	Std. Dev	Mean	Std. Dev
Group A (with intervention) Students = 9	46.44	15.55	59.67	12.82
Group B (without intervention) Students = 6	36.33	26.65	47.5	15.63

As mentioned, to compare the results from the pre and post-tests, the student's T-test was applied alongside the Cohen's D statistic to observe if there were significant differences between the two tests.

Table 2 shows the result for the p-value of the T-test, where a significant difference is considered when a p-value of less than 5% (<0.05) is evident. In the case of group A, a significant difference was observed, which is supported by Cohen's D calculations to measure the impact of the intervention. A value greater than 0.6 is considered to indicate that the intervention had a successful impact. The value achieved for group A was 0.92, indicating that the intervention had a high impact.

Table 2. Significant data in the learner results.

	T-test - p-value	Cohen's D
Group A (with intervention) Students = 9	<0.001	0.92
Group B without intervention) Students = 6	0.1010	N/A

5.2 Time Usage Results

The time of use of the application by each student was reviewed to check how long it took the students to work with the different activities (as outlined in implementation and evaluation). Table 3 displays the average usage times by the students in group A (with technological interventions).

Table 3. Time usage results.

Activity	Average time (minutes)	Standard deviation (minutes)
Write the word	06:29	05:13
Match	07:17	05:27
Fill in the missing letter	05:14	04:03

As the data presents, the average times of each activity is similar to the accompanying standard deviations, approximately one minute apart. However, the matching activity presented the most dispersed times, with a difference of almost two minutes. This may be attributed to two factors. Firstly, the difficulty or lack of previous knowledge of the vocabulary studies, or, secondly, the cognitive load of the student's interaction with the application.

In addition to the usage time of each activity, Table 4 presents the average number of attempts, correct responses, and errors for each activity.

From these results, it is apparent that the average number of correct responses and errors are similar, indicating that a successful outcome upon the first attempt is infrequent.

Table 4. Usages results in regards to attempts, correct responses, and errors.

Activity	Average number of attempts	Average number of correct responses	Average number of errors
Write the word	1	1	0
Match	5	3	2
Fill in the missing letter	2	1	1

The matching activity exhibits the highest average numbers for each finding suggesting that for every five attempts, three attempts will be correct while 2 will be incorrect. While "complete with the missing letter" indicates a ratio of one correct and one incorrect for every two attempts, a fifty percent success rate. Evidently, the best performing activity for children is the "write the word" activity, demonstrating that each attempt results in a correct response.

Overall, this experiment resulted in a significant impact on the learning achieved in the experimental group. The Cohen D resulted in 0.92 with a p-value of <0.001. Furthermore, the analysis of the standard deviation of time usage in each activity provided insights into the difficulty levels supporting modifications of future activities.

6 Conclusion and Future Work

In exploring relevant applications that support English practice for students with ID, a gap was identified that these applications did not support the practice of English as a second language. Thus, the experiment to observe the impact of mobile applications in an SEN school of native Spanish speakers practicing English as a second language was initiated.

Alongside ID specialist teachers, three different types of lessons ranging in three difficulty levels were designed and implemented. Students of both control and experimental groups participated in pre and post-tests to determine the impact of the application.

It was observed that there was a quantifiable impact regarding the learning achieved in the experimental group (Cohen's D = 0.92, p-value <0.001). The results were further analyzed by identifying the standard deviation of the time used in each activity, demonstrating that the matching activity was the most difficult eliciting more attempts with higher errors.

In pursuing the topic addressed by this project, it is evident that a significant impact is achieved when implementing mobile applications in SEN schools of Spanish speaking students with ID practicing English as a second language.

As for future work, we expect to create more activities to address different themes and situations of the English language. Additionally, we expect to integrate activities that promote socialization and self-care through the English language. We want to explore situations in which the activities can be adapted automatically depending on the interaction between the children with ID and the mobile application. Finally, we expect to carry out real case studies that analyze both in-depth and qualitatively [22] how difficult it is for children with ID to interact with the different functionalities designed in the mobile application.

References

1. Stavroussi, P., Karagiannidis, C.: Assisting students with intellectual disability through technology. Encycl. Educ. Inf. Technol. 157–164 (2020)
2. Morash-Macneil, V., Johnson, F., Ryan, J.B.: A systematic review of assistive technology for individuals with intellectual disability in the workplace. J. Spec. Educ. Technol. **33**(1), 15–26 (2018)
3. Paradis, J.: English second language acquisition from early childhood to adulthood: the role of age, first language, cognitive, and input factors. In: Proceedings of the BUCLD, vol. 43, pp. 11–26 (2019)
4. Hyland, K., Hyland, F.: Feedback in Second Language Writing: Contexts and Issues. Cambridge university press, Cambridge (2019)
5. Kung, F.-W.: Teaching second language reading comprehension: the effects of classroom materials and reading strategy use. Innov. Lang. Learn. Teach. **13**(1), 93–104 (2019)
6. First, E.: EF English Proficiency Index. Recuperado Httpswww Ef-Aust, Com Auepiabout-Epi (2017)
7. Sembiring, S.E.: English language acquisation of students with intellectual disabilities at special junior high school in bengkulu. Edulitics Educ. Lit. Linguist. J. **4**(1), 13–20 (2019)
8. Fundación Lovaas, AbaPlanet. http://www.abaplanet.com/es/
9. III Edición Máster Privado Young Autism Program, Lovaas Foundation. https://lovaasfounda tion.es/es/blog/25-blog-formacion/728-iii-edición-máster-privado-young-autism-program. html
10. Caice, C., Raquel, J.: Estudio Comparativo de las Tecnologías de Software y Hardware que permitan la comunicación con personas autistas., BABAHOYO (2018)
11. TalkEnglish, Learn English Speaking and Improve your Spoken English with Free English Speaking Lessons Online!, 2016. https://www.talkenglish.com/
12. SpecialiApps, Palabras Especiales| Special iApps, 2020. https://www.specialiapps.org/es/pal abras-especiales
13. Special iApps (2019). https://www.specialiapps.org/es/palabras-especiales
14. Aprende inglés, Lingvist, (2019). https://lingvist.com/es/. Accessed 08 Feb 2021
15. Lingvist, Somos Lingvist, Lingvist (2019). https://lingvist.com/es/blog/somos-lingvist/
16. Palomino, M.C.P., Ruiz, M.J.C.: PICAA: Aplicación móvil de aprendizaje para la inclusión educativa del alumnado con discapacidad, Migramos Una Nueva Plataforma, **13**(1) (2013)
17. Azahar, Proyecto Azahar (2013). http://www.proyectoazahar.org/azahar/loggined.do;jsessi onid=762671D1FF1475787991E0D5188D0470
18. Constantin, A., Johnson, H., Smith, E., Lengyel, D., Brosnan, M.: Designing computer-based rewards with and for children with autism spectrum disorder and/or intellectual disability. Comput. Hum. Behav. **75**, 404–414 (2017)
19. Dekelver, J., Kultsova, M., Shabalina, O., Borblik, J., Pidoprigora, A., Romanenko, R.: Design of mobile applications for people with intellectual disabilities. Commun. Comput. Inf. Sci. **535**. 823–836 (2015)
20. Rojas, L.A., Macías, J.A.: An agile information-architecture-driven approach for the development of user-centered interactive software. In: Proceedings of the XVI International Conference on Human Computer Interaction, pp. 1–8 (2015)

21. Galkute, M., Rojas, L.A.P., Sagal Maureira, V.A.M.: Improving the web accessibility of a university library for people with visual disabilities through a mixed evaluation approach. Social Computing and Social Media. Design, Ethics, User Behavior, and Social Network Analysis, pp. 56–71. Springer Cham, New York (2020). https://doi.org/10.1007/978-3-030-49570-1_5
22. Rojas, L.A.P., Truyol, M.E., Calderon Maureira, J.F., Orellana Quiñones, M., Puente, A.: Qualitative evaluation of the usability of a web-based survey tool to assess reading comprehension and metacognitive strategies of university students. Social Computing and Social Media. Design, Ethics, User Behavior, and Social Network Analysis, pp. 110–129. Springer Cham, New York (2020). https://doi.org/10.1007/978-3-030-49570-1_9

Student eXperience in Times of Crisis: A Chilean Case Study

Cristian Rusu[1](✉) , Sandra Cano[1] , Virginica Rusu[2] , Nicolás Matus[1] ,
Daniela Quiñones[1] , and Iván Mercado[1]

[1] Pontificia Universidad Católica de Valparaíso, Av. Brasil 2241, 2340000 Valparaíso, Chile
{cristian.rusu,sandra.cano,daniela.quinones,
ivan.mercado}@pucv.cl
[2] Universidad de Playa Ancha, Av. Playa Ancha 850, 2340000 Valparaíso, Valparaíso, Chile
virginica.rusu@upla.cl

Abstract. Customer eXperience (CX) includes all physical and emotional responses during the interactions with the products, systems and services that a company or an organization offers. We can consider a student as a particular case of customer, and Student eXperience (SX) as a particular case of CX. Higher education students are using not only the educational service, but they are interacting with a wide range of products, systems and services that a university offers. Chile was affected by crises since October 2019: a social outbreak crisis first, then the COVID-19 pandemic crisis. They have influenced the way in which students and universities interact, and consequently the SX. We carried out an exploratory study in order to identify how these crises have impacted the SX in the particular case of Escuela de Ingeniería Informática (School of Informatics Engineering) of the Pontificia Universidad Católica de Valparaíso (PUCV), in Chile. The paper presents our preliminary findings.

Keywords: Student experience · Customer experience · Social outbreak · COVID-19 pandemic

1 Introduction

Customer experience (CX) is the most relevant factor when it comes to customer's satisfaction with a company/organization. CX includes all physical and emotional responses that a customer experiences before, during and after coming into contact, directly or indirectly, with a brand/company, during the whole "journey", including the post consumption stage [1]. CX is generated in "touchpoints" (interactions) between the customer and the company (organization), through the products, systems and services that this offers [2].

CX has a highly interdisciplinary nature, and the Human-Computer Interaction (HCI) community is showing a growing interest on CX. Following this trend, in the last years we were expanding are work from User eXperience (UX) to CX. Aligned to Lewis opinion, we think that CX is a natural extension of UX, and could build a bridge between HCI and Service Science [3–5].

G. Meiselwitz (Ed.): HCII 2021, LNCS 12775, pp. 270–285, 2021.
https://doi.org/10.1007/978-3-030-77685-5_22

By considering students as customers of educational services, products and systems provided by a university, we can refer to Student eXperience (SX) as a particularized case of CX. SX is conditioned by the contact between students and their educational institution. Experiences occur every time they interact with any service, product or system that the university provides. Moreover, each experience has a potential impact on future experiences, and all of them are building the holistic SX. Since October 2019, social and health crises have affected Chile. They have influenced the way in which students and universities interact, and consequently the SX.

In October 2019 a social outbreak occurred in Chile; it triggered a series of protests, riots and looting. These incidents rapidly escalated in complexity and violence; a state of emergency was imposed throughout the country, and a curfew was declared in several regions. As a result of this crisis, face-to-face activities in the country's universities were interrupted [6]. Although traumatic, the sudden adaptation of a virtual model allowed universities to be better prepared for the upcoming health crisis, where again restrictions were imposed.

In early 2020, after the wide spread of the COVID-19 virus, the disease was declared as pandemic by the World Health Organization [7]. A series of measures were taken by the Chilean government, including lockdown and curfew. Students were again exposed to a situation that dramatically modified the way in which they relate to the university, and the educational environment in general. Students' social isolation was particularly negative, considering the role of students' social interactions in the academic context. The COVID-19 pandemic affected students and their family and social environment, during and outside of academic hours. It generated anxiety and stress, and students' academic and social performance were affected.

Considering that the SX is generated by the interactions between students and educational institutions, it is logical to think that both social and pandemic crisis had significant impacts on students' experience. It is important to understand how the student – university interaction has changed in times of crisis, and what the impact of these changes in SX was.

In April - November 2020 we carried out an exploratory study in order to understand the impact of the social outbreak and the COVID-19 pandemic crises on SX, in the case of Escuela de Ingeniería Informática (School of Informatics Engineering) of the Pontificia Universidad Católica de Valparaíso (PUCV), in Chile [8, 9]. The department is offering two undergraduate programs in Informatics Engineering: a 4 years program (Ingeniería de Ejecucción en Informática, Operational Informatics Engineering, INF), and a 6 years program (Ingeniería Civil Informática, Civil Informatics Engineerings, ICI). We collected the undergraduate students' opinion in two surveys. Roughly 10% of the students participated in each survey. Students voluntarily participated in the experiment and we did not follow a sampling procedure; so, the results of the study cannot be generalized.

The paper presents our preliminary findings. Section 2 describes the survey regarding the impact of the social outbreak crisis on SX. Section 3 presents the survey regarding the impact of the COVID-19 pandemic crisis on SX. Finally, Sect. 4 highlights conclusions and future work.

2 The Survey Regarding the Social Outbreak

Due to the social outbreak in Chile, since October 2019 a considerable group of public and private institutions decided to close their doors, in order to safeguard the physical and emotional integrity of their workers and customers. The remote work modality was imposed in most of these institutions. Higher education students were not oblivious to this measure. Suddenly, most of the Chilean universities switched from face-to-face activities to online classes. This dramatic change generated stress and anxiety, and a constant feeling of insecurity and uncertainty about the future, into the whole academic community.

We made an exploratory study regarding the impact of the social crisis on SX, among the undergraduate students of the School of Informatics Engineering at PUCV. The survey took place in April 2020.

2.1 The Questionnaire

The questionnaire regarding the experience during the social outbreak is presented in Table 1. It was developed iteratively, and includes three sections:

- Background: the section was kept to minimum, including only 3 questions;
- Perception of online activities during the social outbreak: regarding students' experience with online classes and administrative paperwork during the social outbreak, as well as previously (if applied);
- Recommendations and future intention: suggestions to improve online classes, as well as willingness to enroll in online courses in the future.

Table 1. The questionnaire regarding the social outbreak.

Section	Question	Type
Background	In what program are you enrolled?	INF/ICI
	When did you start your studies?	Year
	In how many courses have you been enrolled in during the social outbreak?	Numeric
Perception of online activities during the social outbreak	How would you rate your experience with online classes?	Likert scale with 5 levels (1 – Very negative, 5 – Very positive)

(continued)

Table 1. (*continued*)

Section	Question	Type
	Did you experience online classes prior to the social outbreak?	Yes/No
	If so, how many courses did you study online prior to the social outbreak?	Numeric
	If so, how would you rate your previous experience with online classes?	Likert scale with 5 levels (1 – Very negative, 5 – Very positive)
	What were your favorite tools when studying online? (More than one option can be marked)	Classes by videoconference/Resources available online/Chatting with professors/Discussion forum/None/Others
	What were the positive aspects of online classes? (More than one option can be marked)	Flexible schedule/Recorded classes/Comfort/Evaluation methods/None/Others
	What were the negative aspects of online classes? (More than one option can be marked)	Professors' attitude/Professors' lack of ability to teach online/Online teaching methods/Lack of planning/Lack of interaction in classes/Level of difficulty/Lack of learning resources/None/Others
	Did you need online administrative paperwork?	Yes/No
	If so, how would you rate your experience?	Likert scale with 5 levels (1 - Very negative, 5 – Very positive)
Recommendations and future intentions	What do you suggest that it should be done to improve future online experience?	Open question
	Would you like to have online classes in the future?	Yes/No

2.2 Quantitative Results

We collected valid responses from 56 students:

- 37 students were enrolled in the INF program (66.1%), and 19 were enrolled in the ICI program (33.9%);

- 15 students were freshmen (26.8%), and 41 were advanced students (73.2%);
- 24 students experienced online classes before the social outbreak (42.9%), having been enrolled in 1 to 5 courses (an average of 1.87 courses);
- 19 students had to do online administrative paper-work during the social outbreak (33.9%);
- Students have been enrolled in 1 to 7 courses during the social outbreak (an average of 4.70 courses);
- Only 23 students (41.1%) declared that they would like to have online courses in the future. The majority rejected this idea (33 students, 58.9%).

We used the Kolmogorow-Smirnow K-S test (using p-value ≤ 0.05 as decision rule), to check the hypothesis:

- H0: the variable perceived experience (EXP) has a normal distribution,
- H1: the variable perceived experience does not have a normal distribution.

We obtained p-value $= 0.008$, so the variable EXP does not have a normal distribution. We used nonparametric statistic tests to analyze data. In all tests p-value ≤ 0.05 was used as decision rule.

We used the Mann-Whitney U test to check the hypothesis:

- H0: there are no significant differences between the perceived experience of two different groups of students,
- H1: there are significant differences between the perceived experience of two different groups of students.

As Table 2 indicates, there are no significant differences between the groups of students, by several criteria. As expected, there are significant differences regarding the perceived experience, between the group of students who would like to have online classes in the future, and the group of those who reject this idea.

Table 2. Mann–Whitney U tests by groups of students.

	INF/ICI	Freshmen/Advanced	Previous/No experience in online classes	Did/Did not administrative paperwork	Would like/Would not like to have online classes in the future
p-value	.819	.984	.712	.186	**.000**

Table 3 shows statistics for variables evaluated with a Likert scale:

- Experience with online classes during the social outbreak (EXP),

- Experience with online classes before the social outbreak (PREVEXP),
- Experience with online administrative paperwork (ADMEXP).

Table 3. Descriptive statistics for variable evaluated with a Likert scale.

Variable	No. of students	Average	Median	Stand. dev.	Min.	Max.
EXP	56	2.30	2	0.893	1	4
PREVEXP	24	3.42	4	1.381	1	5
ADMEXP	19	3.74	4	0.933	1	5

Students have a negative perception on their experience with online classes during the social outbreak (average 2.30, median 2). Their perception ranges from 1 to 4, but none of them indicated a very positive perception. Those who experienced online classes prior to the social outbreak have a slightly positive perception on those classes (average 3.42, median 4). Students that have done administrative paperwork during the social outbreak have a significantly better opinion on this process (average 3.74, median 4), comparing to the average opinion regarding the online classes (2.30).

We performed Spearman ρ tests to check the hypothesis:

- H0: $\rho = 0$, the variable perceived experience (EXP) and number of courses enrolled (COURSES) are independent,
- H1: $\rho \neq 0$, the variable perceived experience (EXP) and number of courses enrolled (COURSES) are dependent.

Table 4 shows a very weak correlation between the two variables.

Table 4. Spearman ρ test for variables EXP and COURSES.

	EXP	COURSES
EXP	1	.084
COURSES		1

2.3 Qualitative Results

Students' favorite tools when studying online where:

- Classes by videoconference (33 students, 58.9%);
- Resources available online (32 students, 57.1%);
- Discussion forum (13 students, 23.2%);

- Chatting with professors (11 students, 19.6%);
- None (9 students, 16.1%).

It is remarkable that 16.1% of the students disliked all online tools that have been used. It shows a real frustration, as some students think the tools were inadequate/insufficient. Some students indicated alternative tools, such as: projects, recorded classes, contact by email with professors.

In spite of their rather negative perception, only 5 students (8.9%) were unable to identify positive aspects of online classes. All positive aspects that we suggested in the questionnaire were confirmed:

- Recorded classes (38 students, 67.9%);
- Flexible schedule (35 students, 62.5%);
- Comfort (28 students, 50.0%);
- Evaluation methods (20 students, 35.7%).

The positive aspects seem to help students to cope with academic overload. In particular, recorded classes and flexible schedule allow them to use their own learning pace. One student also highlighted that online classes help saving money.

Only 3 students (5.4%) failed to identify negative aspects of online classes. All negative aspects that we suggested in the questionnaire were confirmed:

- Professors' lack of ability to teach online (31 students, 55.4%);
- Lack of interaction in classes (26 students, 46.4%);
- Lack of planning (24 students, 42.9%);
- Online teaching methods (22 students, 39.3%);
- Lack of learning resources (20 students, 35.7%);
- Level of difficulty (17 students, 30.4%);
- Professors' attitude (11 students, 19.6%).

In few cases, some other negative aspects were indicated: lack of standarized methods and tools among different courses, academic overload, and high level of exigency. Some negative aspects are related to elements that negatively influence students' motivation.

Student suggestions to improve their future online experience include:

- Activities that would improve their motivation and better interactivity;
- Professors' training for online classes;
- Better classes planning;
- Better infrastructure;
- Improved communication channels;
- More flexibility in attending classes and scheduling evaluations.

3   The Survey Regarding the COVID-19 Pandemic

The COVID-19 pandemic occurred in Chile in the worst possible time. The pandemic crisis overlapped with the social one. Lockdown and curfews were imposed in most of the country's regions. The whole academic activities during 2020 were virtual.

Following the survey related to the social outbreak, we made a follow-up study regarding the impact of the pandemic crisis on SX, among the undergraduate students of the School of Informatics Engineering at PUCV. The survey took place in November 2020.

3.1 The Questionnaire

The questionnaire regarding the experience during the COVID-19 pandemic is presented in Table 5. It was developed iteratively, based on the questionnaire regarding the social outbreak. Some questions were eliminated or adapted; new questions were added. Options available as responses were slightly changed in some cases. The final version includes four sections:

- Demographics and background: the section was kept to minimum; two questions regarding students' infrastructure were added;
- Experience during the COVID-19 pandemic: regarding students' experience with online classes and administrative paperwork during the COVID-19 pandemic;
- Recommendations: suggestions to improve online classes; the question regarding the willingness to enroll in online courses in the future was eliminated;
- Emotions: students were asked about the level of 6 emotions that they may have felt during the COVID-19 pandemic: fear, stress, anxiety, disgust, boredom and joy [10, 11].

Table 5. The questionnaire regarding de COVID-19 pandemic.

Section	Question	Type
Demographics and background	In what program are you enrolled?	INF/ICI
	Gender	Female/Male
	When did you start your studies?	Year
	Quality of internet connection	Scale with 5 levels (1 – I don't have internet connection/2 – Bad/3 – Reasonable/4 – Good/5 – Excellent)
	Devices used for online classes	Smartphone/Tablet/Desktop/Notebook

(continued)

Table 5. (*continued*)

Section	Question	Type
Experience during the COVID-19 pandemic	How would you rate your experience with online classes?	Likert scale with 5 levels (1 – Very negative, 5 – Very positive)
	How would you rate your level of stress?	Likert scale with 5 levels (1 – Very low, 5 – Very high)
	What aspects of life as student were more stressful?	Open question
	What do you feel could reduce your level of stress as student?	Open question
	What were your favorite tools when studying online during the social outbreak? (More than one option can be marked)	Classes by videoconference/Resources available on the e-Learning university platform/ Resources available on other platforms/Discussion forum/Groupwork/Professors' advisory/Tutors advisory/Others
	What were the positive aspects of online classes? (More than one option can be marked)	Flexible schedule/Recorded classes/Comfort/Evaluation methods/Online webinars, seminars, conferences/Others
	What were the negative aspects of online classes? (More than one option can be marked)	Low motivation in classes/Lack of interaction in classes/Online teaching methods/Level of difficulty/Curses lack of planning/Professors' attitude/Evaluation methods/Others
	Did you need online administrative paperwork?	Yes/No
	If so, how would you rate your experience?	Likert scale with 5 levels (1 – Very negative, 5 – Very positive)
Recommendations	What do you suggest that it should be done to improve future online experience?	Open question
Emotions	Fear	Likert scale with 5 levels (1 – None, 5 – A lot)
	Stress	Likert scale with 5 levels (1 – None, 5 – A lot)

(*continued*)

Table 5. (*continued*)

Section	Question	Type
	Anxiety	Likert scale with 5 levels (1 – None, 5 – A lot)
	Disgust	Likert scale with 5 levels (1 – None, 5 – A lot)
	Boredom	Likert scale with 5 levels (1 – None, 5 – A lot)
	Joy	Likert scale with 5 levels (1 – None, 5 – A lot)Yes/No

3.2 Quantitative Results

We collected valid responses from 55 students:

- 25 students were enrolled in the INF program (45.5%), and 30 were enrolled in the ICI program (54.5%);
- 11 students were females (20.0%), and 44 students were males (80.0%);
- 14 students were freshmen (25.5%), and 41 were advanced students (74.5%);
- 28 students had to do online administrative paper-work during the COVID-19 pandemic (50.9%).

Most students used notebooks for their online academic activities (41 students, 74.5%). The second most popular device was smartphone (27 students, 49.1%), followed by desktop computers (19 students, 34.5%). Only 2 students used tablets (3.6%). Regarding the quality of their internet connection, 2 students (3.6%) had a bad connection, 27 students (49.1%) a reasonable one, 17 students (30.9%) a good one, and 9 students (16.4%) had an excellent connection.

We used the Kolmogorow-Smirnow K-S test (using p-value ≤ 0.05 as decision rule), to check the hypothesis:

- H0: the variable has a normal distribution,
- H1: the variable does not have a normal distribution.

We checked the following variables:

- EXP – experience with online classes,
- STRLEV – perceived stress level,
- ADMEXP – experience with online administrative paperwork,
- FEAR – perceived fear as emotion,
- STRESS – perceived stress as emotion,
- ANX – perceived anxiety as emotion,
- DISG – perceived disgust as emotion,

- BORE – perceived boredom as emotion
- JOY – perceived joy as emotion.

As Table 6 shows, most of the variables do not have a normal distribution, excepting ADMEXP, FEAR and DISG.

Table 6. Kolmogorow-Smirnow K-S test for checking a normal distribution.

	EXP	STRLEV	ADMEXP	FEAR	STRESS	ANX	DISGT	BORE	JOY
p-value	.016	.005	.106	.189	.000	.002	.055	.036	.016

We used nonparametric statistic tests to analyze data. In all tests p-value ≤ 0.05 was used as decision rule.

We used the Mann-Whitney U test to check the hypothesis:

- H0: there are no significant differences between the perception of two different groups of students,
- H1: there are significant differences between the perception of two different groups of students.

As Table 7 indicates, there are no significant differences between groups of students, with one exception: regarding variable EXP, between students that did and those that did not administrative paperwork. The experience with online administrative paperwork seems to be a differential factor for the experience with online classes.

Table 7. Mann–Whitney U tests by groups of students.

Variable:	EXP	STRLEV	FEAR	STRESS	ANX	DISGT	BORE	JOY
By program (INF/ICI):								
p-value	.396	.455	.304	.397	.126	.320	.643	.643
By gender:								
p-value	.137	.093	.378	.066	.591	.836	.177	.799
By level (freshmen/advanced):								
p-value	.708	.831	.193	.967	.080	.380	.944	.483
By administrative paperwork (did/did not):								
p-value	.015	.093	.790	.143	.060	.525	.413	.420

We used the Kruskal–Wallis H tests to check the hypothesis:

- H0: there are no significant differences between the perception of students belonging to groups that have internet connection of distinct quality,

- H1: there are significant differences between the perception of students belonging to groups that have internet connection of distinct quality.

As Table 8 indicates, there are no significant differences between groups of students with distinct internet connection quality regarding most of the variables, with two exceptions: ANX and DISGT. The quality of internet connection seems to be a differential factor for the perceived anxiety and disgust.

Table 8. Kruskal–Wallis H tests by groups of students with distinct internet connection quality.

	EXP	STRLEV	FEAR	STRESS	ANX	DISGT	BORE	JOY
p-value	.170	.567	.201	.148	.047	.017	.206	.333

Table 9 shows statistics for variables evaluated with a Likert scale: EXP, STRLEV, ADMEXP, FEAR, STRESS, ANX, DISG, BORE, and JOY. For ADMEXP we had 28 valid data, as only 28 students did administrative paperwork. For all other variables we had 55 valid data.

Table 9. Descriptive statistics for variable evaluated with a Likert scale.

Variable	Average	Median	Stand. dev.	Min.	Max.
EXP	3.00	3	1.054	1	5
STRLEV	3.93	4	1.120	1	5
ADMEXP	4.11	4	0.786	3	5
FEAR	2.85	3	1.407	1	5
STRESS	4.02	4	1.063	1	5
ANX	4.02	4	1.163	1	5
DISG	3.38	3	1.284	1	5
BORE	3.45	3	1.214	1	5
JOY	2.71	3	1.031	1	5

Students' perception on their experience with online classes during the COVID-19 pandemic is neutral (average 3.00, median 2). Their perception ranges from 1 to 5. It worth notice that the average perception improved comparing to the perception during the social outbreak crisis. The perceived stress level during the pandemic crisis is high (average 3.93, median 4). The experience with online administrative paper work was much better (average 4.11, median 4) that the one with online classes.

Regarding the 6 emotions, the results are as expected. The strongest emotions were stress and anxiety (average 4.02, median 4, in both cases). The levels of boredom (average 3.45, median 3) and disgust (average 3.38, median 3) where rather neutrals. As one would expect, the weakest emotion was joy (average 2.71, median 3). The level of fear was also low (average 2.85, median 3). Students' perception of emotions ranges from 1 to 5 in all cases.

We performed Spearman ρ tests to check the hypothesis:

- H0: $\rho = 0$, two variables are independent,
- H1: $\rho \neq 0$, two variables are dependent.

As Table 10 shows, variable BORE is independent of all variables, excepting ANX. There is a weak correlation between the two variables; when students felt anxiety, they also felt boredom. Variable EXP and FEAR are also independent; all other variables are dependent.

As expected, when there are negative correlations between EXP and several variables. When students perceived a high level of stress, and strong stress, anxiety and disgust as emotions, their experience with online classes was negative; but when they perceived joy, their experience with online classes was positive.

As anticipated, the level of stress perceived during the pandemic crisis (STRLEV) is highly correlated with stress as emotion (STRESS); it is the highest identified correlation (.843). When the level of stress was high, students did also feel fear (FEAR), anxiety (ANX) and disgust (DISGT). They did not feel joy (JOY).

As expected, there are negative correlations between emotion joy (JOY) and all other emotions; when students felt fear, stress, anxiety, disgust, or boredom, they did not feel joy. There is also a negative correlation between JOY and STRLEV; when the level of stress was high, students did not feel joy. But there is a positive correlation between JOY and EXP; when students felt joy, they also perceived their experience as positive.

Table 10. Spearman ρ test for variables EXP and COURSES.

	EXP	STRLEV	FEAR	STRESS	ANX	DISGT	BORE	JOY
EXP	1	−.460	Indep	−.480	−.267	−.396	Indep	.467
STRLEV		1	.456	.843	.497	.481	Indep	−.345
FEAR			1	.457	.313	.407	Indep	−.422
STRESS				1	.502	.547	Indep	−.340
ANX					1	.388	.267	−.292
DISGT						1	Indep	−.351
BORE							1	−.023
JOY								1

3.3 Qualitative Results

The level of stress during the pandemic crisis was high, probably even higher than during the social outbreak crisis. Actually, the two crises overlapped, which probably made things worst in Chile, comparing to other countries. Students indicated multiple factors of stress:

- Online methodology; this was especially complicate for freshmen;
- Improper infrastructure (internet connection and/or computational devices);
- Improper workplace in their own residences;
- Social isolation and lack of contact with their classmates;
- Disruptive external factors;
- Tiredness when spending too much time using a computer;
- Difficulties in effective and timely communication with professors;
- Struggles in focusing on their academic tasks and lack of planning;
- Difficulties to coordinate groupwork with their classmates;
- Problems to adapt to online methods of evaluation;
- Lack of free time and excessive academic load.

Students suggest some measures that could relief their stress:

- Carrying out activities with ludic elements, to make classes more motivating and competitive;
- Additional instances in which students can clarify their doubts with professors and classmates;
- Better coordination of evaluations schedule between professors;
- Fewer evaluation instances;
- Additional resources available online;
- Timely feedback from professors.

Students' favorite tools when studying online where:

- Resources available on the e-Learning university platform (38 students, 69.1%);
- Classes by videoconference (35 students, 63.6%);
- Resources available on other platforms (28 students, 50.9%);
- Groupwork (26 students, 47.3%);
- Professors' advisory (26 students, 47.3%);
- Tutors advisory (12 students, 21.8%);
- Discussion forum (3 students, 5.5%).

Comparing to the social outbreak crisis, same two tools are still the preferred ones. Discussion forum lost relevance. New options provided in the questionnaire have a good acceptance (resources available on other platforms, groupwork, and professors' advisory. Students also suggest the wide use of tools that make classes more interactive, engaging and appealing, as Mentimeter or Kahoot.

All positive aspects that we suggested in the questionnaire were confirmed by students, excepting comfort:

- Recorded classes (52 students, 94.5%);
- Flexible schedule (36 students, 65.5%);
- Evaluation methods (17 students, 30.9%);
- Online webinars, seminars, conferences (8 students, 14.5%).

No other aspects were identified. It is interesting that comfort was not considered as a positive aspect in pandemic crisis, contrary to the social outbreak crisis, when 50% of the students indicated it. It is also remarkable the very high acceptance of recorded classes.

- Low motivation in classes (38 students, 69.1%);
- Courses lack of planning (24 students, 43.6%);
- Lack of interaction in classes (20 students, 36.4%);
- Professors' attitude (20 students, 36.4%);
- Evaluation methods (15 students, 27.3%);
- Level of difficulty (14 students, 25.5%);
- Online teaching methods (9 students, 16.4%).

The main negative aspect mentioned by the students refers to the low motivation that the classes generate. It is interesting that in almost equal percentage students perceived the evaluation methods as positive, both also as negative. As suggestions to improve the experience with online classes, some of the ones made in the survey regarding the social outbreak occurred again. Most of the suggestions refer to interactive classes, active learning methodologies, and the link between theory and practice.

4   Conclusions and Future Work

CX is gaining each day more relevance for any company/organization. It is equally important for educational institutions, that offer mainly the educational services, but also associated products, systems and services to their students. Higher education students are a specific category of customers, and SX can be considered as a specific case of CX. When identifying students' needs, designing and evaluating educational services, CX methods can be used, but specific approaches and methods are also necessary. An HCI approach to SX is especially important, especially in times of crisis, when face-to-face classes are replaced by online classes, and software platforms are more important than ever. SX is increasingly important for universities.

Since we are focusing our research on CX for years, it is only natural to focus on SX, as we are also trying to improve our work as professors. Since October 2019, social and health crises have continuously affected Chile, overlapping. They have dramatically influenced SX. The study helped us to better understand the problems that impacted the whole academic community of the School of Informatics Engineering at PUCV, and undergraduate students in particular. It was an exploratory study, with some limitations, as the lack of a sampling procedure, and the relatively small number of participants; however, it offers valuable insights.

The surveys that we conducted offers interesting quantitative and qualitative data. Unexpectedly switching from face-to-face to online classes in October 2019 was very challenging for professors, students, and the whole academic community. Students' perception of online classes during the social outbreak crisis was quite negative. Their frustrations were obvious, and most of them are also professors' frustrations. We learned valuable lessons, and it seems that students' perception of online classes during the pandemic crisis got better, comparing to the social outbreak crisis. However, there is a lot of room for further improvements.

Most of the students' comments, specific problems that they have been identifying, and suggestions that they have been making, confirms our own views. More or less the same issues have been identified by the professors. Surveys' results are also confirmed by interviews to our fellow professors, academic tutors, focus groups, and several activities in the CX courses that we are teaching.

As future work, we would further analyze SX, extending the study to other departments, universities and countries. We would focus not only on SX evaluation, but also on students' needs and SX design.

Acknowledgments. We would like to thank to all students involved in the study. The study has been supported by the project UE2020.12.INV.FIN.INF.02, financed by Pontificia Universidad Católica de Valparaíso (Chile). Authors are participating in the HCI-Collab Project – The Collaborative Network to Support HCI Teaching and Learning Processes in IberoAmerica (http://hci-collab.com/).

References

1. Laming, C., Mason, K.: Customer experience – an analysis of the concept and its performance in airline brands. Res. Transp. Bus. Manag. **10**, 15–25 (2014)
2. Stein, A., Ramaseshan, B.: Towards the identification of customer experience touch point elements. J. Retail. Consum. Serv. **30**, 8–19 (2016)
3. Lewis, J.R.: Usability: lessons learned… and yet to be learned. Int. J. Hum.-Comput. Interact. **30**(9), 663–684 (2014)
4. Rusu, V., Rusu, C., Botella, F., Quiñones, D.: Customer eXperience: is this the ultimate eXperience? In: Proceedings Interacción 2018. ACM (2018)
5. Rusu, V., Rusu, C., Botella, F., Quiñones, D., Bascur, C., Rusu, V.: Customer eXperience: a bridge between service science and human-computer interaction. In: Ahram, T., Karwowski, W., Pickl, S., Taiar, R. (eds.) IHSED 2019. AISC, vol. 1026, pp. 385–390. Springer, Cham (2020). https://doi.org/10.1007/978-3-030-27928-8_59
6. Estallido social genera una explosión del uso de plataformas virtuales para hacer clases. https://www.uc.cl/noticias/estallido-social-genera-una-explosion-del-uso-plataformas-virtuales-para-hacer-clases/. Accessed 01 Jan 2021
7. WHO declares novel coronavirus outbreak a pandemic. https://edition.cnn.com/2020/03/11/health/coronavirus-pandemic-world-health-organization/index.html. Accessed 27 Dec 2020
8. Escuela de Ingeniería Informática PUCV. http://www.inf.ucv.cl. Accessed 31 Jan 2021
9. Pontificia Universidad Católica de Valparaíso. http://www.pucv.cl. Accessed 31 Jan 2021
10. Ekman, P.: Basic emotions. In: Dalgleish, T., Power, M.J. (eds.) Handbook of Cognition and Emotion, pp. 45–60. Wiley, New York (1999)
11. Aiyer, A., Surani, S., Gill, Y., Ratnani, I., Sunesara, S.: COVID-19 anxiety and stress survey (CASS) in high school and college students due to coronavirus disease 2019. Chest **158**(4), A314 (2020)

SCSM in Health and Wellbeing

Social Media During the COVID-19 Pandemic: A Public Health Crisis or a Political Battle?

Ashwaq Alsoubai[✉], Jihye Song[✉], Afsaneh Razi[✉], Pallavi Dacre[✉], and Pamela Wisniewski[✉]

University of Central Florida, Orlando, FL 32826, USA
{atalsoubai,chsong,afsaneh.razi,pdacre19}@knights.ucf.edu,
pamwis@ucf.edu

Abstract. Since the start of coronavirus disease 2019 (COVID-19) pandemic, social media platforms have been filled with discussions about the global health crisis. Meanwhile, the World Health Organization (WHO) has highlighted the importance of seeking credible sources of information on social media regarding COVID-19. In this study, we conducted an in-depth analysis of Twitter posts about COVID-19 during the early days of the COVID-19 pandemic to identify influential sources of COVID-19 information and understand the characteristics of these sources. We identified influential accounts based on an information diffusion network representing the interactions of Twitter users who discussed COVID-19 in the United States over a 24-h period. The network analysis revealed 11 influential accounts that we categorized as: 1) political authorities (elected government officials), 2) news organizations, and 3) personal accounts. Our findings showed that while verified accounts with a large following tended to be the most influential users, smaller personal accounts also emerged as influencers. Our analysis revealed that other users often interacted with influential accounts in response to news about COVID-19 cases and strongly contested political arguments received the most interactions overall. These findings suggest that political polarization was a major factor in COVID-19 information diffusion. We discussed the implications of political polarization on social media for COVID-19 communication.

Keywords: COVID-19 · Twitter · Social media influencers · Information dissemination

1 Introduction

Beginning in late 2019, coronavirus disease 2019 (COVID-19) emerged and spread around the world at an alarming rate, creating a large-scale public health emergency (World Health Organization 2020). It is crucial that public health agencies deliver information to the public in a timely manner during the health crisis. As a result, people turned to social media for news and discussion about this global health crisis. Social media has been widely used to gather and share information following disaster events (Starbird and Palen 2012; Zade et al. 2018). For instance, a report from Hether et al. (2014) suggests that 60% of adult Americans (80% of internet users) use online media as their main

© Springer Nature Switzerland AG 2021
G. Meiselwitz (Ed.): HCII 2021, LNCS 12775, pp. 289–307, 2021.
https://doi.org/10.1007/978-3-030-77685-5_23

source of health information. However, uncertainty and conflicting information have created obstacles for public health communication and posed dangerous consequences to people's lives (Spencer 2020; Zarocostas 2020). Therefore, health authorities have highlighted the importance of seeking credible sources of information related to COVID-19 (Zarocostas 2020). Given the importance of social media during health crises, 'social media influencers' have been considered 'critical actors' during the pandemic, since these influencers deliver timely information about COVID-19 to people who use social media platforms (Abidin et al. 2021). We analyzed influential sources of information on Twitter that people engaged with to understand how the dissemination of information during COVID-19 reflects governments' and public health agencies' efforts to promote credible sources on social media.

In this study, we identified Twitter influencers in the United States by scraping 13,492 Tweets from a 24-h period between June 16, 2020 and June 17, 2020. In the U.S. at this time, reported COVID-19 cases had decreased relative to the preceding spike in March and April[1]. However, during this week, the U.S. Centers for Disease Control and Prevention (CDC 2020) reported that while the number of cases of COVID-19-like illnesses was lower at the national level, cases were increasing in certain regions. Tension between economic and public health concerns led to disputes between health experts and politicians over appropriate government responses to COVID-19, with public health officials warning that reopening the economy could result in a surge in cases (Cher 2020). During this time, U.S. President Donald Trump clashed with health officials, prioritizing reopening and downplaying the risk of increased COVID-19 spread (Forgey 2020). Additionally, Trump received significant attention and criticism for moving forward with a planned campaign rally in Oklahoma, despite a major increase in COVID-19 cases in the state (Shumaker and Schwartz 2020). Meanwhile, reflecting both the uneven impact of COVID-19 across U.S. states, as well as partisan division across the nation, local and state governments took divergent paths when it came to reopening the economy or extending stay-at-home orders and business closures, leading to confusion and uncertainty (Gross 2020; Karimi et al. 2020; Olson 2020). Ultimately, these events culminated in a significant surge in COVID-19 cases nationwide in the weeks and months to follow[1].

A clear identification of the main influential sources of information about COVID-19 on social media can provide insights into the types of engagement and information that people sought for COVID-19 updates and news during the early days of the pandemic. There is a need for research to provide an identification of U.S. sources of information from online digital trace data to better understand this phenomenon. Thus, we pose the following research questions:

- **RQ1:** *Who were the most influential sources (based on interactions) of COVID-19 information on Twitter during the early stages of the pandemic?*
- **RQ2:** *What are the characteristics of these accounts/users and the information they shared?*
- **RQ3:** *How did users interact with these influential accounts and the COVID-19 information they share?*

---

[1] https://covid.cdc.gov/covid-data-tracker.

To answer RQ1, we first created an interactions network demonstrating information diffusion of the collected data to identify which users are the most influential information sources. To address RQ2, we then conducted qualitative and quantitative analyses of the identified influential accounts. For RQ3, we examined the types of interactions received by the influential accounts. Based on our network analysis, we identified 11 influential accounts. The influential accounts included public figures, such as elected government officials and news organizations, along with personal accounts. While the majority of influential accounts were verified with a large following, the influencers also included non-verified accounts with fewer followers. We found the influential accounts varied in the types of interactions they received. Additionally, we found the content receiving the most interactions from these users included news and updates about COVID-19 cases, as well as personal commentary. However, politically charged arguments received the most interactions overall.

By identifying the influential sources of COVID-19 information, we make the following unique research contributions: 1) We highlight the differences in users' interactions with different types of influential sources of information, and 2) We identify the influence capacity of influencers based on the received interactions using the visualized network. At the end, we discuss the implications of our findings for understanding polarization in health communication and provide recommendations for future research on the role of influencers in COVID-19 information diffusion.

2 Related Work

In this section, we explore relevant studies that discussed information diffusion and COVID-19 news diffusion on social media.

2.1 Information Diffusion on Social Media

Information diffusion happens when a piece of knowledge spreads from a source to a recipient(s) or audience through interactions. Zafarani et al. (2014) described the diffusion process with three main components: a sender of the information, a receiver, and a medium. Katz and Lazarsfeld (1955) pointed out that information can go viral through a person-to-person diffusion process. Large-scale of information distribution relies on social media networks. One study showed that people tended to imitate majority behavior in the diffusion process because they believed that the wisdom of the group could help them make the right decision (Levitan and Verhulst 2016). It is important to address how the bigger groups, or hubs, on social media can affect diffusion speed. This is introduced in the Barabási and Albert (1999) preferential attachment model. The preferential attachment model is based on the concept of "rich get richer" where a network is constructed randomly at the beginning. Then, a new node or individual connects randomly to an existing node with a preference to attach to the popular nodes or users. According to Freberg et al. (2011), these popular users emerge on social media platforms as third-party endorsers, or 'influencers.'

Influencers have a significant impact on people's attitudes, behavior, and decisions (Casaló et al. 2020). Influencers' abilities to gain trust and influence other users has become an advantage for them in reaching target users in an effective way (Pestek et al. 2017). Chae (2018) defined influencers as micro-celebrities, since they gained popularity over time using social media. Influencers on social media varied from "unknown actresses and models, fitness trainers and musicians to wealthy people" (Chae 2018). Examining the influencers' following network was one of the ways to identify influencers using social network analysis (Stieglitz et al. 2018). The capacity of influence of these influencers is usually linked with following size (Okuah et al. 2019). However, following size is not the only indication for quantifying influence; valuable interactions can also be considered another successful influence metric (Gräve and Greff 2018). Studies have shown that influencers with a "mid number of followers" can hold more engagement and trust than some influencers with a large number of followers (Pestek et al. 2017). In marketing, for example, the impact of influencers can be quantified by a two-way conversation on a product via social media (Booth and Matic 2011). Level of engagement can be defined by the interactivity of a piece of content shared on social media. Therefore, the influence indication used in this study to identify influencers of COVID-19 discussions was the number of engagements received.

2.2   COVID-19 Information Diffusion via Social Media

Since the beginning of the COVID-19 pandemic, many efforts have arisen to explore the reflection of this major health event in different social media platforms. Researchers have begun to investigate the sources of information related to the pandemic on social media, such as Ko et al. (2020), who were able to identify the sources of information on Twitter based in Taiwan using an online survey. Budhwani and Sun (2020) found that, there was a significant increase in using hashtags related to COVID-19 on Twitter. This resulted in the production of a large scale of data that can help researchers understand public perceptions about COVID-19. Some early research efforts focused on publishing datasets about COVID-19 discussions on social media to the public for analysis. Dimitrov et al. (2020) emphasized the role of Twitter as a tool for the research community to study online conversation dynamics, including information dissemination. The researchers published a publicly available dataset that has potential for analyzing COVID-19-related tweets. One of the major findings from the initial analysis of the published dataset was that it verified that "Twitter discourse statistics reflect major events." It was also observed that verified accounts "are the most active when major events occur."

Studies that involve the creation and/or analysis of datasets of online public postings to identify the influential sources of information are particularly useful in guiding the actions and policies of public agencies. For example, Rufai and Bunce (2020) stated that government leaders and public agencies can leverage pandemic-related studies of online discourse and information diffusion to evaluate the effectiveness of implemented policies and to inform future policy decisions. There was a noticeable trend of conducting sentiment analysis, a methodology that utilizes Natural Language Processing (NLP) to assess the connotation of a given text, on public discussions about COVID-19 on social media. Lwin et al. (2020) explored the sentiments from COVID-19 related discussions focusing on four emotions: fear, anger, sadness, and joy. The researchers found that during the pandemic, there was a significant shift in the public emotions from fear to anger "while sadness and joy also surfaced." Most fear emotions appeared around shortages of COVID-19 tests and medical supplies while the anger was shown in the tweets related to the stay-at-home notices. Sad emotions were shown clearly on topics related to losing friends and family members while tweets including words of gratitude and good health highlighted the joyful emotions. Another sentiment analysis based on positive and negative sentiments was done by Dimotrov et al. (2020) toward four prespecified prominent sources of pandemic-related information: Donald Trump, The World Health Organization, Breitbart, and CNN. Tracking the positive and negative sentiments of the tweets sent to the predefined sources revealed a possible controversy by synchronous increase in positive and negative sentiments in the week of Trump's State of the Union address.

Analyzing major sources of information was also an interest of Rufai and Bunce (2020) who conducted a content analysis on the COVID-19 responses from eight of the Group of Seven (G7) world leaders on Twitter. The analysis yielded 203 viral tweets: 166 (82.8%) were categorized as 'Informative,' 48 (28.6%) had weblinks to government-based sources, 19 (9.4%) were 'Morale-boosting,' and 14 (6.9%) were 'Political.' These studies used predefined lists of sources for analysis, while in this study, we obtained data using a scraper that collects data from Twitter users in the United States and then created a visualized network that illustrates the interactions between users who discussed COVID-19 related topics to identify the sources based on the accounts that received the highest number of interactions.

3 Methods

3.1 Study Overview

We performed an analysis of the interactions between Twitter users who posted tweets related to COVID-19 in order to identify and investigate the main sources of information that people engaged with during the early stages of the global pandemic. This analysis was done based on a visualized network constructed using the collected data (the interactions) and in-depth analysis on the identified sources. Further analysis was performed on the main identified sources of information in order to understand the shared characteristics of these users and extract the different types of accounts. In order to achieve this understanding, we performed a manual analysis on information related to the identified influencers' activity on Twitter based on number of followers, date of account creation, profile description, and whether the account was verified. The visualized network, along with the deep analysis of the identified accounts, allowed us to frame a comprehensive understanding of Twitter sources of COVID-19 information.

3.2 Data Collection

We selected Twitter as the data source for this study because it is a powerful tool for analyzing COVID-19 discussions (Dimitrov et al. 2020). We used the TwitterStreamingImporter on Gephi (Levallois and Totet 2020) to collect COVID-19 related tweets along with the interactions that were recorded for these tweets including mentions, retweets, and quote tweets between the users. Trending hashtags about COVID-19 were used to filter tweets. The terms used for filtering were: "COVID-19," "Coronavirus," "COVID Pandemic," "Covid-19 vaccine," "corona cure," and "corona vaccination." Based on these search terms, we collected 13,492 Twitter user interactions over a 24-h period from June 16, 2020, to June 17, 2020. This allowed us to conduct a detailed mixed method (quantitative and qualitative) analysis of influence within a short period of time. The scraper collected English-language tweets from Twitter users who were in the United States.

Using the same Twitter scraper software, further meta data were extracted for each user for in-depth analysis of the identified sources. This further investigation helped explore more information about the different types of accounts that dominate Twitter during the global pandemic. The meta data that were collected for the sources' analysis are described in the following subsections.

Number of Followers. The number of followers is defined as the number of Twitter users who follow a given user. The number of followers is considered as an influence indicator because the more followers a user has, the faster information can be spread. Therefore, we expected that most of the identified influential sources would be users with a high number of followers.

Profile Creation Date. The creation date of a Twitter profile indicates the date the user created their Twitter account. Based on early Twitter reports, there was approximately a 6% increase of new users accounts on Twitter who engaged in discussions about COVID-19 between November 2019 and March 2020 (Sharma et al. 2020). In this study, we investigated the creation date of influential accounts in order to check whether newer accounts dominate Twitter discussion during the pandemic.

Profile Description. Profile description refers to a short autobiography written by Twitter users to introduce themselves. Using profile descriptions helped us understand the identities behind accounts whose COVID-19 tweets receive the most interactions.

Verified Accounts. Verified accounts are Twitter accounts that have been authenticated by the platform. In this study, we collected a Boolean variable that indicated whether a given user was verified. Verification status may enhance the account's credibility, since González-Bailón and Domenico (2020) confirmed that verified accounts were significantly more visible to other Twitter accounts during events. Usually, these verified accounts were celebrities or public figures (Twitter 2013). This motivated us in this study to explore whether the main sources of COVID-19 news were verified accounts and to compare that with the number of followers to check which factor had more influence on reaching a wider audience. This provided a clear understanding about what types of accounts people would seek and trust for news and updates about COVID-19. Next, we describe the data analysis methods used in this study.

3.3   Data Analysis Approach

We performed network analysis by creating a directed network using Gephi, an open-source network visualization software (Bastian et al. 2009), to better understand the information flows between Twitter users who discussed COVID-19 during the data collection time period (Borgatti et al. 2009). For the visualized network, our aim was to visually identify the Twitter user accounts that were influential sources of COVID-19 information. Two indications used for identifying these sources were node size and edge direction. Twitter users were represented in the network graph as nodes, where node size was an indication of the number of interactions a node (user) had received. Bigger nodes showed a high number of interactions sent to the user and vice versa. The interactions (mentions, retweets, and quote tweets) between the users were represented by the edges' direction. After identifying the main sources of information in the network, we filtered the data in order to explore and deeply analyze these accounts.

In this analysis, interactions received by these accounts along with the previously defined variables (number of followers, profile creation date, profile description, verified account) about users were used in order to explore the different types of users that the public Twitter audience would seek for information about COVID-19. We followed a qualitative thematic approach (Braun and Clarke 2006) to find themes across tweets and extract patterns between the accounts based on the collected features. We analyzed the tweets of the influential sources that were collected during the collection time and received the highest number of interactions. This process started by reading the tweets and discussing what these posts were, how the content could impact the number of interactions received, and what were the topics of these tweets. In the next section, we present our results regarding the network interactions and influential users.

4 Results

In this section, we identify the influential sources of information on Twitter (RQ1), along with their characteristics, including account types, profile creation date, number of followers, and verification (RQ2). We also describe characteristics of the interactions received by the identified influential accounts (RQ3).

4.1 Influential Sources of Information from Engagement Network

Figure 1 illustrates the engagement network that was created based on the collected sample of data from Twitter, where 6707 Twitter accounts were the nodes in the graph and 13,492 interactions (mention, retweet, and quote tweet) between these accounts were the directed edges that connected two nodes (users). The network graph clearly showed dense interactions between users, which took place mostly on the network center. The nodes, or users, who were placed in the outer area showed lighter interactions observed by one interaction between only two nodes. In this study, we focused on the dense interactions between users because analyzing this type of interactions helped us identify Twitter accounts that people interacted with heavily regarding their COVID-19 tweets.

Node size was proportional to the number of interactions a given node received. After filtering the network to focus only on the dense interactions area, the major visualized finding was that most users were found to be small nodes, which indicated that these users interacted with other users, rather than receiving interactions themselves. Another major visualized finding was that we found a small number of large size nodes, denoting that people heavily interacted with these accounts' tweets. To identify influential sources

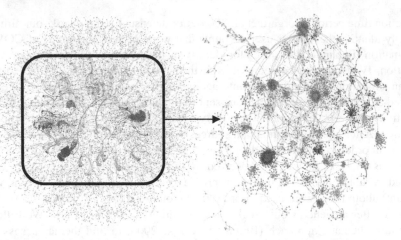

Fig. 1. Twitter users' interactions network where nodes represented users and edges represented the form of interaction between these users.

of information in the interaction network (see Fig. 1), we filtered the large size nodes (sources) along with the other users' that connected to it that are shown in Fig. 1 on the right. Based on the collected sample, the average number of interactions was 70.51. This number was used as a threshold to identify the influencers on the created network. We included usernames for verified accounts, which were all associated with public figures or news agencies. However, we anonymized the identity of the non-verified accounts to respect their privacy. As a result, we found 11 users who received more than 70 interactions (listed in Table 1). We consider these identified as influential, since people not only passively read their tweets, but were also motivated to actively interact with the tweets.

Having a small minority of users as influential sources of information out of the 6707 total users was a notable pattern of information diffusion. Typically, there is a high number of users who provide content to social media, but what we found was the opposite: people tend to be more interactive by responding to tweets posted by a few accounts. Therefore, it is worth navigating through these accounts to understand who these users are and why they received disproportionately greater attention than other users based on the collected sample. By applying the manual iterative approach to qualitatively analyze the top 11 influential accounts, the identified sources were categorized into three main account types: personal accounts (6), news agencies (3), and political authorities (2).

Political and Personal Accounts were the Dominant Influencers. The two political authority accounts were @realDonaldTrump, U.S. President Donald Trump, which was found to be the dominant influencer in discussions about COVID-19, and @SenSanders, who is Bernie Sanders, U.S. Senator of Vermont. Trump and his administration were under pressure to provide a precise plan and clear instructions to inform people about the pandemic in a timely manner (Rufai and Bunce 2020). Trump used his Twitter account to disseminate information about the pandemic by posting tweets and videos daily, which received the most attention from people inside the US. Receiving such a high number of interactions to COVID-19 related tweets demonstrated the importance of the existence

Table 1. Twitter influential sources of COVID-19 information, based on the collected sample of users who received interactions above the mean.

Twitter username	Account type	Number of interactions	Followers count	Verified	Created date
@realDonaldTrump	Political authority	210	**82193259**	TRUE	2009
@thehill	News	182	3817296	TRUE	2007
@anonymized_a	Personal	135	61380	FALSE	2008
@Newsweek	News	110	3448350	TRUE	2007
@anonymized_b	Personal	109	**660**	FALSE	2010
@funder	Personal	88	701056	TRUE	2008
@perlmutations	Personal	86	987380	TRUE	2012
@AP	News	85	14286804	TRUE	2009
@anonymized_c	Personal	82	2444	FALSE	2009
@anonymized_d	Personal	75	4281	FALSE	2011
@SenSanders	Political authority	71	9946708	TRUE	2010

of active government accounts on Twitter during times of crisis. Whether people agreed with Trump's actions or plans, nobody can deny that the usage of Twitter as a medium to provide fast-paced pandemic updates was an advantage. Another government official among the list of influencers was Senator Bernie Sanders (@SenSanders). Sanders received attention from people during data collection based on a posted tweet about COVID-19:

> *@SenSanders: "I'll be damned if when a <u>COVID-19</u> vaccine is developed, more people die because they can't afford to purchase it. Any life-saving vaccine must be free."*

This tweet triggered users' emotions by mentioning that people may die because they cannot afford the COVID-19 vaccine even before the vaccine was developed during a health and economic crisis, which resulted in a high number of retweets as a sign of agreeing with the Senator's demand. The usage of emotional language has shown to be effective in manipulating people, which mostly resulted in a high number of retweets (Stieglitz and Dang-Xuan 2013). Based on Rufai and Bunce (2020), Trump used Twitter as an informative platform to post updates about COVID-19. In our data, Sanders used Twitter to express opinions that generally seemed to be against Trump's actions.

A surprising result was that we found (54.54%) six personal accounts among the influencers who received a high number of interactions for COVID-19 tweets. These accounts varied from private individuals to public figures, such as @funder and @perlmutations. @funder is the account of Scott Dworkin, a political commentator and founder of a super PAC (Political Action Committee). Dworkin is the executive director of the

Democratic Coalition, which was founded with the express purpose of opposing Trump's presidency[2]. Reflecting his partisan preference, Dworkin's tweets about COVID-19 focused on criticizing Trump's decisions and actions during the pandemic. For example, one of Dworkin's most retweeted tweets in our dataset was:

> @funder: "BREAKING: Trump's going to Dallas today to do a photo op, go to a fundraiser, then to his NJ golf resort. We're at the height of a pandemic where over 115,000 Americans have died with over 2 million infected. And he's on vacation. Trump's the laziest, most pathetic failure ever."

Although Dworkin's Twitter account is an active and popular account that mostly publishes political tweets, not all of Dworkin's tweets received as many interactions as the previously quoted example; the reason for this might be the tweet's content, which included the number of infected people and harsh criticism of Trump for being on a vacation during the pandemic. This triggered fear over the increasing number of infected people and anger towards Trump which was reflected by interactions with this tweet. Another public figure in the personal accounts list was @perlmutations, the celebrity actor Ron Perlman. Perlman also used similarly emotional language to express anger against Trump's actions in the following tweet:

> @perlmutations: "Over 118,000 American souls have been lost to the coronavirus and that number is not slowing down. Instead of formulating an actual plan to save lives, the president is tweeting in all caps about the stock market. There's only so much tequila I can drink so please VOTE."

Perlman shared his frustration regarding how the pandemic had negatively impacted the lives of people in the United States while the president was paying attention to other topics and encouraged people to vote in the upcoming presidential election.

Dworkin and Perlman's tweets might have received a high number of interactions because their tweets criticized Trump and prompted anger and fear by juxtaposing the number of COVID-19 cases with examples of Trump's alleged failure to respond appropriately in favor of self-serving interests and actions. This implied that people were not only interacting with Trump's own account, but also with other accounts criticizing Trump during the pandemic. This left us questioning whether the influencers, along with the users interacting with them, were against the Trump administration in general or how Trump responded to the COVID-19 crisis. Since these accounts had a political interest, our results imply that people who were against Trump framed discussions of the pandemic to emphasize Trump's poor management of COVID-19 in the U.S., using the same medium Trump used for posting updates about it. This political debate has concerning implications for health communication, especially during the pandemic.

Next, we looked into the remaining personal accounts that were not public figures (@anonymized_a, @anonymized_b, @anonymized_c, and @anonymized_d) and found that the emerging theme from these users' tweets is that these accounts were also critical of the U.S. government's pandemic response. Most of these personal accounts also amplified news sources in addition to providing their personal views about how the

---

government was handling the pandemic. For instance, @anonymized_a shared political news content from other sources, such as Fox News and MSNBC. One of the users (@anonymized_b) used humor in the form of memes to criticize government responses to the pandemic. Another user, @anonymized_d, shared a persuasive argument on how it is important to stay safe, along with personal commentary criticizing the poor performance of the government to the detriment of public safety. A tweet from @anonymized_d stated the current number of COVID-19 cases in the U.S., then argued that this meant that efforts to reopen only considered economic consequences rather than safety. The user concluded the tweet by claiming those in charge of reopening the economy did not care about people's lives.

Finally, the identified influential accounts only included three official news agencies. Although @AP (Associated Press) has the highest number of followers, it received the lowest number of interactions compared with the other news accounts. @thehill (The Hill), which is a political news account, received the highest number of interactions of the three news accounts, while @Newsweek (Newsweek) had the lowest number of followers out of the three news accounts and had the second highest number of interactions out of the news accounts (with a ranking of 4 out of 11 overall). The news accounts posted informative updates on COVID-19 cases. During the data collection time, news accounts gained interactions on tweets that were mostly about the number of infected people with COVID-19 or Trump's decisions. Below, we present descriptive characteristics, themes, and patterns identified based on our in-depth analysis of the tweets.

Most of the Identified Influencers were Popular Accounts. Based on Table 1, all influencers, regardless of other account characteristics, had accounts that were created over seven years prior to the COVID-19 pandemic. This was the only shared characteristic between all the identified influencers. The number of followers for each identified source were reported during the data collection time. From Table 1 we can summarize that the identified sources had an average of 10,495,420 followers (median = 987,380). This could suggest that all the identified influencers were popular accounts on Twitter; however, Fig. 2 illustrates heavy skewness in the follower counts which affected the mean significantly. We found that @anonymized_b, @anonymized_c, and @anonymized_d, accounts with fewer than 5000 followers, received high attention from users that contributed to the high interaction counts. For example, @anonymized_b, a personal non-verified account with the lowest number of followers (660) out of all the influencers, posted two tweets during the data collection period that went viral and received over 8000 retweets. The tweets included the same cartoon meme image with different captions on the tweets criticizing one state's response to COVID-19. The text accompanying the image mocked a governor for reopening the state while encouraging close contact without masks, only to act surprised when COVID-19 cases increased.

The two meme tweets received much more engagement than the user's other tweets during the same time period that were not about COVID-19 but focused on other social and political issues.

Seven Out of the Eleven Influential Sources were Verified Accounts. Verified accounts constituted the majority of influential accounts in our sample and included

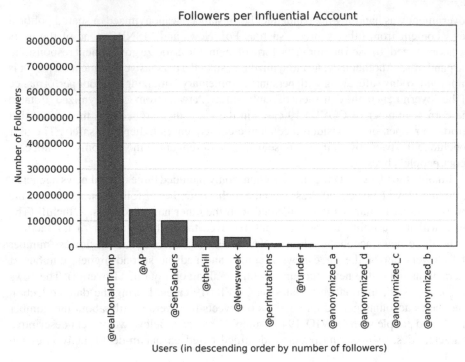

Fig. 2. Follower counts of the identified influencers.

elected government officials, news organizations, and other public figures in entertainment and politics. The four accounts that were not verified appeared to be personal accounts run by individuals who are not acting in any official capacity. Table 1 shows that 7 out of 11 information sources were verified accounts. This aligned with our expectations, since most of the listed accounts were either public figures, such as @realDonaldTrump, @funder, @perlmutations, and @SenSanders, or accounts for major news agencies such as @thehill, @Newsweek, and @AP. On the other hand, we found personal accounts for private individuals, such as @anonymized_a, @anonymized_b, @anonymized_c, and @anonymized_d, were not verified, but people interacted heavily with their COVID-19 tweets. While we might expect that verified accounts with the most followers might also receive the most interactions, this was not always the case. Although the accounts that received the most interactions were verified, there were also verified accounts that received relatively fewer interactions. For example, @AP and @SenSanders were both in the bottom half of interactions received, with @AP ranking 8 out of 11 and @SenSanders receiving the lowest number of interactions of all 11 influencers.

Finally, when examining profile descriptions, the verified influential accounts tended to list their official job positions and affiliations. On the other hand, while two of the non-verified influential accounts also included professional information, only one included specific information about professional affiliation, while the other alluded to be a health-care worker without adding any personally identifiable information. The other two non-verified accounts had the shortest profile descriptions of all of the influencers and also contained the least personal information about the users.

4.2 Interactions Received by Influencers Varied Based on Account Type

We found that among the three forms of interactions (mentions, retweets, quote tweets), there was a tendency to use mentions rather than using other forms of interactions with an average of 46.36 for mentions, 28.78 for retweets, and 37 for quote tweets. Mentions can include direct replies to one's own tweet, indirect replies (which notify a user of a reply to a different user's tweet), and any other mentions in the tweet (e.g., including a user's @ username in the body of a tweet to draw their attention to it). Retweets share another user's tweet to one's own profile, while quote tweets allow users to retweet other content while adding their own commentary to it. Different forms of interactions were found to vary based on the account type.

Another pattern that can be seen in Fig. 3 was that @thehill, @Newsweek, and @anonymized_a have many more quote tweets than retweets or mentions, but for the other accounts (except @realDonaldTrump), they show the reverse pattern, with relatively more mentions and retweets compared to quote tweets. It was expected to find more retweets than quote tweets since retweeting takes less effort than quote tweeting. For the three accounts that received the most quote tweets, this could suggest more people were not only sharing their content, but also adding their own commentary (whether agreeing or disagreeing, such as in the case of a controversial tweet that is shared for the purpose of either supporting or opposing it).

Another major finding was that although the two political authority accounts (Trump and Sanders) were verified and popular accounts with a high number of followers (82,193,259 and 9,946,708, respectively), the types of interactions they received were entirely different. Figure 3 illustrates the number of interactions for each identified influencer per interaction type. One interesting pattern that Trump's account received the highest number of mentions among all accounts. Twitter users sought Trump's account for updates and news about the coronavirus; however, these users tended to mention Trump (by mentioning his username in a tweet or replying to his tweets) rather than using other forms of engagement. On the other hand, Twitter users used a relatively equal number of retweets and mentions to engage with @SenSanders on tweets about COVID-19.

Overall, the major interaction patterns can be summarized in three points. First news-focused accounts (official organization accounts and @anonymized_a, which is a personal account that frequently shares news content) have the highest proportion of quote tweets compared to other interactions (with the exception of @AP). Second, unlike the other influential accounts, @realDonaldTrump received many more mentions compared to the number of retweets and quote tweets received. Third, all other accounts received about equal numbers of retweets and mentions, which made up the majority of their interactions, and very few quote tweets.

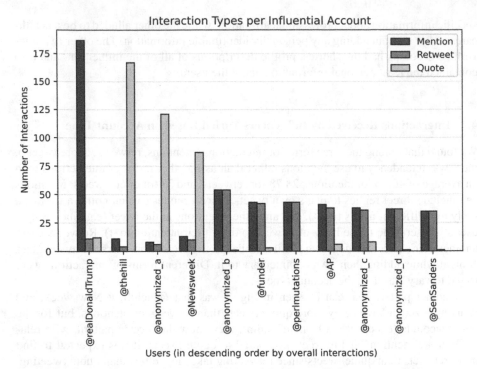

Fig. 3. Interactions rates sent to the influential sources of information on Twitter.

In sum, we discussed in this section that mentions were the most common type of interaction among users overall, yet the relative proportion of mentions to other interactions varied across influencers. We also found that some non-verified users with a smaller number of followers gained visibility through the content they shared, but verified accounts were more common for our identified influencers. In the following section, we discuss broader implications of our study.

5 Discussion

5.1 Social Media as a Source of Information During COVID-19

The COVID-19 pandemic demonstrates the evolving role of social media in public health communication. The most influential sources of information in the dataset included political authorities, news organizations, public figures, and personal accounts. By network analysis we found that most users interacted with other users rather than receiving interactions. This pattern of engagement was expected because people experienced a significant level of uncertainty and anxiety during the outbreak (Steinert et al. 2020). This uncertainty has persisted over time, unlike previous crises where uncertainty is mostly resolved within a few days. In addition, with COVID-19, the situation was ambiguous at all levels from public health authorities to the general public. This high degree of uncertainty can motivate people to speculate, which can affect people's ability to judge the veracity of news (Karduni et al. 2018). Above this uncertainty, certain nonphar-maceutical interventions, such as stay-at-home orders and physical distancing policies, have made the use of social media more crucial than before to connect with others in addition to staying informed about COVID-19 updates. This study showed a relatively high number of mentions, which suggests that people may have been seeking to resolve their uncertainty by replying to the influencers' tweets, as well as connecting with other users to share information with them. The dense network engagement denoted that people absorbed information and decided to diffuse the shared tweets about the coronavirus which had two sides. The positive impact of people's engagement in social networks can be seen in campaigns to help provide awareness, food, and masks for people (Al-Dmour et al. 2020). On the other hand, there was a negative impact of people's dense engagement which made them vulnerable to misinformation, political polarization, and strategic manipulation (Mian et al. 2020). Therefore, it was important to identify who the Twitter accounts people interacted with the most and discuss these interactions with more scrutiny.

5.2 COVID-19 and Political Polarization on Social Media

When examining influential sources of information about COVID-19 on Twitter, we found that users were drawn to controversial politically oriented content, demonstrating the polarization of COVID-19 communication. In fact, our results showed that during the time period we examined, U.S. President Donald Trump's Twitter account was the most influential source of information in our dataset. Additionally, our analyses revealed the overwhelmingly political nature of COVID-19 discussions on Twitter. Because several of the influential users we identified were either political authorities or otherwise engaged in political activity and commentary, especially in a partisan manner, our results may raise concerns about the impact of political ideology on the type of information that is shared about COVID-19. For instance, one of the influential users in our dataset, @funder (Scott Dworkin), received significant interactions in response to tweets harshly criticizing another influential user in our dataset, @realDonaldTrump (Donald Trump). Emerging research has found political ideology predicted perceptions of COVID-19 and belief in COVID-19 misinformation (Calvillo et al. 2020). Future research should continue to investigate the effects of political ideology on the types of information shared during the pandemic, along with polarization of users who engage with this information.

Additionally, the impact of politicized health communication on both social media behavior and public health outcomes needs to be examined further. For example, a recent study by Yaqub (2020) on tweets by Donald Trump over a 159-day period from January 24 to June 30, 2020 found a correlation between the sentiment of Donald Trump's tweets and the number of COVID-19 cases in the United States. They ascertained that the positive tone of President Trump's tweets decreased as the number of COVID-19 cases increased. An area of research that merits further exploration, and to which similar methodologies may be applied (sentiment analysis, statistical methods), is the investigation of the relationships between the sentiment of prominent sources of information regarding certain COVID-19 mitigation measures and public sentiment about those measures. A specific timeframe, source, and social media platform may be selected for study.

Finally, on January 8, 2021, Twitter announced the permanent suspension of @real-DonaldTrump due to "risk of further incitement of violence" following the storming of the U.S. Capitol on January 6, 2021 [3]. Future work should investigate how the suspension of Trump's account and the transition to the newly elected President Biden affect COVID-19 information influencers.

5.3   Heterogeneity of Influencers and Implications for Mechanisms of Influence

One noteworthy finding was that consistent with prior findings (e.g., Gräve and Greff 2018), the high number of interactions received by the influencers in our study cannot be attributed to follower counts alone. This sheds light on the importance of differentiating between the impact of the number of followers and other factors involved in influence. Overall, we observed that during the time period of data collection, the most influential users discussing COVID-19 comprised both verified public figures with a large following, as well as smaller personal accounts. In the latter case, it is possible that the interactions received by these personal accounts were anomalous compared to their typical engagement (e.g., due to receiving a burst of interactions in response to a viral tweet), whereas we would expect to observe the verified influencers receive a relatively high number of interactions in general. This suggests there may be different mechanisms of gaining influence for these different account types. Because we examined interactions within a 24-h time period, we were able to detect different types of influential users in our dataset.

5.4   Limitations and Future Work

Our analyses focused on influential sources of information during a short period of time, so we analyzed Twitter user interactions over a duration of 24 h. This means that the results are not reflective of larger periods of time for user interactions and may not generalize to other social media platforms. For future work, researchers can investigate influencers across larger periods of time and across other social media platforms to have a more comprehensive view of influential sources of information during the pandemic. Our analyses also focused on English-language tweets based in the U.S. Therefore, the interactions and political polarization we observed are only applicable to users in the U.S. Future work can seek to identify the degree to which political polarization related to COVID-19 is occurring in other geographic regions.

6   Conclusion

In this study, we identified influential sources of information during a one-day period of COVID-19 discourse on Twitter. From this, we examined account features to characterize these influential users. During this investigation, we discovered the content of information being shared during this time focused heavily on politically charged discussions. Our findings illustrate the ongoing need to understand the impact of social media interactions and political polarization on public health outcomes.

---

[3] https://blog.twitter.com/en_us/topics/company/2020/suspension.html.

Acknowledgements. Co-authors of this paper were supported by the U.S. Defense Advanced Research Projects Agency under grant FA8650-18-C-7823 and the U.S. National Science Foundation under grant IIP-1827700. The co-authors' sponsors had no role in study design, data collection and analysis, decision to publish, or preparation of the manuscript. Any opinions, findings, conclusions, or recommendations expressed in this material are those of the authors and do not necessarily reflect the views of the co-authors' sponsors.

References

Abidin, C., Lee, J., Barbetta, T., Miao, W.S.: Influencers and COVID-19: reviewing key issues in press coverage across Australia, China, Japan, and South Korea. Media Int. Aust. **178**(1), 114–135 (2021). https://doi.org/10.1177/1329878X20959838

Al-Dmour, H., Masa'deh, R., Salman, A., Abuhashesh, M., Al-Dmour, R.: Influence of social media platforms on public health protection against the COVID-19 pandemic via the mediating effects of public health awareness and behavioral changes: integrated model. J. Med. Internet Res. **22**(8), e19996 (2020). https://doi.org/10.2196/19996

Barabási, A.-L., Albert, R.: Emergence of scaling in random networks. Science **286**(5439), 509–512 (1999). https://doi.org/10.1126/science.286.5439.509

Bastian, M., Heymann, S., Jacomy, M.: Gephi: an open source software for exploring and manipulating networks. In: Proceedings of the Third International AAAI Conference on Web and Social Media. Association for the Advancement of Artificial Intelligence (2009)

Booth, N., Matic, J.A.: Mapping and leveraging influencers in social media to shape corporate brand perceptions. Corp. Commun.: Int. J. **16**(3), 184–191 (2011). https://doi.org/10.1108/135 63281111156853

Borgatti, S.P., Mehra, A., Brass, D.J., Labianca, G.: Network analysis in the social sciences. Science **323**(5916), 892–895 (2009). https://doi.org/10.1126/science.1165821

Braun, V., Clarke, V.: Using thematic analysis in psychology. Qual. Res. Psychol. **3**(2), 77–101 (2006). https://doi.org/10.1191/1478088706qp063oa

Budhwani, H., Sun, R.: Creating COVID-19 stigma by referencing the novel coronavirus as the "Chinese virus" on Twitter: quantitative analysis of social media data. J. Med. Internet Res. **22**(5), (2020). https://doi.org/10.2196/19301

Calvillo, D.P., Ross, B.J., Garcia, R.J.B., Smelter, T.J., Rutchick, A.M.: Political ideology predicts perceptions of the threat of COVID-19 (and susceptibility to fake news about it): Soc. Psychol. Personal. Sci. **11**(8), 1119–1128 (2020). https://doi.org/10.1177/1948550620940539

Casaló, L.V., Flavián, C., Ibáñez-Sánchez, S.: Influencers on Instagram: antecedents and consequences of opinion leadership. J. Bus. Res. **117**, 510–519 (2020). https://doi.org/10.1016/j.jbusres.2018.07.005

CDC: COVIDView summary ending on 20 June 2020. https://www.cdc.gov/coronavirus/2019-ncov/covid-data/covidview/past-reports/06262020.html. Accessed 10 Feb 2021

Chae, J.: Explaining females' envy toward social media influencers. Media Psychol. **21**(2), 246–262 (2018). https://doi.org/10.1080/15213269.2017.1328312

Cher, A.: WHO's chief scientist says there's a "very real risk" of a second wave of coronavirus as economies reopen (2020). https://www.cnbc.com/2020/06/10/who-says-theres-real-risk-of-second-coronavirus-wave-as-economies-reopen.html

Dimitrov, D., et al.: TweetsCOV19 - a knowledge base of semantically annotated tweets about the COVID-19 pandemic. In: Proceedings of the 29th ACM International Conference on Information & Knowledge Management, pp. 2991–2998. Association for Computing Machinery, New York, NY, USA (2020)

Forgey, Q.: 'There is no emergency': W.H. economic advisers shrug off feared 'second wave' of coronavirus (2020). https://www.politico.com/news/2020/06/12/larry-kudlow-coronavirus-sec ond-wave-314904

Freberg, K., Graham, K., McGaughey, K., Freberg, L.A.: Who are the social media influencers? a study of public perceptions of personality. Public. Relat. Rev. 37(1), 90–92 (2011). https://doi.org/10.1016/j.pubrev.2010.11.001

González-Bailón, S., De Domenico, M.: Bots are less central than verified accounts during contentious political events. SSRN Electron J. (2020). https://doi.org/10.2139/ssrn.3637121

Gräve, J.-F., Greff, A.: Good KPI, good influencer? evaluating success metrics for social media influencers. In: Proceedings of the 9th International Conference on Social Media and Society, pp. 291–295. Association for Computing Machinery, New York, NY, USA (2018). https://doi.org/10.1145/3217804.3217931

Gross, T.: Amid confusion about reopening, an expert explains how to assess COVID-19 risk (2020). https://www.npr.org/2020/06/17/879255417/amid-confusion-about-reopening-an-exp ert-explains-how-to-assess-covid-risk

Hether, H.J., Murphy, S.T., Valente, T.W.: It's better to give than to receive: the role of social support, trust, and participation on health-related social networking sites. J. Health Commun. 19(12), 1424–1439 (2014). https://doi.org/10.1080/10810730.2014.894596

Karduni, A., et al.: Can you verifi this? studying uncertainty and decision-making about misinformation using visual analytics. In: Proceedings of the Twelfth International AAAI Conference on Web and Social Media (ICWSM 2018), pp. 151–160. Association for the Advancement of Artificial Intelligence (2018)

Karimi, F., Sgueglia, K., Cullinane, S.: New York could roll back reopening if coronavirus restrictions violated, Gov. Cuomo says (2020). https://www.cnn.com/2020/06/14/health/us-corona virus-sunday/index.html

Katz, E., Lazarsfeld, P.F.: Personal Influence: The Part Played by People in the Flow of Mass Communication. Free Press, Glencoe, IL, US (1955)

Ko, N.-Y., et al.: COVID-19-related information sources and psychological well-being: an online survey study in Taiwan. Brain Behav. Immun. 87, 153–154 (2020). https://doi.org/10.1016/j.bbi.2020.05.019

Levallois, C., Totet, M.: Twitter Streaming Importer. https://seinecle.github.io/gephi-tutorials/gen erated-html/twitter-streaming-importer-en.html. Accessed 2 June 2020

Levitan, L.C., Verhulst, B.: Conformity in groups: the effects of others' views on expressed attitudes and attitude change. Polit. Behav. 38(2), 277–315 (2016). https://doi.org/10.1007/s11109-015-9312-x

Lwin, M.O., et al.: Global sentiments surrounding the COVID-19 pandemic on twitter: analysis of twitter trends. JMIR Public Health Surveill. 6(2), (2020). https://doi.org/10.2196/19447

Mian, A., Khan, S.: Coronavirus: the spread of misinformation. BMC Med. 18(1), 89 (2020). https://doi.org/10.1186/s12916-020-01556-3

Okuah, O., Scholtz, B.M., Snow, B.: A grounded theory analysis of the techniques used by social media influencers and their potential for influencing the public regarding environmental awareness. In: Proceedings of the South African Institute of Computer Scientists and Information Technologists 2019, pp. 1–10. Association for Computing Machinery, New York, NY, USA (2019). https://doi.org/10.1145/3351108.3351145

Olson, T.: Pennsylvania Senate Republicans sue Gov. Wolf over refusal to end coronavirus lockdown (2020). https://www.foxnews.com/politics/pa-senate-republicans-sue-wolf-over-refusal-end-coronavirus-lockdown

Pestek, A., Alic, A., Sadinlija, A.: Use of social media influencers in tourism. In: Proceedings of the International Scientific Conference: TRADE PERSPECTIVES 2017: Specialization and Customer Centered Retailing, pp. 177–189. Faculty of Economics and Business, Zagreb & Croatian Chamber of Economy, Zagreb, Croatia (2017)

Roitero, K., et al.: The COVID-19 infodemic: can the crowd judge recent misinformation objectively? In: Proceedings of the 29th ACM International Conference on Information & Knowledge Management, pp. 1305–1314 (2020). https://doi.org/10.1145/3340531.3412048

Rufai, S.R., Bunce, C.: World leaders' usage of Twitter in response to the COVID-19 pandemic: a content analysis. J. Public Health **42**(3), 510–516 (2020). https://doi.org/10.1093/pubmed/fda a049

Shumaker, L., Schwartz, D.: COVID-19 cases surge in Oklahoma, other states ahead of Trump's Tulsa rally (2020). https://www.reuters.com/article/us-health-coronavirus-usa-idU SKBN23O2T2

Sharma, K., Seo, S., Meng, C., Rambhatla, S., Liu, Y.: COVID-19 on social media: analyzing misinformation in Twitter conversations. arXiv:2003.12309 [cs]. (2020). https://arxiv.org/abs/ 2003.12309

Spencer, S.: Fake coronavirus cures, part 1: MMS is industrial bleach. https://www.factcheck.org/ 2020/02/fake-coronavirus-cures-part-1-mms-is-industrial-bleach/. Accessed 2 June 2020

Starbird, K., Palen, L.: (How) will the revolution be retweeted? information diffusion and the 2011 Egyptian uprising. In: Proceedings of the ACM 2012 conference on Computer Supported Cooperative Work, pp. 7–16. Association for Computing Machinery, New York, NY, USA (2012). https://doi.org/10.1145/2145204.2145212

Steinert, S.: Corona and value change. The role of social media and emotional contagion. Ethics Inf. Technol. 1–10 (2020). https://doi.org/10.1007/s10676-020-09545-z

Stieglitz, S., Dang-Xuan, L.: Emotions and information diffusion in social media—sentiment of microblogs and sharing behavior. J. Manag. Inf. Syst. **29**(4), 217–248 (2013). https://doi.org/ 10.2753/MIS0742-1222290408

Stieglitz, S., Mirbabaie, M., Ross, B., Neuberger, C.: Social media analytics – challenges in topic discovery, data collection, and data preparation. Int. J. Inf. Manag. Sci. **39**, 156–168 (2018). https://doi.org/10.1016/j.ijinfomgt.2017.12.002

World Health Organization: COVID-19 public health emergency of international concern (PHEIC) global research and innovation forum: towards a research roadmap (2020). https://www.who.int/publications/m/item/covid-19-public-health-emergency-of-intern ational-concern-(pheic)-global-research-and-innovation-forum

Yaqub, U.: Tweeting during the Covid-19 pandemic: sentiment analysis of Twitter messages by President Trump. Digit Gov: Res. Pract. **2**(1), 1:1–1:7 (2020). https://doi.org/10.1145/3428090

Zade, H., Shah, K., Rangarajan, V., Kshirsagar, P., Imran, M., Starbird, K.: From situational awareness to actionability: towards improving the utility of social media data for crisis response. In: Proceedings of the ACM on Human-Computer Interaction, pp. 195:1–195:18 (2018). https:// doi.org/10.1145/3274464

Zafarani, R., Abbasi, M.A., Liu, H.: Information diffusion in social media. In: Social Media Mining: An Introduction, pp. 179–214. Cambridge University Press, Cambridge (2014). https:// doi.org/10.1017/CBO9781139088510.008

Zarocostas, J.: How to fight an infodemic. Lancet **395**(10225), 676 (2020). https://doi.org/10. 1016/S0140-6736(20)30461-X

The Covid-19 Crisis: An NLP Exploration of the French Twitter Feed (February-May 2020)

Sophie Balech[1]([✉]) [iD], Christophe Benavent[2] [iD], Mihai Calciu[3] [iD], and Julien Monnot[2]

[1] Picardie Jules Verne University, 10 Venelle Lafleur, 80000 Amiens, France
[2] Nanterre University, 200 Avenue de la République, 92000 Nanterre, France
[3] Lille University, 104 Avenue du Peuple Belge, 59000 Lille, France

Abstract. The Covid-19 pandemic offers a spectacular case of disaster management. In this literature, the paradigm of participation is fundamental: the mitigation of the impact of the disaster, the quality of the preparation and the resilience of the society, which facilitate the reconstruction, depend on the participation of the populations. Being able to observe and measure the state of mental health of the population (anxiety, confidence, expectations, ...) and to identify the points of controversy and the content of the discourse, are necessary to support measures designed to encourage this participation. Social media, and in particular Twitter, offer valuable resources for researching this discourse.

The objective of this empirical study is to reconstruct a micro history of users' reactions to the pandemic as they share them on social networks. The general method used comes from new processing techniques derived from Natural Language Processing (NLP). Three analysis methods are used to process the corpus: analysis of the temporal evolution of term occurrences; creation of dynamic semantic maps to identify co-occurrences; analysis of topics using the SVM method.

The main empirical result is that the mask emerges as a central figure of discourse, at least in the discourse produced by certain social media. The retrospective analysis of the phenomenon allows us to explain what made the mask a focal point not only in conversation, but also in behaviors. Its value resides less in its functional qualities than in its ability to fix attention and organize living conditions under the threat of pandemic.

Keywords: Covid-19 · Twitter feed · NLP methods

1 Introduction

The Covid-19 pandemic that hit the planet offers a spectacular case of disaster management [12]. In this literature, the paradigm of participation is fundamental [7,16] : the mitigation of the impact of the disaster, the quality of the preparation

G. Meiselwitz (Ed.): HCII 2021, LNCS 12775, pp. 308–321, 2021.
https://doi.org/10.1007/978-3-030-77685-5_24

and the resilience of the society, which facilitate the reconstruction, depend on the participation of the populations. Being able to observe and measure the state of mental health of the population (anxiety, confidence, expectations, ...) and to identify the points of controversy and the content of the discourse, are necessary to support measures designed to encourage this participation. Social media, and in particular Twitter, offer valuable resources for researching this discourse.

In the literature on disaster management, three concepts are key and necessary at all stages of a disaster: the first is the state of preparedness for the consequences of the phenomenon and its aftershocks, the second concerns the mitigation of these consequences, which requires the participation of populations, and the third relates to the capacity of each individual to bounce back and embark on the road to reconstruction: resilience.

The modern conception of disaster management, with its emphasis on the participation of populations, questions the factors that encourage or curb it. Material, cognitive and organizational resources are obvious, their mobilisation and preparation are decisive, but in the end, it is undoubtedly the mental health of populations and their level of commitment that make the difference.

The objective of this empirical study is to reconstruct a micro history of users' reactions to the pandemic as they share them on social networks. Despite the volume of data and the technique used, the methodological approach is descriptive and aims to establish a fact: the central and increasing role of the mask in social conversation as it emerges from observation. The general method used comes from a new paradigm [4] which build itself between abundant data (web, social networks, ...) and new processing techniques derived from Natural Language Processing (NLP).

2   Dataset

The dataset is a corpus of Twitter content developed by [2] based on a set of keywords around covid, corona and associated words. The original corpus with nearly 110 million tweets, collected between the end of January and end of Mai 2020 and available in dehydrated form due to Twitter's terms of service was used in order to extract the French tweets. From the resulting 2.156 million posts, whose production over time is shown in Fig. 1, 565,662 have been retained as having contributory content that is original, reply and quote tweets. Retweets have been excluded in order to avoid redundancy.

This corpus is pre-processed by removing account mentions and URLs by the appropriate regular expressions, putting the whole text in lower case, tokenizing, lemmatizing and annotating the text with the "part of speech" with the Udpipe annotator of CleanNLP [1] as well as identifying syntax dependencies. The whole corpus represents 10 million tokens whose only common names were filtered out in order to analyze the topics discussed in the message flow.

The heterogeneity of the content is fully shown in the distribution of the number of tweets per account (Fig. 2). A very small number of accounts produces a large part of all tweets, even if the number of accounts is high: 202,000 distinct

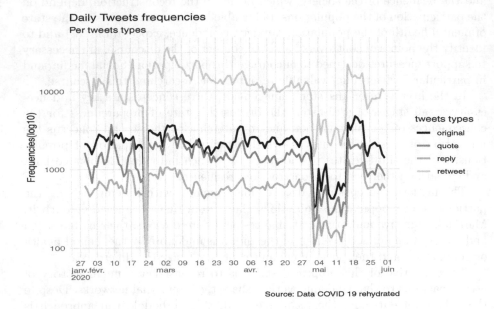

Fig. 1. Number of posts produced per day by type of post (n = 2.2 m)

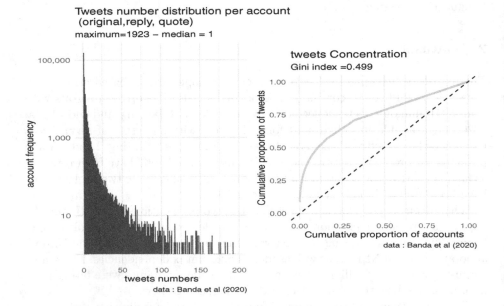

Fig. 2. Tweets distribution per account

contributors. The degree of concentration is high with a Gini index of 0.50. It indicates a huge inequality of contribution: 25% of the 565,662 primary production tweets were created by a minority of about 1000 contributors from a total of 202,000 accounts. We find the major actors: media, politicians, but also activists, journalists, columnists. The extreme heterogeneity of the population and its production is questionable, as is its small size (the number of daily Twitter users is around 4.6 million in France, less than half of whom are active). Although the database claims to be somewhat exhaustive, a certain fragility emerges. On such a scale, small groups of activists can fairly easily find an audience, but at least we have a good reflection of the media arena.

3   Method

We use the tidyverse [15] collection of packages of the R statistical environment [9] to analyze data. Three types of methods are used in a complementary way to highlight the different aspects of chronological variations of the discourse themes.

3.1   Daily Evolution of the Study's Focal Categories

The methods used aim first to capture daily changes in the use of the most frequent vocabulary. A certain number of target terms have been identified, those relating to the epidemic (corona, covid), lockdown and deconfinement, and those naturally linked to barrier gestures (mask, gel, teleworking, ...). To test the consistency of the daily changes, the frequency with which countries are cited is also measured, which gives a coherent picture of the trends. In order to deal with morphological variations in terms and to take into account spelling errors, rather than annotation by lemmas, we use regular expressions. Thus, for the term "hôpital" (hospital), the pattern ".*h([o,ô]—[os,ôs])pital.*" is used, which makes it possible to identify more than thirty variants.

3.2   Dynamic Semantic Maps

Simple semantic maps are used to explore the evolution of discourse on a weekly scale. These maps are obtained by calculating for each of the 22 weeks the co-occurrences between the most frequent words. We are therefore interested here in the joint distribution of terms in the same documents, their proximity resulting from their use in the same texts.

These co-occurrence tables are binary recoded according to the following dualism: existence of relation/absence of relation, according to a predefined threshold, then represented in a small space using Fruchterman and Reingold's algorithm [6]. The implementation of the procedure is carried out with igraph [5]. The elements obtained by the analysis of semantic networks are then the subject of centrality calculations. We retain three centrality indicators:

– the degree of centrality: the number of links each node has;
– the centrality of betweenness: the number of times a node intervenes in a shorter path connecting two other nodes;
– closeness: the sum of the length of the shortest paths connecting a node to the others.

3.3   Analysis of Structural Themes (STM)

Topic analysis is already well known [3], it aims to identify a number of k topics in a corpus by assuming that each document has a probability of corresponding to one or the other of the k topics (n x k matrix of the theta parameters), and that each term has a certain probability to belong to a given topic (m x k matrix of the beta parameters).

Here we use a method that differs from the initial model, and whose characteristics are, on the one hand, to take into account the longitudinal nature of the data by measuring the prevalence over time of each of the topics (and more generally other co-variables that act as independent variables), and, on the other hand, to assume that the topics are correlated, which is reasonable in this situation. This is the Structural Topic Model proposed by [11]. We use its implementation in the stm package [10].

4   Results

4.1   The Mask in First Place for Attenuation Tactics

The first approach to content analysis is simply to count the terms frequency and focus on the most frequent ones. This is what we have represented in Fig. 3. The different forms of corona and covid dominate the ranking. The mask stands in a good position, it is certainly the first evocation in frequency of a means of defence against the epidemic, of a concrete object. It dominates the other means of attenuation. This raw frequency deserves to be described more qualitatively: do we say the same things about the mask at different phases of the epidemic episode? To this end, syntactic dependency annotations are used to identify which terms are grammatically associated with the common noun "mask": adverbs, adjectives, other nouns (some universal Stanford dependencies are used: acl, amod, nmod and appos). We compare the most frequent ones among the 4 months of observations. For each of the terms obtained their density is calculated and the spectrum of meanings is obtained, represented in Fig. 4. The results are clear: 1) the mask protects it' s trivial 2) its shape is surgical rather than ffp2 despite hesitation 3) its distribution and commercialization become more important with time. But the main thing is that it is associated with the "mandatory" aspect. The mask used to be a means, it is now as much a legal norm as a social norm.

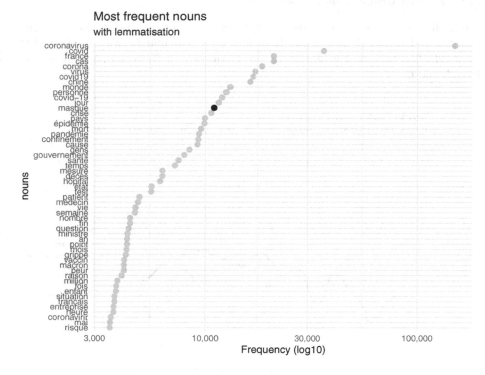

Fig. 3. The mask among the most frequently used words

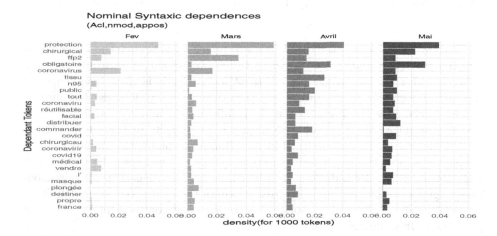

Fig. 4. The most frequent nominal mask dependencies by month (in terms of density $= f_{im}/f_{.m}$ with i = term, m = month). (Universal Dependencies: acl, amod, nmod and appos)

4.2   From Coronavirus to Covid-19

From the frequencies of occurrence of a series of terms representative of the debates and topics of interest, a daily density is calculated, with a smoothing over 7 d. The temporal evolution of the frequency of these terms is shown in Figs. 5 and 6.

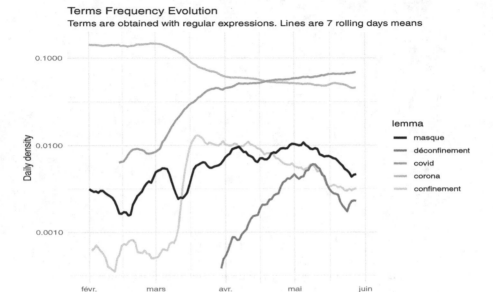

Fig. 5. Changes in the frequency of key terms: corona, covid and lockdown/mask.

The evolution is cristal clear. If from January to February the coronavirus was the star (very dark), the Covid-19 takes over during March and remains in the lead for the rest of the period. In other words, it is the consequences of the epidemic spread of the coronavirus that dominate the debates. The disease weighs directly by the pressure put on public health and by its victims, but also by the measures it provokes to mitigate its impact. In this sense, Covid-19 becomes the social and political incarnation of its biological counterpart the Coronavirus. The change of term marks a change in discourse: the threat that was external is rapidly endogenized, it becomes less the virus than the perturbations it generates (excess mortality, disruption of the health system, redefinition of social relations, economic shock). The moment of confinement is a shift in perspective from outside to inside.

As for the mask, we observe its progressive rise, in successive waves that undoubtedly concern its various polemics, and its quantitative domination over other methods of attenuation: test, hydroalcoholic gel, telework, to mention the

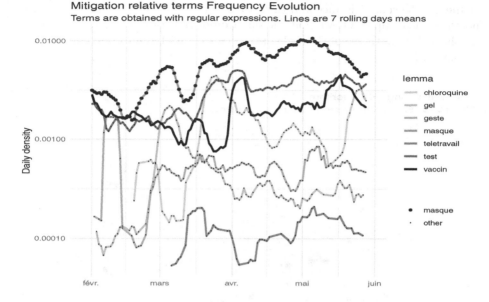

Fig. 6. Means of barrier gestures

most significant ones. The impact of the disaster coming from elsewhere is accompanied by a change of perspective, and a reversal where the mask becomes an increasingly frequent concern.

4.3   The Mask at the Center of the Debate from the Beginning

To report on the conversations and their evolution, a method of semantic maps is applied for each period (22 consecutive weeks). Reading the map is fairly simple: words whose co-occurrences are greater than a frequency determined according to each period's corpus are represented, satisfying a constant proportion across the periods (about 30%). The size of the nodes corresponds to their density in the corpus, that of the arcs to the frequency of the co-occurrence. The relative positions in the plane are calculated by a multidimensional positioning method according to the similarity of the terms. As can be seen in Fig. 7 there is a central theme represented by the macro-component appearing as a network of terms surrounded by more specific and disconnected themes positioned at the periphery.

It illustrates the main discussions during the second week of (first) lockdown. During this period, the peripheral conversations dealt with a variety of topics: chloroquine treatment, the health system, the practical issue of travel certification, and a petition addressed to the president for the use of chloroquine. The macro-component is fairly clearly structured. On an almost horizontal axis, lockdown is at the center of a temporal concern: for how long? At the other end, the crisis of the shortage of masks, in particular, for caregivers, is clearly taking shape. At the center, France and the government are bridging the issues. In the north of the component, we find the question of the state of emergency, in the south the factual theme of the scale of the crisis translated into the daily number of deaths.

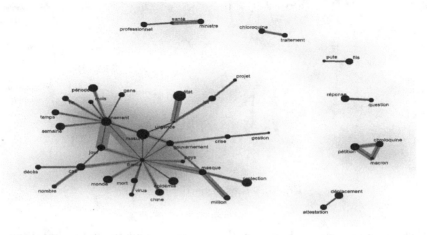

Lexical mapping (FR algorithm)
2020-03-18 : Elections municipales- début du confinement

edge size proportionnal to co-occurences,
vertice size to term density.

Fig. 7. Example of a semantic map (week 12 (16–22 March 2020) beginning of lockdown and municipal election)

By repeating this interpretative analysis over the 22 weeks of data, and thus 22 maps, we can schematically reconstruct the evolution of the discourse.

To validate the hypothesized evolution of the mask object in the social media discourse, we suggest a centrality test (see Fig. 8). One would naturally be curious about the future, but over the observed period there is an undeniable increasing centrality (even if the last few weeks mark a weakening), the mask is connected to an increasing number of conversations. Becoming the lowest common denominator, it becomes the main key through which one can access the different paths of collective thinking. Naturally, the higher citation frequency of the mask compared to other means of attenuation, favours increased variety of associated objects. This is the statistical point of view. We can also consider the hypothesis that being associated with more themes, it is cited more often.

4.4   Confirmation by Topic Modeling

The last approach to appreciate the importance of the mask is to apply a topic model on temporal data (STM model). This type of model integrates variables

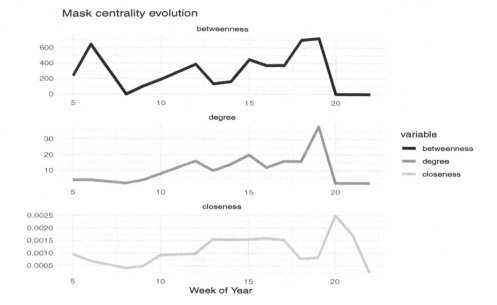

Fig. 8. Evolution of the lexical centrality of the mask (criteria of degree, betweenness and closeness)

that explain the prevalence of topics. Time, translated here as the order of weeks, is assumed to be associated with the prevalence of certain topics; it represents a proxy for the states of the general environment that affect the content of conversations. The model also allows topics to be correlated with each other.

A satisfactory solution seems to support 20 topics, of which it is difficult to give an exhaustive analysis here, but more easily a synthetic presentation based on the most visual representation provided by the model. Figure 9 provides the synthesis. The topics are closer the more they are correlated, the correlations (over 0.15) are represented by the thickness of the segments, and the size of the circles is proportional to the frequency of the topics.

This structure is characterized first of all by a kind of duality, a macro segment seems to be articulated around two components. One is centered on the coronavirus and China, it will be characterized as exotic; the other on the covid and the public issue. We find this idea of a change of perspective. What used to be a foreign body becomes an inner pain.

The advantage of the model is that it makes it possible to represent temporal prevalence, which is shown in Fig. 10. We can clearly identify the topics that are favoured in the first period and then decline, as well as those that rise in the second period.

The beginning of the study period is characterized by the prevalence of questions related to the discovery of the coronavirus, its effects visible through the number of deaths in China, and the situation in France facing an unprecedented virus. Then new themes emerge, related to Covid-19: the development of the

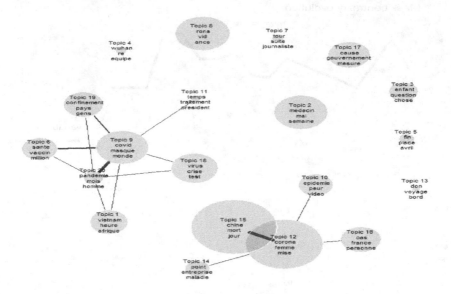

Fig. 9. Correlation network of the 20 identified topics: (r threshold: 0.15 - FR projection))

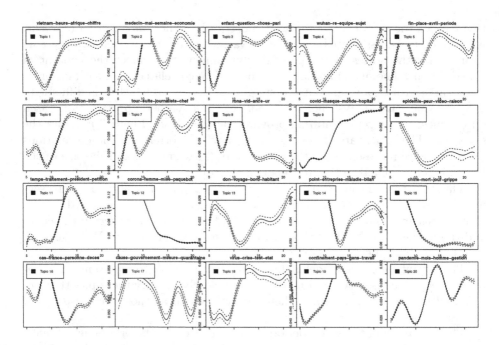

Fig. 10. Time prevalence graphs on the probability of topics (described by the three most distinctive terms)

pandemic, the case of children, announcements concerning future vaccines and potential treatments (with chloroquine at the heart, of course), to end with the state of crisis in the country and its management by the political power. The general trend is that the discussions are moving towards an endogenization of the epidemic, which starts with an unknown Wuhan virus and turns into a disease that devastates France and the French (both economically and medically).

As for the mask, a schema is emerging that clarifies its position. It is not found, as one might have expected, in a large number of themes, but as a central theme closely associated with the disease. This topic is itself associated with a few others, and this configuration defines the new paradigm of discourse which is tied up in the first lockdown.

5   Conclusion

Empirically, the main result, obtained by triangulation of methods, is that the mask emerges as a central figure in Twitter discourse as early as April, with the endogenization of the epidemic. This is the term that seems to articulate the polemics (lack of protection for health workers, supply problems, dissemination of the obligation to wear it). Over the period under study, that of the first lockdown, the obligation is limited, and compliance with its wearing is largely voluntary insofar as voluntary behaviour includes the effects of social standardization.

This result was not obvious at first glance, other figures were candidates: videoconferencing, in which millions of workers, students or professors quickly learned to manipulate interfaces with variable happiness but which does not appear in the contents. The hydroalcoholic gel too, whose distributors spread out over shops, stations and administrations and which pharmacists could not manufacture in time. Tests in particular, whose usefulness was questioned before becoming a central argument for government action and no doubt a factor of success in certain Asian countries. It is finally towards the mask that the discourses of the twittosphere converge.

A posteriori analysis of the phenomenon makes it possible to explain what has made the mask a focal point of conversation, but also of behavior. It is worth less for its functional qualities (continuously discussed even from a scientific point of view) than for its ability to fix attention and to organize living conditions under threat of epidemic. The defended hypothesis is that its phenomenological ambivalence nourishes sufficient interpretative flexibility to polarize the questioning of mismatched social worlds (scientists, politicians and citizens), and provides a common framework within which conventions and norms can be renegotiated. Thus, we can consider the mask as a boundary object [13,14]. Beyond this role of border-crosser, it paradoxically forms the fabric of social relations, the material, ritual and symbolic knots through which social activity is reorganized.

On a practical level, this study underlines the need to consider the means of attenuation (barrier gestures, social distance, use of artefacts ...) not only in terms of their intrinsic and extrinsic effectiveness, respect for compliance and the obligation that provokes resistance, but also from a more anthropological perspective that gives the material objects of (extra) ordinary life a power nourished by their capacity to ritualize social interactions, to symbolically carry the commitment of the actors and even more to give them power over the invisible curse of the epidemic [8]. Even if it does not provide much protection, the mask is as effective as the fetish, it maintains social order when we know nothing about the battles that take place out of our sight. It may well be that getting people to participate requires more than just rational arguments.

Despite the quantitative dimension of our treatments (counting frequencies, densities, probabilities), the analysis conducted in this study is largely exploratory at least in the thematic sense. The ability to quantify the frequency of themes, however, allows us to reconstruct an immediate micro history in a factual manner and to highlight a key phenomenon: the mask is the central figure in twitter discussions. The methodological contribution is straight forward: developing formal methods to deal with massive data contents. Beyond the technical aspects, the general idea is that of building processing procedures that allow the researcher to deal with large volumes of data and to have an objectified representation of the discourse.

The methods of analysis presented in this research are particularly appealing to social network managers: they help identify topics of importance and represent the dynamics of discourse. Applications can be found in the management of online reputation, in the identification of irritants and the responses to solutions implemented to deal with them. Detailed code is available upon request.

The limits of this work are numerous and result from the rush of this research which began exactly a few days after the confinement (March 16, 2020) and ends, at least in the form of this contribution, at the end of October 2020, with the empirical material covering the period from February to May 2020. The main limitation lies in the weak explicitation of the social processes that are invoked without having observed them. We observe only the discursive consequences without describing them precisely, on an object of study limited to social media whose profoundly unequal textual production structure gives the most engaged a disproportionate voice.

The research avenues opened up by this work are numerous, but we can cite two main ones: continuing the study (data being available) over the remaining period to December 2020, and extending it to other countries in order to see wether the same phenomena converge and if the role of the mask is maintained depending on the context.

References

1. Arnold, T.: A tidy data model for natural language processing using cleanNLP. R. J. **9**(2), 248 (2017). https://doi.org/10.32614/RJ-2017-035, https://journal.r-project.org/archive/2017/RJ-2017-035/index.html
2. Banda, J.M., et al.: A large-scale COVID-19 Twitter chatter dataset for open scientific research - an international collaboration. arXiv:2004.03688 [cs], April 2020. http://arxiv.org/abs/2004.03688, arXiv: 2004.03688

3. Blei, D.M., Ng, A.Y., Jordan, M.I.: Latent Dirichlet Allocation. J. Mach. Learn. Res. **3**, 993–1022 (2003). http://dl.acm.org/citation.cfm?id=944919.944937

4. Cambria, E., White, B.: Jumping NLP curves: a review of natural language processing research [review article]. IEEE Comput. Intell. Mag. **9**(2), 48–57 (2014). https://doi.org/10.1109/MCI.2014.2307227, http://ieeexplore.ieee.org/document/6786458/

5. Csardi, G., Nepusz, T.: The igraph software package for complex network research. Int. J. Complex Syst. **1695**(5), 1–9 (2006). https://igraph.org

6. Fruchterman, T.M.J., Reingold, E.M.: Graph drawing by force-directed placement. Softw. Pract. Exper. **21**(11), 1129–1164 (1991). https://doi.org/10.1002/spe.4380211102, http://doi.wiley.com/10.1002/spe.4380211102

7. Horney, J., Nguyen, M., Salvesen, D., Tomasco, O., Berke, P.: Engaging the public in planning for disaster recovery. Int. J. Disaster Risk Reduction **17**, 33–37 (2016). https://doi.org/10.1016/j.ijdrr.2016.03.011, https://linkinghub.elsevier.com/retrieve/pii/S2212420915301680

8. Lemonnier, P.: Mundane objects: materiality and non-verbal communication. Left Coast Press, Walnut Creek, CA, Critical cultural heritage series (2012)

9. R Core Team: R: A Language and Environment for Statistical Computing. R Foundation for Statistical Computing, Vienna, Austria (2019). https://www.R-project.org/

10. Roberts, M.E., Stewart, B.M., Tingley, D.: STM: an R package for structural topic models. J. Stat. Softw. **91**(2), 1–40 (2019). https://doi.org/10.18637/jss.v091.i02

11. Roberts, M.E., et al.: Structural topic models for open-ended survey responses: structural topic models for survey responses. Am. J. Polit. Sci. **58**(4), 1064–1082 (2014). https://doi.org/10.1111/ajps.12103, http://doi.wiley.com/10.1111/ajps.12103

12. Rodriguez, H., Quarantelli, E.L., Dynes, R.R. (eds.): Handbook of Disaster Research. Handbooks of Sociology and Social Research, Springer, New York (2007)

13. Star, S.L., Griesemer, J.R.: Institutional ecology, 'translations' and boundary objects: amateurs and professionals in berkeley's museum of vertebrate zoology, 1907–39. Soc. Stud. Sci. **19**(3), 387–420 (1989). https://doi.org/10.1177/030631289019003001, http://journals.sagepub.com/doi/10.1177/030631289019003001

14. Trompette, P., Vinck, D.: Retour sur la notion d'objet-frontière. Revue d'anthropologie des connaissances, **3**(1), 5 (2009). https://doi.org/10.3917/rac.006.0005, http://www.cairn.info/revue-anthropologie-des-connaissances-2009-1-page-5.htm

15. Wickham, H., et al.: Welcome to the tidyverse. J. Open Source Softw. **4**(43), 1686 (2019). https://doi.org/10.21105/joss.01686

16. Witvorapong, N., Muttarak, R., Pothisiri, W.: Social participation and disaster risk reduction behaviors in Tsunami prone areas. PLOS ONE **10**(7), e0130862 (2015). https://doi.org/10.1371/journal.pone.0130862, https://dx.plos.org/10.1371/journal.pone.0130862

Supporting Students While Shifting to Online Learning During COVID-19: Community College Feedback from Several Computing Courses

Fred Bartlett Jr.[✉] and James Braman[✉]

Community College of Baltimore County, Baltimore, MD 21237, USA
{fbartlett,jbraman}@ccbcmd.edu

Abstract. The shift in educational strategies and modalities brought on by the COVID-19 pandemic has intensified the need for innovative teaching methods. Both students and educators faced numerous challenges caused or exacerbated by the shift to different learning modalities and compounded by limited services and other restrictions. Adding to this complexity is the diversity in student skillset and technology literacy within the community college environment. At the same time, instructors had to manage their own issues related to the pandemic while juggling critical changes in their courses. In this paper, the authors discuss challenges in teaching several computing courses during the shift to an online format during the COVID-19 pandemic. Several challenges and strategies for supporting students in the computer science/information technology department at a large community college will be discussed, in addition to initial feedback gained from students.

Keywords: Online learning · COVID-19 · Community college · Student success

1 Introduction

Over the last several years, there have been significant efforts to create quality online courses that aim to achieve high levels of student engagement and include dynamic course content and relevant materials. While this has been an ongoing effort at many institutions for some time, the abrupt shift in educational strategies and modalities brought on by the COVID-19 pandemic has intensified the need for new innovative approaches for teaching and learning. Not only are educators faced with many pedagogical challenges, but numerous other problems that were caused or exacerbated by the shift from traditional teaching and compounded by limited college services. Adding to this complexity is the diversity in student skillset and technology literacy within the community college environment. In addition, instructors at the same time had to manage their issues related to the pandemic while juggling critical changes in their courses. In this paper, the authors discuss challenges in teaching several computing courses during the shift in modalities during the COVID-19 pandemic. Specifically, challenges and strategies for supporting students in the computer science/information technology department at a

© Springer Nature Switzerland AG 2021
G. Meiselwitz (Ed.): HCII 2021, LNCS 12775, pp. 322–336, 2021.
https://doi.org/10.1007/978-3-030-77685-5_25

large community college. Feedback from a student-centered survey about their difficulties during online learning is presented. Considerations for upcoming semesters based on new strategies and guidance will also be discussed.

The Community College of Baltimore County (CCBC) located in Maryland, USA, is an important part of Baltimore County, collaborating with government, business, and local organizations. CCBC provides an accessible, affordable, and high-quality education that prepares students for transfer and career success. In 2017, the college-educated 61,191 students, including 29,115 credit students and 33,247 non-credit students [1]. With three main campuses and three extension centers, CCBC serves a diverse population of Maryland residents. The computer science/information technology (CSIT) department offers associate degrees in Information Technology, Computer Science, and Computer Science with a concentration in Information Systems Management as well as five credit-based certificates (Database, Information Management, Mobile Development, Programming, and Office Specialist). At the Community College of Baltimore County (CCBC), a systematic approach to evaluating and developing online courses has been in place to ensure quality and consistency [2]. This approach utilizes metrics of quality assurance in combination with Quality Matters (QM) review and rubric.

In March 2020, the COVID-19 pandemic caused worldwide disruptions in many areas of society. It has been an ongoing health concern causing many deaths and various levels of illness. There have been millions of cases worldwide and numerous deaths [3]. Many school systems were forced to close worldwide, facing an array of challenges and ramifications of the COVID-19 pandemic. Multiple solutions were explored, including the quick adoption or expanded use of various learning management systems.

In some cases, publishers and other digital learning platform providers assisted even providing some content and services for free [4]. There were numerous and diverse responses within higher education that varied by country, jurisdiction, and school to meet students' needs [5]. These included various forms of online learning, hybrid formats, and alternative face to face teaching. In any case, these abrupt shifts in teaching strategies were disruptive and required swift, dramatic changes to ensure continued learning while maintaining the same academic rigor.

Students faced a plethora of challenges that have the potential to hinder academic success. The real impact of these difficulties will be hard to measure for years to come. These can be issues related to access to course materials, lack of technology, correct software, lack of Internet connection, or transportation challenges to and from college. Other events in a student's life can cause problems such as the death of a family member or friend, illness or injury, or many other traumatic events. At any time, these challenges are difficult. Changes brought on by the COVID-19 pandemic have amplified these issues exacerbating already challenging times. Added to this already problematic recipe, students are now faced with additional responsibilities at home caring for children or younger siblings and changes in work schedules. Many others were faced with unemployment, changes in income, and lack of basic needs causing added stress while continuing to provide for their families.

2 Methods and Results

2.1 Research Design

Anecdotally, many observations were made during the rapid switch to online learning during the Spring 2020 semester and continued into the summer session of that year. During the Fall 2020 semester, a survey was developed and deployed electronically through SurveyMonkey to a few limited numbers of computer courses within the computer science/information technology department. This was part of a small pilot assessment to gain some insight into challenges faced by students. Courses included for voluntary participation included a limited number of CSIT 101 – Technology and Information Systems, CSIT 120 – Diversity in a Technological Society, CSIT 211 – Advanced Programming, CSIT 214 – C++ Programming. A total of 42 participants responded to the survey, which included 23 (54.76%) computer science majors, 5 (11.90%) listed as general studies, 3 (7.14%) Information Technology major, and 3 (7.14%) listing therapy as their major. Most of the participants, 31 (73.81%), were between the age of 18–24, 8 (19.05%) were between 25–34 age range, 1 (2.38%) participant reported being in the 35–44 age range, and 2 (4.76%) participants were 45–54 age range. No other age ranges were reported. It is important to note that the survey responses were generalized to any course that the participants were taking during the semester and not explicitly related to CSIT courses. After examining this initial feedback, more extensive deployment of the survey is planned.

2.2 Survey Results

After obtaining some necessary demographic information, the survey contained questions to assess participants' internet and computing resources at home. In question 3, the survey asked, "Do you have internet access at home?". All 42 (100%) reporting "yes" that they do have internet access at home. Question 4 asked explicitly about the type of access and is presented in Table 1 below.

Table 1. Internet access type at home

Options	Frequency (n = 42)
Dial-up	0 (0%)
DSL	6 (14.29%)
Satellite	4 (9.52%)
Cable	21 (50.00%)
Fiber Optic	8 (19.05%)
Cell phone only	1 (2.38%)
Other	2 (4.76%)

Next, Q5 asked, "How many other people do you share the internet within your home?". Only one participant (2.38%) responded that they were the only ones using the internet at home and did not share their connection. Five (11.90%) noted that they share their connection with one other person at home, 9 (21.43%) reported sharing with two people, 9 (21.43%) reported sharing their connection with three other people, 10 (23.81%) reported sharing with four people. The remaining 8 (19.05%) reported sharing the connection with five or more people. Also, in Q6, when asked about having children under the age of 18 at home, 30 (71.43%) of the participants reported "no" and 12 (28.57%) reported "yes". Subsequently, 8 of the 12 participants that noted they have children at home, reported having one to three children at home, with the majority having only one child (62.5%), two children (25%), three children (12.5%). We also wanted to learn more about where participants primarily worked on their coursework. Q7 presented the following choices: Public library, Campus, Home, At work, Friends house, other family member, and other. When answering this question, 39 (92.86%) reported primarily working from home, while the remaining 3 (7.14%) reported: "At work". Following was question 9 that asked about participants operating system, which is summarized in Table 2 below.

Table 2. Primary operating system

Options	Frequency (n = 42)
Windows	27 (64.29%)
Mac OS	12 (28.57%)
Chrome OS	1 (2.38%)
Android	1 (2.38%)
iOS	0 (0.0%)
Linux	1 (2.38%)

Next, to assess how other outside time constraints may impact the survey asked in question 10, "Are you currently employed?". Seven participants (16.67%) reported "Yes – Full Time", 19 (45.23%) reported "Yes – Part-Time", and the remaining 16 (38.10%) said "no". A follow-up question was presented in question 11 to gauge how many hours per week participants work per week. Twenty-six responded to this question (61.9%), which revealed, on average working 25.99 h (median: 30). Question 12 asked, "How many courses are you taking this semester?" referred to the Fall 2020 semester. Forty-one of the participants responded (97.6% response rate). Zero participants (0%) reported only taking one course, 8 (19.51%) reported taking only two courses, 11 (26.83%) reported taking three courses, 18 (43.90%) reported taking four courses, 4 (9.76%) reported taking five courses, and 0 (0%) reported taking more than five courses.

The survey then asked, "Has COVID-19 impacted your enrollment or course selection?" through question 13. There was an option for participants to make additional comments, which is presented in Table 3 below. When asked, "Due to COVID-19, are you educating or working with school-aged kids in the home?". Most of the participants, 33 (78.57%) responded "No", and 9 (21.43%) answered "Yes". All participants,

42 (100%) reported taking online or remote synchronous courses during the semester. The survey did not ask about other course formats.

Table 3. COVID19 impact on enrollment or course selection

Options	Frequency (n = 42)
Yes	25 (59.5%)
No	17 (40.5%)
Comments:	
"It affected course availability"	
"Some limitations on course sections"	
"Non-online courses were converted to online with no options"	
"Semester not as expected"	
"I seemed to have missed important things"	
"I was not able to get the classes I wanted to attend in person"	
"I had to take all asynchronous online courses"	
"I primarily retook classes for better grades"	
"Not a lot of time to study/homework"	
"It forced me to take online courses which I really don't like to do"	
"I did not take any classes that would have required any kind of contact"	
"Working from home has proved more difficult in learning the course material"	
"I decided to take some courses I considered easy because I find the online setting difficult"	
"I like being in the classroom and having a physical reminder of my responsibilities"	
"It is tiring to sit behind a computer"	

The survey then asked several questions related to tools used for online learning. In Question 16, the survey asked, "Which of the following have you used for remote or online learning?". Participants could select more than one option. Results for Q16 are presented in Table 4 below. One participant noted they used "Blackboard", the College's Learning Management System (LMS) only. This most likely is due to the participant only taking asynchronous online courses only. As a follow-up question, the survey also asked, "How do you feel about using online meeting tools for class?". This was an open-ended question where the results have been classified in Table 5. Question 18 asked, "How do you feel about meeting online instead of Face to Face?". This was another open-ended question, and the results have been classified and presented in Table 6 below. Participants could list more than one comment about their feeling regarding meeting online versus face to face.

The survey then asked in Q19, "Have your study habits changed since COVID-19?". Most of the participants, 27 (67.29%) responded "Yes", 12 (28.57%) responded "No", and the remaining 3 (7.14%) reported that they were "Unsure". Following in Q20,

Table 4. Online meeting tools

Options	Frequency (n = 42)
Zoom	37
Teams	28
Skype	2
Google Meet	2
Other	1

"Explain how your study habits may have changed since COVID-19?". This was another open-ended question, and the responses are classified in Table 7 below. Participants could write multiple part responses.

Table 5. General comments about meeting tools

Generalized comment topic	Frequency (n = 42)
Great/good/works well/Ok	21
Not as good as in-person/limited interaction	5
Encountered technical problems	5
Prefer face to face	3
Require good internet connection	2
I do not recommend	2
Hard to learn online	2
Not comfortable with online meeting tools	2
Hard to use	2
Convenient	2
I am starting not to like meeting online	1
Meeting online helped me do better in class	1
Not a good user interface	1
Feels draining	1

Next, in Q21, the survey asked, "How do you contact your instructor the most for a course if you have questions? (Select all that apply)". Table 8 presents the responses. The survey then asked in Q22, "Have you experienced any of the following challenges related to completing course work during the COVID-19 pandemic? (select all that apply)". The responses to question 22 are presented in Table 9. As a follow-up, Q23 asked participants to describe any other challenges they have faced since being in school during COVID-19 that was not listed as an option for Q22. This was an open-ended question whose responses are classified in Table 10 below.

Table 6. General feelings about meeting online vs. face to face.

Generalized comment topic	Frequency (n = 42)
Good/Ok/fine	11
Prefer Meeting face-to-face	11
I do not like Meeting online	6
Harder to focus/more difficult meeting online	4
Prefer meeting online	4
I like the convenience of online	4
I just deal with it/Ok for now	3
I am more comfortable interacting online	2
Meeting online is engaging	1
Online is not as engaging	1
Hard to replace hands-on activities	1
Missing personal interaction	1
Online is not as good or beneficial	1
I like that the lectures are recorded online	1

Table 7. Changes in study habits

Generalized comment topic	Frequency (n = 40)
Study time increased	10
No change	10
Diminished/Declined	5
I needed to rely on myself more	5
More distractions	3
I am less motivated to study	3
Needed to spend more time finding supplementary materials	2
Time management is a challenge	2
I procrastinated more on assignments	1
Tried online study groups	1
Unsure	1
Needed to create a distraction-free area to work	1

Next, in question 24, the survey asked, "If you were enrolled last semester, what has been the biggest change?". This was an open-ended question whose responses have been classified in Table 11 below. Participants could list more than one response.

Table 8. Communication methods

Options	Frequency (n = 41)
Email	35
Through the learning management system	25
Video conferencing/Online meeting tool	14
Text message	4
Phone	3
In-person	0
Other	0

Table 9. Challenges related to course work.

Options	Frequency (n = 38)
Poor concentration while working at home	28
Trouble with course format being online or remote	23
Not being able to contact instructor	15
Lack of resources	10
Access to the Internet	10
Trouble accessing course material	7
Access to a computer or tablet	5

In Q25, the survey asked, "Do you plan to take more online or more remote courses in the future after COVID-19?". Forty-one participants responded to this question. Thirty (73.17%) participants reported "Yes" that they would take more online or remote courses in the future, 11 (26.83%) responded "No". Participants were also asked if there have been any positive aspects of taking online courses during the COVID-19 pandemic?". These comments are noted in Table 12. Participants could note multiple responses to this question.

Question 27 asked, "Do any of your courses use interactive simulations or VDIs?". Most of the participants, 38 (90.48%) responded "No", and the remaining 4 (9.52%) reported "Yes". Additionally, it was asked, "Have you had any technical problems with hardware or software?". Twenty (47.62%) reported "Yes," and 22 (52.38%) responded "No". There was an option for participants to note additional comments which included: "Poor internet connection from both my side and the instructor's side". "Lockdown browser crashing and submitting an unfinished exam" (referring to an online proctoring tool), "One of my teachers had plenty of issues using Microsoft teams, like her mic not working well and her sound cutting off on our end.", "Sometimes the internet disconnects, but I have been able to reconnect successfully every time".

Table 10. Additional challenges

Generalized comment topic	Frequency (n = 39)
No/None/Not Sure	29
Could not visit the campus	1
Not having access to the Library	1
Hard to limit distractions	1
Inability to work on problems during synchronous online class	1
Hard to do work without the instructor	1
Feels impersonal	1
Lack of communication	1
Lack of human contact	1
Motivation to do my work	1
Increased time being online	1

Table 11. Comments on biggest challenges

Generalized comment topic	Frequency (n = 39)
Adapting to online	4
Having all classes online	4
More workload	4
Not being able to work with instructor	4
Working from home	3
Study habits/lack of motivation	3
Limited support for disability services	2
Not being able to go to the library/campus	2
Switching to an online format	2
Not being able to go out/being stuck at home	2
Teaching myself	2
More stress	1
Needing more materials to help with classwork	1
Lack of support	1
New working environment	1
Different routine	1
This was my first semester in college	1
Having kids at home	1

Table 12. Positive aspects of online courses during COVID-19

Generalized comment topic	Frequency (n = 39)
No Response/No	14
No Commute/driving/travel	11
Online is convenient/more flexible	8
Yes (noted yes but no detail provided)	2
Instructors have been flexible and helpful	2
Always on time for class	2
Helped with course selection options	1
Became more self-reliant	1
Being able to work from home	1
Learned more	1
Reading more	1
Spending more time with family	1

3   Discussion

Although the student survey was limited in scope and had a low number of participants, the feedback overall was insightful and helpful to understand the challenges that the students have been facing. The survey will also serve as a basis for possible future surveys and studies in the future. Overall, from the data, we could see that although all students reported having home internet connectivity, there were still some that had limitations in speed. Those with limited connection speed would certainly be impacted in courses where instructional material relies on heavy graphics, video, virtual desktop environments, and other simulations. This could also be a problem for courses that require students to connect live through video conferencing tools. A similar problem was revealed through question five when asking how many other people used the same connection. Having numerous devices and users on the same connection will inevitably use more bandwidth. In our small sample, most students did not have children at home, but 28.6% did which may impact both internet connection and provide additional distraction due to their needed care. Additionally, most students have been completing their course work at home as their primary location for schoolwork.

Another issue is the operating system that is being used. In several courses, there have been issues with using specific software. Students would use computers in the classroom, library, and during open labs during a typical semester. With some of the restrictions due to COVID-19, students had limited access and could only use their own systems. Most issues were due to some simulation software used and when using online proctoring software. Question 9 in the survey did confirm that most of those responding were using Windows or Mac OS, with limited use of Chrome OS, or those accessing content through their mobile phones. Although not well represented through this set of participants, there were more reported problems in other sections related to incompatible software for the students operating system and device.

Shifting priorities were also a concern that students were facing. This included employment changes, changing responsibilities at home, and possible job loss due to the pandemic. The survey did not focus on specific employment changes; however, it did ask about employment and time at work to gauge how this time commitment may affect study habits. Related was the number of courses that students were taking. The majority were taking at least four courses, which would require significant time to study. Although all students reported, they were taking online courses (synchronous or asynchronous), which may have been a factor. It was reported that there was an impact on course selection due to the pandemic. Due to many courses being online or remote synchronous, students also needed to learn many new skills, including video conferencing tools. Most of the participants reported using Microsoft Teams or Zoom for their synchronous courses. Overall, the comments were positive or neutral for the overall functionality and use of these tools for the class. A few comments were noting there were some technical problems that were encountered, and several preferred face-to-face interactions for learning. This was confirmed through comments related to question eighteen, where many were Ok with learning online due to the circumstances. However, several participants preferred face to face interaction, and others did not like the idea of meeting online. One interesting aspect that can be later explored is students that chose online or felt more empowered to interact in an online format.

Interestingly, there were several changes reported in study habits during the shift to online learning. This may indicate needed changes to course structure, support, or other aspects of a course to assist students learning materials. Several participants reported that they studied less, had less motivation, had more distraction, or needed to rely more on themselves to keep on track. Others said there was no change at all, while others reported that their study time increased. It was not known from the survey the cause of the increased study time with these students. Is the increase in time due to more reading and taking their time with the material due to a decrease in-class time, due to issues with reading or increases in distraction or other factors? When asked to report on specific difficulties, most participants noted that poor concentration while working from home and difficulty contacting the instructor for courses. The survey was not specific to CSIT courses, which often have a strong technical component for communication. In future iterations of the survey, this question will be adjusted. Participants also noted that they had been contacting their instructors mainly through email, the LMS or through video conferencing. It is unknown through the survey the impact on study habits or learning course materials compared to pre-COVID-19 class interaction.

Another interesting aspect revealed in the survey was that the majority, 73.2% of participants, reported that they would be interested in taking more online courses in the future. This most likely is due to the convenience of online coursework and that many students who would have chosen not to take an online course have become more comfortable with this format. This would be another interesting aspect to investigate further in more detail. Eleven, or 26.2%, reported that not having a commute to campus was a positive aspect of the pandemic, along with 8 (19%) noting that online courses were more convenient overall.

4 Considerations

This pilot study and feedback provided beneficial information about challenges and recommendations to mitigate some of these challenges and issues. The feedback confirmed many of the initial observations of potential problems and ways to improve the courses. The following are several recommendations based on challenges and initial feedback:

- Be mindful of internet connection speeds as this may limit how students connect to live streams and course materials. Instructors should remind students of any connection requirements needed for the course. Consider how this could impact courses that use inclusive textbook programs or rely on the publisher's material.
- Consider the work environment where students are completing their course work. Is it free of distractions? Do they have a desk and a working computer? Be mindful that students may be sharing space and internet connections with other household members.
- Due to possible incompatibility issues with some devices and operating systems – test all software needed for the class thoroughly. Use software that can be used across devices and systems for lessons and assignments. Can cloud technologies be used as well as virtual desktop infrastructure (VDI).
- Consider VDI software and simulations to replace typical hands-on assignments.
- Flexibility – Being flexible with due dates. Students may be experiencing unusual circumstances at home, which may make adhering to original deadlines more difficult. While we are not advocating having deadlines but developing a flexible policy can be helpful. Consider a student that may be taking care of younger children or helping with siblings at home. Perhaps a family only has one computer that must be shared among several people, thus reducing the time allowed to do schoolwork.
- For assignments that could be problematic to complete due to a possible lack of resources or technology, consider alternate formats, requirements, or ways to submit assignments.
- Consider multiple communication modes outside of the learning management system (phone, text, email, social media, chat, virtual worlds, etc.,).
- Due to external and nonacademic challenges, consider checking on students in a friendly way to check on their wellbeing. This could also lead to conversations that could help the students understand course materials or understand problems they may face accessing or interacting with content.
- Similarly, check on your colleagues. Just as students may be having problems, other instructors may be facing challenges. Communication within the department can be useful to share ideas, best practices and to provide assistance.
- As students may have changed course offerings compare to past semesters, consider offering courses in an array of formats. This also ties into flexibility. Provide options for students that need or prefer synchronous or asynchronous formats.
- Have a plan in place for students who become ill or need to take care of sick family members.
- Have a plan in place for students who experience a death in the family related to COVID-19.

- Remind students to take opportunities to get outdoors and to practice self-care. Faculty can even host outdoor sessions and share experiences to help encourage outdoor activities [6].
- Consider electronic options for remote proctoring for tests and quizzes to maintain academic integrity.

5   Innovation Through Virtual Worlds

Lastly, this section describes a potential experimental innovation for student interaction through the potentials of virtual worlds. During the Spring 2020 semester, one of the authors created a dedicated space in the virtual world of Second Life to be used as a meeting space for CSIT 211-Advanced Programming. The class had previously had only been using Blackboard for content delivery. The instructor had primarily used email and phone to communicate with the class outside of the LMS with occasional Zoom meetings as needed. A poll was conducted in March and distributed to the class to see how they wanted to continue with the course after the dramatic shift to an online format. The primary purpose of the poll was related to the course modality. 100% of the students opted for the course to shift to an asynchronous format.

To augment the missing face-to-face interaction in the course where additional notes and information would be presented to the course, the instructor made changes to the remaining modules in the course that were then taught exclusively online. In addition to required readings for each topic, additional notes were uploaded to the LMS along with the presentation notes that would have been discussed in class. Each week the instructor posted an overview of what topics would be most important so if students had limited time, they could at least focus on those components. To offset missing time in class, additional practice questions were posted. Also, links were provided that offered interactive exercises and, in some cases, interactive problems [7]. In addition, each week, mini video lectures were posted on main topics if students needed additional resources.

Virtual worlds have the potential to be a very dynamic and valuable space for teaching and learning. As an educational tool, these spaces can be used for more than just communication or entertainment. At first glance, these worlds may look like a game. However, they can be a serious tool that can be used for engagement. Overall a virtual world is a computer-generated 3D space that can be accessed through the Internet. One does not need to have expensive virtual reality headgear (although that could be the case for some). Instead, these online worlds can be accessed using a typical computer setup with a standard monitor, keyboard, and mouse. A user is represented in the world as a 3D character that can be controlled through the mouse and keyboard, which allows one to manipulate objects in the world and interact with other avatars.

As discussed by [8], there are three major educational benefits from using virtual worlds:

- Virtual worlds give users the ability to carry out tasks that could be difficult for them in the "real world" due to constraints, including cost, scheduling or location.
- Virtual worlds' persistence allows for continuing and growing social interactions, which can serve as a basis for collaborative education.

- Virtual worlds can adapt and grow to meet user needs.

Virtual worlds have already been used in other CSIT courses with positive feedback [9]. More work and design is planned for the use of Second Life in an experimental capacity.

6   Conclusions

Students generally expressed added stressors and anxiety due to the COVID-19 pandemic and the switch to online learning. While there have been numerous challenges, both students and faculty have adapted well. As one student commented separately in the survey, *"I think CCBC did online classes very well considering a lot of the professors had to transition within a week or so. I prefer face to face classes, but my grades haven't suffered so I think the online transition and classes were just fine"*. As this paper notes, there have been challenges, but through continued course improvements, flexibility, and some redesign, education can continue positively and meaningful. With many courses being converted to an online format, educators and students can be flexible and experimental in discovering new ways for learning and presenting materials.

It is planned to expand the survey into other courses in upcoming semesters, survey more students, and ask for feedback from non-computer courses. Many other aspects are important to investigate. This paper has discussed challenges in teaching several computing courses during the shift to an online format during the COVID-19 pandemic and noted strategies for supporting students to overcome these issues. The data collected from the initial feedback can be used to update and improve courses for future semesters.

References

1. CCBC Office of Planning, Research and Evaluation: CCBC Fact Book (2019). http://www.ccb cmd.edu/~/media/CCBC/About%20CCBC/Administrative%20Offices/PRE/ccbc_factbook. ashx
2. Paniagua, F.G.: Quality assurance in online education: a development process to design high-quality courses. In: Meiselwitz, G. (ed.) HCII 2019. LNCS, vol. 11579, pp. 182–194. Springer, Cham (2019). https://doi.org/10.1007/978-3-030-21905-5_14
3. John Hopkins University COVID-19 Dashboard: COVID-19 Dashboard by the Center for Systems Science and Engineering (2020). https://coronavirus.jhu.edu/map.html
4. Teräs, M., Suoranta, J., Teräs, H., Curcher, M.: Post-Covid-19 education and education technology 'solutionism': a seller's market. Postdigital Sci. Educ. **2**, 1–16 (2020)
5. Crawford, J., et al.: COVID-19: 20 countries' higher education intra-period digital pedagogy responses. J. Appl. Learn. Teach. **3**(1), 1–20 (2020)
6. Massey, M.: Encountering Nature: Outdoor Walks to Reduce Stress and Increase Focus in Students. Faculty Focus (2020). https://www.facultyfocus.com/articles/teaching-and-learning/ encountering-nature-outdoor-walks-to-reduce-stress-and-increase-focus-in-students/
7. Braman, J., Vincenti, G., Arboleda Diaz, A.M., Jinman, A.: Learning computer science fundamentals through virtual environments. In: Ozok, A.A., Zaphiris, P. (eds.) OCSC 2009. LNCS, vol. 5621, pp. 423–431. Springer, Heidelberg (2009). https://doi.org/10.1007/978-3-642-02774-1_46

8. Antonacci, D., DiBartolo, S., Edwards, N., Fritch, K., McMullen, B., Murch-Shafer, R: The power of virtual worlds in education: a second life primer and resource for exploring the potential of virtual worlds to impact teaching and learning. ANGEL Learning White Paper (2008)
9. Pigatt, Y., Braman, J.: Engaging students in a computer diversity course through virtual worlds. In: Choi, D.H., Dailey-Hebert, A., Estes, J.S. (ed.) Current and Prospective Applications of Virtual Reality in Higher Education, pp. 170–193. IGI Global (2021). https://doi.org/10.4018/978-1-7998-4960-5.ch008

Life Clock: Developing a Technological Platform to Promote Active Ageing

Milda Galkute[1] ⓘ, Luis Rojas[2](✉) ⓘ, and Erick Folch[3] ⓘ

[1] Pontificia Universidad Católica de Chile, Santiago, Chile
[2] Universidad San Sebastián, Facultad de Ingeniería y Tecnología, Santiago, Chile
[3] Facultad de Ingeniería, Universidad Andres Bello, Santiago, Chile

Abstract. Population is now aging at an unprecedented rate worldwide, which has caused an important concern about the sustainability of health, pension and social protection systems in developed and developing countries. Promoting active aging policies and practices which would improve older adults' autonomy, independency and health status has become one of the priorities of many politicians and practitioners across the globe. In this sense, the new technologies and, more specifically, the field of Human-Computer Interaction can and should play an important role in the promotion of an active aging model within society. Nevertheless, today there is still a very limited amount of devices or services adapted to the characteristics and needs of the elderly, especially in less developed countries. The aim of this research was to introduce a new easy-to-use and accessible mobile application to promote the active aging through the integration of physical, cognitive and social activities for older adults. The proposed mobile application showed an adequate ability to assist end users in achieving a healthier and more participative way of life at older ages, which is essential to foster older adults' empowerment within any society.

Keywords: Active aging · Older adults · Mobile application · Usability · Accessibility · Cognitive and physical activities

1 Introduction

The population is now aging at an unprecedented rate worldwide as a consequence of increased life expectancy and decreased birth rates. In fact, the number of people aged 60 years old or above will double across the globe by 2030, as forecasted by the United Nations [1], which will consequently lead to older adults aged 65 years or over outnumbering those aged under 24 years by 2050 [2].

While Europe and North America have always been the regions with highest population aging rates, several developing countries (i.e. in South America) have been going through important demographic changes too. According to the United Nations [1], the number of people aged over 65 years old is likely to increase from 9% in 2019 to 19% by 2050 and up to 31.3% in 2100 in Latin America and the Caribbean. Such accelerated population aging in Latin America would make it one of the oldest regions in the world by the next century.

© Springer Nature Switzerland AG 2021
G. Meiselwitz (Ed.): HCII 2021, LNCS 12775, pp. 337–351, 2021.
https://doi.org/10.1007/978-3-030-77685-5_26

These striking and unparalleled demographic changes are widely affecting different social, health, and economic settings, including social welfare sector, healthcare sector, and employment trends in both developed and developing countries. Nevertheless, developing countries characterized by profound social and economic inequalities are likely to face even more challenges when dealing with the demands arising from the aging of its population. The overarching presence of informal employment and lack of social protection for most vulnerable groups (i.e. older adults) make the low- and middle-income developing countries especially susceptible to fast-paced population aging [3].

Given the above, promoting active aging policies and practices becomes crucial in order to move from a dependent and passive lifestyle towards an active and dynamic one, fostering the autonomy as well as civic and socio-economic integration of older adults for longer periods of time.

In this context, the development of new technologies plays a key role in promoting active aging. The number of mobile applications aimed at facilitating the lives of older adults has grown considerably over the last decades [4]. There is now a great variety of applications supporting older adults in different life settings, such as encouraging adequate physical activities, helping with the daily medication intake, simplifying online grocery shopping, or facilitating social interaction with friends and family members.

Notwithstanding the increasing number of applications created to ease the everyday life of the elderly, some essential factors are often overlooked in the process of their design and development, such as accessibility and usability issues [5]. Indeed, as stated by [6], a very limited amount of devices or services have adapted to the characteristics and needs of this age group, especially in developing countries where older adults are likely to be excluded by the mobile phone industry and providers, as they are not considered as a potential audience due to higher technological analphabetism rate.

Moreover, it is important to highlight that most applications designed for older adults have mainly focused on promoting one particular area of active aging, whether it is physical, cognitive or social activity. Thus, what has been missing so far is the integration of the three main domains of the active aging model (i.e. physical, cognitive and social activities taken all together) in one single easy-to-use and accessible mobile application. Indeed, it has been acknowledged by some scholars that "multi-component interventions were more effective than standalone app interventions" [7].

Given the above, the aim of this research is to introduce a new technological platform with an interface designed specifically for the use of older adults to promote their active aging. That is, we have developed an easy-to-use and accessible mobile application to encourage physical, cognitive and social activities among older adults. Furthermore, we have formally assessed the usability and accessibility of the proposed platform.

This paper is organized as follows: in the next section we present the theoretical background and related works; we then describe our proposal and tools; next, we discuss the results related to the experimentation with users; finally, we present the conclusions.

2   Theoretical Background and Related Works

World Health Organization (WHO) has been one of the main institutions that started highlighting the importance of an active lifestyle at an older age. In one of their policy frameworks WHO stated that "active ageing is the process of optimizing opportunities for health, participation and security in order to enhance quality of life as people age" [8]. While the term of active aging has often been associated exclusively with physical activity, it is important to clarify that it actually refers to participation in diverse areas, including labor, social, spiritual and other types of settings. More specifically, health conditions, emotional well-being, high functioning in both cognitive and physical dimensions, and social interaction are all closely related to the successful and active people's aging [9, 10]. Thus, the main idea behind the active aging perspective is to move from a passive and dependent way of life in old age towards engaged and dynamic lifestyle [11].

Furthermore, active aging is perceived as beneficial not only for the older person, in terms of remaining "connected" to the society, but is also of great importance for the whole society, as it contributes to its social and economic development. Therefore, active aging can be understood as a two-way giving and receiving policy, because the quality of life of the elderly also improves the quality of life of other people (e.g. family members, friends) in an indirect way.

Given the current accelerated population aging worldwide, there is an increasing need to thrive in health promotion of the elderly as to reduce dependency rates and functional decline, and to improve the overall quality of life of the elderly, enabling in this way more dynamic and active lifestyles. In this sense, the emerging technologies, particularly from the Human-Computer Interaction field, play a crucial role in older adults' engagement with technological advances developed to support active aging.

In recent years, applications have been taking full advantage of the capabilities offered by new technologies and older adults could also benefit from such expansion. It has now been widely acknowledged that technological advances can help older adults avoid loneliness and self-isolation, bring them closer to the socio-cultural environment, and promote their independence [12].

As for physical activity, there are now hundreds of applications designed to encourage exercising among older adults. "Johnson and Johnson: 7 min Workout", "Daily Yoga", "C2K 5k Trainer", "FitOn" or "Freeletics" are just some of the fitness apps for over 60-years old, selected by the Senior Outlook Today team as the best apps in 2020 that offer a wide variety of exercises and workouts for seniors. From helping reduce back pain to increase flexibility or lose weight - the range of offer is very broad today. It seems that physical wellness of the elderly has now been broadly tackled by software developers.

In order to maintain good health the brain needs to be exercised in the same way as the body. Familiados [13] mentions some applications developed by neuroscientists that help maintain the mental abilities of the elderly. For example, "Lumosity" is composed of more than 25 games and a daily training program. This application is designed to expose the brain to gradually difficult challenges, promoting cognitive stimulation for older adults. "Fit Brain Trainer" is another application developed by neuroscientists, which includes more than 360 training sessions in which concentration, memory, capacity of deduction and visual perception are tested.

Despite the continuous expansion of mobile applications to promote healthy lifestyles at older age, an all-inclusive approach that would integrate different active aging settings into one accessible and easy-to-use software has been missing so far. Our proposal is therefore to implement an innovative mobile application to encourage physical, cognitive and social activities in the elderly, considering the specific needs and requirements of this group of population.

3   Proposal

A mobile technological platform is proposed as a solution, which provides adequate physical, cognitive and social activities for the elderly (see Fig. 1). This proposal aims to encourage the well-being of the elderly by promoting active aging. The platform is based on the following elements:

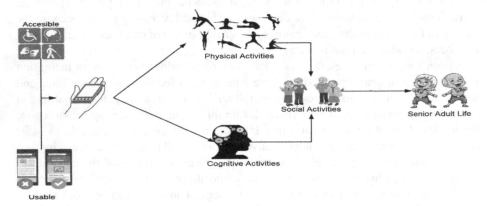

Fig. 1. Proposed solution.

3.1   Process Based on Accessibility and Usability

The process model used in the development of the technology is based on [14, 15]. The main objective is to consider accessibility and usability as pillars in the construction of technology for older adults. On the one hand, in terms of accessibility, adults may present some type of physical or cognitive disability, which is why the criteria established by the WCAG 2.0 guidelines are considered. The aim is to develop a platform adaptable to the physical and cognitive qualities of older adults. To ensure the accessibility of the proposed solution, an automatic evaluation was performed using the W3C Markup Validation Service and the Wave browser extension in Google Chrome. The results of both tools allowed addressing unresolved elements related to alternative text for images, color contrast, empty HTML headers, and the presence of frames.

On the other hand, regarding usability, the platform must consider it in order to provide software that allows interaction in a simple, comfortable and easy way. Therefore, end users (older adults) must have a relationship with the system that is offered, where the effectiveness, efficiency and satisfaction of the platform are a fundamental role for the application to be considered useful.

3.2   Usefulness of Physical and Cognitive Activities

This element corresponds to the usefulness of the physical and cognitive activities integrated in the application. In this case, both routines must develop stimuli in the elderly, strengthening the mind and body. Likewise, the application addresses the social field, promoting the integration of the elderly in events or group activities, thus it is possible to improve the quality of life of the elderly, promoting active aging based on the mobile platform.

The proposed solution is a means to reduce the breakdown in the relationship between technology and older adults, since a mobile application has its argument in the high and growing number of smartphones in the world. Thus, this technology has a great reach and penetration in the population. In addition, the different characteristics that the devices provide to their users, the low cost of product development, scalability, and easy distribution, mean greater accessibility for users. Currently, there is no mobile application that promotes physical and cognitive activities adapted to older adults. Likewise, it should be noted that physical and cognitive activities allow promoting social activities. In this way, participation in social activities can be essential for older adults to develop holistically, staying physically and cognitively active. To achieve the above, the technological platform is based on the following aspects:

Provide Adjusted Physical Activities for Older Adults. For adults aged 60 and over, physical activities consist of recreational or leisure, occupational, chores, games, exercises, or sports scheduled in the context of daily, family, and community activity. Therefore, it is important to consider physical inactivity, given that it is one of the fundamental risk factors for mortality worldwide [16, 17].

According to the data provided by the Catholic University and the Caja de los Andes [18, 19], the performance of physical activities in Chile, one of the most rapidly aging countries in the region, has decreased between 2007 and 2016, reaching 47.3% of older adults who never or almost never do exercises. The most relevant differences are seen in relation to the gender and educational level of the elderly. In this case, women and people with a lower educational level are those who do the least physical activity.

The mobility of the elderly is an indicator of autonomy and maintenance of personal identity, since it enables the preservation of other significant activities [20, 21]. In this way, if the older adult loses the ability to move around, the possibilities of socializing, working, entertaining, etc. are drastically reduced. Therefore, it is essential to facilitate the movement of older adults, in order to promote and prolong their autonomy and independence [22].

The physical activities proposed in the technological platform are based on the recommended National Institute on Aging [23]. The National Institute on Aging [23] indicates 4 main types of activities essential to benefit older adults:

1. Endurance or aerobic activities: Increase respiration and heart rate. Some examples are walking or running, dancing, swimming, and biking.
2. Strength exercises: strengthen muscles. An example is lifting a moderate amount of weight or using elastic bands to strengthen the body.
3. Balance exercises: These help prevent falls.

4. Flexibility exercises: It is used to stretch the muscles and help the body remain relaxed.

People who do solitary training activities prevent muscle problems, joint problems or possible diseases. While by making a social participation, people shorten the progress of progressive deterioration, associated with the decline of functional capacities and self-efficacy of the elderly [24].

Cognitive Activities to Stimulate the Mind of Older Adults. Cognitive impairment is any alteration of mental abilities and is an implicit factor in the person's behavior to carry out activities [25]. This is a limitation in the autonomy and quality of life of the elderly [26, 27]. Therefore, risk factors that cause cognitive deterioration are closely related to dementia.

Cognitive aging corresponds to the deterioration of mental activities carried out by human beings when interacting with the environment, representing the decrease in the essence of the individual's personal adaptation and the social process capable of developing future planning, strategies and evaluations [28].

Cognitive stimulation is a rehabilitation of the processes, carried out by people who are disabled or impaired, together with a professional, family member or community. It is an activity that benefits the mental state of the person [29]. Therefore, the goal is to stimulate the cognitive functions of older adults through meaningful activities that favor integration and active participation in work sessions, helping to maintain or improve the self-confidence of older adults.

A series of cognitive activities have been compiled [30–33] to integrate them into the technological platform. These activities allow to stimulate the minds of adults, such as reminiscence therapies, club for the elderly, reality orientation and cognitive psycho-stimulation programs.

3.3 Final Interface Design

In this section some final interfaces are presented, in order to illustrate some concrete examples of the materialization of the designed activities.

Once authenticated in the system, all the functions and tasks that the platform has can be accessed. The first option presented is the categorization of the different activities proposed for the elderly (see Fig. 2).

In the physical activities section, different types of exercises are provided for coordination, balance and muscle strengthening. Each activity is performed with a run time or by repetitions to execute the exercise. The left image of Fig. 3 shows a physical activity and its instructions in text and images.

In the cognitive activities section, the user can register the preferences that they want to stimulate in cognitive functioning. In this way, the activities are concentrated only for those exercises. After doing one activity, you can do another or go back to do other types of activities. The right image of Fig. 3 presents a cognitive activity to complete popular sayings.

The social activities do not have execution time, they correspond to exercises to carry out social life and get to know the people with whom the activity takes place. The left

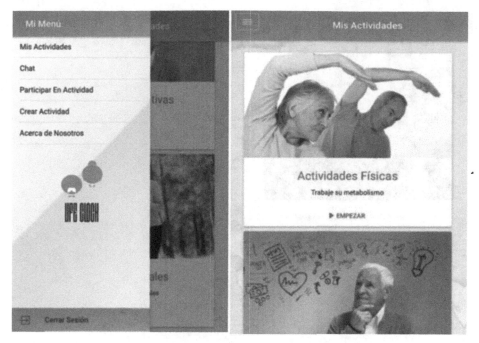

Fig. 2. Categorization of activities proposed for the elderly.

image of Fig. 4 shows one of the social activities that can be carried out between several older adults.

The right image of Fig. 4 shows the module for creating new activities. This module allows other users to view the activities carried out in conjunction with others.

There are 4 types of activities that users can create:

Physical activities: they correspond to everything that is done in constant movement, which allows you to burn calories or simply exercise the body to stay healthy.

Cognitive activities: these are activities that allow to stimulate the mental process through which it captures the aspects of reality, being a stimulation to perceive the environment.

Physical-cognitive activities: they correspond to physical activities that require a certain cognitive effort to carry them out. This type of work is of a slightly more advanced level, since the mind and body respond to sensory stimuli with respect to coordination and memory. For example, raising your arms while doing an addition, squats and saying colors, among others.

Social activities: these types of activities promote non-academic actions, bringing people together in meetings, sports, music, among others. Therefore, different activities can be defined according to the preferences and needs of socialization styles.

Figure 5 presents the data that were defined in the creation of activities. In this tab, users can select one of the activities they want to carry out, review its details and the route from their location to the point of arrival. This module provides various filtering options to organize the display of search results.

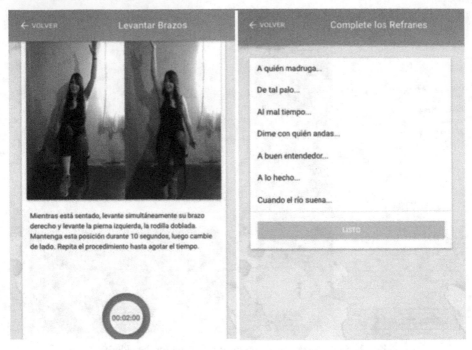

Fig. 3. Demonstration of physical (left) and cognitive (right) activities.

4 Evaluation with Users

The evaluation method is based on the observation and analysis of a group of users using the mobile device platform, in order to carry out usability tests of the technological platform and satisfaction of the proposed activities.

4.1 Evaluation Method

In order to evaluate the proposed solution, the Retrospective Test and Thinking Aloud evaluation techniques have been selected. These two evaluation techniques are classified within the Test evaluation methods, where representative users work on tasks using the system, and evaluators use the results to see how the user interface responds to users in their tasks.

The first evaluation technique selected corresponds to Retrospective Test, which consists of reviewing the video records stored during the users' test. This allows additional information to be collected by reviewing the user test recording [34], allowing more information to be acquired from each test performed. One of the disadvantages is that it takes time, since each test recording must be reviewed at least twice.

The second selected evaluation technique is called Thinking Aloud. This technique, introduced by Clayton Lewis [35], is considered one of the most valuable in usability engineering [36]. It is about having the end user continually thinking out loud while using the system. By verbalizing users' thoughts, the technique enables understanding

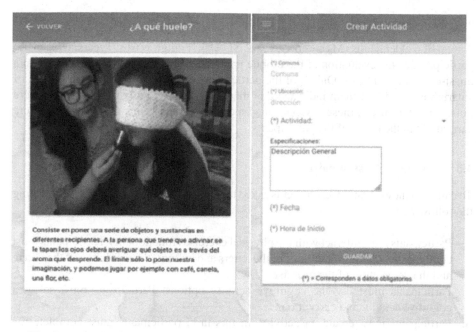

Fig. 4. Example of a social activity (left) and the option to create a new activity (right).

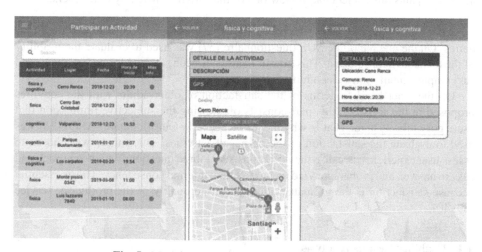

Fig. 5. Module to search and participate in activities.

how end users view the computer system, making it easier to identify misconceptions [34]. For the implementation of this evaluation technique, the participants were asked to indicate their feelings and opinions aloud while interacting with the proposed solution in the performance of a specific task.

4.2 Participants

A total of 6 older adults ($M_{age} = 66.2$ years, $SD = 4.1$, range $= 61$–71years; 67% male) participated in the evaluation of the mobile application. Participants were selected on a quasi-experimental basis. Only 4 of the participants presented basic skills in the use of smartphones and 2 of them indicated that they did not make daily use. The latter were not aware of the use of these devices. One aspect to consider is that the evaluations were carried out in the home of the participants.

4.3 Tasks and Questionnaires

To carry out the evaluation, each user is asked to interact with the application, performing the following tasks:

1. Participants must interact with the physical exercises functionality. Participants must configure the options for the size of the letters and buttons, the resolution of the image and the description of the exercise.
2. Participants must use the cognitive activity options. Participants must select a cognitive activity and carry it out.
3. Participants must create an activity. In this task, participants must complete the requested data associated with a social activity.
4. Participants must select and review one of the activities listed by other users.

After completing the tasks, the participants were asked to complete two questionnaires. On the one hand, the SUS questionnaire [37] was used to evaluate the usability of the technological solution. This questionnaire has been selected for its simplicity and easy implementation in older adults.

On the other hand, in terms of the satisfaction of older adults with the activities proposed in the software, this part consists of showing the subjective impression that users got of the system. That is why the After-Scenario Questionnaire (ASQ) [38] was used to evaluate the satisfaction of the proposed activities. This survey was chosen to assess user experience because the ASQ consists of three questions which are quick and easy to answer, and is characterized by an excellent internal consistency. This is essential because satisfaction is the ultimate validation of the quality of the product or service [39, 40].

4.4 Usability Results Analysis

As indicated above, the SUS questionnaire is used to evaluate the usability of the technological platform. Each question in the questionnaire is evaluated on a scale between 1 and 5 (1 totally disagree and 5 totally agree). The results of the questionnaire were evaluated according to the following ranges: Less than 25 points corresponds to the worst scenario. Between 25 and 38 points, usability is considered poor. Between 38 and 52 points indicates that the usability is acceptable. Between 52 and 73 points usability is considered good. Greater than 85 points the usability is excellent. Finally, between 85 and 100 points is the best possible score.

Table 1 presents the results of each of the participants and associated averages, to determine the usability scenario.

Table 1. Scores obtained by the participants in the usability questionnaire.

Participants	Scores
1	37.5
2	95
3	65
4	92.5
5	62.5
6	57.5
Average	**68.33**
SD	**21.95**

As can be seen in Table 1, participants 1 and 5 obtained the lowest evaluation, 37.5 and 57.5, respectively. These evaluations are due to the difficulty of interacting with the options to create and search activities. Likewise, these participants had problems with the tonality of the images, the size of the letters and the lack of use of the keyboard. Moreover, the participants had to navigate through different pages to carry out the tasks. These participants coincided with those who stated that they did not use their smartphone on a daily basis. However, participant 5 obtained an evaluation considered as good.

It is worth highlighting the evaluation of participants 1 and 4, with a score in the highest range of usability. These participants carried out all the tasks without inconvenience and were also motivated by the proposed activities.

In general terms, the usability results obtained an average evaluation of 68.33 (SD = 21.95), which is considered as good. In addition, it is highlighted that the participants managed to perform all the tasks.

4.5   Satisfaction Results Analysis

As mentioned above, the ASQ questionnaire was used to evaluate the satisfaction of the proposed activities. Each question was rated on a seven-point Likert scale, ranging from 1 (Strongly disagree) to 7 (Strongly agree). Table 2 shows the questions asked as well as the descriptive statistics with regards to each question.

As can be seen in Table 2, participants had positive feedback on subjective satisfaction of the application proposed. The descriptive statistics show that participants' satisfaction with the ease of completing the tasks was the best evaluated aspect, while satisfaction with the support information obtained the lowest score. Nevertheless, the ASQ showed a positive overall impression of the system.

After having completed the ASQ, we also conducted the interviews with each participant to gain a deeper understanding of his/her experience using the application. In particular, the users were asked the following open questions:

Table 2. Descriptive statistics of the After-Scenario Questionnaire

After-scenario questionnaire		
Question	Mean	SD
Overall, I am satisfied with the ease of completing the tasks in this scenario	6.33	0.81
Overall, I am satisfied with the amount of time it took to complete the tasks in this scenario	5.83	0.75
Overall, I am satisfied with the support information when completing the tasks	5.5	1.04

- What would be the advantages and disadvantages of this application?
- What was the most difficult part when using this application?
- Do you believe this application can contribute to promote a more active lifestyle among older adults?

The detailed answers helped us understand the main challenges faced by the participants when using this application. Although the users acknowledged the contribution of the tool developed, most participants agreed that they needed more time to get familiar with the application. Therefore, the organization of information throughout the application is likely to be one of the weakest points of our tool that would require further improvements in the future. All users accepted, however, that the application proposed was an important tool to promote active aging since it combined some of the main features that needed to be addressed in old age.

5   Conclusions

Due to accelerated population aging worldwide, it becomes fundamental to develop technological solutions that help maintaining the wellbeing of older adults. Therefore, this work aimed to introduce a new technological platform with an interface designed specifically for the use of older adults to promote their active aging. By incorporating physical, social and cognitive activities in one easy-to-use and accessible mobile application the proposal of this study can be perceived as a comprehensive approach to encourage healthier and more dynamic aging in the elderly.

The new platform was assessed considering its accessibility, usability and utility for the main users, i.e. older adults. To ensure the accessibility of the proposed solution, an automatic evaluation was performed using the W3C Markup Validation Service and the Wave browser extension in Google Chrome. The results of both tools allowed addressing unresolved elements related to alternative text for images, color contrast, empty HTML headers, and the presence of frames [41]. In terms of usability of the platform, although most users rated the platform below 80 points, the average rating of all users was 68.33 points, making it a manageable application, although with some improvements to be implemented in the future. Then, the ASQ questionnaire was used to evaluate the satisfaction of the proposed activities, showing a positive overall impression of the system.

Therefore, the proposed mobile application showed an adequate ability to assist end users in achieving a healthier and more participative way of life at older ages, which is essential to foster older adults' empowerment within any society.

We believe that this research makes a significant contribution to both scientific community and practitioners. To the best of our knowledge, so far there has been a limited number of platforms that aim to engage older adults in a variety of activities stimulating their cognitive, physical and social parts of life together. Thus, by bringing them all together, we offer an innovative and all-encompassing way to approach active aging from the Human-Computer Interaction field. As for practitioners, we believe that this application can be easily handled not only by older adults themselves but also to be implemented in such settings as care homes where occupational therapists and other staff members seek out new tools to help maintain the autonomy of older adults.

References

1. United Nations: World population prospects 2019: highlights. Department of Economic and Social Affairs, Population Division (2019)
2. World Health Organization: 10 Facts on Ageing and Health (2017)
3. ILO Monitor: COVID-19 and the world of work. Updated Estimates and Analysis (2020)
4. Paiva, J.O., et al.: Mobile applications for elderly healthcare: a systematic mapping. PLoS ONE 15(7), e0236091 (2020)
5. González, C., Fanjul, C.: Aplicaciones móviles para personas mayores: un estudio sobre su estrategia actual/Mobile applications for the elderly: a study of their current strategy. Aula Abierta 477(1), 107–112 (2018)
6. Becerra, T.A.M., Genta, M.I.F.: Comunicación móvil y adulto mayor: exclusión y uso desigual de dispositivos móviles Perspect. Comun. 9(2), 7–29 (2016). ISSN 0718-4867
7. Helbostad, J.L., et al.: Mobile health applications to promote active and healthy ageing. Sensors 17(3), 622 (2017)
8. World Health Organization: Active ageing: a policy framework. World Health Organization (2002)
9. Fernández-Ballesteros, R., Zamarrón, M.D., López Bravo, M.D., Molina, M., Montero López, P., Schettini del Moral, R.: Envejecimiento con éxito: criterios y predictors. Psicothema 641–647 (2010)
10. Limón, M.R., Ortega, M.D.C.: Envejecimiento activo y mejora de la calidad de vida en adultos mayors. Rev. Psicol. Educ. 6 (2011)
11. Walker, A., Foster, L.: Active ageing: rhetoric, theory and practice. In: The Making of Ageing Policy. Edward Elgar Publishing (2013)
12. Casado-Muñoz, R., Lezcano, F., Rodríguez-Conde, M.: Envejecimiento activo y acceso a las tecnologías: un estudio empírico evolutivo= active ageing and access to technology: an evolving empirical study. Envejec. Act. Acceso Las Tecnol. Un Estud. Empír. Evol. Act. Ageing Access Technol. Evol. Empir. Study 37–56 (2015)
13. Familiados: Las 12 mejores aplicaciones para ejercitar la mente de nuestros mayores. Tercera edad. Familiadosnews (2018). https://familiados.com/blog/las-12-mejores-apps-para-ejercitar-la-mente-de-nuestros-mayores/
14. i Saltiveri, T.G., MPIu+ a. Una metodología que integra la Ingeniería del Software, la Interacción Persona-Ordenador y la Accesibilidad en el contexto de equipos de desarrollo multidisciplinares. Universitat de Lleida (2007)

15. Rojas, L.A., Macías, J.A.: An agile information-architecture-driven approach for the development of user-centered interactive software. In: Proceedings of the XVI International Conference on Human Computer Interaction, pp. 1–8 (2015)
16. Fernández-Ballesteros, R., Robine, J.M., Walker, A., Kalache, A.: Active aging: a global goal. Hindawi (2013)
17. de la Salud, O.M.: Envejecimiento activo: un marco politico. Rev. Esp. Geriatr. Gerontol. **37**, 70–105 (2002)
18. Leiva, A.M., et al.: Factores asociados a caídas en adultos mayores chilenos: evidencia de la Encuesta Nacional de Salud 2009–2010. Rev. Médica Chile **147**(7), 877–886 (2019)
19. Fernández, M.B., Herrera, M.S.: Chile y sus Mayores. 10 años de la Encuesta calidad de Vida en la Vejez UC-Caja Los Andes. Programa Adulto Mayor UC Cent. UC Estud. Vejez Envejec. (2017)
20. Cirella, G.T., Bąk, M., Kozlak, A., Pawłowska, B., Borkowski, P.: Transport innovations for elderly people. Res. Transp. Bus. Manag. **30**, 100381 (2019)
21. Wong, R.C.P., Szeto, W.Y., Yang, L., Li, Y.C., Wong, S.C.: Elderly users' level of satisfaction with public transport services in a high-density and transit-oriented city. J. Transp. Health **7**, 209–217 (2017)
22. Theou, O., Blodgett, J.M., Godin, J., Rockwood, K.: Association between sedentary time and mortality across levels of frailty. CMAJ **189**(33), E1056–E1064 (2017)
23. National Institute on Aging: Exercise: A guide from the National Institute on Aging, no. 1. National Institute on Aging (2001)
24. Andrieieva, O., et al.: Effects of physical activity on aging processes in elderly persons (2019)
25. Scarmeas, N., Anastasiou, C.A., Yannakoulia, M.: Nutrition and prevention of cognitive impairment. Lancet Neurol. **17**(11), 1006–1015 (2018)
26. Ren, L., et al.: Investigation of the prevalence of cognitive impairment and its risk factors within the elderly population in Shanghai. China. Sci. Rep. **8**(1), 1–9 (2018)
27. Song, D., Doris, S.F.: Effects of a moderate-intensity aerobic exercise programme on the cognitive function and quality of life of community-dwelling elderly people with mild cognitive impairment: a randomised controlled trial. Int. J. Nurs. Stud. **93**, 97–105 (2019)
28. Salthouse, T.A.: What and when of cognitive aging. Curr. Dir. Psychol. Sci. **13**(4), 140–144 (2004)
29. Knowles, M.S., Holton III, E.F., Swanson, R.A., Robinson, P.A.: The adult learner: the definitive classic in adult education and human resource development (2020)
30. Depp, C.A., Harmell, A., Vahia, I.V.: Successful cognitive aging. Behav. Neurobiol. Aging 35–50 (2011)
31. Forbes, S.C., et al.: Exercise interventions for maintaining cognitive function in cognitively healthy people in late life. Cochrane Database Syst. Rev. (5) (2015)
32. Daffner, K.R.: Promoting successful cognitive aging: a comprehensive review. J. Alzheimers Dis. **19**(4), 1101–1122 (2010)
33. Hatta, A., et al.: Effects of habitual moderate exercise on response processing and cognitive processing in older adults. Jpn. J. Physiol. **55**(1), 29–36 (2005)
34. Nielsen, J.: Usability Engineering. Morgan Kaufmann Publishers Inc., Burlington (1993)
35. Lewis, C.: Using the "thinking-aloud" method in cognitive interface design. IBM TJ Watson Research Center Yorktown Heights, NY (1982)
36. Holzinger, A.: Usability engineering methods for software developers. Commun. ACM **48**(1), 71–74 (2005)
37. Brooke, J.: Sus: a quick and dirty usability. Usability Eval. Ind. **189** (1996)
38. Lewis, J.R.: IBM computer usability satisfaction questionnaires: psychometric evaluation and instructions for use. Int. J. Hum.-Comput. Interact. **7**(1), 57–78 (1995)
39. Badran, O., Al-Haddad, S.: The impact of software user experience on customer satisfaction. J. Manag. Inf. Decis. Sci. **21**(1), 1–20 (2018)

40. Vermeeren, A.P., Law, E.L.-C., Roto, V., Obrist, M., Hoonhout, J., Väänänen-Vainio-Mattila, K.: User experience evaluation methods: current state and development needs. In: Proceedings of the 6th Nordic Conference on Human-Computer Interaction: Extending Boundaries, pp. 521–530 (2010)

41. Galkute, M., Rojas P., L.A., Sagal M., V.A.: Improving the web accessibility of a university library for people with visual disabilities through a mixed evaluation approach. In: Meiselwitz, G. (ed.) HCII 2020. LNCS, vol. 12194, pp. 56–71. Springer, Cham (2020). https://doi.org/10.1007/978-3-030-49570-1_5

Layer Zero: An Approach for Deepening Self-reflection on Instagram Shares

Pelin Karaturhan$^{(\boxtimes)}$, Asim Evren Yantaç, and Kemal Kuscu

Koc University, Istanbul, Turkey
{pkaraturhan13,eyantac,kkuscu}@ku.edu.tr

Abstract. Self-reflection is an essential part of personal well-being and development. One of the strategies to support reflective thinking is to revisit personal recordings. Existing and emerging social media platforms are powerful mediums for self-reflection. However, additional mechanisms may be necessary to support deepening reflective thinking through social media use. We explore the concept; Layer Zero, a tool that helps users record reflective logs when they share on Instagram through a question set, and present them later for reflection. This paper focuses on the data collection phase of Layer Zero. We conducted 2 user studies through Instagram with a total of 29 participants to understand the potential of Instagram shares for reflection and measure the effectiveness of questions on self-reflection. We found that our approach can help users engage in deeper reflective thinking about their motivations, actions and thought processes. The results indicate various design insights for future social media reflection tools.

Keywords: Self-reflection · Social media · Instagram · Personal data

1 Introduction

Self reflection, "a critical or reproachful thought about oneself",[1] is a critical part of our path to personal wellbeing and development. The level of awareness about reflective thinking may significantly effect our progress in life. Humans have been engaging in self-reflection without digital artifacts and technologies. However, digital artifacts and technologies help self-reflection by triggering and regulating reflective thinking. For instance, not knowing what to reflect on may be an obstacle to reflective thinking. Therefore, one of the ways that technology supports self-reflection is by collecting, and presenting people with their own personal information. Having the ultimate aim of increasing life quality through insightful personal information, personal informatics movement in HCI [2] crosses paths with the concept of reflection very often: the stage-based model of Personal Informatics [3] that proposes 5 stages to obtain self knowledge from personally relevant information (Preparation, Collection, Integration, Reflection,

---

[1] https://www.oed.com/view/Entry/175407?redirectedFrom=self-reflection#eid.

© Springer Nature Switzerland AG 2021
G. Meiselwitz (Ed.): HCII 2021, LNCS 12775, pp. 352–372, 2021.
https://doi.org/10.1007/978-3-030-77685-5_27

Action) considers reflection as a standalone stage. However, personal informatics systems tend to focus on one kind of personal data at a time. Therefore, existing studies that highlight the importance of reflection in personal informatics movement are usually very specific as well, such as chronic illnesses [1] or physical activity [4].

Additionally, personal informatics systems mainly rely on tracking devices or dedicated applications, but in today's world many of digital artifacts and technologies collect and store personal data. Even though not all data can provide meaningful insights for self-reflection to occur, information collected from personal e-mail accounts [5], photo archives [6] and music archives [7] have been proven to be sources of reflective thinking. This points out Personal accounts, archives and social media can provide opportunities for self-reflection on a variety of subjects, in addition to what personal informatics systems provide.

The reason behind the rich information on personal accounts is that, people were interested in recording personal information before technology started to do so for them. Diaries are one of the first ways to record personal significant experiences and to reflect on them. With the advancements in technology and emergence of the concept of social media, people now share their personal experiences online. For instance, Instagram is an online photo and video sharing platform with 1 billion monthly active accounts[2] and with over 60% of the users logging in every day[3]. This vast adaptation of social media to people's everyday experiences have allowed Instagram to be a medium that stores personal information in the form of posts and stories, even profile pictures and biographies. As a result, studies related to human conditions such as depression [8], mental illnesses [9], eating habits [10] are conducted through Instagram in HCI research.

Personal information shared and stored on social media can be used not only by researchers, but by the users themselves. Social media became one of the possible systems that can be supportive of self-reflection for general public [11]. Social media channels are aware of their potential: main social media channels such as Facebook, Instagram and Snapchat integrated features, services and push-notifications to encourage users to revisit memories through previously shared personal data (on this day, friendiversary, look back). However, remembering and revisiting are not equal to self-reflection. In order for self-reflection to occur, expression of inner thoughts and feelings are necessary. Studies on social media and reflection highlight certain obstacles to users' shared expressions and emotional statements such as hurting friends, privacy, security, personal image and self-representation concerns [12,13,27]. It is worthwhile to explore the ways to enhance the potential of social media for self-reflection and search for new ways to establish a new relationship between social media and users' self-reflection.

In this paper, we explain our approach to support self-reflection through social media. We propose a tool, Layer Zero, that helps users to create personal reflection logs about their social media shares through a question set, stores

---

[2] https://www.statista.com/statistics/272014/global-social-networks-ranked-by-number-of-users/.
[3] https://www.brandwatch.com/blog/instagram-stats/.

the reflection logs, and presents them back for retrospective self-reflection. The formation of Layer Zero have 2 phases; (1) the process of collection of reflection logs and (2) presentation of collected reflection logs to the users; this paper reports the lessons learnt on the studies we conducted regarding the collection phase.

In the light of the theoretical background on reflection, we compare 2 question sets for users to fill in the reflection logs with our first user study, and we explore how mediation through a reflection log alters users' experiences of sharing on social media with a second user study. This paper presents our design process, *findings on the needs of social media users to be able to engage in reflective thinking*, and their experiences on engaging with a self-reflection tool among with their social media sharing experience. This paper contributes to the HCI community by; (1) contributing to the groundwork for future directions of research for self-reflection through conventional social media channels, and (2) demonstrating the lessons learnt from the use case of applying the Layer Zero concept to Instagram as a reflection medium.

2 Background and Related Work

Below we will first discuss existing work on processes and strategies that support self-reflection in HCI and existing work on using social media for self-reflection.

2.1 Methodologies of Reflection

Reflection is one of the concepts that do not have a generally accepted definition. This makes it harder both for theory and practice to work on the topic. With the increasing interest of HCI on reflection, multiple theoretical approaches are derived from the other disciplines such as psychology, philosophy, and education for the use of HCI community. The theoretical foundations are important as they guide researchers and practitioners in designing more reflective systems. In this section, we give an overview of theoretical work on reflection in HCI and explain how it shaped our approach.

Fleck and Fitzpatrick [14], proposed the first adaptation of existing models to HCI through "Levels of Reflection" framework. The framework consists of five levels of reflection: description, (a non-reflective statement), reflective description (justifications and explanations accompany description), dialogic reflection (thinking activity with a search for new perspectives, alternatives and relationships), transformative reflection (A conscious attempt to accept new perspectives and change existing way of thinking) and critical reflection (consideration of wider implications of thought like social and ethical issues). Further, the authors highlight the importance of reflective questions in encouraging at least low level reflective thinking. Some examples of the use of reflective questions in system designs include Gama, Storytellr, Echo [13], Reflection Companion [4] and FeedReflect [15].

Another theoretical approach is Eric P.S. Baumer's dimensional approach to designing for reflection [16]. The three dimensions he proposes are moments of breakdown, opportunities for inquiry and action for transformation. The explanation behind breakdowns is the process of the disturbance created by surprising situations to the flow of everyday activities. The disturbance allows the creation of moments in which reflection can occur. Additionally, the breakdown moments help people shift from experiential mode to reflective mode [12,17,18].

Layer Zero builds up on both Fleck and Fitzpatrick's and Baumer's approaches. Fleck and Fitzpatrick's definition of a non-reflective statement coincides with statements that users share on media due to obstacles mentioned before, such as security and self-representation. Layer Zero and its reflection logs aim to deepen the self-reflection at least by one level to reach reflective descriptions. Thus, reflection logs should consist of reflective questions to guide users. Baumer's definition of a breakdown moment also presents an opportunity for reflection logs: filling reflective questions while or short after sharing on social media will create a surprising encounter and open up space for self-reflection.

2.2 Reflection and Social Media

In this section, we highlight existing work on social media and reflection, and findings that guide us in designing Layer Zero. Social media has multiple potential uses for reflective thinking [11]. Sun et al. designed procedurally generated postcards that visualize the nutritional values and emotions extracted from user's Instagram posts of their foods [28]. The postcards successfully leveraged the potential of social media posts in terms of self-reflection. One of the concepts where social media content is investigated is reminiscence. Reminiscence is defined as "recalling, investigating and sharing significant memories" and it is closely related to reflection. Our approach differs from reminiscence as we aim to encourage deeper levels of reflections about more day-to-day experiences through mainstream social media content. However, some of the findings about the use of social media content for reminiscence is very relevant our research. Thomas and Briggs [19] conducted a user study with Intel's Museum of Me, a website that creates a short video clip from users' Facebook data. Results indicated that existing data in social media is considered shallow and not enough for meaningful reflection about users' lives. NowandThen is a prototype of a recommendation tool for previously shared social media content to encourage users to positive reminiscing [20]. Revisiting past social media content through NowandThen is perceived well by the users, though some users wanted more information such as associated status and tags, date and time. One of the earliest and influential work on social media and reminiscence is Peesapati et al.'s Pensieve [21]: a system design that emails either past social media content or generic prompts in an unpredictable manner. The system also lets people add written comments to the content shared with them by the system - either through email or website. One of the relevant findings is how personalized triggers (photos from Picasa) collected more responses than generic prompts. Additionally, participants expressed a preference about seeing the metadata along with the photo, such as people, events, place: just like NowandThen's users.

Social media can also be used as a in-situ data collection medium for later reflection. Grafitter [22] is a personal informatics tool that gathers information from the users through tweeting in a specific format. It collects various types of information using the hashtags: therefore in contrast to other personal informatics systems, users have control over what information to collect. The system later presents the collected data visually for reflection. The Grafitter system is inspirational for us since it collects momentary data for reflection through social media and presents users with their own input. Similarly, Andre et al. [23] investigate the value of social media in collecting personal well-being data. Their system Healthii collects the data through users' Facebook and Twitter updates, and Healthii desktop application by having users rate their own busyness, stress, health, and engagement (positive, negative, neutral). Their findings emphasize that providing users with multiple dimensions encouraged both retrospective and momentary reflection. Healthii system uncovered how just inputting personal data can trigger reflection in the moment of experience. Bae et al., takes a similar approach with Ripening Room [12]. Ripening Room is a social media website that creates a 'ripening time' between creating and sharing content. This ripening time acts as an agent of "strategic breakdown of experience" in order to create space for reflective thinking. Their work emphasize the importance if resourcefulness of collected data to encourage deeper levels of reflection and how concerns related to online presence may prevent online self expression. In a very recent work on self-reporting emotional states through Instagram [24], Nave et al. asked their participants to share information about energy and pleasantness ratings (1–9 scale), colors, and emotion labels when they post on Instagram. Although their work mainly focuses on emotional states, participants reported assessing themselves while posting made them get involved in reflective processes and they enjoyed doing so. Even if our work takes a very similar approach, we do not focus on emotions and collect self-reports in a more private manner to avoid online presence concerns.

3   Preliminary Study: Explorations on Reflective Questions for Social Media

3.1   Introduction to the Concept: Layer Zero

In this section, we explain Layer Zero's reflection log collection phase principles. A reflection log essentially refers to a new layer of user generated personal information that is collected in addition to the information shared on mainstream social media channels. Layer Zero adds another layer to the already existing personal information through reflective questions to enable deeper self-reflection. The name is derived from its approach to already existing social media data (such as images, written descriptions, location, date and time, hashtags) as just one layer of the overall information of the experience shared in social media.

By providing another layer, Layer Zero aims to remove the barriers of existing social media systems and encourage users' self-reflection. Below, we explain the two foundations that Layer Zero is built on.

Sharing on Social Media is an Experience to Reflect On. One of the assumptions behind Layer Zero is that both the content on the social media and the experience of sharing on social media are potential sources for reflective thinking. This assumption is rooted in American pragmatist John Dewey's work on experience [25]. Dewey made a distinction between experience in general sense - which may not provide grounds for self-reflection - and having an experience. Roth and Jarnet explain his definition of having an experience as follows: having an experience is *"when an event that we have lived has run its course and comes to a determinate conclusion - a consummation."* [17]. Following Dewey's definition, we believe the use of social media has at least two differentiated experiences: creating, and sharing content. For example, as an Instagram user, while walking you see an instance you want to capture, stop walking, pick a perspective, customize settings, take a picture or more, look at it, and continue walking. After a while, you open your Instagram application, choose the photograph, edit, add a caption with hashtags, add a location marker and share it with your followers. Both of these moments have specific beginnings and endings, and they represent pauses to the everyday flow of activities. Therefore, we believe that both moments have the qualifications of being an experience, and they are reflective instances. In order to capture the additional layer of information about those instances, Layer Zero aims to collect information about the sharing experience just after people are engaged with the experience. This also goes in-line with Baumer's approach as collecting reflection logs while people are engaged will produce a breakdown moment - which, in itself, is reflective.

Questions that Provide New Perspectives Will Produce Resourceful Data for Later Reflection. One of the main obstacles to deeper self-reflection on social media content is the lack of resourcefulness of existing information. Resourceful here means that the statements shared in social media do not represent the overall experience: certain aspects may be self-censored due to the habitual purpose of social media. Therefore, Layer Zero searches for additional information that is valuable for reflection. One of the most reliable ways to gather personal information is just to ask the person: but the way we ask should differ in terms of content to not just replicate, but add on existing information. Following Fleck and Fitzpatrick's [14] comments on the use of technology to nurture reflection through providing new perspectives, and Dewey's approach to an 'experience', we explored how we may shift users' perspectives on the experience of sharing on social media through a set of reflective questions. Many of the existing work in HCI literature (such as [23] and [22]), that aim to understand personal experiences focus on the results of the experience: how certain circumstances make one think, feel or do. In a different manner from these existing approaches, we realized decomposing the experience or understanding the different qualities of an experience holds great potential to make users think deeper and become more reflective.

3.2 Searching for Reflective Questions About Social Media Experience

In this section, we explain two question sets we explored with the aim to decompose the social media experience in two different ways, and how we turned those into reflection logs.

Question Set 1: Group Discussions. Through research group discussions on decomposing experience, we defined three aspects of an experience: pain (a sense of discomfort or negative feeling), pleasure (rewarding positive experience) and security (a positive experience of comfort). Reflection Log 1 had two open ended questions: 'Can you please explain the moment you posted this photo?' and 'Why do you think you decided to post in that moment?'. Those are followed by questions asking the relevance of aforementioned experience to the notions of security, pleasure and pain on a 7 point scale. Following each scale, the participants are asked to briefly explain why and how with open ended questions.

Question Set 2: Dewey's Approach. We turned to Dewey one more time to search for aspects or qualities of 'an experience'. In Technology as Experience, McCarthy and Wright explain Dewey's approach to experience: *"...it encapsulates a person's full relationship - sensory, emotional, and intellectual - with his or her physical and social environment."* [26]. We decided on 4 aspects for question set 2: personal, spatial, temporal, social. Personal aspect also has three aspects: sensory, emotional, intellectual. Reflection Log 2 also had two open ended questions: 'Can you please explain the moment you posted this photo?' and 'Why do you think you decided to post in that moment?'. For personal aspect, the log included questions regarding the relevance of aforementioned experience to the notions "sensory, emotional and intellectual" on a 7 point scale. Following each scale, an open ended question asked for a brief explanation. For spatial, temporal and social aspects, questions asking for explanations with open ended response areas are included.

3.3 Preliminary User Feedback on Question Sets

In order to compare the comprehensibility of two reflection logs, we conducted a preliminary online user study through Instagram. We choose Instagram as our study medium as Instagram comes to the forefront among other social media channels for multimodal sharing (such as images, text, video and sound) of personal data, it has a community using the medium for reflective sharing and it is one of the most actively used social media channels for sharing everyday experiences.

We recruited 18 (16 female) active Instagram user participants through announcements placed on Instagram as posts and stories of researchers, and snowballing. After the recruitment, all the communication is provided via Instagram direct messages. We created a wizard-of-oz setting for our user study. The first author played the wizard role. In order to deliver the logs as soon as possible, first author followed and turned on the post notifications of the participants in order to receive notifications each time they post on Instagram. The Reflection Log is mimicked with an online Qualtrics survey. Every time a participant posted a photo, an online link is sent to the participant along with the photo posted. We asked our participants to fill the logs that are delivered to their Instagram Direct Inboxes after they post a photo during their participation.

Feedback on Open-Ended Questions. Open ended questions helped us gain insights about the timing preferences and underlying motivations behind the act of sharing on Instagram. There were 2 different patterns when describing the moment of sharing. When sharing retrospectively, the answers described the moment of posting apart from the moment of capturing the shared image. Others described the moments of capturing and sharing as a whole: the post is made at the time of capturing or right after.

The open ended questions also revealed motivations of participants to post on Instagram. When they posted momentarily, 2 dominant motivations (that can overlap) raised. One reason was the thought processes triggered by the moment or by the image. Participant 18 stated *"I felt something similar within me. The minster was reflecting my anger as well as my 'child' part in me"* and P8 stated *"I always think the improvement of human being. We are in change and it lasts until we die. If there is no change it means there is no life. Hands and feet show the changes clearly. So i decided to share"*. The other is of aesthetic/visual value of the image (6 answers). P18 stated *"Here there was all the glam and i was all dressed up. Its like 'you have to take a photo and post to Instagram"'* and P11 stated *"Because i saw the sun light on the see. I liked that light colour. It's like a silver."*. In addition to those two dominant motivations, participants who posted retrospectively had various other motivations such as trying to catch attention, not feeling productive, timing concerns and to keep an online presence. P1 stated *"I don't have much time to spend in Instagram so I decided to post a photo while I had the chance. Also I have thought of a really funny caption about our incoming party so it was gonna be a good promotion."*, P2 stated *"I always prepare three images in advance, and post them within 5–20 h of each other. It was time for this one, the third in the series."*.

Although the focus of the survey questions was on reflection about the moment of sharing, P2 - who never posts a photo when he captures it- stood out from rest of the participants for he deliberately preferred answering the questions either referring to the moment of capturing or regarding compositional/aesthetic value of the image. His answers were detailed descriptions of the experience of capturing the image, *"The posting moment was insignificant. I may have been taking a break from actual work. However, to shoot this photo, I remember forcing*

my friends to stop by the side of the Karadeniz motorway between Rize and Tra-
bzon, when I spotted the large ship at a distance surrounded with nothing else for
miles." or meaning through compositional content of the image: "*The photo has*
two subjects: the electrical infrastructure (huge towers rt human scale)and the
sky/sunset (even more huge and contrast-amplified in post). We take electricity
for granted, but the vast towers are consumed here by the epic sunset.".

These results indicate that moments of capturing or posting were already reflective moments before the participants are encountered the survey: when asked to describe the moment of posting and the reason why, their answers contained information regarding the multiple aspects of the experience as well as internal thought processes.

Another important knowledge gained from the initial study is the effect of potential time gap between the moment of capturing and posting on both motivations and reflective thinking. Additionally, case of P2 also provides a valuable insight into reflecting on the moment of capturing rather than sharing. As the moments of capturing were significant for him, he was able to provide detailed information from a past experience. Therefore, giving the users control over which moment to reflect on is an important insight when designing a reflection tool.

Feedback on Reflection Log 1. Our analysis regarding the answers to questions of reflection log 1 revealed that notions other than pleasure were hard to comprehend. Out of 26 answers, 11 answers found security aspect irrelevant or did not understand the question. Similar evidence were present for the pain notion. 13 answers recorded the irrelevance of the concept of pain to their experience.

It suggests that this categorization does not allow the participants to approach to their experiences from multiple and unfamiliar perspectives. It seems like pain and security are too unfamiliar to trigger reflective thinking, as almost half of the time they were found completely irrelevant to the experience. Pleasure aspect is found highly relatable in most of the cases. This is understandable considering the preference of sharing positive experiences on social media platforms. (citation) Therefore, as said before, this approach is observed not to serve the dimensional approach we were seeking.

Feedback on Reflection Log 2. Answers to Log 2 revealed different understandings of the notions of emotional, intellectual and sensory. The notion of emotional was the one that found the most relevant: out of 24 answers, 21 of the recorded answers had points 4 or higher to the relevance rating of emotional aspect.

A variety of understandings of intellectual aspect is observed among participants. One of the understandings of intellectual aspect was thought processes related to using social media: P8 stated "*Little bit intellectual because social media is an id of ourselves in social media. We sometimes just post to show people what we think, what we do, and how we react.*", P13 stated "*I waited for my followers most active hours to post, to boost my profile so i was more thought act. I always know that I'm not a passive user, I'm active who influences other people so i knew that my post was going to reach peoples minds somehow"* and P15 stated *"I try to be thoughtful with my work and I also avoid being solely pleasing."*. Others referenced intellectual aspects of the moment; such as being in a cultural event, having deep thoughts or having an intellectual discussion.

The understanding of sensory aspect had the most diverse answers: motivations behind answers change from posting solely emotionally (P8, rated 0) to having many post-processing steps to the image (P2, rated 7). This is especially interesting since being a visual sharing platform, Instagram by nature is a sensory medium. However, it became evident that users have different understandings of sensory input especially when thinking about their own experiences of posting.

Social aspect was also found relevant by most of the participants. 17 explained social connections either about the moment or the act of posting on social media when answering the social aspect of the experience. Examples include, *"It is fund to observe how people react and reply in each posts via Direct Message in Instagram"*, *"I always ask my friends why they do like a particular photo."*, *"I was with the people I loved around me, it was a time of socially good time"*. Encountering different understandings is not a flaw but a sign of success, since it indicates that participants went through internal thought processes while they were trying to make sense of the questions. The findings indicate that answering questions in survey 3 directed participants to think more, differently, or once more on their experiences of using social media, and their motivations of doing so.

3.4   Lessons Learnt from the Preliminary Study: Layer Zero Logging Methodology

In the light of the insights generated through the preliminary study, we choose Log 2 for data collection of Layer Zero. However, certain adjustments were needed:

- Since there is a distinction between momentary and retrospective shares, the log initially asks if the participant wants to reflect on the moment he took the photo or the moment he shared the photo.
- The first question is a text area with the title "The moment I shared and the reasons why...".
- The log asks for the relevance of the notions of 'sensory, emotional, and intellectual' with a 7-point scale accompanied by open ended question boxes asking why. The wording of 'personal aspect' is removed since it creates confusion.
- Following, written descriptions are asked for the spatial, temporal, and social aspects of the experience.

4   Secondary Study: The Layer Zero Logging Experience

In order to better understand the overall experience of filling reflection logs on social media posts, we conducted a second study with only one set of questions, based on lessons learnt from the preliminary study. We used a phenomenological approach and created a prototypical setup that helps participants to experience filling in logs for two weeks every time they post a feed or a story on Instagram, then discussed the overall experience and their perceptions with them through semi-structured interviews. Phenomenological research approach aims to understand participants' lived experiences of a phenomenon to find commonalities around what participants' have experienced and how they have experienced it [29].

4.1   Procedure

Participants were recruited through e-mail invitations and Instagram open calls shared in stories and posts. In total, there were 11 participants (7 female, 4 male) and their age ranged between 23 and 41 (mean 29). Most of the participants stated that they share on Instagram every week (6 participants) or every 2–3 weeks (5 participants). Due to the language restrictions observed through the initial study, the second study is conducted in the participants' native language, Turkish.

The study is conducted over a two-week period. Different from the initial study, we asked participants to fill the reflection log for their story shares along with their posts. Every time a user shared content on Instagram, the reflection log is delivered to their inboxes accompanied by the content they posted. During the 2-week period, 48 reflection logs are filled by 11 participants (15 posts and 33 stories). After two weeks, semi-structured interviews are conducted with the participants that lasted from 20 min to 1 h apiece. The interview questions are structured in three sections. The first set of questions were related to users' experiences on posting and revisiting on Instagram. The second set of questions were aiming to understand how the question set (Layer Zero Log) is perceived and whether it helps to deepen self-reflection. Lastly, we asked about their overall experience and insights on the design of Layer Zero. To analyze results, interview notes and voice recordings are reviewed to reveal outstanding themes and insights among participants.

4.2   Findings

Our study revealed significant findings around the question set we structured. Here, we present our findings from our interviews.

Instagram as a Reflection Medium. Our interviews reveal that sharing on Instagram is a reflective action. However, the intentions and motivations behind the reflection vary. That is closely related with the fact that users' reasons to share on Instagram is also very different from each other. Some examples are; to communicate (P7), when visiting different places (P10), to use like a photo album (P2), to share information with people (P11). The level of consideration on personal level is somewhat proportional with the perceived level of reflection. Participants those stated that they don't use their Instagram posts to think about themselves still engaged in thinking, while and after sharing. However, their concerns were more related to representation, such as maintaining the visual harmony or checking the number of likes. Regardless of the differing motivations, the decision between sharing a story and sharing a post was mainly made depending on whether the content was worth keeping permanently or not. It should be mentioned that the reasoning behind that decision was also differing among participants, and it was in line with their purpose of sharing on Instagram. For example, P2 had a order on her posts, and had a few story series she is curating. For her, both the stories and posts are curated but the ones posted are selected more carefully. P1 stated that only the announcements, calls and content with communication purposes are shared as stories and posts are the moments she wants to remember. Therefore, a more careful curation was present for posts over stories is observed in participants.

Appertaining to the curatorial concerns, participants often stated that they post not during the experience but after a while; after the experience finishes, a few hours later, whenever they have free time, or after a few iterations on visual effects. This finding is in line with our previous finding on momentary and retrospective shares and differences on the reflections for posting them. When designing the survey, we made the first distinction between 'the moment the photo is taken' and 'the moment the content is shared' to understand users' preferences better. Discounting the participants who take photos and share at the same time, most logs for posts (out of 19, 11) were reflections for the moment that the photo taken. Some participants stated they did not choose that option because the photo is not taken by them. Otherwise, participants preferred to reflect on the moment content is created, rather than the moment it is made online.

Clearly, it is more tempting to think and comment about the moment of experience that is represented in the photo. Even if so, it appears that the questions have the potential to make one think about not just the content but also themselves. Several participants stated answering questions made them think about their sharing habits and preferences. Two participants even thought about questions while they are posting (P5 and P12), before they are presented with the reflection log. These insights illustrate how taking photos and posting photos on Instagram -even those that are not taken by the owner- are both moments of reflection, but the levels and motivations behind the reflective thinking differ person to person.

Question Set as a Reflection Tool. Although some had hard time understanding the dimensions we provide them with at a glance, participants approved that filling the reflection log made them think deeper, or from a point of view

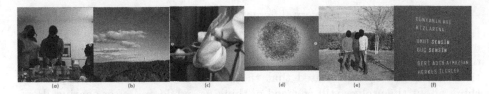

Fig. 1. (a) "A night to remember!" Reflection Log: "I could share the photographs from the evening of New Years Eve when I finished my duties and relaxed. It was a night that I will want to remember, that is why I wanted it to be in my profile, so I shared". (b) two emojis are used in caption. Reflection Log: "The relief I felt because of the finish of my final exams". (c) "Good feelings" Reflection Log: "I took a photo of and shared my orchid which is budding out. It is a moment that I get in return for my full care effort and I feel excited about a new flower, a beginning of a journey. I wanted to share this moment as a post and always keep it alive". (d) "#regularinsanity" Reflection Log: "I liked the chaos of the lines". (e) "Gencers." Reflection Log: "I was at the airport, I was looking at the photos that were taken yesterday and Ive realized that I will not see my brother for at least 5 months". (f) Text translation: "To the rebel girls to the world: you are the hope, you are the power, if you dont step back, everybody moves forward." Reflection Log: "I wanted all the women and girls to read the book I read and I wanted (my story) to be a source of motivation to those who will not read it".

they did not think about before (see Fig. 1 for some examples.[4]) The reactions and perceptions were various. Participants who state that they think thoroughly when posting saw the reflection log as a tool to deepen, organize and record reflections. Furthermore, filling the reflection logs made people question their sharing habits and motivations from a broader perspective. P3 stated *The three categories made me think about how the weight of the categories change amongst my shares and how I usually share with sensory and emotional focus."* and P5 stated *"I realized I share things that will challenge me to motivate myself. ...I've realized this more with the study: I tend to share when I want to talk about something with someone. ...I've asked myself my expectations and thoughts when sharing content with socialization concerns.".* Apparently, the questions made people think critically on their sharing behaviors. For example, P6 explained; *"The questions were interesting in the sense that I've realized I don't think at all when I am sharing, even not focus on the moment. ...When I got the questions, I've realized I could think over it more when sharing."* It is visible that even before being able to look back, answering questions triggered momentary reflection.

Several participants thought regularly using this tool would alter themselves' or other people's posting behavior on social media; it would decrease the number of shares. Furthermore, they considered this as a positive improvement on their Instagram use; either because they feel like they are exposed to unnecessary content or they would not like to share content that would be perceived negatively. Being critical of the people that share frequently on Instagram, P5 argued

---

[4] All content shared with the permission of participants.

"I wondered if even though they don't fill the survey every time, being presented with this questions every time they post would decrease their number of shares". P7 stated even if her decision of sharing probably would not change, she suspect especially facing the questions before sharing would change people's decision of sharing.

One of the possible reasons behind some participants' hard time relating the questions may be because of the fact that not everyone was able to fill the reflection log for the content that is more meaningful for them. That is, given the two weeks of the study time, some participants were only able to fill the reflection log for the stories they share, which do not hold as meaning as the posts do. Indeed, when asked about their preferences on the content they would like to fill the log about, all answered posts. Regardless from the motivation behind, the posts carry more meaningful information than the stories. Some other cases were P2 and P7. P7 explained she would like to reflect on most of the content she shares on Instagram, even for the ones that are related to her personal life but rather current agenda; *I would use such a tool to get to know myself and see the changes in my social circle, my country's agenda, or world's agenda*. P2, when reflecting back to her experience, explained how even for her story shares which mostly have a clear motivation such as raising awareness, she would like to use this tool for recording her current opinion on the subject.

4.3   Contents of the Reflection Logs

Out of 48 reflection logs filled by the participants, 38 logs involved a statement of feelings, emotions or inner thoughts at least once. These statements occurred in different questions. For example, while filling the reflection log for a building photograph, P10 first mentioned about the warm sunlight and the visual pleasantness of the environment. Following, while answering the questions about the emotional and intellectual aspects, she stated; *"My last days at school... (I thought about) the feeling that come from saying farewell."* 10 reflection logs were description based or just involved a statement about the visual pleasantness or having good times. Even though perception of beauty and categorizing an event as 'good' are feelings, we categorized 3 statements that refer only to beauty or visual pleasure since that is one of the intrinsic motivations for social media sharing activity. Out of 10 reflection logs, 6 belong to story shares. An example of description based log is as follows: P7 said she shared this image because it is relatable for her and her friends, and it is entertaining.

Experiencing the Reflection Logs. The overall experience of the study was found interesting by the participants. However, there was a confusion about the aim of the study. Participants were unclear about the benefits of just filling the reflection logs since they did not see any representation of their input. P3 clearly stated that even though the questions did guide him into a deeper reflection, he wouldn't use such a tool without any other motivation than participating to a user study because he did not perceive a remarkable gain just from filling the reflection log. He is not the only one; participants those are not familiar with reflection was skeptical about the benefits and reasons for using such a tool.

All of the participants were interested in the idea of being presented with the collected reflection logs. All of the participants stated they would use such a tool for the content of their choice, if they have the opportunity to see the accumulation of their input. As in any other case, their motivations varied. The most common motivation was to 'see the personal development'. P3 explained how he perceives such a tool as supportive of reflection; *"I will think when I look back at the photos, (having reflection logs) will provide me with key elements that I determine back then (when the content is shared).".* Some participants were much more interested in the ability to see specific periods of time. Motivations raised around remembrance were also present. P4 expressed his motivation as *"If I want to tell the story behind (the photograph), ...what happened, who was there. Characters, place, time; those are important for me. ...I would be attracted to reliving the memory.".* Participant 11 imagined setting a mindset beforehand and start using the tool: "I may use it in times where I will go through a change in my life to track and better understand myself.". It can be concluded that people with various motivations for posting on Instagram differ in levels of reflection and their motivation behind using such a tool, but they agree that such a tool could be used for self-investigation purposes and they would try it.

Furthermore, from the feedback collected from the participants, we observed a potential for this tool to be used as a social communication tool as well. Some of the participants stated they would share their reflection logs -in the moment of creation or after a while passed- with close friends if they feel like it represents things from both of their lives at that time, or their experiences of the moment better. However, all users would prefer to keep overall verbal reflections to themselves while share visual representations of their experience.

Participants also shared more constructive feedback about the design and implementation of the reflection log. 7 point scale is mostly found confusing or unnecessary. For example, P2, talking about the 7 point scale said *"I can't make the distinction between 5 and 6"* and P11 suggested the numbers to have written levels such as low-moderate-high. Most of the participants found the question design a bit confusing at the first sight, and some stated that they would require an explanation for each aspect or more clear questions to better relate with the concepts. P11 suggested rather than having concepts or keywords, it is better to have sentences such as *"what did you think, what did you feel, which senses did it appeal to?"* since keywords made her think more technically. P4, carried the concept one step further and explained: *"I wanted to have more criteria to rate. ...such as feelings like love, togetherness, achievement. ...It is hard to write, if I prefer writing, I wouldn't be on social media, I would have a blog"..* Participants had personal preferences when it came to the delivery time, but most preferred answering questions right after they share content on Instagram.

5 Discussion

Overall, based on the feedback collected through the 2 studies we conducted, we consider Layer Zero's information collection methodology (Namely: Logging) to be successful in accumulating resourceful data for self-reflection based on the emotions, feelings and thoughts mentioned in the reflection logs and participants' statements. Even though this study doesn't involve the presentation of the collected data at this stage, it was very critical for us to learn how users would react to the idea of further logging on the posts they share on social media for self-reflective purposes and if answering a certain set of questions is perceived beneficial or pleasant. Our findings show that reflection logs help users go through a momentary self-reflection or to report their already existing reflections through answering questions. Below, we discuss what we learned for the design of tools for self-reflection through social media; the further iteration of the Layer Zero tool in our case.

Throughout our research, we realized the potential for reflective thinking through social media is highly connected to people's motivations for sharing on social media and their behavioral patterns. For some, the main motivation to post on Instagram is to collect moments that are worth remembering, since the medium provides a permanent storage of memories. The participants' reflection logs revealed that in some cases the post has been created through after a reflective consideration of an experience. In such cases, the logs capture the information that is not shared on social media, but was present on participants' minds. The is a significant difference between the motivations for sharing posts and stories. Since posts are associated more with the concept of remembering, they can provide a better ground for self-reflection. This is validated by users demonstrated preference of filling reflection logs for their posts over their stories. Regardless of being in the form of stories or posts, shares on Instagram are perceived as representative of real world. Participants' comments on how they would use reflection logs for life review reveals that the content they are sharing is affected by what they go through in life. This is a valuable finding since public information in shares does not often reflect such personal information and Layer Zero is an appropriate approach to provide the users an additional medium for recording personal experiences behind their sharing decisions. Several participants' alternative use case suggestions support this perception; one highlighted Layer Zero's possible importance in tracking psychological disorders of patients.

There is no common understanding of what reflection is. It was hard for some participants to relate to the concept when asked about. However, even they commented on spending time understanding questions and answering them. However, time to time, their answers contained details as reflective as other participants who were familiar with the concept. Apparently, being familiar or aware of reflection makes it easier to relate with different aspects when evaluating an experience or a photograph. Therefore, Layer Zero may act as a reflection awareness agent before a reflection support agent. If not, for some of the participants, it may ended up acting like a personal informatics system through which users collect non-reflective information about their shares just to track their "mood", for example. It is interesting to see how lower levels of already occurring self-reflection comes with higher desire of automation. Suggestions about automatic analysis and presentation of the content is generally suggested by people who state that their shares does not make them think about themselves. This supports that users' input is important to make the information resourceful, otherwise it may follow the same logic with all personal informatics systems that does not ensure reflection in any level.

Some other concerns and insights that should be taken into consideration in the future were the cases where some other person takes the photograph or re-sharing content. However, other distinctions should be explored; for example, a participant suggested having another filter for the content between 'related to me' and 'something that I do'.

Layer Zero's reflection log approach allowed us to see reflective activities on various stages of social media use. Through reflection logs, three different processes are observed throughout our research. First, the questions allowed participants to state more emotions and thoughts than their captions on social media, hence would provide a resourceful source for retrospective reflection since expression of thoughts and feelings are crucial for later reflection. Second, there were occurrences where the logs are used to record reflective thought processes that led participants to share social media. This shows, as we claimed, sharing on social media can be a reflective activity itself. And third, answering the questions allowed participants to reflect on their experiences of sharing on social media. Apparently the third activity sometimes allowed participants to thought further than the content they share when answering the questions. However, it was not possible for the users to (i) see their reflection logs after they record them and (ii) answer the questions for a longer time period than 2 weeks. Therefore, their further reflections mostly focused on their thoughts, motivations and reasons for sharing on Instagram. The focus on that momentary reflection may be subject to change or even decrease with a long term deployment of Layer Zero. However, it also exposes a potential for behavior change through the use of Layer Zero.

Aiming to increase awareness would require a slightly different approach and this may again be in line with the feedback from participants. We intentionally did not provide any specific explanation about the sensory, emotional and intellectual dimensions to provoke independent thinking and explore how each participant understands the aspects. However, the participants' experiences with the reflection log could have been more joyful if they were initially presented with neutral descriptions of the aspects or the wording would have been different. This may also support other mentioned use cases of the tool, such as wanting to remember a memory better. The sensory aspect is mostly linked with visual aspects, however if we would have been mentioned the other senses, the users may have been provided information related to other senses. Those suggest that users need prompts when they are answering questions to dig deeper in their thoughts.

It is critical to keep up the motivation to use the tool. Collected data should be presented back in such a way that it would encourage using the tool. Participants were mostly interested in seeing the trends through a certain time when looking back, which is also inline with previous research suggesting technology-mediated reflection is the most suitable when it helps seeing patterns and getting lessons out of the finished events [13]. Therefore, Layer Zero's presentation of reflection logs should allow reading information related to each dimension clearly and in relation with each other. As in the new social media prompts, another option is to present the user with the individual reflection after a while (3 months, 6 months, 3 years), which is also valued by participants. Motivation is closely related for their ability to not being reinforced to use such a tool but it is up to them; with their own preferences.

In conjunction with motivation, personalization is also critical. Such a tool should provide as many personalization options as possible without confusing or overwhelming the users. It is important to allow the users select what to reflect on and when to reflect. Especially the timing of the delivery of the reflection log was a very personal choice, different to each user with different motivations. However, Layer Zero's aim should be collect information on an experience that has just happened, rather than intervening the experience itself. The reason behind is to keep every individual experience intact. One participant, for example, stated that he would like to receive the questions just before posting to re-evaluate his decision. This approach highlights the risk of perceiving Layer Zero as a self-control tool, rather than self-reflection.

6   Conclusion and Future Work

This research proposed a new approach for transforming the social media content and the experience of sharing into a reflection opportunity through providing a tool that collects and presents an additional layer of personal information to its user. The features of the data collection phase of Layer Zero seemed to encourage momentary reflection and hence was successful to extract resourceful information for later reflection. However, the experience of filling the reflection logs showed that its current design can be improved in such a way to increase awareness about reflection in addition to just collecting reflective information. In consideration of the limitations and the participants' suggestions for future design of Layer Zero, there are two worthwhile directions for future work. One is to design the second phase of Layer Zero and the other is to conduct long-term studies to understand the effects of using such a tool on self-knowledge and users' strategies when using the tool.

References

1. Raj, S., Newman, M.W., Lee, J.M., Ackerman, M.S.: Understanding individual and collaborative problem-solving with patient-generated data: challenges and opportunities. Proc. ACM Hum.-Comput. Interact. 1(CSCW), Article 88, 1–18 (2017). https://doi.org/10.1145/3134723

2. Li, I., Medynskiy, Y., Froehlich, J., Larsen, J.: Personal informatics in practice: improving quality of life through data. In: CHI 2012 Extended Abstracts on Human Factors in Computing Systems (CHI EA 2012), pp. 2799–2802. Association for Computing Machinery, New York (2012). https://doi.org/10.1145/2212776. 2212724

3. Li, I., Dey, A., Forlizzi, J.: A stage-based model of personal informatics systems. In: Proceedings of the SIGCHI Conference on Human Factors in Computing Systems, pp. 557–566. Association for Computing Machinery, New York (2010). https://doi. org/10.1145/1753326.1753409

4. Kocielnik, R., Xiao, L., Avrahami, D., Hsieh, G.: Reflection companion: a conversational system for engaging users in reflection on physical activity. Proc. ACM Interact. Mob. Wearable Ubiquitous Technol. 2(2), Article 70, 1–26 (2018). https:// doi.org/10.1145/3214273

5. Gerritsen, D.B., et al.: Mailing archived emails as postcards: probing the value of virtual collections. In: Proceedings of the 2016 CHI Conference on Human Factors in Computing Systems, pp. 1187–1199. Association for Computing Machinery, New York (2016). https://doi.org/10.1145/2858036.2858541

6. Odom, W.T., et al.: Designing for slowness, anticipation and re-visitation: a long term field study of the photobox. In: Proceedings of the SIGCHI Conference on Human Factors in Computing Systems (CHI 2014), pp. 1961–1970. Association for Computing Machinery, New York (2014). https://doi.org/10.1145/2556288. 2557178

7. Odom, W., et al.: Investigating slowness as a frame to design longer-term experiences with personal data: a field study of Olly. In: Proceedings of the 2019 CHI Conference on Human Factors in Computing Systems (CHI 2019), Paper 34, pp. 1–16. Association for Computing Machinery, New York (2019). https://doi.org/10. 1145/3290605.3300264

8. Andalibi, N., Ozturk, P., Forte, A.: Sensitive self-disclosures, responses, and social support on Instagram: the case of #Depression. In: Proceedings of the 2017 ACM Conference on Computer Supported Cooperative Work and Social Computing (CSCW 2017), pp. 1485–1500. Association for Computing Machinery, New York (2017). https://doi.org/10.1145/2998181.2998243

9. Feuston, J.L., Piper, A.M.: Everyday experiences: small stories and mental illness on Instagram. In: Proceedings of the 2019 CHI Conference on Human Factors in Computing Systems (CHI 2019), Paper 265, pp. 1–14. Association for Computing Machinery, New York (2019). https://doi.org/10.1145/3290605.3300495

10. Chung, C.-F., Agapie, E., Schroeder, J., Mishra, S., Fogarty, J., Munson, S.A.: When personal tracking becomes social: examining the use of Instagram for healthy eating. In: Proceedings of the 2017 CHI Conference on Human Factors in Computing Systems, pp. 1674–1687. Association for Computing Machinery, New York (2017). https://doi.org/10.1145/3025453.3025747

11. Thomas, L., Briggs, P., Kerrigan, F., Hart, A.: Exploring digital remediation in support of personal reflection. Int. J. Hum.-Comput. Stud. 110, 53–62 (2018). https://doi.org/10.1016/j.ijhcs.2017.10.002

12. Bae, J., Lim, Y., Bang, J., Kim, M.: Ripening room: designing social media for self-reflection in self-expression. In: Proceedings of the 2014 Conference on Designing Interactive Systems (DIS 2014), pp. 103–112. Association for Computing Machinery, New York (2014). https://doi.org/10.1145/2598510.2598567

13. Isaacs, E., Konrad, A., Walendowski, A., Lennig, T., Hollis, V., Whittaker, S.: Echoes from the past: how technology mediated reflection improves well-being. In: Proceedings of the SIGCHI Conference on Human Factors in Computing Systems, pp. 1071–1080. Association for Computing Machinery, New York (2013). https://doi.org/10.1145/2470654.2466137

14. Fleck, R., Fitzpatrick, G.: Reflecting on reflection: framing a design landscape. In: Proceedings of the 22nd Conference of the Computer-Human Interaction Special Interest Group of Australia on Computer-Human Interaction (OZCHI 2010), pp. 216–223. Association for Computing Machinery, New York (2010). https://doi.org/10.1145/1952222.1952269

15. Bhuiyan, M.M., Zhang, K., Vick, K., Horning, M.A., Mitra, T.: FeedReflect: a tool for nudging users to assess news credibility on Twitter. In: Companion of the 2018 ACM Conference on Computer Supported Cooperative Work and Social Computing (CSCW 2018), pp. 205–208. Association for Computing Machinery, New York (2018). https://doi.org/10.1145/3272973.3274056

16. Baumer, E.P.S.: Reflective informatics: conceptual dimensions for designing technologies of reflection. In: Proceedings of the 33rd Annual ACM Conference on Human Factors in Computing Systems, pp. 585–594. Association for Computing Machinery, New York (2015). https://doi.org/10.1145/2702123.2702234

17. Roth, W.M., Jornet, A.: Toward a theory of experience. Sci. Educ. **98**, 106–126 (2014). https://doi.org/10.1002/sce.21085

18. Danzico, L.: Adding by leaving out: the power of the pause. Interactions **17**(4), 55–57 (2010). https://doi.org/10.1145/1806491.1806505

19. Thomas, L., Briggs, P.: Assessing the value of brief automated biographies. Pers. Ubiquit. Comput. **20**(1), 37–49 (2015). https://doi.org/10.1007/s00779-015-0896-2

20. Nguyen, V.-T., Le, K.-D., Tran, M.-T., Fjeld, M.: NowAndThen: a social network-based photo recommendation tool supporting reminiscence. In: Proceedings of the 15th International Conference on Mobile and Ubiquitous Multimedia (MUM 2016), pp. 159–168. Association for Computing Machinery, New York (2016). https://doi.org/10.1145/3012709.3012738

21. Peesapati, S.T., Schwanda, V., Schultz, J., Lepage, M., Jeong, S.Y., Cosley, D.: Pensieve: supporting everyday reminiscence. In: Proceedings of the SIGCHI Conference on Human Factors in Computing Systems, pp. 2027–2036. Association for Computing Machinery, New York (2010). https://doi.org/10.1145/1753326.1753635

22. Li, I., Dey, A., Forlizzi, J.: Grafitter: leveraging social media for self reflection. XRDS **16**(2), 12–13 (2009). https://doi.org/10.1145/1665997.1666001

23. André, P., Schraefel, M.C., Dix, A., White, R.W.: Expressing well-being online: towards self-reflection and social awareness. In: Proceedings of the 2011 iConference (iConference 2011), pp. 114–121. Association for Computing Machinery, New York (2011). https://doi.org/10.1145/1940761.1940777

24. Nave, C., Romão, T., Correia, N.: Self-tracking emotional states through social media mobile photography. In: Proceedings of the 32nd International BCS Human Computer Interaction Conference (HCI 2018), Article 146, pp. 1–6 . BCS Learning & Development Ltd., Swindon, GBR (2018). https://doi.org/10.14236/ewic/HCI2018.146

25. Dewey, J.: Art as experience. Penguin (2005)

26. Mccarthy, J., Wright, P.: Technology as Experience (2004). https://doi.org/10.1145/1015530.1015549

27. Pirzadeh, A., He, L., Stolterman, E.: Personal informatics and reflection: a critical examination of the nature of reflection. In: CHI 2013 Extended Abstracts on Human Factors in Computing Systems (CHI EA 2013), pp. 1979–1988. Association for Computing Machinery, New York (2013). https://doi.org/10.1145/2468356. 2468715
28. Sun, Z., Wang, S., Yang, W., Yürüten, O., Shi, C., Ma, X.: A postcard from your food journey in the past: promoting self-reflection on social food posting. In: Proceedings of the 2020 ACM Designing Interactive Systems Conference, pp. 1819–1832. Association for Computing Machinery, New York (2020). https://doi.org/10.1145/3357236.3395475
29. Creswell, J.W., Poth, C.N.: Qualitative Inquiry and Research Design: Choosing Among Five Approaches. Sage publications (2016)

Role of Social Media in Coping with COVID-19 Stress: Searching for Intergenerational Perspectives

Najmeh Khalili-Mahani[1,2,3]([✉]), Sasha Elbaz[1,2], Amber Pahayahay[4], and Janis Timm-Bottos[1]

[1] engAGE Living Lab Créatif, Concordia University, Montreal, QC, Canada
najmeh.khalili-mahani@concordia.ca
[2] Department of Psychology, Concordia University, Montreal, QC, Canada
[3] PERFORM Centre, Concordia University, Montreal, QC, Canada
[4] University of Waterloo, Waterloo, ON, Canada

Abstract. The COVID-19 pandemic has accelerated demand for screen-mediated social connections. The drivers of digitization of socialization are often young and social-media savvy individuals who wish to alleviate the stress of social isolation for seniors. To design successful programs, it is important to first consider intergenerational differences in both the experience of COVID-19 stress, and the affordances of technology. In this mixed-methods study, we aimed to investigate perceptual differences in how social media can assist older adults (65+) to cope with the COVID-19 stress. Data was obtained from two sources: A snow-ball survey (conducted between April - Sept 2020, n = 595); and scraping the public comments on mainstream media's articles focusing on senior's coping with the COVID-19 (7 sources, and 3390 valid comments). Quantitative analyses of age-related differences in attitudes towards social media, and changes in media usage after pandemic (in <25, 25–34, 35–54, 55–65, 65+ groups), indicated significant differences in what, why and how different age groups used the social media. Qualitative analyses of the comments revealed some intergenerational misunderstandings about one another's coping needs. In general, older adults were less vulnerable to COVID-19 stress than were the younger, and technology was not their main resource for coping with social isolation. Nevertheless, communication technologies such as Zoom were important for connecting to older parents and grandchildren. These independent studies show that although technology plays an important role in keeping older adults connected, it does not address the stress of losing time to be together in person. These findings suggest that with the exception of Zoom, the usage of other social media for older adults has not changed from before the pandemic.

Keywords: COVID-19 · Older adults · Stress · Social media · Zoom · Intergenerational · Appraisal

© Springer Nature Switzerland AG 2021
G. Meiselwitz (Ed.): HCII 2021, LNCS 12775, pp. 373–392, 2021.
https://doi.org/10.1007/978-3-030-77685-5_28

1 Introduction

1.1 Background

The COVID-19 pandemic has created an abrupt and forceful thrust of several generations into a common stressor: an age-discriminating infectious disease, with age-dependent socioeconomic consequences of mandatory "social distancing". Among the many, social isolation, especially of older adults (defined as those aged 65+) has become a major concern. Indeed, emerging data suggest that social isolation is a remarkable additional health risk [1–6].

In 2020, information and communication technologies (ICTs) accelerated their penetration in the daily lives of many, especially older adults, for whom these technologies have become a necessity for connecting to services and maintaining safe social relations.

We experienced the stress of disconnection firsthand, as the mandatory lockdowns forced us to halt all our participatory-research activities, which specifically aimed to address the question of creating intergenerational communities through various modes of self-expression and communication. In 2019, we set up the 'engAGE Living Lab Créatif' (ELL) in a shopping mall in the Cote Saint-Luc District of Montreal with high percentage of older retired citizens frequenting the mall. The aim of ELL was to serve as a hub to connect university researchers who study different aspects of aging (urban planning, engineering, cognition, healthcare, leisure, public practice arts therapies, etc.) with the stakeholders (seniors and their caregivers).

A cost-free, open-door, inclusive and creative cultural space, ELL was set up to house an Art Hive, a multimedia space equipped with materials for making art (textile, painting, photography, Photoshop), and a Media Spa, for experiencing art (films, games, VRs, magazines). The pandemic forced us to move all our interactive space to Zoom, and social media. In this context, we sought to investigate the potentials and barriers of communication in the digital era, primarily, focusing on intergenerational understandings of the affordances of social media for seniors, in the context of coping with COVID-19 stress and isolation.

1.2 Previous Related Work

The affordances of social media for older adults have been studied extensively. In a mini-review in 2013, Leist showed that at the time, older adults resisted to adopt social media for several reasons ranging from discontent about the (lack of) social norms to concerns about privacy, or personal relevance and control [7]. However, in 2014, a study by Dumbrell and Steel showed that, six months after training older adults to use Skype, Twitter and Facebook, more than 77% of the 110 participants found them beneficial for finding information, 65% found them important for sharing information, and more than 64% found them safe to use (with respect to their privacy concerns) [8].

Connecting with the younger generations is also an important motivation for older adults to use social media. In a qualitative study of Technologies in Later Life (TILL) in 37 rural older adults in 2020, Freeman et al. showed that to remain connected to younger members of their family (be it to share experiences with grandchildren, appease them, or just to stay in touch for practical reasons) was key motivation for using social media [9].

Nevertheless, the TILL study also revealed important impediments in adoption of communication technologies, stemming from inadequacy of interfaces and instructions, as well as from misunderstanding of the actual needs of seniors for such technologies, often introduced to the lives of older adults by their children [9].

In fact, the penetration of social media in older adult population remains low. As the Pew Research Centre's survey [10] illustrates, despite the steady growth of social media use among those 65+, a significant intergenerational gap remains, in the percentage of population that use them (Fig. 1). This raises an important challenge for those who, like us, need to create social media spaces for intergenerational communication.

Social media use by age

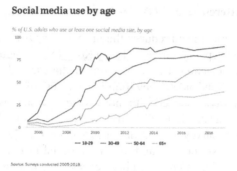

Fig. 1. Age-related differences in social media use. Source: Pew Research Centre. Retrieved Feb 2021. https://www.pewresearch.org/internet/fact-sheet/social-media/

While the question of acceptability of social media is frequently asked, less is done to design modes of interaction that foster comfortable and mutually satisfying intergenerational experiences. Most design studies focus on creating accessible and attractive user experiences in relation to presumed cognitive and physical abilities of older adults [11], or try to maximize their use and gratification–reiterating general assumptions about their cognitive and perceptual limitations [12]. In other words, the question of age is often addressed in either a biological and functional context, or in relation to psychosocial harms or benefits, without attention to the circumstances in which certain technologies become meaningful [13].

1.3 Importance of 'Generationing' in the Context of COVID-19 Stress

Social media is a place where the co-presence of different generations occurs naturally, but this means that this space must respond to needs arising from different life cycles (e.g. school, work, or retirement), accounting for differences in culture (arising from historical memories experienced across generations) [14]. Nicoletta Vittadini emphasized the importance of considering the concept of generation in media studies, as tied to their shared histories, media landscapes and social participation in dramatic life events (e.g. WWII, the fall of Berlin Wall or the 911 attacks).

In the context of this global and unprecedented life event involving an infectious disease, the generational divide is both related to life cycle and to culture. In terms of life cycle, older adults are more vulnerable to contracting COVID-19, the schools are interrupted for the young, and the work-life balance has shifted for the majority of adults who need to care both for the elders and for the young. In terms of culture, older generations have richer historical memories, different communication tools, and different media-grammar styles. Therefore, because the nature of stress experienced by different generations is different, the ways in which they adopt media to cope with those stressors are likely to be different as well.

1.4   Generational Differences in COVID-Related Social Media Use

Social media both exacerbates and reduces the burden of COVID-19 [15–20].

In a cross-sectional telephone survey in Hong Kong (May-August 2020), Wong *et al.* (2021) examined the associations between social media use and anxiety symptoms in 3421 adults aged 60 years and older. They found that the use of social media for COVID-19-related information was associated with more anxiety symptoms that predicted lower social trust in information and higher COVID-safe behaviours [21].

Boursier *et al.* (2021) surveyed a sample of 715 adults (18–72 years) to examine the relation between loneliness, anxiety, and excessive social media use. They found that perceived feelings of loneliness predicted both excessive social media use and anxiety. In their study, excessive social media exacerbated anxiety levels, especially in younger adults [17].

Similarly, Zhong *et al.* (2020) surveyed 2185 participants from 30 provinces across China, who were the first to experience the COVID-19 outbreak in the world, showed that although using social media did not cause mental health issues, it mediated elevation of stress, anxiety, depression, and traumatic experiences, especially in those living in big cities compared to those living in rural areas [18]. An interesting finding of this study was that socioeconomic and demographic factors determined what kinds of support the users sought from WeChat: Younger high-income high-education female participants sought information, but older high-income high-education participants sought more emotional support.

In a survey study in 650 adults conducted prior to COVID-19, Khalili-Mahani *et al.* (2019) found a positive correlation between emotional and perceptual stress and increased dependency on screen-mediated activities, especially social media for younger adults [22]. A follow-up survey in the aftermath of the COVID-19 North-American shutdowns in March 2020, showed that there was a causal relationship between COVID-19 stress and increased usage of certain media technologies, with significant demographic and intergenerational differences in which types of media were preferred for coping. One interesting observation in that study was that while age-related differences in social media dependence were not significant, the differences in appraisal of their usefulness or stressfulness across different age groups were significant [23].

1.5   Research Objective and Rationale

In studying the relation between media use and stress, it is essential to account for interindividual differences in perception of, and coping with any given stressor. Specifically, in designing media-based interventions to relieve the burden of physical or mental stress, we advocate for a process that starts from a data-driven approach to identify the patterns that emerge from voluntary interactions of different people with different modalities that fit their needs or interests [24].

Survey studies are the first informative step as they reveal the commonalities in patterns of specific behaviors or sentiments related to the motivations or outcomes of coping via media. However, survey studies cannot account for specific contexts or perspectives experienced by their participants. Such knowledge is usually obtained from qualitative studies, that explore patterns of salient behaviors or beliefs, emerging from extensive conversations with a small study sample (e.g. [9]) or from small conversations with a larger group of participants in specific programs (e.g. [25]).

In both cases (survey or narrative studies), what participants share is structured and guided by specific research questions and governed by the ethical constraints that frame the implicit or explicit relationships between the researcher and the participant. As such, both participants and researchers are self-prohibiting in what they express. In studying psychosocially contentious issues such as intergenerational relations in the midst of a global pandemic (that threatens different age groups differently), the patterns of 'noise' that emerge in public (somewhat anonymous) discussions on an issue constitute important data. To this end, social media provides an important site for research.

Hence, in order to gain a timely perspective on the issue of using screen-based intergenerational community-building, and communication, we tapped into the mainstream media's response to the question of senior's coping with COVID-19 stress.

Specifically, we sought to investigate the patterns of intergenerational exchanges that emerged around the topic of stress, coping and communication technologies in order to identify the benefits, barriers, and opportunities. To address these questions, we re-analyzed our previous survey [26] with specific attention to age-related differences in avoiding or approaching the social media in relation to COVID-19 stress. We also examined public comments on social media posts addressing the question of senior's coping with COVID-19 stress.

2   Materials and Methods

2.1   Cross-Sectional Snowball Survey Study

Data Collection

Data presented in this report provide a new perspective of the survey study that we published earlier [23]. The minimum sample size (384) was calculated based on a 5% margin of error and a confidence level of 95%. We obtained 595 complete answers. The survey was distributed via email lists and social media.

Social Media Use and COVID-19 Stress

Because it was important to deploy the survey in the early phase of the pandemic, we created a brief survey that took less than 5 min and avoided administering extensive psychometric scales for stress measurement. Instead, we simply asked to rate the level of stress experiences as a result of COVID-19. In addition, we asked participants to rate whether they were worried about physical or mental health of increased screen-usage as a result of the pandemic ('Yes I am worried', 'I am a little worried', 'No, I am not worried', 'I don't know').

To assess attitudes toward social media in the context of COVID-19 stress we asked participants to state their opinions ("Definitely true," "Somewhat true," "Not really true," "Definitely false," or "I don't know") about the following statements: *(1) I use social media to be connected while social distancing, (2) social media connects me to what is happening in the world, (3) COVID-19 news and social media posts overwhelm me, (4) social media spreads false information about COVID-19, (5) Following COVID-19 news gives me a sense of knowledge and control, (6) I try to avoid the COVID-19 news as much as I can.*

In addition, we asked respondents to indicate whether their usage of media (Facebook, Instagram, Twitter, Print Media, Telephone and Video conferencing had changed after the COVID-19 lockdown ('Increased, 'Decreased', 'Stayed the same', 'Rarely use it.').

Age information was collected as a categorical variable: <25 (n = 75, 79% female), 25–34 (n = 131, 75% female), 35–54 (n = 166, 77% female), 55–64 (n = 99, 78% female) and >65 (n = 124, 70% female).

Statistical Analyses

Survey statistics are presented in terms of within-group percentage of response frequencies to each question and results are plotted using Likert charts. One-way Kruskal-Wallis analysis of variance is used to investigate the statistical significance of agerelated differences on dependent variables (COVID-related changes in pattern of usage; and COVID-related attitude towards social media).

2.2 Surveying Social Media Comments

In order to obtain more organic data about the opinions of different users of social media (about helping seniors cope with COVID-19 through technology), we canvased the Internet for any articles with topics related to older adults coping with COVID-19 stress.

Figure 2 depicts a summary of the social media data-mining procedures which involved targeted examination of the general public's interactions with mainstream media accessible to our local community (Montréal). Details are presented below.

Targeted Mainstream Media Search

We searched major media outlets with global readership (such as The Guardian, The Wall Street Journal, New York Times, The Washington Post, CNN, and Fox News), as well as Canadian (The Star and CBC), and Montreal newspapers (Le Devoir, Le Soleile, and The Montreal Gazette).

We searched any articles published between March 2020 and September 2020 (corresponding to the dates of our survey study) with the terms "Senior" OR "Older Adults"

OR "Elderly" AND "technology" AND "coping" AND "COVID-19" AND" < the name of the media outlet > ". The retrieved list is presented in Table 1. Articles that did not have any social media engagement were excluded.

Scraping Social Media Comments
We focused on three sources of public engagement with articles: comments on the Facebook pages of the media outlet, comments on Reddit, and comments on the permanent websites of the articles. Data from Facebook was scraped using FacePager, a python based open-source application for automated data retrieval or on the main article website. Data from Reddit was scraped using Simple Scraper to extract all comments. Comments on the main websites were small and were copy pasted into our datasheets.

Two raters examined all comments and cleaned the data to exclude irrelevant content, such as single response words, advertisements, unrelated political commentary and performed qualitative analysis on the remaining 3390 cases.

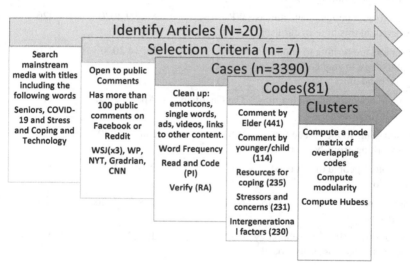

Fig. 2. Overview of social media data mining procedure

2.3   Qualitative Content Analysis

Model-Free Content Analysis
Qualitative analyses were done using NVivo for Mac (2020, QSR Inc.). We first explored the word-frequency of the comments on each article. Because of thematic similarity, we merged comments from two articles dealing with elder isolation. In addition to default stop words (transition verbs, pronouns, adjectives, prepositions), we also removed words like "people", "just", "like" and verbs unless they conveyed a specific meaning in relation to the subject of our inquiry (e.g., "connect", "play", "miss", "lose"). Word frequency

was depicted using word-clouds in order to identify the most salient themes emerging from readers interaction with the content of the article.

Thematic Coding

Comments from each of the included media outlets (3390 cases) were coded at two stages. First, we created the following general categories:

Table 1. Mainstream media articles about older adults coping with COVID-19 (retrieved between April 2020-Sept 2020)

Title	Source	Date of publication	# of comments
Ways older adults can cope with the stress of coronavirus	WSJ	Mar 28 2020	2500
The grandparents who dropped everything to help during COVID	WSJ	Dec 27 2020	315
For isolated older people, pandemic is 'a cruel event at this time in our lives'	WP	May 9 2020	226
These seniors are turning to cutting edge technology to stay connected during the pandemic	CNN	Jul 14 2020	216
Ok Zoomer: how seniors are learning to lead more digital lives	The Guardian	Apr 30 2020	212
It's grandparents to the rescue for stressed working-from-home parents	WSJ	May 5 2020	133
Just what older people didn't need: more isolation	NYT	Apr 13 2020	129
Coronavirus pandemic: How to help senior citizens	NBC	Apr 24 2020	NA
Seniors who struggle with technology face telehealth challenges and social isolation	CNN	Jul 23 2020	NA
Call grandma: survey shows older adults want more family connection during pandemic	MSN News	Apr 13 2020	NA
Elderly citizens stuck in isolation reflects poorly on all Canadians	Toronto Star	May 21 2020	NA
Staying engaged with a parent during isolation just takes a little creativity	Toronto Star	Jun 19 2020	NA
In the pandemic, technology has been a lifesaver, connecting them to the outside world. But others don't have this access	Washington Post	Aug 3 2020	NA
Internet could help isolated seniors out of their loneliness	Deutsche Welle	Mar 7 2014	NA

(continued)

Table 1. (*continued*)

Title	Source	Date of publication	# of comments
From lockdown to loneliness: old age in the age of coronavirus	Haaretz News	May 3 2020	NA
Elderly more worried about others than themselves during pandemic - study	Jerusalem Post	Jun 2 2020	NA
La technologie, remède pour rompre l'isolement des aînés	Le Soleil	Apr 11 2020	NA
La santé des aînés intéresse les géants de la technologie	Le devoir	Jan 21 2019	NA
Se maintenir à domicile grâce à la technologie	Le devoir	May 25 2019	NA
Coronavirus: how can we stay in virtual touch with older relatives?	BBC	Mar 18 2020	NA

Who Commented: 'Elder' node was used to code whether the person who commented considered themselves as targeted by the article as a 'senior'. The 'Younger' node was used to code whether the person who commented referred to examples of a senior person (e.g., their parent, grandparent, older friend, family member, etc.).

Generation: Any comments that referred to one or other form of intergenerational relationship, be it actual care for one another (e.g., grandparents take care of grandchildren, or anyone having an opinion or thought about another generation) were coded under this node.

Resources: Any comments that referred to one or other form of coping mechanisms (be it conceptual, e.g., beliefs, or practical, e.g., specific activities) were coded as resources.

Concerns: Any comments that expressed a skeptical, anxious or worrying opinion about the ramifications of the COVID-19 pandemic were coded under this node.

In the second reading, we coded any specific coping strategies that were explicitly mentioned as such, by the commenter. We also coded concerned generational expectations or interactions as they emerged in the comments.

Emerging Themes from Social Media Comments

We used a network visualization strategy, similar to the method described in [27] in order to examine the overlap in thematic categories emerging from the qualitative content analysis of the comments . The four major themes were further sub-coded to provide a more detailed view of specific topic categories discussed in the comment. This revealed 81 thematic categories (nodes), which we have presented hierarchically in the results section. We then created a node matrix whose cells indicated the number of times that any two theme categories (nodes) were expressed in the same comment. This node matrix can be understood as a correlation matrix which can be represented as a network, with the weight of an edge corresponding to the number of co-occurrences of any two nodes.

We then used the software Gephi 0.9.2 for computing the network modularity (i.e., network components that were more likely to form a community of interconnected nodes). We also computed eigenvector centrality (which is a measure for detecting networks hubs, i.e., nodes that have the highest degree of connectivity, not only in terms of the number of other nodes that are connected to them, but how far reaching those connecting edges go). For the purpose of illustration, network communities are depicted with different colors and the font size of the node label (weighted logarithmically) corresponds to the centrality of the node.

3   Results

3.1   Survey Results

Subjective Perception of COVID-Related Stress

Figure 3 depicts the age-related response frequencies to the questions of subjective feelings about COVID-19. We draw attention to the fact that the number of older adults (65+) taking the survey was larger than the younger older adults (55+) and the youngest respondents (<25). We did not find any statistically significant age-related differences in subjective feelings about COVID-19 ($\chi^2_{(df=4)} = 6.92$, p = .14). In all age categories, more than 91% of the respondents were concerned about COVID-19. However, it is worth noting that reporting themselves as 'Very Stressed' was most frequent in those in 25–34 year age group (36%), and least frequent in the 65+ age category (21%).

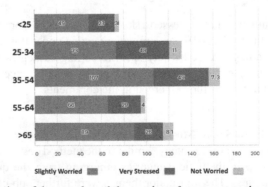

Fig. 3. Age distribution of the sample and the number of responses to the question: "Which one of these statements best describe how you feel about the COVID-19: 'I am...'". We also provided the option of "I am excited about it" (selected by 1 in < 25 and 65+ and 3 in 35–54 categories.

COVID-Related Changes in Media Usage

Figure 4 depicts that patterns of change in media use after COVID-19 lockdowns. Kruskal-Wallis tests did not reveal any statistically significant differences in age groups in relation to the patterns of change in using Facebook ($\chi^2_{(df=4)} = 4.43$, p $= .35$); Telephone ($\chi^2_{(df=4)} = 2.6$, p $= .62$) Across all ages, the likelihood of increasing Facebook use was higher than remaining unchanged or decreasing. However, age-related differences in using Teleconferencing, Twitter and Instagram were all significant ($\chi^2_{(df=4)}$'s > 10, p $= .02$), mainly driven by the fact that these were less used by older groups, with the exception of Print media that was more likely to have increased in older adults ($\chi^2_{(df=4)} = 18.6$, p $< .001$). All age groups significantly increased their teleconferencing activities (Zoom, Facetime, Skype, etc.). Those younger than 35 were more likely to have increased their Instagram use.

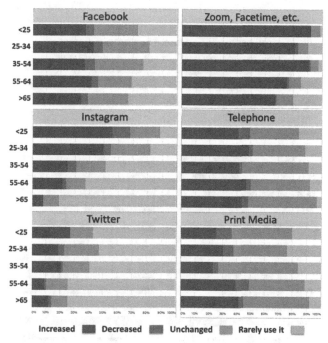

Fig. 4. Patterns of change in media use across different age categories. The Likert chart depicts percentage of responses within each age category.

Age Related Differences in Reasons for Using Social Media

Figure 5 depicts different age-group's relation to social media content related to COVID-19. Kruskal-Wallis test revealed significant age related differences in all questions: Connection to Global News ($\chi^2_{(df=4)} = 25.2$, p $< .001$); Alternative Connection While Social Distancing ($\chi^2_{(df=4)} = 18.5$, p $= .001$); Provides Knowledge and Control ($\chi^2_{(df=4)} = 29.8$, p $< .001$); Avoid COVID-19 News ($\chi^2_{(df=4)} = 29.3$, p $< .001$); Source of Fake and False News ($\chi^2_{(df=4)} = 13.1$, p $= .01$); Overwhelms Me ($\chi^2_{(df=4)} = 42.5$, p $< .001$).

The following age-related patterns are noteworthy:

1. Compared to the 65+ age group, the youngest group had significantly higher reliance on social media for Connection to Global News; for Alternative Connection While Social Distancing. At the same time, compared to the 65+ age group, the <25 group also had significantly higher negative appraisals (Avoid the News, and finding the content Overwhelming, and finding it as a Source of Fake and False News.)
2. Compared to the younger generations, the 65+ age group had significantly higher reliance on social media for gaining Knowledge and Control, and significantly less reliance on it for Alternative Connection While Social Distancing. This was consistent with the observation that more than 45% of this age group did not Avoid the COVID-19 News, and that more than 20% of this age group did not know whether social media was a Source of Fake and False News.

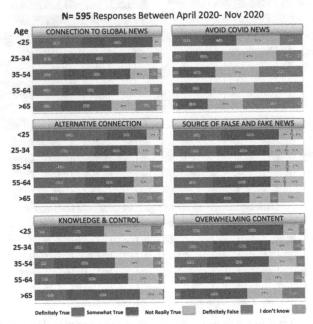

Fig. 5. Patterns of personal beliefs about positive and negative aspects of social media in the context of COVID-19. The Likert chart depicts within-group percentage of responses to the following questions: *Social media connects me to what is happening in the world* (**Connection to Global News**); *I use social media to be connected while social distancing* (**Alternative Connection**); *Following COVID-19 news gives me a sense of knowledge and control* (**Knowledge and Control**); *I try to avoid the COVID-19 news as much as I can* (**Avoid COVID News**); *Social media spreads false information about COVID-19* (Source of False and Fake News); COVID-19 news and social media posts overwhelm me (Overwhelming Content).

Mainstream Media Coverage of the Senior's Stress

Figure 6 illustrates the frequency of words detected in comments on the mainstream media articles. Word clouds are generated from the first 1000 most-frequently used words. The purpose of this exploration was to detect whether there was a high prevalence of referring to social media technologies as a coping strategy. This was not the case. In the WSJ's article providing advice about *Ways Older Adults Can Cope with the stress of Coronavirus,* reading emerged as the most frequently used word (e.g. reading the news, the bible, books, blogs). Even in articles that were specifically talking about technologies of communications for assisting older adults while social distancing (e.g. The Guardian's *Ok Zoomers! How seniors are Learning to lead more digital lives),* discussions focused on Computing (often in the context of rejecting the 'ageist' notion that seniors were technologically naive). In the context of intergenerational connections (WSJ's articles about *The grandparents who dropped everything to help during COVID-19,* or *It's grandparents to the rescue of stressed working-from-home parents,* the usage of technology (mainly Zoom or other teleconferencing tools) was how older generations supported their children and grandchildren (e.g. by virtual schooling or virtual baby-sitting.)

3.2   Qualitative Results: Themes Emerging from Social Media

Our initial coding started from characterizing comments into categories of who commented, intergenerational discussions, resources, and concerns. Figure 7 illustrates the proportional representation of how many comments were coded into each category, as well as the subcategories that emerged from each. In total 81thematics sub-categories emerged.

Who Commented: Proportionately, the majority of commenters identified themselves as seniors. A salient theme emerging from the comments of those who referenced age was relationship to technology, whether to talk about proficiency with technology (Nerdy Elder), disinterest in technology (Luddite), inability to use technology (TechAccess) and also intergenerational relationships.

Generations: When the topic of intergenerational relations was raised in the comments, the most salient theme was the resilience of older adults in the face of the pandemic. Those who identified themselves as the senior audiences of the media expressed more concern for the younger generation, indicated their contribution to de-stressing their children and grandchildren, and also rejected ageist notions that presumed seniors lack self-efficacy. In general, there were more comments about the value of the wisdom gained through living hardships prior to COVID-19, and about the 'weakness' of the young, as well as acknowledgement from seniors that the young working adults bore the brunt of the burden of the pandemic (employment, economy, child-care, and care for older parents--when the comments came from those who identified themselves as a child or caregiver to a senior).

Resources: References to existing and effective coping strategies was the most salient of all themes in the comments. The most common resource was family, friends and

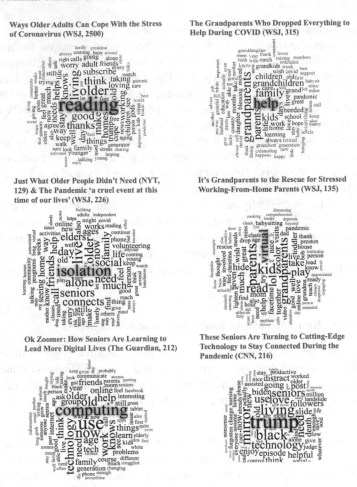

Fig. 6. Word clouds generated from comments.

community. Numerous activities were listed as coping strategies, especially walking, gardening, reading, finding the time to learn new things. Culture (collectivism, mentioned comparatively to individualism) and religion were also mentioned as resources that made going through the pandemic easier. Technology (especially teleconferencing tools such as Zoom, WhatsApp and Skype) were mentioned often as one of the many other tools for coping, with its value being mainly in connecting individuals socially (especially to their families).

Concerns: Relative to the number of comments discussing resources, there were fewer comments about concerns. The most salient concern was lack of social connections, especially loss of time to be together with grandchildren. When the disease COVID-19 was a health or economic concern, it was often in reference to worrying about the well-being of the children in the workforce, or about the acceptance of the necessity of lockdowns for keeping safe or blaming the politicians.

Co-occurring Themes: In order to better understand the interrelations between the emergent themes, we performed a network analysis and partitioned it based on modularity. Figure 8 depicts the themes that were more likely to cluster together. The network modularity was low (0.163) meaning that there were overlaps in edges that connected the nodes of each community. The font size of each node corresponds to the eigenvector centrality of the node, meaning the importance of the node in the entire network. This partitioning revealed three communities:

The first cluster (depicted in orange) included nodes corresponding to comments by elders, resources (Activities, Family, and Wisdom and Resilience). The second cluster included comments by the Younger, Community, Connection and Technology, specifically Zoom, phone, and issues of accessibility of technology to older adults (whether comment by or about Nerdy elders, or inaccessibility of technology). In the third cluster, concerns about Loneliness, Isolation and Lost time co-occurred.

The low modularity of the network suggests that there was a significant co-occurrence of different themes (meaning that the clusters are interdependent). For example, the theme "Ageism" had connections both to the Elder and to the Younger nodes. Or Technology, which was a central hub in the second cluster was also linked with Resources and Generation which were important hubs in the first cluster.

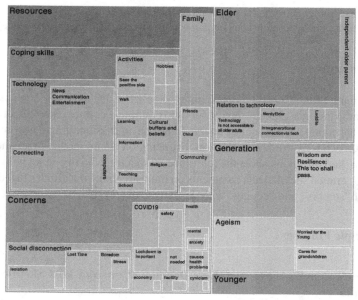

Fig. 7. Hierarchical representation of coded content from Social Media comment scaping.

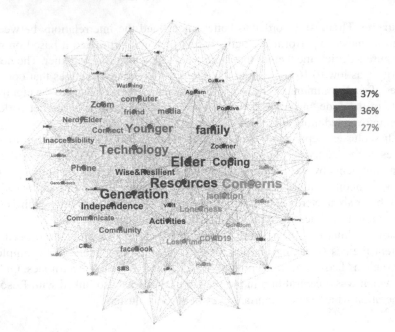

Fig. 8. An exploratory network analysis to assess the overlap between themes. Colors represent network partitions emerging from computing modularity (Q = 0.16, weighted by edge).

4 Discussions

In the aftermath of the COVID-19 pandemic, socializing distantly, via Zoom and social media, became the only available option for us to continue our intergenerational activities in ELL. In that context, we examined intergenerational understandings of how seniors can cope with COVID-19 stress and isolation. Focusing on social media, in an anonymous survey, we asked questions about the relevance of social media to coping with COVID-19. We also scraped social media comments on mainstream media articles that dealt with the topic of "seniors" and "coping" with the "stress of COVID-19".

4.1 Principle Findings

Older Adults were Less Stressed, Less Dependent on, and Less Skeptical About Social Media
We conducted two independent inquiries about COVID-19 stress and social media, and they both showed that older adults were not particularly stressed about COVID-19, nor overly dependent on technology for coping with it.

We observed significant generation-related effects from the survey suggesting that those older than 65 years of age were significantly less stressed than the younger groups, and used social media differently (for knowledge and gaining a sense of control) than the younger group (using it mostly as an alternative source of connection while social distancing.)

Similarly, scraping the social media comments did not reveal any significant expression of feeling stressed; *au contraire*, the pandemic seemed to have provided an opportunity for them to express and communicate their resilience and wisdom in the face of this event). Interestingly, while commenting on social media, there was no explicit mention of it being relevant to coping with the pandemic, but relevant to reading about it.

For example, in the WSJ article *"Ways older adults can cope with the stress of COVID-19"* (which provided a list of coping tools and techniques), the word 'reading' was most frequently mentioned. In the CNN article "These seniors are turning to cutting edge technology to stay connected during the pandemic", an article about potential affordances of VR to facilitate socially-distant communications, the word Trump and cynical comments about the prospect of a Black Mirror world (a Sci-fi TV series about a dystopic machine-dominated virtual future) were most frequent.

Generational Differences in Coping with COVID-19 Stress Determine the Relation to Technology

While a significant portion of older adults increased their usage of Facebook, and teleconferencing tools after COVID-19, older adults are less represented in social media networks (especially Twitter and Instagram) (Fig. 4). But it was not only their inability to access the technology that explained their lower dependence on such media. In the context of coping with the pandemic, it was explicitly their ability to draw on their wisdom and experience from having survived previous stressors.

Our exploratory cluster analysis of the co-occurrence of themes from social media comments revealed an interesting picture, where the important nodes of Technology and Young belonged to the same cluster (which also included references to Facebook, Zoom, and Connection), but nodes Elder, Resource, and Generation belonged to a different cluster that also included Family, Independence and Wisdom and resilience. Yet, the concerns for COVID-19 seem to form a third cluster which also included worrying about the young, and taking care of the young (e.g., by babysitting or homeschooling grandchildren via Zoom).

The fact that technology was not a 'big deal' for older adults was clear in the comments on The Guardian's article that directly dealt with the question of older adults adopting technology after COVID-19. *"Ok Zoomer: how seniors are learning to lead more digital lives"* discussed providing tech support to previously technology-avoiding seniors who are now forced to use tele-conferencing technologies for social connection. This article received many irritated responses by tech-savvy older adults, who emphasized that they were the pioneers of computing in the 60's-80's. Many of those indicated that the reason for not becoming comfortable with recent technologies was because it did not serve a meaning in their already fulfilled life.

Overall, technology was more important to the younger generation for enabling them to connect to their elders. Numerous comments were about parents or grandparents who had picked up Zoom or Facebook to stay connected to their grandchildren.

4.2   Comparison to Previous Work

Our results are not directly comparable to previous studies because we have not undertaken any formal psychometric evaluation to assess anxiety and stress, and instead have relied on subjective self-evaluation (in the case of the survey) and data-driven extraction of expressions of concern about COVID-19. Our findings indirectly support the observations of Boursier *et al.* [17] and Zhong *et al.* [18] who showed a positive association between COVID-19 stress and increased usage of social media (mainly in the younger generation.) Our findings also indirectly support the finding by Yang *et al.* [19] that social media can provide a positive relief from COVID-19 stress. Especially, it provided an outlet for self-expression (as was evident from engagement of seniors with the mainstream media articles) and information exchange (as was evident from the survey), for older adults. Although, neither in the survey nor in the social media comment, did it appear as a major 'hub' in the network of resources for coping.

Our findings strongly support Vittadini's position that 'generationing' is an important consideration when analyzing the social media landscape [14]. While the pandemic is creating an unprecedented opportunity for different generations to experience a global catastrophe in a common social media space, generational divisions still manifest in relation to the past experiences of the older generation, with important generalizations and stigmatizations to overcome--not only those that criticize older adults about their technological ineptitude or praise them for nerdiness, but also those perspectives that disparage the younger generation's wisdom for overrelying on technology for coping.

5   Conclusion

5.1 Summary of Findings

The aim of this study was to examine the intergenerational differences vis a vis reliance on social media for coping with COVID-19 stress. We investigated this question from two angles: 1) A cross-sectional anonymous survey study announced in the context of a specific research study (What Media Helps, What Media Hurts: Coping with COVID-19 Through screens) which did not specifically focus on age-related differences; 2) A targeted but data-driven examination of the public engagement with the question of seniors coping with COVID-19 as presented in the mainstream media.

Both studies gave a similar conclusion: Differences between generations stem from differences in life experiences that change their perception of stress, and as a result, create differences in appraisal of technology as a coping tool.

Whereas the younger generations have a higher expectation from technological solutions to coping with COVID-19 stress (and therefore resort to them more), the older generation (so called seniors) use technology as one of the many other resources for coping that they have developed without initial reliance on technology.

5.2 Limitations and Future Work

Interpretation of the above findings must consider several limitations. First, the interpretation of our results are exclusive to the sample, taken from those who could read English (mainly the US, Canada, and the UK). Second, our sample was biased by those with access to social media, and the ability to fill our online survey. Finally, qualitative research is always subjective. To mitigate investigators' bias, the social media analyses should be repeated by other coders who are blind to the objective of this particular inquiry, to explore what other themes may be present in the data.

Irrespective of these limitations, our mixed methods approach to the question on intergenerational perspectives on social media revealed important gaps in different generations' understanding of each other's needs and preferences. Whereas for the young, technology provides an important tool to remain connected to elders during the pandemic, for the older adults, technology is one of the many other tools for coping with the pandemic, and one that does not replace the loss of time to spend together, physically. Our study also revealed a certain degree of intergenerational bias: Whereas many older adults were acknowledging the financial and emotional stressfulness of this pandemic on younger adults, and tried to assist them, several others blamed the young for 'weakness' and over-reliance on virtual coping (even before the pandemic hit).

In future work, we intend to undertake a qualitative study to ask the opinions of our local community of seniors on the topic of intergenerational connections in social media.

References

1. Ollivier, R., et al.: Mental health & parental concerns during COVID-19: the experiences of new mothers amidst social isolation. Midwifery **94**, 102902 (2021)
2. Medeiros, R.A., et al.: Prevalence of symptoms of temporomandibular disorders, oral behaviors, anxiety, and depression in dentistry students during the period of social isolation due to COVID-19. J. Appl. Oral. Sci. **28**, e20200445 (2020)
3. Robb, C.E., et al.: Associations of social isolation with anxiety and depression during the early COVID-19 pandemic: a survey of older adults in London, UK. Front. Psychiatry **11**, 591120 (2020)
4. Gaeta, L., Brydges, C.R.: Coronavirus-related anxiety, social isolation, and loneliness in older adults in northern California during the stay-at-home order. J. Aging Soc. Policy 1–12 (2020)
5. Maguire, S., O'Shea, F.: Social isolation due to the COVID-19 pandemic has led to worse outcomes in females with inflammatory arthritis. Irish J. Med. Sci. **190**(1), 33–38 (2020). https://doi.org/10.1007/s11845-020-02307-2
6. Pecanha, T., et al.: Social isolation during the COVID-19 pandemic can increase physical inactivity and the global burden of cardiovascular disease. Am. J. Physiol. Heart Circ. Physiol. **318**(6), H1441–H1446 (2020)
7. Leist, A.K.: Social media use of older adults: a mini-review. Gerontology **59**(4), 378–384 (2013)
8. Dumbrell, D., Steele, R.: Social media technologies for achieving knowledge management amongst older adult communities. Procedia. Soc. Behav. Sci. **147**, 229–236 (2014)
9. Freeman, S., et al.: Intergenerational effects on the impacts of technology use in later life: insights from an international, multi-site study. Int. J. Environ. Res. Public Health **17**(16), 5711 (2020)
10. Pew Research Center (2019). https://www.pewresearch.org/internet/fact-sheet/social-media/
11. Quinn, K.: Cognitive effects of social media use: a case of older adults. Soc. Media Soc. **4**(3) (2018)
12. Arfaa, J., Wang, Y.: A usability study on elder adults utilizing social networking sites. In: Marcus, A. (ed.) DUXU 2014. LNCS, vol. 8518, pp. 50–61. Springer, Cham (2014). https://doi.org/10.1007/978-3-319-07626-3_5

13. De Schutter, B., Vanden Abeele, V.: Towards a Gerontoludic manifesto. Anthropol. Aging **36**(2), 112–120 (2015)
14. Vittadini, N.: Intergenerational social media use: expectations of adults and elder users. In: Gao, Q., Zhou, J. (eds.) HCII 2020. LNCS, vol. 12209, pp. 101–113. Springer, Cham (2020). https://doi.org/10.1007/978-3-030-50232-4_8
15. Wong, F.H.C., et al.: Consuming information related to COVID-19 on social media among older adults and its associations with anxiety, social trust in information, and COVID-safe behaviours: Cross-Sectional Survey. J. Med. Internet Res. **23**(2), e26570 (2021)
16. Eden, A.L., et al.: Media for coping during COVID-19 social distancing: stress, anxiety, and psychological well-being. Front. Psychol. **11**, 577639 (2020)
17. Boursier, V., et al.: Facing loneliness and anxiety during the COVID-19 isolation: the role of excessive social media use in a sample of Italian adults. Front. Psychiatry **11**, 586222 (2020)
18. Zhong, B., et al.: Association of social media use with mental health conditions of nonpatients during the COVID-19 outbreak: insights from a national survey study. J. Med. Internet Res. **22**(12), e23696 (2020)
19. Yang, Y., et al.: Social media activities, emotion regulation strategies, and their interactions on people's mental health in COVID-19 pandemic. Int. J. Environ. Res. Public Health **17**(23), 8931 (2020)
20. Cauberghe, V., et al.: How adolescents use social media to cope with feelings of loneliness and anxiety during COVID-19 lockdown. Cyberpsychol. Behav. Soc. Netw. **24**(4), 250–257 (2020)
21. Wong, F.H.C., et al.: Consuming information related to COVID-19 on social media among older adults and its associations with anxiety, social trust in information, and COVID-safe behaviours: cross-sectional survey (preprint). J. Med. Internet Res. **23**(2), e26570 (2020)
22. Khalili-Mahani, N., Smyrnova, A., Kakinami, L.: To each stress its own screen: a cross-sectional survey of the patterns of stress and various screen uses in relation to self-admitted screen addiction. J. Med. Internet Res. **21**(4), e11485 (2019)
23. Pahayahay, A., Khalili-Mahani, N.: What media helps, what media hurts: a mixed methods survey study of coping with COVID-19 using the media repertoire framework and the appraisal theory of stress. J. Med. Internet Res. **22**(8), e20186 (2020)
24. Khalili-Mahani, N., De Schutter, B.: Affective game planning for health applications: quantitative extension of gerontoludic design based on the appraisal theory of stress and coping. JMIR Serious Games **7**(2), e13303 (2019)
25. LoBuono, D.L., Leedahl, S.N., Maiocco, E.: Older adults learning technology in an intergenerational program: qualitative analysis of areas of technology requested for assistance. Gerontechnology **18**(2), 97–107 (2019)
26. Pahayahay, A., Khalili-Mahani, N.: What media helps, what media hurts: a mixed methods survey study of coping with COVID-19 using the media repertoire framework and the appraisal theory of stress. J. Med. Internet Res. **22**(8), e20186G (2020)
27. Pokorny, J.J., et al.: Network analysis for the visualization and analysis of qualitative data. Psychol. Methods **23**(1), 169–183 (2018)

Gamified Mobile Health Interventions for Mental Well-Being of Older Adults

Thuy-Trinh Nguyen[1], Joseph C. M. Chai[5], Øystein Eiring[2], Wenru Wang[3], Ronald R. O'Donnell[4], and Hoang D. Nguyen[5(✉)]

[1] ReML Research Group, Sydney, Australia
`Trinh.Nguyen@reml.ai`
[2] Norwegian Institute for Public Health, Oslo, Norway
`Oystein.Eiring@fhi.no`
[3] Alice Lee Centre for Nursing Studies, Yong Loo Lin School of Medicine, National University of Singapore, Singapore, Singapore
`NurWW@nus.edu.sg`
[4] College of Health Solutions, Arizona State University, Phoenix, USA
`Ronald.ODonnell@asu.edu`
[5] School of Computing Science, University of Glasgow, Singapore, Singapore
`2355338C@student.gla.ac.uk`, `Harry.Nguyen@glasgow.ac.uk`

Abstract. Population ageing has raised major concerns about the prevalence of age-related mental health deterioration which is further intensified amid the COVID-19 pandemic. Mobile health (mHealth) interventions bear promising impacts on alleviating the mental health burden of this vulnerable group. However, mHealth solutions often report a high drop-out rate suggesting a lack of motivation and engagement among users. Also, the limited number of clinically validated mHealth applications indicates an urgent demand for empirical evidence on the subject. This paper proposes a design framework for gamified mHealth activities to enhance mental and cognitive well-being of the elderly. Further, the paper outlines a research protocol to investigate the impacts of the framework on a cohort of 250 older adults in a developing country under a single-subject experimental design. Our social experiment may reveal valuable insights into the potential of mHealth solutions and gamification in this domain.

Keywords: mHealth · Mobile interventions · Mental well-being · Cognitive stimulation · Cohort study · Older adults

1 Introduction

Modern society is facing massive demographic shifts due to population ageing. Projections indicate that the population of people aged 60 or over will outnumber that of the 10–24 age group by 2050 [25]. According to the World Health Organisation (WHO), over 20% of older adults suffer from a mental or neurological disorder (e.g. loneliness, isolation, depression, and dementia) [32]. The

© Springer Nature Switzerland AG 2021
G. Meiselwitz (Ed.): HCII 2021, LNCS 12775, pp. 393–406, 2021.
https://doi.org/10.1007/978-3-030-77685-5_29

WHO report also indicates that apart from common stressors applied to the general public, the elderly are exposed to other age-related risk factors such as the declining socioeconomic status during retirement. Moreover, research has shown that social isolation and loneliness intensify the progression of cognitive decline among seniors [14, 24].

With decreasing fertility rates, decreasing mortality rates, and increasing life expectancy, developing countries such as Vietnam or Thailand are amongst the fastest ageing nations in Asia [25]. The unprecedented ageing has created enormous challenges in securing and allocating health care resources to the elderly population. Although mental health care infrastructure has witnessed considerable progress in the last two decades, resource deficits, lack of mental health policy, and mental health stigma remain major issues in developing regions [17, 29]. Therefore, the aged population is severely underserved in terms of mental health support. With the prevalence of COVID-19, it is urgent to seek such support for older adults due to the negative impact of social distancing on mental well-being [15, 22].

Regarding existing solutions for elderly mental health, mental health institutions and community facilities are not available and affordable in many developing countries, such as Vietnam, where mental health awareness is still limited [17]. Especially during COVID-19, physical mental health services have been deemed secondary due to social distancing measures and the high-risk nature of the elderly population. Another solution to address mental health issues is pharmacological treatment. This type of intervention, however, is restricted to polypharmacy and risk of adverse drug-related events as older adults often consume multiple drugs simultaneously for chronic somatic diseases [11]. Thus, other preventive methods are often sought in trying times. Cognitive stimulation activities such as memory and attention exercises are promising to support seniors with maintaining and improving their cognitive function. Existing brain training interventions, however, often lack engagement with monotonous exercises; therefore, gamification is considered a potential addition to brain gym training to improve engagement and motivational dynamics [5, 7]. A recent systematic review also reports the effect of cognitive games on multiple cognitive functions (i.e. working memory, processing speed, executive function, and verbal memory) among healthy elderly [2].

In this paper, we propose an activity design framework for mobile interventions that aims to enhance elderly mental well-being. The paper provides design guidelines for mobile applications (apps) in mental health support using gamified cognitive training solutions. We discuss the development of multiple elder-friendly games including chess solving and quiz games. Our innovation incorporates various achievement-oriented game elements such as challenges, leaderboard, points and extrinsic rewards. Besides, the app supports social interaction, which is often neglected in gamified mental health applications [7], via cross-platform friend invitation, collaboration, and competition among friends and family members to lessen seniors' social isolation. To emphasise the relaxation effect, the proposed mobile intervention can employ alpha waves (6–12 Hz) as the application background music [33].

We present a cohort study protocol of a social experiment on elderly mental health support under a single-subject approach. Recent systematic reviews on gamification in mental health application highlight (1) the lack of empirical evidence on gamification efficacy in improving mental health, (2) the understudied effect of social interaction game elements [5], and (3) the demand for attention towards vulnerable groups such as the aged population [7]. Our social experiment, therefore, may reveal valuable insights to bridge the stated gaps in the academic body of mental health mobile interventions.

This study also carries useful implications for mental health support practitioners. For healthcare organisers, our mobile solution contributes to the collection of home-based mental health interventions that act as an alternative to offline consultation during COVID-19. For solution designers, our design concepts including brain training games, and various gamification elements are useful references for future applications.

In summary, this paper contributes to the development of mobile mental health interventions in manifolds. First, the paper presents a review of existing mobile solutions for mental health support for the elderly. Second, our paper sketches an open social innovation which is an ecosystem for older adults, healthcare service providers, and platform operators. Third, this paper outlines the research protocol for a social experiment to examine the effect of a mobile intervention on elevating the mental well-being of older adults.

2 Literature Review

According to the United Nations, the number of older adults aged 60 or over worldwide is expected to double from nearly 1 billion in 2017 to 2.1 billion by 2050 [25]. Projections also indicate that population ageing occurs at a more rapid rate in developing countries than their developed counterpart with an estimated 80% of the world's older adults living in developing regions in 2050.

Besides physical ageing, older adults also face psychological and social ageing. The decline in socioeconomic status during retirement and less attention by children result in stress, depression, loneliness, and social isolation among older people [1,8]. Research has shown that mental health issues, including loneliness and social isolation, accelerate cognitive decline [14,24], which is already a prominent late-life condition. Ill health can cause loss of independence, loss of self-esteem and lower quality of life [8]. With the advent of COVID-19, elderly mental well-being is at greater risk. Essential social distancing restrictions limit offline social activities such as physical gathering, travelling, and outdoor hobbies. As a result, recent studies report an increased level of loneliness and distress among the elderly and call for creative measures to support this vulnerable population amid the COVID-19 pandemic [15,22,26]. Considering the urgency of the problem, the ideal elderly mental health support solution needs to satisfy several criteria. First, the solution should be online or home-based to comply with essential quarantine and social distancing measures. Second, the proposed intervention should be elder-friendly and fast to pick up, so that older people feel comfortable to use it routinely. Lastly, the solution should encourage a high engagement rate to deliver the maximum benefit of the program.

In this paper, we review past studies of relevant mobile interventions for mental health support and gamification concepts in mobile health.

2.1 Mobile Interventions for Mental Well-Being

In recent years, the prevalence of digital devices (e.g. smartphones and tablets) and the embedded mobile culture have paved the way for mobile health (mHealth) - smart health care support applications. The elderly population is an emerging but substantial consumer group of this novel technology with an increasing number of mobile phone registrations every day. Findings from [28] show that maintaining social connections and accessing health care information are the primary motivations of elderly mobile phone usage. Recent research also suggests significant benefits of mHealth in mental health support. Firstly, mHealth offers constant availability, immediate support, and greater access to attend to user needs, regardless of time or physical location [18,28]. Furthermore, mobile health interventions can reduce the mental barriers associated with seeking support in-person [12]. In some developing countries such as Vietnam, where the awareness of mental disorders among the community is limited [29], mHealth is a viable option for older adults to avoid the stigma and distress about traditional consultations. Also, several mHealth solutions have positive clinical evidence for behavioural change and mental health improvements. For example, [3,21] report that mHealth can enhance the development of healthy behaviours such as awareness, stress management and balanced nutritional consumption. Wang et al. (2018) advocate the significant impact of mHealth on various mental health domains such as anxiety and stress, alcohol disorder, and sleep disorder [31].

2.2 Gamification in Mobile Health interventions

A promising addition to the standard mHealth interventions is gamification. Gamification refers to game design elements in non-game contexts [6]. Although gamification in mental and cognitive health applications is a premature topic due to its recency, initial studies suggest its potential benefits for mental health support and behavioural change [7]. In addition, the overlap between dimensions of motivation in games and game-based techniques suggests that gamification has engaging potential. In particular, [9] identifies five key dimensions pertaining to motivations of game player: Achievement, exploration, sociability, domination, and immersion. On the other hand, [7,27] suggest that game design elements can also be categorised into the listed motivation dimensions. Table 1 provides examples of game elements and their categories.

A similar trend is observed in both mental and cognitive health domains. Among these features, achievement, domination, and immersion-typed are the most popular in gamified mental health programs, while a promising but underexplored feature as social interaction is only included in a limited number of applications [5,27].

Table 1. Motivation dimensions and related game elements

Motivation dimension	Example of game element
Achievement	Progress bar, Difficulty level, Rewards
Exploration	Unlockable content, Virtual world exploration
Sociability	Community, Collaboration, Competition
Domination	Leaderboard, Challenge
Immersion	Background music, Real-time activity, Virtual avatar

There remains, however, several concerns regarding gamification in digital well-being applications for the elderly. As older adults and the general public have different game preferences, this entails the need for purposeful game design. Also, recent systematic reviews have revealed that the majority of available solutions lack clinical evidence of their efficacy [5,7,31]; therefore, empirical evidence of digital mental health intervention is greatly welcome.

3   Activity Design Framework for Mobile-Based Mental Health Interventions

3.1   Overview

This study introduces an activity framework for designing health interventions using mobile technologies, which is adapted from [19,20], to achieve mental well-being (Fig. 1). It consists of seven components based on the Activity Theory, namely (1) subject, (2) object, (3) outcome, (4) tool, (5) control, (6) context, and (7) communication.

1. **Subject**. The "subject" component depicts the target of our mobile interventions who are mainly older adults, above 60 years old.
2. **Object**. The "object" component reflects the purpose of interventional activities that induce changes in the subject's characteristics. In mental health interventions, the object entails individuals' healthy behaviours, cognitive functioning, and emotional quality.
3. **Outcome**. The outcome is a transformation of the object through activities resulting in improved mental well-being with the use of self-reported measures.
4. **Tool**. The "tool" component refers to the mediation aspects. In mental health support, mobile capabilities, gamification, and health assessment tools help subjects to enhance their behaviours, emotions, and cognition.
5. **Control**. The "control" component depicts various boundaries in health interventions, including personalisation, protocol, affordances, and access control.

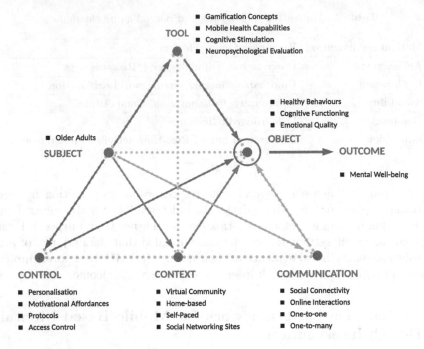

Fig. 1. Design framework for mental health support

6. **Context**. The "context" component depicts the environment or situation in which activities take place. It spans a variety of physical and virtual communities. Moreover, with the use of mobile technologies, subjects have the freedom of participating in mental health interventions at home and at their own pace.
7. **Communication**. The "communication" component highlights the role structure of the subjects as well as the interaction among them. It enables social connectivity and communication styles (e.g., one-to-one or one-to-many messaging).

3.2 Gamified Mobile Health Interventions

In this paper, we propose a gamified mobile application to support seniors' mental health using brain gym solutions. Currently, our innovation targets the elderly population in Vietnam, where there is limited support for this vulnerable group, to ease loneliness, enhance positive moods, and stimulate elderly cognitive functions during the COVID-19 pandemic. In the long run, the app will be extended to serve communities on a larger scale. Our mobile solution is currently in the development stage and will have its first public launch in the third quarter of 2021.

Our innovation utilises popular achievement and progress-oriented game design features including leaderboard, challenges, adjustable difficulty, and rewards. By joining games, participants receive points which can be exchanged for physical goods in our online store. The reward exchange attribute introduces real-life benefits of the virtual application to potentially stimulate engagement among senior users. Beside achievement and domination game elements, the app also focuses on social interaction features including cross-platform friend invitation, collaboration (i.e. Multiplayer mode), and competition (i.e. Real-time challenges among friends). The use of various social cooperation elements is expected to evoke intrinsic motivation and alleviate loneliness among senior users. Another highlight of our solution, in terms of ambience, is the option of alpha brain waves background music to enhance relaxation.

3.3   Activities

Based on our proposed activity framework, we identify five activities to achieve the final outcome of enhancing elderly mental and cognitive well-being. Table 2 demonstrates how key activities of our mobile app employ components of the activity framework.

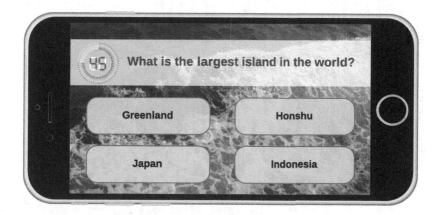

Fig. 2. Quiz game

Quiz Game. Trivia-style is one of the most popular and enjoyable cognitive games among the elderly [10] which can stimulate memory recall and endorse knowledge acquisition. Therefore, we introduce a timed quiz game that tests the user's knowledge on diverse subjects including culture, science, history, geography, and general topic. Each quiz consists of 10–15 multiple choice questions with an increasing level of difficulty. Figure 2 illustrates the user interface (UI) of the proposed quiz game. Points are awarded based on the user's performance, and top players are featured on the leaderboard. In addition, the app allows cross-platform friend invitation and results sharing on other social networking sites (SNSs).

Table 2. Application of activity framework in a gamified mobile solution for elderly mental well-being

Activity theory	Component		Quiz game	Chess solving	Food frenzy	Conversation	Reward store
Control	Personalisation		Topics based on interest	Select between International and Chinese Chess		Personal conversational space	Filter based on interest
	Motivation affordances		Earn points; Compete with friends	Earn points; Compete with friends; Collaborate with friends	Earn points; Compete with friends	Socialise with friends and family members	Exchange points into physical goods
	Protocols		Time limitation; Scheduled games daily	Time limitation; Chess rules	Time limitation; Limited lives per game		Exchange is irreversible
Context	Virtual community		Leaderboard competition	Leaderboard competition; Multiplayer mode	Leaderboard competition	Chat room	
	Home-based		x	x	x	x	x
	Self-paced					x	x
Communication	Social connectivity		Invite a friend; Share game scores	Invite a friend; Share game scores	Invite a friend; Share game scores	Invite a friend	Share results
	Online interaction		Competition	Competition; Collaboration	Competition	Communication	
Tool	Gamification	Reward	x	x	x		x
		Leaderboard	x	x	x		
		Level of difficulty	x	x	x	x	
		Social interaction	x				
		Sound effect			x		
		Virtual avatar	x	x	x	x	x
	Mobile capabilities	Touch motion	x	x	x	x	x
		Swipe motion			x		x
	Cognitive stimulation	Brain waves music	x	x		x	
		Memory	x	x			x
		Attention		x	x		x

Fig. 3. Chess solving

Chess Solving. Chess has long been studied for its impact on cognitive science [4]. Recent research also provides evidence that Chess game can generate a sound cognitive mind for older adults and enhance active thinking, as well as long-term memory span [30]. Thus, a modified version of chess is proposed in our mobile app. In our chess solving game, the users need to arrange chess pieces to recreate the desired chess stage. The game can be played in a single- or multi-player mode, which encourages collaboration or competition among friends. Chess solving offers two options for international (Western) and Chinese chess. Each chess game is limited to 30 minutes. Figure 3 presents the UI of our chess solving game in international chess mode. The reward, leaderboard and cross-platform connections are similar to those of the quiz game.

Food Frenzy. Besides activities that support users' memory and problem-solving skills (i.e. quiz game and chess solving), our mobile solution introduces another interactive game that targets the level of attention and speed of processing of the elderly. Food Frenzy challenges the user to slice flying animated food items using swiping motions. Figure 4 illustrates the interface design of Food Frenzy. This game requires a high level of attention and speed. There are limited attempts (i.e. lives) to finish the game. Users earn points based on their final score, and they are ranked on the leaderboard.

Conversation Space. Although social interactions can create potential intrinsic motivation, these features are substantially underexplored in gamified applications. Thus, our mobile solution provides a personal in-app chat space for users to communicate with their friends and family members apart from other discussed social elements such as multi-player collaboration and competition. Users can invite friends to connect via other SNSs or add contacts using their usernames.

Reward Store. Points earned from games can be exchanged for physical goods in our reward store. This feature will be tested in Vietnam first. The reward store is expected to motivate users to participate and engage in games. The interface of our reward store is shown in Fig. 5.

4   A Cohort Study Protocol for Ageing Population

The study is a social experiment based on a single-subject experimental design with an estimated total of 250 older adults. The participants will complete short assignments before and after each interventional activity that induces changes. In addition, comprehensive mental health assessments will be conducted at three timestamps: Baseline (Time 1), 4-week intervention (Time 2), and a final 3-month intervention phase (Time 3).

4.1   Study Aims

- Primary Aim: To investigate the short-term impact of our mobile solution on the elderly cohort using primary outcome variables including Brief Mood Introspection Scale (BMIS), Repeatable Battery for the Assessment of Neuropsychological Status (RBANS), and 9-item Patient Health Questionnaire (PHQ-9) at each phase.
- Secondary Aim: To investigate the impacts of activity elements on mental and cognitive well-being.

Fig. 4. Food frenzy

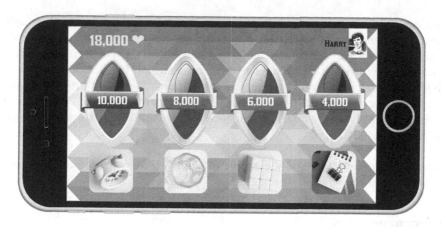

Fig. 5. Reward store

4.2 Including Criteria

Eligible participants should (1) reside in a developing country, (2) be able to read and speak properly, (3) be 60 years old or over, (4) have access to a mobile phone or tablet, and (5) not currently enrol in other intervention trials.

4.3 Recruitment Procedure

After the mobile app's launch event, we will call for participation among an expected total of 10,000 event attendees. Individuals who express interest in the experiment will be screened based on the eligibility criteria. Then, the potential participants will be instructed to sign the consent form and complete the first baseline measurements. 250 participants will be chosen randomly among eligible individuals to participate in the social experiment.

4.4 Data Analysis

The primary variables include BIMS [16], PHQ-9 [13] and RBANS [23]. Besides, activity logs (e.g. the number of completed sessions, total time spent in each game, brain waves music listening usage), and self-reported socio-demographic variables (e.g. age, gender) will be recorded to form a data panel.

Chi-Square test will be conducted to evaluate the impact of the mobile intervention on mental and cognitive well-being by comparing pre- and post-test results of primary outcome variables. To investigate the impact of each activity elements, time series analysis (e.g. regression analysis) will be performed on the prepared panel data.

5   Conclusion

This paper introduces the design concepts of mobile interventions for mental and cognitive health among the elderly. The innovation employs Activity Theory and gamification elements to alleviate the age-related health burden in developing countries, where population ageing is advancing rapidly. We propose a research protocol for a social experiment under a single-subject experimental design to (1) investigate the short-term impact of the intervention via BMIS, RBANS and PHQ-9 measurements, and (2) examine the impact of each activity component on elderly mental and cognitive well-being. Our research protocol contributes to the collection of limited empirical evidence of mHealth in mental and cognitive health domains [31].

Acknowledgement. This study is a part of the ReML research initiative on social AI supported by the IGV Group.

References

1. Azizah, L.M., Martiana, T., Soedirham, O.: The improvement of cognitive function and decrease the level of stress in the elderly with brain gym. Int. J. Nurs. Midwifery Sci. (IJNMS) **1**(1), 26–31 (2017)
2. Bonnechère, B., Langley, C., Sahakian, B.J.: The use of commercial computerised cognitive games in older adults: a meta-analysis. Sci. Rep. **10**(1), 1–14 (2020)
3. Changizi, M., Kaveh, M.H.: Effectiveness of the mhealth technology in improvement of healthy behaviors in an elderly population–a systematic review. Mhealth **3**, 51 (2017)
4. Charness, N.: The impact of chess research on cognitive science. Psychol. Res. **54**(1), 4–9 (1992)
5. Cheng, V.W.S., Davenport, T., Johnson, D., Vella, K., Hickie, I.B.: Gamification in apps and technologies for improving mental health and well-being: systematic review. JMIR Mental Health **6**(6), e13717 (2019)
6. Deterding, S., Dixon, D., Khaled, R., Nacke, L.: From game design elements to gamefulness: defining "gamification". In: Proceedings of the 15th International Academic Mindtrek Conference: Envisioning Future Media Environments, pp. 9–15 (2011)
7. Fleming, T.M., et al.: Serious games and gamification for mental health: current status and promising directions. Front. Psych. **7**, 215 (2017)
8. Fund, U.N.P.: The ageing population in Vietnam: Current status, prognosis, and possible policy responses (2011)
9. Hamari, J., Tuunanen, J.: Player types: A meta-synthesis (2014)
10. Hollander, E.K., Plummer, H.R.: An innovative therapy and enrichment program for senior adults utilizing the personal computer. Act. Adapt. Aging **8**(1), 59–68 (1986)
11. Holvast, F., et al.: Late-life depression and the association with multimorbidity and polypharmacy: a cross-sectional study. Fam. Pract. **34**(5), 539–545 (2017)
12. Kovandžić, M., et al.: Access to primary mental health care for hard-to-reach groups: from 'silent suffering' to 'making it work'. Soc. Sci. Med. **72**(5), 763–772 (2011)
13. Kroenke, K., Spitzer, R.L., Williams, J.B.: The PHQ-9: validity of a brief depression severity measure. J. Gen. Intern. Med. **16**(9), 606–613 (2001)
14. Lara, E., et al.: Are loneliness and social isolation associated with cognitive decline? Int. J. Geriatr. Psychiatry **34**(11), 1613–1622 (2019)

15. Le, X.T.T., et al.: Evaluating the psychological impacts related to COVID-19 of Vietnamese people under the first nationwide partial lockdown in Vietnam. Front. Psych. **11**, 824 (2020)
16. Mayer, J.D., Gaschke, Y.N.: The experience and meta-experience of mood. J. Pers. Soc. Psychol. **55**(1), 102 (1988)
17. Minas, H., Edington, C., La, N., Kakuma, R.: Mental health in Vietnam. In: Minas, H., Lewis, M. (eds.) Mental Health in Asia and the Pacific. ICP, pp. 145–161. Springer, Boston (2017). https://doi.org/10.1007/978-1-4899-7999-5_10
18. Nguyen, H.D., Jiang, X., Poo, D.C.C.: Designing a social mobile platform for diabetes self-management: a theory-driven perspective. In: Meiselwitz, G. (ed.) SCSM 2015. LNCS, vol. 9182, pp. 67–77. Springer, Cham (2015). https://doi.org/10.1007/978-3-319-20367-6_8
19. Nguyen, H.D., Jiang, Y., Eiring, Ø., Poo, D.C.C., Wang, W.: Gamification design framework for mobile health: designing a home-based self-management programme for patients with chronic heart failure. In: Meiselwitz, G. (ed.) SCSM 2018. LNCS, vol. 10914, pp. 81–98. Springer, Cham (2018). https://doi.org/10.1007/978-3-319-91485-5_6
20. Nguyen, H.D., Poo, D.C.C.: Analysis and design of mobile health interventions towards informed shared decision making: an activity theory-driven perspective. J. Decis. Syst. **25**(sup1), 397–409 (2016)
21. Nguyen, H.D., Poo, D.C.C., Zhang, H., Wang, W.: Analysis and design of an mHealth intervention for community-based health education: an empirical evidence of coronary heart disease prevention program among working adults. In: Maedche, A., vom Brocke, J., Hevner, A. (eds.) DESRIST 2017. LNCS, vol. 10243, pp. 57–72. Springer, Cham (2017). https://doi.org/10.1007/978-3-319-59144-5_4
22. Pfefferbaum, B., North, C.S.: Mental health and the COVID-19 pandemic. N. Engl. J. Med. **383**(6), 510–512 (2020)
23. Randolph, C., Tierney, M.C., Mohr, E., Chase, T.N.: The repeatable battery for the assessment of neuropsychological status (RBANs): preliminary clinical validity. J. Clin. Exp. Neuropsychol. **20**(3), 310–319 (1998)
24. Shankar, A., Hamer, M., McMunn, A., Steptoe, A.: Social isolation and loneliness: relationships with cognitive function during 4 years of follow-up in the English longitudinal study of ageing. Psychosom. Med. **75**(2), 161–170 (2013)
25. United Nations - Population Division Department of Economic and Social Affairs: World Population Ageing 2017 (2017). https://bit.ly/2NelZGh
26. Van Tilburg, T.G., Steinmetz, S., Stolte, E., van der Roest, H., de Vries, D.H.: Loneliness and mental health during the covid-19 pandemic: a study among dutch older adults. Series B, J. Gerontol. (2020)
27. Vermeir, J.F., White, M.J., Johnson, D., Crombez, G., Van Ryckeghem, D.M.: The effects of gamification on computerized cognitive training: systematic review and meta-analysis. JMIR Serious Games **8**(3), e18644 (2020)
28. Vroman, K.G., Arthanat, S., Lysack, C.: "Who over 65 is online?" older adults' dispositions toward information communication technology. Comput. Hum. Behav. **43**, 156–166 (2015)
29. Vuong, D.A., Van Ginneken, E., Morris, J., Ha, S.T., Busse, R.: Mental health in Vietnam: burden of disease and availability of services. Asian J. Psychiatr. **4**(1), 65–70 (2011)
30. Wahyu Laksono, W.A., Haryanto, J., Bahiyah, K.: The impact of chess games towards comfortableness of cognitive mind on elderly. Indian J. Public Health Res. Dev. **10**(9) (2019)

31. Wang, K., Varma, D.S., Prosperi, M.: A systematic review of the effectiveness of mobile apps for monitoring and management of mental health symptoms or disorders. J. Psychiatr. Res. **107**, 73–78 (2018)
32. World Health Organization: Mental health of older adults (2017). https://www.who.int/news-room/fact-sheets/detail/mental-health-of-older-adults
33. Yehuda, N.: Music and stress. J. Adult Dev. **18**(2), 85–94 (2011)

Pandemic Discussions in VKontakte: Hopes and Fears

Kamilla Nigmatullina$^{(\boxtimes)}$ ⓘ and Nikolay Rodossky ⓘ

Saint Petersburg State University, 7/9 Universitetskaya Emb., 199034 Saint Petersburg,
Russian Federation
k.nigmatulina@spbu.ru

Abstract. The article is devoted to the reaction of the Russian-speaking audience to news reports about the pandemic in large news groups on the VKontakte platform. Based on five scenarios for the development of discussions, the authors qualitatively researched the messages and comments to them in 30 groups devoted to the local agenda of 10 different Russian regions. The found trends were confirmed by experts from these regions. As a theoretical premise, we used the texts of classic media researchers of our time (such as Jaron Lanier, Geert Lovink and John Keane) and an analysis of how emotions, such as fear and hope, actually manifest themselves in social networks during pandemic. We also used our previous work to reflect the specifics of the Russian-speaking social media ecosystem. The study shows that in both April and November, the dominant scenarios remained the utopian, denying the presence of the virus or its danger, and the realistic scenarios. At the same time, the decrease in general interest in the pandemic agenda did not affect the fact that the emotional context of its discussion became more positive.

Keywords: Social networks · Future scenarios · COVID-19 pandemic · Emotional contagion

1 Introduction

In March 2020, Russia was not an exception in facing the rise of people's activity on social networks. Self-isolation stimulated mainly search for interpersonal communication, stress relief and hopes for the future based on uncertainty. In October–November 2020, hopes and fears have been transformed into a certain set of scripts based on an increased number of "expert opinions". Emotional swing is the main characteristic of discussion patterns – from hopes to fears and vice versa. We may recall that social media are more likely to evoke negative feelings such as anxiety and envy especially during emotional collapse [1]. So-called media literacy [2] is also of a great importance today, being able to grasp the principles of the news feed which affects tremendously on our emotional sphere.

For media researchers this period was especially important as it has been lasting for quite a long period compared to other natural disasters like earthquakes or other viruses studied before. General research questions for the study were:

© Springer Nature Switzerland AG 2021
G. Meiselwitz (Ed.): HCII 2021, LNCS 12775, pp. 407–423, 2021.
https://doi.org/10.1007/978-3-030-77685-5_30

What were the dominant scenarios?
What is the list of major hopes and fears?
Which emotions and key topics dominated discourse?

Emotional patterns in social media discussions were studied by authors before [3], based on Twitter and ethno-political conflicts. In this case study VKontakte platform was chosen as the most used in Russia for posting and private messaging (49 mln authors and 1,3 bln messages in 2019 according to BrandAnalytics). Our previous study [4] has shown that for economically and industrially developed Russian regions VKontakte is the major source for news and exhaust of political sentiments. It is argued that social media may behave decadently misleading citizens about their real helplessness [5]. Compared to Twitter and Facebook, media studies of VKontakte discussions are not well-known for western academia. As for disinformation, VKontakte is actively removing all fake news regarding the pandemic. For example, in April 2020 VKontakte removed more than 800 thousand records of the same type in communities and spam mailings.

Other studies were focused on visualising patterns of Twitter discussions (for example, about Ebola and patterns of disaster scenarios [6]); accelerating facilitation of social change during times of disaster when heightened emotions embolden people [7]; sentiment mining in social media to determine how local crowds react during a disaster [8]; media practices and rituals compared offline and online during natural disasters and crisis management [9]. These and same studies provide different methods for finding correlation between emotions in social media and emotional smoothing in society in general. The open question is to what extent social media discussions reflect emotional interpersonal communication and public opinion both.

There is no dominant theoretical framework except the public sphere concept by Habermas in explaining social media discussions. We find discourse analysis framework (T. van Dijk, N. Fairclaugh) helpful to trace discussion patterns within a certain context in a certain national media system. Discourse analysis is aimed at looking for dynamics, in this case – at discussion waves of different scenarios which struggle with uncertainty. As discourse analysis is not based at fixed methodology, but is qualitative by nature, we mixed topic analysis with expert interviews.

2 Emotions in Social Networks During Pandemic

Speaking of things that help an individual get through the twists and turns of the pandemic safe and sane most of us can recall stable positive emotions, a sense of security and hygiene awareness. All of these as well as the common touch feeling, today, during the quarantine, are primarily distributed, shared, strengthened (but also endangered) by the means of social media.

Geert Lovink [10] noticed that "social networking is experienced in terms of an actual potentiality: I could contact this or that person (but I won't)". This shows the essential feature of social media – its accent on potentiality, its orientation towards the upcoming. This forward-facing perspective makes social media an ideal platform for elaborating future scenarios, discussing tomorrow's possibilities and announcing prophecies. Hope and fear are two emotions that have become especially noticeable in the communication field during the pandemic crisis. They are both directed towards the upcoming and deal with our expectations and they play a very significant role in outlining future scenarios, including those in social media.

It seems quite obvious that emotions expressed by others via online social networks influence our own moods [11]. Overall, we can attribute fear to negative emotions, while hope may be attributed to positive ones. The previous history of social media studies shows that the negative emotions are more likely to be contagious, i.e. they are spread more easily form one person to another via social media posting. Some researchers claim, that this may be due to the very nature of social media, where "people are only a few clicks away from being able to annoy frustrate or upset a whole range of people" [12]. Scientists noticed that in the communicative abundance era there are more complaints about social exclusion and political vulnerability [5].

It is also argued that social media is interested in users expressing emotions regardless of their content. As was observed, "it makes sense for digital companies to try to promote emotion expression because emotions keep people engaged on the platforms and engagement means more opportunities to present ads and gather data... For instance, Twitter messages about cancer that included joy, sadness, and hope are liked more than others, and tweets that contain joy and anger are retweeted more than others" [13]. To keep users engaged social media fulfill the news feed with emotionally contagious messages. But the point is that "negative emotions such as fear and anger well up more easily and dwell in us longer that positive ones... This is true in real life, but it is even more true in the flattened light of algorithms" [1]. It may be also argued that in a state of fear, sadness, or insecure we are more likely to buy goods advertised via social media.

No doubt that fear is one of the most (if not the most) widespread emotions in social media sphere during the COVID-19 pandemic. Different publications claim that fear "has been the most dominant emotion expressed in posts, with all negative views increasing across the English-language world" [14] and "is one of the central emotional responses during a pandemic" [15].

Being a negative emotion itself fear doesn't necessary lead to negative social consequences in the pandemic situation. Some scientists claim that fear may become a powerful and actionable health communication message, and result in wide sharing and engagement across populations [16]. Others point out that fear "increases the likelihood that citizens follow public health advice while hope can induce false optimism which can lead to lower levels of protective behavior" [15]. But in the long term, sustained fear spreading via social media can be dangerous to society and may contribute to societal value change. Researchers suggest that fear for someone's health "may increase the importance of values like security and in turn, decrease the importance of values like tolerance or caring for people outside of their immediate circles" [13].

Hope is another emotion which is commonly associated with the emotions vividly shared via social media during the pandemic crisis. In the situation of compelled social isolation social media prove "life-giving connection as well as kindness and compassion at a time when there are almost no other means to communicate" [17]. Hope is closely connected with the feeling of togetherness, that we all fight the illness as one community, and this is where social media are extremely helpful [18]. It is also argued that hope may be the result of telemedicine especially with the use of social media tools as it helps a lot in diagnostics and "also for reassurance of the patients" [19]. Social media can also be a place where anyone "can disconnect themselves from the stigma of their disease" [20] which is surprisingly common [21].

Some researchers show that emotions of hope and joy, as well as hopeful concepts about life restoration, became dominating in social media after the lockdown release, but not for long: many fearful ideas connected with economic repercussions and new possible outbursts of the virus also emerged [22].

However, hope has its own downside. According to some scientists, it can be extremely dangerous during the pandemic and "might result in a feeling of false optimism, i.e. the notion that the crisis is not as dangerous as it actually is" [15], which obviously leads to neglecting necessary restrictions and recommendations.

It should be added that the "epidemy" of both fear and false hope is spread via fake viral posts, tweets, and memes, which are mostly "inherently detached from reality" [23]. Today, when "there are ten times as many PR agents as fact-checking journalists", internet users should be ten more times cautious applying "crap detector" towards received information [24].

As we mentioned above, hope and fear play a huge role in outlining future scenarios connected with pandemic and post-pandemic situation. As for fear, the first thing that comes in mind is that any form of scenario helps people to cope with fear regardless of its nature. This is something deeply rooted in our psychology since childhood. Studies suggest that "a child who is really afraid of monsters lurking in the dark... may cope with his fear a little better if he can control the unknown monster by trapping him in the story matrix" [25]. This simple mechanism makes it easier for us to get through difficult times but it also is the reason why many conspiracy theories are so popular, including those related to the COVID-19 pandemic.

There were different classifications of business post-COVID world scenarios. One of the earliest suggests the following plots: "The passing storm" (hope that there will be no second wave), "The good company" (a surge of public-private sector partnerships emerges helps to beat the virus), "Sunrise in the east" (Asian states quickly manage to cope with the disease and then help the others) and "Lone wolves" (states isolate from one another, governments get a lot of credentials) [26]. Now we can say that the last scenario was the closest to life. Another set of scenarios points out the most significant factors that will define post-COVID-19 world: virus longevity (how long before viral infections and deaths slow down to the point where isolation policies can be lifted), global mindset (how will people's views of social, economic, and political boundaries be impacted by the virus) and digital adoption (how will consumers react to digital tools and technologies that have emerged because of the virus) [27].

In terms of politics and society there also are different versions of what happens after the pandemic crisis. Some scientists say that the accent on security and isolation might revive exclusivist moral tendencies "that limit civil liberties and reduce social justice for the sake of stability and avoidance of threat" [13]. Another frightening possibility is that government parties which take unpleasant but necessary measures to curb the pandemic will lose their popularity among people leading to populist parties gaining more support. This process is well observed in social media which show that in many societies "populist radical right parties, rather than government parties, succeed in influencing public opinion" [15] during the pandemic. It's quite important to point out that government parties usually rely on fear while populists exploit false hope and optimism. Some researchers argue that the pandemic has intensified such factors like unemployment and inequality which may result (and in different countries did result) in mass protests.

The basic method of emotion strategies analysis is discourse analysis and working with keywords. Scientists usually choose a specific social media platform in a specific period of time to study and then analyze the word usage, which show "the sentimental perusal of the text: whether is it positive, negative, or neutral" [28]. However, the very distinction between positive, negative, and neutral may be not entirely applicable: some classifications (e.g., Ekman's six emotion types and Plutchik's "wheel of emotions") comprise "surprise" as one of the fundamental emotions which cannot be attributed to any of the three [29].

3 Local Communities and Emotional Exchange

Authors claim that social networks offer typical scenarios responding to major hopes and fears: catastrophic, utopic, idealistic, realistic, fantastic. Emotional patterns in discussions do not reflect static opinions, but discursive vectors towards different scenarios. One should be aware of the sources of discourses – officials, professional journalists, amateur content creators. The common aim of grief relief is revealed in different discussion patterns and emotional triggers. With fake news, verified information, memes and numerous opinions social networks create an illusion of continuous communication about life and its scenarios. The very fact of discussion forms an impression of collective connection, compassion, and response to uncertainty.

Social networks show strategic flexibility of emotions and options to deliberate. Along with that, VKontakte tends to be a crucial platform for local authorities in Russia to shape certain discourses, with help of hashtag campaigns and volunteer movement public pages. Lack of intersections between artificially stimulated discussions and "naturally" arisen ones reveals methodological complexity to describe a whole picture of stress relief discourse.

Previous research by authors [4] revealed the complexity of Russian regional media landscapes which are remarkably diverse, including different levels of criticism in social networks. We found that level of criticism depends not only on economical factors and digital development, but on political leaders and their policy in social networks as well. For example, In Udmurt Republic (from the sample of this study) the head of region almost replaces mass media with his personal media in social networks, we see hundreds of complaints and requests in his accounts comparing to low engagements in traditional media accounts. This was once more proved by expert interviews in the new study:

The position of officials determines how acceptable this level of criticality will be, whether censorship elements will be introduced. (Kurgan region).

Spring 2020 was disastrous for traditional media in Russia, at the same time online media and social networks got new audiences and possibilities to engage them after pandemic. News and entertaining formats were in demand, and social networks took an emotional blow from people who lost face-to-face communication.

The circulation of the republican media has seriously fallen, for example, the popular non-state publications Chernovik and Novoye Delo lost up to 3–4 thousand readers. At the same time, the traffic on their sites increased, the traffic of accounts in social networks increased. During the period of self-isolation, news formats were in great demand. (Dagestan).

In this study we also considered large national research by sociological and analytical centers. First, Brand Analytics has calculated the COVID anxiety index in social media in the regions of Russia [30]. In the central regions, residents are more relaxed about the second wave. Anxiety increases with distance from the center. Kurgan region from our sample took the 4th place in top-5 of most anxious regions. Dagestan from our sample took 5th place in top-5 of most relaxed regions. Second, Public Opinion Fund continues to monitor number and tonality of messages in social media. Statistics show that VKontakte remains the main platform for COVID-discussions, followed by "Odnoklassniki" (both belong to Russian company Mail.Ru Group). Number of messages in social networks started to decrease after 5th May 2020, when graphic reached the point of 0,5 mln messages. As experts concluded in the end of 2020, the positive and the desire to adapt to new conditions were at a high level among users of social networks [31]. Monitoring of tonality demonstrated that discussions about consequences of pandemic was mostly positive regarding relationships, lifestyle, partly positive and partly negative regarding job and plans, and mostly negative regarding money and psychological state [32].

Social media (primarily groups in VKontakte) play an important role in the digital transformation of regional media landscapes in Russia. It can be assumed that local news media on digital platforms are focused on the main requests of the mass audience for operational information, social navigation and orientation, mobilization and integration, facilitating communication between the authorities and society, informing about the latest events and the situation with the coronavirus. Another important aspect of the activities of news media on social networks is the satisfaction of the need for communication, which has greatly increased during the forced self-isolation. The openness of digital platforms to critical audience discussions appears to be both a positive and a negative trend. Media experts tend to highly assess the role of social networks in the structure of regional media consumption, while the effectiveness of the audience's contact with the media is assessed ambiguously. Researchers differently assessed the role of news media in social networks in the interaction of local authorities and the population, which is especially important during the pandemic situation.

4 Method

Our sample included 10 Russian regions and their media landscapes on social media. We explored most popular public pages, which are run by professionals, officials and amateurs, and their content in April and November 2020 to find differences in future scenarios expressed in open discussions. Sample included 3 popular accounts (according to VKontakte statistics) in following regions: Mordovia, Kurgan region, Dagestan, Vladimir region, Lipetsk region, Krasnodar region, Udmurt Republic, Astrakhan region, Yamalo-Nenets Autonomous Okrug, Yekaterinburg. The choice was based on diversity principles: we collected data from national republics (Udmurt Republic, Yamalo-Nenets Autonomous Okrug, Dagestan), middle-Russia territories (Vladimir region, Lipetsk region, Kurgan region), economically developed regions (Krasnodar region, Yekaterinburg) and digitally divided ones (Dagestan, Mordovia). In every region we chose either regional city center and its media (e.g., Izhevsk in Udmurt Republic), or small district center and its media (e.g., Rylsk in Kurgan region). Two regions represent top-5 of most anxious and most relaxed regions regarding people's attitude to pandemic situation.

We used Popsters analytical tool to find most engaging posts related to pandemic in April and November – 3 for each month. Then we manually analyzed topics in comments tracing every message, where future form of verbs was used. Thus, we qualitatively processed 180 messages and comments to them in 30 VKontakte groups (see Table 1).

Table 1. List of VKontakte groups included in the sample

Region	Group name	Link
Mordovia	Podslushano Ruzaevka (Overheard in Ruzaevka)	https://vk.com/ruzvk
Mordovia	Doska pozora Saransk (Board of shame in Saransk)	https://vk.com/doska_pozora_saransk
Mordovia	Privet, seichas, Saransk (Hello, now, Saransk)	https://vk.com/saransk_photo
Kurgan region	Interesnoye v Kurgane (Interesting in Kurgan)	https://vk.com/inkgn
Kurgan region	Che Es Kurgan (Emergency in Kurgan)	https://vk.com/chs_kgn
Kurgan region	Podslushano Kurgan (Overheard in Kurgan)	https://vk.com/kurgan.overheard
Dagestan	Moy Derbent 24 (My Derbent 24)	https://vk.com/myderbentplus
Dagestan	Podslushano Derbent (Overheard in Derbent)	https://vk.com/derbent_overhear
Dagestan	Moy Derbent (My Derbent)	https://vk.com/moy_derbent
Vladimir region	Pro gorod (About the town)	https://vk.com/news_vladimir
Vladimir region	Tipichniy Vladimir (Typical Vladimir)	https://vk.com/tipichnyi_vladimir
Vladimir region	Podsluhano vo Vladimire (Overheard in Vladimir)	https://vk.com/podsluhano_vo_vladimire
Lipetsk region	Gorod 48 (Town 48)	https://vk.com/gorod48
Lipetsk region	Che Pe in Lipetsk (Emergency in Lipetsk)	https://vk.com/myregion48
Lipetsk region	Lipetsk lucshiy gorod (Lipetsk is the best town)	https://vk.com/lipa48
Krasnodar region	Tipichniy Krasnodar (Typical Krasnodar)	https://vk.com/typical_krd

(*continued*)

Table 1. (*continued*)

Region	Group name	Link
Krasnodar region	Zhest' Krasnodara i Kraya (Gore of Krasnodar and its region)	https://vk.com/ghestkrd
Krasnodar region	Che Pe in Krasnodar (Emergency in Krasnodar)	https://vk.com/krd_chp
Udmurt Republic	Izhevsk	https://vk.com/gorod_izhevsk
Udmurt Republic	Zloy Izhevchanin (Angry Izhevsk citizen)	https://vk.com/zlou18
Udmurt Republic	Udmurtia	https://vk.com/18udmurtia
Yamalo-Nenets A.O	V Salekharde (In Salekhard)	https://vk.com/inshd
Yamalo-Nenets A.O	Nadym i Nadymskiy rayon (Nadym and Nadym region)	https://vk.com/nadymregion
Yamalo-Nenets A.O	Nadym	https://vk.com/nnadym
Astrakhan region	Astrakhan VKontakte	https://vk.com/volga30
Astrakhan region	Tipichnaya Astrakhan (Typical Astrakhan)	https://vk.com/astra30
Astrakhan region	Astrakhan online	https://vk.com/astr_online
Yekaterinburg	Tipichniy Yekaterinburg (Typical Yekaterinburg)	https://vk.com/te_ekb
Yekaterinburg	Interesniy Yekaterinburg (Interesting Yekaterinburg)	https://vk.com/inburg
Yekaterinburg	Incident Yekaterinburg (Incident in Yekaterinburg)	https://vk.com/incekb

Finally, we connected comments' topics with emotional scenarios, described in advance. This is a list of possible scenarios and their key concepts:

Catastrophic – we will all die, the virus is for a long time, we are being prepared for the worst, the virus is a cover, etc.; Utopian – there is no virus; Idealistic – everything will be over soon, the vaccine is almost completed, the authorities are doing everything right; Realistic – no one knows how long it will last, some measures were correct and some were not; Fantastic – conspiracy theories, government invented coronavirus to boost ratings, the extraterrestrial origin of the virus, etc.

Each of these scenarios contains the potential to discuss both fears and hopes, with varying degrees of denial of both. A realistic scenario is assumed by us as the most acceptable, since it adequately operates with the available verified facts and expert forecasts, does not contain a strong emotional factor and corresponds to the expectations of officials who make valid decisions. Catastrophic and often fantastic scenarios carry many emotions of fear and, as a result, hatred. Fear can contribute to panic, defensive behavior and xenophobia, for instance towards people who returned from abroad or towards citizens of Moscow and Saint Petersburg. Fear can also cause stigmatization of the carriers of the virus. When fear is way too enormous people can turn to conspiracy theories, which clothe their shapeless fear in the framework of the plot (albeit the most bizarre).

At the same time, as we mentioned above, fear (if it's moderate and controlled) can have positive consequences and incline people to a realistic perception of what is happening. A person who has a reasonable amount of fear is more likely to follow government's and medical services' recommendations.

Hope on the other hand can also be helpful in establishing a realistic picture as it helps to cheer up and to stay sane. Meanwhile, hope can lead us down the road of unrealistic planning. Idealistic and utopian scenarios are saturated with deceptive hope completely. These two scenarios can be particularly dangerous for those who share these ideas, and for their family members and colleagues, as well as for the community as a whole.

Media literacy is one of the most important features that help to form and hold for oneself a realistic scenario. Indeed being a news media, regional groups in VKontakte are not usually run by professional journalists or media managers. The content provided by the users themselves is not usually filtered by such managers so a lot of misinformation can be spread via these groups. That is especially true for the pandemic situation. So being able to distinguish facts from fiction and to avoid anxiety is something that is really vital for social network users in terms of building up a scenario.

Discourse analysis was based on interpreting found scenarios in regional context, revealed in expert interviews in sample regions. Through continuous commentary scans, we looked for relevant examples of the development of discussions on key topics within the scenario.

5 Results

The results of the studies carried out in April and November are presented in the following charts (see Fig. 1 and 2). We can observe that most of the scenarios discussed and expressed by users in groups in VKontakte are utopian in both the first and second cases (34.8% in April, 34.1% in November). Realistic scenarios take the second place by a small margin (32.6% and 32.9% respectively). Catastrophic scenarios also occupy a significant, albeit much smaller proportion of users, and their share increased slightly by November (14.6% and 15.3% respectively). We can see that these three types of scenarios demonstrate stability. At the same time, the portion of fantastic scenarios increased from April to November from 10.1% to 15.3%. This growth was due to a decrease in the portion of idealistic scenarios, of which there were a small number in April (7.9%), and an insignificant number in November (2.4%).

The balance of realistic and utopian scenarios may seem surprising, especially given the change in the situation from April to November. Even more surprising is the increase in the proportion of fantastic scenarios against the background of the fall of the idealistic picture of the world, which is associated, among other things, with support of government actions. Perhaps, this is where the general critical attitude of social network users in Russia makes itself felt. "Idealists" often give more preference to television as a news media and live conversation as a means of communication.

With that being said, regional statistics do not always coincide with the general one. Some regions changed their attitude to the pandemic, and these changes took place both towards utopianism and towards realism. In a couple of regions, even catastrophic and fantastic scenarios were topping at some point. We would like to share our observations

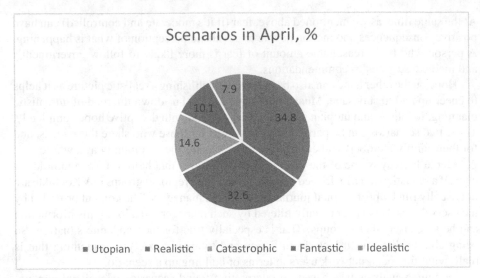

Fig. 1. Types of scenarios discussed in groups VKontakte in April 2020

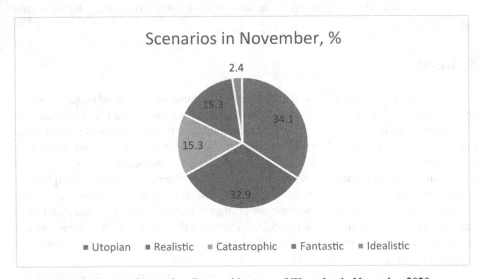

Fig. 2. Types of scenarios discussed in groups VKontakte in November 2020

in Table 2. In some cases, it was impossible to single out one dominant scenario, and we indicated several of them.

Table 2. Dominant scenarios per region in April and November

Region	April	November
Mordovia	Realistic/utopian/catastrophic	Catastrophic
Kurgan region	Realistic/utopian/catastrophic	Realistic
Dagestan	Realistic	Utopian
Vladimir region	Fantastic	Realistic
Lipetsk region	Utopian	Fantastic
Krasnodar region	Utopian	Utopian
Udmurt Republic	Fantastic/realistic	Utopian
Yamalo-Nenets A.O	Realistic	Realistic
Astrakhan region	Realistic/utopian	Utopian
Yekaterinburg	Utopian	Realistic

6   Discussion

The pandemic has become an unusual news item and has really changed a lot in the media consumption of the audience and the work of the media. The main beneficiary of the infodemic is social media, which has seen a dramatic increase in people's engagement. VKontakte statistics show that interest in the main agenda related to the virus faded out rather quickly, but the demand for emotional support only increased. People showed a high degree of anxiety in most of the regions, which resulted in support or opposition to specific scenarios. The bulk of the messages were not contained in professional media accounts, but in large amateur groups, which are not covered by the media law, but only general restrictions on content on social networks. Moderators of such groups do not interfere in the direction of the discussions, which means that their course can be considered relatively natural. Our experts proved the fact that traditional media are "losing the battle" in social platforms' environment.

> *Young people, in turn, prefer to consume content without going to other sites. Therefore, VK public pages, including news, are developing so rapidly. At the same time, the law does not regulate them in any way regarding the reliability of information, which limits traditional media. While the media is checking the data, the VK public has already issued a post and collected all the traffic. This is the pain of regional media professionals. (Kursk region).*

Our research has confirmed that negative scenarios are more "contagious" or generate more attention from the audience. Fear caused by negative scenarios really reduces the level of tolerance towards each other, provokes both a decrease in empathy and, on the contrary, false optimism. Often, the unifying trigger for the participants in the discussions turned out to be a "common enemy" in the form of the state or unknown officials or businessmen, for whom the situation was simply beneficial.

- *Zadolbali, there is nothing more to write about, people are already in a panic.*
- *Lyubov, it is a business, they deliberately create panic. This is a lot of money.* (https://vk.com/wall-39490001_838497).

It would seem that doctors should have become the unifying heroes for ordinary users, but they also received a share of negativity. The comments were related to the possible benefits of doctors who change profiles to get into the red zone, or make "favorable" diagnoses. The doctors were also accused of being unable to protect themselves from the virus and getting sick. In some regions, the official authorities had to carry out work to promote gratitude and tolerance to doctors.

- *The antenatal clinic doctors work in the red zone, leaving their pregnant women unattended, making money!!!! And pregnant women are losing their long-awaited baby!!!! Hate them!!!!* (https://vk.com/wall-108870974_539285).

Another target of hatred was residents of the capital cities, Moscow and St. Petersburg, who were found to be to blame for the spread of the virus due to movements in the regions on the May weekend. Such emotions have become a kind of bridge between the utopia that the virus does not exist and the reality in which people continue to disregard the regime and infect others.

- *Muscovites must be driven back to their anthill. Let them get sick there. And then they ate barbecue on Saturday, and then went to spread the infection.* (https://vk.com/wall-26617714_281937).

The Russian audience shows a high emotional component when discussing sensitive topics, but the set of these topics is difficult to compare with other countries. For example, social media users are sensitive not only to local events, but also to the international agenda. The argument "you want it like in the USA" or "you want it like in Europe" is presented if the reasons from domestic politics run out.

Of particular interest is the catastrophic scenario of the development of events, since it has absorbed the maximum number of variations on the topic of what harm the virus and pandemic will cause. For example, either death from the virus or hunger strike awaits us, it will be worse further; people in masks are like experimental mice, it is not clear why we wear them; this is just the beginning of some more terrible scenario.

- *Maybe it's offtop. It seems to me that this virus will not pass even on April 30. The measures will not get better. If, for example, even people are released to work, there will be infection again. Whatever one may say, either infection or there will be a hunger strike. Result: Either we will go to the next world because of the virus, or from loans and hunger strike.* (https://vk.com/wall-37473293_1528184)
- *80 years ago, Alexander Chizhevsky set up an experiment: he placed the mice under a sealed glass cover and began to supply air into it through a 12-cm cotton filter. A week later, the mice began to behave sluggishly, and 3 weeks after the start of the experiment, the animals fell into a coma, then agony began,*

and, as a result, the last mouse died on day 24. (https://vk.com/wall-55811535_92627)

Some fantastic scenarios are mesmerizing. However, we must say that the growth of conspiracy theories is observed during the pandemic around the world.

– *There is a disease, there is death, BUT! It's a game of Rockefellers, Gates, freemasons... Human life today has no value. They want to enslave us, make us a herd without a name, a surname – a cyborg under a code! On pain of death, we are brought to our knees.* (https://vk.com/wall-108870974_505037)
– *This is a world conspiracy! The people were intimidated, so any death can be attributed to the coronavirus. The circus was staged, word of mouth would have long let know about the real deaths from the coronavirus. Everyone has friends abroad, one could call and find out the fact. Nevertheless, the elections are coming soon, the rating must be raised. Soon to elect the Tsar, this is another term for Vladimir Putin.* (https://vk.com/wall-26617714_281565)
– *The elderly and the sick are exterminated by an artificially created virus... children under the guise of a remote location... let them grow dumb... that's all... stupid herd of surviving slaves... Teach your children before it's too late... explain to them why they do it to us...* (https://vk.com/wall-23684992_475936)

Utopian scenarios boil down to the idea that there is no virus or that it is no more dangerous than the usual flu. At the same time, users criticize the measures taken by the authorities to combat the virus as excessive (which sharply distinguishes these scenarios from idealistic).

– *Doctors will now find a virus in anyone, for this they will immediately receive a premium* (https://vk.com/wall-39490001_803747)
– *Are there any relatives confirming this information about the virus, or neighbors of these infected? For me, there is nothing more than words. Bullshit.* (https://vk.com/wall-108870974_499535)
– *It is a fact that the medical component of this epidemic looks more and more doubtful every day. The disease is obvious, but what kind of disease it is, what is its epidemic threshold, how much more dangerous this particular disease is than "ordinary" and trivial epidemics of influenza is a mystery today. A mystery simply because everything is covered by a wave of panic, hysteria, fear. The fear is irrational, and most importantly – in many ways "induced".* (https://vk.com/wall-23684992_403537)

There are also idealistic scenarios. There are very few of them, especially in November, but in April there are still users who believe that the pandemic will soon end if the recommended sanitary measures are followed.

– *But we will cope with the virus, the main thing is to stay at home, not to spread the virus further and everything will be cool by the end of the month!* (https://vk.com/wall-146919455_614295)

- *If you follow precautions and self-isolation, then I think people will also be able to protect themselves from the new strain of influenza.* (https://vk.com/wall-322 371_212003)

A large proportion of realistic scenarios inspire joy, reasonable hope and even confidence in the future victory over the pandemic. It cannot be said that their number increased from April to November, but, on the other hand, their stability suggests that there are enough people in Russia who are ready to take proper precautions and, most importantly, who have media literacy and are able to distinguish truth from lies.

- *Speaking out against wearing masks is like speaking out against wearing safety helmets on a construction site.* (https://vk.com/wall-101515078_3051176)
- *Guys, is it difficult for you to put on a mask and gloves? You understand that there are children around you, and your parents, and the people in general. Are you forced to carry bags of sugar or something heavier? When will you finally realize this is serious? The whole world is on its head. Well, we are the smartest of all, until we personally are affected!* (https://vk.com/wall-508 02562_934877)

Many "realists" compare the situation in Russia and in other countries and criticize the measures taken in Russia, without falling into conspiracy theories or panic.

- *Because in China they did not become impudent, but strictly observed quarantine! And here, you see for yourself, people are in command, similar to those who comment... The feeling that the people, at best, received three classes of education in the parish.* (https://vk.com/wall-8152398_1461171).

A critical tone is, in principle, characteristic of the carriers of realistic scenarios.

- *For appearing in shops, transport and any other spaces without a protective mask will be fined. This is all great, of course. But there are still no medical masks in pharmacies.* (https://vk.com/wall-32182751_5620768)
- *People were detained on the streets for movement and placed in cramped quarters for many hours. During an epidemic. Thus, a threat was created to the life and health of people, as well as to their family members. This is how our authorities are fighting the epidemic. Forcing dozens of people to spend hours in tight spaces.* (https://vk.com/wall-54825165_252024)
- *Surveillance cameras are being installed in clinics and hospitals in the Kurgan region.*
- *Absolutely f*cked up. We need equipment, medicines, doctors. They put f*cking cameras.* (https://vk.com/wall-57699201_198551)
- *What distance can we talk about if in the morning people go to work like sprats in a can. Carriers, meanwhile, are reducing the number of buses on their routes. Everything for people!* (https://vk.com/wall-39490001_838497)

Following one of the scenarios by the audience created the effect of forming connections within the community on the social networks' platform. However, we believe that this was an illusion based on emotional instability and carrying more communication gaps than a positive effect. The keywords that were found in these discussions conveyed more fear than hope and increased the degree of uncertainty. Even the shift of discussions from utopian to real scenarios does not contain a large number of arguments related to stabilizing the situation. It should also be borne in mind that VKontakte as a platform is not an expert platform like Facebook, here we often meet the opinion of ordinary people who do not possess specialized information, who are not versed in media and infodemic processes, and, as a result, who cannot come to a constructive end to the discussion with a limited set of arguments.

Although it is generally accepted that fear and other negative emotions are more prevalent in social networks, in our sample we see that the dominant scenarios in social networks in Russian regions are utopian and realistic scenarios. In the first, the main emotional component is hope (albeit reckless), in the second, reasonable fear is balanced by reasonable hope and common sense. Catastrophic and fantastic scenarios based on uncontrolled fear are obviously less common. We also saw that communication on social networks often took on a bright emotional connotation. Users felt that they belonged to a particular community, felt their closeness with others, albeit often through opposing themselves to people who believe in other scenarios. This is a feature that should not be underestimated in a pandemic era. Although the arguments of the parties were not particularly logical and supported by unconditional facts, we hope that many users could adjust their ideas towards a realistic scenario by reading the comments in the VKontakte groups.

7 Conclusion

Our research has shown that of the five scenarios that were typical for discussions on various social networks, for VKontakte and the Russian-speaking audience the most engaging were the utopian and realistic in both April and May. At the same time, the idealistic scenario was practically forgotten, and the number of users sharing fantastic attitudes increased slightly. A qualitative analysis of the discussions showed that people were more inclined to intensify fears or to neutralize them through denial and false hopes, and to a lesser extent – to critical analysis and fantastic conspiracy theories. General interest in the topic of the pandemic fell sharply by November, but at the same time the negative emotional background in the remaining discussions increased. Emotional reactions towards medical workers, which in a real scenario have a positive connotation, and in the rest have a negative one, were also ambiguous. The commentators' aggression mainly concerned officials, big business and partly the actions of doctors.

In conclusion, we may say that emotions, primarily fear and hope, can fuel different scenarios of the future. Different types of scenarios, reflecting the expectations of users during a crisis period, can replace each other, collide, become obsolete over time, or, on the contrary, demonstrate a certain stability. The study of these scenarios and their transformations helps to understand the mood of society, and, consequently, to find new ways to coordinate society and government in a pandemic situation.

References

1. Lanier, J.: Ten Arguments for Deleting Your Social Media Accounts Right Now. Henry Holt and Co., New York (2018)
2. Lovink, G.: Overcoming Internet Disillusionment: On the Principles of Meme Design. In: Lovink, G. (ed.) Sad by Design, pp. 13–22. Pluto Press, London (2019)
3. Nigmatullina, K., Bodrunova, S.S.: Patterns of emotional argumentation in twitter discussions. In: Bodrunova, S.S., et al. (eds.) INSCI 2018. LNCS, vol. 11551, pp. 72–79. Springer, Cham (2019). https://doi.org/10.1007/978-3-030-17705-8_7
4. Litvinenko, A., Nigmatullina, K.: Local dimensions of media freedom in Russia: a comparative analysis of news media landscapes in 33 Russian regions. Demokratizatsiya J. Post-Soviet Democratization, **28**(3), 393–418 (2020). George Washington University, Washington, DC
5. Keane, J.: Democracy and Media Decadence. Cambridge University Press, Cambridge (2013). https://doi.org/10.1017/CBO9781107300767.001
6. Lu, Y., Hu, X., Wang, F., Kumar, S., Liu, H, Maciejewskial R.: Visualizing social media sentiment in disaster scenarios. In: Proceedings of the 24th International Conference on World Wide Web, pp. 1211–1215. Association for Computing Machinery, Florence (2015)
7. Al-Saggaf, Y., Simmons, P.: Social media in Saudi Arabia: exploring its use during two natural disasters. In: Technological Forecasting and Social Change, vol. 95, pp. 3–15. Elsevier, Amsterdam (2015). https://doi.org/10.1016/j.techfore.2014.08.013
8. Beigi, G., Hu, X., Maciejewski, R., Liu, H.: An overview of sentiment analysis in social media and its applications in disaster relief. In: Pedrycz, W., Chen, S.-M. (eds.) Sentiment Analysis and Ontology Engineering. SCI, vol. 639, pp. 313–340. Springer, Cham (2016). https://doi.org/10.1007/978-3-319-30319-2_13
9. Hjorth, L., Kim, K.Y.: The mourning after: a case study of social media in the 3.11 earthquake disaster in Japan. Telev. New Media **12**(6), 552–559 (2011). https://doi.org/10.1177/1527476411418351
10. Lovink, G.: What is the social in social media? In: Papastergiadis, N., Lynn, V. (eds.) Art in the Global Present, pp. 97–111. UTS ePress, Sydney (2014)
11. Kramer, A., Guillory, J., Hancock, J.: Experimental evidence of massive-scale emotional contagion through social networks. Proc. Natl. Acad. Sci. **111**(24), 8788–8790 (2014). https://doi.org/10.1073/pnas.1320040111
12. Wakefield, J.: Why are people so mean to each other online? BBC (2015). https://www.bbc.com. Accessed 10 Feb 2021
13. Steinert, S.: Corona and value change. The role of social media and emotional contagion. Ethics Inf. Technol. 1 (2020). https://doi.org/10.1007/s10676-020-09545-z
14. Morrison, R.: 'Fear' is the most widespread emotion on social media for the fourth day in a row as coronavirus continues to spread around the world, study shows. Daily Mail (2020). https://www.dailymail.co.uk. Accessed 10 Feb 2021
15. Widmann, T.: Who Played Down the COVID-19 Pandemic? Strategic Emotional Rhetoric. In: Political Communication and its Impact on the Mass Public (2020). https://doi.org/10.2139/ssrn.3679484
16. Ali, K., Zain-ul-abdin, K., Li, C., Johns, L., Ali, A.A., Carcioppolo, N.: Viruses going viral: impact of fear-arousing sensationalist social media messages on user engagement. Sci. Commun. **41**(3), 314–338 (2019). https://doi.org/10.1177/1075547019846124
17. Waxman, S.: Can Social Media and Technology Come to the Rescue in a Pandemic? WrapPRO (2020). https://www.thewrap.com. Accessed 10 Feb 2021
18. Sheerman, L., Marston, H.R., Musselwhite, C., Morgan, D.: COVID-19 and the secret virtual assistants: the social weapons for a state of emergency. Emerald Open Res. **2**(19) (2020). https://doi.org/10.35241/emeraldopenres.13571.1

19. Waseem, M., Aziz, N.: Role of social media in diagnosis & management of COVID-19: an experience of a pulmonologist. Annals of King Edward Med. Univ. **26**, 233–234 (2020)
20. Payton, F.C., Conley, C.: Fear or danger threat messaging: the dark side of social media. In: Bennet, A. (ed) Social Media: Global Perspectives, Applications and Benefits and Dangers, pp. 23–38. Nova Science Publishers, Hauppauge (2015)
21. Chandrashekhar, V.: The burden of stigma: From leprosy to COVID-19, how stigma makes it harder to fight epidemics. Science **369**(6510), 1419–1423 (2020). https://doi.org/10.1126/science.369.6510.1419
22. Stella, M.: Social discourse and reopening after COVID-19: a post-lockdown analysis of flickering emotions and trending stances in Italy. First Monday **25**(11) (2020). https://doi.org/10.5210/fm.v25i11.10881
23. Lanier, J.: Dawn of the New Everything: A Journey Through Virtual Reality. Penguin Random House, London (2017)
24. Lovink, G.: After the social media hype: dealing with information overload. e-flux, vol. 45 (2013)
25. Grider, S.A.: Children's ghost stories. In: Goldstein, D.E., Grider, S.A., Thomas, J.B. (eds.) Haunting Experiences: Ghosts in Contemporary Folklore, pp. 111–140. Utah State University Press, Logan (2007)
26. The world remade by COVID-19. Recover: Planning scenarios for resilient leaders. Deloitte (2020). https://www2.deloitte.com. Accessed 10 Feb 2021
27. Wade, M.: Scenario Planning for a Post-COVID-19 World. Institute for Management Development (2020). https://www.imd.org. Accessed 10 Feb 2021
28. Dheeraj, K.: Analysing COVID-19 news impact on social media aggregation in international journal of advanced trends. Comput. Sci. Eng. **9**(3), 2848–2855 (2020). https://doi.org/10.30534/ijatcse/2020/56932020
29. Li, Q., Wei, C., Dang, J., Cao, L., Liu, L.: Tracking and analyzing public emotion evolutions during COVID-19: a case study from the event-driven perspective on microblogs. Int. J. Environ. Res. Public Health **17**, 6888 (2020). https://doi.org/10.3390/ijerph1718688
30. Social Media COVID Anxiety Index 2020: Russia, Ukraine, Kazakhstan, Belarus, Armenia, Moldova. "Is there a second wave of discussions?" (in Russian). Brand Analytics (2020). https://br-analytics.ru. Accessed 10 Feb 2021
31. COVID on social media: Summary for 2020. Coronavirus attacked on all fronts, but positive sentiment persisted (in Russian). COVID-fom (2020). https://covid19.fom.ru. Accessed 10 Feb 2021
32. Sentiment Index of Consequences Discussion in Social Media (in Russian). COVID-fom (2020). https://covid19.fom.ru. Accessed 10 Feb 2021

Coaching Older Adults in Health Games: A Goal Oriented Modelling Approach

Zhengxiang Pan[1,2]([✉]), Yaming Zhang[2,3], Hao Zhang[2], and Zhiqi Shen[2,3]

[1] Interdisciplinary Graduate School, Nanyang Technological University, Singapore, Singapore
panz0012@e.ntu.edu.sg
[2] Joint NTU-UBC Research Centre of Excellence in Active Living for the Elderly,
Nanyang Technological University, Singapore, Singapore
{zhangym,zhang.h,zqshen}@ntu.edu.sg
[3] School of Computer Science and Engineering, Nanyang Technological University,
Singapore, Singapore

Abstract. Coaching is a novel integrative method to help older adults with little prior experience with digital technology to interact properly with health games. However, coaching as a practice is rather case-specific and none has attempted to apply coaching into health games. This paper presents a formalized, integrative coaching model that infuses Goal Net with Propp's functions to outline a flow of events that eventually assemble into a "coached gameplay session". With the formalization of the Goal-Oriented Storytelling Model, the role of the coach in a health game session becomes clearer. The study presented in this paper validates GSM-driven coaching as an effective approach to bolster confidence among older adults when they interact with health games. The GSM also makes a generalizable, scalable solution to health game enjoyment possible through facilitating the creation of future digital health game coaches.

Keywords: Health game · Coaching · Storytelling · Goal net · Game literacy

1 Introduction

1.1 Background

The gaming industry is going through an unprecedented rise in in the last decade. The growth rate of global games market is forecasted to increase from 2018 up until 2023 [1]. Commercial video games which provide rich experiences are continuously being released to provide entertainment to the masses, even among the elderly population.

A study by AARP [2] showed a significant rise in gaming among older adults. The number of gamers older than 50 years old has risen by approximately 10 million from 2016 to 2019 (from 38% to 44% of the population). Games' popularity among seniors is also reflected in the money spent on games, from $523 million to $3.5 billion within the same timeframe.

Games' popularity among older adults has created an avenue for practical applications such as serious games. Serious games are games that go beyond entertainment,

G. Meiselwitz (Ed.): HCII 2021, LNCS 12775, pp. 424–442, 2021.
https://doi.org/10.1007/978-3-030-77685-5_31

designed to achieve a meaningful purpose that is significant in the real world. While they typically do entertain, the more valued 'serious' purposes are typically related to transmitting knowledge, developing skills, or inducing healthy behavior change [3].

1.2 Research Problem: Low Motivation for Adopting Health Games

The definitive "serious" aspect of health games can be a drawback as well. To be specific, the need for serious use (e.g. reliability, scientifically proven) has placed a constraint for serious health games in terms of appeal to the players. Lu and Kharrazi [4] conducted a systematic review on the state-of-the-art of health games and revealed the less obvious cracks in the wall. From health games being released from 2018 back to 1983, they have observed:

- More than 84% of health games are designed for the healthy general public, indicating the need for a "health game motivator" which is scalable.
- Games for health have slowed in production since 2014; developing more health games is likely not be the proper way to increase adoption.

Other researchers agree that health games market is still at an early stage with relatively low investments compared to commercial games [5]. When comparing the game experience, health games are generally still limited to offering short-term engagement through extrinsic rewards [6], in contrast to the rich, vast, and varied experiences offered by the commercial game industry which many reported to genuinely enjoy [7].

From the observations above, there is a need to create better health game experiences to motivate the population to adopt health games. This need is especially relevant among the older population where health games are projected to bring the most benefits.

1.3 Research Question: How Do We Systematically Coach Older Adults to Enjoy Health Games?

A research gap exists in exploring health game experiences *outside* the game world. While existing studies place focus on improving the in-game design of health games [8, 9], there is still a need to address the game experience from the player's perspective; after all, for engaging game experiences between health games and older adults to manifest, we need to investigate older adults' ability to understand games too. Unlike the younger generation who grew up with video games, the older generation has to rely on their understanding towards the real world to obtain basic game literacy. Only then, they can start to appreciate digital games and reap the health benefits from serious health games. In short, when the goal is to create positive health game experiences, helping older players increase their game literacy complements existing HCI-focused approaches on health games' design.

A Goal-Oriented Approach to Coaching

Thus for older players, the practice of *coaching* is proposed to cater to this group of "digital immigrants" who may not possess the knowledge nor the ability to interact well with digital games. Coaching as a practice tends to be case-specific with little generalizability. Despite that, several coaching models have been proposed to attempt to identify common practices that produce positive coaching outcomes. According to the Handbook of Coaching Psychology [10, p. 10], coaching psychologists employ more than 28 different coaching models, each of which are typically rooted in psychology theories. The various coaching models typically involve one-to-one sessions between the coach and coachee. Coaching models acknowledge that ultimately, the real-world practices are still up to providing *personalized* aid to the coachee to realize their goals.

To provide consensus on the concept of coaching, Olsen [11] formalized a broader understanding towards the act of coaching by describing it as a focused, goal-oriented process filled with both recurring and evolving methods of progression. We found this practice of coaching to be applicable in health games' context. The systematic, goal-oriented approach of coaching an elderly through an unfamiliar digital realm has potential to yield a fruitful learning experience for them. The ideal implementation of the coaching model would take shape in the form of a personalized, goal-oriented coach which issues help upon facing errors, provides continuous feedback, and impart a constant stream of motivation or encouragement to the player as they play a health game.

Hence this paper proposes a goal-oriented coaching model in order to systematically provide coaching to older adults in health games. The proposed model, structured with storytelling theories, is named as the Goal-Oriented Storytelling Model (GSM). The organization of the paper is as follows: Sect. 2 proposes a general model for GSM, namely how storytelling can be modelled using Goal Net to form coaching scenarios. Section 3 presents a study on how GSM-driven coaching helps enhance older adults' game performance and game literacy, at the same time enjoy better game experience.

2 Concepts of the Goal-Oriented Storytelling Model

The Goal-Oriented Storytelling Model (GSM) is applied on top of an existing health game to generate "coached gameplay sessions": predefined sets of gameplay that players will play through in one sitting with the company of a game coach. Through this model of planning and coaching, it is hypothesized that older adults will find it easier to accept and enjoy health games delivered in such gameplay sessions. Key concepts of the GSM are presented below.

2.1 Storytelling

Propp's theory uses 31 functions [12] to generalize fairytales and folklores that have captivated people through the years. Propp's 31 Functions have been used extensively as story generation models, including stories that aim to promote health or cultivate interest for particular subjects. However, there has been little research on the role of Propp's 31 Functions in describing real life experiences as it happens.

Researchers support the use of storytelling in describing an individual's experience instead of simply telling a story. Studies have shown that the persuasive effect of narrative promoting health behavior is largely influenced by how relatable the story is to the reader's past experiences (i.e. self-referencing) [13, 14]. Logically, the most relatable story that a person can experience is his/her *own* past experiences. This is also known as the *narrative construction of reality*.

This *narrative construction of reality* has also been applied in *narrative coaching* [15], where coachees tell the coach stories about their own experiences to revise, reflect and rechart their behavior through externalizing and vocalizing their thoughts.

In this light, there is enough support in re-applying Propp's functions to describe the health game coaching process. Admittedly, Propp's functions as mere "descriptors of the gameplay process" is still rather abstract. A goal-oriented modelling approach is needed to provide actionable framework so that a better understanding can be established on "what are coached gameplay sessions".

2.2 Goal Net Modelling Approach

Intelligent agents have seen applications in digital games especially in aspects like storytelling and AI controlled characters [16]. Intelligent agents are also starting to be applied in e-health coaching, which typically involves making "smart" decisions on setting motivating goals for the coachee [17]. These agents are usually driven with a model that allows them to make correct or at least convincing decisions given a situation. The Goal Net modelling technique developed by Shen [18] is one such model.

Goal Net emphasizes on having agents achieve the goals that are set out for them. It does so by providing a systematic methodology to capture the dynamic relationship among goals and provide an orderly structure for them. Goal Net modelling encourages us to think in a modular way when breaking down complex goals into simpler achievable goals, which is desirable in helping us dissect the coaching process into different sets of coaching scenarios. A game coach (AI or human) could then follow the coaching model's guidelines to design a health game into manageable segments before deciding how much to put into a single gaming session. This guided approach to conduct "gaming sessions" also helps elderly without prior game literacy to ease into the process by engaging with it as a set of "trainings" or "learning sessions" instead.

Main Components

In Goal Net, four main components have been defined to visualize different implementations: goals, transitions, and arcs. Their relationships are summarized as follows:

- Arcs are arrows that connect the input goal (s1) to the transition (tr1), and the transition to the output goal (s2) (see Fig. 1).
- Each transition is associated to a task list, which defines the possible task(s) that may be performed by the agent to proceed to the output goal.
- Goals are represented as states[1] that the agent transits along. States can be classified into composite states or atomic states.

- An atomic state represents a goal that is deemed specific enough and cannot be further broken down.
- A composite state tends to be a more abstract goal that can be broken down into sub goals, eventually decomposing into atomic goals.

---

[1] In Goal Net, the term *states* and *goals* are used interchangeably.

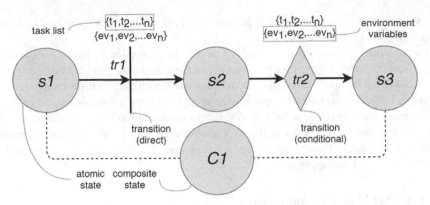

Fig. 1. Basic components of a goal net

Modelling Propp's functions using Goal Net should yield us a logical flow of events that take place during a coached gameplay session. These flows of events are termed as "coaching scenarios" below.

2.3 Coaching Scenarios: Goal Net General Model for Health Game Coaching

4 coaching scenarios are presented in this section. They are essentially Propp's functions modelled together using Goal Net methodology in context of playing health games, and they serve as building blocks for coached gameplay sessions. Thus, "coaching scenarios" provide an essential bridge by grouping the detailed and nuanced Propp's functions together to describe an implementable template for crafting coached gameplay sessions.

Each scenario is modelled in GSM as a composite goal, which each consists of several Propp's functions. After presenting each coaching scenario, the composite goals are then assembled to form a coherent coached gameplay session.

Coaching Scenario 1: Introducing the Game
In Propp's theory, a story typically starts with the Hero being addressed with a request. In the case of playing health games, the coach introduces the health game to the elderly. The Introduction of the health game consists of two states: an "Initial Condition" before commencement of the gameplay session, and the "Interdiction" where the coach introduces the health game to the elderly player (Fig. 2). As part of the coach's preparation, we recommend spending effort on finding the best way to explicitly present the game's health values to the participant. This helps them perceive the health game as personally relevant and useful, which is a key motivator towards health game adoption.

With the Pumpkin Garden game as an example, it may be suitable to highlight it as a Parkinson's Disease rehabilitation game [19] to PD patients. Whereas to non-patients, it is more appropriate to introduce the game's early detection of PD [20] to be more personally relevant.

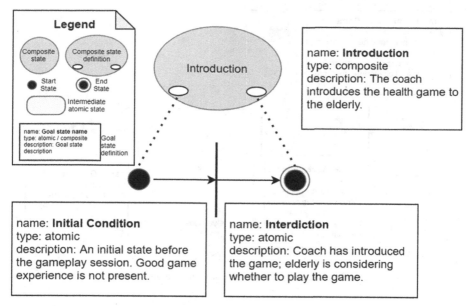

Fig. 2. Coaching scenario 1: introducing the game

Coaching Scenario 2: Completing a Game Goal

A particular stretch of Propp's functions illustrate the Hero's journey to their adventure's destination. The journey is typically less than smooth. Challenges will be encountered and here is where the reader gets engaged with the story as they watch the Hero learn and grow from the numerous challenges they encounter. The health game session acts as a learning journey for an elderly and is similarly not without its challenges.

This scenario illustrates the coaching process when the coach sets a specific goal for the elderly and they start to attempt it (Departure). From here, either the elderly will have no issues in achieving the goal (Guidance), or they will realize that they have missing knowledge that prevents them from achieving the game goal (Absentation). We anticipate that elderlies with little to no prior exposure to video games (i.e. low game literacy) will fall into Absentation more often. After Absentation, 1 or more challenges will be encountered. All challenges must be resolved to complete the current game goal (Guidance), hence the diamond-shaped arrow indicating "all-of" relation [18, p. 53]. The flow of events described above are modelled in Fig. 3.

Coaching Scenario 2–1: Overcoming a Challenge During Goal Completion

In the process of achieving a game goal, one or more challenges may be encountered by the elderly. Here we show the intermediate states that comprises a single challenge. The elderly player is tested (Testing), the coach observes their reaction and determine if help is needed, and they subsequently complete the challenge.

The elderly players can sometimes figure out what to do by themselves. In this case, it is better to encourage them instead of directly helping them; doing is one of the most effective way to learn after all [21], and being able to figure out complex problems are

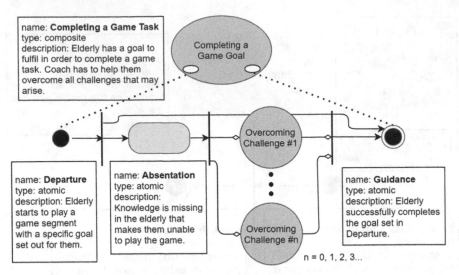

Fig. 3. Coaching scenario 2: completing a game goal

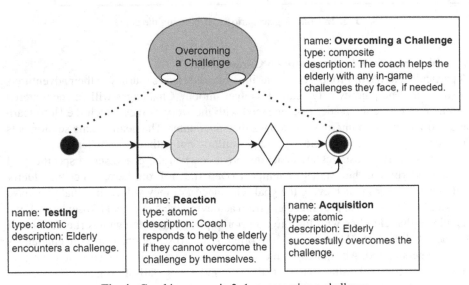

Fig. 4. Coaching scenario 2–1: overcoming a challenge

one of the key satisfactions in gaming. In this case, the elderly immediately proceeds to the Acquisition stage (Fig. 3).

On the flipside, it is expected that older adults who do not have prior exposure to digital games will often not be able to resolve in-game challenges. From a "compassionate" point of view [22], researchers support that digital games can be made easier if it meant providing a better game experience for the elderly [23, 24]. Hence, help should be given to them in a step-by-step and easy to understand format (Reaction). The coach could also consider lowering the passing mark if it means the elderly gets to continue with the rest of the game. The elderly player eventually resolves the current challenge (Acquisition), with or without help from the game coach. The flow of events described above are modelled in Fig. 4.

Coaching Scenario 3: The Final Challenge
One of a story's climax features the Hero facing off an ultimate challenge before claiming Victory. If we re-apply this concept into a coached gameplay session, it means the coach needs to prepare a gameplay segment as a "Final Challenge" to test what the elderly had learnt in the previous game tasks they have completed. The segment should only contain gameplay that is familiar to the player. The level of challenge perceived by the elderly can be increased via gameplay mechanics (e.g. set time limits, require more skills). The coach can also artificially create more challenges by prompting the player for responses instead of giving the usual step-by-step guidance. On the flipside, considering that the elderly player may have reduced ability to complete the game, the increase of challenge should not be overdone; the coach in this case needs to regulate the difficulty through the amount of help provided (Fig. 5).

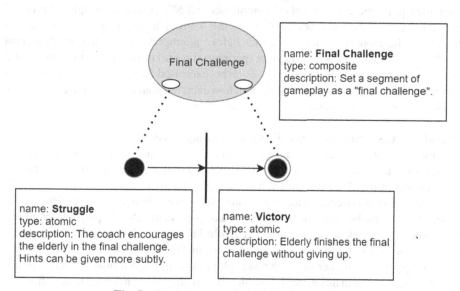

Fig. 5. Coaching scenario 3: the final challenge

If successful, the optimal challenge provided in the gameplay session (with its conception guided by Propp's narrative theory) can help the elderly achieve a psychological need for achievement [25], thereby improving game experience for the elderly.

Coaching Scenario 4: Persuading the Elderly to Continue the Game
It is a well-known issue that non-adherence is a frequent matter when attempting to teach the elderly on using digital products [26]. A similarity exists in Propp's storyline as well: when the Hero is addressed with a request, they may refuse to take on the challenge. Effort is required to change their mind over time, obtaining compliance (Fig. 6).

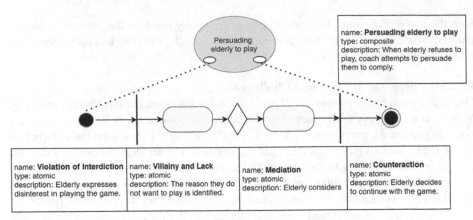

Fig. 6. Coaching scenario 4: persuading the elderly to continue the game

In this case, persuasion techniques can come in useful as part of the coaching process as an attempt to obtain the elderlies' compliance. ELM's central or peripheral route of persuasion can be explored here. Following the 4 Propp's functions above, the coach should first hear out the elderly's reasons before attempting to provide re-affirmation that they will be well guided throughout (peripheral route) or remind them of the health benefits (central route). Flexibility needs to be exercised here to gain cooperation as conversations can be rather context-specific; however, the goal here is to have the elderly decide to give the games another try (Counteraction).

Assembling GSM Sub-goal-Nets into a Gameplay Session
The sub-goal-nets that describe the various coaching scenarios can be assembled into a general model. The general model (Fig. 7 below) outlines the essential components above as part of the GSM-driven coached gameplay session.

A GSM-driven coached gameplay session starts with an introduction of the health game. Then, *n* number of game tasks will be assigned to the elderly player to complete (selection of game task sequence can be fixed, rule-based or random). During this process, the coach may need to persuade the elderly to continue playing if they express disinterest. After completing *n* number of game tasks, players go through a final challenge to test what they have learnt in this gameplay session before they are considered to have finished the gameplay session.

From the general model in Fig. 7 below, the game coach should segment out well-defined tasks from an existing health game. These in-game tasks will then each form a composite goal (see Overcoming Challenge #1 to #n in Fig. 3 above) with clear achievable goals. The coach who designs the gameplay session should also set aside a gameplay segment to serve as the "final challenge". The amount of challenge should be relatively higher in this "final challenge". No new gameplay elements should be introduced, so that the player may focus on reapplying familiar gameplay knowledge gained beforehand. By formalizing a methodology to coach older adults through a health game, it is anticipated that they can become more motivated to play health games from the improved game experience.

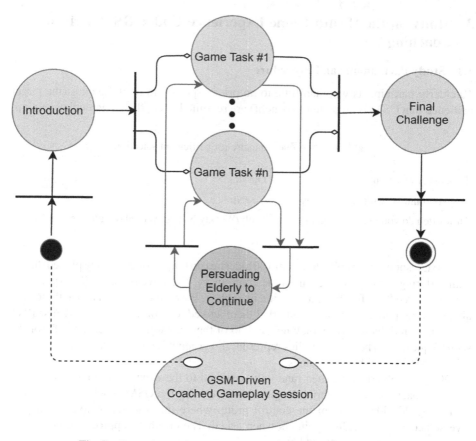

Fig. 7. General model of GSM-driven coached gameplay session

2.4 Summary of the GSM

In Sect. 2, Propp's functions and the Goal Net modelling technique were introduced as existing theories for modelling our coached gameplay sessions for older adults when they play health games. 4 *coaching scenarios* are then modelled into composite goals. The proposed *coaching scenarios* serve as intermediate building blocks that connect the discrete Propp's functions with the coherent flow of a gameplay session. After introducing the coaching scenarios, a general model is proposed to assemble the coaching scenarios into a coached gameplay session. This prepares the game coach to help players overcome in-game difficulties and persuade the player to continue if they want to give up. The GSM-driven approach of health game coaching is then evaluated in a study for its positive effects in creating enjoyable game experiences and fruitful learning sessions.

3 Study on the Health Game Experience Under GSM-Driven Coaching

3.1 Study Participants and Procedure

40 elderly participants who had little to no prior exposure to digital games (the target audience that GSM is projected to benefit) are recruited to conduct a gameplay session.

Table 1. Short questionnaire for participant selection

Pre-survey question	Options
Are you familiar with video games?	Yes/No
How often do you play video games?	Daily/Weekly/Not actively playing/Never played

First, responses are collected from 100 elderlies on how frequently they played digital games during a lucky draw event in the community. Then, we selected 50 respondents who answered "no" for the first question in Table 1. We contacted them to see if they are able to participate in our study, and 40 of them agreed. Out of the 40 respondents, 10 of them answered "not actively playing" and 30 of them answered "never played" for the second question. These 40 elderlies represent the group of elderlies who had little to no prior experience with video games.

20 of the elderlies are then randomly assigned to the experiment group which we actively coach them throughout the game session using the GSM coaching model. The remaining 20 elderlies form the control group where the researcher takes on a passive stance, only providing pointers when asked. The coaching approach used for the experiment group is elaborated below.

3.2 Goal Net of GSM Implementation for the Pumpkin Garden Health Game

The Pumpkin Garden health game for Parkinson's Disease early detection and rehabilitation [19, 20] is used to conduct the study to validate GSM's coaching approach.

For a single session, players play through 3 rounds of the water wheel minigame (using their fingers, the Microsoft Arc Mouse, and the Apple Pencil respectively) and 1 round of the weed clearing minigame. Each minigame consists of 6 rounds with slight variations in-between (e.g. switch hands that turn the water wheel, cut weeds growing in different shapes). Each minigame has 6 rounds. Thus, each minigame forms a *gameplay segment* where the goal for our elderly is to complete 6 rounds in the minigame.

The 4 gameplay segments (minigames) are ordered sequentially, forming a gameplay session, and the "Final Challenge" is defined as the last round in the weed-clearing minigame due to the significantly increased challenges (in the last round, participants have time constraints to clear the weeds on-screen, opposed to the usual static gameplay at the player's own pace in the previous 5 rounds).

The goal net generated from our GSM implementation (Fig. 8 below) features "conducting a coached gameplay session for the Pumpkin Garden health game" as our composite goal. It is then broken down into sub-goals that must be completed in sequence for the main composite goal to be considered complete (the sequential approach is selected for its simplicity as we are validating the coaching model's effectiveness as a whole). The sub goals are the various Propp's functions that represent different story points that our elderly players traverse throughout their gameplay session.

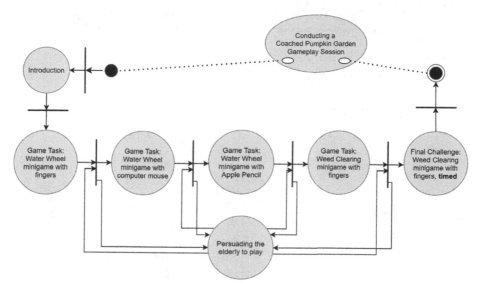

Fig. 8. GSM goal net implementation for study

3.3   Study Goals and Results Collected

We evaluate how GSM coaching can help them better learn about video games and eventually enjoy health games. 3 different metrics are collected to show that GSM coaching improves game performance, game literacy and game experience respectively.

Since increased performance is typically linked to coaching as a desirable outcome, we are interested in measuring whether older players performed better under GSM-driven coaching, compared to the control group. On the other hand, game literacy is deemed important as a learning outcome: Can participants without technology background learn, understand and appreciate gaming as an activity under GSM-driven coaching? Lastly, we are interested whether the whole gaming or learning process is made more enjoyable via the use of GSM-driven coaching. The points above are summarized into 3 hypotheses, measurement tools are elaborated, and results are presented.

H1: GSM-Driven Coaching Improves Players' Performance When Playing Health Games

First, we record participants' game performance in terms of time taken to complete each round. Each participant's time taken to complete each round is recorded (in seconds), and the average scores of 2 participant groups are compared for each round. From the

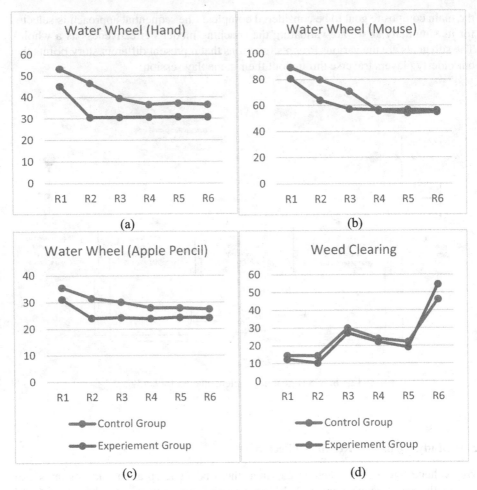

Fig. 9. Time taken to complete each round for the 4 minigames

difference of time taken to complete each round between control and experiment group, we evaluate the effectiveness of coaching on participant's game performance.

Here we highlight key findings for the data:

1. Coaching helps elderlies learn faster: The first round took slightly longer on average to complete, but participants in the experiment group were quickly able to learn the mechanics of the water wheel game when using their fingers. The faster learning speed of participants that went through coaching are shown by the sharp dip in time after the first round in Fig. 9 (a), (b) and (c). On the other hand for the controlled group, their time taken saw slower improvement and only stabilizes until the 3rd or 4th round.

2. Coaching motivates elderlies to achieve game goals faster: Each round in the experiment group is completed in shorter amount of time. For example in (a), the experiment group's playtime stabilizes at 30 s after 1 round while the control group's playtime stabilizes around 37 s after 3 rounds.

3. In (b), players generally experienced a difficulty spike. This difficult segment took the longest time to complete on average (67 and 62 s respectively for control and experiment group). Due to the increased difficulty, 4 participants requested to drop out in the control group (1 after round 2, 2 after round 3, 1 after round 4, not in the graph). In contrary, the experiment group saw no dropouts in this segment. Participants who dropped out tends to be those who spent the most time on in R1-R3 as they expressed to be unfamiliar with the computer mouse. As slower players have requested not to continue, the control group's average time is reduced for R4–R6 to resemble the experiment group more closely.

4. In the weed clearing minigame (d), R1–R2 in took little time to complete, while R3 saw an increase in the time taken to complete. This is because the weeds spawn in a curving shape instead of a straight line from R3 onwards, causing a difficulty increase. For R1–R2 and R3–R5, we still observed a reduction of the time taken to complete a round. In other words, the "learning effect".

    a. Special circumstances emerge for round 6, which was framed as the Final Challenge in coached experiment group. Players chased a continuously growing stream of curving weeds. It is typically cleared either within 10 s or beyond 50 s. Either participants were able to catch up to the growing weeds before they grow off the screen, or they are not able to, and had to spend more time in subsequent screens. The latter group of participants who did not manage to clear the first screen spent a lot of time in subsequent screens, causing the average time to go up.

The observations presented above indicated significant performance boost among the experiment group who received GSM-driven coaching. This provides support for H1.

H2: GSM-Driven Coaching Improves Players' Game Literacy

We evaluate participants' game literacy using a scale constructed by Rosenberg [27] using Exploratory Factor Analysis. Identified constructs as part of game literacy are:

- Information, Learning, Resource Management and System Skills (ISM)
- Exploration and Enjoyment
- Teamwork
- Design
- Socialization

In our study, participants play the Pumpkin Garden game with one-to-one coaching, hence social elements like *Teamwork* and *Socialization* are not used. As the game tasks in Pumpkin Garden game only require players to follow on-screen instructions to complete, they do not suit the *Design* constructs' question items which typically features the player creating their own contents in the game. *Exploration and Enjoyment* is omitted as it will be addressed in H3.

Hence, we only administered the first construct (ISM) to our participants to compare their core game literacy skills [27, p. 67] across the coached group and the control group. As participants only qualify for this study if they do not have prior experience with digital games, we are confident that our sample population possess a relatively similar starting point for game literacy. Since the questionnaire is not yet named officially, will refer to it as the Game Literacy Questionnaire.

Significantly higher mean scores are highlighted in Table 2. Results of the Game Literacy Questionnaire are satisfactory; elderly players who received GSM coaching reported higher confidence and ability in understanding the visual and auditory feedback provided by the Pumpkin Garden health game. This has manifested in their performance results above in Fig. 9 too as they are able to both learn and complete the game slightly faster than the control group. Unsurprisingly, questions like "ease of recalling information", "understanding in-game action consequences" and "exploring how game systems work in-depth" do not present differences that are as significant. This is because reading deeper in game mechanics or recalling game information afterwards are not really required in Pumpkin Garden; these skills are relevant to more sophisticated, captivating games that are for people who are more literate in games. Given our participants' little to no prior experience with video games, they are able to play the Pumpkin Garden game well after simply understanding the basic feedback that games provide.

Thus, questionnaire results support use of GSM coaching to help elderly players with low game literacy to engage and better interact with health games. With H2 satisfied, we look at the effects of GSM coaching on participant's health game experience.

H3: GSM-Driven Coaching Improves Players' Health Game Experience

After the gameplay session, we use the Health Game Experience Questionnaire (HGEQ)[2] to measure their health game experience. The HGEQ is an extension to the Game Experience Questionnaire (GEQ). It factors in health game-specific and elderly-specific constructs to better capture the health game experiences among older adults.

Significantly higher mean scores are highlighted in Table 3. By comparing scores of individual dimensions across the control and experiment groups, we gain better insights into which parts of the game experience are better improved by our GSM-driven coaching. The higher mean scores for *health values* indicated that the game's health values highlighted in the introduction and persuasion process (for some participants) are well-received by participants. Our older players are also able to better identify with human interactions and familiar objects when playing the Pumpkin Garden game under GSM-driven coaching. The higher *competence* suggests that players with presence of coaching have more confidence in their abilities to perform well in the game, thus agreeing with the Game Literacy Questionnaire results in Table 2. Whereas the significantly higher *immersion, post-game positive experience* and *return to reality* suggest a higher level of immersion for the experiment group as they were able to better engage with the game.

---

[2] The paper that details and validates the Health Game Experience Questionnaire (HGEQ) is planned to be published by the author in the future under the title "Developing an Assessment Tool for the Elderly Health Game Experience".

Table 2. Results for game literacy questionnaire - ISM construct

ISM Question Items	Mean Score	
	Experiment Group	Control Group
It is easy for me to obtain information in or about games.	2.40	1.70
I can successfully monitor inputs, meters, points, and other sources of information that video games present. *	2.65	1.85
It is easy for me to recall information about games after the gameplay experience.	2.50	2.15
It is easy for me to look up information about games after the gameplay experience.	2.30	2.20
I am confident in my ability to analyze information and feedback presented by video games. **	2.65	1.75
I am able to appropriately implement information from or about games. *	2.60	1.95
I am able to assess the quality of the information I receive from video games. **	2.45	1.80
I am good at explaining information from or about games to others.	1.95	1.95
I pick up the rules of most games fairly quickly. **	2.65	1.90
I am good at understanding the consequences of my in-game actions.	2.10	1.60
I tend to explore how the systems (including rules) of a game work in-depth.	2.05	1.70
When the situation changes, I actively attempt to update my information.	2.20	1.75
I build on my knowledge of games to better my understanding and/or proficiency.	2.25	1.90
I understand the more complicated parts of games because of the simpler actions that built up to them.	2.40	1.85
I know how to manipulate virtual environments.	2.20	1.85
I know how to navigate virtual environments. **	2.65	1.70
I am proficient at controlling games. **	2.35	1.65
I am proficient with the interfaces in games.	2.35	1.90

*. T-test is significant at the 0.05 level (2-tailed).
**. T-test is significant at the 0.01 level (2-tailed).

Conversely, players who did not receive coaching reported higher amounts of challenge, tension and feeling of tiredness after the game (**bolded and underlined** in Table 3). These may have originated from the less fruitful game session that they had: unintuitive gameplay and lack of direction that makes them not know what questions to ask in the first place. Hence, the HGEQ results in Table 3 support the effects of health game coaching in producing better game experiences for older adults, satisfying H3.

Table 3. Results for health game experience questionnaire

HGEQ Construct	Experiment Group Mean Scores	Control Group Mean Scores
Core Constructs		
Positive Affect	2.650	2.240
Competence**	2.720	2.120
Sensory and Imaginative Immersion*	2.650	2.033
Flow	2.450	2.020
Negative Affect	1.025	0.950
Challenge*	1.430	**2.010**
Tension*	1.601	**2.167**
Health Values*	2.690	1.930
Familiarity*	2.883	2.168
Identification of Human-Like Properties*	2.840	1.970
Post-Game Constructs		
Positive Experience*	2.692	1.809
Negative Experience	1.075	1.268
Tiredness*	1.200	**1.850**
Return to Reality**	2.550	1.584

*. T-test is significant at the 0.05 level (2-tailed).
**. T-test is significant at the 0.01 level (2-tailed).

3.4 Summary

The time taken to complete each round, Game Literacy Questionnaire and HGEQ results provides proof that GSM coaching improves the gameplay quality and game experiences of our elderly participants who had little to no exposure to video games before the study. With the validation of H1, H2 and H3, we are confident that the GSM coaching methodology can produce fruitful learning experiences for older adults when playing health games.

4   Conclusion

Storytelling and the Goal Net modelling methodology go hand in hand in the development of the Goal-Oriented Storytelling Model as a model for coaching older adults to play health games. The study presented in this paper demonstrated that GSM-driven coaching can successfully improve health game performance, game literacy and game experience for older adults with little prior experience with digital technology. The GSM can be further explored in future AI-based implementations, which yields us a digital health game coach which is widely accessible. This can hopefully encourage health game adoption or, for rehabilitation's case, adherence among older adults.

Acknowledgements. This research is supported by the Interdisciplinary Graduate School, Nanyang Technological University, Singapore. This research is also supported, in part, by the National Research Foundation, Prime Minister's Office, Singapore under its IDM Futures Funding Initiative and the Singapore Ministry of Health under its National Innovation Challenge on Active and Confident Ageing (NIC Project No. MOH/NIC/HAIG03/2017).

References

1. Wijman, T.: The World's 2.7 Billion Gamers Will Spend $159.3 Billion on Games in 2020; The Market Will Surpass $200 Billion by 2023, Newzoo, 28 May 2020. https://newzoo.com/insights/articles/newzoo-games-market-numbers-revenues-and-audience-2020-2023/. Accessed 24 Nov 2020
2. Gaming Attitudes and Habits of Adults Ages 50-plus. AARP research (2019)
3. Xun, G., Ifenthaler, D.: Designing engaging educational games and assessing engagement in game-based learning. In: Handbook of Research on Serious Games for Educational Applications, pp. 253–270. IGI Global, Hershey, PA (2017)
4. Lu, A.S., Kharrazi, H.: A state-of-the-art systematic content analysis of games for health. Games Health J. Res. Dev. Clin. Appl. 7(1), 1–15 (2018)
5. Kaleva, J.-P., Hiltunen, K., Latva, S.: Mapping the full potential of the emerging health game markets. Sitra, the Finnish Innovation Fund, vol. 72 (2013)
6. Sardi, L., Idri, A., Fernández-Alemán, J.L.: A systematic review of gamification in e-Health. J. Biomed. Inform. 71, 31–48 (2017)
7. de Lima, L.G.R., Salgado, A.d.L., Freire, A.P.: Evaluation of the user experience and intrinsic motivation with educational and mainstream digital games. In: CLIHC 2015: Proceedings of the Latin American Conference on Human Computer Interaction, Córdoba, Argentina, (2015)
8. Ijsselsteijn, W., Nap, H.H., de Kort, Y., Poels, K.: Digital game design for elderly users. In: Future Play, Toronto, Canada (2007)
9. Marston, H.R.: Design recommendations for digital game design within an ageing society. Educ. Gerontol. 39(2), 103–118 (2013)
10. Palmer, S., Whybrow, A.: Coaching psychology - an introduction. In: Palmer, S., Whybrow, A. (eds.) Handbook of Coaching Psychology, pp. 1–20. Routledge, London (2007)
11. Olsen, J.M.: Health coaching: a concept analysis. Nurs. Forum Independ. Voice Nurs. 49(1), 18–29 (2014)
12. Propp, V.: Morphology of the Folktale: Second Edition, University of Texas Press (2010)
13. Chen, M., Bell, R.A., Taylor, L.D.: Narrator point of view and persuasion in health narratives: the role of protagonist-reader similarity, identification, and self-referencing. J. Health Commun. 21(8), 908–918 (2016)
14. de Graaf, A.: The effectiveness of adaptation of the protagonist in narrative impact: similarity influences health beliefs through self-referencing. Hum. Commun. Res. 40(1), 73–90 (2013)
15. Ho, L.: Narrative coaching and psychology of learning from multicultural perspectives. In: Palmer, A., Whybrow, A. (eds.) Handbook of Coaching Psychology, pp. 174–192. Routledge, London (2007)
16. Yu, H., Shen, Z., Miao, C.: A goal-oriented development tool to automate the incorporataion of intelligent agents into interactive digital media applications. Comput. Entertain. 6(2) (2008)
17. Mohan, S., Venkatakrishnan, A., Hartzler, A.L.: Designing an AI health coach and studying its utility in promoting regular aerobic exercise. ACM Trans. Interact. Intell. Syst. 10(2) (2020)
18. Shen, Z.: Goal-Oriented Modelling For Intelligent Agents and Their Applications. Nanyang Technological University, Singapore (2005)

19. Liu, S., Shen, Z., Yuan, Y., Ji, J., McKeown, M.J.: Pumpkin garden: a tablet game platform for Parkinson's disease rehabilitation. Int. J. Inf. Technol. **9**(1) (2003)
20. Liu, S., Miao, C., McKeown, M.J., Ji, J., Shen, Z., Leung, S.: Pumpkin garden: a mobile game platform for monitoring Parkinson's disease symptoms. In: Human Aspects of IT for the Aged Population. Applications in Health, Assistance, and Entertainment (2018)
21. Schank, R.C.: What We Learn When We Learn by Doing (Technical Report No. 60), Institute for the Learning Sciences Northwestern University (1995)
22. Bayrak, A.T.: Compassionate game design: a holistic perspective for a player-centric game design paradigm for games4health. Int. J. Adv. Intell. Syst. **13**(1 & 2), 1–18 (2020)
23. Ogomori, K., Nagamachi, M., Ishihara, K., Ishihara, S., Kohchi, M.: Requirements for a cognitive training game for elderly or disabled people. In: International Conference on Biometrics and Kansei Engineering, Takamatsu, Kagawa, Japan (2011)
24. Gerling, K., Schulte, F.P., Masuch, M.: Designing and evaluating digital games for frail elderly persons. In: Proceedings of the 8th International Conference on Advances in Computer Entertainment Technology (2011)
25. Ke, F., Xie, K., Xie, Y.: Game-based learning engagement: a theory- and data-driven exploration. Br. J. Edu. Technol. **47**(6), 1183–1201 (2016)
26. Namazi, K.H., McClintic, M.: Computer use among elderly persons in long-term care facilities. Educ. Gerontol. **29**(6), 535–550 (2003)
27. Rosenberg, K.A.: Gaming Literacy: Construct Validation and Scale Construction, University of South Florida (2011)

Isolation and Use of Social Media by Autistic Individuals During Covid-19 Lockdown: Perceptions of Caregivers

Oronzo Parlangeli[1]([envelope]) [iD], Sonia Grifoni[1], Paola Palmitesta[1] [iD],
Alessandro Andreadis[2] [iD], Paul M. Liston[3] [iD], and Stefano Guidi[1] [iD]

[1] Department of Social, Political and Cognitive Sciences, University of Siena,
P.zzo san Niccolò, via Roma 56, Siena, Italy
{oronzo.parlangeli,paola.palmitesta,stefano.guidi}@unisi.it,
sonia.grifoni@student.unisi.it
[2] Department of Information Engineering and Mathematics, University of Siena, via Roma 56,
Siena, Italy
alessandro.andreadis@unisi.it
[3] Centre for Innovative Human Systems (CIHS), School of Psychology, Trinity College Dublin,
Dublin, Ireland
pliston@tcd.ie

Abstract. This study explores the extent to which social media manages to meet the relational needs of individuals diagnosed with Autism Spectrum Disorder (ASD) during Italy's first COVID-19 lockdown (March – May, 2020). To this end 22 caregivers of people with ASD completed a questionnaire investigating the living conditions of the affected people during this time, their use of social media/communication tools, their anxiety levels, their perception of the usefulness of social media, and the types of cognitive and/or relational dysfunction. The results show that social media did not prove useful, even in situations of obvious need such as those experienced during the lockdown. Caregivers, however, viewed social media in a positive light only for those individuals with ASD who had used them already prior to the lockdown. Further studies are therefore needed to better design social media for the needs of people with ASD.

Keywords: ASD · Social media · Lockdown · Caregivers

1 Introduction

Autism Spectrum Disorder (ASD) relates to various cognitive and motor difficulties, problems with social interaction and communication (verbal or otherwise), and often the commission of repetitive behaviors [1]. Methods for the diagnosis of this disorder have evolved greatly over the past few years. It is now possible to diagnose autism around the age of 3, usually following the appearance of symptoms in the previous months. But the progression of symptoms is not always linear. Some children develop problems as early as their first few months, while others show typical development up to a certain

G. Meiselwitz (Ed.): HCII 2021, LNCS 12775, pp. 443–455, 2021.
https://doi.org/10.1007/978-3-030-77685-5_32

age and then there is a regression of motor and language skills around 15–30 months [2]. The cause of this regression is still unclear [3] but this makes it difficult to identify the disorder before symptoms have stably manifested themselves.

In order for a person to be diagnosed with an autism spectrum disorder, four conditions must be met:

- Persistent deficits in social communication and social interaction in multiple contexts;
- Repetitive behavior patterns;
- Presentation of symptoms in the early period of development;
- Symptoms cause clinically significant impairment in social, occupational, or other important areas of daily life [4].

Much research has highlighted how social relationships are of fundamental importance for persons with ASD, and it emphasizes how the difficulties related to these can create further problems in emotional and cognitive development. Observable negative consequences are varied, ranging from failure to achieve adequate levels of performance in education, to peer marginalization [5, 6]. Problems such as the generation of anxious states can also impair social relationships. People with the autism spectrum generally show a greater predisposition to suffer from anxiety disorders which seem, in fact, very present in adolescents and young adults due to the fact that these periods of development are characterized by attempts to understand their role in the world and interpersonal differences [7, 8].

If they assume a positive function, however, social relationships can facilitate the development of many skills and also have a protective role against aggressive contexts: through their support and presence, people with whom there is a relational bond can, for example, shield or completely prevent the occurrence of bullying [9] or cyberbullying [10, 11].

More than the number of relationships, what seems important is their quality. There is evidence to suggest that even one or two friends - those who can be defined as true friends - may be enough to facilitate the development of reactive skills to stressful events and lead to the achievement of higher levels of self-esteem and independence [12]. For years, therefore, specific training programs for individuals diagnosed with ASD have focused precisely on facilitating relational skill development. Through the development of relational aspects there is a tendency to facilitate the development of cognitive and emotional skills, as well as to promote the formation of contexts that are inclusive and therefore able to hinder marginalization [13–17].

It is clear that the well-being of individuals with ASD is dependent on the possibility of living in, and interacting with, contexts which mitigate the difficulties of social interaction [18]. Some scholars have wondered if social media can be considered a means for fostering adequate social relationships, in particular as possible moderators of anxiety [19]. It should be pointed out that the development of social media almost never takes into account the user requirements of people who manifest forms of disability. For example, the attention problems that often occur in people diagnosed with ASD create difficulties in interactions with stimuli and interfaces which, for their effective use, must be recognized in their entirety [20, 21]. In fact, people with autism show a tendency to analyze details rather than overall configurations [22]. Indeed eye tracking studies recommend that web pages should not insert too many images and videos, and should make the structure simpler with the most important information being associated with those elements that best attract attention [23].

Furthermore, people with autism who manage to access these platforms often misuse them. Some studies show that individuals diagnosed with ASD can easily develop addictions that lead to loss of control and interpersonal and intrapersonal conflicts. It should be noted that this association between autism spectrum disorders and internet addiction was mainly measured in young adults rather than adolescents [24].

Addiction also leads to other types of problems such as an increase in depression and social anxiety [25], although there is ample evidence to suggest that people with greater anxiety and depression use social media more to boost self-esteem [26]. Van Schalkwyk and colleagues [19] instead highlighted how many autistic individuals have reduced anxiety through the use of social media and how they have managed to increase and improve the quality of their friendships.

The findings from all these studies do not seem to be pointing in the same direction. The question regarding the usefulness of social media as a means to integrate social relationships and to facilitate the development of cognitive and emotional skills in individuals diagnosed with ASD, without negatively impacting anxiety states, still seems far from a solution. This issue therefore requires an urgent solution precisely in moments of isolation - that is, when it is difficult or impossible to have face-to-face social relationships. In these circumstances, it could easily be assumed that social media would provide an opportunity to foster relationship opportunities and that this could be particularly beneficial. However, the social isolation associated with the use of social media may have a negative impact, as online social contact can negatively impact and limit real social relationships which were difficult to establish for persons with ASD in the first place. Adult caregivers of persons diagnosed with ASD face many challenges in their daily life: lack of a support network in their community, isolation, physical and mental fatigue [27, 28]. These problems are exacerbated in exceptional situations such as those that occurred in Italy between March and May 2020 due to the lockdown associated with the COVID-19 pandemic. For all these reasons, it was important to investigate how social media was used by persons with an ASD diagnosis in a period of isolation, and to examine whether their caregivers perceived social media as beneficial for the ASD individuals.

2 The Study

The study was conducted in Italy in September 2020 and involved the administration of an online questionnaire to adults who are the parents or relatives of an individual diagnosed with ASD. The main purpose of the study was to assess whether, at that particular time, social media had been used by subjects with ASD and whether they had been able to sustain face-to-face relationships that, due to social distancing restrictions, had been interrupted. To this end, information was collected on the living conditions of the caregivers in that period, and therefore of the individual with ASD. It was also considered necessary to explore the use of social media, the levels of anxiety and the degree of perceived usefulness of social media.

2.1 Method

Participants. Our sample consisted of 22 individuals who spent the March to May 2020 COVID-19 lockdown period of isolation with low-, medium-, and high-functioning autistic spectrum children or adults. To recruit them, we sent an email to three associations in the Siena and Florence areas that are involved in providing support to families who have people diagnosed with ASD.

In 81.8% (n = 18) of cases the caregivers were mothers of the individual with ASD, in 13.6% of cases the fathers (n = 3) and in one case the sister. The mean age of the caregivers was 52.9 years, and 27.3% of them had other persons with special care needs (e.g. newborn, elderly people), 50% had children (40.9% one, 9.1% two). The majority of caregivers lived in a household with two (54.6%, n = 12) or three (40.9%, n = 9) other persons.

Information on the 22 individuals with ASD was collected from their caregivers. The average age of the individuals was 23 years (sd = 8.7), and all but one were males. On average, they were diagnosed with ASD at 4.8 years of life (sd = 4.1), and 63.6% of them received the diagnosis within their first three years of life. They were cared in their households by a range of 1 to 4 people.

Materials. Each member of our sample completed an online questionnaire with 4 sections. In some cases the respondent was answering for themselves, in others from the point of view of the person diagnosed with ASD, while in others the questions were duplicated to obtain answers from both points of view. Before participating in the study the objectives, the methods of collecting and processing data, and the data storage protocols were explained and outlined to participants. The questionnaire took approximately 20 min to complete.

The first section of the questionnaire consisted of 26 items gathering demographic data such as age, gender and information relating to the caregivers' occupation. In the second section, consisting of 26 open questions and statements with Likert scales from 1 to 5, opinions were solicited on the technological devices used, the internet connection, and information was sought relating to the activities carried out both by the caregiver and by people diagnosed with ASD during the lockdown in Italy between March and May 2020.

In the third part, two scales were used to measure the level of anxiety and the use of social media by the person diagnosed with ASD. The first scale was the multidimensional ASC-ASD scale (Anxiety Scale for Children- Autism Spectrum Disorders), structured to measure anxiety levels and highlight the different symptoms in children with autism spectrum [29, 30] across 4 subscales: uncertainty, anxiety arousal, separation anxiety, and performance anxiety. This scale has 24 statements to be rated using a Likert scale ranging from 0 (Never), 1 (Sometimes), 2 (Often), 3 (Always). The maximum score, given by the sum of the scores for each item, is 72 and there is a score that suggests a symptomatology of significant anxiety when this is greater than 20, while if it exceeds 24 points there may be a specific indication of problems with anxiety. There are two versions of this scale, one for parents, the other for children with ASD; here the parent version was used. The other scale is the SMES (Social Media Experience Scale) in which there are 11 items [19]. 6 items allow us to identify the perception of usefulness of social media, that is, if social media tools are of any help, and another 5 measure the anxiety perceived by their use. Also for this reactive, the answers were collected on 4-point Likert scale ranging from 1 (Absolutely No) to 4 (Absolutely Yes). An additional question investigated the perceived usefulness of social media during the lockdown, again using a 4-point Likert scale. Finally, in the last part of the questionnaire data relating to the diagnosis and development of the disorder were collected with 9 open questions and a Likert scale from 1 to 5.

Following the specification of the questionnaire described above, ethics approval was sought from the Ethics Committee for Human and Social Sciences of the University of Siena (CAREUS) on August 16, 2020. Approval was subsequently issued (approval number 13/2021, date 07/01/2021).

2.2 Results

Table 1 reports the average scores of the ratings of the severity of different clinical symptoms (concerning difficulties exhibited by the individuals in 4 different domains), and of the measures of anxiety (the ASC-ASD total and subscales) collected from the participants.

Table 1. Average scores for the measures of anxiety in the ASD individuals (ASC-ASD Parent Anxiety Scale) and of the difficulties in different life domains (clinical symptoms).

Variable	Mean	Sd	Range (min-max)
ASC-ASD: Total score	26	12.1	46 (5–51)
ASC-ASD: Uncertainty	11.5	5.6	21 (1–22)
ASC-ASD: Anxious arousal	2.8	2.2	8 (0–8)
ASC-ASD: Separation anxiety	5.5	3.7	12 (0–12)
ASC-ASD: Performance anxiety	6.1	4.5	15 (0–15)
Issues: Relationships with people	3.2	1.2	4 (1–5)
Issues: Adapation to change	3.3	1.0	4 (1–5)
Issues: Verbal communication	3.2	1.3	4 (1–5)
Issues: Non-verbal communication	2.7	0.9	3 (1–4)

The average score of the individuals on the ASC-ASD anxiety scale (parent version) was 26 (sd = 12.1), corresponding to a significant anxiety level, and indeed the majority of individuals had a score above the threshold (19/20) for detecting the presence of significant levels of anxiety (4 individuals with a score between 20 and 24, and 11 with a score of 25 or above). The analysis of the correlations (Fig. 1) revealed that the scores on the Uncertainty subscale were significantly correlated with those on the Anxious Arousal ($r = 0.62$, $p < .001$) and the Separation Anxiety ($r = 0.6$, $p < .001$) subscales, which were also significantly correlated among them (r = 0.49, p < .05). The average scores for the ratings of the different ASD clinical symptoms were all located around the midpoint of the scale (3). The ratings about the difficulties with verbal and non-verbal communication were significantly correlated (r = 0.69, p < .001), those about the difficulties in relating with other persons were significantly correlated with the total ASC-ASD scores (r = 0.52, p < .05) and with the ASC-ASD Anxious Arousal scores (r = 0.62, p < .001), while difficulties with adapting to changes were significantly correlated with the ASC-ASD Uncertainty scores (r = 0.48, p < .05). The severity of the clinical symptoms was not significantly correlated with the age of the individual at diagnosis or with their current age.

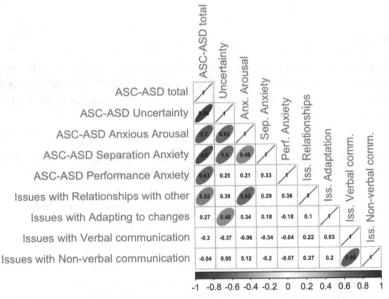

Fig. 1. Correlations among measures of anxiety and of the severity of clinical symptoms in the ASD individuals. Ellipses represent statistically significant correlations.

Living and Working Conditions During Lockdown. Participants reported a moderate increase in the overall number of things to do (for work, family and friends) during lockdown (mean = 3.8, sd = 1.1). Sixty-four percent of participants reported that during lockdown they had needed help to achieve all the tasks that they had to do, more often (50%, n = 11) or much more often (13.6%, n = 3) than usual, and among them 35.7% had all the support they needed, while 14.3% did not at all, and 66.7% of them had looked for help outside of their household. The ratings of the increase in the overall number of things the caregiver had to do daily during lockdown was significantly correlated with the ratings about the degree to which they needed extra help (r = 0.81, p < .001).

Figure 2 plots the distributions of the responses about the features of the environment in which participants and ASD individuals spent the lockdown periods.

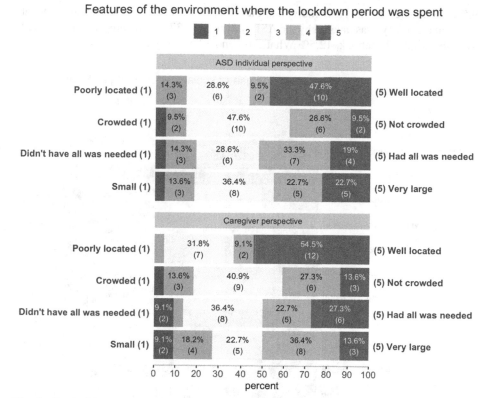

Fig. 2. Stacked frequencies bar plots of the responses concerning the features of the household where participants and ASD individuals lived during the lockdown. In the upper plot the responses are relative to the needs of the ASD individuals, while in the bottom plot are relative to the needs of their caregivers.

Almost all participants and ASD individuals (90.9%, n = 20) had access to a computer or a tablet during lockdown, of which they had exclusive use in 65% (n = 13) of the cases. The computer's features were deemed adequate for the ASD need in 80% of the cases (n = 16). The majority of the ASD individuals also had a smartphone (68.2%, n = 15). All the caregivers reported that an internet connection was available in the household, and only a minority of them (22.7%, n = 5) said it was not adequate for their connectivity needs or for those of the ASD individual.

Activities and Use of Social Media by the ASD Individual During Lockdown. In Fig. 3 (below) the distribution of responses about the frequency with which the ASD individuals were involved in several activities during the lockdown period according to their caregivers are plotted. It is clear from the plots that the most frequent activity was watching TV (mean = 3.4, sd = 1.2 on a 1 to 5 scale), followed by browsing the internet (mean = 3.3, sd = 1.3), and playing games (mean = 3.1, sd = 1.4). The least frequent activity (mean = 1.5, sd = 0.98) was interacting with other people on social networks, an activity which 86% of participants reported that was never (76.2%) or almost never

(9.5%) conducted by the ASD individual they cared for. As to the question about what social media, if any, was favored by the ASD individuals, 37.5% of caregivers responded YouTube, 18.8% Facebook, 12.5% WhatsApp and 12.5% Skype.

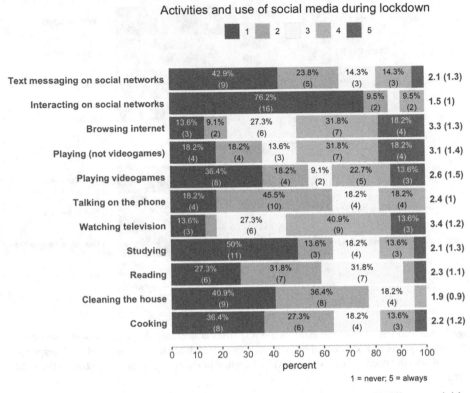

Fig. 3. Distribution of the responses from participants about the frequency of different activities during lockdown by the ASD individuals. The numbers reported on the right side of the plot along the y axis are the mean and standard deviations of the ratings for each activity.

We analyzed the correlations between the frequencies with which the different activities were conducted. A plot of the correlations is presented in Fig. 4 below. As is clear from the plot, the frequency of reading was significantly correlated with the frequency of studying ($r = 0.46$, $p < .05$) and browsing the internet ($r = 0.52$, $p < .05$). The amount of time spent studying was negatively correlated with the time spent interacting with other people on social networks ($r = -0.44$, $p < .05$). The time spent interacting on social networks was also strongly correlated with the time spent sending text messages on social networks ($r = 0.77$, $p < .001$), which in turn was positively correlated with the time spent talking on the phone ($r = 0.61$, $p < .001$). Negative significant correlations were also found between the time spent watching television and the time spent talking on the phone ($r = -0.62$, $p < .01$) and cleaning the house ($r = -0.57$, $p < .01$). The time spent cleaning was also negatively correlated with the time playing videogames ($r = -0.43$, $p < .05$) and positively with the time spent cooking ($r = 0.64$, p

< .01). Finally, an additional analysis revealed that the time spent interacting on social networks was negatively correlated with ratings of the extent to which the household was well-located with respect to the needs of the ASD individual (r = −0.52, p < .05). Conversely, the time spent studying was positively correlated with the ratings of the extent to which the household was well-located (r = 0.53, p < .05).

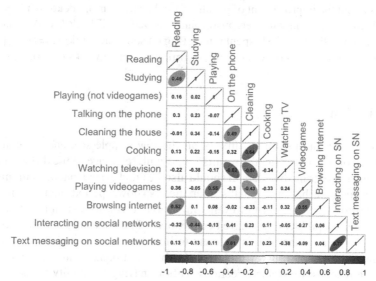

Fig. 4. Correlations among the time spent by the ASD individuals on different activities during lockdown. Ellipses represent statistically significant correlations.

Effects of Lockdown and Perceived Utility of Using Social Media. 41% (n = 9) of participants reported that the psychological health of the ASD individual had neither worsened nor improved during lockdown, 36.6% (n = 8) reported that it had worsened (n = 6) or much worsened (n = 2), and only the remaining 22.7% claimed that it had improved (n = 3) or much improved (n = 2). The ratings about the improvement of the psychological health of the ASD individuals were significantly correlated with the ratings about the size of the location in which the lockdown was spent from the point of view of the individual (r = 0.48, p < .05), and of the extent to which the location was well-located from the point of view of the caregiver (r = 0.48, p < .05). They were also positively correlated with the amount of time the individuals spent studying (r = 0.48, p < .05) and negatively correlated with the total ASC-ASD score (r = −0.59, p < .01), and with the ASC-ASD factors *Uncertainty* (r = −0.56, p < .01) and *Anxious Arousal* (r = −0.5, p < .05).

The majority of participants (n = 11, 57.9%) reported that social media were not (n = 5, 26.3%) or absolutely not (n = 6, 31.6%) useful for the ASD individual (mean = 2.3, sd = 1.1, on a scale from 1 to 4) during lockdown. The average scores on the Social Media Engagement Scale's factors concerning, respectively, the perceived *utility* of using social media for the ASD individual, and the perception of the possibility that social media can induce *anxiety* in the individual, were indeed, for both subscales, quite low (SMES-Utility: mean = 1.7, sd = 0.56; SMES-Anxiety: mean = 1.4, sd = 0.54). The scores on two SMES factors were significantly correlated (r = 0.64, p < .01). The ratings of the overall usefulness of social media during lockdown were positively correlated with the amount of time spent on the internet (r = 0.46, p < .05), with SMES *Utility* (r = 0.69, p < .05) and *Anxiety* (r = 0.5, p < .05), and negatively correlated with the ratings about the improvement of psychological health during lockdown (r = −0.49, p < .05). Positive correlations were also found between SMES *Utility* of social media and the amount of time the ASD spent interacting on social networks (r = 0.58, p < .01) and sending text messages on WhatsApp or similar social networks (r = 0.63, p < .01).

3 Limitations

The study has several limitations, first of all the low sample size and the consequent impossibility of differentiating the results found with reference to the different expressions of autism spectrum disorders. It should also be emphasized that the administration of the questionnaire began 4 months after the lockdown period, and this may have impacted respondents' memory of events in various ways, for example by improving the assessments of problems that have been resolved in the meantime, or by remembering difficulties in a manner that is different to how they were experienced at the time. Furthermore, the use of a survey tool, namely the questionnaire, may have altered the value of the responses in some directions without having the ability to balance these results with evidence from other survey methods such as interviews or ethnographic observations.

4 Conclusions

This study highlights some aspects of the relationship between individuals diagnosed with ASD and the use of social media that appear problematic. These means of communication, in fact, failed to meet the relational needs of the individuals in our sample who had a period of social isolation forced upon them by the COVID-19 pandemic.

The reasons for this are different. It is evident, for example, that some individuals - those with greater relational difficulties and those characterized by high social anxiety - usually prefer to engage in activities that do not involve the use of mediated means of communication that involve relationships with other people. Housing conditions, especially the location of the house, can instead make a difference for those who seem to have a particular need for direct interactions. Conversely, the users who interact most with social media do so, at least in part, because their homes are in less advantageous locations. But from this they do not derive an improvement in the state of well-being which instead seems more related to the housing conditions.

All in all, the use of social media did not seem to change as a result of the momentary state of need, and was rated as useful only if respondents were already users of the internet, social media and instant messaging programs.

Clearly, therefore, social media as it is now designed is not a suitable means of communication for individuals with ASD. It should probably be designed with particular attention to people with these needs, as has been attempted with Social mirror, a social media site specifically designed to facilitate the development of greater autonomy for adults with autism thanks to the support provided by close people, such as family or friends [31]. Within this social network, people share their calendar of daily activities and can share pictures or ask for advice by writing down their main problems. In this way a social network of people will be formed around the individual who can help them at any time. Despite being a social network open to anyone, it aims to be a safe place since close people can watch out for strangers who could post offensive comments or words. That said, the increased use of this tool has raised questions about privacy - as all the activities of a person's day are shared [31] - and the possibility to create a sort of disorientation amongst users – related to the expression of numerous opinions from close people that may sometimes be in contrast with each other. As shown by research in other sectors, problems related to ethical behaviours can originate precisely from dysfunctions in relationships between peers [32].

Finally, it should be emphasized that social media created specifically for people with autism are aimed only at those with high functioning autism because they require the exercise of cognitive skills that are not always typical of individuals diagnosed with ASD. Similarly, evaluating the usability of these social media with reference to the abilities of each individual affected by ASD is perhaps the preliminary step that, for cognitive and implementation reasons, has not yet been carried out in a sufficiently informative manner.

References

1. Lord, C., Bishop, S.L.: Recent advances in autism research as reflected in DSM-5 criteria for autism spectrum disorders. Ann. Rev. Clin. Psychol. 11, 53–70 (2015). https://doi.org/10.1146/annurev-clinpsy-032814-112745
2. Williams, K., Brignell, A., Prior, M., Bartak, L., Roberts, J.: Regression in autism spectrum disorders. J. Paediatr. Child Health 51(1), 61–64 (2015). https://doi.org/10.1111/jpc.12805
3. Baird, G., et al.: Measles vaccination and antibody response in autism spectrum disorders. Arch. Dis. Child. 93(10), 832–837 (2008). https://doi.org/10.1136/adc.2007.122937
4. APA: DSM-5 Diagnostic and statistical manual of mental disorders. Fifth Edition, pp. 57–58. American Psychiatric Publishing, Washington DC (2014)
5. Bellini, S., Peters, J.K., Benner, L., Hopf, A.: A meta-analysis of school-based social skills interventions for children with autism spectrum disorders. Remedial Spec. Educ. 28(3), 153–162 (2007). https://doi.org/10.1177/07419325070280030401
6. Rotheram-Fuller, E., Kasari, C., Chamberlain, B., Locke, J.: Social involvement of children with autism spectrum disorders in elementary school classrooms. J. Child Psychol. Psychiatry 51(11), 1227–1234 (2010). https://doi.org/10.1111/j.1469-7610.2010.02289.x
7. Tantam, D.: Psychological disorder in adolescents and adults with asperger syndrome. Autism 4(1), 47–62 (2000). https://doi.org/10.1177/1362361300004001004
8. White, S.W., Oswald, D., Ollendick, T., Scahill, L.: Anxiety in children and adolescents with autism spectrum disorders. Clin. Psychol. Rev. 29(3), 216–229 (2009). https://doi.org/10.1016/j.cpr.2009.01.003

9. Mazurek, M.O., Kanne, S.M.: Friendship and internalizing symptoms among children and adolescents with ASD. J. Autism Dev. Disord. **40**(12), 1512–1520 (2010). https://doi.org/10.1007/s10803-010-1014-y

10. Parlangeli, O., Marchigiani, E., Bracci, M., Duguid, A.M., Palmitesta, P., Marti, P.: Offensive acts and helping behavior on the internet: an analysis of the relationships between moral disengagement, empathy and use of social media in a sample of Italian students. Work **63**(3), 469–477 (2019). https://doi.org/10.3233/WOR-192935

11. Parlangeli, O., Marchigiani, E., Guidi, S., Bracci, M., Andreadis, A., Zambon, R.: I do it because i feel that… moral disengagement and emotions in cyberbullying and cybervictimisation. In: Meiselwitz, G. (ed.) HCII 2020. LNCS, vol. 12194, pp. 289–304. Springer, Cham (2020). https://doi.org/10.1007/978-3-030-49570-1_20

12. Buhrmester, D.: Intimacy of friendship, interpersonal competence, and adjustment during preadolescence and adolescence. Child. Dev. **16**(4), 1101–1111 (1990). https://doi.org/10.2307/1130878

13. Howlin, P., Goode, S., Hutton, J., Rutter, M.: Adult outcome for children with autism. J. Child Psychol. Psychiatry **45**(2), 212–229 (2004). https://doi.org/10.1111/j.1469-7610.2004.00215.x

14. Romanczyk, R., White, S., Gillis, J.: Social skills versus skilled social behavior: a problematic distinction in autism spectrum disorders. J. Early Intensive Behav. Interv. **2**(3), 177–193 (2005). https://doi.org/10.1037/h0100390

15. White, S.W., et al.: Development of a cognitive–behavioral intervention program to treat anxiety and social deficits in adolescents with high-functioning autism. Clin. Child. Fam. Psychol. Rev. **13**(1), 77–90 (2010). https://doi.org/10.1007/s10567-009-0062-3

16. Camargo, S.P.H., Rispoli, M., Ganz, J., Hong, E.R., Davis, H., Mason, R.: Review of the quality of behaviorally-based intervention research to improve social interaction skills of children with asd in inclusive settings. J. Autism Dev. Disord. **44**(9), 2096–2116 (2014). https://doi.org/10.1007/s10803-014-2060-7

17. Yamada, T., et al.: Examining the treatment efficacy of PEERS in Japan: improving social skills among adolescents with autism spectrum disorder. J. Autism Dev. Disord. **50**(3), 976–997 (2020). https://doi.org/10.1007/s10803-019-04325-1

18. Jones, K.K.: Social engagement versus isolation in the well-being of individuals with autism spectrum disorder. Journal of Childhood & Developmental Disorders, vol. 5, no. 2:9 (2019)

19. Van Schalkwyk, G.I., et al.: Social media use, friendship quality, and the moderating role of anxiety in adolescents with autism spectrum disorder. J. Autism Dev. Disord. **47**(9), 2805–2813 (2017). https://doi.org/10.1007/s10803-017-3201-6

20. Parlangeli, O., Roncato, S.: Draughtsmen at work. Perception **39**(2), 255–259 (2010). https://doi.org/10.1068/p6500

21. Guidi, S., Parlangeli, O., Bettella, S., Roncato, S.: Features of the selectivity for contrast polarity in contour integration revealed by a novel tilt illusion. Perception **40**(11), 1357–1375 (2011). https://doi.org/10.1068/p6897

22. Eraslan, S., Yaneva, V., Yesilada, Y., Harper, S.: Do web users with autism experience barriers when searching for information within web pages?. In: Proceedings of the 14th Web for All Conference on the Future of Accessible Work, pp. 1–4. Association for Computing Machinery, New York, NY, USA (2017)

23. Eraslan, S., Yaneva, V., Yesilada, Y., Harper, S.: Web users with autism: eye tracking evidence for differences. Behav. Inf. Technol. **38**(7), 678–700 (2019). https://doi.org/10.1080/0144929X.2018.1551933

24. So, R., et al.: The prevalence of internet addiction among a Japanese adolescent psychiatric clinic sample with autism spectrum disorder and/or attention-deficit hyperactivity disorder: a cross-sectional study. J. Autism Dev. Disord. **47**(7), 2217–2224 (2017). https://doi.org/10.1007/s10803-017-3148-7

25. Kawabe, K., et al.: Internet addiction and attention-deficit/hyperactivity disorder symptoms in adolescents with autism spectrum disorder. Res. Dev. Disabil. **89**, 22–28 (2019). https://doi.org/10.1016/j.ridd.2019.03.002

26. Woods, H.C., Scott, H.: # Sleepyteens: social media use in adolescence is associated with poor sleep quality, anxiety, depression and low self-esteem. J. Adolesc. **51**, 41–49 (2016). https://doi.org/10.1016/j.adolescence.2016.05.008

27. Weitlauf, A.S., Vehorn, A.C., Taylor, J.L., Warren, Z.E.: Relationship satisfaction, parenting stress, and depression in mothers of children with autism. Autism **18**(2), 194–198 (2014). https://doi.org/10.1177/1362361312458039

28. Nik Adib, N.A., et al.: Perceived stress among caregivers of children with autism spectrum disorder: a state-wide study. Int. J. Environ. Res. Publ. Health **16**(8), 1468 (2019). https://doi.org/10.3390/ijerph16081468

29. Den Houting, J., Adams, D., Roberts, J., Keen, D.: Exploring anxiety symptomatology in school-aged autistic children using an autism-specific assessment. Res. Autism Spectr. Disord. **50**, 73–82 (2018). https://doi.org/10.1016/j.rasd.2018.03.005

30. Rodgers, J., Wigham, S., McConachie, H., Freeston, M., Honey, E., Parr, J.R.: Development of the anxiety scale for children with autism spectrum disorder (ASC-ASD). Autism Res. **9**(11), 1205–1215 (2016). https://doi.org/10.1002/aur.1603

31. Hong, H., Kim, J.G., Abowd, G.D., Arriaga, R.I.: Designing a social network to support the independence of young adults with autism. In: Proceedings of the ACM 2012 Conference on Computer Supported Cooperative Work, pp. 627–636. Association for Computing Machinery, New York, NY, USA (2012)

32. Parlangeli, O., Guidi, S., Marchigiani, E., Bracci, M., Liston, P.M.: Perceptions of work-related stress and ethical misconduct amongst non-tenured researchers in Italy. Sci. Eng. Ethics **26**(1), 159–181 (2020). https://doi.org/10.1007/s11948-019-00091-6

Infusing Motivation into Reminders for Improving Medication Adherence

Yaming Zhang[1,2]([✉]), Yang Qiu[1,2], Zhengxiang Pan[1,3], Xinjia Yu[1,3], and Chunyan Miao[1,2]

[1] Joint NTU-UBC Research Centre of Excellence in Active Living for the Elderly, Nanyang Technological University, Nanyang, Singapore
{zhangym,qiuyang,xinjia.yu,ascymiao}@ntu.edu.sg,
panz0012@e.ntu.edu.sg
[2] School of Computer Science and Engineering, Nanyang Technological University, Nanyang, Singapore
[3] Interdisciplinary Graduate School, Nanyang Technological University, Nanyang, Singapore

Abstract. The treatment of chronic diseases commonly includes the long-term use of medication. However, patients typically do not accurately or continuously take their medications as prescribed. Building on medication reminders, this paper conceptualizes the term "Motivational Reminders" for enhancing reminders' effects among unmotivated people who may "intentionally" forget to adhere to their medication. The design approach pulls in existing practices and arranges them on the internalization process outlined in the Organismic Integration Theory (OIT), one of the sub-theories of Self-Determination Theory (SDT). Based on the proposed motivation reminder system, we designed a prototype that helps the users internalize the new behavior of taking medications regularly, timely and persistently.

Keywords: Medication adherence · Reminders · Motivation · Self-Determinant theory (SDT) · Organismic integration theory (OIT) · Internalization

1 Introduction

One of the practices of effective chronic diseases is taking medications correctly [1]. The degree of chronic disease patients takes their medications as prescribed and recommended by the doctors in known as medication adherence [2]. However, approximately 50% of patients do not comply with their long-term prescribed medications precisely [3]. Medication non-adherence brings about the worsening of one's health condition, which may result in poor quality of life, rise in healthcare cost, further complications in treatment, comorbid diseases, and possibly premature death. Thus, the World Health Organization has placed priority on resolving the issue of medication non-adherence [4].

Medication adherence is a complex health behavior and very substantial literatures are available to describe its predictors and influencing factors [5]. The socio-demographic factors of age and gender tend to be weak predictors of adherence, whereas socio-cognitive factors of illness perceptions and health beliefs have been recognized as more

© Springer Nature Switzerland AG 2021
G. Meiselwitz (Ed.): HCII 2021, LNCS 12775, pp. 456–471, 2021.
https://doi.org/10.1007/978-3-030-77685-5_33

powerful predictors [6]. Such studies have found that patients' conscious decisions to medication adherence is more useful than exploring practical barriers. At the heart of these conscious decisions is the element of motivation, which induces satisfaction in medication-taking behavior. According to Easthall and Barnett [7], medication non-adherence can be viewed as an intentional or unintentional human behavior.

- Unintentional non-adherence relates to practical barriers, such as physical deficiencies or memory problems. Although this group of patients is willing to take their medications regularly, they are unable to, as practical impediments reduce their capability or opportunity to do so. Solutions that can strengthen their prospective memory (e.g. reminders) can be explored to curb these cases of non-adherence.
- In contrast, patients who have the ability to adhere but make conscious decisions not to take medicines are known to be not adhering intentionally due to perceptual barriers. Intentional non-adherence can be understood as unmotivated individuals "conveniently" forgetting their medication schedule, which then require more rigorous interventions or "behavior change regimes" (e.g. health coaching) to overcome.

Medication non-adherence may require more integrative approaches that can simultaneously address both intentional and unintentional factors. When unhealthy behaviors or refusal of healthy behaviors is intentional, we need to find ways to *motivate* healthy behaviors. Whereas when the above acts are unintentional, we need to design effective methods to *remind* them. From this angle, the intersections between motivation and reminders are substantial.

Motivational Reminders. Designing reminders with motivational approaches is a promising way to curb cases of forgetfulness, which can be intentional, unintentional or a mix of both. It is hypothesized that *motivational reminders* can be suitable for enhancing adherence to reminders, especially among those with "intentional forgetfulness".

This paper puts forward a design methodology for implementing motivational reminders. Topics of self-determination theory are reviewed and then positioned into reminder applications that was originally meant for enhancing prospective memory. This combination of SDT and reminders creates the term *motivational reminders*.

The organization of the paper is as follows. Section 2 presents the literature review that features the internalization process in SDT, a process that is deemed important for motivational reminders. Section 3 details a sub theory of SDT and formalizes a set of design recommendations for motivational reminders. Section 4 summarizes the recommendations using the Goal Net modelling methodology and provides a future research direction.

2 Literature Review

This chapter evaluates existing research that we refer to when conceptualizing the term "motivational reminders".

2.1 Reminders: The Base

Reminders serve the purpose of alleviating cases where prospective memory failures occur. Alarms, handphone notifications, written lists are examples of reminders that attempt to ensure planned tasks are fulfilled.

Reminders appear to be the ideal solution for unintentional forgetfulness among motivated individuals who just need an additional nudge. However, the same cannot be said for less motivated individuals. Patients who require medication adherence may not object the use of reminders when they are asked to do so, but rates of "conveniently" ignoring reminders are expected to be higher among such unmotivated individuals.

Existing research supports use of rewards as motivators to enhance adherence to reminders. Walter and Meier [8] showed in their review that prospective memory can be enhanced in a *rewarded* condition. In this case, the reward serves as the motivator for carrying out prospective tasks. When an extrinsic reward (e.g. cash rewards) is promised upon completion of prospective tasks, it causes the tasks to be perceived as being more important. The effects of rewards are validated with control groups where the same rewards are not promised [9]. Results show that extrinsic rewards motivate people to strategically monitor for cues to obtain the reward, while more intrinsic forms of motivation encourage automatic retrieval of the prospective task. The same paper [8] concludes that extrinsic and intrinsic motivations work in different ways to encourage adherence to reminders, and both types of motivations should be further evaluated to create better reminders. Therefore, the Self-determination Theory is more extensively explored in this paper to find out applicable aspects to make reminders more motivational.

2.2 Self-determination Theory: The Motivational Element in Reminders

Self-Determination Theory (SDT) highlights the importance of humans' evolving personalities as an inner resource for achieving behavioral self-management [10]. While the definition of an "self-determined" individual may vary, many can agree that a decision made by the self generally lasts for longer on top of generating better psychological health and effective performance [10]. This human need for self-determination is a popular research topic when the goal is to first *initiate* then *maintain* healthy behavior change [11].

Intrinsic Motivation. Researchers have taken interest in boosting individuals' level of perceived self-determination by its 3 dependent variables: autonomy, competence and relatedness, which according to SDT, produces *intrinsic motivation* that allows longer lasting and resistant healthy behavior.

- Autonomy focuses on the individual's need to feel in control of one's behaviors and goal. The individual is able to satisfy this autonomy by taking decisions independently without being forced by any external influence or pressure [12].
- Competence in SDT describes an individual's need for mastering tasks and learning different skills. The need of competence is achievable by practicing a certain skill regularly [13], which enables individuals to attain desired outcomes.

- Relatedness focuses on the need to feel a sense of belonging and attachment with other people through their behaviors. The affectionate relationship with others is effectuated by making friends and creating trusting relationships [14].

These psychological needs are considered essential for understanding the what (content) and how (process) of behavioral change [15]. Individuals who have these psychological needs fulfilled are considered to be "highly self-determined" and have high *intrinsic motivation*, which is often associated with better psychological health and effective performance [10].

Extrinsic Motivation and the Internalization Process. On the other side of the coin is extrinsic motivation. These forms of motivation often come in the form of immediate rewards which provide instant gratification, with the upside of being straightforward to understand being easy to administer. While some studies criticize extrinsic motivation to undermine intrinsically motivated behavior [16], there appears to be more that supports strategic use of extrinsic motivation to minimize its adverse effects.

Since behavior must first be *initiated* then *maintained* [11], providing extrinsic rewards provides an easier starting point when attempting to initiate new, healthy behavior like medication adherence. For subsequent long-term behavior maintenance, extrinsic rewards then give way to other solutions that can bring more intrinsic motivation. This process is described in SDT as the "internalization process", where the individual achieves higher self-determination through various ways that can increase their autonomy, competence and relatedness [17]. Throughout the internalization process, different classes of motivation are proposed (and validated) to describe different psychological qualities exhibited by individuals [18, p. 2]. This broad class of motivations are categorized under extrinsic motivation, indicating that it is more than just a singular concept.

2.3   Implications

The term "motivational reminders" can be literally dissected and understood from its parts. Motivation is used as an augment for reminders to become more effective when encouraging adherence to certain uninteresting but necessary activities. Motivational reminders fill in the behavioral intention gap when attempting to cultivate healthy activities that often appear to be uninteresting at first glance.

This paper explores how motivational reminders can be crafted to encourage the *initiation* of adherence, then facilitate the internalization process to help them *maintain* the said healthy behavior [11].

3   Designing Motivational Reminders

From [2] above, it is common for researchers to include some sort of extrinsic reward in their reminders to promote enhanced adherence. However they rarely go beyond those extrinsic rewards and find new ways to facilitate the internalization process of the healthy behavior. Here we look into the Organismic Integration Theory (OIT), a sub theory of SDT. With understanding towards how OIT breaks down the internalization process into certain stages, we can then design reminder applications that adapt to different OIT stages to facilitate the internalization process.

3.1 Organismic Integration Theory (OIT)

According to Deci and Ryan: *"The term internalization refers to the process through which an individual acquires an attitude, belief or behavioral regulation and progressively transforms it into a personal value, goal, or organization."* [19, p. 130]. The OIT is proposed by Deci and Ryan [20] as part of the SDT, specializing in describing different qualities that individuals exhibit when they internalize a new behavior. OIT posits that extrinsic motivation can be broken down into 4 stages. Each stage describes different forms of regulations that individuals use to drive their behavior at various different levels of self-determination. The stages describe a continuum, ranging from behaving under full external control to a predominantly self-determined state where behavior is autonomous and self-initiated. Figure 1 illustrates the 4 stages of the internalization process as proposed and categorized by the OIT.

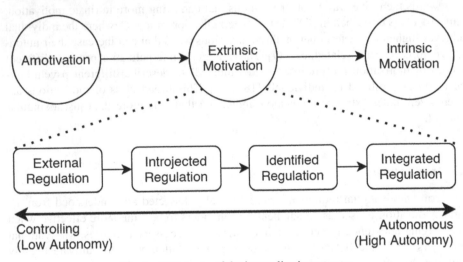

Fig. 1. OIT stages of the internalization process

When cultivating healthy behavior, individuals first start in a motivation which indicates a lack of interest towards carrying out the desired behavior. Then, reminders act as the first step to initiate the healthy behavior, playing the role of an external mediator that requests users to perform certain tasks (such as taking their medications on time). This *externally regulated* form of behavior is driven by desire for reward and avoidance of threats or punishments [21]. Implementing extrinsic rewards or punishments in reminders has seen significant improvements in medication adherence rates as recent studies have shown [22, 23]. Unfortunately, extrinsic rewards (i.e. positive reinforcement) diminish over time and a steady increase of the said rewards are required to maintain interest, which may incur additional costs [23, pp. 7–8].

3.2 OIT in Reminders for Medication Adherence

Subsequent stages in the internalization process are, however, currently less explored in reminders for medication adherence despite being thought to help in the maintenance of healthy behavior [17] after the initiation stage. Below we present some thoughts on their interpretations and implications for medication reminders:

1. Introjected regulation represents a fear- or anxiety-driven state to act. When compared to the previous state where the regulation is completely external, individuals care about their medication habits enough to feel "guilty" or "bad for themselves" whenever they are unable to adhere to their medication schedule. It appears that individuals in this state have a "noisy ego" to calm and appease [24]. Reminders could theoretically help alleviate this psychological need by boosting self-worth using rewards which do not necessarily have extrinsic, real-world value. This is slightly different from the *external regulation* stage which often feature monetary rewards. After all, detaching from real-world rewards means that basic needs have transformed into psychological needs, indicating a step up in Maslow's Hierarchy of Needs [25]. Since SDT constructs are deemed suitable as replacements for the "higher levels" of Maslow's Hierarchy [26], introjected regulation may actually describe progression in terms of basic or psychological needs. In extension, the kind of rewards provided by reminders can adjust accordingly.

2. Identified regulation appears to be a significantly greater step forward in the internalization process. This stage is often described as the start of self-determined behavior [27, Fig. 1] that is deemed to produce higher levels of wellbeing, as a result of volition replacing external or self-inflicted pressure. Individuals in this state typically start to understand and identify with the values behind their actions, eventually using the actions' outcomes to motivate their own behavior. In the case of medication adherence, reminder recipients know to consume medicine on time because they understand its importance. In order to reach this state, reminders have to serve an educational role; the valuable aspects behind MA should somehow be presented to the user on top of the usual notifications or alarms.

3. Integrated regulation signifies the most self-determined state for adhering to these types of externally imposed behavior. The new behavior is now held as part of one's identity, which is consonant with other existing personal values of the individual [18, p. 3]. It is fair to ask: Can reminders help an individual reach this state of value-integration? Looking back on how each previous approach works:

   a. External regulation focuses on initiating new behavior through use of instantly gratifying valuable rewards, creating an artificial reason for people to follow an imposed behavior.

b. Introjected regulation focuses on positive or negative reinforcement that have less extrinsic value, which empathizes with the user and answers "why should I listen to you".

c. Identified regulation focuses on having reminders convey a certain educational message on "what are the benefits of medication adherence", aiming to get users to adhere because it is important.

The approach in each stage of the internalization process goes from satisfying "why" (in a, b) to answering "what" (in c). In line with Sinek's model of inspirational leadership [28], showing the "how" is a promising final act to have the user personally endorse the act of medication adherence. Directly addressing "how does ideal medication adherence look or feel like" or "how can you too achieve it" is a logical approach to invite users to take action, thereby enabling them to perform well under guidance and empowering them to build their identity around personal achievements.

The 4-stage OIT framework has uncovered some design insights for motivational reminders. The following section proposes some broad approaches to facilitating transition between each different stage of the internalization process.

3.3 Formalizing Design Recommendations for Motivational Reminders

The role of reminder systems in helping individuals internalize their motivations is explained using the OIT. Specifically, the transitions between different states of motivation helped us derive several different design approaches to make reminders more motivational.

Amotivation → External Regulation: Obtain Adherence via Extrinsic Rewards

Adherence to a certain behavior is a main outcome that reminders try to achieve. Medication adherence may not be enjoyable in their own right, but individuals can be motivated to adopt healthy behaviors if immediate benefits are perceived. Thus, when initiating new healthy behavior, messages presented need to serve its role as the "external motivator"; the call to action. This may be able to encourage willing (albeit forgetful) individuals to carry out the tasks successfully. However, more incentives may need to be paired with the reminders for individuals who were less motivated to get them started.

This used of mixed methods intervention to improve medication adherence is supported by a recent meta-analysis. According to Wiecek et al. [29], several components exist to classify medication adherence interventions:

- Technical components simplify the medication-taking process, with reminders being a prime example.
- Reward components are self-explanatory; users get rewarded with incentives whenever they adhere to their medications.

The meta-analysis which includes 249 studies has provided solid evidence that the combination of *technical* and *reward* components consistently improves medication adherence over other intervention types/combinations with statistical significance. Other intervention components show a promising way forward as well:

- The *educational* component is another interesting component that informs the medication, disease state or importance of adherence.
- The *attitudinal* component refers to approaches that aim to modify beliefs.

Addition of the *educational* and *attitudinal* components onto existing technical components (i.e. reminders in our case) has been shown to produce long-lasting effect on adherence [29, p. 11], which supports our proposed approach to have reminders adapt to later stages of the internalization process.

From the findings above, the following directions are explored: Gamified rewards can be the eventual addition for reminders to slowly modify *attitudes* via introjection, and *educational* values (what is medication adherence, and how to successfully carry out medication-taking behavior) can become important when helping individuals identify and integrate the behavior.

External Regulation → Introjected Regulation: Provide Sense of Achievement via Gamified Rewards

In this stage, the messages displayed by the reminder becomes more oriented towards fulfilling psychological needs. Individuals who are under introjected regulation do things to avoid guilt and shame from the peer pressure [30, p. 285]. The contrary can be true when designing reminder messages; individuals can receive rewards that bolster their ego and self-worth.

Gamification is a concept that excels in reinforcing psychological needs. Gamification refers to the act of motivating beneficial (albeit uninteresting) behavior through rewards like badges, points and achievements [31] without much compromise to the behavior's requirements. These gamified elements are a prime example of psychological rewards; they are not as tangible compared to real world items, but they still create enough affirmation for the individual that can motivate them to maintain a healthy behavior.

The practice of gamification is closely related to the Self-Determination Theory (SDT) [32]. Various studies which uses SDT have retrofitted gamification elements onto cultivating healthy behavior [33] or education [34] with certain success. Prior research supports the notion that gamification helps users introject the external demands of the task by providing rewards that affirm their efforts [35, 36]. Thus, it is fair to imply that these extrinsic forms of rewards provide a sense of satisfaction that is partially intrinsic to the individual, as they become invested into the "feel good" experience that is ultimately extrinsic. Reminder systems could utilize gamification at this stage to help users introject new healthy behavior that they still perceive to be fully extrinsic (i.e. only for the benefits) up until now.

Introjected Regulation → Identified Regulation: Cultivate Health Values
While incentives and gamified rewards presented above are relatively extrinsic, health values can be explored as a form of intrinsic reward. The gamification approach proposed in the previous section is still relevant. It is believed that incorporating goal setting and health values into gamification help us design reminder messages that is supportive towards individuals' autonomy. This maximizes users' chances of reaching the Identified Regulation stage and subsequently, establishes a long-lasting *regulatory schema* within the user, reinforcing the behavior as a persistent habit.

To reach this stage, the reminder system has to help users identify the value of their action outcomes [17] instead of having them simply follow along out of submission (external) or self-worth (introjected). In the case of healthy behavior change, the user needs to understand the health values behind the healthy behavior they all the while have been led to do and set goals which are more related to their real-world health condition instead of arbitrary gamified rewards. The values behind actions are a key differentiator for this transition that makes it significant.

At this stage, messaging content shifts away from *rewarding* the user and towards *initiating action* for the user. Users should be encouraged to set their own health goals in this stage. The reminder system can then provide timely reports of their health goals achievement process. Incorporating goal setting and positive health values into reminder messages help explicate the positive consequence of their actions, how their actions have benefitted them, and eases them out from the relatively "controlling" rewards provided by gamified elements without context. While the user may keep up their behavior to obtain gamified rewards in the Introjected Regulation stage, they now start to learn about the health benefits through the same process, and how their own participation and "investments" directly relate to their own beliefs.

Identified Regulation → Integrated Regulation: Form Imagery of Role Models
When participants have identified with the values behind their healthy behavior, the last role for reminder systems is to help users visualize how they might perform well in behaving healthily, on top of curbing cases of forgetfulness. The rationale of choosing this approach is simple: once users agree it is personally important for them to achieve certain behavior, if they can see the how an ideal role model behave, they are able to simply follow. It is important to note that this transition focuses on the "how" instead of the "why" in the 1st transition above.

Imagery interventions have been successful in improving levels of Integrated Regulation in encouraging people to exercise [37]. It is generally a well-accepted strategy for enhancing performance in the domain of sports. One of the sub-types of imagery intervention is centered around creating motivation through imagining flawless execution, scoring specific goals, along with the associated positive experiences felt upon success [38, p. 9]. Reminder messages for a certain healthy behavior could utilize these visualizations to encourage the user to take action, derive satisfaction from tasks done well, and ultimately "integrate" the healthy behavior as part of themselves. Thus, questions like "how would an ideal 'me' look like if I can perfectly adhere to my medication" may be helpful when designing reminder messages that helps with developing integrated regulation.

Exclusion of Integrated Regulation → Intrinsic Motivation in Reminders for Medication Adherence
Intrinsic Motivation is described as doing something out of pure satisfaction with full self-determination. For maintaining healthy behavior, it is widely considered the ideal final source of motivation. However, studies are still inconclusive whether individuals are able to achieve full Intrinsic Motivation on an externally imposed behavior. From Deci and Ryan's own attempt to redefine the distinction between the two states:

"Integrated forms of motivation share many qualities with intrinsic motivation, being both autonomous and unconflicted. However, they are still extrinsic because behavior motivated by integrated regulation is done for its resumed instrumental value with respect to some outcome that is separate from the behavior, even though it is volitional and valued by the self... Yet, as implied above, this does not mean that as extrinsic regulations become more internalized they are transformed into intrinsic motivation." [39, p. 62]

Achieving full intrinsic motivation appears to be both out of reach and unnecessary for reminder applications. It is likely that *integrated regulation* is sufficient to produce the desired long-lasting behavior change the case of medication adherence. Logically when designing reminders, the states of Integrated Regulation and Intrinsic Motivation should not be differentiated. In other words, we consider *integrated regulation* to be the ideal the final state to aim for.

4   Proposed Motivational Reminder Framework

This step-by-step approach using OIT stages throughout the internalization process provides a framework that is goal oriented. In each stage we attempted to answer: what should reminders show, and what other forms of interventions are viable on top of reminders, so that the user can progress to the next stage?

The Goal Net modelling methodology [40] lay out a few handy concepts that help summarize the design recommendations above:

- Complex goals can be broken down into sub-goals. Similarly, extrinsic motivation can be broken down into an internalization process which proved to be valuable foundation for the design of motivational reminders.
- Each goal should be accompanied by an action list that, upon execution, brings the situation to the next state. Similarly, this paper proposed the use of incentives, gamified rewards, health values and role models at different internalization stages.

Thus, a preliminary high-level goal net is presented in Fig. 2 below to summarize the design recommendations discussed in this paper.

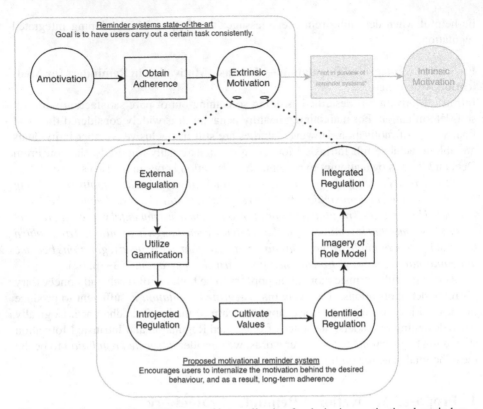

Fig. 2. Roadmap of using OIT stages of internalization for designing motivational reminders

5   Application of the Proposed Motivational Reminder Framework

A mobile app is currently being developed with a reminder function, utilizing the proposed motivational reminder framework. This chapter explains the concept walkthrough of remainder mechanics.

To motivate medication adherence intrinsically through SDT, the app considers the following to be goals that it aims to achieve:

1. Reward the users for good medication-taking behavior.
2. Produce a sense of guilt or obligation for users who missed their medications.
3. Help users understand the possible consequences and related complications caused by medication nonadherence.
4. Enable the users to share their health values to motivate others.

The app's functions aim to motivate users so that they improve their medication adherence. The patient-centered design tries to ensure that users' needs, and goals are the primary consideration at every stage of the reminder functions. Thereby, the design philosophy consists of two main components. First, the three psychological needs of SDT are mapped into "Message" (tasking), "Setting" (goal setting), and "Connect" (social support) modules, which correspond to autonomy support, perceived competence, and relatedness. With these basic modules in place, the four stages of the internalization process are then used to design different reminder messages (Fig. 3).

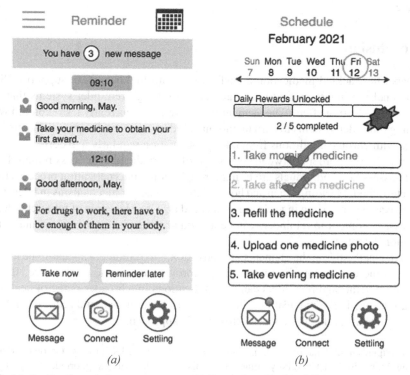

Fig. 3. Motivational reminder app prototype (a) Reminder tab with different messages and tasks to the user; and (b) User's schedule table with reward given for completing their daily medication.

In line with Goal Net's idea to "make goals actionable", the reminder messages presented in the app emphasizes the need for structured support to promote sustainable medication-taking behavior. Message contents are dedicated to produce the four transitions detailed in Sect. 3.3 above. The general messaging guideline for each transition are drafted based on as below:

1. Obtain adherence — present critical facts about medication adherence;
2. Utilize gamification — reward scores, badges and achievements to players who performed well in adhering to the reminders;
3. Cultivate values — educate users to understand the values behind their actions;
4. Imagery of role model — help users integrate their motivation by showing them how to do it.

Compared to existing reminder systems (e.g. Google Calendar), the proposed app is hypothesized be more effective for motivating medication-taking behavior by several methods to facilitate the internalization process. The proposed motivational reminder system presents greater autonomous self-regulation for medication-taking behavior and greater opportunities to reduce medication non-adherence. While SDT generates motivation, it also mediates the associations between perceived need for support and adherence outcome.

6 Conclusion

This paper has tackled medication nonadherence with the theoretical support of SDT. Motivational reminders present a new approach to design reminder systems that produces a longer lasting effect. The element of motivation is currently less explored when designing reminder systems to curb intentional medication nonadherence. This prevents patients with chronic conditions from taking medication regularly and correctly.

Currently, the borders between each stage of internalization process remain fuzzy. Ways to assess how individuals are faring throughout the internalization process are yet to be determined. Deciding when and how to introduce newer mechanisms in later stages (e.g. cultivate values, showing role models) could also be a key area of research interest. The message content in reminders can be a good starting place for implementations of motivational content.

In a nutshell, adding the elements of motivation into reminders appear to be a viable method to increase their effectiveness for improving medication adherence. If well-designed, motivational reminders can see applications in a broader range of healthcare applications outside of medication adherence. Further studies should refine each design approach to truly evaluate the workability of this approach.

Acknowledgements. This research is supported by the Interdisciplinary Graduate School, Nanyang Technological University, Singapore. This research is also supported, in part, by the National Research Foundation, Prime Minister's Office, Singapore under its IDM Futures Funding Initiative and the Singapore Ministry of Health under its National Innovation Challenge on Active and Confident Ageing (NIC Project No. MOH/NIC/COG04/2017 and MOH/NIC/HAIG03/2017).

References

1. Cramer, J.A., Benedict, Á., Muszbek, N., Keskinaslan, A., Khan, Z.M.: The significance of compliance and persistence in the treatment of diabetes, hypertension and dyslipidaemia: a review. Int. J. Clin. Pract. **62**(1), 76–87 (2008). https://doi.org/10.1111/j.1742-1241.2007.016 30.x
2. Lam, W.Y., Fresco, P.: Medication adherence measures: an overview. Biomed. Res. Int. **2015**, 1–12 (2015). https://doi.org/10.1155/2015/217047
3. Brown, M.T., Bussell, J.K.: Medication adherence: WHO cares? Mayo Clin. Proc. **86**(4), 304–314 (2011). https://doi.org/10.4065/mcp.2010.0575
4. World Health Organization, "Adherence to Long-Term Therapies: Evidence for Action," World Health Organization. https://www.who.int/chp/knowledge/publications/adherence_Section1.pdf. Accessed 25 Dec 2020

5. Horne, R., Weinman, J., Barber, N., Elliott, R., Morgan, M.: Concordance, adherence and compliance in medicine taking, December 2005. https://www.researchgate.net/profile/Ian_Kellar/publication/271443859_Concordance_Adherence_and_Compliance_in_Medicine_Taking/links/54cfdb790cf298d65665b4d4.pdf
6. Kardas, P., Lewek, P., Matyjaszczyk, M.: Determinants of patient adherence: a review of systematic reviews. Front. Pharmacol. **4**, 91 (2013). https://doi.org/10.3389/fphar.2013.00091
7. Easthall, C., Barnett, N.: Using theory to explore the determinants of medication adherence; moving away from a one-size-fits-all approach. Pharmacy (Basel) **5**(3), 50 (2017). https://doi.org/10.3390/pharmacy5030050
8. Walter, S., Meier, B.: How important is importance for prospective memory? a review. Front. Psychol. **5**, 657 (2014). https://doi.org/10.3389/fpsyg.2014.00657
9. Shanker Krishnan, H., Shapiro, S., Prospective and retrospective memory for intentions: a two-component approach. J. Consum. Psychol. **8**(2), 141–166 (1999). https://doi.org/10.1207/s15327663jcp0802_02
10. Deci, E., Ryan, R.: Motivation, personality, and development within embedded social contexts: an overview of self-determination theory. The Oxford Handbook of Human Motivation, January 2012. https://doi.org/10.1093/oxfordhb/9780195399820.013.0006
11. Rothman, A.J.: Toward a theory-based analysis of behavioral maintenance. Health Psychol. **19**(1), 64–69 (2000). https://doi.org/10.1037/0278-6133.19.suppl1.64
12. Evans, P.: Self-determination theory: an approach to motivation in music education. Musicae Sci. **19**(1), 65–83 (2015). https://doi.org/10.1177/1029864914568044
13. Patrick, H., Williams, G.C.: Self-determination theory: its application to health behavior and complementarity with motivational interviewing. Int. J. Behav. Nutr. Phys. Act. **9**, 18 (2012). https://doi.org/10.1186/1479-5868-9-18
14. Nicholson, S.: A RECIPE for meaningful gamification. In: Reiners, T., Wood, L.C. (eds.) Gamification in Education and Business, pp. 1–20. Springer, Cham (2015). https://doi.org/10.1007/978-3-319-10208-5_1
15. Taylor, G., et al.: A self-determination theory approach to predicting school achievement over time: the unique role of intrinsic motivation. Contemp. Educ. Psychol. **39**(4), 342–358 (2014). https://doi.org/10.1016/j.cedpsych.2014.08.002
16. Warneken, F., Tomasello, M.: Extrinsic rewards undermine altruistic tendencies in 20-month-olds. Dev. Psychol. **44**(6), 1785–1788 (2008). https://doi.org/10.1037/a0013860
17. Ryan, R., Patrick, H., Deci, E., Williams, G.: Facilitating health behavior change and its maintenance: interventions based on self-determination theory. Eur. Health Psychol. **10**(1), 2–5 (2007)
18. Legault, L.: Intrinsic and extrinsic motivation. In: Zeigler-Hill, V., Shackelford, T.K. (eds.) Encyclopedia of Personality and Individual Differences, pp. 1–4. Springer International Publishing, Cham (2016). https://doi.org/10.1007/978-3-319-28099-8_1139-1
19. Deci, E.L., Ryan, R.M.: Intrinsic Motivation and Self-Determination in Human Behavior, 1st edn. Springer, US (1985). https://doi.org/10.1007/978-1-4899-2271-7
20. Deci, E.L., Ryan, R.M.: Toward an organismic integration theory. In: Intrinsic Motivation and Self-Determination in Human Behavior, 1st ed., Springer, US, pp. 113–148 (1985). https://doi.org/10.1007/978-1-4899-2271-7_5
21. Olanipekun, A.O.: Applying the self-determination theory (SDT) to explain the levels of motivation for adopting green building. Int. J. Constr. Manag. **18**(2), 120–131 (2017). https://doi.org/10.1080/15623599.2017.1285484

22. Alshammari, F., Tearo, K., Orji, R., Hawkey, K., Reilly, D.: MAR: a study of the impact of positive and negative reinforcement on medication adherence reminders. In: 2020 IEEE 8th International Conference on Serious Games and Applications for Health (SeGAH), pp. 1–8 (2020). https://doi.org/10.1109/segah49190.2020.9201781

23. Liu, X., Varshney, U.: Mobile health: a carrot and stick intervention to improve medication adherence. Decis. Support Syst. **128**, 113165 (2020). https://doi.org/10.1016/j.dss.2019.113165

24. Niemiec, C.P., Ryan, R.M., Brown, K.W.: The role of awareness and autonomy in quieting the ego: a self-determination theory perspective. In: Transcending Self-interest: Psychological Explorations of the Quiet Ego. American Psychological Association, Washington, DC, US, pp. 107–115 (2008)

25. Mcleod, S.: Maslow's Hierarchy of Needs- Simply Psychology, vol. 1, pp. 1–8 (2007)

26. Rasskazova, E., Ivanova, T., Sheldon, K.: Comparing the effects of low-level and high-level worker need-satisfaction: a synthesis of the self-determination and Maslow need theories. Motiv. Emot. **40**(4), 541–555 (2016). https://doi.org/10.1007/s11031-016-9557-7

27. Legault, L., Green-Demers, I., Grant, P., Chung, J.: On the self-regulation of implicit and explicit prejudice: a self-determination theory perspective. Pers. Soc. Psychol. Bull. **33**(5), 732–749 (2007). https://doi.org/10.1177/0146167206298564

28. Sinek, S.: How great leaders inspire action. https://www.ted.com/talks/simon_sinek_how_great_leaders_inspire_action. Accessed 16 Jan 2021

29. Wiecek, E., Tonin, F.S., Torres-Robles, A., Benrimoj, S.I., Fernandez-Llimos, F., Garcia-Cardenas, V.: Temporal effectiveness of interventions to improve medication adherence: a network meta-analysis. PLoS One **14**(3), e0213432 (2019). https://doi.org/10.1371/journal.pone.0213432

30. Hagger, M.S., Chatzisarantis, N.L.D., Biddle, S.J.H.: The influence of autonomous and controlling motives on physical activity intentions within the theory of planned behaviour. Br. J. Health Psychol. **7**(1), 283–297 (2002). https://doi.org/10.1348/135910702760213689

31. Botte, B., Bakkes, S., Veltkamp, R.: Motivation in gamification: constructing a correlation between gamification achievements and self-determination theory. In: Marfisi-Schottman, I., Bellotti, F., Hamon, L., Klemke, R. (eds.) GALA 2020. LNCS, vol. 12517, pp. 157–166. Springer, Cham (2020). https://doi.org/10.1007/978-3-030-63464-3_15

32. Aparicio, A.F., Vela, F.L.G., Sánchez, J.L.G., Montes, J.L.I.: Analysis and application of gamification. In: Proceedings of the 13th International Conference on Interacción Persona-Ordenador – INTERACCION 2012, Elche, Spain, pp. 1–2 (2012). https://doi.org/10.1145/2379636.2379653

33. Schmidt-Kraepelin, M., Warsinsky, S., Thiebes, S., Sunyaev, A.: The role of gamification in health behavior change: a review of theory-driven studies. In: Presented at the Hawaii International Conference on System Sciences (2020). https://doi.org/10.24251/hicss.2020.155

34. Shi, L., Cristea, A.I.: Motivational gamification strategies rooted in self-determination theory for social adaptive e-learning. In: Intelligent Tutoring Systems, pp. 294–300 (2016). https://doi.org/10.1007/978-3-319-39583-8_32

35. Wintermeyer, A., Knautz, K.: Meaningful implementation of gamification in information literacy instruction. In: Information Literacy: Moving Toward Sustainability, pp. 350–359 (2015). https://doi.org/10.1007/978-3-319-28197-1_36

36. De-Marcos, L., Ortega, A., García-Cabo, A., López, E.G.: Towards the social gamification of e-learning: a practical experiment. Int. J. Eng. Educ. **33**(1), 66–73 (2017)

37. Duncan, L.R., Hall, C.R., Wilson, P.M., Rodgers, W.M.: The use of a mental imagery intervention to enhance integrated regulation for exercise among women commencing an exercise program. Motiv. Emot. **36**(4), 452–464 (2012). https://doi.org/10.1007/s11031-011-9271-4

38. Cumming, J., Ramsey, R.: Imagery interventions in sport. In: Advances in Applied Sport Psychology: A Review, pp. 5–36 (2009)
39. Ryan, R.M., Deci, E.L.: Intrinsic and extrinsic motivations: classic definitions and new directions. Contemp. Educ. Psychol. **25**(1), 54–67 (2000). https://doi.org/10.1006/ceps.1999.1020
40. Shen, Z.: Goal-Oriented Moedling For Intelligent Agents and Their Applications. Nanyang Technological University, Nanyang (2005)

Author Index